THE
AMERICAN
CITY

THE AMERICAN CITY
From the Civil War to the New Deal

Giorgio Ciucci
Francesco Dal Co
Mario Manieri-Elia
Manfredo Tafuri

Translated from the Italian by
Barbara Luigia La Penta

GRANADA
London Toronto Sydney New York

First published in Great Britain, 1980, by
Granada Publishing Limited - Technical Books Division
Frogmore, St Albans, Herts AL2 2NF
and
3 Upper James Street, London W1R 4BP
866 United Nations Plaza, New York, NY 10017, USA
117 York Street, Sydney, NSW 2000, Australia
100 Skyway Avenue, Rexdale, Ontario M9W 3A6, Canada
PO Box 84165, Greenside, 2034 Johannesburg, South Africa
CML Centre, Queen & Wyndham, Auckland 1, New Zealand

Published in the USA, 1979, by The MIT Press, Cambridge,
Massachusetts 02142

Originally published in Italy under the title *La città americana dalla guerra civile
al New Deal*, © 1973 by Guis, Laterza & Figli, Spa, Rome. This translation of
the 1973 edition © 1979 by The Massachusetts Institute of Technology.

ISBN 0 246 11368 5

Printed in the United States of America

Granada ®
Granada Publishing ®

CONTENTS

PREFACE

The four essays brought together in this volume are the fruit of a period of research and discussion on a single common theme: the city in the United States as a problem of historical criticism. Nevertheless, the reader would search in vain in these pages for even the simplest outline of a general historical analysis of the American City from the Civil War to the New Deal. Nor, indeed, has it been our intention to offer a comprehensive historical synthesis. From the necessity of treating certain common arguments and, at times, identical historical periods and events, some specific interrelations do exist among these four studies. What really unites our work are not these individual overlaps but our effort to confront a single problem from different perspectives and using different arguments.

This method arises largely from the particular circumstances of the problem we have posed for ourselves. In fact, a history of the American city has still not been written, although an enormous quantity of information has been collected and a vast literature on the subject exists. What has most generally affected the efforts made up to now, however, is not this particular lack—which leaves open the fascinating possibility of a work that will eventually fill the lacuna—but, rather, the dearth of interpretive viewpoints, of perspectives on the problem other than those traditionally adopted.

The difficulties arising from this situation explain the incompleteness of the historical literature on the American city, which is nevertheless rich and extensive. The works aimed at a comprehension of the urban phenomenon that is neither exclusively sociological nor exclusively technical are many and varied. Among them are studies that bring together as much information as possible, diligently and patiently collected and often presented with a remarkable philological depth and exactness. Such works have the great merit of making accessible a vast range of data that would otherwise be difficult to obtain. They do not, however, guarantee the completeness of the data, and they set forth the essential and the purely marginal in the same uniform light, ultimately offering a simple "collection" of information. In any case, within this philological and reconstructive perspective, studies such as those of Mel Scott and John W. Reps provide a fundamental service.

Another type of historical contribution proffers, instead, a strongly partisan interpretation of the facts, aiming more at the demonstration of a general thesis, usually of a "progressive" stamp, than at completeness of information. The phenomena are presented according to critical criteria based on a priori judgments. Works of this type—eminent among which are those of Lewis Mumford—are lively and stimulating; they are also notable for the marked selectivity of the facts dealt with and for the weight of their interpretive theses. But while the viewpoint is always quite clear and the judgments can thus be interpreted easily, readers must be on guard against distortion of the facts that results from omissions or from the emphasis placed on particular episodes.

Yet another category of American criticism, which can be extended to include the writings of James Marston Fitch as well as those of Vincent Scully, attempts a total reconstruction of the phenomena of architecture and urban planning. As a totality, however, already reconstructed, such criticism can be used only after a laborious operation of decomposition.

In addition to these works of a synthetic nature, American literature on architecture and urbanism is exceedingly rich in specific and specialized contributions. The classification of such a vast body of material is nearly impossible, but its breadth and importance may be grasped by the reader who has the patience to peruse the notes to these four essays, which have been compiled as a bibliographical guide and aid to further study.

It seems to us that two principal features of the present work set it apart from any of the types of writing outlined here. First, we have been concerned with verifying a critical hypothesis matured over a long period of time and frequently applied. The problem of the city as revealed in these four essays has forced us to test once again the validity of the hypothesis constructed on the highly important, but nevertheless partial, reality represented by the "great apocalypse" of European bourgeois culture. Certain schemes developed within this line of criticism appear inconsistent and largely irrelevant and are often misleading when confronted with the history of the New World. What, in effect, we have discovered with our research, is not a differing history but certainly another history. It has therefore been necessary to find other, new interpretive keys and search out other tendencies—another reason why we have written four essays and not a general history. This search for new insights does not mean that we are questioning a method or critical conviction already long matured. Rather, it simply reflects the need for new bases of judgment and new arguments, the need to reveal yet other movements and trends, which may even be contradictory but which are in any case present and operative in the reality we have sought to analyze.

These particular circumstances of the problem give rise to the second fundamental characteristic of our work. A series of critical formulas are simply taken for granted here, on the assumption that, because of our emphasis on certain aspects of the phenomena and our specification of certain tendencies and not others, the facts we have reconstructed can, in themselves, indicate the interpretive key we wish to provide. In these essays the reader will find narrative passages, historical reconstructions pure and simple, and schematic references to complex facts and realities; the choice of those references, events, and hypotheses is intended to demonstrate just where our discourse leads.

In a youthful work Leon Trotsky spoke, perhaps for the first time among modern critics, of the necessity of a class point of view in the criticism of art and the criticism of the values of bourgeois culture. The construction of such a class point of view, derived from Marxian matrix, is not to be understood as the creation of a ready formula on the basis of which to pronounce the merits and the faults of bourgeois intellectual products. The problem is to bring this point of view up to date in terms of the historical levels of the material analyzed by continually applying criticism to both the complex of phenomena and the criticohistorical acquisitions that the values of bourgeois culture present and interpret.

The need for critical updating is particularly urgent in the historical study of American society and in the analysis of the multiple aspects in which the products of its culture are manifest. Academic disdain for the banal in this culture and acritical disparagement of its products are both positions to be rejected, not because they are wrong but because they are useless in explaining trends over time; they do not help us to understand, because they tend to eliminate phenomena and problems the forms of which may leave us indifferent but the mechanisms of which must be continually recognized.

It is precisely these mechanisms to which we wish to call the reader's attention with the studies presented here—even at the price of neglecting more attractive and usual arguments. Our efforts have been directed at demonstrating how the levels of integration of cultural products and ideologies is based not only on an implicit vocation but also on a well-defined complex of techniques, which, in turn, is even partly shaped by the intellectual production as a whole. The direct transformation and utilization of ideology and culture as a technique—even where the ideology is the most regressive, the culture weakest, and the technique least evident—appears to us the most important fact to emerge from our studies. In American society, the span of time within which the idea becomes technical, and at a very advanced level, is much shorter than that encountered in the crucial period of European bourgeois culture. An understanding of the brevity of this time span has seemed to us a more decisive contribution than the very questionable attempt to write a comprehensive history of the American city.

The American city is thus revealed as an enormous, form-defying product of technique. The causality behind this particular urban formalization is one possible starting point for an analysis of the historical process of the city in the United States. The creative structure, the mechanisms, and thus the scientific efficiency of this causality will never be clarified, however, if those writing history continue to ignore the connections that turn the disciplines of architecture and city planning into agents of the ponderous process of transformation set in motion by the American capitalist system in determining the urban structure. It is, in fact, from the historical and functional connection with a complex process, in which architecture and urbanism play at most very marginal roles, that urban culture itself becomes a technique of transformation—at the lowest level, in the formation of consensus and through control over the labor force; at the highest, by programming new social equilibriums. In order to identify and examine these tendencies, however, not as ideas but as determining historical factors, it is clearly necessary to understand the effect such transformation exerts on the intellectual product, and, at the same time to use means of historical interpretation that can be continually brought up to date.

Of the four essays in this book, the first and the last deal with the city as it is and as it becomes through the action of those who actually run it and the "official" culture linked to them. The alternation of boss rule and reformist interventions in the city of laissez-faire, which constituted the dialectical continuity of the capitalist development of the American city, is a theme that relates the first two essays. The second and third treat the American "tradition" and the various attitudes toward the city that derive from it.

Very generally, it is the great economic crises that tend to structure our treatment of the material. The laissez-faire period drew to a close in 1893-94 with the severe depression and the Pullman strike. Coinciding with this period of change, which prepared the way for the Republicans' advent to power, was the sudden shift within the field of urban planning itself that produced the Columbian Exposition—the first real attempt to integrate architectural planning, up to that time compromised by urban chaos, and "uncorrupted" landscape. The period from the Republican victory to the economic crisis of 1907-09 was a period marked by imperialist politics and witnessed the creation of the great plans for Washington, San Francisco, and Chicago. These plans were products not of the progressive culture of the country, which instead condemned them, but of the "official" culture bound to the economic and political power that conditioned their ends and forms. The City Beautiful as exemplified in the work of Daniel H. Burnham, which forms the subject of the first essay of this book, was to assume a place within the Open Door policy, becoming the design for the "imperial city."

The road followed by progressive thought, to which the second essay is dedicated, was completely different. This study presents a great deal of material about phenomena that were largely unknown in Italy before the original edition of this book was published: the mystic utopias of the eighteenth and nineteenth centuries that testified to the moment when the ethic of work chose nature as its fundamental reference; the work of Frederick Law Olmsted; and the regionalism of the 1920s, in which progressive thought sought to establish a positive contact with reality. This complex of phenomena, extending through the period terminated with the crash of 1929, is here interpreted as the "tradition" of the New Deal.

The ideology of nature had other channels of expression, however. The third essay examines the myth of the frontier, which formed an integral part of the American tradition and was a constant factor in American thought from transcendentalism to the back-to-nature movement of the 1920s. The essay also brings into focus the various agrarian movements and their confluence in what may be considered the most original and important individual effort to recover the "humanistic" aspirations of architecture: the work of Frank Lloyd Wright. The study of Wright's work within this context shows that between Broadacres, despite its regressive ideology, and the Tennessee Valley Authority project there existed historical points of contact that subtly connect the otherwise contrasting regionalist and "naturalist" hypotheses.

The final essay of the volume addresses "the city of scrambled alphabets" in its process of becoming chaotic. In respect to this process the skyscraper is seen as perhaps the most contradictory attempt to impose a formal control—the skyscraper as an "event," as an "anarchic individual," as a striking object of publicity, as the expression of technological power. While the progressives campaigned for better building and urban standards and for a solution of the urban problem on a regional scale, the great business enterprises, with more immediate effect, found in the city on the eve of the great crash occasions for massive investments in building construction.

It should be clear from the outset that many important arguments have not been touched upon and many critical hypotheses still remain to be tested. This book is presented as a first series of results of an investigation that we consider open to further development. The original Italian text, published in 1973, has not been revised for the English language edition, but a sporadic and inevitably incomplete attempt has been made to bring the bibliographical references up to date.

Our research had its beginning in 1969. In the academic year 1969-70, some faculty members of the Institute of the History of Architecture of the University of Venice Institute of Architecture organized a series of courses centered upon the historical problem of American architecture and urbanism. This instructional work led to partial studies that were published before the present volume. The pursuit of this research was also made possible by the financial aid provided by the Italian National Research Council.

Our essays are the fruit of a continual exchange of information and viewpoints, and we should like to thank all those who joined in our discussions and aided us with their criticisms and suggestions. A large majority of the bibliographical and documentary material for our research was gathered from libraries and archives in Italy, Germany, Britain, and the United States. Without the valuable collaboration of several American research institutions, in particular, it would have been impossible to obtain any significant results.

We wish to express our gratitude to all those who assisted us. Among them we would particularly like to thank the friends who materially aided our studies. First we are grateful to Professor Giancarlo de Carlo, who made possible a long period of study in essential American archives and libraries. Also of great importance to us were the aid and advice of Professors John W. Reps and Oswald M. Ungers of Cornell University, Kurt Junghanns of the Bauakademie in East Berlin, George R. Collins of Columbia University, Edward Shapiro of Seton Hall University, Roy Lubove of the University of Pittsburgh, Peter Harrison of the Australian National University in Canberra, and Carlo Doglio of the University of Naples and of Dr. Georges Teyssot of the University of Venice.

During our research we received many critical suggestions, together with material assistance, from Dr. Anna Chiara Danieli, whom we wish to thank along with Elena and Lesley Madhjoubian. We owe a special debt of gratitude to the late Clarence S. Stein, who graciously allowed us, with the kind assistance of Wilma Breit, to consult his personal archives. Other information, principally about the Regional Planning Association of America, came from Professor Stuart Chase and Charles S. Ascher.

The kind and attentive collaboration of the directors and personnel of the Collection of Regional History and University Archives of Cornell University, particularly its curator, Herbert Finch, was fundamental to our work. The staff of Olin Library and the Library of Fine Arts of Cornell University, of the New York Public Library and the New York Historical Society, and of the Department of Microfilms of the Library of Congress offered invaluable assistance in the collection of bibliographical material. Others who helped us collect similar material and who deserve grateful recognition include Elda Colombo and Sylvia Arrigoni of the Chicago Public Library, Harley P. Holden and M. Ellen Reardon of the Harvard University Archives, May M. Stone of Avery Architectural Library at Columbia University, Patrick M. Cadell of the National Library of Edinburgh, and Alessandra Pinto Surdi of the Italian Center of American Studies in Rome. Interesting information was also furnished by Mary E. Osman, assistant editor of the *Journal of the American Institute of Architects*.

The material for the initial phase of our research, contained in American libraries, was collected in 1970 by Luisa Dal Co, to whom we express particular thanks. The preparation of part of this volume was enormously facilitated by the kindness and generosity of Lewis Mumford. Without his help, information, and interest, the results of our research would certainly have been limited.

Finally, the organizational work required for the preparation of these four essays was greatly alleviated by the intelligent collaboration of the personnel of the Institute of the History of Architecture in Venice, to whom, as always, we express our friendship and thanks.

Giorgio Ciucci   Mario Manieri-Elia
Francesco Dal Co   Manfredo Tafuri

THE
AMERICAN
CITY

MARIO MANIERI-ELIA

Toward an "Imperial City": Daniel H. Burnham and the City Beautiful Movement

Introduction: The Laissez-Faire City

The social and organizational developments that characterize the United States in the last quarter of the nineteenth century are related, directly or indirectly, to the phenomenon of urbanization, here understood to include both major movements toward the city: that of the American rural population and that of the foreign immigrants. In the population growth and economic development of the American city, these two movements constituted a continual influx, activated by the evolution of the relations of production. Like the native American newcomers to the city, the foreign immigrants came generally from rural areas; they were peasants drawn from distant lands by the great attraction of the American city.

It is precisely in the American city at this moment when it was becoming a metropolis that documentation offered in stable and measurable physical structures permits a series of phenomena related to the formation of modern capital to be studied. Here I will adopt an approach intended to clarify the organizational and ideological mechanisms that accompany this economic evolution, of which urbanization is the most conspicuous phenomenon. From such a perspective architecture is the expression of an intellectual elite and its immediate significance lies in its relationship to the broader frame of reference of the building industry and the processes of urban development.

The laissez-faire American city can be compared in its general formal structure to the bourgeois European city; in both, commerce and manufacturing were concentrated in the center and an ample and elastic labor supply on the periphery. There were, however, notable differences, resulting, on the one hand, from long-established European urban forms and the inertia of the "values" connected with them, and, on the other, from the general adoption in America of the grid plan, which functioned as a neutral support for capital's free exploitation of the city soil. Another significant difference stemmed from the management of the American city; through at least the whole of the last century, it was in the hands of construction bosses over whom no authority comparable to the European prefects was capable of exerting even partial control. This pattern was undoubtedly also related to the other great difference that distinguished cities such as New York and Chicago from London or Paris. The fact is that Europe experienced nothing comparable to the dynamics of urban development in the New World, particularly that of the 1870s and 1880s, the decisive years in the formation of the American metropolis.

If, indeed, it is true that colonization toward the Pacific and immigration from across the Atlantic were comparable, respectively, to the European processes of colonial expansion and the movement of rural populations to the city, in the United States these two phenomena met with no resistance and proceeded with an optimal rhythm and a success unknown in Europe. The continual acquisition of wealth from the West, in the form of land taken from the Indians, and the corresponding arrival there of low-cost labor from the East were easily maintained at maximum yield. This success was due, in turn, not only to the vast proportions of the two processes but, above all, to the ease with which the dosage of each could be controlled—on the one hand, by control over the construction of railroads to the West and, on the other, by control over European immigration into the East. Maximum profits were also maintained by the system's simultaneously permitting the arrival of low-cost labor from Europe but preventing, through a sagacious policy of protectionism, the arrival of low-cost merchandise.

When the Civil War gave the industrialized North political control of the country and the frontier was still something more than a myth, colonization and immigration thus functioned as inexhaustible mechanisms for the primitive accumulation of capital and for ensuring the labor supply. From them arose not only an extraordinary industrial development but also the remarkable growth and congestion of the American cities.

The racial aspect of the discord between Yankee and immigrant has often obscured its structural nature. Actually, it was comparable to the conflict in the Old World between the unionized working class and the proletarian and subproletarian populations newly arrived in the cities. Once again the situation in America made it easier to handle this conflict—first of all because of the complete lack of communication between these two categories of workers in America, but also because the immigrants, thirty million uprooted people ready to work for limited wages and accept a standard of living far below the rest of the population, could be much more effectively manipulated as a mass maneuver against strikes than in Europe. The American-born workers, for their part, excluded the immigrants from their unions and perpetuated their own privileged position with a social and political rupture.

The two classes had to be controlled and kept in proper balance. The hardships faced by the immigrants could not be allowed to reach the point of turning them into a subversive, anarchic force, nor could the political power of the unionized aristocracy rise far enough to threaten laissez-faire itself. The division between these classes, essential to the establishment, was reinforced ideologically by two new, opposing figures who characterized the period, the boss and the reformer, whose reciprocal functions were essential factors in the history of the city.

The boss was the organizer of the immigrant masses. He saw to it that the burdens of the immigrant's work were kept within the limits of endurance; he reduced the immigrant's compensation to a minimum necessary for subsistence but also guaranteed this minimum; and he consented to the immigrant's continuing the practices and social customs of the old country, thereby naturally reinforcing the immigrant's segregation. The boss managed to make the immigrant's situation livable—livable only at the very lowest level, but still better than conditions for the blacks, to which the white immigrant was never to sink. In practice the boss introduced into the production cycle, then slowly into the social system, a mass of disinherited people of the most diverse cultures, prevented insofar as possible any manifestations of discontent, and maintained instinctive desires for justice at a personal, elementary level.

The boss's field of action was obviously the city—the city as residence, the city as the place of production and exchange and of political struggle and strikes, the city as the labor market. The phenomenon of the boss has been described many times.[1] Essentially, what he did was to mediate the immigrant's contact with the American production system by offering him a series of services, which also had the effect of providing psychological support. He limited the difficulties arising from differences in language and from chauvinistic and racist movements, offered legal protection with no questions asked, and participated in the social customs and native ceremonies of the immigrants to the extent that he came to know them individually. In return, he asked for the personal loyalty that secured him their votes. His political power was generally limited to the city government; if he had a key position, he could offer employment in building construction and public works, quick naturalization, social services, and recommendations to the local authorities. By managing this instable material of the city, he was able to give credibility to his ideology. Corrupting the government within which he operated naturally formed an integral part of his method. He therefore became the principal target of the muckrakers; these crusading journalists represented the extreme of the reformers' ideology, which directly opposed that of the bosses.

The reformers were the native progressives among the forces operating on the city; their role was to defend democratic institutions, keep public opinion aroused, and see that high moral standards were met by those in office. Rather than personal loyalty, the reformers wanted to create a kind of public loyalty; their aims were efficiency, openness, stability, and legitimacy in government. On the side of the reformers were the heads of the elite unions, men such as Edward A. Ross and John R. Commos, who were capable of expressing the harshest racial condemnation of the immigrants as those responsible for the grave damage being inflicted on the native working class. These native workers were naturally marshaled behind the vindicatory position of the Noble Order of the Knights of Labor or, later, the American Federation of Labor,[2] and were horrified by the abysmal conditions in which their new compatriots managed to live. Their instinctive repugnance found ready and authoritative confirmation in the ideology of the progressives, while it was roused to aggressive action by the actual opposing forces.[3]

The boss—almost never a Yankee, often an Irishman—was thus the only connecting link between the "system," represented by the reigning forces of the laissez-faire city, and the confused mass of immigrants. It was precisely as a connecting link that he could guarantee a flexible relationship between these two elements and could manage to ease the stresses and strains, transmitting them only after making their solution possible. The social condition of the immigrant, segregated but connected with the rest of society by means of a controlled system of mediation, naturally installed him as a resident of the ghettos, compact slums, neither better nor worse than those of London and Berlin. Cut off from the city, although within and surrounded by it, connected to it only through obligatory routes, the ghettos were the formal reflection of the immigrant's social condition. The obligatory routes were the connecting junctures of the city, which was made up, on the one hand, of gray areas, reservoirs of labor governed by the bosses, and, on the other, of organizational structures that, aided by the dynamics of the developing economy, were capable of providing a supporting frame for the whole.

Before long it would become obvious that the organizational structures required planning, but in the gray areas the construction boss would continue to reign with respect for nothing but the law of maximum profit. The grid plan was the neutral support for his freedom of action, the logical spatial scheme in which his completely arbitrary operations were legal. It was also the factor that guaranteed a basic, vital efficiency. The principle of order and rationality on which the grid plan rested was an elementary planning device, intrinsic to the city and beyond the boss's range of influence; it had actually orginated from ideas of efficiency. The progressive reform elements generally intervened in the city once structures were established; their denunciations, crusades, and exposés of scandals functioned as warning signals and served to moderate exploitation in the city. Ultimately, their appeal for quality promoted architecture.

The patron of the architect was not the boss, whose occasional concessions to culture never went beyond mere ceremony or the adoption of an imported stylistic tradition at the most conventional level. Nor was it the reformer, who was usually inept at the management of capital. In the laissez-faire period, the patron of architecture was generally a particular sort of converted boss, a progressive businessman, or one of the outstanding figures of the world of finance and industry, for whom an architectural undertaking represented an occasion to give luster to his firm and, with it, to the city. Patrons thus felt a need for culture and sought it where it was to be found, that is, among "progressive" intellectuals.

From its very beginnings Chicago was a typically American city, free of any nostalgia for European conventions. Thus urban architecture developed there on the basis of completely native, enlightened, and progressive concepts; it was founded on the principles of cultural independence and individualism expounded by transcendentalist philosophy, which in the laissez-faire period corresponded to economic protectionism.[4] While they did not overlook efficiency, the architects of the Chicago school—who in their heyday created the first skyscrapers, famous for their undeniably high quality and fascination—were dedicated to originality. Although their work may have been constrained by an inevitable inferiority complex with respect to Europe, their objective was the foundation of a uniquely American architecture, one whose debt to Europe would be no more than that of any innovative architecture to tradition.

They pursued this objective in terms of the individual building, respecting the lot assigned to it within the grid. The urban character of this architecture was therefore conditioned by the rigid, two-dimensional nature of the ordinary grid of streets; thus the margin of volumetric liberty—certainly very fully exploited—consisted exclusively in the third dimension. Apart from the rare cases of designs created with exceptional dedication and diligence, however, this third dimension had no organic, proportional relationship to the other two. Nor would its development have been possible without contesting the law of maximum yield and its corollary, which was precisely the grid plan. To explain the skyscraper, however, it is necessary to take into account the mentality of the boss, for whom height, in addition to making possible the full exploitation of the city land, could be a means of obtaining quality through quantity.

The Chicago Loop is the perfect product of the laissez-faire city and its "system": a regular grid and an assemblage of prismatic buildings the height of which is determined by the investment of capital. As has been noted more than once, these two basic elements are arithmetical results—the first of division, the second of multiplication.[5] In such a city form is obscured, and the only really perceptible characteristics are, instead, the signs of consumption, the movement of the crowd and its dress and behavior governed by the laws of consumption. The exceptional dedication of the masters of the Chicago school was probably prompted in part by the enormous challenge this city posed; armed solely with the means of design, an exceptional effort was needed to combat this "distracted perception," which the sociologists were soon to demonstrate as typical of the metropolis. This condition was, in fact, carried to the extreme in Chicago because of the exceptional rapidity of its development and also because of its particular type of boss rule, in which there was no one dominant figure capable of centralizing power in the city.

View of Chicago from Lake Michigan in 1892. The overall grid plan extends as far as the eye can see. Near the port at the center of the illustration is the Loop, where the first skyscrapers were concentrated. Visible on the lakefront is the Auditorium with its tower (Adler and Sullivan, 1889) and, in the center of the Loop, the Masonic Temple (Burnham and Root, 1891). The shore is occupied by the railroad lines.

View of a section of the Chicago Loop in about 1890. Left to the management of the bosses, the laissez-faire city grew chaotically on the basic grid plan.

New York, although it too developed very rapidly, bears the signs of a completely different type of city management, one dominated by a single boss. William Marcy Tweed, however, had attached himself to a long-established tradition of boss rule, Tammany Hall, which as early as the mid-nineteenth century completely controlled the labor market and the organization of the city.[6] When Tweed came to absolute power, the streets of New York were widened, the transport services—with monopolized concessions—were coordinated and became efficient, and the construction of Central Park went forward. As soon as the city government fell irreparably into debt, the bankers sent the boss to prison. Shortly thereafter, however, the Democrats won the elections and the Tweed machine, this time without Tweed, resumed work more or less as before. What happened in New York in 1871 is analogous to events in Philadelphia ten years later. The only difference was that Philadelphia boss James McManes was a Republican; the democrats attacked him and, when his hour came, they defeated him.

A unique boss, with remarkable control over construction and real estate speculation, was Alexander Shepherd in Washington. Because of the lack of industry in that city and the law, passed in 1871, that made the administration of the nation's capital practically nonelective, the boss did not have the popular, familiar character he had in other cities. In the District of Columbia, in reality, the urban administrative machine coincided with national political power. In Shepherd's time, national power was held by the Republicans and, in particular, by President Ulysses S. Grant. A friend of the President's, Shepherd soon became governor of the District of Columbia. In this case, far more than elsewhere, the urban project undertaken was a thorough and unified operation and anticipated mechanisms that were to be developed by the City Beautiful movement. Even in Washington, however, the operation finished in bankruptcy. The work was not controlled by a plan, and completely arbitrary decisions were unchecked except by violent political attacks that could provoke sudden reversals. This crude but effective system was well adapted to the unscrupulous haste of the 1870s and 1880s, but with the crisis of 1893 it became clear to all that some more stable and less primitive equilibrating mechanism was indispensible.

In the city described here, one made up of organizational structures and neutral areas left to the unhampered will of the bosses, the latter were never to be eliminated, but beginning in the late nineteenth century the organizational structures became the object of increasingly decisive urban action. These projects had a notable ideological content, but they were also of importance for the new scale of their technical organization, as well as for their social and economic implications.

Urban design as developed in such projects is the subject of this essay. The period covered opens with the White City of the Chicago World's Fair, which, to the regret and vexation of some, marked a sudden change of direction and the beginning of a new conception of the city in the United States; it extends to the executed and unexecuted projects related conceptually to the City Beautiful movement in its most ambitious and conspicuous version, that dominated by the work of Daniel H. Burnham. My principal objects are to demonstrate Burnham's fundamental importance and to clarify his precise role in the ambiguously defined City Beautiful movement.[7]

Chicago in the 1890s and the Idea of the Fair of 1893

Historians seem to be unanimous in accepting the World's Columbian Exposition of 1893 as the point of demarcation between two epochs.[8] Many have even sought to pinpoint the moment at which the idea of the fair came into being. John W. Reps, for example, indicates 1882, just six years after the international exposition in Philadelphia.[9] By a remarkable coincidence, 1882 is the date William Appleman Williams assigns to the end of the Indian wars.[10] Actually, the maturation of the conditions that gave rise to this extraordinary reaffirmation of American prestige and power, with Chicago as its focal point, can be placed at about 1887, a date that corresponds to the end of the West's position of dependence on the East.

Until this time an essentially colonial relationship had persisted between East and West, and the frontier towns had been forced to make money to enrich the centers of economic power on the Atlantic coast. Julian Ralph wrote: "That . . . is why men in Chicago have talked only 'business'; that is why Chicago has had no leisure class, no reservoir of home capital seeking investment."[11] As early as the 1880s, however, the situation began to change. After the Civil War, the American economic cycle pivoted on Chicago, the seat of the largest productive force, which offered the greatest potential for the working-class struggle. The tension that grew as Chicago acquired strength gave rise to the clamorous episodes of the Gould strike of 1885, which registered a dangerous success of the unions, and the Haymarket incident in the following year. These events were the alarms that opened the phase of violent and systematic repression of labor. Despite the size of the working-class organizations—the unions at this time numbered a million members—capital was by now strong. The fortunate economic cycle of the frontier period had multiplied it, and, by prompting competition between the states at the highest level, the new production equilibrium between East and West was now consolidating its development.

The years from the Haymarket riot of 1886 to 1892 were years of reorganization. On the one hand, an intense reorganization of the labor movement took place during this period of truce initiated by the unions; new alignments and new unions developed, and the Knights of Labor, which represented the elite old guard of privileged workers, gradually collapsed. On the other hand, political and economic reorganization prepared the way for the imperialist policies of the new century.

Josiah Strong was the prophet of this new course.[12] He sounded the alarm against socialism and declared that the people of the United States, because of their Anglo-Saxon racial superiority, were destined to civilize the world. Strong's preaching was to influence Henry Cabot Lodge and Theodore Roosevelt, among many others. By 1890 the time was ripe for the great change; the foundations of the new system, destined to replace laissez-faire, had already been laid. In the 1880s James J. Hill's vast railway holdings, the Cambodia Iron Works in Pittsburgh, and the economic empires of Rockefeller, Morgan, and Carnegie—with their diversity and tendency toward impersonality—had, in fact, anticipated the advantages that would later characterize the corporations, even in their political management of union disputes. Power did not actually pass into the hands of the representative of the new system until the election of William McKinley to the presidency in 1896 and the institution of the imperialist Open Door policy. First, however, the country had to readjust and overcome the serious economic crisis of 1893-94.

The Columbian Exposition can be interpreted as a final energetic outburst on the part of the American economy, particularly of the rapidly developing West, on the eve of the crisis. Seen in this light, Chicago was the necessary site for the fair. Among the competing cities—New York, Saint Louis, Boston, and Philadelphia—Chicago stood out as a miracle of the American economic system. This prodigiously developing city was living proof of the advantages of capitalism in its heroic, unimpeded form.

In reality, the end of economic isolationism and protectionism and the institution of the Open Door policy were to give much less of a boost to Chicago than to New York and San Francisco, cities far more favorably situated in respect to the new transoceanic markets. At the time of the fair, however, the Republican foreign policy had not yet been put into practice; in any case, its dangers did not occur to Western businessmen while they were still gathering the fruits of their labors.

"Chicago expects to become the largest city in America," Ralph wrote in 1893. "In the heart of Chicago . . . the crowds convey the idea that Broadway is a deserted thoroughfare as compared with . . . the corner of Clark and Jackson streets."[13] There was no end to the statistics on this miraculous city. A twenty-fifth of the world's railways converged there, thirty million people found Chicago the most easily reached of the world's large cities. It already had two dozen skyscrapers in 1890; they were higher and more modern than even New York's. A completely new technology had made this construction possible; 7,000 offices were already functioning, and another 7,000 were being built on the eve of the fair. A prodigious metropolitan development was underway, and no limits were in sight. Its difficult period now in the past, Chicago indulged in luxury: Louis Sullivan's Auditorium, like John W. Root's Rookery, expressed the opulence acquired through laissez-faire. The important public and commercial buildings were magnificently decorated; vast surfaces were covered with tapestries, arabesques, mosaics, marbles, onyx, and gold leaf.

Thus one might say that Chicago itself was the fair. Writing at the time, Ralph predicted, "Chicago will be the main exhibit at the Columbian Exposition of 1893."[14] But the fair also had to indicate a new course, a completely different development; it had to express an America no longer proud of its isolation but, instead, eager to extend a hand to the most distant peoples, cultures, and markets. For this reason, in the architecture and general cultural trend it promoted, the fair radically contradicted the architectural and cultural developments that were then taking place in Chicago.

Even if they were not the dominant figures the architectural historians have made them out to be, the architects of Chicago were present at this historical juncture. They had individual names and styles, and they differed from the architects of the East, as well as from each other. They were distinguished from the Eastern architects, such as Richard Morris Hunt or Charles F. McKim, by their greater independence from European tradition and their rejection of eclecticism. Among themselves, they differed in their cultural upbringing and in their capacity to adapt to the changeable reality within which they had to work.

The more original and creative among them, such as Sullivan and Root, who felt themselves heirs of H. H. Richardson and inheritors of his mission to found a specifically American architecture, were the least elastic, the least adaptable to the evolution of the architect's role, which was nonetheless a reality and did not permit ideological crystallization. Thus, although Richardson's, Sullivan's, and Frank Lloyd Wright's "glorious" pursuit of quality earned them places of honor in the history of architecture, it was actually men like William Le Baron Jenney and Daniel H. Burnham who most fully carried out the role of the American architect. Without setting their own ideologies against that of the system, these men were able, within the limits of architecture, to affect the reality of the city to a far greater extent.

The costly stylistic experiments of Sullivan and Root found places in the congested world of Chicago precisely because the task of stylistic research had been delegated to each of these architects by partners of great value, who, although certainly capable of participating in at least the conceptual phase of design, were disposed to assume more purely managerial roles. On the contrary, Wright, who refused to work with Burnham after Root's death, was essentially never to build within the city of Chicago proper. Similarly, when Sullivan worked alone in his later years, his rare, exquisite banks found sites only far from the center of the capitalist fray.

If Dankmar Adler was no more than Louis Sullivan's strong shoulder,[15] Burnham was surely a match for his associate, a fact that, naturally, became clear only in the works produced after Root's death. In fact, Burnham not only maintained a very high level of quality, but all his production subsequent to his partner's death is so homogeneous, despite the many able designers constantly at work in his vast studio, that it demonstrates beyond doubt his own personal ability, even on the formal level. It is more difficult to establish the nature of

Auditorium Hotel dining room, Chicago,
by Adler and Sullivan, 1899.

Auditorium Hotel, detail of exterior.

Monadnock Building, Chicago, Burnham
and Root, 1891.

Burnham's contribution in works executed together with Root, but there is a good reason for attempting to do so. In the designs to which we have some real reason to believe that Burnham's personal contribution was greater than usual, it is possible to discern a particular sensitivity to the urban scale.[16] Typical in this respect is the Monadnock Building, one of the most admired skyscrapers at the time of the fair and still a highly esteemed work today. Its sheer quality has often led historians to attribute it to Root, eliminating all mention of Burnham in some cases.

Regardless of the wide range of Root's stylistic experiments, which he himself acknowledged,[17] it does not seem possible that the designer of such works as the Phoenix Building, the Art Institute, the Rookery, the Masonic Temple, and the Women's Building could have designed the Monadnock Building in the same years. Actually, the production of the firm of Burnham and Root was so vast—over sixty buildings in five years in Chicago alone—that the significant contribution in many of the designs could not always have been that of one of the two titular members. In the firm's earlier work it is possible to find precedents for the Monadnock—the Argyle and Pickwick Apartments, the Chemical Bank, the Rand McNally Building, and, above all, the Great Northern Hotel, all since demolished—in which the molded wall and the use of bricks or bay windows clearly relate to the Monadnock Building.

Montgomery Schuyler, the most authoritative and objective critic of the time, unhesitatingly attributed the Monadnock to "the individual design of Mr. Burnham."[18] If this attribution is accepted, the experimentation in the buildings just cited can be seen as a precedent to the extraordinary Flatiron Building in New York, which was executed by Burnham ten years after Root's death. In fact, apart from a certain stylistic resemblance, which has little weight in the present argument because of the large number of designers habitually at work in Burnham and Root's studio, these buildings show a similarity in the "urban" character of their conception, that is, in the reciprocal relationship between building and street. Precisely because of this relationship, the skyscraper is no longer a closed architectural object composed according to a hierarchy of parts, as it is in Root's and Sullivan's work in Chicago or often in the earlier works of Eastern architects such as Bradford Gilbert or George B. Post. By doing away with the self-contained character of the skyscraper and acknowledging the role of the street as a fundamental urban element, the Monadnock Building became part of the organizing structure of the city. This was a real and significant step forward. It overturned one old idea of counteracting the undifferentiated character of the grid plan and the banal form of the building lot through the expressive emphasis of a single, individual work. Instead, in an attempt to indicate a different urban structure, the volumetric design of the Monadnock was deliberately simplified and given a continuous treatment in terms of a simple rhythmic wall; what was here but an attempt was to be a goal fully achieved in the Flatiron Building.

Unlike Sullivan and Wright, Burnham has left no autobiography, nor did he, like Root, have an enthusiastic sister-in-law ready to write his biography after his death. Charles Moore, historian of medieval architecture, member of federal commissions on the arts, and closely associated with Burnham in his more official undertakings, published a biography of Burnham after his death that is much less romantic and, perhaps for this reason, much less known, but that reveals an American reality intimately related to the social, political, and economic structures and their continual process of evolution.[19]

In the early part of his life Daniel H. Burnham was a typical restless Yankee. He did badly in school and failed the entrance examinations for both Harvard and Yale, then worked for a while in a store until his father arranged for him to enter William Le Baron Jenney's studio. Burnham was not the type to become a draftsman, however, and left for Nevada to make his fortune in mining. When he failed in this aim he turned to politics, although for what party is not clear. Biographies and obituaries are all discreetly silent on this period; still not twenty-five, Burnham, like Kafka's Karl Rossmann, was struggling in the limbo that stretched between those who counted in Grant's America and the chaos of all the rest.

In 1871, Burnham decided on architecture, but the studio he had just set up with Gustave Laureau was reduced to ashes by the Chicago fire in that year. Still, his decision had been made, and the following year Burnham was at work in the Chicago studio of Carter, Drake and Wright. Here he met John W. Root, a Georgian who was already the chief draftsman of this New York firm and who was in Chicago for the reconstruction of the city. In 1873 Burnham induced Root to leave the firm and set up a studio with him; they were joined by William Holabird and Clinton J. Warren.

Work came to the group, and they tried to make contact with the world of those who counted in the city. A friend of Root knew the rich stockyard owner John B. Sherman and recommended the young architect for the new residence Sherman wanted built. It was Burnham, however, who was more convincing and able in such situations and who presented himself, instead of Root, at the meeting with Sherman and obtained the commission for both. Shortly thereafter, Burnham married Sherman's daughter. Prosperity was now assured for the thirty-year-old Burnham. From this time on, Burnham and Root, in competition with the other Chicago firms, were frequently at work designing the tallest building in the city. Each time they installed their studio on the top floor, only to be overtaken by Jenney or Adler and Sullivan. They moved from the 7-story Grannis Building to the 10-story Montauk Building ("the first skyscraper") and finally established themselves in the Rookery, a prestigious building that was to be overshadowed only in 1889 by Adler and Sullivan's Auditorium.

The moment when Burnham would be able to demonstrate his full abilities was still to come, however, and was to coincide, by a trick of fate, with Root's death. Burnham had always prepared himself for a great step forward to a position of power and to enterprises of unprecedented scale, something that for other architects, such as Sullivan, would have been fatal. Indeed, he made no secret of his ambition. As early as 1874, in the building yard of the Sherman house, he told Sullivan, "I'm not going to stay satisfied with houses: my idea is to work up a big business, to handle big things, deal with big businessmen, and to build up a big organization." And the sight of Root too diligently employed at his drafting table provoked Burnham to advise, "Delegate, delegate, delegate!"[20]

The moment Chicago was chosen as the site of the fair, it was inevitable that Burnham be recognized as just the man to organize the project architecturally in the form such an initiative demanded: a forceful proposal for a new development, the novelty of which would consist principally in its difference from the current character of Chicago's architecture. The bitter resentment and ferocious condemnation of Burnham's stylistic "betrayal" and the denunciation of the fair as the consecration of the worst sort of academicism, promoted by Sullivan in his autobiography,[21] do not take account of the historic reality the fair expressed. What, indeed, would Sullivan have done had the choice of the fair's architectural style fallen to him? He would most likely have given free rein once again to the myth of the individual genius and the ideal of an autonomous American architecture. He would probably have proposed a series of interesting Richardsonian buildings of a Beaux-Arts character mixed episodically with fantastic and Oriental motifs, situated in a park designed by Frederick Law Olmsted. History, of course, cannot be written with "ifs," but Root's design for the fair's buildings, published by Monroe, certainly gives a far from inspiring idea of what the autonomous Chicago architecture would have wanted or been able to produce. It would have been the final fair of the old-guard, individualistic, anticlassical, and anti-European intellectuals of the West.

The fair of 1893 had to represent a very different ideology, however. Whatever its genesis the first decisive show of faith in the initiative came from Wall Street in response to the needs of developing capitalism. The fair would demonstrate to the world the prodigiousness of American capital and the quality of its products; it would establish new financial and commercial contacts with distant countries, exhibit America's efficiency, productive capacity, and progress, and refute the old accusation of provincialism. In addition, the fair itself could be economically productive if it were big—bigger than any other and, especially, bigger than the last European exposition, held in 1889. The movement and influx of people would mean the sale of a great quantity of merchandise, transportation profits of every kind, an impetus to the further extension of the railway system—a fundamental factor of development—and a boost to construction.

These were the advantages seen by Wall Street; those counted on by the Chicago financiers who proposed to manage the undertaking were even more direct. These men saw the fair not only as a stimulus to industrial and commercial activity but also as a means of increasing real-estate values, within

Design by John W. Root for the World's
Columbian Exposition, published by
Harriet Monroe in 1896.

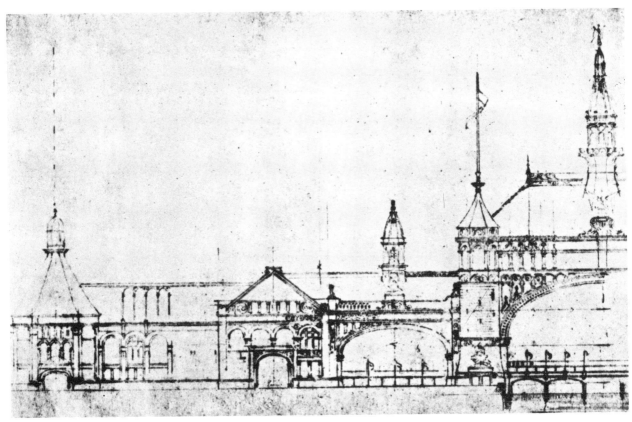

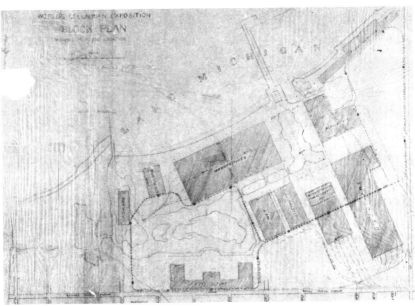

Plan of the Court of Honor for the Chicago
fair, from the archives of Frederick Law
Olmsted (see note 28).

the general scheme of managing the city's urban development. And this was precisely the area in which Burnham set to work.

While the Paris Exposition of 1889 was still going on, a commission of experts led by Edward T. Jeffery, president of the Illinois Central Railway, was charged with the task of studying it and preparing a report. At the same time, even before Chicago was definitely chosen as the site of the fair,[22] Burnham was moving among the men who held the economic power in Chicago—or in other words among the members of the Commercial Club—trying to settle the question of where to put the fairgrounds. This issue was lengthily disputed, and to resolve it James E. Ellsworth, president of the South Park Commission, proposed consulting Olmsted. Of the seven sites in question, three on the lake and four inland, the elderly Olmsted inclined toward Jackson Park—reluctantly, however, because many years earlier, in 1871, he and Calvert Vaux had created a design for this park that was never executed. On the occasion of the fair, he hoped finally to see it realized, at least in part. In September 1890, with Burnham in charge of construction and Olmsted of landscaping, the operation got under way. Burnham brought in Root as consulting architect, and Olmsted was seconded by his assistant Harry Codman. This now seems the logical and natural choice, but it was not made without further complications and dissension.

While the site for the fairgrounds was still undecided, the organizers were inundated with architectural proposals. Among these, one that attracted some attention was that of E. S. Jenison, about whom almost nothing is known today. The design he presented to the Chicago Real Estate Board proposed a unitary solution: a remarkable structure in the form of an umbrella covering 193 acres, an area ten times that covered by the London Crystal Palace, which had boasted an extent four times greater than the surface covered by St. Peter's. "The [glass] roof at the central circle . . . would be 700 feet above the heads of the visitors on the floor. By day it would be a cloud. By night it could be made by electric lights a constellated sky."[23] The initial success of this proposal was very soon quashed by the American Institute of Architects, with which Burnham had certainly already begun to negotiate. In any case, there was a certain obvious provincialism in Jenison's proposal; an immense greenhouse is fascinating precisely because of its schematic quality, and it is the direct solution of a single problem, the necessity of a roof. Many years later Buckminster Fuller was to propose something similar on a still larger scale—covering the entire city of New York.

The limit of such designs lies in their narrow functional conception and rigidly technological ideology. They were admissible, indeed appropriate, in Europe, where the international fairs, especially the French ones after the London exposition of 1851, presented opportunities for technology, masked and impeded in the old cities, to triumph in its most obvious and authentic qualities. In America the situation was just the opposite; the cities already demonstrated the advancement of technology, and the fairs were occasions for filling the

Design for the Chicago South Park system by
Frederick Law Olmsted and Calvert Vaux,
1871.

Sectional view of proposed building for
the Columbian Exposition by E. S.
Jenison, published in the *Chicago Tribune*,
March 9, 1890.

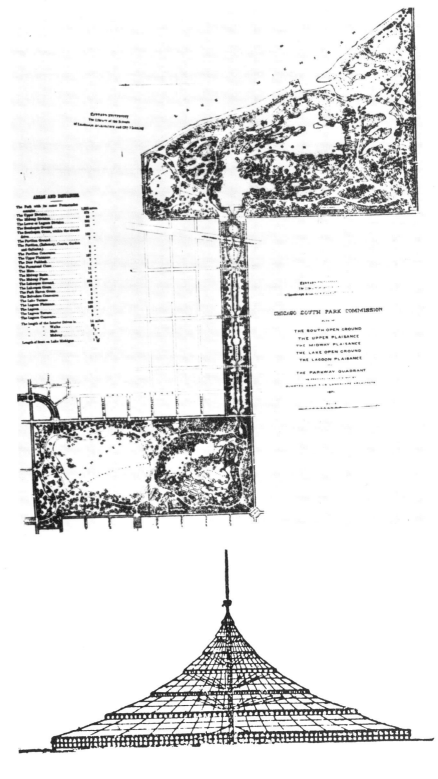

cultural void that results from the absence of historic centers. The concepts that the Columbian Exposition was called on to express were thus many and complex. First and foremost, however, it had to affirm Illinois's new position as a state no longer isolated but, rather, eager to ally itself with the forces of the East and to establish relations on the widest possible scale.

The *Chicago Tribune* of May 10, 1890, carried the first notice of a policy aimed at eliminating any improvisations: "The Jenison or any other building can be killed in face of the endorsement of the [Chicago Board of Directors of the Fair]. The directors are only an advisory organization. . . . Summed up, the [National] Commission has the powers: 1) to select the site, 2) to plan the buildings, 3) to determine the plan and scope of the exposition." In July the Chicago journal *Inland Architect* stated, "It is too soon to speak of the buildings, except that there will be no competition of any sort, but those architects who have shown decided ability in particular classes of work will be appointed from among the members of the profession throughout the country."[24] Jenison and his proposal were no longer discussed. The plan to commission nationally noted architects, which was the plan supported by Burnham, prevailed.[25]

The decision to seek the collaboration of the organizational and cultural centers of the East, particularly New York and Boston, may have been made when Chicago was selected as the site of the fair and may thus have been a policy imposed at the federal level. If so, Burnham's direct responsibility for the brusque stylistic reversal proclaimed by the architecture of the fair, so greatly emphasized by his detractors in their search for a Judas, would be considerably less.

Furthermore, the American Institute of Architects surely exerted the major influence in the decision to dispense with any competition and select outright certain major figures in American architecture. In such negotiations, of which Burnham was, of course, a part, the AIA, presided over by Richard Morris Hunt, obviously pressed for the selection of its own outstanding members (Western architects had been slow to join the AIA, in general). Burnham was the one to carry out the decision, but this fact, to my mind, does not make him a "traitor."[26] His role may more justly be defined as that of an increasingly convinced and enthusiastic mediator; otherwise the whole course of his subsequent activity is incomprehensible.

The preponderance of Eastern architects and their receipt of the most prestigious commissions were related to the choice of classicism as the architectural style of the principal buildings of the fair. This was an eclectic classicism, quite open to heretical motifs but conditioned by a supraindividual order that was reinforced by the consistent use of white. As opposed to the neomedieval style of laissez-faire, classicism signified stability, the end of the insecurity of the heroic period, and faith in the achievements of the established institutions. It also signified a relationship with the European architectural tradition, and one now free of the old sense of inferiority. Classicism provided American architecture—already certain of its power to surpass Europe in quantity—with the opportunity to prove itself qualitatively, on common stylistic grounds.

Finally, classicism meant consistency of building types and thus economy of design and efficiency of production. It also meant that the individualism of the hero-architects was replaced by the discipline of coordinated work required for control of the urban scale. Charles Zueblin later went so far as to claim that "The White City was the most socialistic achievement of history, the result of many minds inspired by a common aim working for the common good."[27]

The choice of the classical style, so sharply criticized by historians sympathetic to Sullivan's bitter condemnation, was thus an extremely coherent choice and perhaps even a necessary one. It went hand in hand, however, with the other fundamental choice, the importance of which has never been emphasized. This was the decision to construct temporary buildings that would appear to be very permanent. The choice of such a procedure reveals the remarkably lucid business sense of the men of Chicago. According to the law of maximum yield, efficiency depends on the precise definition of the relationship between end and means. If the end is to impress through both quantity and quality in a fair that lasts only a few months, the return will be maximized by cutting down on durability. At its most extreme, this principle calls for constructing as many buildings as possible and making them as monumental as possible at minimum cost—that is, building them of lath and plaster rather than of long-lasting materials.

In this way the fair became a performance of prestige and monumentality acted out by businessmen-magicians. Once the show was over, they just dismantled everything. There comes to mind the finale of Kafka's *Amerika*, in which young girls disguised as angels, with trumpets and great wings, balance on top of high hidden pedestals. The Columbian Exposition was undoubtedly kitsch, but it influenced twenty of the most significant years of American urban design.

The Marvels of the Fair

The most important area of the exposition architecturally was to be situated on the lake in Jackson Park, a vast, unconstructed trapezoidal terrain of 550 acres, including some wooded areas. The fairgrounds also extended inland through the other areas of the South Park System; among these were the long strip of the Midway Plaisance, where the foreign exhibitions, curiosities, and amusements were to be situated, and the 370-acre rectangle of Washington Park.

In Olmsted's unexecuted design for the South Park System, made in 1871, the rigid disposition of these three areas was disguised by the casual, fluid course of roadways and bodies of water. Jackson Park, the most beautiful part, was so enriched by a series of little lakes that it was renamed Lagoon Park. In the last months of 1890 this earlier plan was overridden by the necessity of constructing the huge block of the fair's principal buildings in this lakeshore area. It was apparently Codman who took over at this point and redesigned the layout of

Jackson Park, resolving the problem of the relationship between water and buildings by taking Venice as his model. Descriptions of the fair indeed invariably refer to Venice and even the idea—pure American kitsch—of importing authentic gondolas and gondoliers may have derived from Codman's inspiration.

The differences between Burnham, interpreter of the necessity of the largest possible block of buildings, and Olmsted, defender of his Lagoon Park, were resolved in concrete form in a large-scale drawing, in black and white pencil on brown paper, prepared by Codman and Root. This detailed plan, presented to the National Commission on December 1, 1890, was approved and "essentially" respected.[28] Root died in January 1891 and therefore could not defend the plan in the course of its execution. He would not have been able to do so in any case, however, because Burnham's letter commissioning the Eastern "masters," specifically stated, "Our consulting architect, Mr. Root, would act as your interpreter when you are absent without imparting into the work any of his own feelings."[29] By coincidence, in January 1893, Harry Codman too died before the inauguration of the fair.

Less care was given to devising a unified design for Midway Plaisance and Washington Park, decidedly secondary areas in comparison to the pretentious official quality of the Jackson Park complex. This very difference indicates a precise programmatic intention of establishing a contrast between the New World and the Old, in which the New was naturally favored. The United States section of the fair was the place of order, size, and efficiency, a marvel of grandeur and stability. The other sections were varied and interesting but not up-to-date, characteristic but not relevant to an evolved society.

The entire *mise en scène* confirmed and reinforced this effect. The immense complex of buildings in Jackson Park, the entrance area of the fair, immediately expressed hospitality and munificence. After the shock of admiration came the curiosities; once overwhelmed, the visitor could go on to make comparisons. Moreover, it was perhaps not simply by chance that the Women's Building was placed just at the point of contact between Jackson Park and the Midway, that is, just as one passed from the official area to that of the amusements. The strikingly evolved concept of this exhibit provided the sharpest contrast with the feudal wonders of the old civilizations displayed in the area just beyond.

Quality, in the highest sense of the term, and "values," simultaneously traditional and progressive, since they were taken from the noblest conventions of the past and directed toward the future, were confined to the American area of the fair, in Jackson Park. There their expression was entrusted to the grandiloquent equilibrium of symmetrical architectural masses, arranged on orthogonal axes, to the timeless prestige of the classical architectural orders, and to the vast dimensions of the spaces, volumes, and basins of water. The creation of all this was, in turn, entrusted to the sure hands of recognized New York architects who, through Burnham's mediation, held the dominant positions in the principal complex.[30]

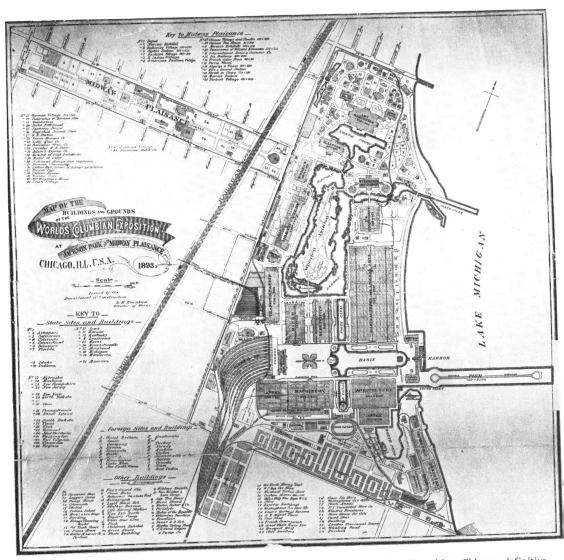

Columbian Exposition, Chicago, definitive plan of Jackson Park and Midway Plaisance, 1893.

Richard Morris Hunt, who was still president of the AIA in 1891,[31] received the most prestigious commission—the temple, so to speak. This was the Administration Building, a mammoth edifice on a centralized plan and covered with a dome, which constituted the compositional pivot of the Court of Honor. Because of its situation in respect to both entrances and to the rest of the exposition, it assumed the multiple functions of portico, central vestibule, and backdrop. The principal entrances to the fair faced west, for those arriving by rail, and east, for those arriving from Chicago by steamboat on the lake. The Court of Honor was laid out longitudinally precisely to connect these two distant points of access.

The Administration Building, located near the railroad station, presented an impressive foreground plane to visitors arriving from the west; as soon as they entered the monumental building, they discovered its immense interior void and, through its broad openings, grasped the principal compositional axes of the fair. Looking straight ahead, toward the lake, they discovered the imposing architectural space of the court, with its long basin of water, bridges, and fountains, and in the distant background glimpsed a view of Michigan.

The offices, stairs, and functional services of the octagonal Administration Building were confined to its perimeter, especially within its four huge piers. This arrangement allowed the visitor fully to appreciate the height and width of the dome; like that of Christopher Wren's St. Paul's, it was composed of an outer and an inner structure, the latter measuring 50 feet in diameter and rising 190 feet above floor level.

For those arriving by water, the effect was more gradual. On the lakefront two immense buildings served as scenographic wings framing the entrance of the Court of Honor. They were designed by the most authoritative of the New York architects, McKim, Mead and White, the designers of the Agricultural Building, and George B. Post, of the Manufactures Building. The monumental entrance-ways to the Court of Honor, opposite the steamboat pier, was the work of another New York architect, Charles B. Atwood, who was taken on after Root's death to fill his place. Atwood's work gave great luster to the classical style of the fair.

The other buildings on the Court of Honor were entrusted to Peabody and Stearns of Boston, the architects of the Machinery Building, and Van Brunt and Howe of Kansas City, designers of the Electricity Building. The only part of the Court of Honor entrusted to a Chicago architect was Solon S. Beman's Mines and Mining Building, which occupied the least prominent position.[32] The work of the other Chicago architects, among them figures of no less fame than Adler and Sullivan, and Jenney, the old master, were relegated to secondary positions outside the Court of Honor and on none of the dominant axes.

Sullivan's architectural talent and inventive capacity were unquestionably superior to those of the Eastern architects, with perhaps the exception of Post, but his resounding artistic vitality, recognized by everyone, was generated by a myth and a view of the architect's role that were no longer operative. Adler and Sullivan had expressed reservations about participating in the fair. The serious problems encountered in the construction of the Auditorium, the tower of which gradually settled and continued to sink for eleven years, had destroyed Adler's resilience and greatly weakened Sullivan's. It was inevitable that in respect to their eternal rival, Burnham, their position in the fair would be a weak one. At first Burnham assigned Sullivan the Music Hall, situated just at the entrance to the Court of Honor on the lakefront; later this commission was retracted and he was left with nothing, until Burnham proposed that Sullivan design the Transportation Building. According to Wright, this project caused Sullivan the "most trouble of anything he even did. . . . I had never seen him anxious before, but anxious he was then."[33] Certainly he must have regretted not having the strength to refuse Burnham's offer flatly.[34] (Root might also have been tempted to refuse, if he had still been alive.) Sullivan's rejection of white and of the classical style and his insistence on a formal experiment in the use of a large, splayed, semicircular portal, decorated with mosaics (a concept that was not new to him), placed him in a contentious minority. From this position he was to reemerge only with great effort and for only a brief period before he accepted his relegation to such a secondary role.

The immense polychrome arch of his Golden Door, interpreted by some as the architect's sunset,[35] is a stimulating and fecund image in the forceful simplicity of its geometric statement, which so frankly proclaims its existence as an object of attraction. In the complex of the fair, however, the Transportation Building must have appeared to be a curiosity to the common visitor; this may ultimately be a historically accurate evaluation of the architectural value of this work, which was so far inferior to Sullivan's other buildings. In the context of the architecture of the fair as a whole, it was an unusual and highly interesting expression of a culture that has been superseded but retains a sentimental attraction.

What triumphed, instead, in this context was Atwood's work. Together with Burnham, the general coordinator of the undertaking, he was the true protagonist of the fair, who designed all the key buildings of the main complex except for Hunt's Administration Building. Atwood's work included the monumental entrance on the lakefront, a structure comprising the Columbus Portico, the Casino, and the Music Hall, and, at the end of Jackson Park, the Fine Arts Building, which concluded the area celebrating American prestige. Described by the sculptor Augustus Saint-Gaudens as the most beautiful edifice "after the Parthenon," Atwood's Fine Arts Building was the only one eventually made permanent by replacing the lath and plaster with solid cement and limestone.[36]

After Root's death, when Burnham had been in need of a new right arm William R. Ware suggested Atwood, a Harvard graduate and a designer with the Boston firm of Ware and Van Brunt. Atwood's knowledge of the "Greek style" was acquired not only from his training in the school of classical design but also from his own personal studies. The man who was unanimously acclaimed and whose influence was preponderant in the fair (if it is true that he designed over sixty works for it) was not, like Hunt or McKim, a student of the Beaux Arts but, rather, a young man educated in the elite schools of the United States. Atwood's versatility would be demonstrated, moreover, by his work on one of the most extraordinary edifices of the Chicago Loop, the Reliance Building.

The most impressive architectural work of the fair was undoubtedly that of Post.[37] The Manufactures Building, it was stipulated, would be an enormous block, 1688 × 788 feet (an area of over 30 acres), the height of which was fixed at 60 feet from ground to cornice according to a rule established for all the buildings on the Court of Honor. Like all the other buildings on the court, it had to be in the classical style, but a block with these proportions would inevitably appear flattened in its volume, so that its compositional treatment could in no way conform to the terms of a classical palace.

Post accepted these disconcerting specifications, and, rather than dividing the block into compositional parts of more usual and workable proportions, he took the stipulated conditions to the extreme and resolved the architectural problem by rethinking the building types of classical antiquity. In this way, he came to realize the working possibilities contained in the image of the ancient city wall—not inappropriately, since one of his building's roles was to delimit the White City on the lakeside. Post conceived a long wall through which a garden was to be glimpsed, arranged within a vast open rectangular court at the center of the block. In defining this concept architecturally, Post derived his long facades from the continuous rhythm of the regularly arched Roman aqueduct. For the axial entrances he borrowed the motif of a triumphal arch with three openings as in the Arch of Constantine; for the architectural solution of the angles, an arch with a single opening such as the Arch of Titus. The idea of a walled court held up until it became necessary to increase the exhibition space within the building. Even this alteration did not ruffle Post; despite the gigantic dimensions of the court, 1287 × 387 feet, he decided to cover it with an iron and glass vault, which retained the effect of a central opening. This solution, of course, had precedents in the Paris expositions of the second half of the nineteenth century.

Post's method was described with great lucidity, as well as with a certain naiveté, by his colleague Henry Van Brunt: "Indeed, this design as a whole admirably illustrates the fact that reservation rather than expenditure of force is the secret of the noble art. The modern architectural mind is an archaeological chaos of ideas inherited from Egypt, from the Far East, from Greece and Rome, from the middle ages, and from the Renaissance. Under these circumstances the highest virtue which can be exercised by the educated architect of today is self-denial in the use of his treasures."[38]

Columbian Exposition, Chicago, general
scheme in a contemporary print.

Columbian Exposition, Chicago, looking
toward the entrance of the Court of
Honor from the lake.

Columbus Portico, Columbian Exposition, Chicago, forming the entrance to the Court of Honor from the lake, designed by Charles B. Atwood.

Columbian Exposition, Chicago, view of the main complex.

The compositional scheme of the much-praised and much-damned White City, was, like this statement by Van Brunt, rather rigid and ingenuous. The implicit attempt to create, as if by magic, a fragment of an ideal, "historical" city failed for lack of anyone who was able really to form and control the external spaces. Root had never demonstrated this ability, and, in any case, he died too soon. Codman, according to Burnham, had a "knowledge of formal settings . . . greater than that of all the others put together. . . . He never failed."[39] But Codman's contribution seems to have been limited to the detailed design and decoration of the free spaces, rather than the disposition of the large volumes. And Burnham had not yet acquired, or at least did not yet make use of, the notable skills he was later to demonstrate as a town designer. The difference between the capabilities of the landscapers and those of the architects is indeed striking. Olmsted and Codman showed consummate skill in the handling of roadways, water, and greenery. Clumsy and awkward by contrast were the spaces between the large buildings, where the water was rigidly configured in wide canals bordered by the Venetian-inspired walkways running along the water at the foot of the buildings.[40] These external spaces, voids between closed building blocks, appear to have been conceived without any clear and convincing system of structural relationships.

The compositional scheme was based on several perspective axes, but except for the main one passing through Atwood's entrance and Hunt's Administration Building, all were very indistinct. Because of the centrally placed canals, moreover, visitors could not walk along the principal axes, and their layout was thus difficult to grasp. Passing along the walkways bordering the canals, the visitor was instead brought up close to the gigantic buildings; stunned by the overwhelming effect of the nearby architectural elements he perceived the other volumes and facades as a confused and endlessly projected reflection. The scheme of Venice, valid in the continuous urban structure without perspectives for which it was created, had quite evidently betrayed the designers of the White City.

The visitors' descriptions that have come down to us often seem to respond to the impossibility of raising the eyes from the ground without receiving a shock from the extraordinary, disconcerting mass of the buildings, rather than from their formal impressiveness and authority. The sense of bewilderment, of "it's too much for me," they expressed must ultimately have stemmed from the impossibility of grasping the general layout and consequently from complete disorientation.

In this confusion, what actually became most evident, most readily perceptible, was the more craftsmanlike work of the sculptors (almost all Italians) who had reproduced, with incredible rapidity and on a gigantic scale, models made by American and French artists. Absolutely essential in this maze was the work of Frank D. Millet, chief of decorations, who controlled the scenic "effects" of the whole exposition. Millet coordinated tones and colors as well as the infinite variety of decorations, pennants, flags, lights, and water displays; in short, he planned the kitsch.

Among the critics, the most feared were not the Americans, all of whom were involved to some degree in the heroic undertaking, but the Europeans. Indeed, men such as Joseph Stübben surely did not allow themselves to be taken in.[41] Comparison with Europe was the constant objective of the reporters and immortalizers of the fair, who incessantly found analogues of the dimensions and characteristics of the various pavilions in European historical monuments: the Manufactures Building was three times as large as St. Peter's and four times as large as the Colosseum; the dome of the Administration Building was 42 feet higher than that of Hardouin-Mansart's Invalides, 45 feet higher than that of Soufflot's Pantheon, almost the same height as the dome of Wren's St. Paul's, and only 90 feet lower than that of St. Peter's.

The most tempting comparison, however, was with the most recent Parisian exposition and its extraordinary Eiffel Tower. Once Jenison's striking proposal had been rejected, however, this comparison was not easy. Nevertheless the reference was made. Ralph wrote, "The Manufactures Building, designed by Mr. George Post . . . will bear the same relation to this Exposition as the Eiffel Tower did to that of Paris of 1889." The statement was naturally followed by the comparative dimensions.[42] Another structure that aspired to this crucial comparison was the Ferris Wheel. Indeed, it was created in direct response to Burnham's public challenge to the civil engineers of the country to create something to rival the Eiffel Tower. What George Washington Gale Ferris proposed and built with great difficulty was a wheel similar to that of a bicycle, 250 feet in diameter, on which rotated thirty-six cabins, each capable of carrying forty people.[43] A proposal also exists for a gigantic tower designed by George S. Morison but never built, which was to be 1,135 feet high and thus 150 feet higher than the Eiffel Tower.[44]

In reality the work most comparable to the Eiffel Tower—and it is difficult to say whether or not its author was conscious of the fact—was Hunt's Administration Building. Its position within the great court and its basic structure of four huge piers bring to mind, especially in the plan, the Parisian tower of 1889. Thus the hand symbolically extended to foreign countries by the fair was quite clearly ready for an accord as well as a conflict; in this respect the fair resembled the Open Door policy that McKinley would institute a few years later and that would function, to all intents and purposes, as imperialism.

The participation of foreign countries, even the smallest and most distant, was, indeed, very extensive; the only notable absentees were Italy and Portugal. Diplomatic relations between Italy and the United States had been broken off in the early months of 1891, after a mass lynching in New Orleans that resulted from an outburst of hostility against the Italian immigrants.[45] Diplomatic

Ferris Wheel, Columbian Exposition,
Chicago, designed by the engineer George
Washington Gale Ferris. The wheel was
250 feet in diameter and carried thirty-six
cabins, each capable of holding forty people,
who could thus be raised rapidly to a great
height.

relations were restored the next year when an American commission was sent to Italy, but by then the most that Italy could do was to send gondolas and gondoliers, Murano glass, and the queen's lace.

Countries toward which the Open Door policy would be particularly directed participated in large numbers. This was the case notably of Japan that had been well represented even at the 1876 exposition in Philadelphia and had now sent to Chicago, among other things, an impressive wooden temple. This structure, "ready made in Japan," was the Phoenix House, which actually survived until destroyed by a fire during the Second World War. Russia, too, was conspicuously represented with a crafts exhibition. Among the European nations, Germany, absent in Paris and now wishing to regain its position, participated impressively.

The organizers succeeded admirably in blending together all the foreign material, from the most serious and prestigious to the curiosities and horrors from the underdeveloped countries. As in Paris in 1889, the Middle Eastern countries presented reconstructions of characteristic streets with artisans' shops and minarets from which a muezzin called the public of the fair to prayer; they also sent belly dancers, who were a novel and unexpected feature and represented, for the times, a shocking display of wantonness. Scorpion eaters and snake charmers mingled in the Midway Plaisance with popcorn vendors from New York, who made $100,000 in sales, and the chewing-gum sellers, who apparently fared no worse.

Among the curiosities, which were certainly the most popular and amusing aspect of the fair, the gondolas on the water and the Chinese rickshaws in the squares and on the roadways must have been a great success. Even in the amusement area, situated principally along the Midway, the objects displayed to the public were of two types: testimonies of the Old World, which were intended to create an archaic, fablelike atmosphere through surprise or horror, and New World artifacts intended to surprise visitors in a different way, generating admiration for the technological miracles that had produced them. This was the ultimate aim of the Ferris Wheel, which made it possible for tens of thousands of people to be raised far above this flat terrain and finally view the whole of the fair, together with the skyscrapers of the Loop. Similar was the impression made by the Circular Railway Tower, placed exactly at the entrance to the long strip of the Midway, immediately after the Women's Building; along a spiral track a train powered by electricity ascended the tower and descended by means of gravity.

One foreign "marvel," however, was certainly not in keeping with the Old World's assigned role of providing amusement. The Krupp works exhibition presented a threatening technical display of such unexpected dimensions and weight that—to the embarrassment of the organizers—the material (cannon, naturally, and other armaments) could not be unloaded in the port of New York. To find an adequate berth, the ship carrying the exhibit had to go on to Sparrows Point, Maryland; the cannon, which were said to weigh 122 tons, ultimately arrived in Chicago in railway cars specially built by the American companies according to Krupp's design.

Among the United States displays, the Naval Exhibition, the architecture of which was probably not of great importance and which has been overlooked by most historians, produced a strong effect on the visitors. The building, which was shaped exactly like a ship, completely equipped, was designed by Frank W. Grogan, under the direction of the high level naval officials. The guide books of the epoch extolled the absolute originality of this building, but it was not actually unique. Since 1891 an extraordinary building in the form of a ship had existed practically in Chicago—more precisely, in Michigan, about half a mile from the lakeshore—though it was largely unknown. It housed the exclusive Argonaut Club, which listed the most famous names of the world of finance among its members. Establishing the club in a real anchored ship was made impossible by a treaty with England, which forbade the presence of naval forces on the Great Lakes. Apparently it was Root's idea to build a cement and masonry ship with two habitable floors and an attic; along with Burnham, he was a member of the club. Its exclusiveness helps to explain its omission from the guide books and the critics' silence about this structure, which was one of Root's last works and today no longer exists. If drawings relative to this project could be found, their study might provide interesting information about Root's innovative design concepts and his sources of inspiration.[46]

The greatest surprise of the fair, however, and probably the most "progressive" in the view of many visitors, was the Women's Building. This pavilion was the result of a highly successful organization of feminists, nationally as well as in Chicago, led by Bertha Honoré (Mrs. Potter) Palmer, a Chicago society leader and wife of one of Chicago's financial giants who was also an outstanding figure in the Democratic party. Fourteen women, all under twenty-five, entered the competition for the design of the pavilion. The winner was the twenty-one-year-old Sophia G. Hayden of Boston, a graduate of the Massachusetts Institute of Technology, who submitted a staid and elegant design in the classical manner of an English architectural handbook, with a profusion of sculptural decoration. The execution of this decoration was entrusted exclusively to women sculptors,[47] selected competitively from all the states of the Union. The project gave a great boost to the feminist movement everywhere; in fact, the whole initiative was a move on the part of the "liberals," who were certainly viewed with disapproval in the Southern states and among the immigrants but were tolerated by the Republican organizers of the fair.

In this case as in others, the wonders of technology were provided as means of convincing dissenters: demonstrations of model kitchens, mechanized household appliances and modern furnishings; an enormous functioning kindergarten where mothers could leave their children in order to enjoy a more serene visit to the fair; a hospital perfectly equipped for any eventuality; displays of books written or edited by women; and even an exhibition of technological inventions by women.

Agreement about the technical progress that had been made, whether it was the work of female or of male hands, was complete; conservatives and progressives, Republicans and Democrats were of one mind about the duty of demonstrating the United States' advanced technological standing to the rest of the world. It was therefore only natural that the exhibit of the Electricity Building should assume a great importance; this department was directed by Professor J. P. Barrett of Nevada, who had been curator of the electricity pavilion at Frankfurt in 1891 and who enlisted Thomas A. Edison as one of his collaborators. The building for the exhibit, designed by Van Brunt and Howe of Kansas City, was a disconcerting conglomeration of Italian architectural styles, including ancient Roman, Renaissance, Venetian and Roman Mannerism, and Roman Baroque (Van Brunt put aside his theories about good architecture in his work for the Fair). At night the building, with its many towers, became a marvel of light. It contained the best the contemporary electrical industry had to offer, including washing machines and electrical household equipment of every type, but it also included less practical items, such as a minaret made entirely of Bohemian glass and illuminated like a huge lantern. Everywhere in the building the visitor was accompanied by the sounds of a large orchestra performing in New York, transmitted over telephone lines.[48]

Telephones appeared again, connected with all parts of the world, in a room of the department of publicity and promotion. This department, directed by the famous journalist Major Moses P. Handy, was the center of all information services at the fair. One of the most basic was the dissemination of printed images of the fair itself; the official edition of these, sold by the hundreds of thousands, made use primarily of a series of watercolors by Charles Graham, rather than of photographs.

Among the technological marvels were pyramids of extraordinarily white salt and an exhibition of models and actual functioning equipment demonstrating Bessemer's original system for manufacturing steel, all in the Mines and Mining Building designed by Beman. The Fisheries Building, the exterior of which was designed in the Romanesque style (and therefore not in the Court of Honor), gave the Chicago architect Henry Ives Cobb an occasion for decorating his capitals with tangles of algae and fish of every kind. The total water capacity of the various aquariums was 140,000 gallons. In order to secure the supply of 80,000 gallons of salt water necessary for the marine aquariums, sea water was evaporated to about one-fifth to facilitate its transportation and expanded to its proper density by adding fresh water supplied from Lake Michigan. Technical data of this sort were promulgated by the publicity department and, often in exaggerated form, became part of the fair's mythology. Thus 138,218 electric bulbs were said to have been lit every evening, or the quantity of steel necessary to cover the immense court of Post's building was stated to be enough to build two Brooklyn Bridges.

Another objective of the fair, rather more timidly expressed, was to demonstrate to the rest of the world that America too had a history. A recent history,

German Pavilion, Columbian Exposition,
Chicago.

English Pavilion, Columbian Exposition,
Chicago.

Fisheries Building, Columbian Exposition,
Chicago, designed by Henry Ives Cobb.

but still inseparably connected, according to Herbert Spencer's philosophy of evolution, to the rest of the history of mankind. A great deal of material expressing this idea was concentrated in the Transportation Building, collected from all over the world by Willard A. Smith, the dynamic director of the department. Egyptian canoes, Chinese, Brazilian, Eskimo, and Viking boats, Roman chariots, and endless other vehicles traced the evolution of transportation down to the Vanderbilt railroad system, the New York Central, which exhibited a full-scale replica of its first station as well as an example of a fully equipped and completely modern one.

Assessments of the Fair: Sentimental and Critical

"Everyone says one ought to sell all one has and mortgage one's soul to go there, it is esteemed such a revelation of beauty. People cast away all sin and baseness, burst into tears, and grow religious." Such was the ironical comment of the fair attributed to William James.[49] For Henry Thurston Peck, on the other hand, the fair "revealed to millions of Americans, whose lives were necessarily colorless and narrow, the splendid possibilities of art, and the compelling power of the beautiful."[50] Hundreds of thousands of visitors were subjected to an aesthetic and cultural shock; thus Paul Bourget described "many merry faces . . . but everywhere the serious attention of minds imperfectly grasping new ideas."[51]

Obviously, an objective assessment of the fair cannot be based on the enthusiastic views of those, such as Ralph, who were dedicated to the undertaking from the outset. Equally unacceptable, however, are the preconceived and biased judgments of its debunkers, whose comments on the fair were almost always made years later.[52]

Among the optimistic voices was the graciously measured judgment of Alice Freeman Palmer, who had been president of Wellesley College; for her the fair was an achievement of brotherhood, a lesson in "obedience, sympathy, dignity."[53] She also noted the educational aspect of the fair and the American people's extraordinary capacity and will to learn. Almost all the balance sheets on the fair emphasized the optimistic prospects it opened for the future: the previously unhoped-for possibility of an ordered, coordinated organization that in turn could make possible a better life. This organization was seen not as something imposed from without but, rather, as the result of authentic American capabilities. Mrs. Schuyler Van Rensselaer, the noted art critic, writing on the "artistic triumph" of the fair, exclaimed: "We have done it—we ourselves, the American people, without foreign help or counsel. . . . We ought never again to be tempted to commit the unpardonable sin—to 'despair of the Republic'— having seen that the Republic is capable of supremely successful effort in intellectual as well as in political paths."[54] The achievement of a new unity in American culture and practice, which would also serve as a lasting model for the future, was credited to the fair even by those who had reservations on the way it was obtained.

It is indeed in this sense that Zueblin spoke of the White City as a "socialistic achievement." His enthusiasm, like that of Charles Eliot Norton, Sylvester Baxter, Edward Everett Hale, and Olmsted himself, was part of a trend of nationalist thought, based on a collectivist ideal that had found its expression in Edward Bellamy's *Looking Backward*. What, in fact, could be better for a middle class shaken by the class struggle (Bellamy's novel appeared just two years after the Haymarket incident) than a utopia based not on the rejection of capitalism but, rather, on its perfection and development? Bellamy foresaw the possibility of prosperity within a peaceful, happy, efficient cooperative system, where the loyalty and productivity of the workers are guaranteed by the militarization of industries and where the end of free competition coincides with the defeat of all conflict and violence. Julian West, Bellamy's protagonist, is incredulous; is it possible, he wonders, to pass from a condition of nearly complete chaos to perfect order and ideal stability in a little more than a hundred years?[55] His host in the year 2000, Dr. Leete, is able to reassure him, however; the achievement is guaranteed by the transformation of human society into a single great corporation.

The White City could well represent the physical form of the peaceable, rational future world that Bellamy describes: "We might ... have much larger incomes, individually, if we chose so to use the surplus of our product, but we prefer to expend it upon public works and pleasures in which all share, upon public halls, and buildings, art galleries, bridges, statuary, means of transit, and the conveniences of our cities, great musical and theatrical exhibitions, and in providing on a vast scale for the recreations of the people." The "large open squares ... with ... statutes ... and fountains" and the "public buildings of a colossal size and ... architectural grandeur" that Julian West sees in the America of 2000 share a common expressive intent with the architecture of the fair.

The publication of *Looking Backward* and the Columbian Exposition were, in fact, two of the most popular and successful events in the United States in the late nineteenth century. Undeniably, their outlook was identical. It is in terms of this outlook that we can understand Olmsted's judgment of the fair, which certainly dealt more with its content than with its form: "Comparing this experience with some in my earlier professional life, I can but think that it manifests an advance in civilization."[56]

The voices of the debunkers, on the other hand, were uncompromising, and precisely by this fact they are revealed as the expressions of a minority. Sullivan was the author of the most provocative and best-known condemnation of the fair, which culminated resoundingly: "Thus did the virus of a culture, snobbish and alien to the land perform its work of disintegration; and thus ever works the pallid academic mind." The crowds came and looked and, according to Sullivan, went away carrying a contagion. "For what they saw was not at all what they believed they saw, but an imposition of the spurious upon their eyesight, a naked exhibition of charlatanry in the higher feudal and domineering culture, conjoined with expert salesmanship of the materials of decay." Like all the other condemnations of the fair and of Burnham, however, Sullivan's famous prediction that "the damage wrought by the World's Fair will last for half a century . . . if not longer" was expressed only thirty years later.[57]

An ethical criticism reminiscent of Ruskin came, also very late, from Claude Bragdon: "All was a simulacrum: the buildings, the statues and the bridges were not of enduring stone, but lath and plaster . . . the civic guards and chair-men were impecunious students, and the crowds were composed not of free citizens of the place, but the slaves . . . of the Aladdin's lamp of competitive commerce."[58] If Bragdon is denouncing the system and if his last phrase is true, is not all the rest then absolutely coherent? The White City's Hollywood-style spectacle of "eternal values" in lath and plaster was an essentially popular conception, far more readily accessible than the cosmic ideology of the rising (or setting) sun of Sullivan's Golden Door. Whose triumph is represented by this golden arch if not Sullivan's own? It is a symbol too aristocratic, too lacking in irony, for the crowd of "slaves" of the system, who must, even if only for the weekend , have felt like *cives romani.*

Emblematically, Sullivan's circular arc expressed his dedication to the intellectual heritage of the transcendentalists, which he was to transmit to a new generation (that is, to Frank Lloyd Wright). Another circular arc, this time with a six-mile radius, was to be traced around Chicago sixteen years later by Burnham. Responding to the reality of production, with all its contradictions, this other controversial master was to explore the limits of formal control on the far vaster scale of urban design. Both—and this is the fundamental point—remain in the architectural history books. A comparison of the two is of interest, however, for the different degrees of detachment from or acceptance of reality it reveals in their respective ideological positions.

Sullivan's Transportation Building was nevertheless a success with the most feared critics, the French masters of the Ecole des Beaux Arts.[59] They were, however, very hard on the Court of Honor, which they considered an overly ambitious attempt with deluding results. *"On me dit que les bâtiments sont des anciens concours des Beaux Arts,"* commented a well-known French painter whom Schuyler quotes but does not identify.[60] And, in Sigfried Giedion's words, "the 'beauties' of the Fair were taken out of the preserve jars of the Académie des Beaux Arts, where they had been laid up during what was certainly its worst period."[61] Rather than continue with such attacks on this first Yankee foray into the "great world of culture," however, it seems more interesting to note the uniqueness of the experiment actually undertaken: the transposition onto a massive scale, for the ephemeral purposes of the fair, of the results of the specialized endeavors of many generations of Europe's architectural elite.

Transportation Building, Columbian Exposition, Chicago, by Adler and Sullivan, which represented Sullivan's protest against the fair in its rejection of the unifying directive that called for the use of white and the classical style.

Golden Door of the Transportation Building, extravagantly decorated in mosaic and gold, interpreted by some as "Sullivan's sunset."

This reflection, possible from the vantage point of modern historical studies, could not, however, be expected from the contemporaries of the Chicago exposition. Instead, the only work that appeared at the time to compete with the French "masters" was Sullivan's Transportation Building. The French, in fact, honored him for it, but the medals Sullivan received from the Union Centrale des Arts Décoratifs were certainly not granted in recognition of his "functionalism," which was to be so greatly praised by Lewis Mumford and Giedion, but rather for his ornamentation. The admiration of the French critics did not entirely please Sullivan, who omitted any mention of the medals from his autobiography.[62] They did, however, provide the basis for Bragdon's reckless conjectures about the American origins of Art Nouveau and the impact on Paris of casts, drawings, and photographs smuggled out of Chicago.[63]

Bourget was more circumspect, like all those writing under the influence of recent impressions of the exposition; he advanced the theory that the fair was the starting point of something different: "The White City of Jackson Park . . . is not an apotheosis, it is a hope. It is not an end, it is a commencement. It is not a result, it is a promise. . . . These enormous splendid palaces of a day . . . do not realize the absolute originality of Emerson's dream, but they prove that the merely colossal, unaccompanied by grace and symmetry, can no longer satisfy the taste of their builders."[64]

The concept of the fair as the herald of a new coordination in American life was also to inform Henry Adams's interesting evaluation. Writing in 1918, he recalled his bewildering impressions of the fair in 1893: "Since Noah's ark, no such Babel of loose and ill-joined, such vague and ill-defined and unrelated thoughts and half-thoughts. . . . One sat down to ponder on the steps beneath Richard Hunt's dome almost as deeply as on the steps of the Aracoeli, and much to the same purpose."[65] Yet he concluded his recollections with this significant, terse judgment: "Chicago was the first expression of American thought as a unity; one must start there."[66]

What is implicit in the apparent contradiction between Adams's impressions and his conclusion was stated more explicitly by Charles Eliot Norton: "The great Fair was indeed a superb and appropriate symbol of our great nation, in its noble general design and in the inequalities of its execution; in its unexampled display of industrial energy and practical capacity, in the absence of the higher works of the creative imagination; in its incongruities, its mingling of noble realities and ignoble pretences, in its refinements cheek-by-jowl with vulgarities, in its order and its confusion—in its heterogeneousness and its unity."[67] For Norton, whose views did not lack lucidity, the value of the fair lay in its most conspicuous aspect, that of an amusement, a great exterior show of staged effects. Schuyler also emphasized this aspect in his contribution to the controversy over the exposition, written immediately after its closing, in which he characterized its architecture as "holiday building" as opposed to "work-a-day building." "The White City," he continued, "is the most integral, the most extensive, the most illusive piece of scenic architecture that has ever been seen. . . . It is the capital of No Man's Land. . . . In Turner's fantasies we have its prototype."[68]

Schuyler was a serious critic who analyzed the facts and avoided prophecies. Nevertheless, almost without intending it, he anticipated the City Beautiful idea when he spoke with alarm of the possibility of copying the fair's architecture and producing for one's hometown "a miniature plaza, with a little Administration Building and a little Machinery Hall." Schuyler preferred judgments based on proven principles to prophecies and reflected, "Those of us who believe that architecture is the correlation of structure and function, that if it is to be real and living and progressive, its forms must be the results of material and construction, sometimes find ourselves reproached with our admiration for the palaces in which this belief is so conspicuously ignored and set at naught." Many years later Fiske Kimball was to pronounce a similar judgment on the architecture of the fair: "The issue, whether function should determine form from within or whether an ideal form might be imposed from without, had been decided for a generation by a sweeping victory for the formal ideal."[69] It is clear that the losers were Sullivan and the whole "organic" tradition.

Schuyler defended Sullivan when Burnham accused the experimentalists of the Chicago school of designing "incoherent originalities."[70] Any such interpretation of the Transportation Building must be emphatically rejected, he argued, basing his views on principles completely different from those of the eulogizers of Sullivan and his famous Golden Door (by which Schuyler, moreover, was not persuaded). Instead, for Schuyler, the Transportation Building was not incoherent, because, unlike all the other buildings of the fair, it did not deny its structure of lath and plaster but expressed it. According to Schuyler's interpretation, which no one else seems to have shared, what Sullivan had consciously produced was an authentic architecture in plaster, inspired by the only style offering such a prototype, that of Saracen interiors. Even in Saracen architecture, however, the exteriors were not of plaster. Thus Sullivan's deflection from current stylistic conventions in this work, Schuyler argued, was due not to incoherent originality but, rather, to the fact that "there is no such thing as an exterior architecture of plaster in the world."[71]

It is difficult to judge the acuteness of Schuyler's observations from the photographs that remain. In any case, the Transportation Building must have been a questionable work. Indeed, Sullivan himself seems to have doubted its validity: Years later he wrote: "It was here that one man's unbalanced mind spread a gauze-like pall of fatality. That one man's unconscious stupor in bigness, and in the droll phantasy of hero-worship, did his best and his worst, according to his lights, which were dim except for one projector by the harsh light of which he saw all things illuminated and grown bombastically big in Chauvinistic outlines."[72] Perhaps the initial uncertainty expressed by the defenders of the "old" Chicago school stemmed from the limited success of Sullivan's building. The young men of the "new" school were inspired and stimulated less by the Transportation Building than by Ho-o-den, the little Japanese pavilion on Wooded Isle in the lake in Jackson Park.[73]

Sullivan, however, avenged himself with the publication of his autobiography in 1923. In 1931 Lewis Mumford, not yet born at the time of the fair, was to write, "The continuity of American architectural tradition was broken, and instead of advancing solidly toward modern forms, our architects wandered for forty years in the barren wilderness of classicism and eclecticism."[74] This thesis reigned for several decades; any different interpretation of the facts, even when pronounced by authoritative voices, remained without echo. A case in point was the interesting and little-known interpretation of Werner Hegemann, who discerned a "truth" exactly the opposite of that seen by Mumford, Giedion, and Bruno Zevi. Writing in 1936, Hegemann sharply criticized the masters of the "native" school—Richardson, Root, and Sullivan—and, along with them, Mumford himself, whom he severely reproached for his ideological viewpoint and the partiality of his judgment, which had ordained the absolute primacy of Frank Lloyd Wright.[75] More recently, even critics of very different persuasions, such as Leonardo Benevolo and Vincent Scully, have moderated both the enthusiasm for the fair and the condemnation of it by avoiding the exclusively ethical interpretation to which "martyrdom" (in the case, Sullivan's) so often dangerously inclines historians.

The achievement of a new coordination and unity, which opened the way to a practice of urban design that would soon make its first experiments, was a positive result of the fair and recognized even by many of its detractors, such as Bragdon.[76] In opposition to this positive and stimulating aspect, however, the fair also promoted the completely ideological, pathetic and ambiguous intellectual attempt to resuscitate "eternal values," or, in other words, to recover the "aura" that Walter Benjamin defined the specific characteristic of the art of the past. In this case, however, the "aura" was without permanence, that is, it lacked the authority possessed by genuine works of the past to indicate unequivocally a time and place. On the contrary, the fair was not governed by the dimensions of reality; its appearance was attributed by a great many writers to Aladdin's lamp. It also disappeared as if by magic; no one seems to have drawn attention to the strange fire that, on January 8, 1894, destroyed almost everything.[77] Except for the works exhibited, which in some cases were authentic masterpieces brought from the Old World, everything newly created was kitsch—kitsch on a giant scale that altered the very "value" of the objects displayed, affected even the authenticity of the public, and, indeed, deformed history itself. The Indians who replaced the traditional barbarians in the reliefs of the triumphal arch of Atwood's entrance became comic-strip characters.

The closing of the Fair generated responses typical of the end of a momentous event, such as this editorial comment that was reprinted in *Public Opinion:* "That those superb buildings, on which so much labor, ingenuity and skill have been expended, should be doomed to speedy destruction, that those magnificent collections of statuary, painting, bronzes, precious exhibits of all sorts, those archaeological and scientific treasures, brought at such trouble and expense from all quarters of the globe, should be disarranged and dispersed, never certainly to be all collected again, is reason enough to give a pathetic coloring to the memories of the Great Fair."[78] Seen in this light, the closing of the fair was a farewell to the world of "values," a sort of bonfire of ideologies on a global scale, after which nothing would be as before; other, new roads would now have to be followed.

In his role of proud guardian of the old Emersonian individualism, Sullivan naturally inveighed against this indicated change of direction. Burnham, on the other hand, had for some time been seeking the new roads that now opened before him. He was convinced that the Beaux Arts provided the correct course, as demonstrated by his attempt to send the young Wright to the Ecole des Beaux Arts, in order to make him into the greatest designer of cities of modern times.[79] This story is recounted by Wright himself and must therefore be essentially true. Who, in fact, could have been a better replacement for Root than Wright?

Burnham asked Edward C. Waller, a noted businessman, to invite Wright to his home, and together they tried to persuade the young man, whose natural rebellious spirit had already taken a radical turn under the influence of Sullivan. When asked if he was aware of the immense success of the fair and the lasting impression it had made on the public, Wright replied that Sullivan was not of the same mind and that Root and Richardson would not agree either if they were alive. But, Burnham insisted, architecture was going to follow a different path from the one indicated by those men, and he was therefore offering to send Wright to Paris—at his expense—to study at the Beaux Arts; he would even support Wright's family in America for the whole four-year period (according to Burnham, nothing less than four years could cancel out the influence of Richardson and Sullivan). On Wright's return, he would join Burnham's firm on a permanent basis. "I saw myself," Wright wrote years later, "influential, prosperous, safe; saw myself a competent leader of the majority rule. . . . It was all . . . too easy and unexciting." No, Wright could not "run away"; it was a question of "keeping faith"—that is, of keeping faith with Usonia, the name Wright was later to give to the myth of an America that does not exist.[80]

Burnham, of course, did not work for that myth, and the episode demonstrates the determination and foresight with which he strove to achieve his own goals. If he had not been almost fifty, he would himself have gone to study in Paris. He was, however, to undertake something very similar, a series of carefully planned trips in the Old World. Without this experience, he felt himself unprepared for the great undertaking he had fixed upon.

It is significant, although the fact has never been emphasized by historians and critics, that Burnham was not himself the architect of any of the fair buildings. He could certainly have reserved for himself—at least with Root, who was still alive when the commissions were given out—the design of one of the important buildings. Instead, Burnham accepted the role of coordinator and in this position he also unhesitatingly accepted classicism, imposing it as the norm and thus opening the way for its further development. Yet he himself remained an experimentalist of the Chicago school, as he was to demonstrate immediately after the crisis of 1893, when, with Root's place filled by Atwood, his designs for buildings in the Loop created for Chicago two of the major works of the "old school": the Reliance Building of 1895 and the Fisher Building of 1896.

Like the Monadnock Building, the Reliance Building poses a problem of attribution, since a first design had been made by Root in 1890. In this case, however, contemporary documentation leaves no doubt; only the ground floor, in granite, follows Root's design.[81] Atwood is designated as designer in this project, which probably means he was responsible for the working drawings. Despite his collaboration, Burnham was not induced to classicism in the Reliance Building, even if in these same years his studio did produce a bank in the Greek style.[82] On the contrary, it was Atwood who was here persuaded to participate in keeping with the boldest anticlassical principles of the "old" Chicago school. Nor would the skyscrapers subsequently designed by Burnham's firm contradict this tendency.

In the meantime, a second-hand classicism, the inspiration for which was attributed not unjustly to the fair, was spreading ever more widely in American architecture, but affecting naturally only routine production and not the work of the qualified studios. Sullivan described the phenomenon caustically: "By the time the market had been saturated, all sense of reality was gone. In its place had come deep-seated illusions, hallucinations, absence of pupilary reaction to light, absence of knee reaction—symptoms all of progressive cerebral meningitis: the blanketing of the brain."[83] And Schuyler amused himself by publishing in the *Architectural Record* a satirical advertisement that was nonetheless surprisingly plausible:

Prospectus
of the
Classic Design and Detail Co.
(incorporated)
Capital -------- $1,000,000
You Get the Job, We Do the Rest

To the Architectural Profession:
It is well known that the chief drawback of the successful practice of architecture in the United States is the enormous burden imposed upon the architect by his office expenses. . . .

Photographs of the construction of the Reliance Building in Chicago, designed by Charles B. Atwood of D. H. Burnham and Company, published in the *Architectural Record*, Jan.-Mar. 1895.

This condition of affairs is entirely unnecessary, in the actual condition of architecture in this country....

Thanks to the beneficent influence of "The White City" at Chicago, and the increasing number of graduates of the Beaux Arts embarking in the profession, the classic revival in the country is now securely established. . . . It is no longer necessary for an architect to design anything.[84]

Burnham certainly did not succumb to the attraction of facile routine. The dimension of classicism he wanted to exploit was that of urban design, but he knew too little and had seen too little in America. Thus on January 28, 1896, together with his wife and her parents, the Shermans, he departed from the Old World; on February 7 he passed the Pillars of Hercules. His itinerary began with visits to the Riviera, Carthage, Malta, Alexandria, and Cairo. In Egypt he met Mr. and Mrs. Harry W. Oliver, with whom he visited the Pyramids.[85]

Burnham's observations on the Great Pyramid, entered in his diary, reveal him as a sensitive, attentive observer of the architectural essence of what he saw: "The architects chose that high bank of sand, the commencement of the Libyan Desert, because it formed an architectural base or terrace for the mighty monument, and because they would not here be in competition with the mountains themselves."[86] What he seems to have drawn from this experience is the aspect most useful in design, the relationship between architectural object and its environment, and he indicates the specific role played by the natural plateau.

After visiting Beirut and Jerusalem, Rhodes and Smyrna, he arrived on March 10 in Istanbul, where Hagia Sofia left him indifferent. Classical antiquity fascinated him, however, and in Athens he wrote, "I have the spirit of Greece once and forever stamped on my soul." The Acropolis taught him much about conceiving architecture as a whole in relation to the natural setting and reciprocal visual axes. This first trip ended with brief visits to Naples and Rome.

Determined as he was to become the leader of architectural culture in Theodore Roosevelt's America, Burnham made many other such tours. Each time the places he visited, the people he encountered, and the observations he recorded seem to have been part of a precise program of self-preparation. His services would soon be required and within the atmosphere created by the Open Door policy his travels would be sponsored by the government.

After Root's death Burnham had set up a new firm, which in addition to Atwood, who was to die prematurely in 1895, included also Edward C. Shankland. Following the fair the first natural development of the urban-planning activity of the new firm of D. H. Burnham and Company was the plan for the Chicago lakefront that extended the layout of Jackson Park along the water. Burnham's friend James E. Ellsworth presented the project to the Chicago magnates, among them George Pullman, Marshall Field, and Philip D. Armour. The interest and support of these powerful men encouraged Burnham to launch a publicity campaign, and he presented the South Shore Drive project to various cultural and commercial clubs in Chicago.

The project, begun in 1894 and final designs presented in 1896, was actually quite ingenuous if compared with later plans prepared by Burnham's firm. Rather than showing the influence of the White City or indicating what was to develop as the City Beautiful movement, the lakefront project showed a dependence on the only movement that had even really been tried in American city planning—that stemming from Olmsted. The South Shore Drive project called for the removal of the old railroad lines on the shore and the creation of a strip of park along the lake that would be connected to the urban traffic system by a limited number of roads. The typical Olmsted element was the long, irregular lagoon, connected with the little lakes of Jackson Park, running along the length of the shore between the lakefront and the city and extending to the basin of the port opposite the Loop. In his admirable program for improving a lakefront that had been degraded and disfigured by the existing railroad lines, Burnham added a cultural touch inspired by his recent trip to the Mediterranean. He spoke of archaeological fragments scattered through the park, pedestals with vases and statues, fountains, and terraces with "seats made in the old Greek pattern" or "with here and there old Greek resting places, some curved into the banks, out of which should flow fountains of water."[87] His emphatic optimism in proposing the project was remarked with irony in the *American Architect and Building News* in 1897:

Mr. Burnham is leaving no stone unturned to arouse enthusiasm in his scheme, and enthusiasm in the idea that he is the man to do it, irrespective of the fact that the two men who, as his partners, made the name of the firm noted for its artistic work are now beyond giving any help in making Chicago a beautiful city. Mr. Burnham may have discovered some other genius whose work will some day delight us as that of Mr. Root's and Mr. Atwood's has done, but it would seem a little risky to trust such a tremendous undertaking as this would be to less tried hands.[88]

The City Beautiful Movement: Washington

In the presidential race of 1896 William McKinley defeated William Jennings Bryan by a very small margin (7,100,000 to 6,500,000). The historical significance of the Republicans' electoral victory (led by Theodore Roosevelt and William Howard Taft, they were to hold power until the eve of World War I) is directly related to the crisis of 1893 and the social tensions of 1894. These were the tremors that accompanied the country's settling down to a new economic equilibrium. The Columbian Exposition itself was a sign of this readjustment; an event of purely Republican stamp, in its aim of establishing new international relations, it indicated the trend of the party's foreign policy. In their domestic policy the Republicans would undertake an anti-inflationary program, but on this issue they had to come to terms with a strong union movement.

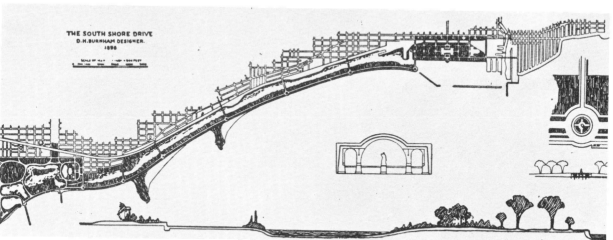

The Chicago lakefront in 1893. The shore is
occupied by railroad lines, behind which
extend Grant Park and Michigan Avenue.
Visible at the right are the Auditorium,
the Studebaker Building, and the Art Institute.

Design made by Burnham and Company in
1896 for the South Shore Drive project,
from Jackson Park to Grant Park on the
Chicago lakefront, showing plan and transverse section of the strip of park along the
lake with its road, lagoon, and area of
greenery.

The crisis of 1893 greatly increased the tension in this conflict. The thorough reorganization of the labor movement in the years immediately preceding the crisis had made the unions strong. Indeed, all the most important edifices of the Chicago school, up to and including its final products, the Reliance and Fisher buildings, were intimately connected in their creation with the relations of production conditioned by the elite old-guard unions. The construction union, the Building Laborers, came into being in 1890.

It is highly unlikely that mere coincidence accounted for the choice of May 1 for the inauguration of the Columbian Exposition. After the Haymarket incident in 1886, the first of May, day of the American workers' combat, had been adopted after their example by the Second International of Paris in 1889, in the name of all the workers of the world, as the day to celebrate the revolution. Tensions on this date were too great for the choice to have been purely casual. An article by Charles Dickens, which appeared on April 29, 1893, just two days before the inauguration of the fair, is indicative: "Compared with the Mayday of the poets, and with that depicted by the analysts of ancient sports and customs, the Mayday of our present era shows a curious contrast. 'Preparations for Mayday' which formed the headline of paragraphs in the daily papers last year, have no connection with May poles, garlands, Morris dancers, or festive milkmaids. The preparations are in the way of massing troops and police about the chief public resorts of the capital cities."[89]

In the choice of this day, the pacifying intentions of those sponsoring the fair take on something of the arrogant self-confidence that characterized the politics of the Republicans, now near to gaining power, and in any case the leaders in the initiative for the exposition. The choice of May Day was, however, ambiguous. On the one hand, the general ideological view promoted by the fair certainly opposed the inflationary tendencies and protectionist stand of the unions, and the City Beautiful movement that the fair anticipated was to introduce into construction work systems and practices favorable to the occupation of nonspecialized labor. On the other hand, however, the delicate execution of the fair buildings themselves required a very large percentage of skilled workers.

In Chicago the fair attenuated the disastrous effects of the economic crisis, but the strike against the Pullman works in 1894 and the resulting financial panic hit the city hard. The period of truce instituted by the unions throughout the country after the military intervention ordered by President Grover Cleveland to surpress the Pullman strike was also a period of horrible depression. In this situation the Republicans' anti-inflationary and stabilizing policies inevitably gained favor and popularity, particularly in the face of the extreme misery suffered by the great mass of immigrants.

The men who had anticipated the organizational needs of the new order that had come into being with the Republican victory were naturally in a favored position. In his own field, Burnham was certainly among this group. He was in constant contact with the leaders of the new regime, on both the local level (for instance, through his friendship with Edward T. Jeffery)[90] and the national (through his future biographer Charles Moore, for example, who was to be very important for Burnham's career). Moreover, a certain degree of government involvement supported the development even of the City Beautiful movement itself, which had made its precocious debut at the Columbian Exposition. An interesting editorial in the *Architectural Record* underlined the fair's importance as a lesson in methodology for official government building. The writer lamented the mediocrity of the design practices of the supervising architect of the Treasury, in comparison with the high quality of private building enterprises. As valid models for public building, he indicated not the insignificant Government Building but Cobb's Fisheries Building, McKim, Mead and White's Agricultural Building, and Atwood's Fine Arts Building. The editorial concluded by recommending that the Senate approve the bill, already passed in the House, that would open the design of public buildings to private initiative through competitions.[91]

The City Beautiful movement was not concerned merely with the design of important public buildings, however, although in the great majority of cases, at least within the United States, its effects were limited to this area. So much confusion has arisen in the definition of the term *City Beautiful* and its use in historical writings, both old and new, that the use of the term here should be clarified.

Although landscape remained outside the city throughout the nineteenth century, Frederick Law Olmsted's design for Central Park and his later projects represented a decisive attempt to organize urban greenery into a "system" within the diverse, confused, and unpredictable structures of the developing metropolis. Part of the importance of the Columbian Exposition was that it afforded a common working ground to the architect, involved with the magma of urban construction and inevitably compromised by the lack of any real control over the urban scale, and the landscape artist, uncorrupted missionary of designed nature within the fabricated confusion of the city.

The meeting of these two figures gave rise to the greatest attempts at spatial control of urban centers—and in Chicago in 1909, of the whole metropolitan area. This attempt was launched triumphally in the Senate Park Commission's plan for Washington, D.C.; among its protagonists were men such as Burnham and McKim. Despite the high-flown "cultural" tone of the principal buildings of the urban show places, where the town designers defined their classicist concepts architecturally, their line of action owed its partial successes, even after Washington, to its own realism, to compromise, and to the close contact maintained in all phases of the projects with those actually holding economic or political power, understood to be the only real patrons.

The other line of development stemming from progressive concepts was very different.[92] Its adherents scorned the Columbian Exposition, classicism, and monumentality and, instead, aimed directly at obtaining a better standard of living. They defied the managers of the chaotic city and sought an ideal patronage in the citizenry, to whom they directed passionate campaigns for civic action. These two positions tended to diverge until that of Burnham and his followers exhausted its productive and ideological role. The landscapers and the proposals of civic improvement were to go on to develop their ideas in the nascent field of city planning.

The two lines of action just described, so different despite their obvious interrelatedness, have often been indiscriminatingly labeled *City Beautiful*; the result has been a confusion of terminology that I wish to avoid in this essay. The movement that interests me here is the more ambitious and realistic one, that practiced principally by Burnham, whose plans were inspired by Paris, and which affected the urban structure even in the purely architectural sense.

In contrast to Olmsted's work and theories, Burnham's was a new movement, which took account of progressive, reform ideas by making them welcome even to the real-estate speculators and reconciling them with the interests of the bosses. In the words of Mumford, its harsh detractor and a supporter of the Park movement that descended from Olmsted, the City Beautiful movement "was a sort of municipal cosmetic" that "reduced the work of the architect to that of putting a pleasing front upon the scrappy building" and made him "a creator of land-values."[93] Undeniably, a plan such as Burnham's for Chicago (which will be discussed at length later in this essay), side by side with the ostentatiously designed and formally qualified public structures, leaves private initiative a density and mass of construction sufficient to satisfy the appetite of even the most avid boss.

The distinction between the City Beautiful and the Park movement specified here, and reinforced by Mumford's accusations, has lead to a recurrent misinterpretation: the conviction that Olmsted's great work was a crusade for safeguarding greenery and was thus substantially antiurban. Certainly, this was not the famous landscape architect's intention. Olmsted not only understood the necessity of the metropolis but accepted the economic mechanism that determined the concentration of commercial activities in the center, to the extent that he explicitly proposed the removal of residential areas from the center to the suburbs. It is true, however, that, becuase of the irrationality of spontaneous urban development, the use made of Olmsted's theories was almost always partial and not organic; it was usually limited to the creation of a certain number of parks organized more or less into a system.

Thus it is not incorrect to view the City Beautiful movement as practiced by Burnham as having descended from Olmsted, insofar as Olmsted's theories rationalized the basic dynamic structure of the city; indeed, in this sense, Olmsted's theories and work had a direct, clearly discernible relationship, beyond City Beautiful, with city planning. It is nevertheless necessary to distinguish between urban projects related to the ideology of the Parks and Boulevards movement and the more properly architectural projects of City Beautiful.

The foregoing considerations and distinctions can help in evaluating the claims of priority over the Columbian Exposition's Court of Honor in regard to the birth date of the City Beautiful movement, which have been made for certain American cities, such as Kansas City.[94] These claims are based on the thesis of Thomas Adams,[95] who considered the White City not a beginning but, rather, the result of twenty years of study and work led by Olmsted and put into operation in Kansas City immediately after 1890. Actually the work of George E. Kessler, an engineer on the board of the Kansas City Park System from the 1880s on, constitutes an important episode in the history of progressive planning; it was not, however, part of the City Beautiful movement as the term is used here.

Furthermore, the writings of Charles Mulford Robinson, widely considered a theoretician of City Beautiful, are in my view more properly related to the movement for civic improvement, which, as already noted, was to bear fruit in the development of city planning. Robinson's articles in the *Atlantic Monthly* and his book *Improvement of Towns and Cities,* published in 1901, do not go much beyond a handbooklike treatment of solutions for street layouts and urban beautification.[96] His writings amplify and systematize ideas already advanced by the various municipal art societies, which had formed in the 1890s and held their first national conference in Baltimore in 1899.[97] At the base of all these movements was the ideology of civic education and participation, with all its intrinsically positive, as well as ambiguous and negative, aspects, including the extreme cases of voluntary efforts at improving urban decor promoted by women's clubs and entrusted to the zeal of the citizens.[98]

From the point of view of this essay, the most valid precedent for the City Beautiful concept as practiced by Burnham remains the White City, the first executed project based on a controlled coordination and aimed at producing results completely different from the grid-plan city of laissez-faire. It was this control that Zueblin defined as a "socialistic achievement." Somewhat later Zueblin assessed the fair and its influence more specifically: "The movement for scientific city planning needed a more powerful impulse. This came in the spectacular achievement of the Chicago World's Fair." As a result of the "scientific" planning stimulated by the fair, "almost every municipal function was better performed because coordinated in a comprehensive scheme. Street paving and cleaning, water supply, sewage disposal, garbage and refuse removal, fire, police, and health protection have been performed at the dictates of science, not of bosses."[99] Zueblin here obviously tends to equate "scientific" city planning with the City Beautiful movement. Frederick Law Olmsted, Jr., summed up the movement's specific concerns more precisely: "First, the sizes, shapes and slopes of the streets; second, the sizes and character of the buildings and their location in respect to each other and the street spaces; third, the distribution of the unbuilt land not included in the streets; and, fourth, the surface treatment of the unbuilt land both with and without the street limits, and the character and distribution of objects that rise from these surfaces, whether trees, telegraph poles, fences or what not."[100]

This program, described by Olmsted in 1910, by which time it was possible to make a real assessment, is significant; three of the four points concern unbuilt areas. As noted earlier, however, giving attention to unbuilt or special areas, according to the elder Olmsted's theories, did not signify that plans were aimed essentially at safeguarding greenery. On the contrary, it meant concentrating organizational and formal control in a limited number of key points and structural channels within the city, while the areas destined to be built up by private enterprise—obviously the more extensive—were governed by an essential minimum of controls. Regulation in this case was aimed only at maintaining the full efficiency of the basic structure of the roadways and areas of public use, the definition and formalization of which was given priority.

Seen in this light, the City Beautiful movement is equivalent not to city planning as a whole but rather to a particular method of planning—the only one, in my view, that could actually have been put into practice at the time. The identification of the source of the City Beautiful movement as the White City, therefore, makes sense when that project is considered for its significance as a designed and coordinated work of town planning rather than for its stylistic significance as an affirmation of classicism. Viewed in this way, even the tendency of some historians to attribute the paternity of the City Beautiful movement to American Beaux-Arts architects, especially Hunt, has a certain validity. The old master's stylistic eclecticism apart, his architecture, in fact, reveals a certain concession to the city, for which Frank E. Wallis gave him generous credit.[101] By comparison, however, Post would appear much the more likely candidate.

The situation becomes much clearer if it is agreed that for Americans of the period, and for Burnham especially, the real City Beautiful was Paris—the Paris of Napoleon I and Napoleon III, the plan of which Burnham kept constantly on his work table.[102] And the real City Beautiful in the United States was Washington, that in a certain sense, was the only one on national territory; the stability of "values" could be expressed completely only in the capital. Before Washington there had been only partial or unexecuted projects, among them James H. Windrim's design for the Philadelphia Parkway from City Hall to Fairmount Park, contemporary with the Columbian Exposition;[103] the 1895 competition for the civic center in Cleveland; and Julius F. Harder's 1898 plan for New York, which will be discussed later.

Washington offered the occasion for actually carrying out the great task of creating a City Beautiful; it was the fruit of the mature phase of economic stabilization that followed the Republican's affirmation of power and preceded Roosevelt's aggressive imperialism. The capital city was especially addicted to the construction boss. As mentioned earlier, an urban planning operation had been attempted in Washington without success by boss Alexander Shepherd after the Civil War. In 1900, as part of the celebration of the centennial of the capital, a new project was inaugurated. Washington had only 218,000 inhabitants and was sparsely constructed, and the cost of land, which the new plan would bring up to a normal level, was still much lower than in other cities. It was an exceptionally suitable occasion for the equivocal marriage between bosses and reformers, for which the situation was now ripe. After all, even Pierre Charles L'Enfant's plan for Washington, made in the 1790s, had involved a notable compromise, that between classical grandeur and Jefferson's antiurban ideology, which, however, the President was disposed to put aside for the creation of a symbolic urban place in which to express the idea of the Union. [104]

The cardinal elements of the old plan had already been built—essentially, the Capitol, at the extreme east of L'Enfant's great L; the White House, at the extreme north of the short arm of the L; and the Washington Monument, at the ideal point of encounter of the two axes, toward the Potomac. [105] Because the old program had been interrupted, these monuments hardly assumed their intended symbolic significance. Moreover, despite their exceptional character, they appeared very distant from and unrelated to each other. The only evident urban structure was the oblique artery of Pennsylvania Avenue, which connected the Capitol with the White House. Furthermore, certain elements tended to deform the unity of the basic layout—especially the immense obelisk of the Washington Monument, constructed between 1848 and 1884, which was off axis, strikingly in respect to the White House and slightly in respect to the Capitol. The engineers had evidently been more concerned with finding solid ground for the foundations of the monument than with its accurate placement in relation to such distant elements. L'Enfant's scheme was distorted and degraded above all, however, by the construction of the Alexandria and Washington Railroad, which arrived from the southwest, and crossed the Potomac at the Long Bridge as early as 1854, and had been extended along Maryland Avenue toward the Capitol and, as a result of a disastrous decision made in 1872, along Sixth Street toward the Mall. The fundamental axis of the whole layout, that connecting the Capitol to the Washington Monument, was thus cut in two by the bleak sight of the yards of the railway terminal. A series of brick buildings, constructed at the end of the nineteenth century, constituted an equally unwelcome intrusion on the Mall.

The idea of saving the Mall came to the fore at the end of the century, at which time a series of arbitrarily conceived and partial projects were presented. Among these was a project by Franklin W. Smith, a well-intentioned would-be architect who, at the same time as Chicago was selected for the site of the fair, proposed that a gigantic gallery of history and art be built in Washington, occupying an immense area between the White House and the Potomac. [106] It is interesting to note that this project originally required the station built beneath

View of Washington, D.C., area of the Mall
in 1882: *right,* the Capitol, *left,* the White
House. Note the terminal station on Sixth
Street, which cuts across the monumental
axis of the Mall.

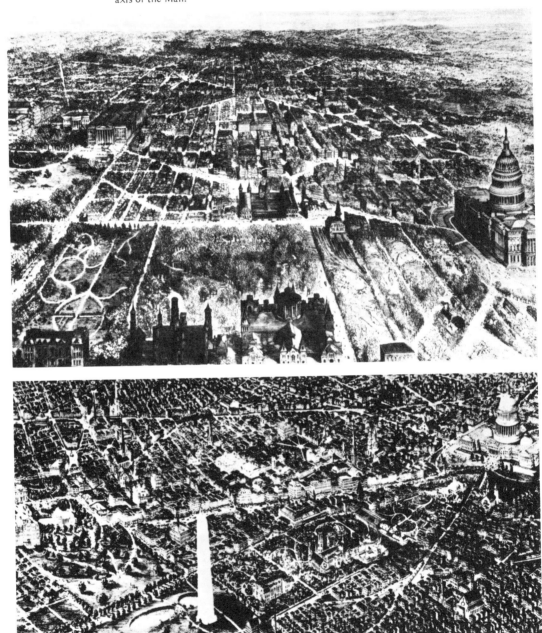

View of Washington, D.C., the Mall area,
in 1892: *right,* the Capitol, *left,* the White
House. The immense obelisk of the Washington Monument has been erected, but the
axes connecting the three major monuments in an L are obscured and interrupted
by numerous nineteenth-century constructions, including the railroad.

the Capitol to be moved back in order to free completely the strip destined for the Mall. Negative reaction to this solution on the part of the powerful railroad men, however, must have been immediate, because the version of the project prepared by Smith himself and presented in 1900 no longer called for such a move.

In 1898 Washington, like many other American cities at this time, formed a committee of illustrious citizens to promote the renewal of the show places of the city. This effort brought forth numerous projects for various partial layouts, public buildings, and parks. An attempt at a comprehensive plan was drawn up by Senator James McMillan, but the press attacked it so ferociously that the senator himself was quickly convinced of the need for expert technical and cultural direction for such a project.[107] At first it seemed that Theodore A. Bingham was the man capable of handling the problem. Since 1867 Bingham had directed the office of public buildings and grounds of the Army Corps of Engineers; as a diplomatic attaché, he lived in Berlin and Rome (later, from 1906 through 1909, he served as police commissioner in New York). An engineer who scorned architects, Bingham designed two plans based on reinforcing the Capitol-obelisk axis and on prolonging New York Avenue beyond the White House and across the Potomac by means of a monumental new bridge.[108] For the design of the Mall park, Bingham requested the collaboration of Samuel Parsons, Jr., who had been involved in the work on Central Park in New York. Parsons designed a bewildering series of quadrilobed roadways passing through the Mall, none of which took account of the principal transverse axes dominated by major monuments.

The fundamental merit of Bingham's work was that he recognized the necessity of moving back the railroad station then encumbering the Mall; the change was called for in both his designs. Bingham's plan was destined to fail, however, as the result of an attack carefully prepared by the architects and organized by a scholar and man of culture, Glenn Brown, author of the history of the Capitol and, beginning in 1898, secretary of the American Institute of Architects.

As a sharply contrasting alternative to Bingham's work, Brown persuaded Robert S. Peabody, then president of the AIA, to hold the institute's annual congress in Washington, with that city as its subject. In the first months of 1900, possible speakers for the program were contacted; they included Cass Gilbert, Paul J. Pelz, George O. Totten, Jr., and Edgar V. Seeley, who concerned themselves more with designing plans for the capital than with preparing reports. Brown published his own plan in August in the *Architectural Record*; his can be considered the first satisfactory solution to the problem of creating an organic urban design for Washington. [109]

On December 12, 1900, on the occasion of the presentation of proposals for the enlargement of the White House as part of the celebration of the centennial of the capital, Bingham's project for the Mall met with organized opposition.

Brown's attack was hard, authoritative, and erudite; his speech was a detailed indictment of Bingham's work and focused principally on the bridge lengthening New York Avenue, which was oblique in respect to the fundamental axis of the Mall, and on the design of the park. In addition, Brown presented the official opposition of the AIA and fifty other United States art associations to Bingham's project.

At the annual meeting of the AIA, a series of alternative projects and some important reports, among which the fundamental one by Frederick L. Olmsted, Jr., were presented. The group's decisive action forced President McKinley to reconsider his favorable view of Bingham's plan and to lean instead toward a solution in keeping with the AIA proposals. This shift in policy led to the formation of a commission made up of prestigious figures in the field of landscape architecture, including at least two obligatory nominations, those of Daniel H. Burnham and Frederick Law Olmsted, Jr. On March 8, 1901, the Senate adopted a resolution filed by McMillan, which authorized the Committee of the District of Columbia to engage experts and produce a plan for the entire Park System of the district; thus the Senate Park Commission came into being. Olmsted's name was suggested by McMillan and Burnham's by Charles Moore. Apparently it was Burnham himself who brought in McKim, the man who had so greatly impressed him by his culture, personality, and ability during the fair.

Burnham had learned much from McKim; that he had also succeeded in remaining independent of him is demonstrated by his subsequent designs for skyscrapers, a type of building condemned by McKim but very congenial to Burnham. During their work on the fair, there had never been any friction between the two concerning the leadership of the project; this harmony may have resulted from the participation of so many authoritative Eastern architects, but it was also certainly due, at least in part, to McKim's respect for Burnham's unfailing and phenomenal capacity for work.

Faced with the task of the City Beautiful, Burnham felt that America could not do without McKim, but he had no intention of depending on him culturally. It was therefore necessary to acquire, with the rapidity of which only Burnham was capable, as much information and as many ideas as possible in a single journey. He requested and was granted a trip for preparatory study in Europe; the members of the Senate Park Commission, Burnham himself, McKim, Olmsted, the sculptor Augustus Saint-Gaudens, and its secretary, Charles Moore, were to participate. Because of ill-health, however, Saint-Gaudens did not make the journey.

What was to be looked for in the Old World? Once again, as in the time of Jefferson, the models of despotism and absolutism could be expropriated and adapted to modern, atemporal use, becoming pure representations of "values" in a society developing so rapidly that it would inevitably be the first to destroy values. The basic conception of Washington had not changed since L'Enfant's plan; it was not a city of commerce but an abstract, collective symbol. As the

Plan for the Mall, Washington D.C., designed by Samuel Parsons, Jr., at the request of Theodore A. Bingham, 1900. The railroad station is moved back on Maryland Avenue in order to clear the monumental axis. The elaborate road layout masks the dislocation of the obelisk in relation to the axis.

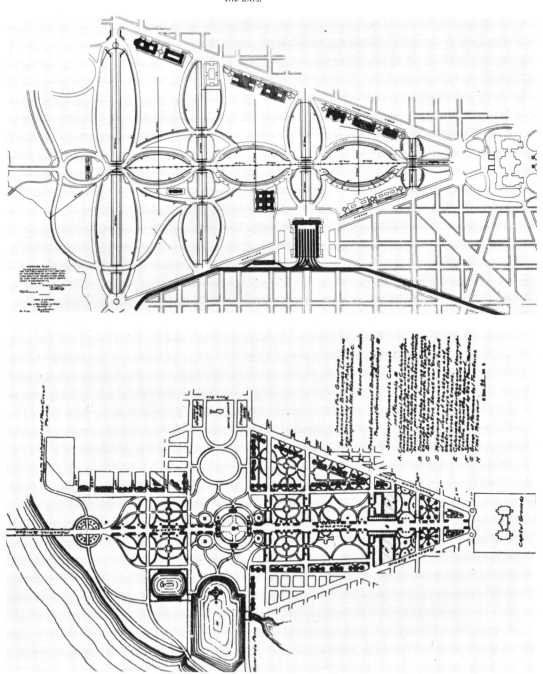

Plan for the Mall, Washington, D.C., by Glenn Brown, 1900. The railroad is entrenched and screened off, and the axial boulevard passes over it, extending to the obelisk. In these projects the complex for the first time becomes symmetrical.

seat of power of a constantly changing, dynamic society, incessantly in search of an impossible equilibrium, Washington still had to be an allegorical representation of stability—"a timeless, indisputable, completely positive Olympus."[110]

As City Beautiful, Washington would offer to the entire United States the same "compensation" that City Beautiful projects elsewhere offered to individual cities. In Mumford's words, "Our imperial architecture is an architecture of compensation: it provides grandiloquent stones for people who have been deprived of bread and sunlight."[111] For fear of a different reality that could too frequently question and endanger the nation's institutions, the capital city had to be an unreal citadel of authority and stability. The different, dangerous reality was that of urbanized society; Josiah Strong considered it the breeding ground of humanity's great ills, which he identified as immigration, Roman Catholicism, and socialism, as well as wealth, poverty, and intemperance.[112]

Even before its time, as noted above, City Beautiful was the guise chosen for Bellamy's equilibrated society of the future: "At my feet lay a great city. Miles of broad streets, shaded by trees and lined with fine buildings, for the most part not in continuous blocks but set in larger or smaller enclosures, stretched in every direction. Every quarter contained large open squares filled with trees, among which statues glistened and fountains flashed in the late afternoon sun. Public buildings of a colossal size and an architectural grandeur unparalleled in my day raised their stately piles on every side."[113] The architectural form of Bellamy's utopia was a prefiguration; although its influence is difficult to evaluate, it was surely substantial in the architectural conception of both the White City and Washington. Curiously, the similarity between a model of the future, which was a product of foresight, and the models of the past, which the most "advanced" architects of the time sought in Europe, was not felt to be a nonsensical contradiction.

The Senate Park Commission began its trip abroad on June 13, 1901. Paris was the first goal; from there the group traveled to Rome by train and car. Venice, Vienna, and Budapest followed. They then returned to Paris by the Orient Express and revisited Lenôtre's gardens. From Paris the commission moved on to Frankfurt to see the new station, which Alexander J. Cassatt, president of the Pennsylvania Railroad, as well as of the Railroad Association, had described as the best in the world. Finally, they visited Berlin. On the return trip they stopped in London, visiting Hampton Court and Oxford. On July 26, without having had time to visit Saint Petersburg, as they had wished to do, they departed for home.

During the stop in London, Burnham learned from Cassatt, who also happened to be in England at the time, that the thorny question of Union Station in Washington had been resolved. It was the end of a long and controversial investigation, during which Burnham, who had been charged with designing the station, constantly enlarged the sphere of his concern by attacking the problem of the station's placement in relation to the entire urban structure. Burnham's

zealous involvement in this dispute with one of the strongest powers of the
"system," the railroads, derived not merely from the motives that had induced
others before him to recommend moving back the station that encumbered the
Mall but also from his concern with the organic significance of the City
Beautiful. In fact, Burnham did not limit his efforts to freeing the Mall of the
station; instead, he suggested a structural alternative based on a more complex
conception of the city, in which the station itself played a fundamental role. The
railroad station became what Mumford would later define as the point of
attachment of the umbilical cord connecting the city to the region. It was
essential from the functional point of view and, by Burnham's lights, also a
significant monument in the City Beautiful.[114]

Burnham's solution called for the radical repositioning of the station to the
north of the Capitol, on the site of the already existing station of the Baltimore
and Ohio Line. In London, Cassatt told Burnham that his proposal had been
made feasible by Senator McMillan's assurance that Congress would make
available $1.5 million for the construction of the necessary railroad tunnel under
Capitol Hill. In addition to this decisive offer of funds, according to Reps, the
acceptance of Burnham's proposal had also been influenced by the personal
aesthetic taste of this important railroad magnate brother of the Impressionist
painter Mary Cassatt.[115] It seems more likely, however, that it was the
importance of the urban role given the station in Burnham's solution that really
made it convincing.

The Mall had to be a monumental void, an accompaniment to the most
important visual axis in America, which itself had to be treated with an almost
sacred, ritualistic continuity and could certainly not be interrupted by a ganglion
like the railway terminal. The station, moreover, was an outlet, an entrance into
the city, and it therefore presupposed an axis leading out from it and concluding
in a distant focal point. The relation between station and Mall, two key elements
of the urban structure, could not be brusque and direct, as it would have been
even in the plans that merely called for moving the station back or for placing it
underground. Instead, their relation had to be mediated by a monumental pivotal
point—nothing less than the Capitol itself.

As the "gateway" to the city, Union Station had to be and became the point
of departure of a system of axes, the first of which would lead to the Capitol
Building, the most prestigious focal point of Washington and, in turn, the point
of departure and belvedere of the monumental axis of the Mall. The Capitol thus
took on a role similar to that of Hunt's Administration Building at the Chicago
fair, where it had served as the vestibule to the Court of Honor. As part of the
classical rhetoric of the City Beautiful, the station could not be in just any style;
to conform to its role it had to be classical and Roman. It was thus for reasons
of coherence that Burnham, an architect of the Chicago school, was disposed to
produce a classical edifice, the prototype of the City Beautiful railroad
station.[116] Among those that were to follow, the most important were McKim,
Mead and White's Pennsylvania Station in New York, built in 1906-10, and

Grand Central Terminal, designed by Reed and Stem together with Warren and Wetmore, also in New York, which was finished in 1913.

The exhibit of the Senate Park Commission's plan for the Mall, which opened on January 15, 1902, was prepared under McKim's personal direction. The 197 graphic panels were exceptionally elegant and much appreciated by the taste of the time. The open structure of L'Enfant's original plan, two axes converging in an L on the Washington Monument, now became a closed figure by completing symmetrically the principal axis leading from the Capitol. The resulting layout was an immense cross of three equal arms and a fourth longer one. To L'Enfant's two terminal points, the Capitol for the greater axis and the White House for the lesser, were added two others, the Lincoln and Jefferson memorials. At the point where the arms of the cross converged, slightly off center in respect to the two axes, stood the gigantic obelisk of the Washington Monument. All around, to connect the extremities of the arms of the cross, were boulevards laid out in polygonal formations. The aim at this point was clearly a balanced, static image, free of any critical points and with all elements related to the unified whole—a metaphor of the definitive resolution of all conflicts.

What was remarkable in these designs, and later in their execution, was the progressive rarefication of elements toward the center of the cross. Here the surreal presence of the immense, smooth, white obelisk is enhanced by a surrounding expanse of flat terrain, an elegiac architectural landscape that creates an unreal memorial in the metaphorical center of the ideal city. The equilibrium of a radial symmetry around a void was, of course, a statement simultaneously abstract and, in its scenic quality, representational, but its creators were not concerned with masking such conventionality. Indeed, it is difficult to say to what extent Burnham and McKim were conscious of the subtle equilibrium between real and unreal in their designs, and yet if there was ever an occasion for such a composite conception to take actual form, it was in the layout of the Mall, of which they were very conscious.

The greatest care was taken in preparing the presentation drawings, particularly by McKim, who oversaw the graphic execution of the project in a studio set up especially for this purpose in New York. Careful attention was given to the selection of the draftsmen for the perspective drawings, in order to assure that they would convey the designers' intentions even to nonspecialists. Jules Guerin and Charles Graham were chosen; Glenn Brown also actively participated in preparing the panels and models for the display. At the exhibition, Brown and Charles Moore served as guides to the officials.[117]

Theodore Roosevelt, newly inaugurated as President after the assassination of McKinley, expressed some reservations; together with Secretary of State John Hay, however, he declared his enthusiasm for the striking ideological concept of aligning the plan on the fundamental axis of the Capitol, Washington Monument, and Lincoln Memorial. This time the press was in agreement and came out openly for the adoption of the plan. Its favorable reception resulted in part from

Plan for Washington, D.C., by Cass Gilbert
(1900), in which the axis of the White House
is four times its present length. The scheme
thus becomes markedly asymmetrical, and
the area of development is doubled.

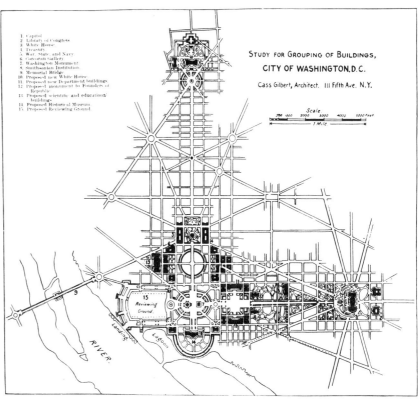

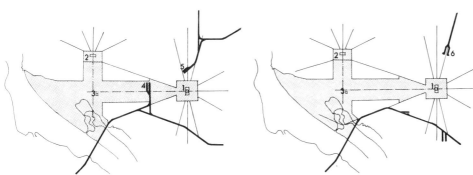

Schemes of the Mall and the railroads as
they existed at the end of the nineteenth
century and as replanned by the Senate
Park Commission: (1) Capitol; (2) White
House; (3) Washington Monument; (4)
Terminal of the Alexandria and Washington
Railroad; (5) Baltimore and Ohio Station;
(6) Union Station, by Daniel H. Burnham.

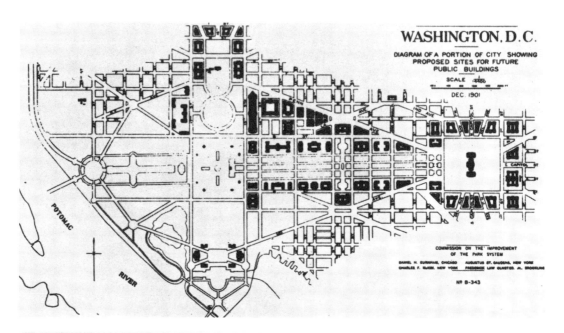

Plan of the Mall in the Senate Park Commission's plan for Washington, D.C., 1902.

Bird's-eye view of the Senate Park Commission plan for Washington, D.C., 1902, prepared in tempera for the official presentation.

The Senate Park Commission's plan for the
Mall, Washington, D.C., 1902.

The Senate Park Commission's Plan for
Washington, D.C., showing the Washington
Monument, 1902.

the prestige of the people involved in the initiative and from their obvious and universally acknowledged disinterestedness, which made the whole operation appear a complete departure from the practice of the bosses, which had prevailed up to now.

Even Montgomery Schuyler, writing in the *New York Times* on January 19, 1902, offered his authoritative, if somewhat ambiguous, approval: "The point is to have a plan that you believe in, that is based upon study of what has been found most admirable in its kind in the world. . . . That without doubt the commission have triumphantly attained. Whatever it will cost Uncle Sam to do all this, it will cost him nothing to say now that he believes in it, that he means to do it."[118] Later in that year, Schuyler discussed the plan again in the *Architectural Record*, this time approving it without reserve.[119]

The cultural significance of the plan was underscored in another architictural journal, which defined it as "the most important work of artistic significance ever projected in the United States. It marks an epoch in our national progress. It educates."[120]

Two Faces of Urban Design: Cleveland and the Flatiron

Historians have expressed surprise at the fact that Burnham was content to earn very little from his plans, for which he often received only reimbursement for the expenses involved in the designing, while their promotion and realization always necessitated fantastic personal expenditures on entertainment and other public-relations activities, of which the interminable series of trips and dinners recorded in his diary afford some idea. In moving from one city and one meeting to another and back and forth across the ocean, however, Burnham met the important people who formed the clientele of the more strictly professional and lucrative side of his architectural activity.

Burnham's patrons were often political figures, men of considerable financial resources, who also had cultural ambitions. In some cases they were typical "reform bosses," the term Charles N. Glaab and A. Theodore Brown have given to the able financial managers and public administrators whose activities were still linked to electoral politics and the apparatus for obtaining votes but who were by now above the moralistic attacks of the muckrakers and the investigations promoted by the reformers.[121] Of the three "reform bosses" cited by Glaab and Brown, at least two were actually patrons of Burnham: Hazen S. Pingree, mayor of Detroit, for whom he designed the Hotel Building in that city, and Tom L. Johnson, patron of the civic center that was to transform Cleveland into a City Beautiful. In other cases his clients were potentates of industry and finance in search of prestige but also of maximum efficiency, usually the men who, like Harry W. Oliver of Pittsburgh, commissioned skyscrapers.

"Probably Cleveland has come nearer to 'finding itself' than any other large city on the continent," wrote Frederic C. Howe in 1903. "It is becoming organized. It is acquiring a capacity for political sacrifice. It is learning to think as a municipality."[122] Cleveland was considered the Sheffield of America, since it was not only an industrial city par excellence but also destined to give positive form to Carnegie's prophecy that the area south of Lake Erie would become the most important in the world for iron and steel. Conscious of this destiny, the administrations governing the city alternated with exceptional alacrity between bosses and reformers, making Cleveland appear particularly scandal-ridden until the advent of Johnson. Johnson was a former railroad boss who became a follower of Henry George after reading his *Progress and Poverty*; together with others of George's followers, Johnson even built him a house. In this new progressive guise he became mayor of Cleveland in 1901 and was reelected three times. Johnson remained a boss, but a democratic and reforming one; Newton D. Baker describes him as "the most spectacular liberal in the public life of America from 1890 to 1910."[123]

An elected boss, one who becomes mayor, must necessarily have obtained a wide consensus, and this public approbation of his administration had to be maintained and put to the test every two years. Even if, on the one hand, Johnson had managed to create a perfect political "machine" in Cleveland by being able to dispose directly of something like 2,500 jobs in his executive department, on the other hand, in his more public activities, he had to be a benefactor to the city. In 1902, Burnham was commissioned to design the railroad station on the Cleveland lakefront. At the same time, Arnold W. Brunner was charged with designing the post office. In Johnson's program, however, the construction of a building or two was not enough. He felt a need for the ideological promise of a City Beautiful, a Cleveland of the future that would be a little Washington. He therefore set up a commission of architects, officially nominated by the governor of the state, to plan a civic center; Burnham and Brunner, already engaged, were joined in the project by John M. Carrère, who had been chief architect for the Pan-American Exposition in Buffalo in the previous year.

The commission's proposal was presented in August 1903. The title and tone of the accompanying report are indicative of the courtly ceremony adopted in relations with the munificent boss, the Honorable Tom L. Johnson.[124] The preparation of the design, which took slightly more than a year, was carried out in a studio set up expressly for this purpose in New York, which Burnham visited frequently at this time in order to direct work on the Flatiron Building. In the words of his colleague Brunner, Burnham "was unquestionably ... leader" of the project and was "always adding fresh inspiration and proving himself to be a designer as well as a more than intelligent critic. In writing the report ... Mr. Burnham contributed largely to its presentation."[125]

The area of the city designated for the civic center complex was actually a miserable slum, a place of crime and corruption that would be eliminated; thus the project may be considered a precocious example of slum clearance. The plan was based on an axis of symmetry perpendicular to the lake and obviously inspired by that of the Court of Honor of the Columbian Exposition; it also called for a large open space laid out longitudinally, with its short end toward the lake, which in the report was actually referred to as the "Court of Honor or Mall." The principal problem involved in the project was the railroad, which as usual ran along the lakeshore. The solution proposed by Burnham from the very beginning was intelligent and realistic: the radical repositioning of the railroad was simply not feasible; the station could not be too far removed from the core of the city; thus the most logical solution was to make the station a focal point, its entrance facade dominating one end of the principal axis of the civic center complex.

This idea reflected the prestige that railroad stations had by now acquired within the urban scene and was probably also quite congenial to the mayor, a former railroad boss himself.

Such a solution, however, was bound to cause a certain amount of perplexity, particularly since Burnham had fought so hard for an apparently contrary end in Washington, where his plan demanded the complete removal of the station from the area of the Mall. Thus in order to make his plan for Cleveland more convincing, he resorted to the subtle strategy of presenting two alternative schemes, the first of which, scheme A, was intended to meet with serious objections and make the adoption of scheme B more likely. Scheme A called for a costly rerouting of the railroad and the construction of a park along the lakefront, like the one created in Chicago. The description of this plan in the report concludes with the following highly discouraging observations: "A large park . . . with a northern exposure fronting on such a large lake, would be very difficult to make attractive, and during many months of the year it would certainly be a most dreary, unattractive and useless feature." In addition to the great difficulty and enormous cost of rerouting the railway, the report continued, "it would not be desirable to have the station a mile or a mile and a half farther east and so inaccessible from the business center of the city."

The unwanted solution thus disposed of, the report described all the advantages of scheme B, not the least of which was the ample space left open to speculation. The report admitted, however, that the development of the long sides of the so-called court of honor or mall, left to private enterprise, "may be very difficult, if not impossible to control." In the face of this potential problem the authors merely express the hope "that by city ordinance, by public spirit and general interest in the matter, these buildings can be developed on coordinated and harmonious lines."

The form of the public buildings, on the other hand, could be controlled, and they were planned to provide the basic structure of the complex. The railroad station, viewed against the lake, formed the focal point of the principal axis. Opposite the station, at the other end of the mall, were two identical buildings, the post office and the library, their combined width corresponding to the width of the mall. Finally, at the end toward the station, the mall terminated in two important edifices, the city hall and the court house. These two buildings, together with the station, gave great monumentality to the axis crossing the

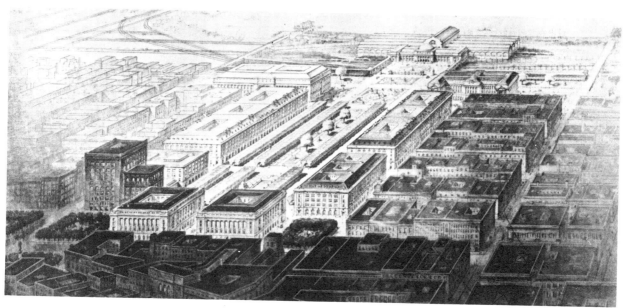

Plan by Daniel H. Burnham for the new civic center in Cleveland, perspective view toward the railroad station and lake, 1903.

European examples cited in Daniel H. Burnham's report on his proposed plan for the monumental complex in Cleveland, 1903.

Plan by Daniel H. Burnham for the monumental complex in Cleveland, 1903.

complex at this point; where the railroad permitted, this axis faced on the lake and was thus called the esplanade. Rows of evergreens and a ground-level layout created a "park effect." A monumental fountain between the post office and the library marked the axis of the mall at this end. In the report the station is explicitly referred to as the "city gate," a "beautiful vestibule to the town," a "magnificent entrance," and compared to the Gare d'Orléans. The esplanade and mall were compared to the Champs Elysées and the esplanade of Nancy. The building style, of course, would be classical Roman.

The distribution of the public buildings allowed for a play of symmetry and axial organization in which care was taken to permit a glimpse of the lake at the north, while vistas from north to south and south to north each included an impressive monumental enclosure. With four public buildings establishing the four corners of its large open space, the mall could probably hold up against the inevitably arbitrary development of the long sides, which was left to private enterprise.

Despite all this realism on the part of Burnham and the other architects, the plan was to be carried out only in part and very slowly. The post office was built in 1911, the court house in 1912, the city hall during the First World War, and the library only in 1925.[126] Burnham's whole concept finally collapsed when the Van Sweringen brothers, who had bought the Nickel Plate Railroad, decided to build the station in another place. In 1931, the stadium was built on the intended site of Burnham's "magnificent entrance." Cleveland thus demonstrated how slight the possibilities were of ever seeing a unified urban plan actually carried out. In fact, Johnson's munificence did not go much beyond offering the project, which during all his terms in office remained far from being put into operation. In such cases, which were far from infrequent, the City Beautiful project was viewed a failure only by the architects, who had the air of believing doggedly in their proposals. The patrons of these projects plainly did not; conscious of the political and social advantages they derived from the mere existence of the plan, they found the proposal useful in itself. This was especially true when, like Tom Johnson, the patron held an elective position.

Private patronage, on the other hand, was essentially limited to commissions for a single building, which in the most outstanding cases was a skyscraper. The Fuller Building in New York—called the Flatiron because of its particular type of metal structure and also, more popularly, for its resemblance to an old-style iron—was certainly one of the most remarkable skyscrapers of America. Contemporary with the plan for Cleveland, it seems to indicate the extent to which it was possible to develop architectural concepts on the urban scale, which Burnham was apparently bent on pursuing at any cost, even in the case of a single building.

On April 30, 1902, in a postscript to a letter about Union Station in Washington, McKim wrote to Burnham, "The only other building higher than your Fifth Avenue-23rd Street building that I have ever heard of is the Tower of Babel. They are adding at the rate of about a story a day, and there are four more stories, they say, to go."[127] The McKim, Mead and White office at 160 Fifth Avenue faced the building yard, and the ponderous mass designed by McKim's dynamic colleague was certainly not the most welcome of daily sights to him.

During this period, McKim and Burnham—the former at the height of his fame, the latter ascending rapidly, experienced the advantages and difficulties of a high-level collaboration on the project for Washington. Moments of friction were not absent,[128] but on the whole reciprocal respect prevailed. Burnham's skyscraper enterprises were certainly the point of maximum disparity in their respective viewpoints; they were occasions for the master of the Chicago school to assert his independence from Beaux-Arts culture. These were thus special works, the designing of which demanded his particular, personal involvement. The Flatiron, in fact, was created as a challenge and from the very beginning it was an enormous success, even if the method that led to its conception was not destined to bear fruit.

In England to receive the gold medal awarded him by the Royal Institute of British Architects, McKim had the not altogether pleasant surprise of hearing Edward VII declare that he would like to revisit America, where he had been forty years earlier, in order to see the Flatiron Building. [129] Baedeker's guide to the United States, published in 1904, compared the sight of the "daring" Fuller Building, "seen from a distance, up Fifth Avenue," to "the prow of a gigantic ship underway." To this description was added the following alarming information: "This building has a curious effect in increasing the violence of the wind at its apex, so that, during a storm, people are sometimes whirled off the side-walk and plate-glass shop-windows shivered." And in 1905 the cover of the Christmas issue of *Life* portrayed Santa Claus colliding in the sky with the soaring angle of the Flatiron Building and tumbling down into the city, together with sleigh, reindeer, and all his gifts.

Nevertheless, it is not true, as McKim, Moore, and many others claimed, that the Flatiron was the tallest building in New York at the time. With 20 stories rising to a height of 300 feet, it was one of the tallest, but in 1903 there were others still taller. The American Surety Company Building at Broadway and Pine streets and the American Tract Society Building at Nassau and Spruce streets both had 23 stories and were 306 feet high; the St. Paul Building at Ann Street and Broadway, 26 stories and 308 feet; the Astoria Hotel at 344-350 Fifth Avenue, 16 stories and 312 feet; the Manhattan Life Insurance Building at 64-68 Broadway, 17 stories and 348 feet; and finally, the Irvins Syndicate or Park Row Building at 12-21 Park Row had 29 stories and the notable height of 382 feet.[130] Yet from these buildings no echo has come down to us of anything like the strong sensations aroused by the Flatiron.[131]

Site of the Flatiron, New York, photograph
taken from the north looking downtown:
right, Fifth Avenue, *left*, Broadway. The
tiny cylindrical tower, barely visible at the
forepoint of the triangle of low constructions situated between the two streets,
prefigures the curve of the acute angle
of Burnham's future buildings.

View of the New York Club, situated opposite the Flatiron between Broadway and
Fifth Avenue.

Site of the Flatiron, view of Broadway
from the south, just before its intersectio
with Fifth Avenue.

Santa Claus and his reindeer colliding with
the soaring height of the Flatiron Building
(cover of *Life*, December 1905).

The impression made by Burnham's building must therefore have been caused by factors other than height; it can be explained by examining New York City as it was at the beginning of the century. Of the twenty-six buildings standing at the time that rose higher than 200 feet and can thus be considered skyscrapers, only three—all of them barely above this minimum height—were located north of the Flatiron. Indeed, almost all the skyscrapers were situated on the southern tip of downtown Manhattan, around Wall Street. Viewed from the north, that is, from the residential part of the island, the Flatiron must have appeared to be an isolated skyscraper, with its acute angle pointed toward the viewer; like the prow of the financial district, it advanced toward the city and towered over the surrounding construction, which reached only half its height. From this vantage it was also a herald of the future commercial development of midtown Manhattan.

Is it possible to say that this was the effect Burnham had counted on? Probably it was, but it would be wrong to imagine him satisfied with merely amazing his contemporaries, including McKim. A more complete appreciation of Burnham's intentions can be gleaned from Julius F. Harder's forgotten plan for New York, published in *Municipal Affairs* in 1898[132] and therefore certainly well known to the Chicago architect.

Harder, inspired by L'Enfant's plan for Washington and Haussmann's Paris, submitted to the New York City Board of Public Improvement a scheme for transforming grid-planned Manhattan into a radial city. Harder's stelliform system of arteries had its center in Union Square and was thus a first indication of the northern development of the city. Only four of the new oblique streets called for in his plan were actually built (one of them, Christopher Street, still exists in large part). Broadway, which already existed and ran obliquely, easily furnished two more of the radii, running north and south from the system's hub at Union Square. The result was an irregular star of ten arms, the fundamental structure of a new urban organism, providing rapid connections between the new center and the two bridges over the East River toward Brooklyn, as well as with the ferries to the east and west of midtown.

Harder justified the introduction of a series of functional channels into the consistent grid of Manhattan on the grounds of the necessity, to which, laudably, he explicitly referred, of creating a workable urban center around which a metropolitan area with a fifty-mile radius would eventually gravitate.[133] Certainly the required demolition was also intended to improve some of the more cramped and dangerous quarters of the city, where easy access for the forces of order, particularly the firemen, would be welcome indeed. There is no doubt, however, that beyond sharing these functional motives Harder wished to create a core within Manhattan's rigid network of streets by indelibly impressing a radial stamp on the city. In this aim he was prompted by nostalgia for the rich and varied urban scene of the European city—the oblique perspectives, the framing wings, and the corners that must be treated as the hinge points between two perspectives, according to the classical model.

The Flatiron Building was one of these corners, one of the few available, since Harder's plan was never executed. Moreover, it suggests that research in Burnham's archives might reveal radial schemes for New York related to the Flatiron commission. Indeed, the site offered such a striking opportunity in this regard that one might well imagine that the very choice of the location was not extraneous to such intentions. Thus, in addition to the interest afforded by its exceptional technical effiency, its height accentuated by its isolation, and its form extended toward the area of future development of the midtown area, the Flatiron can be considered a proposal for a new urban structure, for a formal matrix intended to evoke a different image of the city. In other words, in Burnham's deliberate extension of the term, an element of a new City Beautiful.

That the architectural form itself was inspired by this intention is clear in the sober elegance of the fenestration and the rusticated walls, as well as in the attenuated emphasis of the lower stories and the accentuated horizontal lines of the crowning structure. The building took its form from the existing curve of the acute angle of the building lot, which had, in turn, resulted from the presence at this point of a tiny cylindrical tower, visible at the center of the old photograph of the site reproduced here. By following this curve Burnham gave the angle of the building volumetric consistency without resorting to the use of an independent vertical structure, as was the usual practice for corner angles. There are, in fact, no vertical lines of any significance at all; the result is the absolute continuity of the two walls enclosing the volume, which form a single, inseparable unit. The effect is therefore quite different from certain buildings by Sullivan or others attributable to Root, created as a montage of a limited number of independent motifs. Even the crowning structure of the Flatiron, so striking and ostentatious in its form, was not, like those of Sullivan or Wright, conceived as a sort of capital to accentuate the individual, organic independence of the building. Rather, its design was intended as a forceful perspective accentuation of the divergence of the two streets; it refers precisely to the two deviating lines of recession that form the structural matrix of the building, which, in turn, suggest an unlimited extension of its volume along the streets.

The similarity of the method adopted here to that used in the Monadnock Building in Chicago is evident. Furthermore, it is impossible to attribute this characteristic to Graham's presence in Burnham's studio; the buildings that Graham constructed after Burnham's death never had the fundamental relationship with the urban scale recognizable in the Flatiron. It may therefore be said that with his design for the Flatiron Building Burnham tried to resolve a dilemma inherent in American architecture in the years before the First World War: the dichotomy between the conception of the single building and the realization of larger complexes according to a unified and coordinated plan. As Burnham wrote in 1903, "There are two sorts of architectural beauty, first, that of an individual building; and second, that of an orderly and fitting arrangement of many buildings. The relationship of all the buildings is more important than anything else."[134]

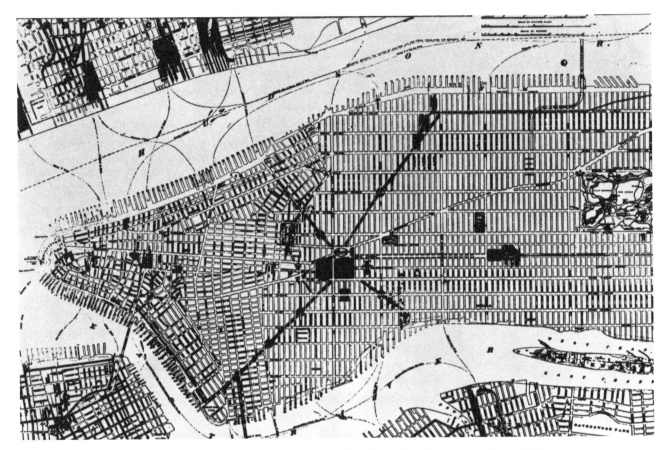

Plan of New York by Julius F. Harder, 1898.

View of the Flatiron in the period
it was built.

This dualism was to remain unresolved for the time being. Nevertheless, coordinated projects and attempts to escape, through order, from what Patrick Geddes called "pandemonium city"[135] and to construct at least a piece of the city of 2000 as described by Bellamy became a general trend in the early years of the century. Certainly this trend was indicative of the ideology of institutional stability. It was, however, also indicative of an actual economic situation and, in particular, of an economic mechanism by which the coordination of urban projects and the return to a type of architecture that was heavily monumental, not only in its taste but likewise in its construction methods, became part of the vital processes of the city in its making.

The City Beautiful under Imperialism

The decisive change from laissez-faire to the domination of the corporations took place, according to Williams, in 1897, with the accession to power of McKinley's Republican administration.[136] Even in the fields of city management and construction the shift gave rise to a different production organization. The private concessionary companies that provided public services for the cities began to merge; in Philadelphia, for example, there were thirty transport companies in 1880 and only one in 1895.[137] Technological development itself demanded such mergers. Holding companies brought together the public utilities of various cities under unified management. Along with the new organization of public services went a rational reorganization of the road networks. The unification of such vast and complex undertakings signified a type of management and a financial organization that only companies of considerable strength could provide.

In addition, the Republicans' anti-inflationary and antiunion policies favored the scheme of production that had been established by the bosses, which was that based on the wide use of unskilled labor and a carefully controlled proportion of skilled labor, a formula that managed to avoid an open clash between opposing interests. The relationship between such production policies and the widespread trend toward monumental architecture, heavy in both its taste and its construction techniques, is quite obvious: the technological specialization required in the construction of skyscrapers was avoided, and it became possible to make use of masses of unskilled workers in a quantity flexibly gauged to resolve the employment problem.

Technological development was actually not the prime goal of the rational reorganization that took place in all areas of production at this time.[138] The principal aim, instead, was the replacement of individual, specialized enterprises, competing among themselves and thus weak in face of the class struggle, with more complex and depersonalized organizations, which could defend themselves from both the pressure of the unions and the force of public opinion aroused by the muckrakers.

In the field of building construction, the City Beautiful movement as an ideology and as an activity would serve to promote those pacifying and stabilizing policies that were now felt to be necessary and of which Theodore

Roosevelt would become the prime interpreter. His domestic politics were based on good intentions toward the worker but absolute intolerance of strikes, on combatting corrupt bosses but opposing even more fiercely the muckrakers,[139] and on encouraging efficiency and rational organization but guarding against the trusts' gaining power over the government.

Even before it came to serve the imperialist politics of the United States, City Beautiful expressed a utopian order achieved by composing the most disquieting contradictions in a harmonious monument to the state. Still earlier, the White City had been intended on an ideological level as a reconciliation of contrasts, not only the East-West conflict in the field of architecture but also the opposition of the two political parties that found a common ground in the fair. Even the radical differences between the Park movement and Beaux-Arts monumentalism, as well as those between the liberal antiurban concepts and the city, were not nearing a resolution. And in the field of building construction proper, City Beautiful, particularly as practiced by Burnham, implicitly extended to the whole city a proposal to overcome the long-standing conflict between bosses and reformers.

In opposition to all the goals of the City Beautiful movement was the contemporary House Beautiful movement, the principles of which were fully set forth in 1896 in Frank Lloyd Wright and William C. Gannett's book *The House Beautiful* and in the periodicals of various radical associations which were first published in just these years.[140] These intellectual initiatives remained on the margins of political and economic life; along with Wright their supporters accepted expulsion from the city. From inspiration they looked to the European Arts and Crafts movements,[141] and while waiting for their views to gain influence in the future development of city planning—through the doctrines of Patrick Geddes, for example—these dissenters identified their untimely aspirations with those of such men as Sullivan.

At this time, moreover, the overtly imperialist turn taken by American politics gave rise to doubts that seriously motivated dissension. The reaction of America's "progressive" intellectuals did not really go much beyond doubt, however; their position remained one of uncertainty. Opposition to Roosevelt's bellicose policies came, in fact, not from the Democrats but from the conservatives of Wall Street, who, unlike the progressives advanced precise arguments against the war. As Richard Hofstadter has written, "War has always been the Nemesis of the liberal tradition in America. From our earliest history as a nation there has been a curiously persistent association between democratic politics and nationalism, jingoism, or war."[142]

On April 19, 1898, after barely a year of Republican rule, Congress had approved armed intervention against Spain in Cuba. Under the idealistic cover of liberating the Cubans lay the immediate objective of putting an end to a civil war that was damaging to the large American landowners' interests on the island. The occupation of Cuba was followed by that of Puerto Rico and by George Dewey's attack on the Spanish in Manila. In 1898 Hawaii was annexed. In 1900 the

United States participated with the more powerful European nations in repressing the Boxer Rebellion in China and consolidated their power in the Philippines. When Roosevelt succeeded McKinley, America became a mediator in the Russo-Japanese conflict, sent a threatening fleet around the world, and, with the usual pretext of liberating the insurgent natives, took the Panama Canal question in hand.

Roosevelt's imperialist actions in Latin America were justified by a rather strained extension of the old Monroe Doctrine of noninterference between America and Europe: United States intervention was necessary in order to prevent acts of domination by European nations in the Western Hemisphere. Intervention was also justified by the necessity of reestablishing order and efficiency. In Santo Domingo, anticipating an eventual military action, the United States intervened to defend the little republic against its European creditors. When it occupied Panama, in a move that Williams has termed "imperial landgrabbing,"[143] it did so "to stop endless talk and get the work done."[144]

Such enterprises were naturally accompanied by an elaborate ideological program that presented the Americans as missionaries of order and civilization and thus by right the arbiters of all controversies. Architecture was to play an important role in providing a cultural mask for the bolder operations of America's Open Door policy. The creation of such an architecture was a task eagerly accepted by Burnham. First, however, he was to experience some failures, among them his plan for West Point, through which he came to realize the limits to the application of the principles of City Beautiful.

Burnham, along with others, was invited by Elihu Root, Roosevelt's secretary of war, to participate in the competition for the improvement of West Point.[145] By now a celebrated architect, Burnham was initially hesitant about submitting a proposal; there was no guarantee that the work would ever be carried out, and the remuneration was very small. McKim, Mead and White had already refused because of the jury's known bias in favor of designs in the neogothic style, similar to the existing buildings by Hunt.

Burnham decided to participate after all when he found that he could count on the assistance of Edward H. Bennett, of Post's studio in New York, whose able collaboration he was henceforth never to do without. Visiting the site with Bennett one morning in the spring of 1903, Burnham gave particular attention to the natural axes of the terrain, according to a Beaux-Arts method of approach that had come alive for him through his direct knowledge of the monumental complexes of ancient Greece. The method is explicitly described in his report on the project:

A study of the ground on which the United States Military Academy is located, leads to the belief that there is one main axis superior to all others for a monumental treatment of the post. . . . It begins on the east side of the river, and, passing across the water, bisects the plateau which forms the parade ground, and then passes upward toward the mountains of the background through a dip between the foothills that lie at their feet.

It has seemed wrong to neglect the course to be pursued when Nature herself has so plainly indicated it. It therefore becomes a question whether one should adopt any compromise offering an inferior solution to the problem; and it would be a compromise to attempt to retain many of the buildings already erected, when an ideal design is plainly possible for both the practical and the beautiful sides of the problem. And because this work is to be for all time, we have, after much hesitation, come to the conclusion that, we should present that scheme which will ultimately bring about the noblest results, rather than one which at best must ever be unequal to it. The main reason for this choice lies in a conviction that order and system of a high quality surrounding a young soldier will strengthen within him a respect for law, so far as environment can affect him.[146]

Burnham and Bennett treated the project for the Military Academy at West Point as an opportunity to design a town plan from the beginning, unhampered by preexisting structures. Their declared intention of adapting the plan to the natural environment, far from conditioning the design naturalistically, actually determined the principal lines of its layout. The central plateau, destined for the parade ground and the other official functions of the institution, is characterized by the stateliness of a severe and strictly axial composition. The offices and all the essential administrative functions of the Academy are located along the slope of the hill, but every building is connected to the central area by a rigidly designed road system laid out like the arms of a machine, according to a direct and simple logic that thoroughly resolves all problems of communication. Instead, the living quarters, situated on the opposite side of the central plateau, are extended along the decline, in a looser, more open layout which seeks an equilibrium between geometry and nature.

The project was to remain an academic exercise, however. The architects had failed to measure their plan against the intentions of the patrons and the extent of their cultural interest; moreover, they had flatly proposed the destruction of the existing buildings designed by Hunt, who had died only seven years earlier. Burnham had probably counted on the support of two of the members of the jury, George B. Post and Cass Gilbert. But it was not possible to ask so much even of them, particularly when he had proceeded with such arrogance and lack of respect for the rules of the game, one that McKim had had the foresight not to enter.[147]

Just over a year after the West Point defeat, on April 24, 1904, another secretary of war, the future president William Howard Taft, summoned Burnham to Washington and invited him to go to the Philippines to study plans for renovating the old capital of Manila and for the new summer capital of Baguio. The popular uprising against the occupation of the American "liberators" had been crushed and an "organic" law had been adopted in the archipelago by which autonomy would be granted to the inhabitants in exchange for order. Independence would be conceded by degrees.

This moment was a natural one to sound the trumpets of ideology. In 1901, immediately after Dewey's victory over the Spanish and the first insurrection, Secretary of War Root had, in fact, proposed that the Washington Park Commission should go to the Philippines to offer advice after their European

IMPROVEMENTS
AT
WEST POINT

GENERAL PLAN

PARADE GROUND

Plan for West Point prepared by Daniel H.
Burnham and Edward H. Bennett for the
competition in 1903.

trip. As Burnham later wrote, "No sooner had the United States come into the possession of the Philippine Islands than the War Department set about adapting the capital city of Manila to the changed conditions brought about by the influx of Americans, who are used to better conditions of living than had prevailed in those islands."[148] The real problem was quickly to find cultural formulas to impose that would make the existing ideological structures ineffective in forming any concrete opposition. Seizing on urban design as a means of undermining the historical authority of local traditions, the Americans had to demonstrate a ready ability in psychosociological manipulation. This ability had already been demonstrated in the Americas at the time of the Spanish colonizers.[149]

The native uprising in the Philippines had interrupted the ideological crusade and had been put down with less persuasive but more rapid methods than those architecture. Once calm was reestablished, Burnham was recognized as the man to take the architectural operation in hand. Nevertheless, the choice of Burnham for this task came about less directly than one might suppose. The real story of the appointment has been brought to light by Thomas S. Hines, who has assembled the documents relating to the intricate commercial and missionary interests of all those involved in the affair.[150] The story of Burnham's appointment goes back to his friendship with W. Cameron Forbes, nephew of Ralph Waldo Emerson and future governor of the Philippines. The mature architect admired the young man and heartily approved of his desire to work in government service abroad. In 1903 Burnham recommended him to Theodore Roosevelt for a post as envoy in Panama; in 1904 Forbes was sent to the Philippines and thus the task of finding a celebrated architect fell to him. After having contacted Frederick Law Olmsted, Jr., who was too busy with other projects, he wrote independently to both McKim and Burnham. Quite unexpectedly, since this was an unpaid appointment, both accepted, Burnham very readily, McKim with more circumspection. Taft's intervention was needed to resolve the rather embarrassing situation in which Forbes now found himself. Burnham was in any case recognized by all involved as the man best suited to the job.

Burnham, in turn, found in America's imperial policies the perfect outlet for what he most believed in: the possibility of order and the usefulness of beauty. Through his tools of design he was confident of commanding the power of American capital: capital by far more fully evolved and readily controlled than that which had provided Haussmann with the means of transforming Paris. Nor was he impeded by social or sociological scruples; as a good reader of Kipling, he seems to have considered these newly conquered people "half devil and half child" and, on the whole, a rather surly lot.

Before departing for the Philippines, Burnham initiated the plan for the city of San Francisco. In a letter to Charles Moore written in August 1904, he spoke of the projects for San Francisco and Manila and declared, "The work now in hand is delightful."[151] He was about to leave for California, where between

September 20 and October 12, together with Bennett and Willis Polk, he would begin work on the plan for San Francisco, concluding a promotional campaign he himself had begun two years before with his design for the Merchants Exchange Building, which had now been taken over by the Association for the Improvement and Adornment of San Francisco. As in other cases, Burnham's planning for San Francisco was almost unremunerated, but it was a project of great prestige, which allowed him to open, with Bennett and Polk, a branch office of his studio in that rapidly developing city. Immediately after his work there was completed, he was scheduled to embark on the *Mongolia*, headed eventually for the Philippines. On the ideological level, Burnham seems to have felt no difference between these two projects, except, perhaps, the greater messianic spirit he attached to the latter.

As on his other trips, he gathered together a whole party, including his wife, his daughter Margaret, and this time even a general. They stopped in Honolulu and then in Yokohama, where the rickshaw that took them to their hotel was hardly a surprise for anyone after the Columbian Exposition. On October 31, they arrived in Tokyo by train. At dinner they met the Japanese ministers of war, of the navy, and of foreign affairs, as well as other dignitaries. Tourist outings, such as that to Lotus Lake, alternated with military parades; at one, eight thousand men filed in review before the Mikado. The month of November was given over to a peculiar official vacation, certainly an integral part of the complex diplomatic relations between the two countries. In the midst of the Russo-Japanese War, and at the moment when Port Arthur was about to fall, Burnham's delegation was a notable manifestation of partiality in spite of Roosevelt's official policy of neutral mediation.

In December they arrived in Manila, where Burnham and his collaborator in this project, Pierce Anderson,[152] were received by Forbes and Governor Luke E. Wright.[153] In the Philippines, the round of official ceremonies continued at a steady pace. To the marathon of dinners and fiestas were added the long trips into the mountains, by foot and horse, to select the site for the summer capital. This direct and onerous encounter with the landscape, which tried Burnham's Yankee temperament,[154] was not without influence on his work. He wrote to Moore in 1905, "It surprises me to find how much this trip has modified my views, not only regarding the exteme East, but regarding ourselves and all our European precedents. It will take time to get a true perspective of it all in my mind."[155]

This salutary uncertainty can perhaps be felt in the less accentuated imperial character of the plan for Manila and in its designer's more attentively receptive attitude toward the social, cultural, and natural context in which he was working. Burnham's concern for the preexisting architecture was concentrated on the Spanish monuments; in recommending the preservation of the narrow, shaded streets in the center of the city, however, he extended this concern to the older architecture. The plan is full of details and suggestions calibrated to the climate and the sociological situation; its principal structural elements result not from a priori decisions but, rather, from an attentive and sensitive examination of the existing city and its monuments. Burnham prescribed the conservation and restoration of the city walls and proposed that the moat surrounding them be transformed into a belt of parks. Rather than superimposing the new administrative center upon the existing official structures, he placed the new complex beside the old, implying a certain equivalence.

In Manila, City Beautiful tended to become more properly city planning, in part also because of the long period of time over which the plan was actually carried out, under the direction of William E. Parsons. [156] All Burnham's earlier works, from the White City to West Point, even the plan then in progress for San Francisco, were far removed from Manila in their methodology; they were now part of the past.

The plan for Baguio lacked the many sensitively studied details that characterized the plan for Manila. According to Burnham himself it was merely preliminary, a scheme for directing the overall growth of the town. Baguio was conceived as an official, administrative city that would not exceed 25,000 inhabitants, to be built in a completely wild area 5,180 feet above sea level. There were no conditioning elements; in fact, at the time Burnham drew up his plan, he had no idea of the routes to be taken by the roads and railway connecting the summer capital with Manila and the rest of the country.

Within the irregular terrain that Burnham and his technicians found so difficult to explore on foot, three level areas were selected for the site of the town. According to the plan these were to be connected by a geometric system of streets that, as Burnham specified, would have to be adapted insofar as possible to the ungeometric contours of the Baguio valley. The concept of order established in opposition to the existing natural context was asserted in the report on the plan less as a means of ideological expression than as a technical precept of urban design, applicable not only to natural chaos but also to the artificial chaos of the laissez-faire city. Certainly at Baguio the City Beautiful method is fully affirmed; the heights become structures from which to enjoy the view, the valleys are dominated by symmetrical axes, and the public buildings are the compositional nodes of the urban design. Burnham's plan was exactly what his patrons wanted. The secretary of war was delighted and did not fail to express his gratitude to Burnham for his thorough and disinterested work. [157]

The plans for Manila and Baguio, completed by Anderson after Burnham's departure, were carried out under Parsons's creative control. Parsons's work in the Philippines is itself of interest from the purely architectural point of view. Through an accurate study of the islands' traditional forms and techniques, he managed, while following the indications of the plans, to imbue the architecture with his own geometrizing interpretation, similar in style to the contemporary work of Irving Gill in California. [158]

With Burnham's initial impetus and under Parsons's constant and intelligent direction, the actual construction proceeded smoothly—so smoothly it surprised Burnham himself, who was used to the slowness and delays of "democracy." In colonial regimes, obviously, designs were carried out. This efficiency, of course, also resulted from the fact that colonial practices coincided with the City Beautiful method in disregarding the urban needs of the population; in both cases, the neglect of such problems was masked by the attention given the city's official structures. This suggests that underdeveloped countries, with their particular type of political system, were the places destined for the actual realization of the City Beautiful. Manila and Baguio were capital cities, however, and it was largely because of this particular institutional significance that architectural ideology was given greater importance than in other cities and also favored in its realization on an urban scale, as had occurred earlier in Washington and would occur later in Canberra and New Delhi.

Burnham's prestige derived from his urban projects, while the prestige of other architects, such as McKim, stemmed principally from particular buildings. From his work on the Washington project to his death in 1909, McKim remained on the crest of the wave, but Pennsylvania Station, the restoration of the White House, and the enlargement of the Metropolitan Museum, all works executed in the first years of the century by McKim, Mead and White, did not transcend the architectural scale.

In Washington, Burnham had personally designed Union Station, but this was an exceptional case. In his work on isolated buildings, he usually behaved in a much more strictly professional way and, at least after the Flatiron, probably participated very little in the actual design, delegating this work to his collaborators, above all the highly qualified Ernest R. Graham.[159] Works such as the Ford Building in Detroit, designed in 1908, demonstrate a professional standard of the highest order, as does the firm's other Detroit skyscraper, the Dime Building (1910). The design for the latter used two towers with a common base, a scheme that would later be repeated in the Equitable Building in New York, Graham's masterpiece. The same scheme was ultimately adopted in a heretical and thoroughly exceptional version in the recent World Trade Center in New York.[160]

Burnham's whole career seems to be based on a precise and conscious plan, which earned him fewer medals and honorary degrees than McKim during his lifetime and less space in the history of architecture afterwards but which had the merit of being clear. On the one hand, he had his strictly professional activity, conducted according to production practices (and not always the most advanced) and keenly attuned to the laws of competition and the market; on the other, culture, prestige, and ideology, which allowed space for rhetoric and grandiose gestures as well as for a lordly display of disinterestedness that hid the obvious promotional advantages of this more public area of activity for the acquisition of new commissions in the strictly professional area. In the professional area the situation could be realistically assessed in a few words; the production of skyscrapers was the right course to follow and the rule of prodecure was to delegate and divide the work involved. In the public area Burnham played a favored role in the limelight of culture, the academy, and "imperial" urban design.

Thus an extraordinary coherence and continuity appear in Burnham's activity from the days of the Chicago school onward—not so much in his stylistic expression, which in this case is not essential, as in his mental attitude. In terms of his involvement in the projects there is a marked and sudden difference between his initial commissions for skyscrapers, where he left his partner, Root, a free hand, and his concern and vigilance over the White City, in essence a metaphorical capital of the New World. This change corresponds exactly to his different attitudes toward his strictly professional activities, delegated to Graham, and the plans for West Point or Baguio, unquestionably products of his own hand and works eminently endowed with "values."

It is in the face of such lucidity and realism that we can fully understand the painful inevitability of Sullivan's professional failure. All Sullivan's ardent dedication to quality and ideology was wasted on works in the field of commercial construction, where "values" are not recognized. In comparison with Sullivan, even McKim's cultured professionalism seems more coherent; his rejection of the skyscraper and his insistence, instead, on works of an official or cultural character made him an architect of the highest order, in the manner of the great French architects. Nevertheless, even McKim's extraordinary success was at times overcast by the unresolved contradiction between an activity completely dedicated to professional production (that is, to architecture as opposed to urban design) and his presumptuous refusal to compromise with his patrons when his classical ideal was involved. This paradox was a source of great anxiety for McKim, who suffered not only the criticism of the press,[161] but even the reproaches of the highest American official of the time; Theodore Roosevelt, provoked by McKim, felt bound to uphold "criticism . . . against the profession of architects by reason of their delay."[162]

At the time of the San Francisco earthquake and fire, Burnham was in Europe on one of his frequent cultural expeditions.[163] A telegram urgently summoned him back; the events might be decisive for his plan for the city. The enormous destruction automatically aroused the hope of finally applying the emphatic theories of the City Beautiful to a developing metropolis. The *Craftsman* published an article entitled "Destruction of San Francisco Brings Burnham Plan into Fresh Prominence." Even if precedents as remote and as recent as London and Chicago contradicted this hope, the architects in Burnham's office made an attempt. The moment had arrived when the ideological and the strictly professional approach to design, hitherto practiced separately, were to be combined in a single effort. Although the fire had passed so near that many drawings had been destroyed, they managed to work quickly enough to deliver the final plan on May 21, 1906, just a month after the earthquake.[164]

On paper, the plan for San Francisco is probably the most elegant ever to bear Burnham's name. Bennett, his principal collaborator, was a master designer, as his activity after Burnham's death demonstrates.[165] Burnham's contribution to the project was limited to its first phase, during which the basic layout was

Plan of Manila by Daniel H. Burnham and
Pierce Anderson, executed between 1905
and 1914 by William E. Parsons, showing
the two faces of Burnham's activity—the
cultural and the professional.

Plan of Baguio, summer capital of the
Philippines, by Daniel H. Burnham, 1905.

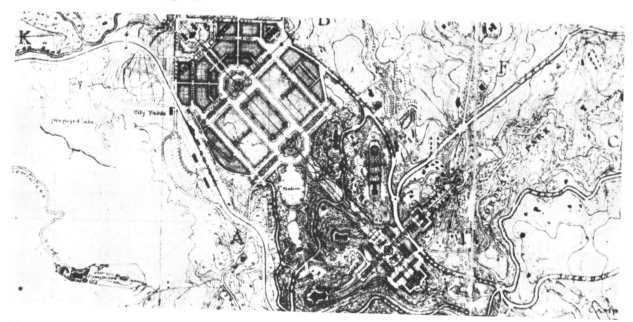

Ford Building, Detroit, by Burnham
and Company, 1908.

Dime Building, Detroit, by Burnham
and Company, 1910.

Plan for San Francisco by Daniel H. Burnham,
Edward H. Bennett, and Willis Polk, 1906.

established, but the structural logic of his method made it possible to delegate its execution. Indeed, since there were no requests for changes between the first phase of the designing and its completion—changes that only Burnham would have been able to make—the plan offers a perfect demonstration of his concept of City Beautiful. That is, it demonstrates how a disorganized conglomeration of grid-planned areas, abutting at diverse angles and interrupted by the irregularity of the terrain, can be brought into a miraculous formal equilibrium by the imposition of a different logic, which is comprehensive and abstract in respect to the ordinary scale of spontaneous alterations of the urban fabric.

The method is clear. The conglomeration of grid-planned areas is the basic material; the places where the irregularities of nature interrupt the grids, the junctions of diversely proportioned grids, or the angular abutments of grids are the occasions for a formal solution, which, however, has reference to a scale far greater than that controlled by the individual grid-planned areas themselves. From disorder arises order; from confusion, clarity.

The task is thus to seize on and exploit, in the most inventive and consequential way possible, certain points already fixed within the context. In the plan of San Francisco, this aim is accomplished with a theoretical exactness that is almost excessive. The unconstructed heights become parks, designed in the manner of Olmsted with elegantly irregular, winding roads. The parks ultimately offer both lofty points from which to view the city below and, inversely, sites for monuments that form the distant foci of the long perspectives of the principal urban thoroughfares. The lines of juncture between grid-planned areas become boulevards, their axes carefully directed toward worthy focal points. The junctions of the boulevards constitute new key points that must be made to emerge with distinction; these are the sites of large public buildings and monumentally designed squares.

The whole is connected in a unified structure, based on the typical urban forms of the City Beautiful, forms given to canonical and predictable solutions, characterized by an emphasis on visual gratification. According to Reps, Burnham's San Francisco plan had "more merit as an abstract design than as a serious proposal for public improvement."[166] Later on, however, Reps attributes the failure of the plan to the hurry in reconstructing the city. Instead, its failure has a more exact and realistic explanation. The idea that it would be possible to realize the plan as the result of the fire was in itself fallacious. The fire destroyed and damaged the buildings but in no way changed the minutely divided structure of the land as it existed legally in the city's land registry; yet it was precisely this structure that would have had to have been changed in order to realize Burnham's plan. In the absence of any power capable of effecting such a transformation, Burnham's plan could not but remain an "abstract design."

The Plan of Chicago

It was certainly not mere happenstance that an unprecedented enterprise like the planning of Chicago came into being in 1907. This was both the first complete plan for an American metropolis and the first to involve the whole metropolitan region. The other City Beautiful plans, including that of Washington, had been concerned only with the urban center or parts of it. That a group of financiers decided to promote the study and preparation of such a plan, donate it to the city, organize an unprecedented publicity campaign around it, and finally create an elephantine organization to execute it and that all this was undertaken in the very year of the financial panic is a coincidence that must be explained.

This economic juncture indicated a change of course no less decisive than that of 1893. Theodore Roosevelt wrote, in 1906, "I do not at all like the social conditions at present. The dull, purblind folly of the very rich men; their greed and arrogance, . . . the corruption in business and politics, have tended to produce a very unhealthy condition of excitement and irritation in the popular mind, which shows itself in part in the enormous increase in the socialist propaganda."[167] It was this preoccupation that prompted Roosevelt to play the role of "tamer of trusts" and to seek both a certain rapprochement with Bryan's views and the passage of important laws such as the Hepburn Act, which granted the federal government control over the railroads. The middle class's loss of faith in the system was, in fact, the most evident aspect of the widespread crisis into which the United States had been driven by the long and increasingly organized class struggle led by the unions. Although the crusades of the muckrakers and the denunciations made by the intellectuals could direct labor's discontent along the lines of a nonrevolutionary protest,[168] the situation could certainly no longer be resolved merely by moral condemnation and a reversal of tendency limited to the appeasement of a specific grievance.

During McKinley's presidency and Roosevelt's first term in office, economic development had been continually stimulated, while immigration and the employment of unskilled immigrants had increased steadily.[169] That the wholesale-price index continued to rise despite the Republicans' anti-inflationary efforts, however, proves the existence of strong union pressure.[170] The Open Door policy and the international investments that absorbed a large part of the capital of American corporations from 1904 on now posed the problem of new outlets for production. Growth became increasingly difficult to maintain, and the tightness of credit finally made it virtually impossible. European investments in the United States briefly sustained employment, but the flow of credit became steadily weaker; by September 1906, the banks were in default and the Treasury Department had to intervene. The panic of 1907, like that which had been rapidly checked in 1903, was a panic among the big investors. The railroads, involved in enormous development programs that had been blocked by the Hepburn Act, vainly sought funds from the banks and in March 1907 began to sell their holdings; the first bankruptcies were declared in the late spring. Toward the end of the year, the steel magnate J. P. Morgan managed to restore stability.[171]

The situation in the construction industry was no better than in other areas of production. From 1899 to 1904, with the lowering of technical standards and the employment in construction of great masses of freshly immigrated, unskilled workers, the price of steel gradually declined. In 1905, however, it began to rise; in exchange for order and social stability, the countries subjugated by the Open Door policy demanded efficient transportation systems; this meant the building of railroads and bridges and a consequent rise in the demand for American steel. Building production peaked until 1906, when it declined rapidly. The panic of 1907 was followed by a depression and a marked decline in steel production. Prices rose by a third, and unemployment became a menacing problem. The general improvement of the situation in 1909 was not sufficient to restore the health of the construction industry; no sooner did it begin to pick up than it was hit by the new depression of 1910.

During these years any risk was worth taking that might force the economic cycle upward again—preferably remaining within the possibilities of national resources and relying above all on building construction. Many cities bet on just this plan of action. Among them was Chicago; with the impetus of the new plan it seemed that the city might be about to regain the central role it had played in the 1880s.

Since that time the Open Door policy had favored New York and San Francisco, cities turned toward Europe and Asia. With the limelight of history directed elsewhere, Chicago had become fertile ground for a vital political and social activity impeded in other cities by the dynamics of development. It became the center of the crusade for the eight-hour day, and it was in Chicago, in 1905, that the Industrial Workers of the World was founded. This significant political agitation corresponded to a more virulent dissension on the part of the Chicago intellectuals. Indeed, at the beginning of the century, Chicago could boast of being the most progressive city in the country—demonstrated by the group of intellectuals who gathered around Jane Addams and by the Department of Sociology founded at the University of Chicago as early as 1892, from which the Chicago school of sociology would descend. [172]

In this atmosphere and faced with such grave economic problems, the city's big businessmen decided to give new life to an old idea, making use of the discipline of city planning, but on an unprecedented scale. Burnham's lakefront improvement project had been ready since 1896, but what these men now foresaw was a plan for the entire metropolitan area of Chicago.

Planning projects were being enthusiastically undertaken everywhere at the time. Geddes had launched the concept of the city as an organism. The City Beautiful movement had given rise to widespread interest, even economic interest, in planning. Between 1906 and 1908—the blackest years of the economic crisis—plans were made for Denver, Oakland, Dubuque, Ridgewood, Savannah, Roanoke, San Diego, Utica, Columbus, Hartford, and Milwaukee. A whole new generation of town planners, among whom John Nolen was to be one of the most significant, began their activity during these years. At the base of this planning fervor was the principle, dear to Andrew Carnegie, of increasing production capacity during the bad times in order to be ready for the good times when they come: "The man who has money during a panic is the wise and valuable citizen."[173]

As early as 1906, the two clubs to which the financial leaders of the city belonged, the Commercial and the Merchants', saw clearly the utility of extending Burnham's project and charging him with the preparation of a general plan for the whole metropolitan area. The following year, merged under the name of the Commercial Club, they organized a committee for the plan, headed by Charles D. Norton, with Charles H. Wacker as vice-chairman.

Burnham set up a special studio for the project at the top of the Railway Exchange building and, as usual, immediately and energetically dedicated himself personally to his new great task; in this case, he was assisted by both Bennett and Graham. Continual meetings with his patrons during the first phase of the project made possible the formation of a realistic basic program. In addition to Norton's and Wacker's, the names that recur in Burnham's diary are those of Frederick A. Delano, Edward Butler, Walter Wilson, Franklin McVeagh, Clyde M. Carr, John V. Farwell, and Cyrus and Harold R. McCormick. The patrons of the plan were a group of private individuals with the power and intention of taking the development of the city in hand by imposing on it a coordination that was now considered a necessity. They behaved like the owners and future operators of the new plan. The city was literally managed by this group of men, and all decisions resulted from agreements and negotiations at its highest level.

Burnham worked full time on the Chicago project for the first three months of 1907, establishing the basic layout of the plan derived from discussions with the committee. Once he had arrived at a clear idea of the structural scheme, Burnham left the field to his highly qualified collaborators; he had experimented with and theorized about the delegation of work, and no one knew how to do it better than he. Important commissions required his presence elsewhere: two buildings in Pittsburgh for Harry W. Oliver, the New Orleans Terminal, and the Cleveland viaduct.

A run-in with McKim had served in the end to keep Burnham on the Washington Park Commission Consultation Board, despite his constant absence.[174] By now the two men were inevitably vying for cultural leadership in their field. McKim, master of the Beaux-Arts technique, collector of honorary degrees and medals, former champion sportsman in Paris and prince of the French salons, was not ready to step aside for what he considered a rather crude and certainly inferior culture and taste, not to be scorned, but certainly not to be feared. He admired and respected Burnham's dynamism and his incredible enthusiasm and capacity in promoting and organizing projects, but on the cultural level McKim felt himself superior. Thus he was not anxious about a direct confrontation on the subject of the design for the Washington Cathedral. Both men naturally aspired to the prestigious commission, an enormous catch professionally, on which they just as naturally held opposing views. The patron of the new cathedral, Bishop Henry Yates Satterlee, favored the English Gothic style from the very start. McKim, eternally ready to battle for his ideal, fought for a church in the classical style. Burnham's position, and his behavior through the affair, is interesting to follow.

In January 1906, Satterlee had invited McKim, Burnham, Bernard Green, Sir Caspar Purdon Clarke, and Charles Moore to become members of an advisory commission. At its first meeting, in February of the same year, Burnham was absent; he had left for Europe, apparently to study Gothic cathedrals. McKim found himself alone among the members in his fight for the classical style; he tried in every way, however, to get Burnham on his side, and in this he finally succeeded by describing the classical style as necessary to the environmental uniformity of the Mall, as well as by historical logic. In June 1906 Burnham wrote to the bishop in favor of his colleague's thesis, arguing that classicism, as a discipline, opposes order against the arbitrary. [175]

In this same letter, however, Burnham mentioned the possibility of finding someone other than McKim capable of producing a valid design—Edward H. Bennett, for instance. In proposing his own collaborator, he assured the bishop that he himself would not be involved in the project in any way. In August the bishop answered Burnham with two letters sent simultaneously, one official and the other personal; Satterlee discouraged Burnham from persisting in his defense of the classical style, which he described as notoriously less religious than the Gothic, "the distinctively . . . Christian style of architecture." In November he communicated to Burnham the names of the future designers of the NeoGothic cathedral, George F. Bodley of London and Henry Vaughan of Boston. Burnham responded curtly, washing his hands of the whole affair.

In April 1907, however, trusting in the ability of his collaborators, Burnham left Chicago and spent three months in Europe systematically studying the French and English Gothic styles. In June 1907 Bishop Satterlee sent copies of the proposal for the cathedral project to the members of the advisory commission. Burnham's response reveals the motive for his sudden return trip to Europe. His letter is an incredible attempt to oust the architects already engaged and, as an obstinate point of pride, to impose his own views, which differed from McKim's and were based on a superior cultural principle.

On July 27, 1907, Burnham wrote to the bishop, saying in essence that he had repeated the trip he made in 1906 and, together with two young scholars (one of whom was his son Hubert, then studying at the Ecole des Beaux Arts), had revisited the Gothic cathedrals of France and England, carrying with him the works of the French, English, and American authorities; he had "come home feeling that the architects of Chartres, Amiens, and Nôtre Dame were among the greatest artists that ever lived." He knew now, Burnham said, exactly what the cathedral ought to be like; before he committed any further errors, the bishop should "let the designing rest on its oars" and restudy the whole field in company with an American Gothic scholar (Burnham suggested Charles Moore).

In conclusion he declared the real Gothic to be that of France and insinuated that while no Englishman of the time could imitate it, an American could.[176] This remarkable affair had a lugubrious ending. Within a few months of Burnham's letter and the bishop's embarrassed reply, both the bishop and the English architect Bodley died. Vaughan died nine years later, leaving the cathedral uncompleted.[177]

During the depression and the consequent lull in construction work Burnham dedicated himself to the cultivation of his cultural role, in which he was no longer overshadowed by anyone.[178] Collecting elements for the plan of Chicago, he was again in Europe in the autumn of 1908. He visited Port Sunlight and, in London, met Frederick Law Olmsted, Jr., and Frank Foster of the Chicago Park Commission, with whom he visited the London parks and those in and near Paris. He then went on to Frankfurt, Jena, and Berlin and finally to Rome, where the prestigious initiative of the American Academy was in difficulty because of the indisposition of McKim, the real founder of the institution and, together with Burnham, its principal supporter.[179]

Meanwhile, work on the plan for Chicago was proceeding. The criteria for all important decisions were efficiency and realism. Nonetheless, Burnham's attentive and foresighted patrons did not overlook the aesthetic aspect; to this, with faultless business sense, they appropriated a precise percentage of the total cost, once again according to the principle of maximum yield.

The structure of the plan came into being as a basic layout for transportation routes, conceived on a regional scale, a network of highways and railroad lines disposed radially and concentrically in relation to the city's economic center. The location of this center was a serious issue, which gave rise to much discussion. The dispute went back at least to the time when the site for the Columbian Exposition was chosen; the selection of Jackson Park had had the effect of moving the economic axis of the city southward. This move was already reflected in Burnham's 1896 designs for the lakefront, in which Congress Avenue became the axis of symmetry for Grant Park. At that time, the skyscrapers and famous buildings of the Chicago school, signs of the economic center of the city, were invariably situated to the north of Congress Avenue.[180] Surely, it would be absurd to attribute Burnham's choice of Congress Avenue as the axis of symmetry to mere professional jealousy—that is, to the fact that its inevitable widening would have meant destroying the most striking part of Louis Sullivan's Auditorium Building.[181]

The urban center was already shifting southward in the 1890s. Legal problems of property division inhibiting real estate speculation in the existing area of development were surely only partly responsible for this tendency; given the great freedom of movement allowed the powerful, such problems could easily be overcome. The real reason for the development to the south was the existing layout of the railroads; together with the mouth of the Chicago River, they formed a barrier on the north that extended to the wharfs on the lake.

Burnham's 1896 scheme for the lakefront, its subsequent editions, and the 1909 plan all accepted the location of the railroads as a determining factor. Indeed, they emphasized it by echoing, in the symmetrical layout of Grant Park, the curve formed by the two arms of the railroad that extended toward the lake.

In the official publication of the Chicago plan, the various plans in color clearly show the railroad system to be a major element, occupying with its lines and yards areas well within the center of the city. The railroads were thus the most conspicuous real estate capital with which the plan had to deal. Essentially and significantly, however, the removal of the urban axis to the south was to remain on paper, and with it the huge civic center Burnham had designed as the hub of his radial plan. It is quite clear, in retrospect, that a dichotomy existed between what the plan expressed and what was actually carried out within a short span of time. This disparity does not show that the plan was a bluff. Rather, it was a kind of ceremony, a promise that reality would reshape and redimension, but that served, in the meantime, to mobilize popular enthusiasm for the inspiring objectives of beauty, order, and prestige.

The new, monumental, civic center was the spectacular high point of the plan as presented. F. Janin's large perspective drawings of the complex, dominated by an immense dome, were persuasive in direct proportion to the improbability of their execution. They represented something to be hoped for, an indication of a new level of quality; just as the historic cities of Europe had their St. Peter's, Nôtre Dame, the Louvre, St. Paul's or Westminster, Chicago, too, would have its place of "history."[182] What really made the construction of the civic center unlikely, however, was not its architecture but its decentralized location. Was this an error? On the contrary, this spectacular complex was part of the illusionistic aspect of the plan. A civic center situated so far to the south and, above all, so far from the lakefront and, at the same time, so credible in its formal coherence and its structural necessity to the plan as a whole would naturally make the surrounding areas highly attractive for real estate speculation. The plan indeed foresaw a high density of construction around the complex and eventually, minus the spectacular civic center, this became a densely constructed peripheral area of the city.

Another element fundamental to this illusionistic aspect of the plan was the lakefront. Creating a park on the degraded land along the lake, occupied by the railroad yards, meant extending the desirability of the area around Grant Park for several miles south to Jackson Park and north to Lincoln Park. The plan called for more than six miles of continuous park along the lakefront; it would become, in a sense, the diameter of the huge semicircle designed by Burnham that centered on the intersection of Congress Avenue and La Salle Street. Although it would enclose extensive suburban areas, this semicircle was the metaphorical limit of the city, which served, by means of an efficient radial system of roads, as the center of gravity for a region with a sixty-mile radius.

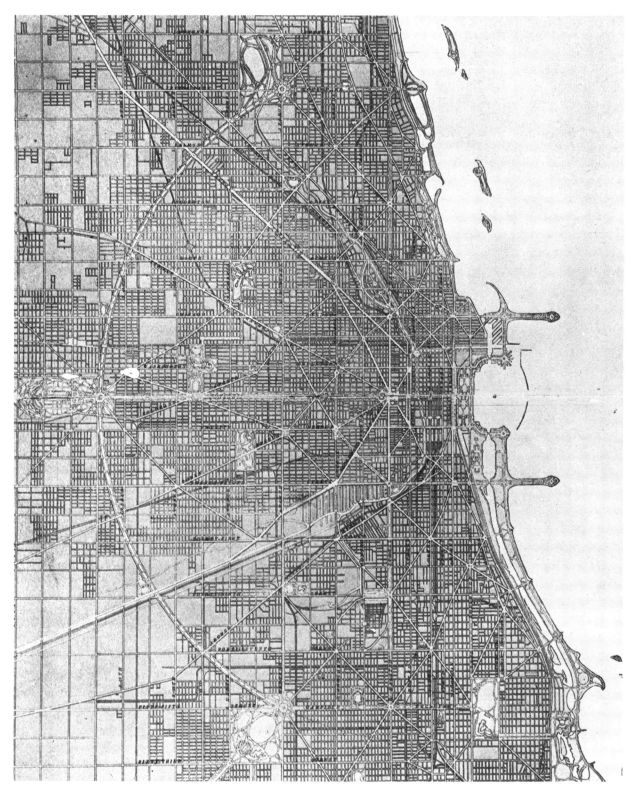

Plan by Daniel Burnham and Edward H.
Bennett for Chicago, 1909, the urban area.
The grand boulevard around the city forms an
arc with a six-mile radius.

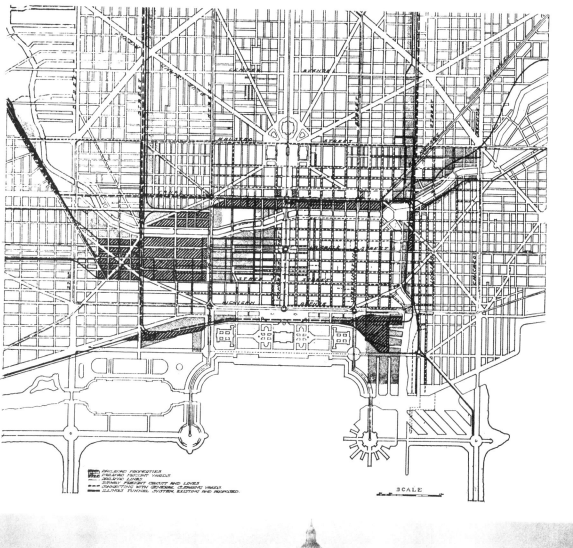

RAILROAD PROPERTIES
RAILROAD FREIGHT YARDS
RAILROAD LINES
SUBWAY FREIGHT CIRCUIT AND LINES
CONNECTING WITH GENERAL CLEARING YARDS
ILLINOIS TUNNEL SYSTEM, EXISTING AND PROPOSED.

SCALE

Plan by Daniel H. Burnham and Edward
H. Bennett for Chicago, 1909, street network
and railroad system between the port and
the civic center.

Plan by Daniel H. Burnham and Edward H.
Bennett for Chicago, 1909, architectural
view of the never-executed civic center.

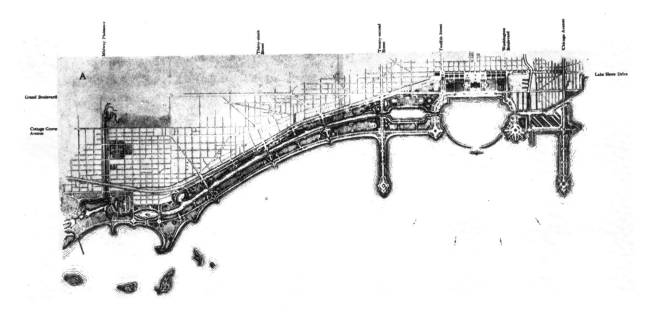

Plan by Daniel H. Burnham and Edward
H. Bennett for Chicago, 1909, the lakefront
park. If it had been built according to the
plan, the park would have extended the
high center-city real estate values all the
way to Jackson Park. From Jackson Park
to Lincoln Park it would have continued
for over six miles, constituting the diameter
of the immense arc with a six-mile radius,
within which Burnham enclosed the city.

This immense semicircle was the third of the fundamental structures conceived by Burnham. Of the three, only a part of the lakefront was ever to be realized and only much later.

Nevertheless, the plan remained in force over a long period; the various portions of it actually realized were, in fact, carried out largely after the period of depression and even after the First World War. This persistence would seem to indicate that between the formal proposals (even those here termed illusionistic) and the organizational decisions based on objective realities there existed a structural coherence, within which the formal proposals could remain, at least in part, purely theoretical enunciations. This coherence undoubtedly arose from the unity of the design, provided by two principal features: the park system, in which existing and projected parks were related by an organic logic to the general structural elements of the plan; and the radial road system that, encountering the existing urban grid, created structural relations on a scale far greater than the grid, therefore giving prominence to the forceful new lines of connection between outstanding elements in the center as well as on the periphery of the city. Thus the general scheme did not suffer unduly when individual elements, even fundamental ones, were not executed, since their projected functional role tended, in any case, to survive. The huge semicircle, for instance, was never built, but its function was eventually assumed by other, albeit less fluid, bypass roads.

In another case this persistence of the projected structural role of a major element that was never executed brought about a remarkable transformation at the very core of the plan; many years later a gigantic, multilevel traffic interchange was constructed where the civic center was to have risen. This substitution provides further astonishing proof of the continuing validity of Burnham's plan, since the transformation is not as radical as it may first appear. In fact, Burnham's huge square was actually conceived as an enormous traffic intersection. The architecture would have masked this function; instead, the development of the urban organism brutally reaffirmed it.

Thus, consciously or unconsciously, the urban design had a double function. The first was the technical one of supporting the theoretical scheme as a whole and defining the scale of its major elements; all local solutions were referred back to the overall scheme, and the adaptation of the formal proposals was left to be worked out during the phase of execution according to the dictates of reality. The second function was ideological, to give sense to the plan as a finished product in itself, on paper, capable of mobilizing the citizenry on its behalf. Burnham's lucid versatility is evident in the clarity with which the plan of Chicago pursues these two functions with equal conviction and competence. Despite the limitations imposed by the task itself, Burnham, by now sixty, masterfully maintained equilibrium between the ideological and the technical aspects of the plan, imbuing both with the maximum power of persuasion.

The intermediate element between the two levels of the plan was, as on other occasions, the park system. Park systems had by now been studied and experimented with for more than half a century and, according to Olmsted's model, provided a clearly defined element that was "sanctified" by use and that was adopted with increasing frequency through the years as a barrier of greenery against the onslaught of the muckrakers. Greenery had indeed become a highly useful element in city plans; it was easy to promote, easy to replace with something else, and, even if carried out only in part, as in Chicago, extremely effective as propaganda.

"City planning work in all its practical essentials is a work of promotion-salesmanship. . . . It is a problem of arousing interest, creating human desire, stirring the spirit for better things and inspiring human action," wrote Walter D. Moody, chief of the publicity office for the Chicago plan, whom Robert L. Wrigley has called the "master salesman of city planning."[183] In 1911, Moody was given the title of managing director of the plan, and it was he who organized the incredible publicity campaign aimed at explaining the importance of the Commercial Club's initiative.

In 1909 the plan was sumptuously presented to the public. Jules Guerin's perspective drawings in watercolor and F. Janin's in pencil, together with the technically perfect and absolutely clear plans personally overseen by Bennett and Graham, produced the impression that some magic force had created order out of chaos. Through the spontaneous munificence of the financiers and the skill of their technicians what Sullivan called "this foul spot on the smiling prairie"[184] was about to become a new Paris, created in the spirit of the Enlightenment and improved by the technology of the future.

In the same year, the report on the plan proposal was published in a lavishly illustrated volume containing reproductions in color of all the exhibition panels.[185] Only 1,650 copies were printed, and at the high price of $25 it was certainly not widely read. In 1911, however, at the end of the depression Moody initiated an enormous editorial campaign. He prepared a 93-page brochure entitled *Chicago's Greatest Issue—An Official Plan*, which was clearly written and cleverly dedicated to the "Owners of Chicago," Moody's term for Chicago's property owners and all persons paying a monthly rent of $25 or more, to whom the 165,000 printed copies were sent free of charge. Moody also wrote a book for students, *Wacker's Manual of the Plan of Chicago*, which contained numerous clear illustrations and which was adopted in 1912 as a textbook by the Chicago Board of Education.

To arouse public interest further Wacker and Moody organized a bureau to give illustrated lectures on city planning in general; the idea, as Wrigley notes, was to present the public with something that would have the appeal of a Burton Holmes travelogue. At the time, illustrated lectures were something quite new and complicated, but they managed nevertheless to put together a collection of two hundred slides, many of them hand colored. The lectures were generally held in school auditoriums, and invitations and tickets were sent out in a number twice that of the seating capacity of the hall. Over a seven-year period, 400 lectures were given and attended by about 175,000 persons. Motion pictures, these too a novelty at the time, were also used in the publicity campaign; *A Tale of One City* had a gala opening and was subsequently shown in sixty theaters. [186] The book *Chicago's World Wide Influence in City Planning* appeared in 1914. In 1916, *Fifty Million Dollars for Nothing* was published; its aim was to arouse public support for the lakefront project. [187]

Wacker proved to be no less skillful a salesman than Moody when in 1909 he published his first article on the plan, containing a detailed descriptive text and the plans of the whole project, as well as plans of the individual parks of the system enclosed within neat rectangular areas taken out of the hands of the real estate speculators. Within these rectangles the parks were laid out as freely designed crystalline compositions in which naturalistic elements were balanced by a complicated geometry, bringing to mind Sullivan's late decorative designs. In his article, Wacker cited statistics on American tourism in Paris printed in August in a French newspaper and showing an overall income of 10 million francs for the months of June and July: "Would it not be a profitable investment for Chicago . . . to be in a position to attract at least part of this travel from other parts of the United States, and even from other parts of the world?" [188] The plan, in its role of a finished product, had to demonstrate that the model—Paris—could readily be matched. Like the utopian city of the year 2000, it was just a step away.

Certainly Charles W. Eliot had Bellamy and the progressive notions frequently aired in times of depression in mind in 1910 when he listed the merits of the plan. Eliot contrasted it with practices that had prevailed up to that time in the development of the city, "whose phenomenal growth has not been guided by far-looking intelligence." In the plan for Chicago, however, one could "see in action democratic enlightened collectivism coming in to repair the damage caused by exaggerated democratic individualism." [189] Eliot considered it an outstanding achievement of the plan that it covered the entire area within a sixty-mile radius around the city center; crossing it required a trip of little more than an hour, given the efficiency of the road network and the rapidity of the available means of transportation. He felt that laws like those already passed in Massachusetts should be enacted to tax suburban residents for a part of the cost of the facilities provided by the city from which they benefitted. Finally, Eliot criticized the plan for its lack of zoning standards governing the density of construction.

The plan was, in fact, very vague in this regard. According to the City Beautiful method, control was limited to the governable elements of the city, that is, essentially to the system of spaces and public works—streets, boulevards, squares, and public buildings. As for the blocks of construction that lined the planned streets, it was already a real accomplishment if uniformity could be imposed for the facades along the main arteries. Behind the facades lay the jungle of the construction bosses. The large perspective drawings of the plan show a consistent density of construction divided by the ably handled layout of streets; this generous construction density was offered to speculation without too many questions asked. Rational control could not be excessive. Construction—in its double role as instrument for forcing the increment of real estate values and as economic stabilizer through its absorption of large quantities of unskilled labor—still required, as it would for a long time to come, a certain vagueness in controls, a flexible program, and space for improvisations.

Eliot, whose criticism of the plan suggests that he supported a more mature and thoroughgoing type of planning, gave great importance to the decor of the streets as a democratic element, because the streets would be the same in the poor as in the rich quarters and because "men, women, and children should be brought out of the crowded houses into the better air of the streets."[190] Thus even he clearly accepted the rows of building blocks that lined the "democratic" streets as the impassable limit of rational control. The report on the plan merely recommended that "provisions be made . . . to ensure . . . as much light and air as possible."[191] As in the days of the nineteenth-century grid plans, those who held the economic power in the city essentially wanted nothing more than a logical basic structure in which to move freely. Thus, as Mumford has observed, the old and the new form of planning were "equally superficial." Mumford's judgment becomes even sharper, however, when referred directly to Burnham, whom he terms a "creator of land values . . . like the merest salesman or advertising agent."[192] It is indeed true that in his treatment of the old grid layout as in the application of the City Beautiful concept Burnham limited his planning operations according to the dictates of the two economic systems governing his work: that of laissez-faire, which permitted no real control of any kind, and that of the powerful corporate interests, which could sustain more organically conceived urban projects and allow him to pursue the City Beautiful idea. Even working within the latter system, however, although the creation of the City Beautiful naturally necessitated rather extensive control, it could not be absolute.

The various projects that turned parts of the plan into reality continued through the years to confirm the validity of its basic concepts. The only portion Burnham was to see carried out before his death in 1912 was the beginning of the enlargement of Michigan Avenue. Work was hindered, but not stopped, by the depressions and the war. In 1920, when Moody died and the great publicity campaign came to an end, many parts of the plan were already in operation, and the most important phase of its execution was about to begin.

Three stations of the new railroad system had already been built—the station on Twelfth Street at the south of the Loop and two farther inland, beyond the Chicago River, Union Station and Northwestern Station. These last two transformed Canal Street, which was enlarged, and had the effect of extending the area of development toward the inland section of the city beyond the river.

Plan by Daniel H. Burnham and Edward H.
Bennett for Chicago, 1909, Twelfth Street
with the layout of the railroad station and
solutions for the railroad intersections
at Michigan and Ashland avenues. Note
the consistent density of the construction
left to private initiative.

The Chicago Plan Commission. Daniel H.
Burnham is at far left.

In connection with building the station, Twelfth Street (present-day Roosevelt Road), running perpendicular to the lakefront, was also enlarged and improved for over two miles at a cost of $8 million. Canal and Twelfth, the first two streets to be reconstructed in accordance with the plan, met at right angles and had the important function of connecting the three new stations with a bypass road outside the Loop.

Michigan Avenue, which formed the limit of the Loop on the lakefront, was enlarged from Randolph Street to Jackson Boulevard at a cost of $15 million. This would become Chicago's spectacular promenade, with its grand display of skyscrapers along one side of the street, which, in turn, forms a terrace on Grant Park and the lake. Other projects early undertaken concerned the outlet of the Chicago River and the area around the port.

In addition to improving the railroad system, the initial application of the plan for the greater metropolitan area involved systematically laying out two large streets situated well inland and running parallel to the lakefront, two chords of Burnham's great semicircle, Ashland Avenue and Western Avenue. Both streets communicated directly with the center, as both crossed the highly important Twelfth Street, running to the lakefront and passing over the railroad crossings.

This first series of projects carried out in accordance with the overall plan included the creation of one of the large diagonal arteries, Ogden Avenue, which was intended to serve the whole northern section of the city from Ashland Avenue to Lincoln Park on the lake; its cost amounted to $4.5 million. Various works along the lakefront, amounting to $20 million, were also undertaken at this time. [193]

The choice of the first projects was only partly governed by a systematic program of procedure; the policy governing the relative financial investments is thus difficult to reconstruct. The tendency to widen the range of action without waiting for any one part of the plan to be completed is nonetheless clear. As a result, within a very few years and without investing excessive sums of money, hundreds of square miles of city land were involved in the operation, and the consequent increase in real-estate values exceeded expenditures by many times. An account of costs made in 1925 showed, for example, that investments in the work executed according to the plan on Michigan Avenue totaled $16 million, while the corresponding increase in the value of property fronting on the street was $100 million. [194]

According to Wrigley, [195] the factors that made the plan for Chicago a milestone in city planning were that it was promoted, donated, and managed by a group of private individuals; that it was the first general plan for a metropolis in the United States; and that it was carried out by a commission established and paid by the promoters of the plan themselves. [196]

From City Beautiful to City Planning

As early as 1910, the plan of Chicago was criticized for lacking certain "good elements of city planning,"[197] and mention has been made of the widespread interest in planning during the economic depression. If, as John L. Hancock has asserted,[198] city planning was born in 1907, its early years overlap with the decline of the City Beautiful movement in general, as well as in the more organic and ambitious version practiced by Burnham.

John Nolen was different from Burnham not only in his methods but also in his cultural formation. From the very beginning, Nolen strongly condemned laissez-faire practices and adhered to the American Economic Association's aims for reform. He shared the innovating spirit expressed by Bellamy and Geddes, which the new generation had made its own. This spirit and these aims had notable reverberations among the young, elite theoreticians of city planning and animated their encounters with the more skeptical working professionals. The national conference on city planning held in Washington in 1909 was an occasion for just such a confrontation—the first, in fact, of historical relevance. The papers delivered at the conference make it clear that during the depression the idea had developed among certain groups that "city planning offers a great social service" capable of mediating "the conflict between communism and individualism."[199] The equivocal implication of this statement is hardly surprising to those who know the history of the Modern movement in European architecture. It also reveals the ideological tendency of the conference, as well the reasons for its organization: if city planning was a mission and, particularly, if it was an instrument for social progress, then the problem was one of giving the municipalities the political power actually to manage and control it.

Once again European examples were carefully examined, but they were no longer Burnham's models—the Europe of the past, with its grand monumental layouts, or present-day Europe, limited to English landscaping. In Washington in 1909, all the speakers referred to the most recent European experiments in city planning, principally those in Germany. Their interest naturally implied a criticism of American enterprises and thus of the City Beautiful movement, but the only reaction came from Bennett: "Although we have an immense amount to learn from Europe, and especially Germany, in regard to city planning, it would be very foolish for us to copy blindly what has been done there."[200] Nolen, however, hit hard. To the question "What is needed in American city planning?"—the provocative title of his report—he replied, "Everything. For with few exceptions, our cities are lacking in almost all those essentials of convenience, comfort, orderliness, and appropriate beauty."[201]

If, however, City Beautiful was not yet city planning,[202] as is now generally accepted, what exactly was the difference between the two? Considering the period, it would not be incorrect to say, very briefly, that the difference lay principally, but not exclusively, in their intentions. In its more ambitious version, City Beautiful corresponded to a practice of urban design and building construction in which the domination of the corporations realistically left room for a range of very unprogressive enterprises, carried out within a belated system of laissez-faire. The projects that were part of the unified design, in which the urban layout was directly determined by the economic structures—location of industries, railroad lines, services—followed the City Beautiful method, while the neutral areas within the network of the layout designed for the city were deliberately left, as stated earlier, to real-estate speculation. When a similar method was extended to produce a plan such as that for Chicago, conceived on a regional scale, its application necessarily included methods proper to city planning. Yet the fundamental presupposition of realism and its corollary—the correspondence between the plan and a program of investments—set a limit beyond which it was not possible to proceed. This was the limit reached by Burnham and the movement he led.

Burnham was not present at the Washington conference, where the young, "progressive" speakers so insistently expressed ideas that indirectly condemned his work. He would have had to defend the "showy civic centers of gigantic cost" and respond to the accusation that City Beautiful was based on outmoded concepts that "assumed without question that the first duty of city planning is to beautify." Nor would he have enjoyed the moral attack on City Beautiful that was insidiously formulated in the question "Is not external splendor a mockery when cloaking congested slums?"[203]

In reality, however, the actual possibilities for municipal control over private investment at the beginning of the century were practically nonexistent. It is well known that Roosevelt's crusade against the domination of the trusts was impeded by the contradictions inherent in capitalist democracy, one of which was precisely the problem of controlling the increment of real-estate values. In the cities of the time, the law could only be that accepted by Burnham: control over the more organized investments of the corporations and reduction to a minimum of the obvious physical form of the minor private investments and their economic and social implications. This system reflected the ideology as well as the realism of Burnham and the City Beautiful movement. It is evident, moreover, that when the City Beautiful method was applied to the regional dimensions of the plan for Chicago it could not be fully realized except on paper. Those parts of the plan that were in keeping with the real possibilities of its instrumentation, however, could be put into operation. The progressiveness of the city planners, on the other hand, would not be given any real space in the city for some time to come. Nonetheless, from their extraneous position they continued vociferously to denounce errors and horrors, with the result that denunciations and divorcement from operative reality eventually came to appear integral components of the discipline of city planning.

Nevertheless, City Beautiful had reached the end of its cycle and the era of city planning had begun, just as Charles R. Taylor's principles of production organization now had to give way to sociology and romantic literature to naturalism, and just as formalist philosophy had to submit to the attacks of John

Dewey's empirical pragmatism. Even faith in the untouchable American institutions was undermined by the new, open-minded interest in America and Americans aroused by the investigating mentality of the muckrakers. Journalism had become a mass phenomenon.[204] The materialist interpretation of history had gained ground and historians like Charles A. Beard systematically attacked the traditional symbols, sparing neither Constitution nor founding fathers.[205]

The design for Chicago's monumental civic center remained on paper as evidence of the most outmoded aspect of Burnham's ideology, even if it took no more than its replacement with an equally large traffic interchange to demonstrate the plan's validity. With similar ambiguity, Burnham himself survived as the repository of a tradition borrowed from Europe and applied on an American scale. As such, he attended the Town Planning Conference in London in 1910, where he presented his sumptuous plans for Washington and Chicago. Burnham's presence at this conference, organized by the Royal Institute of British Architects as an official summing up of half a century's work in city planning throughout the world, has been considered a confrontation between the two fundamental approaches to urban planning: the sociological approach of the Garden City movement of Geddes and Ebenezer Howard and Burnham's formal-classical approach.[206] This, however, is an American interpretation of the evolution of planning, which considers Walter Burley Griffin's plan for Canberra as an outgrowth of Burnham's plan for Chicago; it is reasonable in an essay such as this, which examines the Beautiful movement, but is much less valid in a general discussion of the evolution of architecture and urban planning.

As Americans, Burnham and Charles Mulford Robinson were marginal figures, or at least isolated exceptions, at the London conference. At the opening meeting in the Guild Hall, the succession of official toasts by Leonard Stokes, the president of the RIBA, John Burns, Member of Parliament,[207] and other important personages made no mention of the United States. Indeed, their references were exclusively to British planning. The organized visits were all to garden cities. The most prestigious personalities were the Britishers Geddes and Howard and the Germans Joseph Stübben and Rudolf Eberstadt. The Germans, moreover, were convinced of their avant-garde position and openly expressed their conviction that they had surpassed not only the French but British as well.

Stübben recounted the history of German planning, which up to 1880 had been dominated by French influence in its symmetrical layouts and rectilinear and radial streets; subsequently, naturalistic and serpentine forms had become dominant, along with the medieval character of the urban layout; finally, according to Stübben, German planning embraced a more rational conception that combined the two methods. The greater part of Stübben's address dealt with the problem of planning streets according to well-defined types, rather than with the city plan as a whole. Eberstadt went beyond the phase of development discussed by Stübben and stated, "The English admiration for our street-planning system came at the very moment when we wished to do away with it."[208]

The exhibition of Burnham's projects, however, was something that could hardly go unnoticed. Remarkable in their graphic elegance and mounted in London with great care by Bennett's assistant Ben Holden, Burnham's plans for Washington and Chicago were striking achievements for both their scope and their practical applicability.[209] Burnham, moreover, knew how to make the most of his accomplishments. Aware of the objections that the architectural content of his plans might arouse, in his speech he concentrated on political considerations and on the dimensions of his technical organization. His eagerly anticipated address opened with a touch of irony that surely hit home with the high priests of European planning: "All of us belong to the profession of prophesy and are prone to play the part of oracle." After expressions of modesty and respect and admiration for the other speakers, Burnham's address continued:[210]

In the United States we have full popular government under universal suffrage. . . . Will our democracy persist? Many students of history are inclined to doubt it, and to think that the United States are already passing into known and well-understood phases of national life which have hitherto invariably ended in revolution and return to despotic control; but we think that their arguments have never given due weight to the effects of education and the growth of intelligence. I am aware that Spencer doubted our being able to escape the back-swing of the political pendulum. . . . Nevertheless, there are good reasons for hope that our democracy will live on: they spring from some considerations which are not given as much weight by historians as by philosophers perhaps, but which cannot be ignored by the former. The people of the United States are a new mixture of bloods in new environments; this will produce a human crystallization in Nature's test-tube which must differ from all preceding ones; and for this reason, if for no other, a form of government that could not long endure in Greece or Rome may persist in the New World on the broad continent of North America. Moreover, there is another element present which did not exist in old so-called democracies, and which cannot but work in favour of the continuance of popular government: it is "publicity," which, although unknown in older times, now exposes everything in the United States to open view. Our thoughts are headlined in the Press almost as soon as they are formed in the brain. . . .

In a continuing democracy nothing will be done illegally: if conflict between purpose and law arises, the latter will be changed before the former is carried into effect, for a democracy cannot continue unless the people are intelligent, and real intelligence is, first of all, appreciation of law and order.

After this description of the American system, Burnham arrived at the specific subject of city planning, citing the Columbian Exposition as the first significant act of this descipline. The fair, according to Burnham, was a typical case of a new law come into being to meet the needs of a new aim, and he emphasized the role it played as propaganda on a worldwide scale for the "law and order" of planning. "As the result of the object lesson the government took up the torch and proceeded to make a comprehensive plan for the future development of the capital." Thus the first American planning commission had come into being, and hundreds of planning commissions had since taken up work. It was not difficult for Burnham to present himself as a constant protagonist and leader of the significant events in the history of American planning. He spoke of the plans for Manila, Cleveland, San Francisco, and Chicago. Whenever possible, he made much of the fact of public patronage, but he also spoke about the private sponsorship of the last two projects and even cited the costs of preparing his plans.[211]

But the most significant aspect of this new phase of life in the United States lies in the kind of men who are actively engaged. They are the best and strongest men of affairs we have. In Chicago in three years there were two hundred meetings of the General Committee, at which hundreds of public men—engineers, architects, sanitary, railroad, city transportation, and other experts—were present. . . . The town-planning men in every city are the ablest in the community. . . . In Chicago there is now a semi-official City Commission, consisting of four hundred men, appointed by the Mayor and confirmed by the Common Council. . . . Four hundred of your best men animated by one purpose are like a Greek phalanx, which was irresistible against barbarians.

Burnham hardly spoke at all about architecture and presented himself strictly as a planner. He referred to technological innovations in transportation and other services as additional rationalizing elements of an advanced, coordinated, specialized, and collective work. In concluding, he spoke of creativity:

The question always arises when a given town is under consideration whether it would be wisest to limit suggestions to present available means, or, on the other hand, to work out and diagram whatever a sane imagination suggests. If the first be made your limit, your work will be tame and ineffectual and will not arouse that enthusiasm without which nothing worth while is ever accomplished. . . . You may expect support for a great cause, whereas men will yawn and slip quietly away from the merely obvious and commonplace. . . . Remember that a noble logical diagram once recorded will never die; long after we are gone it will be a living thing, asserting itself with ever-growing insistency, and, above all, remember that the greatest and noblest that man can do is yet to come, and that this will ever be so, else is evolution a myth.

Before the masters of the new discipline, to which he was essentially extraneous or at least in a theoretically outmoded position, Burnham pointedly played up the vast dimensions of planning operations in his country. He spoke not a single word in defense of classicism or monumentality, which had played such a great part in his plans displayed on the walls. Instead, just as he had done thirty-five years earlier before the young Louis Sullivan in the building yard of the Sherman house, Burnham spoke of "organization," thus inevitably arousing admiration for the "big things" he had been able "to handle . . . and build up."

In the end, however, he did not fail to honor creativity. Burnham astutely avoided discussing the rhetorical and stylistic elements of his plans and emphasized their most valid aspect, their structure. His "noble logical diagram" is not deduced from an objective observation of reality; it has an autonomous value quite beyond its function and exists through a logic of its own, so that it retains its validity despite changes in function. Here the detachment from the organic conception and Sullivan's late interpretations of it is complete; Burnham's "diagram" is something quite other than function and its vitalist expression.

This final assertion of pride by the man who had designed an arc with a six-mile radius around Chicago probably impressed his audience less then the sheer size of his organizational apparatus, the costs involved in his projects, and the quantity of work they represented. These were dimensions, not conceivable in purely theoretical terms, with which an evolved Europe would now have to deal; they involved not only the development of production but also, most important, its sociopolitical corollary: in speaking repeatedly of a government of the people, Burnham intended to convince his audience about the capitalist utopia of democracy.

The next address and the discussion that followed demonstrate the audience's attentive interest in this particular argument. L. Cope Cornford's entire speech was an attack on American "collectivism" and a defense of individualism, the "home," and art:

The chance that the individual citizen may obtain his peaceful, solid little home depends entirely upon the measure in which Mr. Smith understands that architecture is an art. . . . because collective intelligence is always inferior to individual intelligence. . . . What Mr. Smith really wants is a home to live in. That is all he asks, and that is precisely what is denied him. He may have churches, Parliaments, schools, museums, baths, workhouses, and the key to the street—and welcome. But a home of his own—no. By no means. Yet Mr. Smith is willing to pay for his house. Still it is denied him. [212]

Cornford's insidious tone reveals the intolerance felt by supporters of the Garden City movement toward Burnham's views. Ardent supporters of these views immediately made themselves heard during the discussion period, however. Richard Paget, certainly the most brilliant of this group, commented, "Mr. Cornford suggested that architecture was a material excretion of the mind. I should like to offer an alternative—namely, that the architecture of a city is the clothing of the body politic." After asserting the importance of concentrating business in the metropolis, Paget made a plea for the formal control of the city with a forceful, imaginative image:

How would it be if, by a stroke of magic, we were to re-plan those sky-scrapers of New York, make them all uniform in shape, make them in form like magnificent and perfectly proportioned pillars, and regroup them so that they formed one single magnificent and stupendous temple of industry and commerce in the centre of the city? Should we not in that way have produced a building before which Karnak would pale into absolute insignificance? It would be four or five times as big and a thousand times as useful, and it would have been produced at a lower cost than that at which the sky-scrapers of New York could be produced—an advantage apparently in every way, wholly unconnected with ornament, and of a beauty solely dependent upon its magnificence, simplicity, and utility. [213]

The discussion continued with Ebenezer Howard's sober remarks in favor of the rival concepts of individualism and the home in a natural setting expressed by Cornford. Howard cited "the growing love for Nature which is calling our people back to the now deserted fields, and the clearly seen possibility of there doing all that is so impossible to be done in the crowded city" and referred to Letchworth, goal of one of the trips announced in the program. [214]

In a long speech, Francis S. Swales attempted to demolish the ideas advanced by Cornford and Howard from both technical and political points of view, remarking also on the limits of Britain's unsatisfactory Town Planning Act. In place of Cornford's middle-class Mr. Smith, who could pay for his "solid little home," Swales offered the example of "Mr. Brown (brickie) or Mr. Jones (navvy), who has not and never will have 'a little 'ome of 'is own,' and who, left to his own choice, will, when the land is full of garden cities, still live in the most crowded part of the biggest town, and regard the cottage as the paradise of fools." Swales repeatedly referred to the housing problem and the hypocrisy and fraud behind the ideology of the "home"; he concluded by affirming the necessity of specialized planning and the development of technicians of the stature and experience of Burnham and his collaborators.[215]

The attacks on Burnham did not, however, come exclusively from the conservative wing of the supporters of the antiurban ideology. He was also strongly criticized from the "left" by Matt Garbutt:

Mr. Cornford . . . hit the nail on the head when he said that the tendency to-day was . . . to substitute for the benevolent despotism of the great landlords an organised democracy. That would appear to be what Mr. Burnham wants, and, to my thinking, it is one of the very worst things that could possible happen to the people. If you have your individual tyrant, and he does wrong, it is possible for a revolution to smash him up; but if the tyrant is the vast majority of the people, it is a tyranny hard to overthrow.

Ironically quoting Burnham, Garbutt added, " 'Four hundred of the best men' are not exactly 'the democracy.' " Instead of the "gigantic architectural schemes" produced by "the tyranny of the big democracy," Garbutt indicated the wholesome example of the small English garden cities.[216] Garbutt's criticism is further proof that, in regard to the political issue, demarcation was not clear-cut between the schematically opposed positions of British and American planning. His remarks, however, were considered too subversive by Councilor Marr, who immediately intervened to urge full respect for Burnham's "democracy."[217]

It cannot be said that the London Conference constituted the opening of a mature phase of planning; instead, it presented an account of different positions, studies, and achievements at a time when America had become a major participant by virtue of projects actually executed and Germany had assumed the avant-garde position. In addition, because of the polemical nature of this confrontation, it clearly did not produce immediate results. As the Washington conference had demonstrated, the American situation could be far more precisely and pertinently criticized by Americans themselves. Burnham, of course, did not represent the most advanced views among American planners. In London he expressed neither the doubts nor the progressive, innovative spirit that had animated the Washington meeting the year before. Instead, with his plan for Chicago, what he presented was a final achievement, the ultimate accomplishment of his long years of activity. The Flatiron in New York and the great arc planned for Chicago, the first an urban object and the second a "diagram," assured him a place in the history of town design, one that only Sullivan's formidable attack ten years after his death would challenge.[218]

The discussion of Burnham and the City Beautiful movement might well end here, but the development of its basic concepts in underdeveloped countries, which makes it possible to identify the City Beautiful with the "imperial city," became clearer with the creation of Canberra and New Delhi. Of particular interest in this essay is the new Australian capital, which seemed on the eve of the world war to open a new, ambiguous road to "architectural" city planning.

The Plan of Canberra

At the London conference in 1910, the Australian delegate, John Sulman, announced a competition for the federal capital city of Australia and spoke enthusiastically about the great opportunity it offered. A capital city to be created from the ground up is indeed a rare occurrence; the next such occasion would not come about until Brasilia in the 1950s. The event was to prove decisive for the career of an outstanding figure in American architecture, Walter Burley Griffin, who was to attach his name definitively to the development of the new Australian city, practically disappearing from the professional scene in the Occident.

Griffin's victory was aided by the RIBA's decision to prohibit its members from participating because of the insufficient guarantee of objectivity and impartiality offered by a jury composed exclusively of Australians (the AIA also disapproved of the competition but did not officially prohibit the participation of American architects). This decision eliminated adversaries of the stature of Leslie Patrick Abercrombie, Geddes, and Edwin Landseer Lutyens in England and Burnham, Bennett, Nolen, and Frederick Law Olmsted, Jr., in the United States. Participation was nevertheless extensive; when the projects were submitted on January 31, 1912, the jury had 137 designs among which to choose. The final decision, which made Griffin the winner and gave Eliel Saarinen and D. A. Agache the second and third places, was not unanimous. Thus although the judges were but three, they pronounced not only this majority decision but also a minority decision, which granted first place to W. S. Griffiths of Sydney, second place to Arthur C. Comey of Cambridge, Massachusetts, and third place to Nils Gjellerstadt of Stockholm. The competition's controversial outcome once again revealed the two contrasting positions confronted at the London conference; that of the City Beautiful was the choice of two of the three judges.

Griffin, however, was not a City Beautiful architect in the sense described so far. Nine years younger than Frank Lloyd Wright,[219] he initially worked with him, following and strongly supporting the Prairie House movement. It seems, however, that he was also early interested in "scientific" planning; in 1899 he received his degree from the University of Illinois, where he had written a thesis on planning in which he lamented the lack of scientific publications, except for those in German. This interest in German developments may have been derived from his professor, Harold Hansen, a Swede who had previously taught at the Preussische Bauakademie in Berlin. Furthermore, the chairman of the department of architecture at the university was Nathan C. Ricker, who had also been at the Bauakademie, where he had collected many books that were eventually translated in America.[220] In 1900, along with other members of the Steinway Hall group, Griffin was greatly impressed by the lectures given by Patrick Geddes, who was in America for a lecture tour on city planning and was then the guest of Jane Addams at Hull House. In 1906, Griffin was commissioned by the Chinese government to prepare a plan for restructuring the center of Shanghai. His skill as a planner was subsequently confirmed by numerous projects for residential areas in the United States.[221]

For Griffin, as for many of the other competitors, Canberra and Australia apparently held a fascination that was related to the more general attraction of the Orient. The Far East, previously perceived as an arena of imperialist domination, such as Burnham had known in the Philippines, had become a place of mystic attraction, in keeping with the increasingly widespread doctrines of the Theosophical Society.[222] Griffin eventually became a member of a theosophical association, and the fact that he worked in Shanghai as well as in Australia, where he decided to pass his life, and died in India is probably not without significance.[223] Geddes, too, felt the attraction of the Orient. During his first trip to America in 1900, he was reportedly eager to meet Vivekananda,[224] and he was to spend the years from 1915 to 1925 in India.

The project for Canberra prompted Griffin to adopt a method close to Burnham's but animated by quite a different spirit. Undoubtedly Griffin, too, sought to create a "logical diagram," but his was based on geometry of a higher order, which through the complexity of its laws was capable of absorbing the most varied elements into a structure that was also partly inspired by the natural setting. The classical conception of Burnham's "diagrams" is left far behind in Canberra. Griffin's city is based on a concatenation of stelliform systems, composed of organizational axes and a widely-spaced grid layouts. Because of the slightness and ambiguity of the angling of the various structural elements, neither the axes nor the grids dominate the design. Thus each of the widely varied geometric configurations—octagons, hexagons, and triangles—appears within the plan as a whole both perfectly free and strictly controlled.

Only two of the many axes of the plan for Canberra meet at right angles, and they are specifically related to the regional setting, which gives them the names land axis and water axis. The land axis leads out from the summit of Mount Ainslie, a hill at the north-northeast limit of the city, directed toward the 5,780-foot peak of Mount Bimberi, some thirty miles to the south-southwest. The water axis runs from the summit of Black Mountain, a hill at the extreme west-northwest, and follows a portion of the course of the Molonglo River, artificially shaped by a radical manipulation of its bed. The land axis forms the axis of symmetry of the official quarter of the city, where it bisects the equilateral triangle that contains the Government Group and at its southern vertex encounters the Capitol. The water axis is not a compositional axis, but it marks the limit of the whole central governmental area of the city on the water.

Plan for Canberra by Walter Burley Griffin,
1912. Griffin created a "diagram" of stelliform systems, connected by complex and
elastic relationships based on the equilateral
triangle and oriented on a visual axis that
refer to prominent elements of the surrounding natural setting. Even the water assumes
a role as mediator between the geometry
of the designed structure and nature.

The north side of the triangle is, in fact, delimited by a basin of water geometrically shaped with the water of the Molonglo into two circular basins connected by a quarter-moon form, laid out symmetrically in respect to the land axis.

These two axes, which are given maximum importance in the plan as organizational axes referring to the natural elements of the site, are in reality scarcely perceptible within the city and do not correspond to any street. Thus the spatial organization in respect to the surrounding heights can be appreciated only from these heights or from the axis of the Capitol. Furthermore, the street axes that connect one star-shaped system with another are invariably laid out at an angle to the major symmetrical axes, and their intersection is marked by no formal focal point. There is also no "parade" axis terminating in a monumental perspective. It could be said that Griffin dissolved the hierarchical structure of the City Beautiful, so pointedly ideological in its conception and so particularly adapted to the architecture of a capital city, in a succession of concentric structures that tend to contest the absolute axial organization befitting the center of power. The result is an endless, animated overlapping of geometric intentions, which seem most authentically expressed in the preliminary plan executed in Griffin's own hand.

If one forgets the water axis and the land axis and their reference to the larger territorial setting, the characterization of the stelliform systems according to their functions becomes clear. Three of the systems are particularly distinguished—the first, the Capitol, the most eminent and emphatic, and the other two, the civic center and the market center. These three centrically planned radial systems are precisely related; each is a vertex of the same equilateral triangle, which is cut by the chain of water basins but perfectly marked on its sides by wide traffic arteries. The other stelliform systems have essentially residential functions, while the northernmost center is industrial. They are connected to the principal equilateral triangle according to geometric laws. The result is a different way of perceiving the city: by triangles and by functions. Thus Griffin's plan, certainly not unintentionally, had the added merit of satisfying the expectation of the judges in regard to the theory of zoning.

Another major factor contributing to the richness of Griffin's scheme is the use he made of water. The system of geometric basins, designed according to the play of symmetric circles framing the government triangle, is continued with still other bodies of water toward the east-southeast and west-northwest. These, too, are created by manipulating the bed of the Molonglo River; unlike the geometrically configured basins, however, these lakes have an irregular, naturalistic design in keeping with the undulating unevenness of the terrain. Thus even in the use of water the design is varied and ambiguous or, rather, ambivalent. Griffin apparently sought to guarantee his design on all fronts, creating an urban structure that was clear and strong in its street network but also sufficiently flexible to be easily developed according to functions that might vary and a density and distribution of construction that could not be wholly foreseen. Certainly strongly marked perspective axes can indeed by referred to the City Beautiful model, but primarily on a perceptual level, because of the great distances they open to view, rather than by reason of their formal structure, which does not obstruct the elasticity of the open system of triangles.

Griffin thus attacked the nearly insoluble problem of a plan for a completely new city with the instruments of the City Beautiful method, enriched by the knowledge of Howard's nuclear planning schemes, which he also interpreted in terms of a formal "diagram." The risk involved in such a project quite evidently lies in the rigidity of the plan in the face of the necessarily undetermined programs of development. It was precisely this risk that made Agache's plan, for example, so plainly abstract and impracticable. Griffin attempted to avoid this danger by means of interruptions, variations in angles, freely connected junctures, and the superimposition of diverse systems in a layout in which only the central triangle, formed by the fixed vertices of the Capitol, civic center, and market center, is really considered constant.

This formally definitive central triangle is a City Beautiful element, but it assumed a character very unlike that of Burnham's designs because Griffin absolutely rejected the old idea of the necessity of the classical, a style Wright's progressive collaborator excluded from his repertory. At the center of the composition, the inevitable dome of the Capitol was replaced by a curious covering with horizontal stepped elements rising in the form of a square-based pyramid, constructed in reinforced concrete. Buildings of an orientalizing character are inserted in the general perspective drawings of the project, executed by Griffin's wife, Marion Mahony. With its ambiguously interconnected triangles, circles, and axes, the design as a whole has something mysterious about it, something of an occult ritual that, together with the buildings of Oriental flavor that appear in the perspective drawings, can perhaps be related to Griffin's theosophical beliefs.

The complexity and novelty of the design, its many modern elements, and its obvious rupture with Beaux-Arts methods were not, however, enough to make the plan of Canberra acceptable to the severe British and German critics. Councilor Wernekke, for example, writing in *Der Städtebau*, did not conceal his reservations about the outcome of the competition. To all three prize-winning projects he preferred that of Gjellerstadt,[225] "who as a Swede represents the Germanic element in the competition and has consequently treated the problem according to completely different suppositions from the prize-winning competitors."[226] Wernekke described the formal solutions of Gjellerstadt's project in detail, noting particularly the absence of any axis of symmetry and the naturalistic, nongeometric street layout.

It is, however, interesting to observe that the one geometrically designed element of Gjellerstadt's plan was the area destined for the city's skyscrapers, which was perfectly square despite the fact that it was certainly inspired by the

Daniel H. Burnham (*right*) in the spring of
1912 during his last trip in Europe, from
which he was never to return.

Chicago Loop. In other words, in this case where his model was an eminently spontaneous urban element, Gjellerstadt, on the contrary, planned it with geometric precision. The paradox had a significance of its own; it affirmed the rejection of City Beautiful America and the acceptance in its place, precisely in the terms of formal planning, of the America of the skyscrapers.

Griffin's victory was enthusiastically acclaimed by the American architectural press,[227] which considered him the master capable of a successful synthesis of the contrasting British and American accomplishments in planning. Ricker offered him the chair in civic design at the University of Illinois, which his work in Australia did not permit him to accept and which was filled instead by Robinson. In Europe, on the other hand, despite the anticlassical and antitotalitarian character of Griffin's design, Canberra was considered a City Beautiful plan, pure and simple. Geddes hoped that Australians would not remain "contented with Canberra, however monumental a Washington it may become" but that they would find inspiration for new planning activities in their own traditions and natural landscape.[228]

In the same tone, Geddes criticized Lutyens's plan for New Delhi, which had become the capital of India.[229] "New Delhi in its imperial way," he wrote, "can but be a greater Canberra" because "city planning has ever been a part of imperial policy."[230] Geddes's attack on the "imperial city" was also directed against Burnham's City Beautiful, identifying it once again and unequivocally as a product for export to underdeveloped countries and an element of imperialist politics—as in the cases of Manila and Baguio, so for Canberra and New Delhi. Similarly, much later, underdeveloped countries would in a certain sense accept the products of designers of "architectural" cities, like Le Corbusier and Louis Kahn.

Burnham, in any case, was no longer in the fray. After the London conference in 1910, his activity as a designer of "imperial cities" came to an end. His last great effort was the building of the mammoth Wanamaker Building in Philadelphia.[231] In the complex problems created by its dimensions—a single block 275 feet high, covering about 3.5 acres—this undertaking seems to have anticipated the need for the kind of managerial coordination of all aspects of the project that was later instituted at Rockefeller Center and that tends inevitably, in practice, to exclude a designer such as Burnham.[232]

By this time Burnham's desire was to dedicate the rest of his life to perfecting his own culture. As a member of the Federal Commission of Fine Arts, Burnham had great authority, but his eternal reverence for an imported classicism was no longer so widely accepted in the United States as at the time of the Open Door policy.

In a letter written in April 1912 to Frank D. Millet, the renowned chief of decorations at the Columbian Exposition and also a member of the Commission of Fine Arts, who was in Rome at the time to resolve the difficulties brought about at the American Academy by McKim's death, Burnham announced to his friend that they would shortly cross each other at sea. Burnham was to sail to Europe on the *Olympic;* Millet, unfortunately, would embark on the *Titanic* for his return voyage. Burnham's letter expressed his great concern over the Lincoln Memorial project: "The argument I made before the Lincoln Commission was that the whole world is looking on and confidently expecting us to do something merely striking and picturesque and not nobly ideal; and that we must disappoint them and rise above their expectations as we did in Chicago. . . . the decision is going to be a vital one, setting for a long time the status of the fine arts in this country."[233] He was particularly concerned about the appointment of a designer and begged his friend to intervene in the affair. Lewis Mumford's subsequent judgment of this monument and the men of the "Imperial Facade" would be severe:

The American that Lincoln was bred in, the homespun and humane and humorous America that he wished to preserve, has nothing in common with the sedulously classic monument that was erected in his memory. Who lives in that shrine, I wonder—Lincoln, or the men who conceived it: the leader who beheld the mournful victory of the Civil War, or the generation that took pleasure in the mean triumph of the Spanish-American exploit, and placed the imperial standard in the Philippines and the Caribbean?[234]

American progressive thought was not then and would never be able to accept either the realistic attitude toward economic power or the uncritical employment of an imported style that are at the base of the page of American history examined here. For Mumford, the "imperial" development of City Beautiful architecture and its export to underdeveloped countries as part of the ideology of power clearly revealed the low ethical level (and thus, according to progressive concepts, the lack of a real historical interest) of the whole affair.

Nevertheless, from a different perspective, it is undeniable that the most extensive attempts made at an organic and spatial control of the city, and thus also the largest urban architectural enterprises designed or actually carried out by American architects at the time, were precisely Washington, San Francisco, Manila, Chicago, and Canberra. None of them, it must be emphasized, was produced by virtue of progressive concepts; rather, all were created under the aegis of the cynical "offical culture." Nor was this sponsorship at all contradictory, since the recognition culture obtains is always granted to it by power. In America in the early years of this century the stabilizing domestic policies of the Republican administration and the corresponding foreign opening generated by their imperalist politics gave rise to one of the rare moments in which power actively wanted to give organic form to the city, at least within certain limits. This period came to an end with the modification of institutional structures that took place between the financial panic of 1907 and the First World War. It is not by chance, moreover, that during the same period progressive concepts became strong enough actively to reverse the prevalent tendencies and to prepare the way for the fervid planning initiatives of the 1920s.

The sinking of the fabulous *Titanic*, during the night of April 14-15, 1912, made a strong impression in America, undermining faith in the sumptuous enterprises of high finance. The event seemed to portend the crisis of the world of Burnham and the "imperial city."

Among the signs of the crisis that marked the closing of the period discussed here, the tragedy of the *Titanic* assumes emblematic significance. The *Titanic* was a traveling city, built to carry the proud message of capitalism arrived at maturity but not yet shaken by the crash of 1929; a miracle of technology in its unequalled size, efficiency, and comfort; a floating City Beautiful in the regal organization of its decks and its grand salons, in its expression of stability and security, as well as in its class structure, which was based on a strict hierarchical division between the emigrants crowded below near the hold and the people who counted, in their sumptuous apartments in Empire style situated above, near the bridge. When this technological colossus collided with an iceberg and was easily and inevitably overcome by a colossus of nature, the self-confidence of the Republican America of Roosevelt and Taft seemed to waver.

Burnham experienced this drama from nearby. He waited in vain for his mid-ocean encounter with Millet, who drowned miserably in the night, together with others Burnham knew.[235] A few days after this mournful event, which shortly preceded his own death, Burnham wrote, "It will seem an empty world with no Frank in it . . . The old World's Fair crowd is thinning out."[236]

NOTES

1

The literature is vast. A few of the most important words on the subject are Harold Zink, *City Bosses in the United States* (Duke University Press, Durham, N.C., 1939); Charles N. Glaab and A. Theodore Brown, *A History of Urban America* (MacMillan, New York, 1967); Richard Hofstadter, *The Age of Reform. From Bryan to F. D. R.* (Knopf, New York, 1956).

2

The Noble Order of the Knights of Labor was formed in Philadelphia in 1869 and was originally a secret society. In 1878 it began to organize skilled workers and achieved its maximum membership —700,000— in 1886; it declined rapidly with the development of the American Federation of Labor, which was formed in Pittsburgh in 1881 and achieved a membership of 2 million by 1905, the year when the Industrial Workers of the World was founded.

3

On the position taken by the great union leader Samuel Gompers in regard to the immigrants, see Arthur Mann, "Gompers and the Irony of Racism," *Antioch Review*, 1953, pp. 203-214.

4

On the relationship between transcendentalist and posttranscendentalist ideologies and American architecture, see Mario Manieri-Elia, "Louis H. Sullivan, epigono di un'ideologia," introduction to Louis H. Sullivan, *Autobiografia di un'idea ed altri scritti di architettura* (Officina, Rome, 1970).

5

Leonardo Benevolo, *Storia dell'architettura moderna*, 3rd ed. (Laterza, Bari, 1971), p. 320. Benevolo cites Emilio Cecchi, who defines the skyscraper and the method of dividing the building lots as arithmetical operations of multiplication and division; see Cecchi, *America amara*, 6th ed. (Sansoni, Florence, 1946), p. 13.

6

On Tammany Hall and Boss Tweed, the literature is ample; see Theodore Roosevelt's interesting *New York City 1890-1895* (Longmans Green, New York, 1918); Seymour Mandelbaum, *Boss Tweed's New York* (Wiley, New York, 1965); Alexander B. Callow, *The Tweed Ring* (Oxford University Press, New York, 1966); Gustavus Myers, *The History of Tammany Hall* (Dover, New York, 1971); and the works cited in n1.

7

The original Italian edition of this book appeared before the publication of Thomas S. Hines's monograph *Burnham of Chicago* (Oxford University Press, New York, 1974).

8

Since the publication of the original Italian edition of this book, a work has appeared dedicated entirely to the subject of the fair; see David F. Burg, *Chicago's White City of 1893* (University Press of Kentucky, Lexington, 1976).

9

John W. Reps, *The Making of Urban America* (Princeton University Press, Princeton, 1965), p. 498: "The idea of a world exposition to commemorate the four hundredth anniversary of the discovery of America originated as early as 1882 when Dr. T. W. Zaremba suggested it to a group of New York leaders.... In 1886 Dr. Zaremba renewed his suggestion at the meeting of the American Historical Society in Washington. The soceity established a committee to meet with the president and obtain his support."

10

William Appleman Williams, *The Contours of American History* (World, Cleveland and New York, 1961), p. 321.

11

Julian Ralph, *The Chicago World's Fair* (Harper and Brothers, New York, 1893), pp. 14-15.

12

Josiah Strong was a Congregationalist home missionary. His *Our Country: Its Possible Future and Its Present Crisis* was first published in 1885 (Baker and Taylor, New York) and appeared in an enlarged edition in 1891.

13

Ralph, *Chicago World's Fair*, p. 8. In *Picturesque Chicago and Guide to the World's Fair* (Woodward, Baltimore, 1892), the story of Chicago was compared to the miracle of Aladdin's lamp.

14

These are the opening words of Ralph's *Chicago World's Fair*.

15

Adler's role as designer in the years in which he was active in the firm of Adler and Sullivan is naturally controversial. See Hugh Dalziel Duncan, "Attualità di Louis Sullivan," *Casabella*, no. 204, Feb.-Mar. 1954, pp. 7-30. An accurate study of Adler's work is Rochelle S. Elstein, "The Architecture of Dankmar Adler," *Journal of the Society of Architectural Historians* 26, no. 4, 1967. John W. Root expressed his opinion of Adler's role in an anonymous article that appeared in a special issue of the journal *America* 5, Dec. 1890, republished in the *Inland Architect and News Record* 16, Jan. 1891: "Among the highest of all the profession stands Mr. Adler, for some time after the fire a partner of Mr. Burling, and 'designing' member of the firm. Of late Mr. Adler has passed the artistic crayon to Mr. Sullivan, but work designed by him in earlier days ... shows a strength, simplicity and straightforewardness, together with a certain refinement, which reveal the true architect." The article is also contained in Donald Hoffmann, ed., *The Meanings of Architecture, Buildings and Writings by John Wellborn Root* (Horizon Press, New York, 1967), p. 236.

16

I presented this thesis—which will certainly meet with disagreement on the part of Burnham's detractors, among whom are such authorities as Lewis Mumford, Henry-Russell Hitchcock, and Bruno Zevi—in a lecture at the Galleria d'Arte Moderna in Rome in April 1971; it was published as "Scuola di Chicago: il mito e la realtà," *Rassegna dell'Istituto di architettura e urbanistica*, no. 19, Apr. 1971.

17

Writing in an anonymous article Root observed: "Burnham and Root, occupying a high position, have been very uneven in their work. Mr. Root, upon whom largely devolved their designing, seems to have been too facile always to carefully reconsider his designs, and to have been to a large extent the victim of his own moods" (Hoffmann, *Meanings of Architecture*, p. 236).

18

This unequivocal attribution was made in Montgomery Schuyler, *D. H. Burnham & Co.*, separate monograph no. 2, pt. 2 of the Great American Architects Series published by *Architectural Record*, Feb. 1896, p. 49; it is reprinted in William H. Jordy and Ralph Coe, eds., *American Architecture and Other Writings by Montgomery Schuyler* (Atheneum, New York, 1964), p. 193. The fact that such a precise statement has not been accepted as decisive reflects the widespread disfavor in which Burnham has been held by critics ever since the publication of Sullivan's autobiography in 1923—a critical position still maintained by some American scholars. In fact, Jordy, in his edition of Schuyler's writings (p. 34), considers the attribution of the Monadnock to Burnham as just an error on Schuyler's part and reaffirms this thesis in his own book; see William H. Jordy, *American Buildings and Their Architects. Progressive and Academic Ideals at the Turn of the Twentieth Century* (Doubleday, New York, 1972). Yet Schuyler was not only a contemporary witness, but his critical position in regard to Root was certainly not that of a detractor. At Root's death he wrote, "I don't know any greater loss that could have happened to the architecture of this country and to the architecture of the future"; see "The Point of View," *Inland Architect and News Record* 17, Feb. 1891, reprinted in Jordy and Coe, *American Architecture*, p. 60.

Furthermore, other contemporary writers agree about the attribution. Charles Moore, Burnham's biographer, definitely placed the Monadnock among the buildings executed by Burnham alone, without the participation of Root; see Charles Moore, *Daniel H. Burnham, Architect and Planner of Cities* (1921; reprint ed. Da Capo Press, New York, 1968) 2, p. 209. In an article written immediately after Root's death, Henry Van Brunt, a diligent and attentive critic, cited all Root's important works but did not include the Monadnock; see William A. Coles, ed., *Architecture and Society, Selected Essays by Henry Van Brunt*

(Harvard University Press, Cambridge, Mass., 1969), pp. 214-224. Even Harriet Monroe, Root's sister-in-law and biographer, considered biased because infatuated with her brother-in-law, did not succumb to the temptation of attributing the building already considered the most beautiful in Chicago to Root. According to her account, Root made a design that the client considered too ornate. During Root's absence Burnham changed the design radically; on his return Root was furious, but he finally adapted himself to the idea and made a contribution himself. See Harriet Monroe, *John Wellborn Root. A Study of His Life and Work*, (1896; reprint ed. Prairie School Press, Park Forest, Ill., 1966), pp. 141-142.

Moreover, the letters written by Owen F. Aldis, the Chicago representative of Peter Brooks of Boston who commissioned the Monadnock, do not really prove anything concerning its paternity. Donald Hoffmann, in his critical edition of Root's writings, *Meanings of Architecture*, attributed the Monadnock to Root; in support of this thesis Hoffmann also published a selection of Aldis's letters in an article entitled "John Root's Monadnock Building," *Journal of the Society of Architectural Historians*, Dec. 1967. Root's name is indeed frequently mentioned in the Aldis letters, but this is hardly surprising since Root was a personal friend, for whose firm Aldis had procured three commissions: the Montauk Building, the Monadnock Building, and the Rookery. The frequent mention of Root also reflects Hoffmann's tendency to exclude Burnham from his otherwise very valuable critical studies. In the selection of letters published by Hoffmann, what to me seems significant is that in precisely the final and definitive phase of the designing, that is, in letters dating from 1889, mentions of Root as designer are lacking.

Finally, it should be noted that the Egyptian inspiration of the Monadnock, so often described as a new and original idea attributable to the hand of Root, can be found in at least three earlier buildings by the firm: the Burlington and Quincy Office Building, the Atchison, Topeka and Santa Fe Office Building, and the Counselman Building, all from 1883-84.

19

See Moore, *Daniel H. Burnham.*

20

The two quotations are from Louis H. Sullivan, *The Autobiography of an Idea*, published serially in the *Journal of the American Institute of Architects* in 1923 and in book form in 1924 (reprint ed., Dover, New York, 1956), pp. 285 and 291.

21

Elsewhere I have shown that Sullivan decided to attack Burnham and the fair only in 1923 and at the specific insistence of his publisher; see Manieri-Elia, "Louis H. Sullivan," p. 10. See also from Charles H. Whitaker to Sullivan, December 22, 1922, quoted in Sherman Paul, *L. H. Sullivan. An Architect in American Thought* (Prentice-Hall, Englewood Cliffs, N.J., 1962), p. 135; Whitaker to Sullivan, June 15, 1923, quoted in David H. Crook, "L. H. Sullivan and the Golden Doorway," *Journal of the Society of Architectural Historians* 26, no. 4, 1967.

22

The bill establishing Chicago as the site of the fair was passed by Congress on April 9, 1890, and signed by President Harrison on April 25.

23

A section drawing of the building, together with the comment from which the quotation is taken, appeared in the *Chicago Tribune*, March 9, 1890, p. 11. See also Titus M. Karlowicz, "D. H. Burnham's Role in the Selection of Architects for the World's Columbian Exposition," *Journal of the Society of Architectural Historians* 29, no. 3, 1970, p. 250. The idea of a single enormous roof for the fair seems to have been proposed first by Bruce Price; see Burg, *Chicago's White City*, p. 79.

24

Karlowicz, "D. H. Burnham's Role," p. 249.

25

In an interview made many years later and published in the *Architectural Record*, Jan. 1913, pp. 34-44, Burnham described his own important role in this initiative and the extent and limits of his power: "Late in the year, December, I believe, I grew very impatient, and told the committee that we must have action—get together a force of men and begin work. It was agreed that I should select five Chicago architects and five outside architects. I made my selection and went before the committee of seven members, three of whom were in political life. The committee could not come to an agreement, the politicians desiring to keep me from making the selection. Finally Gage put the motion—four voted for and three against me."

26

Once the plan of action was settled upon, decisions were made rapidly. A memorandum dated December 9, 1890, directed to the Grounds and Buildings Committee and signed by Burnham, Root, Olmsted, and the chief engineer A. Gottlieb, listed four possible ways of selecting the architects: (1) a commission to a single architect, (2) a public competition, (3) a competition by invitation, and (4) direct selection of a certain number of architects. On December 12, just three days later, Burnham was able to send letters, signed by him as chief of construction, commissioning five groups of architects, all Eastern, to design "the main group of buildings at Jackson Park." The architects were Richard Morris Hunt, McKim, Mead and White, and George B. Post, all of New York, Peabody and Stearns of Boston, and Van Brunt and Howe of Kansas City. The letter stated: "It is intended to place the problem in your hands as to the artistic aspects only—first, of the group as a whole, second, of the separate buildings. . . . I realize the hesitation you may feel in assuming the responsibility for a design when you do not fully control the execution of it. The committee feels, however, that strict economy of the two essentials, time and money, will be best subserved by keeping the actual control of the work in the hands of one man and his bureau; and I can assure that your intents and purposes of design, once agreed upon by the Committee, shall be carried out as you wish." For the relevant documents, see Moore, *Daniel H. Burnham*, 1:37ff. The Chicago architects were named only later.

27

Charles Zueblin, *A Decade of Civic Development*, (Chicago, 1905), p. 61. Later in this essay I shall examine this statement and try to give it a just interpretation.

28

In the archives of Frederick Law Olmsted is a preparatory plan, dated 1891, showing some differences in the building blocks and their positioning; it has been published in Julius Gy. Fabos, Gordon T. Milde, V. Michael Weinmayr, *Frederick Law Olmsted, Sr. Founder of Landscape Architecture in America* (University of Massachusetts Press, Amherst, 1968), p. 94. In the interview published in 1913 (see n25), Burnham stated that he participated in the preliminary drafting of the plan, together with Codman and Root, and that he still had many of the drawings made at that time.

29

The letter is that of December 12, 1890, cited in n26. Burnham's statement evidently responds to a precise demand from the Eastern architects for absolute autonomy in regard to the studies already carried out by Root.

30

Henry Van Brunt wrote: "The architects to whom the five buildings on the great court were assigned constituted a family, by reason of long-established personal relations and of unusual close professional sympathies. Of this family Mr. Hunt was the natural head; two of its members, Post and Van Brunt, were his professional children; Howe, Peabody, and Stearns, having been pupils and assistants of the latter, may be considered the grandchildren of the household; while McKim, who had been brought up under the same academical influences, was, with his partners, of the same blood by right of adoption and practice." See "Architecture at the World's Columbian Exposition," *Century Magazine* 44, 1892, contained in Coles, *Architecture and Society*, p. 236.

31

The first presidents of the American Institute of Architects were Richard Upjohn (1857-76); Thomas U. Walter (1877-87); Richard Morris Hunt (1888-91); Edward H. Kendall (1892-93); Daniel H. Burnham (1894-96); and George B. Post (1897-99).

32

Solon S. Beman was the designer of the town of Pullman; his work in Chicago included the Pullman Building, the Studebaker Building, and Wisconsin Central Station.

33
Frank Lloyd Wright, "Louis Sullivan: His Work," *Architectural Record* 56, 1924, p. 29.
34
Sullivan was forced to comply immediately with a command from Burnham that he displace his monumental portal from the axis of his building in order to make it correspond with the axis of Post's. See Burnham to Sullivan, February 11, 1891, quoted in Crook, "L. H. Sullivan and the Golden Doorway," p. 256.
35
Jessie Heckman Hirschl, in "The Great White City," *American Heritage* 11, Oct. 1960, p. 75, quotes the phrase "Sullivan's sunset in the golden glow of the door of the Transportation Building," without indicating its source.
36
Louis Sullivan was of a different opinion and described it as "of them all, the most impudently thievish." (*Autobiography of an Idea*, p. 322).
37
George B. Post, like Atwood, was educated in the United States. He received a degree in engineering in 1858 and joined Hunt's studio in 1860. During the Civil War he was made a colonel; in 1868 he set up a studio of his own. His architectural production, especially from 1874 on, is of great interest for the variety of building types it covered, which seem to have offered models even to the Chicago architects. See Winston Weisman, "The Commercial Architecture of George B. Post," *Journal of the Society of Architectural Historians* 31, no. 3, 1972, pp. 176-203; see also Manfredo Tafuri, "The Disenchanted Mountain: The Skyscraper and the City," this volume, n27.
38
Van Brunt, "Architecture at the World's Columbian Exposition," p. 255.
39
See Burnham interview, *Architectural Record*, Jan. 1913, pp. 34-44.
40
In this work on the fair, however, an attempt was made—and would be carried further by the City Beautiful movement—to reach a compromise between the two methods of design, which had resulted earlier, in the construction of Central Park in New York, in a direct clash. Olmsted had designed the park together with Vaux; when Hunt received the commission for the entrances in 1863, a heated controversy broke out. Hunt's design, inspired by the Napoleonic Tuileries, the construction of which he had witnessed in 1854, was rejected by the designers in the name of a "democratic" ideal of a park without emphatic demarcations; see Albert Fein, *Frederick Law Olmsted and the American Environmental Tradition* (Braziller, New York, 1972), pp. 11-14.
41
In Chicago at the time of the fair, Joseph Stübben presented his artistic principles for city planning in readings from his *Der Städtebau*, which had been published in 1890 and by 1895 was to have been translated in three languages. Stübben termed American planning "execrable," with the sole exception of the Park movement. See George R. and Christiane Crasemann Collins, *Camillo Sitte and the Birth of Modern City Planning* (Random House, New York, 1965), pp. 86-88.
42
Ralph, *Chicago World's Fair*, p. 123.
43
George Washington Gale Ferris (1859-1896) was an engineer and builder of bridges. The construction of his wheel proved enormously difficult, and it was ready only after the inauguration of the fair; the axle of the wheel was said to be the largest piece of steel ever worked up to that time. See Edna Yost's entry on Ferris in *Dictionary of American Biography* (Scribner's Sons, New York, 1943). The Ferris Wheel was the model for the wheel of the Prater in Vienna, built in 1898.
44
See "The Columbian Tower," *Scientific American* 66, Jan. 1892, p. 9. Burg describes a series of incredible proposals, among them that of transporting the Colosseum from Rome stone by stone; see *Chicago's White City*, pp. 79-81.

45

On March 1, 1891, eleven Sicilians accused of assassinating the New Orleans police chief were lynched by a mob. The tense climate of hostility toward immigrants in general increased political support for new laws against immigration, which were, in fact, soon passed. Italy recalled its ambassador and requested damages from the federal government. Diplomatic relations were not reestablished until 1892. The principal concern of the commission sent to Italy was that Italy contribute to the good international reputation of the fair and that the king grant it his official recognition.

46

See Ralph, *Chicago World's Fair*, chap. 6, which is devoted to the Argonaut Club.

47

Among them were Enid Yandall of Louisville, who modeled the caryatids beneath the cornice, and Alice B. Rideout of San Francisco, who won the competition for the decoration of the attic. See ibid., p. 163.

48

The idea seems to have come directly from the portrayal of the future in Edward Bellamy's *Looking Backward, 2000-1887.* Bellamy's utopian novel (Houghton Mifflin, Boston, 1888) described the music room of a house in the year 2000, equipped with an invisible, automatic system of sound transmission: "She made me sit down comfortably, and, crossing the room, so far as I could see, merely touched one or two screws, and at once the room was filled, not flooded, for by some means, the volume of melody had been perfectly graduated to the size of the apartment."

49

Quoted in Sigfried Giedion, *Space, Time and Architecture*, 3rd ed. (Harvard University Press, Cambridge, Mass., 1954), p. 392.

50

The statement was made fourteen years after the fair in Harry Thurston Peck, *Twenty Years of the Republic*, 1907, p. 350.

51

Paul Bourget, "A Farewell to the White City," *Cosmopolitan* 16, Dec. 1893.

52

For an economic assessment, which seems to have been very positive even in its direct and immediate returns, see Franklin H. Head, "The Fair's Results to the City of Chicago," *Forum* 16, Dec. 1893, pp. 524-526.

53

Alice Freeman Palmer, "Some Lasting Results of the World's Fair," ibid., pp. 517-523.

54

M. G. Van Rensselaer, "The Artistic Triumph of the Fair-Builders," *Forum* 14, Dec. 1892, p. 539.

55

West declares, "We felt that society was dragging anchor and in danger of going adrift. Whither it would drift nobody could say, but all feared the rock."

56

Frederick L. Olmsted, "A Report upon the Landscape Architecture of the Columbian Exposition to the AIA," *American Architect and Building News* 41, Sept. 1892, p. 151, quoted in Fein, *Frederick Law Olmsted*, p. 65.

57

The quotations are from Sullivan, *Autobiography of an Idea*, pp. 322, 325. Giedion, writing in 1941, took no notice of the late date of Sullivan's famous phrase and wrote, "At the time this may have seemed only the exaggerated expression of an outraged artist; it turned out to be a precise prophecy of what was actually to follow" (*Space, Time and Architecture*, p. 392). See also n21.

58

Claude Bragdon, "Architecture in the United States, II. The Growth of Taste," *Architectural Record* 26, July 1909, p. 38.

59

"At that time few hoped to rival Paris; the artistic capacity and experience of the French made us distrustful of ourselves" (Monroe, *John Wellborn Root*, p. 218), See also Prof. A. D. F. Hamlin, "The Influence of the Ecole des Beaux Arts on our Architectural Education," *Architectural Record* 23, Apr. 1908, cited in Giedion, *Time, Space and Architecture*, p. 393, n15.

60

Montgomery Schuyler, "Last Words about the World's Fair," *Architectural Record*, Jan-Mar. 1897, contained in Jordy and Coe, *American Architecture*, p. 218.

61

Giedion, *Space, Time and Architecture*, p. 393.

62

On these awards and Sullivan's silence, see Crook, "L. H. Sullivan and the Golden Doorway." Willard Connely, author of the biography *Louis Sullivan as He Lived* (Horizon Press, New York, 1960), writes that the architect was not pleased with the motivations for the awards. The motivations are stated in "Rapport de M. Jules Macier, vice-president de la commission," *Revue des Arts Décoratifs* 14, 1894, p. 324.

63

Claude Bragdon, "Art Nouveau and American Architecture," a lecture delivered at the convention of the Architectural League of America, October 5, 1903, and published in *Architectural Review*, Oct. 1903, pp. 141-142.

64

P. Bourget, "A Farewell to the White City," p. 186.

65

Henry Adams, *The Education of Henry Adams. An Autobiography* (Houghton Mifflin, Boston, 1918), p. 340.

66

Ibid, p. 343.

67

Charles Eliot Norton, "Art in America," a lecture given in 1898, quoted in Moore, *Daniel H. Burnham*, 1:87.

68

Schuyler, "Last Words." These and the following quotations are taken from this article.

69

Fiske Kimball, *American Architecture* (Bobbs-Merrill, Indianapolis, 1928); quoted in Coles and Reed, *Architecture in America*, p. 194.

70

"The intellectual reflex of the Exposition will be shown in a demand for better architecture, and designers will be obliged to abandon their incoherent originalities and study the ancient masters of building." Schuyler ("Last Words," p. 277) quotes Burnham's words from "a Chicago newspaper," which it has not been possible to identify more precisely.

71

Ibid., p. 275

72

Sullivan, *Autobiography of an Idea*, p. 321.

73

Grant Carpenter Manson, *Frank Lloyd Wright to 1910. The First Golden Age* (Reinhold, New York, 1958), p. 34, defined the Transportation Building as "Adler and Sullivan's agonizingly small share of the total layout of the 'White City.'" Manson develops the thesis—denied by Wright but undoubtedly not unfounded—of the influence of the Japanese buildings and prints seen at the fair on Wright and his contemporaries. For these young men the really provocative edifice of the exposition was not the Transportation Building but Ho-o-den.

74

Lewis Mumford, "The Chicago Fairs," *New Republic* 65, Jan. 1931.

75

Werner Hegemann, *City Planning Housing* (Architectural Book Publishing, New York, 1936) 2, pp. 343-394. See also Francesco Dal Co, "From Parks to the Region: Progressive Ideology and the Reform of the American City," this volume, n59. Bruno Zevi, in *Storia dell'architettura moderna* (Turin, 1950, p. 398), describes the fair in this way: "The abysmal disaster of a culture marked by the hundreds of columns of an exposition comparable for its irresponsible anachronism only to that prepared in Rome for 1942." Zevi's words reveal the emotional response of one who has recently come out of a nightmare, referred to here in his mention of the Fascist exposition. It is also evident that such a comparison, certainly arbitrary, can only lead to an ethical judgment.

76

After accusing the fair of falsity and degenerateness, Bragdon admits, "The Science of Cities, that is, the conception of cities as coherent organisms, with many diverse and highly specialized functions. . . . dates from the Chicago Exposition" ("Architecture in the United States," p. 39). That the fair gave birth to city planning was to become a commonly accepted idea.

77

This fact, which it has not been possible to confirm, is supplied by Gordon Carruth in *The Encyclopedia of American Facts and Dates*, 6th ed. (Crowell, New York, 1970); he speaks of the almost complete destruction of the buildings and a damage of $2 million. Were they perhaps insured?

78

"Pathetic Aspects of the World's Fair," *Public Opinion* 16, Nov. 1893, p. 195.

79

If Burnham failed in this attempt with Wright, he was to insist with others—for example, Pierce Anderson (see n152); he also later sent his son Hubert to study in France.

80

Frank Lloyd Wright, *An Autobiography* (Duell, Sloan and Pearce, New York, 1943), pp. 127-128. It may here be recalled that at the time of the fair, or immediately thereafter, Wright designed the Milwaukee Library (1894) in a strictly classical style akin to Atwood's.

81

Four photographs of the work in course of construction were published in "A White Enameled Building," *Architectural Record* 4, Jan.-Mar. 1895, p. 299. The first shows clearly that only the ground floor had been built previously. The article states:

Chicago has been treated to a most novel sight. On one of its most crowded thoroughfares a sixteen-story building has been in course of erection, the two lower floors of which are occupied by one of the largest dry-goods establishments in the city, and the daily routine of business goes on without interruption while the fourteen upper stories of steel fire-proofing and cream-white enameled terra cotta climb up into the sky to a height of 200 feet. It is the Reliance Building at the southwest corner of Washington and State streets, 55 feet on State street by 85 feet on Washington, and the plans come from the office of D. H. Burnham and Co. Mr. Charles B. Attwood [sic], architect; Mr. Edward C. Shankland, M.A.S.C.E. and M.I.C.E., of London, engineer.

Some five years ago there had been a five-story building on this site of very heavy masonry construction, the lower floor of which was occupied by a National Bank. The leases of the upper floors did not expire until May 1, 1894, but on the removal of the bank to its own building it was deemed desirable to arrange the first floor for store purposes, plans were made in 1890 for a sixteen-story building by Mr. John Root, and the foundations and first story of this new building were put in, the upper four stories of the old building being held up on screws, while the first story of the new building was slipped in under them. This spring, when the leases ran out and it became possible to proceed with the work, the original plans underwent radical changes, and Mr. Attwood conceived the idea of using cream-white enameled terra cotta for the exterior, with the exception of the first story already completed, which is of polished Scotch granite. The somewhat limited ground space and the great height of the building present difficult problems to the architect who attempts to produce an attractive structure, and with its plate-glass foundations, which the shopkeeper demands, it is hardly to be supposed that even the designer will consider it a masterpiece. Still there is one most important feature which, regardless of the architectural beauties of the structure, must be considered, and which will make this building stand out as a conspicuous mark in the history of architecture in America, namely, the use of enameled terra cotta for the exterior. The question of being able to obtain this material was a serious one. However, the Northwestern Terra Cotta Co. was able to guarantee the required conditions.

82

This was the Illinois Trust and Savings Bank, built in Chicago in 1898 (see illustration opposite p. 92 in Moore, *Daniel H. Burnham.* Sullivan was probably referring ironically to this building in his *Kindergarten Chats* when, after a long exposition by the "master" on good and bad architecture, the "disciple" interrupts by exclaiming, "My goodness! What a light that throws on the bank!" "What Bank?" "You know." "Bank me no banks—that has neither form nor function here." See Louis H. Sullivan, *Kindergarten Chats (Revised 1918) and Other Writings* (Wittenborn, New York, 1947), p. 44.

83

Sullivan, *Autobiography of an Idea*, p. 324.

84

Montgomery Schuyler, "Architecture Made Easy," *Architectural Record*, Dec. 1897, pp. 214-218; contained in Jordy and Coe, *American Architecture*, pp. 298-299.

85

Burnham was to construct several important buildings for Harry W. Oliver in Pittsburgh between 1902 and 1906. His choice of the Pyramids as the first goal of his diligent career as traveler seems to suggest the possible influence of Henry Adams, whose haughty and "enlightened" conservativism was certainly dear to Burnham; in particular, it suggests the closing words of Adams's *Democracy, an American Novel* (1881): "I want to go to Egypt. . . . Democracy has shaken my nerves to pieces. Oh what rest it would be to live in the Great Pyramid and look out forever at the polar star!"

86

The quotations from Burnham's diary are taken from Moore, *Daniel H. Burnham*, 1:123, 127.

87

Ibid., 2:106.

88

Quoted in Mel Scott, *American City Planning since 1890* (University of California Press, Berkeley and Los Angeles, 1969), pp. 38-39.

89

The Dickens article is quoted in Robert Minor, "The Story of May Day," *Liberator* 5, May 1924, p. 8. Minor demonstrates that according to tradition, principally Anglo-Saxon, May 1 was a festal day of a particular significance; the death and rebirth of nature were celebrated metaphorically as the killing of the king and the institution of a new social order. It was the Baltimore organization of the Knights of Labor that proposed that May 1, 1884, be set as the day to begin labor demonstrations in the fight for the eight-hour day. Interestingly enough, this date was rejected by the union leaders precisely because of its too rebellious significance. Subsequently, at the 1886 convention of the Federation of Organized Trade and Labor Unions (predecessor to the American Federation of Labor that was founded in this same year) May 1, 1886, was established as the date for the beginning of the national strike for the eight-hour day. The bloodshed in Chicago during the 1886 strike (on May 3 four workers were killed by the police; at the protest meeting in Chicago's Haymarket Square on May 4 a policeman was killed and others wounded by a bomb) and the terroristic repression that followed, indelibly stamped this day in history with all its significance for the class struggle throughout the world.

May 1 is given as the date of the opening of the Chicago fair by the majority of sources consulted: James Truslow Adams, *Dictionary of American History* (Scribner's Sons, New York, 1940); Carruth, *Encyclopedia of American Facts;* Hirschl, "Great White City." On the other hand, Gilbert and Bryson, *Chicago and Its Makers* (Chicago, 1929), give May 31 as the day the fair opened.

90

In *Autobiography of an Idea*, p. 319, Sullivan noted, "Burnham and Jeffery loved each other dearly. The thought of one was the thought of both." Jeffery, an influential railroad executive, had been chairman of the grounds and building committee of the fair.

91

"Architectural Aberrations. The Government and the World's Fair," *Architectural Record* 2, Mar. 1893, pp. 333-336.

92

See also Dal Co, "From Parks to the Region," this volume.

93

Lewis Mumford, *Sticks and Stones. A Study of American Architecture and Civilization* (Norton, New York, 1924), pp. 130-131.

94

See William H. Wilson, *The City Beautiful Movement in Kansas* (University of Missouri Press, Columbia, 1964).

95

Thomas Adams, *Outline of Town and City Planning* (Russell Sage Foundation, New York, 1935), pp. 173-175. See also the issues of the Kansas City *Star* edited by William R. Nelson from 1881 on.

96

Charles Mulford Robinson, *The Improvement of Cities and Towns* (New York, 1901). The trip to Europe that made it possible to write the book was undertaken for *Harper's* magazine. In 1900 Robinson formed the National League of Improvement Associations, which banded together in 1904 with the American Park and Outdoor Art Association, of which J. Horace McFarland became secretary.

97

For a summary of the Baltimore conference see *Municipal Affairs* 3, no. 4, Dec. 1899.

98

Loring Underwood, "The City Beautiful: the Ideal to Aim At," *American City* 2, May 1910, pp. 214-218. Education was a central theme at the Universal Exposition in Saint Louis in 1904, which included a whole pavilion dedicated to the subject; there the visitor could compare the educational methods of all civilized peoples. See David R. Francis, *The Universal Exposition of 1904* (Saint Louis, 1913); cited in Scott, *American City Planning.*

99

Charles Zueblin, *American Municipal Progress* (Macmillan, New York, 1918), p. 353. At the time, Zeublin was president of the American League of City Improvement.

100

Frederick Law Olmsted, Jr., "The Limits of City Beautification," *American City* 2, May 1910, p. 209.

101

Frank E. Wallis, "Richard Morris Hunt, Master Architect and Man," *Architectural Review* 22, Nov. 1917, pp. 239-240; cited in Christopher Tunnard, *The Modern American City* (Van Nostrand, Princeton, 1968), pp. 127-129. In Wallis's, opinion no architect "except possibly Wren, or Da Vinci, or Michelangelo, had such complete control of mass and of a problem as a whole as did Hunt." Hunt helped finance the *Architectural Review* and in 1888 advised the editor of the journal to emphasize classical principles rather than those of the picturesque movement.

102

This fact is explicitly mentioned by George Kriehl, "The City Beautiful," *Municipal Affairs* 3, no. 4, Dec. 1899, pp. 594ff. Also cited as models were Vienna and Berlin.

103

This project was proposed in the early 1890s. Windrim's design, approved and then put aside because of its excessive cost, was taken up again in 1904. In 1907 Paul Philippe Cret and others worked on the problem; finally, in 1917, the Frenchman Jacques Gréber produced a design executed in 1919, for the present-day Benjamin Franklin Parkway.

104

See Manfredo Tafuri, *Architecture and Utopia, Design and Capitalist Development* (M.I.T. Press, Cambridge, Mass., 1976), p. 33.

105

The most complete work on the city of Washington is John W. Reps, *Monumental Washington. The Planning and Development of the Capital Center* (Princeton University Press, Princeton, 1967). The most accessible source material is found in the two books by Charles Moore, *Daniel H. Burnham* and *The Life and Times of Charles F. McKim* (Houghton Mifflin, Boston, 1929).

106

The actual design of Smith's proposal was by the architect James Renwick. The plan of Renwick's complex followed the type of the Forum of Trajan (See Reps, *Monumental Washington*, fig. 40). In Conjunction with the Columbian Exposition and the return to Classical planning, Glenn Brown discovered L'Enfant's original design for Washington; see Glenn Brown, *History of the United States Capitol* (Government Printing Office, Washington, D.C., 1900).

107

See the Washington *Evening Star*, Mar. 3, 5, 6 and May 3, 1900. See also Reps, *Monumental Washington*, p. 76.

108

Bingham's plans bear the inscription "compiled and drawn by Frederick D. Owen."

109

Brown's plan was the matrix of that of the Senate Park Commission. It was based on a large cross formed by the axes leading out from the Capitol and the White House and crossing at the Washington Monument; it also foresaw both the symmetry of the two radial arteries departing from the Capitol toward the White House and the Jefferson Memorial and the creation of a plaza around the obelisk. The station on the Mall was to be placed underground.

110

Tafuri, *Architecture and Utopia*, p. 36.

111

Mumford, *Sticks and Stones*, p. 147.

112

Strong, *Our Country*.

113

Bellamy, *Looking Backward*.

114

The monumental conception of railroad-station architecture had its beginnings around 1890. Union Depot, Detroit (Isaac Taylor), Union Station, Saint Louis (Theodore C. Link and E. D. Cameron), and Broad Street Station, Philadelphia (Frank Furness) are the most notable examples; all were built between 1889 and 1894 and all in medieval style.

115

Reps, *Monumental Washington*, p. 98.

116

It is significant that in Pittsburgh, a totally different type of city, at almost the same time (1898-1902), Burnham built an extraordinary railroad station that was hardly classical in character at all.

117

The preparation of the plan was carried out in three offices: in New York, where McKim was joined by Brown and the very young William T. Partridge; in Brookline, Massachusetts where Frederick Law Olmsted, Jr., was situated; and in Washington, where Moore and Senator McMillan handled the official activities. Burnham, who assumed the role of coordinator of the project, made a monthly round of the three. A list of the meetings and their dates is given in Reps, *Monumental Washington* p. 99, n21.

118

Montgomery Schuyler, "The Nation's New Capital," *New York Times*, Jan. 19, 1902, supplement, pp. 4-5.

119

Idem, "The Art of City Making," *Architectural Record* 12, May 1902, pp. 1-26. Both articles are cited in Reps, *Monumental Washington*, pp. 142-143.

120

American Architect and Building News, Feb. 1902; cited in Reps, *Monumental Washington*, pp. 142-143.

121

Glaab and Brown, *History of Urban America*, p. 213. The examples cited are Hazen Pingree of Detroit, Samuel M. Jones of Toledo, and Tom L. Johnson of Cleveland.

122

Frederic C. Howe, "Cleveland—A City 'Finding Itself,' " *World's Work* 6, Oct. 1, 1903, pp. 3988ff.

123

Newton D. Baker, *Dictionary of American Biography*; see also Tom L. Johnson, *My Story*, ed. Elizabeth J. Hauser (Huebsch, New York, 1913).

124

Daniel H. Burnham, John M. Carrère, and Arnold W. Brunner, *The Group Plan of the Public Buildings of the City of Cleveland. Report Made to the Honorable Tom L. Johnson Mayor and to the Honorable Board of Public Service* (Cleveland, Aug. 1903).

125

From a long passage describing working procedure on the Cleveland project quoted in Moore, *Daniel H. Burnham* 1, p. 202, apparently from a letter written years later in which Brunner supplied Moore with information for his biography of Burnham. From Martigni, on May 20, 1912, Burnham was to write Brunner what was perhaps the last letter of his life. This short note was apparently unoccasioned and concluded with the words: "I just thought I would send you a line to say on paper, as I am sure you have long ago guessed, that I do think a great deal of you" (ibid. 2, pp. 156-157).

126

After 1911, the work was directed by Brunner. Carrère, who died in an auto accident the same year, was replaced by Frank B. Mead of Cleveland. After Burnham's death in 1912, his place was filled by Frederick Law Olmsted, Jr.

127

McKim to Burnham, in Moore, *Daniel H. Burnham*, 1:280.

128

Moore records some of these incidents, and in particular an angry letter, dated Feb. 6, 1903, to Burnham from McKim, who was fed up with the constant difficulty encountered in trying to meet with his colleague; see *Daniel H. Burnham* 1, p. 198.

129

Edward VII's remark was often ironically repeated by McKim; see ibid. 1, p. 200.

130

Data on the height of buildings are from K. Greven, *New York und Ungebungen* (Albert Goldschmidt, Berlin, 1903); according to this work the New York buildings over 200 feet high were the following:

Flatiron Building, 300 feet, 20 stories, Broadway and 5th Avenue
American Exchange Bank, 232 feet, 16 stories, Broadway and Cedar Street
American Surety Company, 306 feet, 23 stories, Broadway and Pine Street
American Tract Society, 306 feet, 23 stories, Nassau and Spruce Streets
Astoria Hotel, 312 feet, 16 floors, 344-350 5th Avenue
Bank of Commerce, 270 feet, 20 stories, Nassau and Cedar Streets
Bowling Green, 272 feet, 19 stories, 5-11 Broadway
Commercial Cable, 255 feet, 21 stories, 20-22 Broad St
Dun Building, 223 feet, 15 stories, 290-294 Broadway
Gillender Building, 273 feet, 16 floors, Wall and Nassau Streets
Home Life Insurance, 280 feet, 16 stories, 256 Broadway
Hotel Netherland, 220 feet, 17 stories, 59th Street and 5th Avenue
Hudson Realty Company, 205 feet, 16 stories, 32-34 Broadway
Irvins Syndicate, 382 feet, 29 stories, 12-21 Park Row
Johnston Building, 205 feet, 15 stories, 30-36 Broad Street
Manhattan Life Insurance, 348 feet, 17 stories, 64-68 Broadway

Mutual Life Insurance, 210 feet, 15 stories, Liberty Street

New York Life Insurance, 270 feet, 12 stories [sic], 346-348 Broadway

New York Realty Co., 203 feet, 15 stories, 9-13 Maiden Lane

O. B. Potter Trust, 292 feet, 20 stories, Broadway and Rector Street

Pulitzer Building, 257 feet, 22 stories, Park Row

St. James Building, 204 feet, 16 stories, Broadway and 26th Street

St. Paul Building, 308 feet, 26 stories, Ann Street and Broadway

Standard Oil Building, 263 feet, 15 stories, 24-30 Broadway

Vincent Building, 205 feet, 14 stories, Broadway and Duane Street

Washington Life Insurance, 273 feet, 19 stories, Broadway and Liberty Street

The small number of stories of the New York Life Insurance Building, in proportion to its height, would appear a typographical error, but I have been unable to find more precise information.

131

The impression aroused by the Flatiron lasted down to the mid-1920s. John Dos Passos did not forget it in his *Manhattan Transfer* of 1925 and inserted it in Jimmy's fantasies: "On roller-skates . . . magic roller-skates . . . up the brick walls of the houses, over roofs, vaulting chimneys, up the Flatiron Building, scooting across the cables of Brooklyn Bridge."

132

Julius F. Harder, "The City's Plan," *Municipal Affairs* 2, 1898, p. 45; cited by Scott, *American City Planning*, who has brought Harder's plan once again to the attention of scholars.

133

Harder, "City's Plan."

134

Burnham to L. M. Shaw, secretary of the treasury, June 1903, quoted in Moore, *Daniel H. Burnham*, 1:206.

135

Geddes to his wife, 1899, included in Philip Mairet, *Pioneer in Sociology: The Life and Letters of Patrick Geddes* (Lund Humphries, London, 1957).

136

Williams, *Contours of American History*, p. 321.

137

Glaab and Brown, *History of Urban America*, p. 148.

138

Between 1900 and 1910, 240 books were published in the United States on the subject of business management; see Hofstadter, *Age of Reform*, pp. 235-237.

139

The term *muckraker* was apparently first used by Theodore Roosevelt.

140

On the book by Wright and Gannett, see Giorgio Ciucci, "The City in Agrarian Ideology and Frank Lloyd Wright: Origins and Development of Broadacres," this volume, n45. *House Beautiful* first appeared in 1896; the *Ladies' Home Journal*, in 1900; the *Craftsman* and *House and Garden*, in 1901; the *Western Architect*, in 1902; and *American Home and Garden*, in 1905.

141

The model was the English journal the *Studio*, first issued in 1893. On relations with the Arts and Crafts movement, see David Gebhard, "C. F. A. Voisey to and from America," *Journal of the Society of Architectural Historians* 30, no. 4, 1971; H. Allen Brooks, "Chicago Architecture. Its Debt to the Arts and Crafts," ibid.

142

Hofstadter, *Age of Reform*, p. 272.

143

Williams, *Contours of American History*, p. 416.

144

Charles A. and Mary R. Beard, *A Basic History of the United States* (Country Life Press, Garden City, N.Y., 1952, p. 352.

145

The other competitors were Cope and Stewartson of Philadelphia, Hines and La Farge of New York, Carrère and Hastings of New York, Charles C. Haight of New York, Peabody and Stearns of Boston, Cram, Goodhue and Ferguson of Boston, Eames and Young of Saint Louis; see Moore, *Daniel H. Burnham* 1, p. 190.

146

Ibid. 1, p. 192.

147

The competition was won by Cram, Goodhue and Ferguson, whose design was in the NeoGothic style of the preexisting buildings by Hunt.

148

Daniel H. Burnham and Edward H. Bennett, *Plan of Chicago* (Chicago, 1909; reprinted, Da Capo Press, New York, 1970).

149

Manfredo Tafuri called the cities of the Spanish colonization in Mexico "machines for conversion" in a course in the history of architecture, given in 1969-1970 at the Institute of Architecture of the University of Venice.

150

Thomas S. Hines, "The Imperial Façade," *Pacific Historical Review* 41, Feb. 1972, p. 33. See also idem, *Burnham of Chicago.*

151

Burnham to Moore, August 26, 1904, Moore, *Daniel H. Burnham* 1, p. 233.

152

Pierce Anderson, like Frank Lloyd Wright, had been advised by Burnham to study at the Ecole des Beaux Arts after he had won attention at the fair as a gifted engineer. Anderson went to Paris and returned with his diploma in 1899.

153

Wright, from Memphis, was governor of the Philippines from 1904 to 1906. He later became ambassador to Japan and, finally, served from 1908 to 1909 as Theodore Roosevelt's secretary of war.

154

According to his diary, Burnham was ill on December 18; while he was working at Baguio he wrote that he was too tired to sleep; see Moore, *Daniel H. Burnham* 1, p. 239

155

Burnham to Moore, March 13, 1905; see ibid, 1:245.

156

Parsons remained in the Philippines from November 1905 until February 1914.

157

Letter from the War Department in Washington to Burnham, October 13, 1905, signed by William Howard Taft; see Moore, *Daniel H. Burnham* 1, p. 177.

158

On Parsons's work in the Philippines, including the designs of two other cities, Cabu and Zamboanga, see A. N. Rebori, "The Work of William E. Parsons in the Philippine Islands," *Architectural Record* 41 no. 4, Apr. 1917, pp. 305ff., and no. 5, May 1917, pp. 423ff.

159

Ernest R. Graham, Burnham's assistant at the fair in 1893, remained with him in the new firm of D. H. Burnham and Company established in the same year, which included also Atwood and Shankland. After Atwood's death and Shankland's departure from the firm, Graham remained as a titular collaborator. In 1908 he took over the general direction of the studio, which was divided into three sections: designing, working plans, and superintendence, controlled respectively by Pierce Anderson, Edward Probst, and H. J. White. In 1910 Hubert Burnham and Daniel H. Burnham, Jr. entered the firm. After Burnham's death in 1912, the firm took the name of Graham, Burnham and Company.

160

The precedents for this building type were the Post Building of 1880 and the Mills Building of 1882, both by George B. Post and both in New York. Among the numerous examples, all of which arose as solutions to the problem of providing light and air to the interior parts of buildings, which would otherwise be too deep, are the New York Life Building in Kansas City (McKim, Mead and White, 1888-90) and the very beautiful Union Trust Company Building in Saint Louis (Adler and Sullivan, 1892-93).

161

The *New York Times* of March 1, 1904, reported an attack on McKim in the Senate for his enlargement of the White House. The January 14, 1908, Washington *Evening Star* carried a cartoon entitled "Group of Le Notre-McKim Tree-Butchers and Nature-Butchers," representing McKim in the lead, with Burnham, Glenn Brown, Green, Hornblower, and Donn behind, all marching toward the Capitol armed with axes and followed by men carrying squarely trimmed, potted trees; see Moore, *Daniel H. Burnham, 2,* p. 65.

162

The episode was recounted by William Howard Taft, secretary of war, at the McKim memorial meeting of the AIA on December 15, 1909. Moore states, in *Daniel H. Burnham 1,* pp. 227-228:

The Mall was Mr. McKim's chief anxiety lest Congress should forget that important part of the plan of the improvement of Washington. The cellar and foundation for the Agricultural Department building had been begun, and some $8000 or $10,000 expended when it came to Mr. McKim's knowledge that the building, if erected according to that plan, would be a few feet too high and a few feet too near the center; and he came to prevent it. The Secretary of Agriculture was not disposed to regard that variation from the plan as substantial, and was very much opposed to the change.

Mr. McKim came to me, after Mr. Root left the Cabinet, as his only true sympathizer and friend, and asked me to speak to the President, whom he also regarded as a friend and sympathizer, but one who at times needed convincing. So I went to see the President and explained to him the situation, and he at once agreed that we ought to change it. "But," said he, "the trouble is with Uncle Jimmy, who has a real cause of complaint. He says that these architects have delayed too long, and the public money cannot be wasted and expended in this way."

"Well," said I, "can't we call a council, or something of that sort, and solemnly sit on the subject, and then finally reach the right conclusion?"

He said, "We can, and we will," and we did. Mr. McKim was of counsel and Mr. Green and two or three others. The President took Mr. McKim to task at once on the audacity of architects who wait thirty and sixty days, until plans have been completed, and then come in and attempt to make a change. Well, that was not a very good beginning, and I am afraid that our brother McKim thought the jig was up. But it so suited the Secretary of Agriculture that when there appeared a suggestion from an engineer that possibly not $10,000, or $5000 would be sacrificed, but an economy might be introduced in another way, the Secretary, at the suggestion or the invitation of the President, said that he thought possibly it might be worked out that way, but the President insisted that if we did, we did not intend to waive the criticism that we had to make against the profession of architects by reason of their delay. And so we separated.

The Agricultural building was moved. McKim and I walked up the steps of the War Department. I said, "Mr. McKim, I congratulate you on your victory." He turned and looked at me a moment and said, "Was it a victory? Another such and I am dead." But it was a victory, and it illustrates his character in quietly pushing and pushing and pushing for the highest ideals of his art."

163

The trip this time included Wells, Salisbury, Wincester, and Hampton Court. He again went to France, Paris, and Italy and visited Tuscany, the region of Venice, and Milan with a rented car.

164

See Reps, *Making of Urban America,* pp. 514-517.

165

Edward H. Bennett was one of the founders of the American Institute of Planners, established in 1917.

166

Reps, *Making of Urban America,* p. 517.

167

R. Hofstadter, *Age of Reform,* p. 239.

168

In this period novels of social protest, such as those of Upton Sinclair and Jack London, had an enormous success.

169

Between 1898 and 1907, annual immigration totals constantly increased (except for a slight decrease in 1904) from 250,000 to 1,300,000. During the same period, the number of unskilled immigrants employed rose from 100,000 to 300,000. See U.S. Bureau of Labor Statistics, Bureau of Immigration, *1820-1932 Immigration and Naturalization Service*, Bulletin no. 651 (Government Printing Office, Washington, D.C., 1968).

170

See U.S. Bureau of Labor Statistics, *Handbook of Labor Statistics*, (Government Printing Office, Washington, D.C., 1950).

171

In the autumn of 1907, the New York Street Railway and Westinghouse Electric Company both failed. With the collapse of the Knickerbocker Trust Company on October 22, the panic exploded. Together with some other financiers, J. P. Morgan found the money to acquire enough gold in Europe to stabilize the situation temporarily.

172

The Department of Sociology of the University of Chicago was headed by Albion Small. Until 1920 its work reflected European sociology, following first Spencer and social Darwinism and later Durkheim and Simmel. In this milieu were developed the protagonists of the Chicago school of sociology, which was to make its important contributions after 1920. See Robert E. Parks, Ernest W. Burgess, and Roderick D. McKenzie, *The City* (University of Chicago Press, Chicago, 1925).

173

Quoted in Bertrand Russell, *Freedom and Organization, 1818-1914* (Allen and Unwin, London, 1934), p. 374.

174

At the end of January 1907, McKim wrote to Burnham: "Although not well, I with much reluctance consented to serve only because it seemed a moral duty to do so. . . . With you a thousand miles away, with Bernard Green a sick man, Saint-Gaudens a sick man, and I not yet strong . . . I, therefore, write now to ask if it will not meet your approval to join with us two more men . . . namely Charles Moore and Frank Millet." On February 4, Burnham responded curtly: "I have to-day telegraphed to the President that I have resigned. . . . This will leave you entirely free to fill my place." McKim immediately telegraphed Burnham: "Without you existence of Board impossible." It took the intervention of Charles Moore and William Howard Taft to make him withdraw his resignation. This correspondence is reprinted in Moore, *Daniel H. Burnham* 2, pp. 16ff.

175

In a letter to McKim, dated June 12, 1906, in response to his solicitations for support of a cathedral in the classical style, Burnham, still in favor of the Gothic, rather ironically asked, "Will you tell me where to find the illustration of one English Renaissance church which you consider beautiful?" Nevertheless, on June 25, 1906, Burnham wrote to Bishop Satterlee, "I believe that Mr. McKim is entirely right and the style of the cathedral should be Classic Renaissance." See Moore, *Daniel H. Burnham*, 2, pp. 52, 56.

176

Burnham to Bishop Satterlee, July 27, 1907, in ibid., 2:64-65.

177

After Vaughan's death, the work was finished, with modifications, by Frohman, Robb and Little.

178

In January 1908, at the age of sixty-two McKim left the studio of McKim, Mead and White and retired from professional activity; he died the next year. William Rutherford Mead, who also acted as manager of the firm, died in 1928. Stanford White, artist, designer of villas, churches, and monuments, had died in 1906, killed while dining on the roof of Madison Square Garden by a man named Harry Thaw, apparently for reasons of jealousy.

179

The American School of Architecture in Rome was founded in 1894 at McKim's initiative. The model was the French Academy, founded by Louis XIV and located since 1801 in the Villa Medici. Its main financial backers were McKim himself and Burnham. The school's first quarters were in Palazzo Torlonia; in 1895 it moved to the Villa Aurora on the Pincio. In 1897 the American Academy was formally incorporated, with McKim as its president. In 1905 the academy acquired as its residence the Villa Mirafiore on the Via Nomentana. A month after McKim's death on September 14, 1909, Mrs. Clara Jessup Heyland bequeathed the Villa Aurelia on the Janiculum to the institution. The present building was constructed between 1912 and 1914 according to a design by McKim, Mead and White. See Moore, *Life and Times of McKim; idem, Daniel H. Burnham.* The essential data are also given in Norman Newton, *Design on the Land. The Development of Landscape Architecture,* (Harvard University Press, Belknap Press, Cambridge, Mass., 1971), chap. 27.

180

The correspondence among the patron, Peter Brooks of Boston, his representative in Chicago, Owen F. Aldis, and the Burnham and Root firm, on the Monadnock Buildings demonstrates that before 1890 the site of the building, although two blocks farther north than Congress Avenue, was still too far to the south of the business center. As Hoffmann has written, "The project came to a halt while Brooks waited for commercial development to move closer to the site. He advised Aldis in a letter of March 16, 1886: 'There is little chance of the Monadnock block being begun before three years' " ("John Root's Monadnock Building," p. 272).

181

All the designs required the demolition of a slice of the Auditorium along Congress Avenue, including the tower, on the top floor of which Sullivan had his studio until 1909.

182

"The architectural studies made for the buildings at this civic center are of course only suggestions; for the precise form of the buildings must be determined hereafter by the requirements for city, county, and national offices. The designs are only intended to suggest the order, dignity, and beauty which should stand forth at the heart of a great city. The old cities of the world possess historical monuments which worthily represent their dignity and unity. For a great American city of the future the present generation ought to design new structures which will represent its intellectual and moral quality, just as St. Peter's stands for Rome, Nôtre Dame, the Louvre, and the Tuileries for Paris, and St. Paul, Westminster Abbey, and the Parliament Houses for London" (Charles W. Eliot, "A Study of the New Plan of Chicago," *Century Magazine* 74, Jan. 1910, pp. 429-230).

183

Walter D. Moody, *What of the City* (McClurg, Chicago, 1919), quoted in Robert L. Wrigley, "The Plan of Chicago, Its Fiftieth Aniiversary," *Journal of American Institute of Planners* 26, Feb., 1960, p. 34.

184

Sullivan, *Kindergarten Chats,* p. 109.

185

Burnham and Bennett, *Plan of Chicago.*

186

All the data on the publicity campaign are given in Wrigley, "Plan of Chicago."

187

Still later, at the time of the 1933 World's Fair, *The Chicago Plan in 1933, Twenty Years of Accomplishment* (Chicago Plan Commission, Chicago, 1933) appeared. There was also a flood of articles in specialized journals, particularly in the *American City,* first issued in the very year 1909.

188

Charles H. Wacker, "The Plan of Chicago," *American City* 1, no. 2, Oct. 1909, p. 52.

189

The passage continues, "This Plan suggests on nearly every page the urgent need of combining differing individual interests for a common end, of procuring the cooperation of competing corporations, and of bringing to bear the public opinion of the multitude to effect the execution of the Plan. It suggests, in short, a large social or collective work, planned in the interest not only of the present generation, but of many generations to come. . . . The democracy will be able to work toward the best ideals through the agency of groups of intelligent and public-spirited citizens who know how to employ experts to advantage" (Eliot, "New Plan of Chicago," p. 418).

190

Ibid., p. 427.

191

Burnham and Bennett, *Plan of Chicago*, pp. 97-98.

192

Mumford, *Sticks and Stones*, p. 132. Just the year before, Sullivan, who certainly influenced Mumford, had defined Burnham as "a colossal merchandiser"; see Sullivan, *Autobiography of an Idea*, p. 292.

193

Moore, *Daniel H. Burnham* 2, pp. 114-115.

194

The data on Michigan Avenue are from Thomas Adams, *Outline of Town and City Planning*. See also Homer Hoyt, *One Hundred Years of Land Values in Chicago* (Chicago University Press, Chicago, 1933).

195

Wrigley, "Plan of Chicago," p. 32.

196

The Chicago Plan Commission, referred to here, was composed of 328 members, who worked from 1909 to 1917.

197

Eliot, "New Plan of Chicago," p. 431.

198

John L. Hancock, *John Nolen and the American City Planning Movement* (University Microfilms, Ann Arbor, 1964).

199

The quotation is from the paper delivered at the Washington conference by Robert Anderson Pope, a New York City landscape architect; see *Proceedings of the First National Conference on City Planning*, Washington, D.C., May 21-22, 1909, in *City Planning: Hearing before the Committee on the District of Columbia, United States Senate* (Government Printing Office, Washington, D.C., 1910), p. 79.

200

Edward H. Bennett, in ibid., p. 70.

201

John Nolen, in ibid., pp. 74-75.

202

Hancock, *John Nolen*, p. 160.

203

Pope, in *City Planning: Hearing*, pp. 75-79.

204

In 1870 there were 574 daily newspapers; in 1899, 1,610; and in 1909, 2,600. During the same period daily circulation rose from 2,800,000 to 24,200,000. See Alfred McKlung Lee, *The Daily Newspaper in America* (New York, 1937), pp. 716ff, cited in Hofstadter, *Age of Reform*.

205

Charles A. Beard, *Economic Interpretation of the Constitution of the United States* (Macmillan, New York, 1913).

206

As Mark L. Piesch has stated, "It is particularly interesting to study the reports of the London Conference of 1910 as a cross-section of the international activity in the field of town and city planning. The ideas of Geddes and Howard represented the sociological

approach to town planning, while the ideas of Burnham expressed the formal and artistic approach. The difference between city planning in Britain and the States could be seen in a comparison of Letchworth or Welwyn Garden City with the Burnham plan for Chicago"; see *The Chicago School of Architecture* (Phaidon, London, 1964; Random House, New York, 1965), p. 106.
207

It was John Burns who had presented the Town Planning Act of 1909 in Parliament.
208

For speeches of Stübben and Eberstadt, Royal Institute of British Architects, *Town Planning Conference, London, 10-15 October 1910. Transactions* (London, 1911), pp. 306-333. Eberstadt was opposed to nuclear, concentric schemes of the type used by Howard; instead, he favored a radial scheme in which the radial arteries developed as autonomous systems as they proceeded from the center. See Giorgio Piccinato, *La construzione dell'urbanistica. Germania 1870-1914* (Officina, Rome, 1973).
209

The space occupied by Burnham's two plans—one of the nine rooms—was all that was allotted to the United States. The exhibition rooms were distributed as follows: I. Italy and England; II. English Colonies; IIa. English Garden Cities; IIb. History of Edinburgh; III. America; IV. Holland, Belgium, Scandinavia, and Austria; V-IX. Germany and France.
210

All quotations from Burnham's discourse, entitled "A City of the Future under a Democratic Government," are from RIBA, *Town Planning Conference*, pp. 369-378.
211

A year of work on the preparation of the Washington project, $50,000; two years on San Francisco, $25,000; four years on Chicago, $100,000 up to that time.
212

L. Cope Cornford, in RIBA, *Town Planning Conference*, pp. 379-382.
213

Richard Paget, in ibid., pp. 383-384.
214

Ebenezer Howard, in ibid., p. 385.
215

Francis S. Swales, in ibid., pp. 387ff.
216

Matt Garbutt, in ibid., pp. 394-395.
217

Councilor Marr, in ibid., pp. 395-398.
218

Sullivan, *Autobiography of an Idea*. The attack on Burnham was made in one of the last installments of the autobiography, in the August 1923 issue of the *Journal of the American Institute of Architects*. In September of the same year, an authoritative defense of Burnham appeared in an English journal in the form of a review of Charles Moore's biography; see Thomas Adams, "*Daniel H. Burnham, Architect and Planner of Cities:* by Charles Moore," *Town Planning Review* 10, Sept. 1923.
219

Griffin was born on November 24, 1876, and died in India on February 13, 1937. See James Birrell, *Walter Burley Griffin* (University of Queensland Press, Saint Lucia, Brisbane, 1964).
220

In 1873 Ricker (1843-1929) was the first graduate in architecture of the University of Illinois. He later served for many years as the chairman of its department of architecture, which was founded in 1868, the second in the United States after the department at the Massachusetts Institute of Technology, founded in 1865. In 1901, in the *Brickbuilder*, Ricker published his translation of Otto Wagner's *Moderne Architektur*. See Ricker, "Story of a Life," 1922, typescript in Urbana Library, Urbana, Ill.; see also Peisch, *Chicago School of Architecture* .

221

Between 1911 and 1913, Griffin designed the Allen Place Scheme; Idalia, Lee County, Fla.; Trier Center Neighborhood, Winnetka, Ill.; Ridge Quadrangles, Chicago; and Emery Hills, near Chicago.

222

The Theosophical Society was founded in New York City on November 17, 1875, with Helena P. Blavatsky as secretary and Henry Steel Olcott as president. On the sect's theoretical principles and ways of life, see Helena P. Blavatsky, *The Secret Doctrine* (1888; reprint ed., Theosophical University Press, Pasadena, Calif., 1974). See also N. Sri Ram, *An Approach to Reality* (Theos Publishing House, Wheaton, Ill., 1968); Anna Kennedy Winner, *The Basic Ideas of Occult Wisdom* (Theos Publishing House, Wheaton, Ill., 1970).

223

According to Birrell, in 1921, Griffin became an active member of the Anthroposophic Society, a theosophical group attached to Rudolph Steiner. In 1928, Griffin is recorded as delivering an address to the Theosophical Society of Sydney, in which he strongly condemned the changes made in his plan of Canberra in the course of its execution by the Australian government, whom he accused of violating its harmony. See Birrell, *Walter Burley Griffin*, pp. 10, 115.

224

See Carlo Carozzi's preface to Patrick Geddes, *Città in evoluzione* (Il Saggiatore, Milan, 1960), p. 17; this work is an Italian translation of Geddes, *Cities in Evolution* (Williams and Norgate, London, 1915). Vivekananda's real name was Narendranath Dutta, born 1863 in Calcutta, died 1902 in Belur, a disciple of Ramakrishna. Vivekananda founded the Vedante movement in the United States in 1893. The Ramakrishna Mission, which he founded in 1897, became a worldwide organization, the goal of which was the great meeting of the Orient and the Occident. See R. Rolland, *Prophets of the New India* (New York, 1930).

225

Nils Gjellerstadt, born in Germany, placed third in the minority decision. At the 1910 London conference, he had presented the plan for Halsingborg.

226

Councilor Wernekke, "Der Wettbewerb um eine Bebauungsplan für die Bundeshaupstadt von Australien," *Der Städtebau* 10, nos. 7-8, 1913, pp. 73-77, 86-89.

227

See "The Plan of Australia's New Capital," *American City* 7, no. 1, July 1912; "Canberra, the Proposed New Federal Capital of Australia," *Architectural Review* 18, no. 8, Aug. 1912; "Canberra, the New Capital of Australia," *Architectural Record* 33, no. 5, Nov. 1912.

228

Geddes, *Cities in Evolution*, p. 239.

229

Until December 12, 1911, Calcutta was the capital of India. Sir Edwin L. Lutyens's plan is modeled on L'Enfant's Washington, with a central mall and diagonal avenues. Around the center of the city the suburban residential area is laid out in broad hexagons.

230

Geddes, *Cities in Evolution*, pp. 240-241. The passage continues, "But this is not permanently limited to the expression of the powers and glories of the ruler or the state, as on the whole from imperial Rome to modern Paris or Berlin, and from Whitehall to New Delhi. The people, in all cities alike, must increasingly ask, with homely directness, 'Where and when are we to come in?' "

231

"A Modern Department Store," *Architectural Record* 29, no. 3, Mar. 1911.

232

On Rockefeller Center see Tafuri, "Disenchanted Mountain."

233

The letter, dated April 12, 1912, was to have been delivered to Millet on his return to the United States; see Moore, *Daniel H. Burnham* 2, p. 151.

234

Mumford, *Sticks and Stones*, pp. 141-142 The quotation is from a chapter entitled "The Imperial Facade," the whole of which is a ringing denunciation of the White City and the City Beautiful.

235

The *Titanic* sank during the night of April 14-15, 1912. At 0:15 hours, for the first time in history an SOS was sent out from sea by means of Marconi's wireless. Among the many who drowned Burnham knew Major Archibald Butt, Taft's military secretary, who was traveling with Millet, Benjamin Guggenheim, John Jacob Astor, and Henry Sleeper Harper.

236

Quoted in Cass Gilbert, "Daniel Hudson Burnham, An Appreciation," *Architectural Record* 32, no. 2, Aug. 1912, p. 176. Burnham's trip continued with the usual endless rounds of visits, even some he had already seen: the Pyrenees, Provence, Florence, Lake Maggiore, the Lake of Geneva, Basel, and Strassbourg. Word of Griffin's victory in the competition for Canberra, announced on May 25, did not reach Burnham; he died in Heidelberg, Germany on June 1, 1912

FRANCESCO DAL CO

From Parks to the Region:
Progressive Ideology
and the Reform of the American City

To my parents

Introduction

The term *Progressive Era*, commonly applied to the period of United States history between 1900 and 1914, is valid particularly if considered from a certain political point of view, without attributing to it a general significance. Yet it must be admitted that full expression was given to the need for reform in all aspects of American life, cultural as well as political, during the middle years of this period. A date that is emblematic of this tendency is 1912, when Woodrow Wilson and Theodore Roosevelt contended for the presidency on the basis of two doctrines, New Freedom and New Nationalism, both of which, although in different ways, expressed a progressive ideology.

In the course of this essay I shall consider briefly the political content of both New Freedom and New Nationalism. It must be emphasized first, however, that both Wilson and Roosevelt were the interpreters—and their political platforms the consequences—of the end of the laissez-faire era. The basic issue of the election campaign of 1912 was how to found a modern state in keeping with the dynamics of development of the American enterprise system, after the defeats and failures of laissez-faire. It would be wrong, however, simply to equate this political awareness with the progressive movement and its tradition. In fact, American progressivism had a dynamic of its own that should in no way be identified with political achievements, which almost always came later. During the nineteenth century, progressive democratic thought developed a critical point of view and advocated alternative practices to those of the laissez-faire government, but its activities had little actual effect in the political and institutional sphere. Progressivism did, however, achieve a certain force in the cultural sphere of urban planning.

In the pages that follow I shall try to reconstruct some of the principal contributions of the tradition of progressive planning, which came into being in the nineteenth century and bore its final fruit during the New Deal years. My aim is not, however, to write a history of American urbanism but, more simply, to use significant examples to trace the basic concepts, as well as the contradictions, of a few of the major trends of this particular area of American culture.

The progressive component that I shall analyze as one of the fundamentals of American urban planning arose together with the first affirmation of industrialism. Along with the industrial city the criticism of urbanization came into being; in the particular case of the United States such criticism has often been considered a further expression of the antiurban ideology. Although this interpretation has been often and validly justified within the extensive literature on the development of the American city, it will receive only limited attention here, not because I believe such a viewpoint fruitless but because I wish, instead, to demonstrate how certain intellectual attitudes, traditionally considered antiurban, were actually fundamental hypotheses of urban reform and how certain concepts belonging to the progressive tradition can be detected behind the romantic and arcadian myths.

In my view it is not possible to speak of American progressivism in terms of a philosophical system; rather, it can be discussed only as an attitude, primarily intellectual and moral rather than political and founded on the assumption of a dynamic series of problems and contradiction that collectively express a grave but optimistic concern about contemporary society, its forms of development, and its functioning. My choice of terms is deliberate: *forms*, not *development; functioning*, not *system*.

The following words from Herbert Croly's famous book can perhaps make this clearer: "From the beginning Americans have been anticipating and projecting a better future. From the beginning the Land of Democracy has been figured as the land of Promise. Thus the American's loyalty to the national tradition rather affirms than denies the imaginative projection of a better future."[1] Its relationship with tradition is a further fundamental component of American progressivism, which can help to explain the persistence of the antiurban and agrarian myths within an urbanized culture; tradition guarantees the future in the *Promise of American Life.* Faith in the future was the most original product of the intellectual and religious revival of what Mumford has referred to as the Golden Day of American culture. Progressive ideology has a monument in the *Pequod*'s last desperate chase of the white whale, in that mythic narrative, constructed like a whaling manual, that contains its reason in itself.

Significantly, Lewis Mumford, one of the major modern interpreters of what I mean by the "progressive spirit" and one of its true inheritors, considers Herman Melville's work the highest expression of this tradition. As Mumford has written, Melville does not teach the avoidance of the white whale: "not tame and gentle bliss, but disaster, heroically encountered, is man's true happy ending." The tradition is epitomized in the battle with the whale; by accepting the irrationality and "futility" of the encounter, one discovers the road to progress:

There is no triumph so petty and evanescent as that involved in capturing the ordinary whale: the nineteenth century made this triumph the end and object of all endeavour. . . . By the same token, there is no struggle so permanent and so humanly satisfactory as Ahab's struggle with the white whale. In the defeat, in that succession of defeats, is the only pledge of man's ultimate victory, and the only final preventive of emptiness, boredom, and suicide.

Battles are lost, as Whitman cried, in the same spirit that they are won. Some day the physical powers of man may be commensurate with his utmost spirit, and he will meet Leviathan on even terms.[2]

Preparing themselves for the encounter with evil—crying with Whitman that every defeat is a promise of victory—the progressives and reformers, in the spirit of Melville, took to the sea where the new white whale, industrial-urban America, had appeared. The battle was undertaken in the conviction that the goal was not merely the patient plotting of the defeat of the "urban leviathan" (the "Dinosaur City," as Clarence S. Stein was to call it) but that, as the literary whaler had taught in "the best handbook of whaling," one could thus again find the "tragic epic of modern times" and also discover poetry.[3]

Ahistorically, then, even if nobly, a "new scale of values" was laid over the structural realities of society, in the dynamics of which it was preferable to concentrate on the endurance of perennial heroic images, rather than on the bitter and irreconcilable contradictions.

Urban Reform from the Golden Day to the City Beautiful

In the field of architecture and urban planning, progressive ideology produced its most outstanding results at the end of the nineteenth century and during the first two decades of our own. As early as the 1820s, concepts began to take shape that were eventually to form some of the basic components of modern urban planning, which emerged as part of the general renewal of American culture that drew its strength from the religious revival and was imbued with a solid civic conscience.

This process of cultural evolution came to maturity in the years of the Golden Day, in the works of the great transcendentalist masters and in the fervor of the Unitarian church. This tradition is of the utmost importance in defining the first attempts at urban reform. In the early nineteenth century a new sentiment toward nature and a new estimation of its values came into being—not only through the concepts of the transcendentalists. Thus the first experiments in planning should be viewed as part of an ideology aimed at reestablishing an organic relationship between the environment and the processes of urbanization, within the context of a romantic return to the genuine values of nature. Before the role of romantic naturalism in the first attempts at a new urban form is considered, a few of the peculiar characteristics of the culture of the Golden Day should be reviewed at least schematically.

Nature between Reason and Ethics

Vernon L. Parrington has written that the European individualism and liberalism of the second half of the eighteenth century was transplanted to New England in Henry David Thoreau.[4] Certainly, as Mumford's description of the search for the white whale suggests, individualism was a major component of progressive culture and its attitudes. More generally, however, the progressive intellectual tradition was a native product generated by the American Renaissance, the masterpieces of which were produced between 1850 and 1855; the five most important literary works of nineteenth-century America were written between

Ralph Waldo Emerson's *Representative Men* and Walt Whitman's *Leaves of Grass*. In his classic study of this period, F. O. Matthiessen has described a common denominator in the works of the masters of the 1850s: in different ways all expressed the need to unify culture and society, intellectual work and manual labor, culture and production.[5]

Matthiessen's study presents the typical romantic and utopian ideal of the era of the bourgeois division of labor and the rise of industry. It is not by chance that transcendentalism was a product of New England. With its free and independent forms of trade consolidated with an economy favored by its monopoly over transatlantic commerce, the New England community played an important role in the transformation of American capital. The Golden Day was contemporary with the primitive phase of industrialization, and rather than judging the industrial system, it expressed a moral rejection of the "horrors" of this stage of capitalist development.[6]

This attitude was typical of Emerson, among others. In his essay "Politics," this "Plotinus-Montaigne," as Matthiessen has defined Emerson, stated that "there is an instinctive sense, however obscure and yet inarticulate, that the whole constitution of property, on its present tenures, is injurious." Elsewhere, however, he wrote, "Property keeps the accounts of the world, and is always moral." These two apparently contradictory statements are typical of Emerson's thought, which never arrives at an internal criticism of the laws of the system but forcefully attacks their determinate historical forms. For him property was a moral given that became immoral to the extent that it did not serve the pursuit of natural ends. From this view arises his stand against the concentration of wealth and means of production, since such concentration robs the individual of his rights and the effect of his personal skills in order to subjugate him to a supraindividual system. The concentration of wealth and property is thus seen as negating the state of nature, rights, and ethical principles.

The "distorted" industrialism of the paleotechnic era was a continual threat to the "state of nature," since it disrupted the form of the original relationship between man and nature—work. In "Man the Reformer," Emerson wrote, "We must have a basis for our higher accomplishments, our delicate entertainments of poetry and philosophy in the work of our hands. We must have an antagonism in the tough world for all the variety of our spiritual faculties, or they will not be born. Manual labor is the study of the external world."[7] Freedom of production, manual labor, and crafts refined and elaborated by tradition were the alternatives to the anonymity of specialization and the mill. In an epoch in which beauty appeared to be banished from the environment and human life, its moral and material advantages could be recaptured only through the teachings of nature. In this sense, "the spirit of Concord" offered the first synthesis of the romantic love for craftsmanship professed by Ruskin and the physiocratic tradition of Jefferson.[8]

This concept of work also clarifies the meaning of the constant call to nature. Anonymous work does not lead to knowledge; the mill separates man from the countryside, preventing the individual from exercising his free will to learn the moral rules that only "an antagonism in the tough world" can teach. In 1843 Emerson noted in his journal, "The world has since the beginning an incurable trick of taking care of itself, or every hilltop in America would have counsel to offer. We sit and think how richly ornamented the wide champaign and yonder woodlands to the foot of those blue hills shall be, and meanwhile here are ready and willing thousands strong and teachable who have no land to till."[9] Thus nature is not only the source of spiritual joy and physical health; it also affords abundant practical instruction and holds the secrets of a just and rational order. These gifts cannot be possessed immediately, however; they must be won, as Whitman affirmed, with science and with love. Thus the philosophy of nature was transformed into a moral struggle and the ethic of work. The latter was the finest expression of transcendental individualism and was directly related to the romantic defense of the manual production of the craftsman; in subjective work, internalized as a mission of conscience, man becomes moral and can apply science to dominating nature by loving its secrets.

The theory of nature, conceived as the necessary premise to the fusion of ethical principles with reason, and individualism were ultimately expressed in what might be described as the active and moral participation in a project for the full achievement of democracy. "I shall use the words America and democracy as convertible terms," wrote Whitman.[10] The American Renaissance was not only a cultural refoundation. It was also something real. Thoreau searched for Homeric suggestions and Helenic beauty along the shores of the Hudson, and Whitman affirmed that America did not yet have a culture but that the essence of its culture existed in the interchangeability of the terms *America* and *democracy*. Whitman further maintained that the culture of the New World was born not from the end of the Middle Ages but, rather, from the continual encounter with nature and the search for an ethic, in other words, from a project for achieving democracy.

These assumptions clearly demonstrate that all the great critical and polemical themes of the Golden Day were "internal." The transcendentalists expressed their disapproval of the amorality of paleotechnic industrialism, the dissolution of religion, and political corruption in much the same way. In all these areas their criticism was directed to the forms of a system the structure of which remained hidden and unknown. Moreover, as a criticism of forms, the "philoso- phy of nature " went beyond the merely apparent forms of man's relationship with nature and gave rise to the continual construction of *values*. Principal among these was the ethic of work, the premise of the moral principle of individual responsibility that was considered the basis for the "equitable" redistribution of social tasks and the recovery of the moral relationships of society. This moral principle was translated into a project for overcoming the irrational "anarchy" of the producers and for organizing work organically and rationally. In the 1830s the great preacher Theodore Parker spoke in similar terms, advocating "planned industrial democracy."[11]

The culture of the Golden Day was a new culture. Thoreau looked to Homer and not to Rousseau or Defoe; conscious of creating a history, he wished to go back to the primary sources of myth, to the origins of history. Mumford has written, "The *new* America saw the possibility of a fresh integration in culture, which would carry into the modern age the spirit that had created the great cultural epochs of the past."[12] Transcendentalism was the original expression of the New World. Mumford is perfectly right in asserting that the American architectural tradition was first defined, during the Golden Day, on the printed page rather than in constructions of "sticks, stones and steel." Thus even the architectural tradition was created before the fact from a theoretical need for history rather than from a direct confrontation with possibilities and current needs; it arose from an ideological system of values rather than from the real relations of society and of production. Transcendentalism also gave rise to a particular attitude toward the city.

Whitman defined the city as the principal product of American democracy. The creation of an efficient, healthy, and democratic urban environment was the challenge the new culture made to America. Generalizing, Mumford has spoken of the transcendentalists' acceptance and comprehension of new triumphs of technology and the machine. His thesis is not shared by all critics, but an understanding of the real position of the culture of the Golden Day toward industrialism considerably clarifies the significance of both the "return to nature" and the whole question of the antiurban tradition in America. Much energy has been spent on this problem and many pages written, but no completely satisfactory explanation has thus far been offered. The unqualified identification of the origin of modern, post-Jeffersonian, antiurban ideology in transcendentalist thought bespeaks a superficial reading of the literature of the period. Furthermore, it leads to the assertion that this tradition was substantially indifferent to industrial development.

In *Walden*, Thoreau wrote, "Our inventions are wont to be petty toys, which distract our attention from serious things. They are but improved means to an unimproved end, an end which it was already but too easy to arrive at."[13] The problem cannot be solved by limiting its scope to the naturalistic component of transcendental thought and examining only this aspect. Rather, one must delve further and try to understand how transcendentalism implied a consistent consideration of the uses of technology and of the ethics of the ends pursued by the machine. To be considered first of all is the fact that the transcendentalist opposition to the city was an ideological project of the paleotechnic era, and as such it was directed against the degraded form of associative life produced in the city by the distortions and irrationalities of this primitive phase of industrialization. It did not automatically imply a criticism of the city as an institution but, rather, as an accumulation of contradictions, as an unrealized aspiration.

The true content of transcendentalist thought is a comprehensive, idealistic project for social reconciliation and it is in this sense that transcendentalism "believed" in the city. Transcendentalism indeed believed in the city not as a static institution but as a dynamic place, capable of being modified and restructured. Certainly its contradictions had to be studied and understood; more than an encounter with them, this comprehension required comparison—in other words, Thoreau's "need of history" and what Emerson saw as the teeachings of nature. The urban reformer, the "Man of the City," needed the same will to understand and the "man of the city," needed the same will to understand and dominate that animated the "man of the woods." From this point of view, transcendentalism expressed a new and different "civic con-science": nature teaches the great ideals of liberty, justice, and equity, but it is in the city that these cease to be mute values and become ethical principles and democracy.

The Utopian Communities

The religious revival of the nineteenth century not only inspired the writers and thinkers of the Golden Day but, more directly, gave rise to the establishment of a large number of utopian communities, particularly in the earlier part of the century. The history of the American utopias is an extraordinarily interesting subject that has unfortunately been given little attention in Europe. The era of utopian experiments in the United States extended roughly from 1632, when Roger Williams and Anne Hutchinson founded a colony in Rhode Island based on complete religious freedom, through 1932, when the Amana Society disbanded. Recent studies, however, have extended the history of such settle-ments to our own day. In the period discussed here, Christopher Tunnard and Henry Hope Reed have calculated more than a hundred such communities with the total number of about 100,000 inhabitants.[14] These few facts alone demonstrate the phenomenon's considerable scope and longevity, characteristics that in themselves indicate the differences in structure and influence between utopian communities in America and those in Europe.[15]

The utopian projects of nineteenth-century Europe have at times been considered, mechanistically, as the real beginnings of modern European urban planning. The socialist communities, in particular, have been seen as symbolizing an alternative to the city and to the system of development created by the industrial revolution. This interpretation, however, does not go beyond the rather obvious fact that the utopian projects broke away from Baroque and eighteenth-century canons of architecture and planning. Furthermore, it takes little account of the analysis of utopian thought made by scientific socialism and decisively made by Marx, who revealed the theoretical schemes of the socialist utopias for what they were. The criticism of ideology as a whole and, above all, the Marxian theory of value have demonstrated that utopia is ultimately not an alternative to the organization of the class struggle but a design for the orderly progress and possible planning and programming of productive forces.[16] From the historical point of view, as an urban project that placed the relations of industrial production at the center of its system, the European socialist utopia was neither an alternative to seventeenth- and eighteenth-century urban planning or a criticism of it but, quite simply, something else. Moreover, the utopian proposals were no more decisive or important in the creation of modern planning than the contemporary changes in the system of urban administration, the development of new categories of technician, the application of new construction techniques or systems of financing, or other factors, all of which took place outside the realm of utopia.

The clash between two epochs that, in general, gave rise to urban transformations in both Europe and America did not, however, in the specific case of utopian communities, provoke the same immediate clash of ideologies and urban formulas in the United States that it did in Europe. The reasons for this difference are complex, but a few are easily singled out. In the first place, the libertarian tradition, evolved in the New World by social groups who had suffered religious persecution in Europe, created conditions more favorable to utopian experiments. Second, the socialist-derived utopias, transplanted from Europe to the United States, revealed even more clearly their limitations and the abstractness of their conception than they had in Europe. In addition, the American utopia did not have to oppose a formal tradition as strong as that of the bourgeois European city; instead, it took its place within the native tradition, resuming and rationalizing the schemes of the earliest settlers' free communities.

The most significant and enduring utopian experiments in the United States were not those of the lay movements but, rather, those with a religious inspiration. The European socialist utopia, conceived as a protest against an urban situation established for centuries, had no tradition in the New World; when transported there, it proved to be static in face of the developmental dynamics of American capitalism. As Mumford has written, "When Stendhal wrote 'L'Amour' the American love of comfort had already become a by-word."[17] More generally it can be said that in America, "the land of utopia," the impact of the phenomenon on society was naturally different.

That America was the Promised Land was a concept that took firm hold in the eighteenth century. In his *Advice to the Privileged Orders,* published in 1792, Joel Barlow affirmed, "The word *people* in America has a different meaning from what it has in Europe. [In America] . . . it means the whole community, and comprehends every human creature; [in Europe] it means something else, more difficult to define." And the entry on New England in the 1797 edition of the *Encyclopaedia Britannica* reads: "It may in truth be said, that in no part of the world are there people happier . . . or more independent than the farmers in New England."[18] The real heirs of this tradition in the United States were not the lay utopias of European origin but the communities founded by religious sects. In fact, among America lay utopias, the disastrous conclusion of the experiments of the Icarians and Owenites indicates clearly that the relative success of the Fourierist movement was an exception.

The North American Phalanx founded in 1893 in Monmouth County, New Jersey, actually lasted for about ten years. Its economic success encouraged the formation of other Fourierist communities, such as the Wisconsin Phalanx. It was principally in terms of propaganda and cultural agitation, however, that Fourierism proved the most vital of the lay movements of European derivation. This success was due mainly to Albert Brisbane and Horace Greeley, who made such publications as the *New York Tribune* available to Fourierist propaganda. The influence of the movement was indeed considerable, as demonstrated by the fact that in 1844 Brook Farm, the community that numbered Emerson and Thoreau among its members, took the name Brook Farm Phalanx.[19]

Even the successes of Fourierism were insignificant in comparison to the results obtained by the religious sects. Apart from the Mormons, who remain an exception, the most significant experiments were those of the Shakers, the Rappites, the Separatists of Zoar, the Perfectionists of Oneida, and the Eban-Ezers of Amana. The common ownership of property and wealth in most of these communities naturally led to an extreme development of the principles of mutual assistance and democracy and the sense of community, influencing even the urban layout of the settlements, which centered on the communal buildings and social services. The rationalization of services and workshops, the introduction of labor-saving processes, administrative efficiency, and an assiduous concern for the education of the young and the spiritual equilibrium of the members of the community were typical of many of these utopias.

Mystical and often religious fanaticism pervaded every aspect of communal life, which in certain cases was purposely kept separate from the rest of the world. Some communities were transformed into a kind of capitalist enterprise and instituted a system of trade with the external economy; its laws, however, in no way contaminated those of the utopian society. Religion was often used repressively, and the Bible was a guide not only for spiritual life but also for social behavior. At the same time, religious aims were ultimately identified with the attainment of prosperity for the community, which led to a forceful affirmation of the ethic of work, not only as a duty imposed by the principle of mutual assistance but also as a means of self-fulfillment and liberation from passions. The sexual repression of the Shakers, which derived from mysticism and, in their case, from a belief in the bisexuality of Christ, let them to a rigid discipline in work, the only activity really possible other than religious practice. For this reason the Shakers nourished the conviction that matrimony and property were signs of an inferior civilization, and prohibited tobacco, games, and books in the community.

Quite beyond its reaffirmation of the work ethic, the religious structure of the mystic utopia contained an embryonic general design for universal reconciliation. This indeed was the aim of John A. Etzler, whom Arthur E. Morgan has identified as the first American utopian. In 1833 Etzler published *The Paradise within Reach of All Men, without Labor, by Powers of Nature and Machinery,* which describes a future society in which the forces of nature, appropriately utilized, would replace human labor. In his mystical vision Etzler—whom Thoreau read—foresaw a society where perfect harmony would exist between man's spiritual ends and a benevolent nature disposed to alleviate his every burden. Etzler's was a society solidly bound to the right of land ownership and regulated by the development of industry; it was thus a society in which all contention between the urban and the rural fell away.[20]

A theory such as Etzler's, antedating by almost twenty years the works of the Golden Day, demonstrates the fact that the relationship between the religious utopia and transcendentalism was not limited to their common affirmation of the work ethic. The concept of nature as a source of fundamentally progressive teachings, which was not extraneous to the mysticism of the religious utopias, was already present in Etzler's work. A precursor of Edward Bellamy, Etzler was already fully aware that in a free and happy society the human settlements had to be conceived as parts of a single program of natural social equilibrium.

Looking even briefly at the maps of some of these utopian communities, one cannot help noting certain peculiarities that demonstrate how much their social and religious theories influenced the urban form of their settlements. Even from the formal point of view, the utopian experiments represented a factor of continuity in the American tradition of urban reform. Among the American utopias the most striking urban model was produced by the Mormons. In Joseph Smith's 1833 plan for the City of Zion, the lots formed by the grid were disposed around an axial system centered on a common area of greenery. In the various cities constructed by the Mormons along their road to the West, green spaces were organized around the communal buildings and precise norms regulated the architectural standards and limited the extraurban development of the community. The regularity of the grid plan, hinged on the green spaces, symbolized both the Mormons' belief in the coming of the reign of Christ on Earth and the postulate according to which the city could not expand beyond a certain optimal size. This dimensional control was central to the regulations governing the principal architectural and planning aspects of the Mormon towns.

In Salt Lake City, founded in July 1847, geographic conditions did not permit the use of the classic Mormon scheme of four urban squares. Nevertheless, the principles of Mormon planning were adopted there with an even greater degree of refinement as the guiding elements of the urban design.[21] The planners of Mormon towns employed these means in a particularly coherent and organic manner, according to a practice that can be traced back to William Penn and that has still other sources outside the utopian tradition. Yet similar principles, even if adopted with less refinement, appear in other utopian settlements. In the diagram of the village of Amana, a rotary organization around the church rationally integrates services, residences, and places of work. The 1805 plan of George Rapp's Harmony has a rigid axial structure with a hierarchical distribution of buildings; at New Harmony and Economy, green spaces and parks provide the central organizing element of the urban structure.

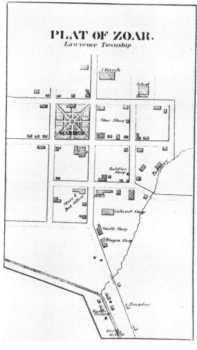

Map of 1876 for the Harmony Society's community of Economy, Pennsylvania.

Map of 1875 for the Separatists' community of Zoar, Ohio.

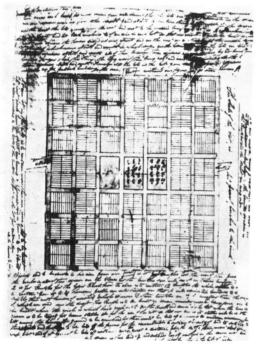

Plan by Joseph Smith, founder of the Mormon sect, for the City of Zion, 1833.

The Mormon town of Salt Lake City, Utah, in a scheme of 1870.

An instructive example of utopian town planning is the design for the Separatist community of Zoar, Ohio. Within the traditional grid plan, the outstanding element is the park, slightly off center, as are the principal buildings. In this two-and-a-half-acre park a red fir surrounded by twelve other trees symbolizes salvation and the apostles.[22] Parks, trees, and nature here become the emblems and physical elements of a just and harmonious urban life. As symbols of faith, the gifts of nature take the place of constructed monuments. It almost seems that nature itself is about to become the architect of the town. Actually, however, nature was used here in a concrete way, both as a moral tonic and as an instrument of urban planning. The utopian community thus came close to achieving the dominion over nature projected by the culture of the Golden Day. The question now to be answered is how nature penetrated urban-industrial America.

The First Experiments: Rural Cemeteries

In the United States the utopian communities did not have so marked an influence on urban planning as the socialist utopias had in Europe. As already indicated, in America even the utopias were essentially part of the planning tradition; thus the urban innovations they introduced were not nearly so radical as those that directly reflected certain important aspects of transcendentalist thought and civic commitment and certain attitudes prompted by the religious revival, particularly among the Unitarians. These were by far the more significant innovations, even if derived formally from European models.

The first examples of landscaping in America, the Nichols Garden in Salem, the estates of the large plantation owners, the work of Thomas Jefferson, and that of André Parmentier on the banks of the Hudson, were all related—logically, since they expressed a culture that wished to be erudite—to certain European examples, particularly English landscape gardening. American culture was intuitively attracted to English romanticism; in fact, the work of Humphrey Repton and J. C. Loudon inspired the initial attempts at landscaping in America, and this relationship with England would be a constant factor in the development of American urban planning. It is interesting to recall that one of the principal figures of American planning of the Progressive Era, John Nolen, edited the Boston edition of Repton's *Art of Landscape Gardening*, issued in 1907.

The American tradition of landscape architecture began in the eighteenth century, and Guston Hall and Mount Vernon may be considered the first examples of a line of development in which Jefferson's work was an important episode. At Monticello utilitarian considerations still dominated the organization of nature surrounding the villa. In the design of the campus of the University of Virginia, however, the natural surroundings were considered an integral part of the architectural organization of space. There Jefferson probably created the beginnings of a language specific to landscape architecture. Similar experiments were carried out at several estates near Boston and on the shores of the Hudson.[23] These early efforts, which would have a worthy following, bore fruit in the 1820s. On the model of the society founded in London in 1804, a number of horticultural societies were established in the United States. One of the most important was the Massachusetts Horticultural Society, founded in Boston in 1829. Indeed Boston became the main center of development in this first phase of landscape architecture.[24]

Cemeteries were among the objects of concern of these associations, which were opposed to the traditional graveyards around the city churches. The interest aroused in this problem had its first important result in Massachusetts in the 1820s, where the horticultural society promoted the creation of a rural cemetery, the Mount Auburn Cemetery in Cambridge. The social and cultural motivations behind the creation of this new type of cemetery are indicative of the way in which landscaping contained some of the important premises of urban planning. Significantly the Mount Auburn project was directly inspired by the Harvard botanist Jacob Bigelow, who was also a physician and an adherent of the theory—typical of the philanthropic epoch—of the influence of environment on health. The spirit animating this concern about cemeteries was actually a manifestation of the civic participation evoked by the contemporary religious revival. The cemetery became a special place in the city. The Egyptian entranceway to Mount Auburn Cemetery emblematically established the separation of a "place of quality" from the rest of surrounding nature and the city. No longer casually present within the city as a *memento mori* but, rather, dispersed within "constructed" nature among classical allusions, the testimonies of death were exorcised. Nature seems to prevail over death in these cemeteries designed and planned as a public service. In their visits to the Cambridge cemetery, members of the public were aided by a printed guide; the same was true of the other rural cemeteries created in the years that followed.

There was, however, nothing naive about this mediated return to nature. It was founded on cultural and religious motivations that brought up to date the peculiarly American myth that Scully has characterized as a "tendency to equate physical dispersion with political freedom."[25] Mount Auburn met with great success and served as a model for similar projects elsewhere. By the 1850s, ten such cemeteries had been built. The map of Mount Auburn or, even better, the view of Greenwood Cemetery in Brooklyn shows clearly how completely the religious intentions animating these projects agreed with their social ends. It is in this sense that one can speak of a new-born language of urban planning in the process of defining its ends and means.

In the cemetery the visitor passed through what was essentially a park and, by "entering" nature, could meet symbols of death that had been freed of any concrete expression of anguish. The mystical intent was expressed in terms of Emerson's richness of the gift of life rather than in somber suggestions of its end; even the images of death, solemnly commemorative and erudite in style, became elements of the "naturalistic decor." The rural cemeteries called forth hope in the present rather than reflections on the imminence of the future. This spirit is

Plan of 1901 for Mount Auburn Cemetery, Cambridge, Massachusetts.

Gate Lodge, Llewellyn Park, West Orange, New Jersey, designed by Alexander Jackson Davis.

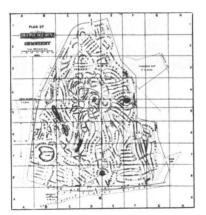

Panoramic view of Greenwood Cemetery, Brooklyn, New York, in 1852.

Plan of 1859 for the northwestern part of Llewellyn Park, West Orange, New Jersey.

clearly expressed in the reverent respect of the layout and the structures for
geographic conditions and the forms of the natural environment. Compared with
the appearance of the industrial cities that were rising at the time, Greenwood
was a romantic dream. The irregularity and subtly designed sinuousness of the
roads and paths, which adapted their courses to the water basins and wooded
areas, were strikingly different from the rigidity of the grid structure of the
cities; one senses in these new forms an intellectual rejection of the reigning
urban dreariness and an assertion of the ethical position inspired by the
Unitarian revival. For Theodore Parker, "industrial democracy"—a recurrent
term in his writings—implied a polemical criticism not so much of the city of
commerce and industry as of a typical product of its society: the predatory elite,
ignorant of tradition and devoid of religious spirit. It was in this social class that
"industrial democracy" encountered its principal obstacle. Democracy as the
realization of a divine order among men had to be based on just institutions, an
equitable distribution of wealth, an upright religious faith, and an appreciation
of the teachings of nature.[26]

The respectful use of nature that guided the design of the rural cemeteries was
actually the first affirmation of an alternative to the shabbiness of life, the
indiscriminate plundering of resources, and the indifference to beauty of the
paleotechnic civilization. Ideologically, the cemeteries expressed hope for a
world that succeeds in annulling the sense of death through the establishment of
a divine justice. At the same time they offered the first example of a type of
urban project that promised to resolve the "distorted and amoral nature" of the
city in terms of a system that was rational, efficient, and beautiful.

The tradition that was evolving in these first experiments was to have great
importance for the future development of American planning. As John W. Reps
has written, "While romantic planning was accepted for cemetery design with
astonishing rapidity, the use of the same landscape principles for suburban
residential districts lagged some twenty-five years behind. These concepts of
large scale planning were to be used next in a different aspect of the urban
scene."[27] Mount Auburn, John Notman's Laurel Hill Cemetery in Philadelphia,
and Greenwood are only the most significant examples of the affirmation of the
discipline of landscape architecture. In American landscape architecture the
formal teachings of romanticism were integrated with the search for values
typical of Parker's sermons, on the basis of which the deranged society of steam
and steel could be regenerated. These were the values of the American
democratic tradition, but it is symptomatic of the new motivations of the period
that from the moment they formed the basis of an urban project they were not
identified with the classicism but interpreted according to a new formal
expression. In the middle years of the nineteenth century Alexander Jackson
Davis became one of the most sought-after and influential architects in America.
Davis's adoption of the Gothic style at the height of the Greek revival testifies to
the growing influence of romanticism and the need for a formal expression

appropriate to religious sentiment. Writing in the *North American Review* in 1836, Henry Cleveland maintained that the Gothic was the major expression of the Christian faith.

As opposed to the static quality of all styles based on the classical canons, the Gothic satisfied the desire for compositional liberty as well as the need for expressive coherence. The historical significance of this fact in American architecture has been aptly defined by Wayne Andrews:

> Rebelling against the symmetrical façades of the great architects of France and Italy, and against the colonial perpetuation of the ideal, [the romantics] were naturally drawn to the asymmetrical opportunities of the Gothic revival. And even if they—at first—failed to sense that the Gothic tradition was based on the structural integrity which the Renaissance had sacrificed in the quest for perfection of proportions.... they at least reminded America of the Gothic past and so were the godfathers of the organic architecture of the twentieth century which springs from Gothic sources.[28]

The America of Washington and Jefferson had found in neoclassical forms the means of expressing its achievement of republican independence. The architecture of Jefferson, Bulfinch's Boston, the work of Latrobe, and, finally, L'Enfant's plan for Washington were the monuments of a nation affirming its right to existence. The American republic did not wish to be inferior to Europe and produced its own monuments, utilizing the classical language in schematic fashion. Nothing demonstrates better than the plan for Washington, the work of Latrobe, or, indeed, the architecture of the new republic in general the exactness of Marx's old analysis of the phenomenon: "Unheroic as bourgeois society is, it nevertheless took heroism, sacrifice, terror, civil war, and battles of peoples to bring it into being. And in the classically austere traditions of the Roman Republic its gladiators found the ideals and the art forms, the self-deceptions that they needed in order to conceal from themselves the bourgeois limitations of the content of their struggles and to keep their enthusiasm on the high plane of the great historical tragedy."[29]

European visitors' ironical reactions to the sight of Washington in Jefferson's time was no more than historical blindness toward a country beginning to consume with extraordinary rapidity cultural models that came largely from Europe. Neoclassical America was the agrarian and preindustrial America of the great myths of the nation's infancy; the classical schemes and the Greek revival were the products of an age seeking dignity and tradition. This, however, was an age that quickly ran its course. In 1820, shortly before his death, Benjamin Henry Latrobe wrote in his journal, "Our religion requires a church wholly different from the temples, our courts of justice buildings of entirely different principles from their basilicas; and our amusements could not possibly be performed in their theaters and amphitheaters."[30] With such thoughts the first phase of American architecture and planning came to an end.

The classical schemes hindered the creation of an original language. This deterrent was to be eliminated with the Neogothic style and romantic planning, both of which express values more religious than civic and thus closer to the native tradition. Significantly the English translation of Georg Moller's work on the origin and development of Gothic architecture, a book that was important for Emerson as well as for Greenough, was published in 1824.[31] And it is sufficient to study the work of Alexander Jackson Davis, the principal interpreter of this phase of stylistic transition, to understand the importance of the Gothic experience.

In this sense, Davis's work for Llewellyn Park in West Orange, New Jersey, is exemplary.[32] Llewellyn Haskell, a businessman who belonged to the Perfectionist sect, chose Davis and Eugene A. Baumann as the architects of what Tunnard has defined as "the first romantic suburban community." Even if this was actually a project for a residential settlement, in its general conception Llewellyn Park is related to the style of the rural cemeteries. The eclecticism of its architecture, as well as the romantic layout of its roadways and the attempts made by its designers to adapt their plan to the forms of the natural environment were expressions of the growing taste for the picturesque. This same tendency is apparent in the Gate Lodge of Llewellyn Park, where the eclectic and romantic forms of the structure blend with the natural elements. The effort to adapt to the environment created a picturesque effect of considerable suggestive tension, which explicitly indicates a cultural attitude unknown to the stylistic revivalism of the eighteenth century and which, instead of ignoring the native tradition, drew fertile inspiration from it. In this way the Gothic revival was to architectural forms what romantic landscaping was to urban forms; the fusion of the two gave rise to picturesque planning.

Parks and Beautiful Cities

The examples of landscape architecture just discussed, the work of Parmentier and Joseph Jacques Ramée, the villas, and the rural cemeteries were only the beginning of a picturesque language that was to find an outstanding interpreter in Andrew Jackson Downing. Downing was intimately involved in the work of the horticultural societies. In 1846 he became editor of the journal the *Horticulturalist*, and editions of his *Fruits and Fruit Trees of America*, first published in 1845, eventually reached the notable number of fourteen. Downing's first book, published in 1841 and entitled *A Treatise on the Theory and Practice of Landscape Gardening Adapted to North America*, combined romanticism with the scientific attitude of the horticulturalist and was one of the most significant texts in the history of American landscaping.

From a study of Downing's writing, it is clear that he tried to define an organic aesthetic of architecture and picturesque landscaping. He followed Henry Cleveland in recognizing the Gothic as the true and perfect expression of Christian Brotherhood in architecture, and many of his works can be considered expressions of the Gothic revival. Nevertheless, he explicitly opposed the indiscriminate use of a single style. To the extent that he rejected simple repetition of a model and sought instead to understand its content and aesthetic laws, Downing made a substantial contribution to the creation of an eclectic language, based on principles such as promotion, symmetry, variety, and harmony, which formed the grammatical structure of a picturesque aesthetic.[33] Moreover, Downing's concept of beauty contained protofunctional ideas—for example, his disapproval of any imitative artifice in the treatment of the architectonic material and the functions it interprets. Architecture must not hide the reality of the constructive material and, at the same time, must assertively adapt to its environment, two convictions stemming from a single theoretical and formal propensity. Downing's interest in the problem of adaptation to the environment, while expressing an aesthetic tendency, originated in the study of nature, "with science and with love," and in his concurrence with transcendentalist and Unitarian thought.[34] Environmental adaptation was certainly an important concept in the architecture of small buildings, but it became absolutely decisive for landscape architecture. In this sense it is significant that Downing explicitly recognized the importance of the rural cemeteries. In an essay written in 1849, he affirmed that they were both a demonstration of the mature taste of the American people and a palliative for the lack of green spaces and parks in the city.[35]

In 1850 Downing made a trip to Europe and returned to the United States accompanied by Calvert Vaux. In the following year he submitted a design for the Washington Mall, commissioned by President Millard Fillmore. Downing's project for Washington was a typical example of picturesque landscaping, enriched by some eclectic elements. The road system within the park, although it reached gently down to the banks of the Potomac, was purposely separated from the surrounding system of streets by a continuous curtain of greenery around the four principal selections of the area, as if the park were intended as an enclosed entity, an alternative to the city. To emphasize merely the elegance of Downing's proposal is not enough. In Albert Fein's words, his design for the Mall "was indicative of the improvement that had taken place in national opinion regarding large-scale urban planning. Downing had become—in an incredibly short period of time—the nation's most influential figure in translating a natural image of religious and social significance into landscape theory and practice."[36] As already noted, Downing's work was an attempt to define the aesthetic canons of the picturesque, but it did not yet fully express an organic theory of the use of landscape as an instrument of urban planning. In indicating the importance of the rural virtues for the process of urban growth, Downing essentially interpreted what Leo Marx has termed America's regret at the loss of the "naive and anarchic primitivism" that drew its arguments in favor of parks from literary sources.[37]

The Park movement first became effective in the 1840s. Between 1843 and 1845 Robert F. Gourlay prepared plans for projects in Boston and New York. In 1844 Downing's friend William Cullen Bryant began a campaign for urban parks in the *New York Evening Post*, which was echoed in Downing's own journal, the *Horticulturalist*. The concept of the public park had come into being with the reformism of the 1830s and 1840s and, as Mumford has written, took a firm hold through the study of European works, a knowledge of which was widely diffused through Bryant's assiduous efforts. London and England became the examples to imitate; the London parks and Paxton's projects were the symbol of utilitarian planning.[38] "Land of our poets! Home of our Fathers! Dear old mother England!" exclaimed Frederick Law Olmsted in *Walks and Talks of an American Farmer in England*. His trip to England in 1850 was of great importance for Olmsted's development. In 1848 he had begun to manage a model farm on Staten Island and, like Downing, was initially prompted to visit England for reasons related to his agricultural activity. During these years, Olmsted was also in contact with intellectual groups in New York. The success of the two editions of his *Walks and Talks* led Henry Raymond, in 1852, to commission Olmsted to prepare a series of articles on the conditions of life in the South for the *New York Times*. Olmsted's writings on the South combine a severe criticism of slavery with a lucid perception of the inevitable consequences of the socioeconomic dualism and sectionalism of the United States. This recognition gave rise to an important declaration on planning, which he saw as a means destined to resolve the striking social contradictions of the degraded environment of the slave-holding South. In 1855, Olmsted joined the avant-garde *Putnam's Monthly Magazine*, as financial supporter and editor. During the Civil War, he was secretary of the United States Sanitary Commission.[39]

From this brief and partial account of his interests and activities, one can sense the complex motivations behind Olmsted's work. His ties with the utopian tradition, particularly Fourierism, his relationship with such exponents of the Unitarian faith as Henry Whitney Bellows, and, finally, his decided stand against slavery make Olmsted a typical figure of American progressivism. In his intellectual development and his convictions are brought together many of the formative elements of the planning tradition. In the early 1850s men like Greeley, Bryant, and Bellows, all in some way connected with Olmsted, succeeded in transforming the utopian and literary debate on the creation of parks into a political issue. In this work they were aided by the publicity given to the first medical investigations—especially those carried out in England—of the effects of urban congestion on public health.

In 1851 the long-debated park issue produced its first important result. On July 11, the municipality of New York passed the first Park Act, which authorized the acquisition of Jane's Wood between Third Avenue and the East River from 64th Street to 51st. In the pages of the *Horticulturalist*, Downing severely criticized the choice of the site, the inadequacy of which was implicitly recognized by the approval of the Amended Park Act of July 21, 1853. The new law authorized the acquisition of the area between Fifth and Eighth avenues from 59th to 106th Street; in 1859 it was extended to 110th Street. In 1853 the first commission for the construction of Central Park was created; it was followed in 1857 by the Board of Commissioners, of which Egbert Viele was chief engineer and Olmsted superintendent. In the same year a competition was opened for the design of the park, in which thirty-five designers participated. In 1858 Olmsted and Vaux's "Greensward" project won first prize, and Olmsted was appointed chief architect. In the course of the work on Central Park, the story of which is too long to be recounted here, Olmsted and Vaux frequently clashed with city administrators and Tweed politics and more than once resigned from their posts.[40]

Despite the innumerable difficulties faced by the architects and the changes made in their plan, the Central Park project and the whole story of its realization were of paramount importance in the history of American planning. After the 1850s, in fact, city parks became a major issue in the controversy over public spending in the creation of social services. The construction of Central Park also stimulated new forms of administrative organization and different relationships between politicians and architects; thus it became, in progressive circles, a constant point of reference in the controversy over ways of operating on the urban structure. Moreover, Olmsted's project marked the attainment of a new qualitative level in the very function of planning, in its philosophy and its technique. As Mumford has written, "Olmsted had done something more than design a park, battle with politicians—he resigned at least five times—, struggle with insolent and rascally city appointees and protect his fantasies against vandals: he had introduced an idea—the idea of using landscape creatively. By making nature urbane he naturalized the city."[41]

Olmsted and Vaux's written description of their "Greensward" plan sheds still further light on the significance of Central Park. In their report the architects emphasize the attention they gave to European works, referring explicitly to Regent's Park and the gardens of the Tuileries. The European examples, particularly the boulevard structure, are criticized and rejected as models, however, because they allow the unity of design and intention to be disrupted by functional exigencies. It is in terms of such considerations that Olmstead and Vaux demonstrated the originality of their proposals, above all in regard to the layout of roads; the system of roads passing through the park and the functional demands of the city do not disturb the compositional unity of the park or the hierarchical order of its internal road network. The separation of road systems, the noninterference of different types of traffic, and the picturesque treatment of roads and pedestrian paths were new solutions that would strongly influence the planning tradition. The principle of separating road systems, in particular, was to be taken up by progressive planning; Central Park has, in fact, been indicated as the model adopted by Henry Wright and Clarence S. Stein for the plan of Radburn.[42]

The purely formal aspects of the design of Central Park were on the whole related to the English picturesque and the canons of Downing, and it was principally its functional aspects—the road systems—and the relationship instituted between park and city that made the project a milestone in American

Plan by Andrew Jackson Downing for the
Mall, Washington, D.C., 1851.

Central Park, designed by Frederick Law
Olmsted and Calvert Vaux, in a map of
about 1870.

An aerial view showing Central Park inserted
in the grid plan of Manhattan.

planning. Central Park reversed the tendency of the rural cemeteries, which were programmatically situated outside the city—arcadian utopias providing a contrast to the materialism and disorder of urban civilization. In this way Olmsted went beyond Downing, who had sought to resolve the evils of the city by introducing into it not only rural values but also rural methods.

Olmsted and Vaux's description of the plan reveals their constant concern for the relationship between park and city, expressed not only in the road layout but also in their attempts to find instances and formulas of mediation between the area of the park and the surrounding city. Notable in this regard is the care with which the entrances to the park are identified as joining elements, as well as the treatment of the external perimeter of the park as a screen through which calculated openings make it possible to view nature within; the passerby senses its aura while remaining immersed in the urban atmosphere. Similar picturesque solutions characterize the composition of elements that provide a gradual passage from urban life to designed nature.[43]

Olmsted was thoroughly convinced of the inevitability and progressive value of urban development. Referring specifically to Central Park in one of the two remaining fragments of his autobiography, he wrote, "Our country has entered upon a stage of progress in which its welfare is to depend on the convenience, safety, order and economy of life in its great cities. It cannot prosper independently of them; cannot gain in virtue, wisdom, comfort, except as they also advance."[44] An integral part of this conviction was the recovery of nature. In the reconstruction of a degraded environment, nature was not only the means to a greater efficiency and better hygienic conditions—and, as such, synonymous with a more mature civic and social conscience; it was also the fundamental means of recreating a comprehensive unity. The park filled a serious void in the moral pursuit of American democracy by contributing to the construction of an environment that was natural and organic. As Albert Fein has observed, the park took the place of the religious building that had symbolized the community spirit in the early settlements; organized around green spaces, the lay symbols of bygone community, the city recovered its lost coherence. For Olmsted, however, the park was also synonymous with social justice and participation in the democratic process; in the park, nature was accessible to all, and the lower classes were no longer segregated within the city. Thus parks were a means of social leveling and of educating the populus in their collective responsibility for well-being. Finally, the creation of parks was a first step in a more comprehensive program of physical and social planning; Olmsted considered the park not only a demonstration of the moral health of the people but also an instrument in the fight for the banishment of congestion and the redistribution of wealth.[45]

If Central Park was a symbolic episode in the development of landscape architecture and in the assertion of certain principles basic to the progressive spirit, Olmsted's subsequent work demonstrates how a series of other concepts were first concretely defined within the work of the Park movement. After the

Civil War, Olmsted resumed his collaboration with Vaux. In 1865 he prepared a
report on the project for Brooklyn Park at Prospect Hill. Unlike the proposal
made by Egbert Viele four years earlier, Olmsted's tended to turn the park
project into a comprehensive planning operation. Olmsted and Vaux's proposal
seems, in fact, to treat the internal layout of the park as a secondary
consideration. In difference to their plan for Central Park, in the Brooklyn
project attention was directed entirely to the relationship between park and
urban structure. In the earlier work, the road system had remained essentially
"internal," clearly indicated but subject to the dictates of the park itself; in
Brooklyn the park expands into the city by means of a system of roads that
become quite directly the determining factor of urban development. The *Report
of the Brooklyn Park Commission from January 1874 to December 31, 1879,*
published in 1880, proposed a reorganization of the road structure through the
creation of a system of parkways. These parkways served not only as the basis
for restructuring the traffic system but also as the axes of future urban
development. The architects' solutions for the park were so intrinsically related
to this comprehensive urban program that, in their view, the development of the
park could be financed from the increase in real-estate values that would result
in residential areas bordering the parkways. Describing the Prospect Hill project
in one of his writings, Olmsted clearly revealed his convictions. The park was a
symbol of a new community life, and he spoke of it in Emersonian terms as a
place of joy where one might cultivate all the spiritual activities the city made
impossible: "I have never seen such joyous collections of people." At the same
time, however, the park was an urban planning project justified on the basis of
purely functional and economic considerations. Moreover, this aspect of the
park was not separate from the first but thoroughly integrated with it; indeed, it
stemmed directly from ethical and ideological considerations of its social
function.[46]

The park was no longer an "addition," no longer an exceptional undertaking
in the city. As the typical expression of American democracy, it was the
fundamental structure of the urban environment. From this basic concept,
Olmsted also drew the originality of his work in the suburban community.
Urban civilization leads to a separation of work and residence, to congestion, to
the division between city and country. In Olmsted's view, all these problems
could be resolved through the efficient planning of urban services, an adequate
use of technology, and the creation of suburban neighborhoods, not cut off
from the city and provided with all the necessary services.[47]

Similar principles were applied in the Chicago suburb of Riverside, designed by
Olmsted and Vaux in 1868-69 for the Riverside Improvement Company. As
Reps has justly observed, certain passages of the *Preliminary Report*, submitted
by the designers to their sponsors in 1868, sound like a manifesto of the
romantic planner, the kernel of which is the conviction that the development of
suburban settlements was by now a permanent part of metropolitan life: "It

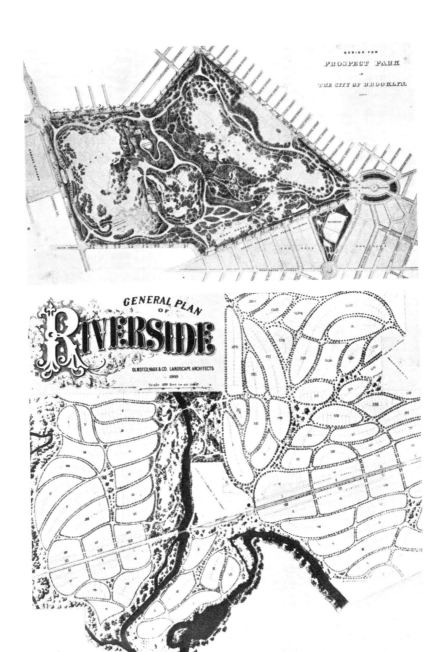

Plan by Frederick Law Olmsted and Calvert Vaux for Prospect Park, Brooklyn, New York, 1870.

Plan by Frederick Law Olmsted and Calvert Vaux for the suburb of Riverside, near Chicago, 1869.

would appear then that the demands of suburban life, with reference to civilized refinement, are not to be a retrogression from, but an advance upon, those which are characteristic of town life, and that no great town can long exist without great suburbs."[48] Olmsted did not use landscaping to create something separate and distinct from the city; instead landscape architecture was transformed in his hands into a precise instrument of urban planning. The parks were the tools of a philosophy that aimed at reforming conditions of life through a highly developed design technique; the city in its totality had now become the scale of urban planning operations. Llewellyn Park had been the prototype of the romantic suburb, a utopian settlement isolated from the city and the fruit, at least in part, of the religious convictions of its founder. Riverside was the product of what had become a widespread movement, with its origin in Olmsted's conception of the suburban neighborhood not as an urban utopia but as a natural and necessary outgrowth of the metropolitan reality.

The observations on Olmsted's work and its significance made so far are clarified still further by his work in Boston, the city perhaps most responsive to the new theories on urban parks. In 1872 Robert Morris Copeland published *The Most Beautiful City in America. Essay and Plan for the Improvement of the City of Boston,* in which he analyzed the conditions of the city and proposed the creation of an integrated system of parks that would be adapted to the favorable geological conditions of the area and make rational use of its water resources. In 1874 the Boston City Council reported favorably on the construction of a park complex, and in 1875 the Park Commission Act was passed. The same year, Olmsted, active in Boston since 1867, when he had been summoned there by Charles Eliot Norton, became consultant to the Park Commission. The commission's plan for the city parks was based on six principal projects, coordinated in the east-west direction by a system of parkways. In 1877, once the necessary property had been acquired, a competition was announced for the plan of the first project, that of the Back Bay area. The inadequacy of the designs presented, which took no account of the particular geological features and water resources of the area, led the Park Commission to entrust a revision of the plan to Olmsted; his project was accepted in 1879.

The Back Bay Fens improvement project was not merely part of an integrated park system. As Olmsted himself affirmed in 1881, the term *park* was not sufficient as a description of this project: "The continued application of the term *park* to an undertaking of the character thus indicated tends to perpetuate an unfortunate delusion, and to invite unjust expectations and criticisms."[49] Before all else, Back Bay Fens was a nodal point determining the organization of the surrounding urban structure; the park area did not represent a break in the urban network but, rather, served to integrate it, tending to expand toward Commonwealth Avenue and Beacon Street up to the Charles River embankment. That Olmsted was concerned less with the internal design of the individual parks than with their continuity is expressed in his definition of this integrated system extending from the Boston Common to Franklin Park as "the Parkway."

Olmsted's work in Boston demonstrates the enormous progress made since the 1820s, when the urban problem was first raised by the horticulturalists. The Boston park system was the first expression of the need to formulate a comprehensive urban plan on the basis of new principles; as such, it was the product of a society that had passed the stage of merely announcing needs and decrying insufficiencies and was taking upon itself the task of devising realistic solutions to the problem of restructuring the city. The Boston project also contained the first indication of a new scale for urban planning; in its tendency to exert comprehensive control over urban development, it tacitly involved the relationship between the city and its surrounding territory, between the city and the region. As early as 1872, Copeland had realized the need for this kind of scope in planning projects. Defending the foresightedness and realism of his own proposals for Boston, which involved the whole metropolitan area, he wrote, "The sole difference, or hindrance to such planning, is that we have not been accustomed to plan in this way. We have supposed that, for some unnamed reason, planning for a city's growth and progress could only be done as it grows; that no one can foresee sufficiently the future requirements of business to wisely provide for them. This is a fallacious belief."[50]

In 1892 the Boston Metropolitan Park Commission controlled roughly 27 miles of parkways, 30 miles of river embankments, and 10,000 acres of park. The secretary of the commission was Sylvester Baxter, one of the leading members of the Nationalist Club of Boston and closely connected with Olmsted and Bellamy. In the 1880s Boston had become a dynamic center of progressivism from which its ideas radiated. Bellamy's utopia achieved enormous success; by 1890 many thousands of copies of *Looking Backward* had been sold, and sales continued at an impressive rate. From Boston the Nationalist movement spread along the East Coast; its official journal, the *Nationalist*, was founded by the First National Club of Boston in 1889. A factor that favored the progressive movement in general was the city's highly evolved religious organization, which was particularly concerned with civic problems. Boston was thus a sort of laboratory where the many and diverse components of the progressive impulse were brought together and where they acquired considerable influence on public opinion and the municipal government and promoted administrative reforms. Boston, indeed, seemed to have inherited the original American tradition.

Baxter was the principal promoter of an active accord among Bellamy's utopia, Olmsted's work, and the political aims of the Nationalist clubs. In the words of Fein:

While the utopian message of the late 1880s was identical to that of the 1850s, the governmental structure and physical form of the city to be were not. The romantic decentralized idealism of the 1850s had been transformed into a highly structured, centralized form reflected in monumental buildings contained within a regular pattern of public squares and uniform blocks. Bellamy's principal argument was that the organization of industry, which had revolutionized American life, would become the basis for restructuring the American city. Most appealing to Olmsted and others was the hope it offered of freeing the professional planner and designer from political interference, as, indeed, industry and business had been freed during the second half of the nineteenth century. A most direct link between the application of Bellamy's theory and Olmsted's work was Sylvester Baxter, a devoted disciple of Bellamy, who saw in park, city, and regional planning the most immediate application of Nationalist theories.[51]

Olmsted's work not only provided a series of models that were taken up and transformed at the end of the nineteenth century but also established principles that would recur in the proposals of progressive urban planning, above all in regard to the socioeconomic structure of the city. Planning was no longer a marginal theory interpreting simple romantic ideals. While the planner continued to pursue his own ideals of democracy and liberty, his work was not abstract or divorced from the reality of social conditions but, rather, a response to that reality; his work also had an educational purpose. By pursuing and teaching respect for the great democratic virtues, first among which is love and consideration of nature, planning sought to ensure that nature would not be harmed by the human environment but would, instead, take its place as an organic, constructive element of it. Finally, urban design and urban reform had to be entrusted to "qualified" technicians who were free from external—expecially political—interference, and planning had to become a precise, scientific discipline. These principles were amply developed in the subsequent decades. They would even pervade the architectural and urban-planning activities of the 1920s, thus demonstrating the persistence of a tradition essentially that of civic responsibility and endeavor, which had its origins in the culture and spirit that Mumford and Van Wyck Brooks have identified in the American Renaissance.

Olmsted was active as designer or consultant in numerous American cities and towns, including New York, Chicago, San Francisco, Washington, Detroit, Buffalo, Cincinnati, Boston, Pawtucket, Tarrytown, Newark, Newport, Bridgeport, and Albany. He also planned various campuses, such as Stanford, Berkeley, Harvard, and Vassar, and collaborated on diverse occasions with the principal exponents of the Park movement and with some of the most famous architects of the period, in particular with H. H. Richardson.[52] One exponent of the Park movement who maintained close working relations with Olmsted was Jacob Weidenmann, important above all for his journalistic activity and his work as superintendent of parks in Hartford, a post he assumed in 1864. In collaboration with Olmsted or alone, Weidenmann carried out numerous works, the most significant among them the layout of the Schuylkill Reservoir in Philadelphia and the environmental design for the Capitol in Des Moines.[53]

As it is obviously impossible to discuss here all the projects of the Park movement, many interesting figures must be bypassed in order to examine briefly the works of Olmsted's two principal followers, Horace William Shaler Cleveland and Charles Eliot.

The nephew of Robert S. Peabody, educated at Harvard, Eliot was the heir and interpreter of the work initiated in Boston by Olmsted. After a trip to

Diagram of the entire Boston metropolitan park system in 1899, indicating the work carried out by Frederick Law Olmsted and Charles Eliot.

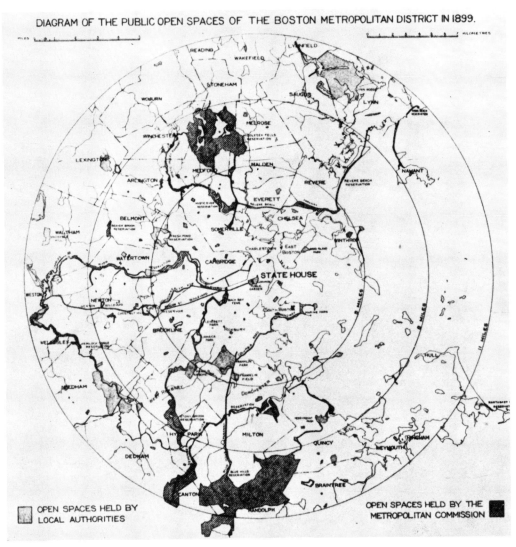

DIAGRAM OF THE PUBLIC OPEN SPACES OF THE BOSTON METROPOLITAN DISTRICT IN 1899.

OPEN SPACES HELD BY LOCAL AUTHORITIES

OPEN SPACES HELD BY THE METROPOLITAN COMMISSION

Plan by Frederick Law Olmsted for Back Bay, Boston, 1879.

Plan by Frederick Law Olmsted for Franklin Park, Boston, 1885.

Observatory, Franklin Park, Boston. The influence of H. H. Richardson, who designed some buildings within Olmsted's system, is evident in this structure.

Entrance to Franklin Park, Boston, from Forest Hills.

England and Europe he opened his own professional office in Boston, establishing contacts in the same circles in which Olmsted was active. Through the Appalachian Mountain Club, Eliot became promoter of a project for the entire area of Boston and its surroundings, based on the development of a metropolitan park system, in which he had the support of many of the same organizations and individuals who had backed Olmsted's proposals, particularly Sylvester Baxter. In 1891 Baxter published a small booklet entitled *Greater Boston*, in which he outlined a reform of the government institutions and the services in the metropolitan area and proposed the creation of an extensive belt of parks around the whole of metropolitan Boston. In 1882 the Boston Metropolitan Park Commission was formed, with Baxter as secretary and Eliot as landscape architect. The "federated metropolis" of which Baxter spoke found expression in the report prepared by Eliot in 1893. The same year, Eliot became an associate of Olmsted and the firm of Olmsted, Olmsted and Eliot became consultants to the Park Commission.

Eliot's work led to a massive enlargement of the nucleus of urban parks foreseen by Olmsted. In this he was aided by urban legislation, such as the Boulevard Act of 1894, that was quite advanced for the times. The plan was no longer urban in scale but aimed at the creation of an integrated system of parks involving the whole surrounding territory, as demonstrated by the undertakings called for. These included a systematic layout along the shore from Revere Beach to Quincy and along the banks of the Charles River up to Weston; in addition, Olmsted's continuous system of parks, which already stretched from Boston Common to Franklin Park was to be extended by continuing it through West Roxbury to Hyde Park and the Blue Hills. Two types of parks, urban and metropolitan, were thus integrated in an area 11 miles in diameter, connecting by means of a kind of greenbelt and an internal parkway system the two great lungs of metropolitan Boston, the Blue Hills and the Middlesex Fells.

In 1919 the Boston Metropolitan Park Commission presented a final accounting of this work; it had involved an expenditure of $21 million, the acquisition of 7,400 acres of land, the construction of 59 miles of parkway, the systematization of the shore and river embankment for 57 miles, and numerous other minor undertakings,[54] but the full importance of Eliot's work is not shown by these impressive results alone. The plan for the Boston metropolitan park system was more than a project for the creation and systematic layout of green spaces; it was a program of comprehensive urban reform, as Eliot himself affirmed: "There seems to be no remedy for this state of things except the establishment of some central and impartial body capable of disregarding municipal boundaries and all local considerations, and empowered to create a system of public reservations for the benefit of the metropolitan district as a whole." Baxter echoed these words in claiming the principal theme of the plan to be the systematization of communications, an assertion certainly confirmed by the attention with which Eliot studied technical solutions to the problem of the roads and considered the probable economic effects of the parkway system.[55] All the obstacles encountered in Eliot's work stemmed from a lack of understanding about the ultimate aims of his plan and from the difficulty of simultaneously effecting institutional reforms in line with the scale of the project. The scale of the undertaking was, in fact, not solely a matter of size; it also involved the willingness of the political powers to resolve the problems of the urban structure comprehensively, in terms not only of planning but also of institutions.

Eliot died on March 25, 1897, and Harvard instituted the first courses in landscape architecture in 1900, in his memory. The event was symptomatic of the transformation that had taken place during the nineteenth century in the romantic concepts that had first motivated the Park movement. It also demonstrated the recognition being granted to new professional categories and the growing awareness of the urgency and validity of problems that work such as Eliot's had brought to the fore. The campaign for city parks had finally become synonymous with urban reform.

H. W. S. Cleveland's career was not unlike Eliot's. Beginning in 1855, Cleveland worked with Copeland in Boston; he subsequently collaborated with Olmsted and Vaux in Chicago, becoming landscape architect of the Chicago South Park Commission in 1872. During these early phases of his career he wrote three works of some importance: *A Few Words on Central Park*, published in 1856, a study written with Copeland that probably exercised a certain influence on the Central Park Commission; *The Public Grounds of Chicago*, published in 1869, in which, like Olmsted, he criticized the grid plan so common to American cities; and his most important book, *Landscape Architecture as Applied to the Wants of the West*, published in 1873. When compared with his first book, this volume demonstrates the advances made by landscape architecture since the 1850s. In it the space dedicated to purely formal problems is limited, and the author's attention is concentrated wholly on planning, on the urban significance of landscape, and on the characteristics and prospects of the town-planning profession.[56] Cleveland's actual work as designer was thoroughly in keeping with this change of approach that had come about in landscape architecture, and it brought to maturity certain characteristics of the planning profession.

In 1883 the city of Minneapolis approved the formation of a Board of Park Commissioners, which in turn, engaged Cleveland to prepare a plan for a metropolitan complex of green spaces. In its approach and aims Cleveland's proposal as presented in his report clearly bespeaks the professional town planner. He maintained that Central Park proved that a park system amounted not to an unproductive expense for the community but to a clear financial gain and affirmed that in New York the value of the taxable area surrounding the park increased by $54 million after the decision was made to create Central Park. Cleveland also emphasized the programmatic significance of his proposal: a master plan meant not only the possibility of coordinating the various individual projects but also made it possible to plan the order in which work would be carried out; thus it provided strategic control over urban development. "Look forward for a century to the time when the city has a population of a million, and think what will be their wants," was Cleveland's advice to the park commissioners of Minneapolis.[57]

The plan of Minneapolis was once again a comprehensive project for restructuring the city, based on an integrated system of green areas and the construction of 20 miles of parkways. Schematically, a large boulevard traces a rectangle around the periphery of the city and connects the various projected urban and extraurban parks. Composed of public spaces and an ample layout of connecting roads, this system not only proposed an alternative to the existing urban structure but also provided a direct indication of the future development of the city. As Cleveland was to affirm in his 1885 proposal for the neighboring city of Saint Paul, the system was, in fact, the axis on which to program the metropolitan development of an urban continuity unifying two cities.[58]

The ideals motivating the Park movement had thus developed into aims of far greater scope than before and gave rise to full-fledged planning projects. This fact is demonstrated not merely by the scale of undertakings like Eliot's and Cleveland's but also by the scientific attention these men began to devote to the social and economic aspects of urban development. Furthermore, the romantic interest in parks had been transformed into projects that now came face to face with mechanisms governing land and real-estate values; as the attempt was made to foresee and plan changes affecting these mechanisms, administrative reform became another necessary objective, one that involved urban planners in controversies over systems of taxation and the role to be assumed by local governments in financing public works and services. Finally, by approaching the problem of urban planning on the larger, metropolitan scale, the Park movement came into contact with the other important formative movement of American planning, that of conservationism, which will be discussed in the next section.

At the end of the nineteenth century, the first protagonists of the Park movement began to disappear. Harry Codman died in 1893 and Eliot, in 1898; in 1895 Olmsted retired from active practice. By this time, however, the new professional image of the landscape architect had come into being, and universities began to offer regular courses in the field. In 1897 the first professional association, the American Park and Outdoor Art Association, was founded. Two years later, in the New York office of Parsons and Pentecost, a group that included Samuel Parsons, Jr., George F. Pentecost, John Charles Olmsted, Frederick Law Olmsted, Jr., Warren H. Manning, Nathan F. Barrett, Downing Vaux, and Charles N. Lowrie founded the American Society of Landscape Architects. In the course of fifty years, the Park movement had substantially changed the perspective of American urban reform. Its romantic and literary interest in nature had developed into a complex ideology, capable of

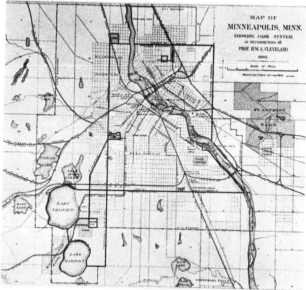

Map of Minneapolis, showing the park system
designed by Horace William Shaler Cleveland,
1883.

Map of Kansas City, showing the development of the park system designed by George
E. Kessler, 1915.

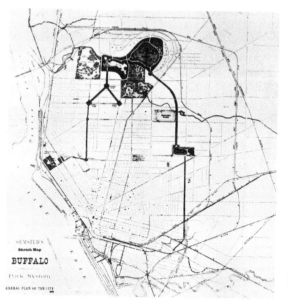

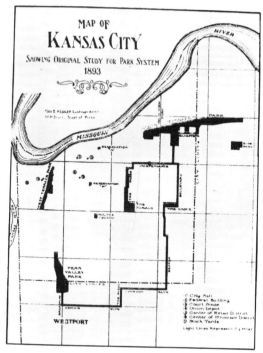

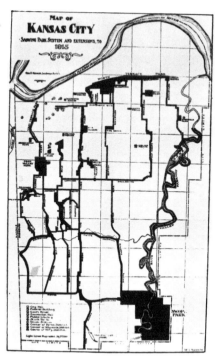

Map of Buffalo, showing the park system,
1876. Only part of this project was the work
of Frederick Law Olmsted.

Map of Kansas City, showing the park system
in George E. Kessler's original study, 1893.

expressing itself with scientifically motivated proposals that aimed at the comprehensive planning of urban development.

This aspiration was hindered by the structural limitations of nineteenth-century planning; indeed, except for a few rare examples of picturesque landscaping, the Park movement did not succeed in achieving spatial control over the urban structure. In other words, the means offered to urbanism by landscape architecture were two-dimensional and did not control the structure of the city in terms of the interrelationship of layout and architecture. This complex dimension of spatial control was to be achieved not by the pioneers of American planning but by the architects of the City Beautiful movement.

The scope of my discussion does not extend to the City Beautiful movement, to which the first essay in this volume is dedicated. Nevertheless, a few brief remarks are necessary here. It would be possible to debate at length the form of the White City of lath and plaster of the Columbian Exposition that opened in Chicago in 1893. What is of interest in this context, however, is that the White City was the product not only of an evident stylistic and formal compromise but also of an interdisciplinary effort of architecture and landscaping experimenting with a new global manner of design. Montgomery Schuyler affirmed that the fair was "first of all a success of unity, a triumph of 'ensemble.'" The principal value of the fair was thus not its architecture but the spatial whole created, the comprehensive control and unity achieved despite so many and such grave formal discrepancies; this objective was guaranteed by the plan and the program, rather than by the architecture as such. Schuyler continued, "The landscape-plan is the key to the pictorial success of the Fair as a whole, and, as we say it generated the architecture of the watercourt by supplying indications which sensitive architects had no choice but to follow. In no point was the skill of Mr. Olmsted and his associate more conspicuous than in the transition from the symmetrical and stately treatment of the basin to the irregular winding of the lagoon."[59]

The interdisciplinary collaboration tried out in Chicago was carried a step further in 1901 by the work of the Senate Park Commission in Washington in which Frederick Law Olmsted, Jr., Daniel H. Burnham, and Charles F. McKim participated. The Park Commission's aim was clearly expressed in the words of Senator James McMillan, one of the principal supporters of the plan for Washington: "The city which Washington and Jefferson planned with so much care and with such prophetic vision will continue to expand, keeping pace with national advancement, until it becomes the visible expression of the power and taste of the people of the United States."[60] Werner Hegemann was to criticize this project severely, describing the Park Commission's plan as no more than an attempt to transplant the Chicago fair to Washington: "Constitution Avenue is the most destructive of all of the crimes yet committed against L'Enfant's plan." L'Enfant had not dreamed of "a beautiful court of honor, but a beautiful city."[61]

Despite Hegemann's radical criticism, however, Washington remains an example of fundamental importance in the history of American urbanism. The accusation that the Park Commission operated on the basis of a model borrowed from Haussmann rather than on an indigenous American design can impress only moralists or formalists. Quite aside from any formal considerations, Washington is a "monument" that corresponds to the objective enunciated by Senator McMillan. Thus what may have appeared anachronistic at the beginning of the twentieth century was the ideals inspiring the project and not the architecture that expressed them. The Park Commission plan, apart from the retrospective ideology it interpreted, has a precise historical significance for the development of American urban planning. Reps has written, "Perhaps Washington is both the testing ground and the symbol of change in our approach to city development."[62] This new approach to the city was not expressed only in "imperial cities," the plans of Burnham, or the buildings of McKim. The Chicago World's Fair of 1893, the Washington of 1901, and the Chicago of 1909 were merely the most conspicuous results of a widespread process, the consequences of which became ever more manifest in the early years of this century.

From what has been said thus far it should be clear that the critical scheme that treats the Park movement as something quite separate from the City Beautiful movement is not operative in the viewpoint taken here. Not only does the interdisciplinary work of the 1890s demonstrate the artificiality of this separation, but the examination of projects such as George E. Kessler's in Kansas City clearly indicates that many motivations of the Park movement merged with the ideals of the City Beautiful. In 1893 Kessler presented his plan for the system of parks to be inserted into the rigid grid of Kansas City. The two green lungs of the city, North Terrace Park and Penn Valley Park, were connected by parkways extending into the city center; the large boulevard, The Paseo, and the space in which it terminates, The Parade, became the characteristic features of the city. Thus the park system was integrated with one of the principal goals of the City Beautiful—the monumental and scenic restructuring of the center of the city.

Kessler was perfectly aware of the consequences and implications of his urban proposals, and his method of procedure was typical of the progressive mentality: "His rhetorical encomium of rural living did not blind him to the city's social needs."[63] The parks did not only offer the possibility of reconciling the health advantages, joys, and community spirit of the country with the city; they were also the rationalizing principle of the urban structure, separating congested functions, establishing rules for efficient communication between functionally diverse areas, between residential and commercial zones, between residence and place of work.[64]

In presenting the advantages to be foreseen from his plan, Kessler did not fail to emphasize that the creation of green spaces would bring with it an increase in real estate values in the surrounding areas; once again, Central Park was the example cited in support of this thesis. Kessler furthermore described the proposed improvements as the foundation for a comprehensive project of urban renewal; as designed, the parks explicitly contested the city's grid-plan structure and established the premises of a redistribution and restructuring that affected not only the monumental areas but also the degraded and obsolete districts of the city.[65] Kessler's proposals fused concerns specific to the Park movement with objectives typical of the City Beautiful, as is evident, for example, in the care with which Kessler studied problems of viability. This was, in fact, one of the major subjects of what was to become a real manual of urban planning, Charles Mulford Robinson's *Improvement of Towns and Cities*, which appeared in 1901 and was reprinted three times in the course of a year. Nothing testifies better than the success of this book to the growth of the movement for urban reform in America. Robinson's "civic art"—"Altruism is its impulse, but it is older than any altruism of the hour, as old as the dreams and aspirations of men"[66]—was intimately related to the "progressive impulse." America was by this time accepting the idea that even democracy had need of plans. This was the ideological concept behind which the practice of architecture and planning was constantly drawn toward a comprehensive model, a model that was unrealizable given the historical contingency—a model that only the prefect Haussmann had had the "power" to put into operation.

The Conservation Movement

From 1840 through the 1880s, the limit of American colonization remained fixed at about the ninety-eighth meridian. The Great Plains continued to be inaccessible until the industrial revolution began to create the instruments and technologies capable of opening this last portion of frontier. In the years following the Civil War, a large body of literature devoted to the subject of the Great Plains appeared. Explorers investigated the nature and resources of this arid land, which had been crossed and left behind during the rush to the West. These studies, which had an important influence on planning and regionalist concepts, formed a tradition that was expressed in the Conservation movement.[67]

A pioneer of this movement was Major John Wesley Powell, who directed the survey of the Rocky Mountain regions and later headed the United States Geological Survey. In 1878 Powell published his classic study, *Report on the Land of the Arid Region of the United States*, in which, on the basis of rainfall statistics, he indicated the hundredth meridian as the western limit for the extension of agriculture. The scientific findings of this report, prepared for the Department of the Interior, indicated a new basis for colonization policy. The principal recommendation contained in Powell's study was that the availability of water, rather than the physical extent of an area of land, should be adopted as the legal basis for portioning out lands. This recommendation implied a complete revision of the land laws for the West, as well as a polemical position in regard to the Eastern politicians' tendency to apply provisions based on the experience of their own regions to the unknown lands of the frontier.[68]

Revision of the Hamiltonian foundations of American agrarian policy had been initiated with the requests of the Free Soil Party in 1840 and continued with the Homestead Act of 1862; Powell's theories now called for even further changes. Powell sought the creation of two different types of land grants, according to whether the lands to be colonized were irrigable or suitable only for pasturage; the amount of land granted to the settler under the Homestead Act would thus be 80 acres in the case of irrigable land and 2,560 acres in the case of pasturage land.[69] The principle of the availability of water resources provided a far more rational basis for subdivision than did the undifferentiated tracing of rectangles of land, the procedure currently followed under the provisions of the Homestead Act. On the basis of this principle, Powell elaborated a sort of colonization program and called for the enactment of necessary legislation, rules for the distribution of water resources, and the preservation of forests. Ultimately, Powell defined the role of the government in this vast work: "I say to the Government: Hands off! Furnish the people with institutions of justice, and let them do the work for themselves."[70]

Along with this typical affirmation of the liberalism and individualism of laissez-faire, Powell actually formulated certain theories that would directly influence regionalist conceptions. On the one hand, Powell outlined a type of territorial development based on the control of resources, particularly water, and, on the other, he set forth in embryonic form certain principles that would eventually guide regional analysis. Powell defined the region in terms of hydrogeological characteristics and the availability of energy sources and conceived its structure as a series of communities of limited size located so as to ensure the most efficient utilization of resources. He summarized his proposal in these words: "This, then, is the proposition I make: that the entire arid region be organized into natural hydrographic districts, each one to be a commonwealth within itself. . . . Each such community should possess its own irrigation works. . . . The plan is to establish local self-government by hydrographic basins."[71]

The importance of such concepts needs little emphasis or explanation. Safeguarding natural resources was to become the central principle of the Conservation movement. The analysis of hydrogeological conditions and the definition of hydrographic basins has much in common with regionalist classifications. And Powell's views on the system of land distribution and the emphasis he placed on the cooperative self-sufficiency of the community were among his most important contributions to the birth of an organic theory of planning. All these ideas were to be greatly respected by the regionalists. Mumford, for example, grants Powell a dominant place among those who contributed fundamentally to the development of organic conceptions of planning.[72]

Another interesting personality from this point of view was Elwood Mead, who, a few decades later, like Powell, investigated problems of the utilization of water resources in relation to agricultural colonization.[73] In Mead's work concepts typical of conservationism, such as the protection of natural resources and their programed utilization, reappear. In a colonization project for California, however, concentrating his analysis on the role of the government, Mead demonstrated that the theories of the movement had evolved since the time of Powell's staunch laissez-faire position. Mead maintained that the state government had a responsibility not merely to provide just institutions but also to establish a precise norm of operation and assume an active and impelling role through a system of credit, as well as by creating colonization services and managing them directly. The *Report of the Commission on Land Colonization and Rural Credits of the State of California*, submitted in 1916, declared: "The State Agricultural College should make systematic provisions for giving advice and information regarding farm management and cultivation. . . . The state should, by contract, build houses, level land for irrigation or loan money to settlers on insurable improvements carried out under the direction and to the satisfaction of the authorities in control, a conservative maximum limit to be fixed."[74]

The proposals contained in the report of the commission headed by Mead indicate that the mentality and outlook of the Homestead tradition was being superseded. The model of colonization on which Mead based his proposals derived, in fact, from the study of new experiments, particularly those carried out in Australia and New Zealand, which had a direct influence also on the theories of urban reformers in America. Mead was among those who contributed most to generating an interest in these particular foreign experiments, which became a point of reference for other conservationists, such as Benton MacKaye.[75] Concerning the role to be assumed by the government, the report of the California commission contained concepts and principles forming part of a theoretical and political trend that would ultimately lead to some of the most important undertakings of the New Deal.

The origin of the conservationist ideology, however, is not to be sought in these examples but, rather, in George P. Marsh's *Man and Nature, or Physical Geography as Modified by Human Action*, published in New York in 1864. Marsh's influence on regionalism was considerable, and Mumford has spoken of *Man and Nature* as the first scientific analysis of the historical consequences of the indiscriminate spoliation of natural resources. In his book Marsh reconstructed the disintegration of the great classical civilizations of the Mediterranean basin, relating their dissolution to the deterioration of organic methods in the utilization of resources, and, in particular, to the indiscriminate destruction of the great forests.[76] A similar attitude toward nature characterized the Park movement; H. W. S. Cleveland and those urging the creation of nature reserves were to find in Marsh's work a valid precedent. Moreover, Marsh's studies were produced in a period when federal policy on natural resources was changing; the years between 1870 and 1890 witnessed the creation of the great national parks, such as Yellowstone, Yosemite, and Sequoia.[77]

The most important heir of this tradition and the link between the Conservation movement and twentieth-century regionalism was Benton MacKaye, whose work is one of the most singular products of the cultural tradition traced in this essay. A typical Yankee, born in Stamford, Connecticut, in 1879, MacKaye passed his youth in New England. Between 1900 and 1910, as a member of the Appalachian Mountain Club, which had been founded in Boston in 1876, MacKaye made a series of expeditions. These trips were the origin of the project that, after being reconsidered and discussed with Clarence S. Stein and Lewis Mumford at Hudson Guild Farm, was presented in 1921 in an article in the *Journal of the American Institute of Architects* entitled "An Appalachian Trail: A Project in Regional Planning."[78] The project will be specifically discussed later in this essay, but what is of interest at this point is the significance the tradition of the Conservation movement acquired in MacKaye's work.

MacKaye was not an isolated ideologist of the movement; he was active in progressive circles, collaborated with the Department of Labor, and was a friend and working colleague of men such as Gifford Pinchot, Stuart Chase, William Stoddard, and Louis Post.[79] His *Employment and Natural Resources*, published in 1919 by the Department of Labor, is a significant document of conservationism. MacKaye's study is divided into sections dealing with various aspects of colonization policy and the utilization of resources, and it sets forth principles shared in large part by regionalism and progressive planning. It is significant that MacKaye's study, which was surely an important contribution, was published at a moment when the first experiments in economic planning, which had come into being as part of an emergency war economy, had still not been repudiated by the American government.

In the introduction to his book, MacKaye set forth two important principles. The first concerns the role of social services and transportation as means of conditioning the localization of production. MacKaye affirmed that initiating a policy of employment development depends not on transferring the worker but, rather, on attracting industry to a particular location by making available transportation facilities and other services. The second principle, equally clear but hardly new in this period, was that the expansion of employment depends on the reduction of work, "upon the increase of efficiency and saving of labor. Increased efficiency, through improved machinery or otherwise, can be used if so desired, to reduce labor time without reducing wages."[80]

These two principles, the sources of which can be found in Patrick Geddes and in French regionalism, are at the base of the main proposals contained in MacKaye's book, which concern the use of natural resources. Forests are the principal subject of his analysis, and MacKaye speaks of lumbering as an industrial activity: "The forest industry requires the building of logging railroads, the improvement of drivable streams, the erection of sawmills and other plants. In order that this industry may provide permanent and profitable employment it must be organized upon a stabilized basis and run under the

Movement of the frontier in the United
States between 1790 and 1880.

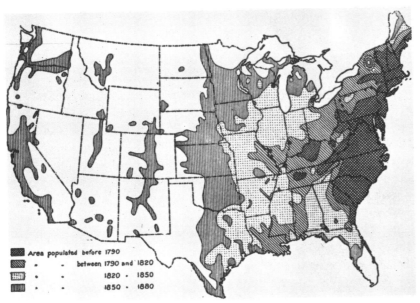

Area populated before 1790
" " between 1790 and 1820
" " 1820 - 1850
" " 1850 - 1880

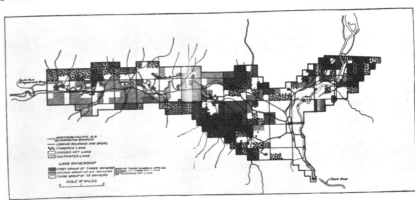

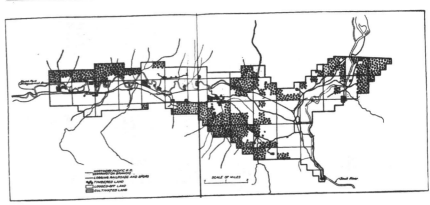

Analyses of the uses of the soil and the structure of land ownership in the Darrington
Valley, Washington, in relation to a proposal
for the location of settlements (from Benton
MacKaye, *Employment and Natural Resources*, U.S. Department of Labor, Washington, D.C., 1919).

methods of forestry and timber culture, and not, as at present, under those of
ordinary lumbering and 'timber mining.' "[81] MacKaye further maintained that a
rational plan of utilization could contribute to resolving difficulties in labor
relations and could limit the enormous territorial mobility of the labor force,
which resulted in inordinate percentages of turnover. In order for the timber
industry not to become an "industry of homeless men," MacKaye asserted that
measures had to be taken so that the population finding employment in this
field of production would have "real communities and not mere shack towns."[82]

The concept of creating autonomous settlements and planning self-sufficient
territorial systems did not, in MacKaye's case, signify embracing the principles of
the decentralists and sectionalists. On this score he left no doubt. Although he
favored certain aspects of decentralization and a policy of decisional autonomy,
he had a precise idea of what the role of the federal government should be:

> There is no question that matters affecting solely the interests of any one local community
> should be controlled by that community. Most local affairs, however, affect national affairs,
> and this is so particularly in the matter of using national resources. What happens to the
> soils, the forests, the ores, or the water powers in any one State affects the people of the
> entire Nation. The opportunity of utilizing land in any State affects not only the workers of
> that State; it affects every worker in America.[83]

Thus the theory of resource planning was not resolved with the assumption of
a purely decentralist position. On the contrary, it implied the necessity of
reforms whereby the federal government, through the financing of transportation systems and other services and the managing of energy resources,
would assume the direction, planning, and control of economic development.
When these ideas are combined with MacKaye's concept of "working units," the
importance of his study for the history of American planning is clear.[84] Only
with the New Deal's Tennessee Valley Authority would such principles finally be
developed and organically applied.

Thus Benton MacKaye, old-style New Englander, founder and honorary president of the Wilderness Society, made a notable contribution to the transformation of the Conservation movement. Mumford has spoken of him as the heir of
the spirit of Thoreau; this literary characterization seems particularly apt when
one recalls MacKaye's affirmation that "the function of planning is to render
actual and evident that which is potential and inevident."[85] Nature was no
longer a romantic dream but a means for producing—a power to be won over, to
be rendered efficient, to be planned. MacKaye's 1919 study makes it clear that
his principal concern was the "plan." Working efficiency, discipline, and
productivity were impossible without a definite rejection of any myth of
laissez-faire; half a century of social struggle, labor upheavals, and economic
instability ended by recognizing the necessity of modifying the ways of growth
and the management of the system. Quite apart from the outdatedness or
modernity of the individual proposals, what is of interest here is the insistence
with which such reforms were viewed as the only possible salvation for the
insecure and vacillating social order. This is the very essence of the phenomenon

discussed in this essay; whatever the methods used, it was only by fighting for the survival of the system that the world the new Yankee had drawn from the bourgeois "epic" of Concord could be perpetuated. This aim is what motivated MacKaye, the student of Thoreau, after teaching at Harvard, to enter into the work of the United States Forest Service, the United States Department of Labor, the New York State Commission of Housing and Regional Planning, the Tennessee Valley Authority, and the Rural Electrification Administration.

Transforming the City, 1893-1920

In his famous essay of 1893, "The Significance of the Frontier in American History," Frederick Jackson Turner spoke of the conquest of the frontier as the determinant factor in the shaping of an American people. Although the history of the United States had begun on the Atlantic coast, according to Turner, it had been written in the plains of the West. The frontier was the first era in American History; eighteen years after writing his classic essay, Turner described the second era in the civilization of the United States, beginning with the "revolution" of the years 1890-1910.[86] The history of this new era was no longer being written in the plains but in the cities; the metropolis had become the new terrain to be conquered. As Arthur M. Schlesinger has written, "The city, no less than the frontier, has been a major factor in American civilization. Without an appreciation of the role of both the story is only half told."[87]

In the preceding section it has been seen that both the Conservation movement and regionalist theories had at least one of their sources in the colonization of the Great Plains. In the pages that follow, I shall attempt to focus on the "progressive spirit" in its response to the transformation of the agrarian order into urban-industrial America. The complexity and internal contradictions of the processes that characterize the course of this new phase of American development are so great, however, that it is necessary first to consider, at least briefly, several economic, political, and cultural factors that may help to clarify the intricate problems under consideration.

Urban-Industrial America

Industrialization took firm hold in the United States, in the view of some historians, between 1840 and 1850, but it was only in the 1860s that a stable relationship began to be established between the development of productive capacity and urban growth. By 1910 the phase of industrialization was essentially completed, even if enormous imbalances still remained, and it was during this very period that the agrarian order entered into definitive crisis.

In the course of fifty-four years, from 1860 to 1914, the value of the national industrial product had grown by roughly a factor of twelve, and the number of wage earners increased five and a half times over. In 1860-1910, while the total population grew by 193.2 percent, the number of urban residents increased by 575.6 percent. During the same fifty years the population of New York increased six times over; that of Chicago, twenty times; and that of Pittsburgh, from 49,221 to 1,044,143.[88]

Indeed, from the late 1850s on, a sort of physiological exchange was established between the development of productive capacity and urban growth. As Shigeto Tsuru has demonstrated, "external economies provided by the city in giving locational convenience for industrial establishments were of unique importance in the early stage of capitalist development.[89] As a market, the city offered decisive external economies, above all in services but also in the mass consumption of goods. At the same time, the city acted as a stimulus in the development of new fields of production by prompting a general acceleration in the acquisition of new techniques and the circulation of productive knowledge.[90]

American urbanization may be considered in terms of cycles related to the particular economic forms that developed from what Paul A. Baran and Paul M. Sweezy have defined as the three "epoch-making innovations": the steam engine, the railroad, and the automobile. The phenomena of urbanization induced by the growth of the railroad system will be discussed briefly later in this essay. Here, however, it is necessary to examine summarily the consequences of the enormous absorption of capital by railroad development on American society and the transformations it wrought in the labor market and the composition of the labor force.

The railroads provided the principal stimulus for the concentration of productive factors and capital. In the last twenty years of the nineteenth century, their development absorbed more than half of all private investment and thus induced an acceleration in the trend of capital formation, as demonstrated in Simon Kuznets's analysis of the period from 1869 to 1913. This monopolistic concentration, brought about and accentuated by the railroads through the first decade of the twentieth century, was accompanied by marked irregularity in the business cycle and a restrained increase in real wages.[91] Economic development created a new, continually expanding geography; the monopolistic concentration needed land in order to grow stronger, and this expansionist tendency, which directly affected the mechanisms of urban growth, remained constant in respect to the concentration of capital in the railroads. With variations, but without substantial fluctuations, the rhythm of investment in the railroad industry remained constant until the crisis of 1907. As Baran and Sweezy have written, "It was in 1907 that the greatest external stimulus in capitalist history lost its tremendous force."[92]

This date marked an arrest in American economic development; without the stimulus of the war and the first period of motorization, the years immediately following the end of the era of the railroads and laissez-faire would have been years of depression. The era of the automobile began in 1911; between 1915 and 1929 the number of motor cars registered increased from 2,300,000 to 23,100,000, and the economic boom was founded on this field of production. The automobile stimulated a whole series of important phenomena, including the territorial diffusion of settlements, the development of suburbs, and the construction of new roads. It is interesting to analyze the trend in building construction in the same period, which reveals a significant anomaly in comparison with trends in the leading fields of production.[93]

If the railroads had needed the plains for their development, the automobile accentuated the American capitalist system's hunger for land. Together, the conquest of new lands and urbanization gave rise to a system of increments in land values and to speculative processes unequaled in extent and aggressiveness. Along with the era of the railroads had ended that of laissez-faire; the various nineteenth-century attempts to establish antitrust legislation and control over the concentration of capital had all been related in some way to the railroad industry and formed the basis for the ultimate defeat of the policies of laissez-faire.[94] The end of laissez-faire was also determined, however, by another phenomenon related to the railroads—the continual agitation of the labor movement from the 1860s on, which had indeed focused on the railroad industry.[95]

Late in the 1860s, the first important labor leader, William H. Sylvis, appeared, along with the first large labor organization, the National Labor Union, destined to disappear with the depression of 1873. That same year wages were cut severely. When wages were again reduced in 1877, labor uprisings broke out in principal cities. At the head of the movement were the Knights of Labor, whose numbers grew during the 1880s, and who led the first fight for the eight-hour day. In 1886 the American Federation of Labor was founded. The first national strike for the eight-hour day, which began on May 1, 1886, resulted in the incident in Chicago's Haymarket Square and the severe repression of the labor movement. In contrast to the syndicalism of Samuel Gompers and the A. F. of L. were the individual trade unions, which drew their strength from the railroad workers. After the 1893 strike in Buffalo, the American Railway Union broke away from the A. F. of L. The Railway Union's president was Eugene V. Debs, the future socialist adversary of Roosevelt and Wilson in 1912.[96]

Again in Chicago, on June 27, 1905, the most singular, romantic, and militant of American labor organizations, the Industrial Workers of the World, came into being. The IWW was an experiment through which passed some of the most important figures of the American labor movement, including Debs, Daniel De Leon, Vincent St. John, Big Bill Haywood, William Trautmann, Elizabeth Gurley Flynn, Joe Hill, Arturo Giovannitti, and John Reed.[97] The history of the IWW offers a key to the study of the increased aggressivity of the class struggle in America and to understanding how this greater militancy was related to a fundamental change in the composition of the labor class. Corresponding to the progressive disappearance of the professional craft worker—the component of the working force described by Jack London in *The Iron Heel* as an ally of the "plutocracy"—was a progressive increase in both insubordination and the mobility of workers. The accelerated transformation of the production system was due in no small way to the effect of this double trend.

In the 1890s, two great events awaited the American trade unions. In June 1892, in the vicinity of the steel plants of Homestead, Pennsylvania, the Amalgamated Association of Iron and Steel Workers clashed with Andrew Carnegie's private police. Two years later, in the town of Pullman, Illinois, the American Railway Union was to face the supreme ordeal. The bloodshed at Homestead and the long fight of the Pullman workers marked the end of the first phase of American unionism. An organization such as that of the American Railway Union could not bear up in the face of the scope and political consequences of the struggle undertaken. Nevertheless, the battles fought by the unions in the 1880s and 1890s dealt a decisive blow to laissez-faire.

Out of this complex of social contradictions, the concepts put forward by progressive thought emerged again with renewed force, often conflicting with and in general confusing the real contradictions that had been brought to light by the recurrent social struggles and labor upheavals. At the same time, the unions had been worn out by the long fight and the most militant labor organizations had been forced to dissolve. Their work had nonetheless brought to the fore all the structural problems of the new order, which included the territorial development of industrialization, the processes of concentration, immigration, and the working conditions in the factories and sweatshops of the large cities. All these problems, from which the principal concerns of progressive thought also stemmed, revealed the fragility and inadequacy of the social structure, which was far from monolithic and, in certain aspects, nonexistent. Meanwhile, however, American democracy seemed bent on reducing the entire territory to a slum, despite the frequently repeated declarations of good intentions.

During this period of struggle it became clear that the problem progressivism had raised in the course of the nineteenth century—the role of the public institutions and the priority of public intervention over private interests—was central to the preservation of the system. In other words, the "business agency" of the laissez-faire era had to be replaced by a modern government. As Sidney Fine has written, "Although the reformers and reform groups of the 1880's and 1890's differed in their estimate of the reforms that the existing situation required, they tended to agree that the functions of the state should be expanded and that a more positive use of the powers of government was essential to promote what in their view was the common interest. Thus did the quest for reform lead away from laissez faire and toward the general-welfare state."[98]

Thus, although it was the fruit of a generally confused ideology, the role played by progressivism can hardly be put aside as purely reactionary. On the contrary, progressive thought and actions—in their varying expressions, among them those that have merited the term *collectivist*—served, not indifferently, to ease and integrate the contradictions. Their efforts at strengthening public institutions and their assertion of need to create organs to mediate between the power and the people, while they served to postpone any ultimate clash, prefigured the solution to the problems in terms of "progress," "order," and the involvement of the class interests in the myth of collective well-being and the "benefit of the people."

The need for economic development founded on collective interests rather than on the exigencies of accumulation of individual business enterprises gained strong support from a new cultural discipline that began to be applied to the city in the decades around the turn of the century. The nineteenth-century social-science movement had its origins in the transformation of the agrarian order brought about by industrial development and urbanization; it thus had significant points of contact with certain principles central to the progressive tradition. Although American sociological thought stemmed originally from religious motivations and an agrarian culture, it was in the city that the movement found its real working ground. European sociology had evolved through the German sociologists' analysis of the *Grossstadt* as a general examination of the "system." The German accomplishments formed the point of departure for American sociologists and, in particular, for the group that was to form the Chicago school. What they added was an analytic basis, derived less from philosophical reasoning than from philanthropic and scientific considerations about the consequences of the degraded form and life of the city as analyzed by the nineteenth century reformers. As time went on Chicago became the subject of studies and analyses that made significant progress in the application of scientific methods of investigation to the urban realities and in the comprehension and description of the phenomena and mechanisms inherent in the structuring of associative and institutional forms of metropolitan life.[99]

One of the most typical products of urban culture was the phenomenon of muckraking. In the opening years of the century, the muckraking journalism attracted the attention of the American public, turning the printed page into an instrument of agitation and denouncement. From an essentially populist point of view, the muckrakers exposed and denounced the system of urban-industrial America.[100] Between 1903 and 1912, more than two thousand muckraking articles appeared in popular American magazines. Among the authors were such famous names as Lincoln Steffens, Ray Stannard Baker, Upton Sinclair, Robert Park, Charles E. Russell, and David Graham Phillips; socialists were also numerous. Along with the classic themes of realistic literature, the muckrakers concentrated their attention on two problems: the rapacity of modern business and the corruption of the city administrations. The attack on corruption was given striking expression in Lincoln Steffens's *Shame of the Cities* (1904); similarly, in his novel *The Jungle* (1906), Upton Sinclair unleashed his Christian socialism on contemporary evils.

The significance of muckraking was not limited to the denunciation of the alliance between business rapacity and political inefficiency. By transforming the city into a real and current problem for every reader—just as it had been for some time for the cultural elite[101] —the muckrakers, in fact, publicized the ideals and concerns of progressivism. The struggle of the laborer, the workings of the trusts, the status of racial minorities, the condition of women in society, political corruption, and the weakness of public institutions were all recounted, exposed, and submitted to a harsh examination, often without taking account of the intrinsic differences and structural peculiarities of the matters treated. Certainly, however, the muckrakers' criticism was in no way nostalgic or retro-gressive. Despite all its weaknesses, as Chalmers has written,

The wielders of the muckrake exposed corruption in order that it might be corrected. Their analysis of national life probed deeply into the vast changes that had taken place during the previous half-century. Collectively they presented one of the first comprehensive descrip-tions of the business civilization that had become the ideal and the motive force of the American nation. With their criticism the muckrakers helped lay the groundwork of public concern which resulted in many of the reforms of the next half-century. In addition, these journalists had positive views to express and were able to do so in the popular magazines for more than a decade.[102]

An editorial in the January 1903 issue of *McClure's Magazine*, entitled "Con-cerning Three Articles in This Number of McClure's," summed up the spirit of muckraking. In essence it described this new literature as seeking among the refuse of the city the great lost values of law, justice, liberty, religion, and culture that had become the palpable symbols of the state of moral degradation, inefficiency, and corruption into which the American people had fallen. Ulti-mately what emerges from this denunciation is the primary importance of what Richard Hofstadter has defined as the most typical of the values of progres-sivism, the ethic of individual responsibility. The editorial concludes, "We have to pay in the end, every one of us. And in the end the sum total of the debt will be our liberty."[103]

Muckraking's populism could have no other outcome; the most violent de-scriptions of degradation, exploitation, and corruption ended with an invocation to the people "as individuals," rather than to individuals as a class. In this pattern is manifest the parallelism of such literary realism with the most aristocratic expressions of the progressive spirit. Both ultimately fought for a "world of ethics" and in the "world of evil," which both had chosen as the object of their concern, neither could discover a solution that was primarily political rather than moral. Within the vague concept of "the people," both were equally incapable of discerning a class perspective.

In the 1910s, the era of laissez-faire ended and progressive criticism found political expression. On August 31, 1910, at the dedication of a public park honoring the memory of John Brown in Osawatomie, Theodore Roosevelt delivered his famous New Nationalism speech: "New Nationalism puts the national need before sectional or personal advantage. . . . This New Nationalism regards the executive power as the steward of the public welfare."[104] The principal concepts of this doctrine expressed some of the most characteristic points of progressive ideology, regarding federal government control of business, the role of public institutions in labor controversies, and a different use of public funds and credit policy. Herbert Croly spoke explicitly of Roosevelt's New Nationalism as an attempt to revive Hamiltonian ideals and definitively overcome the Jeffersonian heritage. Similar concepts were also part of Woodrow Wilson's New Freedom; indeed, the economic reforms carried out during his presidency strongly tended to bring the politics of the Democratic Party into line with the progressive position. [105]

Although in different ways, both Wilson and Roosevelt interpreted the expansionist needs of the American economy, which the laissez-faire state could not satisfy; indeed, the problem of the state was the core of both their doctrines. In recent years the relationship between the affirmation of corporate capital and progressive theories has been studied extensively, and their reciprocity has become quite clear. This relationship can indeed be gathered directly from Roosevelt's Osawatomie address or from the pages in which Wilson set forth his "philosophy." [106] In its understanding of the primary importance of public intervention and the role of government institutions, progressivism was the only tendency that interpreted the process of transformation of the agrarian order economically, politically, and ideologically.

New Freedom and New Nationalism—even if the one bespeaks the thought of Turner and the other that of Croly—were ultimately the fruits of a single tradition formed in the nineteenth century, one that was constructively critical of the laissez-faire society. The persistence of the tie with this tradition or, indeed, with tradition plain and simple, was another essential aspect of progressivism. The Osawatomie address ended with the words "Our public men must be genuinely progressive." Commenting on his doctrine in 1910, Roosevelt declared, "What I have advocated . . . is not wild radicalism. It is the highest and wisest kind of conservatism." [107] Matching Roosevelt's words was Wilson's affirmation, "If I did not believe that to be progressive was to preserve the essentials of our institutions, I for one could not be a progressive." [108]

Both these statements reveal the essence of the progressive spirit, which was expressed not in a philosophical system but in ethical aspirations that drew their force from the native Yankee tradition of democracy, with all the pitfalls and contradictions it contained and implied. The offspring of Protestantism, strengthened by an expansionist adventure unequaled in modern history, progressivism made its most important contribution in creating a civic consciousness that revived a deeply rooted conviction of the New World, the ethic of individual responsibility. Taking upon himself that grave but optimistic concern about contemporary society, each individual assumed the responsibility of fulfilling, in the forms of democracy, the "promise of American life." But this "promise"—or, rather, this still dormant hope (as described by Whitman in the passage quoted below, which demonstrates, among other things, the relation between the ideology of American democracy and the sentiment toward nature)—must have been viewed much less optimistically by the American laborer and by those peoples on whom American imperialism had recently bestowed the gift of the *Pax Americana*. It was surely difficult for them to imagine that the "sleep" of which Whitman speaks could be interrupted by the dawning of a different day:

We have frequently printed the word Democracy. Yet I cannot too often repeat that it is a word the real gist of which still sleeps, quite unawaken'd, notwithstanding the resonance and the many angry tempests out of which its syllables have come, from pen or tongue. It is a great word whose history, I suppose, remains unwritten, because that history has yet to be enacted. It is, in some sort, younger brother of another great and often-used word, Nature, whose history also waits unwritten. [109]

The City as Factory from the Industrial Revolution to the Crisis of Laissez-Faire: Lowell and Pullman

The idea of building towns around factories in order to house the workers came into being with the earliest industries; in the United States, as part of an economic outlook inspired by Hamiltonian ideas, the practice began to take hold at the end of the eighteenth century. The company town was the utopia of a capitalism striving to build an economic system founded no longer on land but on the machine; it was an ideal that made explicit the incipient transformation of the economic basis of the American nation and a model that interpreted the myth, typical of early capitalism, of a "perfect" society in the service of industry.

The company town represented a drastic break with the American tradition; indeed it aimed to create a community in which the traditional social components tended to disappear. As an urban model, it was completely different from the historical city, not so much in its formal structures as in the fact that it had a new, single motive for its development: the factory. Having no aim other than maximum productive efficiency, the company town created a monocultural economy and society.

On the basis of these preliminary considerations and the examples that will be discussed, it is possible to risk a hypothesis on the company town that could fill a gap in the critical study of the antiurban tradition of American urbanism. The ideal of the company town was, in fact, strongly antiurban—not only in its ideology and form but, above all, in the social and economic structures to which this particular type of "utopia" gave rise. First of all, it was opposed to the city because of the continuity of economic development and social forms that the city represented. It also opposed the city because it is urban civilization itself that makes possible a reciprocal development of economic and social forms, while the company town tends to create a life model in which the economic motivations entirely subsume the social. Indeed, the company town seems to have been the product of an ideology that sought to annul the city through the factory, to integrate the "urban" into the "productive." The Civil War seriously undermined this paleotechnic utopia, but some of its principles lingered on in the company towns of the laissez-faire era and became a precise policy in this new capitalist system, serving as a typical internal economic instrument in the process of accumulation. One of the first examples of this type of community was Paterson, New Jersey, created at the end of the eighteenth century by the

Hamiltonian-inspired Society for Establishing Useful Manufactures and designed first by Pierre Charles L'Enfant and Nehemiah Hubbard and subsequently by Peter Colt.[110] The example that best illustrates my thesis, however, is Lowell, Massachusetts.[111]

In the early years of the nineteenth century, the number of manufacturing concerns was steadily increasing in America. For the most part, they were small mills located by streams that offered limited productivity and were thus not capable of attracting sufficient capital to create a real industrial system. Only with the introduction of new machinery were the mills transformed into real factories, becoming a remunerative investment for capital of commercial formation and urban origin. In the case of the textile industry, this transformation took place when Francis Cabot Lowell introduced the power loom into his factory in Waltham, Massachusetts.

Lowell was a typical New England businessman. In contact with the intellectual currents that made this region the heart of the American Renaissance, he was animated by a certain sensitivity to social problems. He thought of creating an ideal community dedicated to work, concentrated around productive activities, and motivated by the sole aim of creating an industrial system of maximum efficiency. As John Coolidge has written, "He conceived of the town as made up of two distinct groups, the employees and citizenry; their ways of life would be quite different, the one wholly controlled by the corporation, the other free, at least up to a point."[112]

In 1822, five years after Lowell's death, his work was continued with the formation of the Merrimack Manufacturing Company, the director of which, Kirk Boott, took up the idea of creating an industrial community and began construction in 1823. Forming the central nucleus of Boott's plan for the town of Lowell were the factories, situated so as to guarantee maximum advantages from the water power of the Merrimack River and from a system of artificial canals within the area of the settlement.[113] Such an installation had become usual for nineteenth-century factories but at Lowell it acquired much greater significance and became a decisive factor for the entire urban layout. In other words, the form and development of the community were based not on organic laws of growth or, as in the case of the utopian manufacturing societies, on certain dominant social considerations but directly on the productive requirements of the industrial plants. That the town had no other motivation for its development than to be an appendage to the manufacturing system is clear from the company's initial policy, which aimed at exercising absolute control over the employees and creating its own labor market. Because it was to guarantee an absolutely stable base for productive development, this market had to be rigid and free from any exterior influence.

The company did not however, exercise an absolute monopolistic control on the land and, above all, did not turn it into a massive speculative venture. Land was largely reserved for the development of the manufacturing plants, and any excessive concentration of locked-up capital was avoided except for activities directly related to production.[114] In my opinion, this policy, which was pursued in the early years of the town, was not due, as Coolidge maintains, to a simple error of judgment or lack of foresight. Rather, it stemmed from the "philosophy" animating this phase of business enterprise: capital was reproduced by work and machines and could not be diverted into land investment. Moreover, the concept of the town as a factory meant that residences and urban services were considered the simple and direct consequences of work, integral factors in the policy of controlling the labor market and guaranteeing the social stability of the workers, rather than remunerative outlets for investment and means of creating an internal system of capital yield. This outlook resulted in an extremely rigid urban structure, reflected in the class divisions of the employees, who resided in dwellings furnished by the company that were separated from those of the other inhabitants of the town.[115] Thus the town existed by reason of the processes rationalizing production and as a comprehensive design for maintaining exploitation at maximum level.

Very soon, however, the requirements of development that had brought about the transfer of Francis Cabot Lowell's factories from Waltham to Lowell also changed the characteristics of the "perfect" system imagined by Boott. The rate of immigration increased rapidly, and the slums populated by Irish immigrants became part of the panorama of Lowell. At the same time as investment increased, the number of inhabitants rose considerably, and new building solutions gradually replaced the anonymous constructions of the original settlement.

Boott's death in 1837 ended the first phase of the history of Lowell, which had coincided with the era of puritanical paternalism. The ideal of the perfect labor market showed itself for what it was, a "pure utopia." Such a design proved vain in face of the varied origins of the new workers and the new problems of production generated by competitive expansion. Even the development of the factories met with difficulties when the natural availability of land suitably situated in relation to water power began to run out, and the location of new plants imposed an increased economic burden—caused not only by the reduced availability of land but also by a town that numbered 30,000 inhabitants in 1845.[116] In the meantime, in order to take hold of a source of income that had been purposely ignored by the founders of the community, new types of dwellings were developed. The Irish immigrants replaced the Yankee girls in the factories, and the puritan dormitories in which New England farmer's daughters had been housed were hardly suitable for the newcomers.[117] The initial consequences of this transformation of the socioeconomic role of the dwellings was the construction of the first complex of row houses. The subsequent irregular and chaotic development of new residential areas would clash with the regular plan of the original community.

The industrial utopia of Lowell was based on the ideological myth of the complementarity of class interests and on the masking of a thorough exploitation of the labor force, as well as on two economic corollaries: the stable availability of water power and the annulment of the labor market. The first corollary encountered a serious obstacle in the factor of land; competitive expansion ultimately gave rise to problems of location and induced the formation of an active land market. At the same time, the growth of the town brought into being all the problems of an urban character that constantly condition the labor market. Lowell declined when the economic consequences overcame the idealistic premises. After the Civil War, the transportation system and the use of coal as the principal source of energy annulled one of the economic factors that had motivated the development of the town. Primarily, however, the system collapsed when the cost of labor became the determining element of industrial development.

If Lowell was unusual as a company town, its singularity was due less to the solutions adapted there than to the ideals that motivated it. As an industrial "utopia," Lowell was an exceptional example of a typical phenomenon, which ended with the birth of laissez-faire. It served, however, as an important precedent for numerous nineteenth-century company towns, which were surely less animated by utopian ideals but far more deeply rooted in the economic reasoning of laissez-faire.

Lowell was not without a sequel in the first phase of industrialization. In the late 1840s, the town of Lawrence on the Merrimack was acquired by the Bay State Mills and the Essex Company, while settlements in New Hampshire, such as New Ipswich and New Market, became significant industrial communities. Among the company towns of the period before the Civil War, the most interesting, other than Lowell, were Manchester, New Hampshire, where the Amoskeag Manufacturing Company operated beginning in 1836; Chicopee, Massachusetts, created in 1823 by the Chicopee Manufacturing Company; and Holyoke, constructed along the Connecticut River on land acquired in 1847 by the Hadley Falls Company. [118]

Another phenomenon characteristic of this period was the development of towns by the mining industry. In addition to the coal towns, the history of the oil towns is especially interesting. One of the most famous was Pithole, Pennsylvania, which sprang up in 1862 and grew to 15,000 inhabitants in just three months. The settlements that grew up along the expanding routes of the railroads can also be considered company towns, whether they were preexisting communities revitalized by the arrival of the new transportation lines or new villages created directly by the railroad companies. One of the best examples is Cairo, Illinois, situated at the confluence of the Mississippi and Ohio Rivers, a town for which the first plan was prepared in the late 1830s by William Strickland and Richard Taylor and was followed by Henry C. Long's plan in 1850. [119] Another community of this type was Tacoma, Washington, built by the Northern Pacific Railroad Company, for whom Frederick Law Olmsted prepared an interesting plan in 1873; Olmsted's plan was not used, however, and the town was actually constructed on a grid layout.

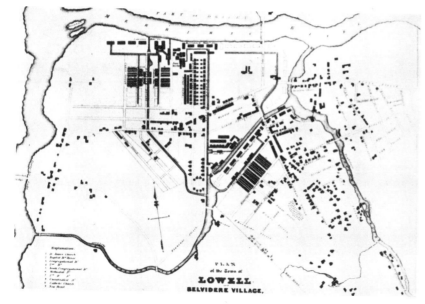

Plan of Lowell, Massachusetts, in 1832.

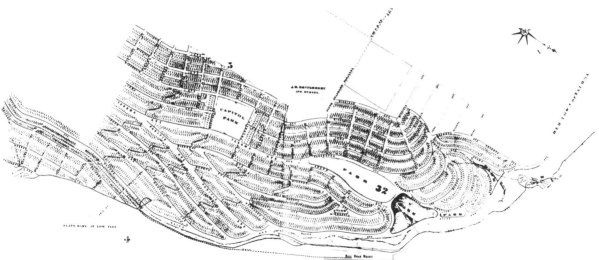

Plan by Frederick Law Olmsted for Tacoma,
Washington, prepared for the Northern
Pacific Railroad Company, 1873.

Plan by Frederick Law Olmsted and John
Charles Olmsted for the town of Vander-
grift, Pennsylvania, prepared for the Apollo
Iron and Steel Company, 1895.

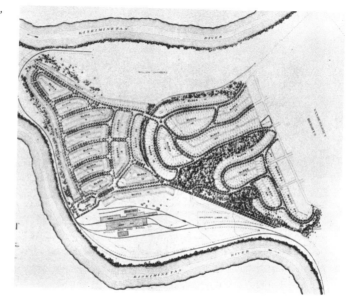

The most important event in this field during the laissez-faire era, however, remains the construction of the town of Pullman in the immediate vicinity of Chicago. Its founder, George Pullman, was born in 1831 to a Universalist family. In 1864 he built his first sleeping car, auspiciously named the Pioneer, which was almost immediately successful and in the brief span of two years assured its builder a monopoly on this type of railroad car in the Midwest. In 1867 Pullman became president of the newly formed Pullman's Palace Car Company, which succeeded in producing 114 cars in 1880.[120] Through the critical years toward the end of the century, Pullman continued to expand his activity by differentiating his production, aiming at high technical standards, and pursuing a policy of stable prices. Some of the cars constructed in these years, such as the Wahsatch, were of historical importance in the progress of American railroads. After the depression of the 1870s, Pullman decided to expand his enterprises; on the advice of Jim Brown, he acquired more than 4,000 acres of land near Lake Calumet. The move from Chicago appears to have been motivated by two fundamental considerations; one was the growing instability of the labor market in the city, severely troubled in the 1870s by frequent strikes; the other, the progressive increase in the cost of land within the city limits.

Pullman was an outstanding figure in Chicago. As a member of various civic associations and of the Commercial Club, he was not indifferent to the new theories on the necessity and utility of substantially improving workers' living conditions.[121] In Chicago, in fact, the living conditions of the working class had gradually become symptomatic of life in the slums. Philanthropy was not the only concern prompting a new interest in and search for solutions to the residential problems of the poorer classes, however. There was also the fact that "during the decade from 1870 to 1880 Chicago did not experience a year free of labor disturbances. The danger present in this situation became obvious in July 1877, when disorders touched off by a strike on the Baltimore-Ohio Railroad occurred in a score of cities. In Chicago conflicts between mobs and police persisted for four days and left thirteen men dead and hundreds injured. The local news-papers reported the trouble under such flaming headlines as 'Civil War,' 'Horrid Social Convulsion,' and 'Red War.' "[122] The betterment of the workers' living conditions appeared to the more enlightened industrialist the first necessary step toward the solution of a situation that had become insupportable. George Pullman was among the first to understand this necessity; although he spoke of the new community he was about to create in terms of pure economic convenience, it is clear that the calculation of the "social costs" and the possibility of stabilizing the labor market had considerable weight in this undertaking.

Along with the town of Pullman, a system came into being. As explained in the booklet distributed by Pullman's Palace Car Company at the Transportation Building at the Chicago World's Fair, this system was based on three thoroughly integrated operations: the production of railroad cars, the experimentation of a model management, and the construction of the town. The last had little that was philanthropic about it; it was good business. As Richard T. Ely observed, "We may feel inclined to shrug our shoulders at the philanthropy which demands a good round sum for everything it offers, but certainly it is a great thing to have demonstrated the commercial value in a city of laborers."[123]

In 1880, construction was begun on the town in accordance with the plan prepared by Solon S. Beman and Nathan F. Barrett; in June of the following year, it welcomed its first 650 inhabitants. The planned construction of the dwellings made standardization and thus significant economies possible, and work proceeded so rapidly that the factories could begin to produce in 1881. In 1884 the town of Pullman had absorbed an investment of $8 million and had a population of 8,500. The structures that had been built included the commercial center, the principal public buildings, the church, and a theater considered to be the most beautiful in the United States until the inauguration of Louis Sullivan's Auditorium.[124] The policy pursued in regard to the labor force was one of the most important aspects of life in Pullman. Three-quarters of the employees were specialized workers, who had to pass a strict examination, in which even the candidates' inclination to alcohol was ascertained, before being hired. This concern for the "moral character" of the workers, praised by the commentators of the time, was coupled with a rigid discrimination in regard to workers' belonging to labor organizations.

The town was managed with an extreme discipline; the power of the company was absolute—"Here is a population of eight thousand souls where not one single resident dare to speak out openly his opinion about the town in which he lives"[125]—and one could escape from it only by emigrating. In fact, the policy of refusing the inhabitants the right to own their homes, which centered all credit and commercial operations in the hands of the company, ended by accelerating turnover. During the 1880s the Pullman industry continued to prosper, despite the increasingly insistent criticism of the town's Bismarckian rule. In 1893—year of the opening of the Columbian Exposition, to the financing of which George Pullman contributed $100,000, and year that saw the rise of Debs's American Railway Union—the number of employees at the Pullman factories was reduced for the first time. In addition, workers' wages were seriously cut in 1893; not only was the hourly wage reduced, but the pay rate was also lowered for piece work, which became a progressively more common form of remuneration. Within a year, despite a brief rise in the employment level, wages diminished by an average of 25 percent.[126] The workers whose wages had been cut became indebted to the company, which ran the banks and commercial enterprises and did not lower the prices of these social services it furnished. Rents remained the same, as did interest rates on loans, so that the worker was doubly exploited through reduced wages and the extraction of "social costs."

The situation soon could not be sustained and the strike that broke out at Pullman drew into a definitive struggle the enlightened dreams of laissez-faire

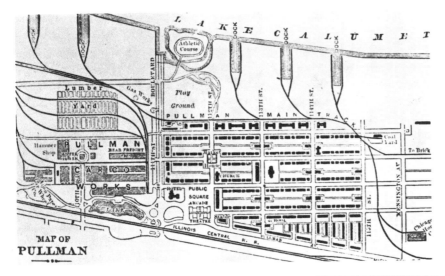

MAP OF
PULLMAN

Map of Pullman, Illinois, planned by Solon
S. Beman, with the collaboration of landscape architect Nathan F. Barrett, and begun
in 1880.

View of Pullman, Illinois, showing the church
and the market building surrounded by the
dwellings.

and Debs's recently formed union. To bring about a decisive turning point in the strike, the American Railway Union resorted to a national boycott of the Pullman railroad enterprises, and the strike gradually involved not only the workers of Pullman but of all Chicago. This united action was an indication of the homogeneity of workers as a class and as such it was the first symptom of the collapse of the company town ideal, the internal contradictions of which were no longer those of the paleotechnic era but comprehensive problems of the whole institutional structure. Demonstrations of solidarity with the striking workers were widespread, and the dream of the 1880s, of a "contained, model town" dedicated to work, dissolved in face of the new organized strength of the working class and the contradictions inherent in the system, which decent residential standards and the prohibition of alcohol could no longer assuage.

Debs's union had been drawn into a fight for which it was not prepared, however, and it was forced to confront a concentration of capital capable of resisting the wearing struggle on a national scale for a very long time. [127] The union came out of its ordeal reduced to exhaustion; the decline of the American Railway Union began, in fact, with the Pullman strike. Also defeated, however, were the dream of laissez-faire and Pullman's enlightened paternalism. "Utopia" did not bear up under the rhythm of industrial development for more than ten years. The findings of the federal Strike Commission, established at the termination of the strike, were quite amazing in regard to the conditions of life in this model town. The level of aesthetic and sanitary standards was high, but so, too, were the rents in Pullman—20-25 percent higher than in nearby Chicago. [128] The "moral town" cost too much—certainly for the workers but, in terms of policy, also for the owners. What collapsed in George Pullman's system was the basic concept itself: the interdependence of town and factory.

President Grover Cleveland sent troops to garrison the town during the strike, but this was not the principal lesson to be learned from Pullman, nor was it a definitive solution. In drawing their conclusions about events in Pullman, the Strike Commission and alert critics such as Florence Kelly emphasized what had, indeed, been made most evident by the course of the strike—the inability of the federal government to take an active role in labor controversies. At Pullman the dreams of laissez-faire revealed their impotence in resolving the internal contradictions of the industrial system, but it was above all the laissez-faire government that showed its weakness under the strain of this strike. The lessons of 1894 were not slow to produce at least partial results. Numerous political groups took up the fight for legislation granting the government an active role in labor relations, and this effort, in which Cleveland himself energetically participated, led to the Arbitration Act of 1898.

Despite some declarations of good intentions, the long strike at Pullman was followed by a period of repression, during which—unsurprisingly, given the frequently demonstrated complementarity of the two phenomena—the principal ideals of progressivism were further strengthened. The great issues of the law and the role of the government had been made still more urgent by the experience of the strike; they were now put forward in a way that went far beyond the enlightened paternalism that in 1880 had led George Pullman to his ambitious undertaking. It was over these issues, over the possibility of making the power of public institutions operative and efficient amid the great contradictions of urban civilization, that twentieth-century progressives would call on American democracy to prove its validity.

The urban civilization the company town had wished to reject as an anomaly in its segregated world dedicated solely to work and production actually decreed the failure of laissez-faire. Among the reasons for this failure was the fact that the model of life-enlightened paternalism sought to impose had little in common with tradition. As Ely observed, "The conclusion is unavoidable that the idea of Pullman is un-American."[129]

The Criticism of Urban-Industrial America

It is not possible to discuss the progressive movements in the United States in the first twenty years of this century without referring at least briefly to the work of three important critics of the world of laissez-faire: Henry George, Edward Bellamy, and Thorstein Veblen. Although their positions in regard to the laissez-faire system were not at all the same, the legacy of these three men's thought is found in various forms in the ideas and work of numerous exponents of the movements, associations, and opinion groups that, beginning in the opening years of the twentieth century, fought for reforms in the field of city planning and administration.

Henry George was born in Philadelphia in 1839, and his life was a fascinating succession of the most disparate activities and of relations with movements, people and associations of the most varied tendencies. In 1880 he published *Progress and Poverty*, a work destined to make history, which procured its author enormous fame not only in the United States but in Britain and had a notable influence on progressive thinking and among reformers in general.[130] Negatively influenced by evolutionist theories, George evolved a harshly polemical argument against the doctrines of Malthus, which occupies the whole second book of *Progress and Poverty*. Together with this polemic, on the basis of certain cardinal principles drawn from physiocratic thought and fused, as Joseph A. Schumpeter has noted, with a contestation of the validity of the wage-fund theory, George proposed a new economic order based on the confiscation of all yield deriving from the increment of land values. This system of taxation of land—and not the confiscation of the land, as has often been claimed—should, according to George, replace all other forms of taxation, hence the term *single tax*. The single tax was therefore not a system of expropriation; it did not question the right to property. Rather, it was a comprehensive instrument of economic equilibrium and a direct means of public control over the economy.

The idea of taxing the yield derived from the increased value of land was not absolutely new in classical economics; it could be found in John Stuart Mill and would be treated most thoroughly by the marginalists. Furthermore, the solutions to the administrative problems arising from such a proposal were not at all clear in George's theories. [131] Indeed, as an economic theory the single tax probably did not merit all the clamor and interest it aroused; its greatest merit was that it revealed and denounced the distortions of the reigning economic system. A valid judgment of the historical significance of George's work is offered in this pithy statement by Mark Blaug:

> ... *Progress and Poverty*, a wonderful example of old-style classical economics, was 30 years out of date the day it was published, and the idea of confiscating the income of a leading social class was deeply shocking to a generation bred on Victorian pieties. [132]

Once this premise is clear, one can better understand the pertinence of George's thought to a certain spirit of progressivism; it derived principally from the basic ideology of *Progress and Poverty* rather than from the economic mechanisms it defined, which, in fact, remained within the system of laissez-faire. This ideology was expressed in a rigid pyramid of values, at the apex of which were morality and justice. Human reason, George affirmed, had to create institutions modeled on divine justice, from which all the fundamental laws of human life are derived. The exploitation of the private ownership of property through land-investment yield distorts divine law, which has established that each man should possess according to what he produces by his own labor, and causes injustice and the slowness of economic and social progress.

It was not only because of its attack on property yield, however, that *Progress and Poverty* gained numerous followers who were disposed to propagate its principles and make George a figure of veneration. The book also polemically confronts a whole series of issues that clearly correspond to those pursued by the progressive movements, despite George's more radical accent—for example, his continual criticism of monopolies, his proposal for abolishing the army as well as the diplomatic service, and, above all, his hypothesis of a new and different type of government institution, of a government called on to create just laws that would guarantee the management and equitable distribution of wealth and sources of well-being.

On the whole, George's thought expressed the expectations of progress unhindered by "archaic" restraints and a proposal for economic development capable of realizing the existing potential of the industrial system: "Wages in all branches of industry are not what they ought to be. That increase in productive power that comes from discovery and invention does not raise wages as it ought to do." [133]

Edward Bellamy's *Looking Backward* is dedicated in large part to a discussion of the structure and functioning of a perfect industrial society. In this novel, published in 1888, Mr. West, awakening from a sleep of more than a century, finds himself suddenly immersed in the everyday life of Dr. Leete and his family and quickly discovers that in the year 2000 all the contradictions and social evils he habitually encountered every morning on leaving his well-to-do Bostonian home at the end of the nineteenth century had disappeared. The fantastic and utopian world through which Mr. West passes if founded on a perfected industrial system. As Mumford has written, "In 2000 'the labor army' is not a figure of speech: it is an army indeed, for the nation is a single industrial unit, and the system upon which the working force is recruited is universal compulsory industrial service."[134]

In Bellamy's words, "The epoch of the trusts had ended in the Great Trust." In *Looking Backward*, there is no room for preindustrial regression; the world of 2000 is a single unit carrying out mass production of goods, with the whole society rotating around the imperative of production. The well-ordered city Mr. West visits opens to the view of the attentive visitor in a series of grand perspectives typical of a "city beautiful"; large tree-lined streets are dominated by colossal public buildings, the vital nerve centers of the management of the "perfect society," which, in their monumental forms, represent the all-encompassingness of the public power.

As David Riesman has asserted, Bellamy's utopia is actually the hypothesis of a refounding of society, in which the public economic sphere prevails for the purpose of furnishing a common basic prosperity and well-being to every citizen in the form of services.[135] The society of services is the product of the omnipresence of the Great Trust that runs and rationalizes all economic activity—it is the impersonal consequence of the free but obligatory work of the citizens, of a system based on the most drastic reproducibility of merchandise and a compulsively stimulated interest in work. In the city of Dr. Leete, there are no strikes; the individual can desire only better work or an award for the assiduity with which he has pursued the community's well-being. In Bellamy's utopia, well-being and bureaucracy make the social classes and struggle for power futile, but what is obviously left out is the problem of labor. What the "labor army" ultimately represents is not the solution of a classless society but the negation of nothing less than the ideal scheme on which *Looking Backward* is based. The irresoluable internal contradiction is such that this utopia becomes only a literary fantasy; despite the comparison attempted by Mumford, it is difficult to find any real relationship between Bellamy's literary construction and Walter Rathenau's ideas of socialization.

Bellamy's utopia is significant mainly for certain concepts regarding the structure of the political power—in the bureaucratic sense of the term—that governs his future society. These were not the ideas of greatest interest to progressive thought, however. What progressivism drew from *Looking Backward* was the principal points of its implicit polemic against the evident aspects of social degradation under laissez-faire. Bellamy's novel provided the progressives with yet another demonstration that the evils they were denouncing were not at all "natural" results of the growth of the reigning system but, instead, the consequences of an erroneous conception of industrial development and of the weakness of the public institutions. Indeed, Bellamy is responsible for one of the most suggestive—and, of course, wholly literary—images of the state of things in this epoch. In *Looking Backward*, the old nineteenth-century order is compared to a long voyage in a stagecoach with the rich comfortably seated on the lurching vehicle and the poor, like a draft team, bent in the effort to draw it along.

The central idea of Thorstein Veblen's *Theory of the Leisure Class* is that, in the age of the machine, industrial efficiency is the basic condition of existence of society; if modern society wishes to survive, it must know how to adapt its forms to the development of productive capacity. [136] This fundamental concept takes its place within a theoretical perspective that can be related to the principles of institutionalist economics, correlated, in Veblen's case, with various evolutionist concepts that strongly oppose the neoclassic theory of prosperity. Veblen's two principal works, *The Theory of the Leisure Class* (1899) and *The Theory of Business Enterprise* (1904), affirm that in modern capitalism a sharp conflict is destined to develop between the production of money and the production of goods, between the economic management and the technical management of enterprises.

... There is a class struggle under capitalism, not between capitalists and proletarians but between businessmen and engineers. Pecuniary habit of thought unites bankers, brokers, lawyers, and managers in a defense of private acquisition as the central principle of business enterprise. In contrast, the discipline of the machine falls on the workmen in industry, and more especially on the technicians and engineers that supervise them. [137]

Thus does Mark Blaug summarize the terms in which modern industrial civilization is described by Veblen, whose analysis has certain inflections that would be interesting to compare with the concepts of Charles Fourier.

These convictions were related in many ways to the basic hypotheses of certain progressive and reform currents engaged in the fight for efficiency in public institutions, particularly in regard to municipal administration. Furthermore, Veblen attributed a role of values to the institutions, inasmuch as the institutions are crystallizations of determined "schemes of life," the same schemes the progressive spirit was trying to change on the basis of democratic tradition and "participation." Finally, Veblen's writings also contain a forceful criticism of the distortions of the financial system of industry. In pointing out the structural contradiction between financial management and industrial management, Veblen's theories offered support to certain basic concepts of progressivism. The progressives, indeed, vociferously denounced such contradictions, not only in their general fight for "efficiency" but very explicitly in their pleas for a "technocratic" policy of control over finance. This aspect of Veblen's theories also contributed solidly to the antimonopolistic ideology of an epoch in which voices of protest were being raised ever more insistently against the growing "Morganization" of the American economy, despite the passage of the Sherman Antitrust Act in 1890.

Business versus *industry*: between the two terms there was no space for the problem of *labor*. This particular limitation of the "problem" afforded a reassuring contradiction, "in the family," and its correspondence to a similar limitation in the battles fought by the more radical form of progressivism need hardly be emphasized. In Veblen, the urban reformers of the turn of the century found ideas of great significance for their own "antipredatory" actions, with which they intended to oppose the spreading power of laissez-faire's system of finance over the world of the city.

Veblen, Bellamy, and George represent three substantially different ways of confronting the evils of American society at the end of the nineteenth century. Rather than concentrating on the objective differences among them and the diverse motivations behind *The Theory of the Leisure Class, Looking Backward,* and *Progress and Poverty,* I have preferred to focus on a certain common ground in the thought of the three authors. While this consonance of motives and solutions is obviously only a matter of tendency, it is nevertheless symptomatic that it occurs precisely in relation to certain concepts and issues of central importance to the phenomenon I am attempting to analyze and reconstruct here. It is this nucleus of common themes that must be borne in mind in order to comprehend the *modus operandi* of the progressive movements in regard to urban reform. These writers must also be referred to in an attempt to understand how it came about that, in the course of the first decades of this century, the comprehensive unity of the nineteenth-century "progressive impulse" split, even on the issue of the city, into two positions that were ultimately to prove antithetical: the one, traditionally progressive, the other, inventively reformist.

The New Impulse of Urban Planning in the Progressive Era

The matters considered in the preceding pages became topics of much study and debate in the first years of this century. Approached in different ways and from different perspectives, they appeared in such publications as Richard T. Ely's *Monopoly and Trust* (1900) and the works of William Ripley, and they left their traces in the policies of Theodore Roosevelt as well as in the politics of Woodrow Wilson. They proved most congenial, however, to the fight for reform in urban administration.

The necessity of questioning and resolving the way in which the American city was managed was brought to the fore by a long series of publications, among which were Frank Parsons's *The City for the People* (1900); Ely's *The Coming City* (1902), and Frederic C. Howe's *The City: The Hope of Democracy,* as well as the writings of Albert Shaw, founder of the *American Review of Reviews.* At the turn of the century numerous civic associations, of local as well as national scale, were also created; they aimed at the improvement of living conditions in the cities and ultimately exercised a notable influence in effecting the first urban reforms. In addition to the Women's Municipal League, the most significant organizations of national scale were the National Municipal League, founded in 1894, the American League for Civic Improvement, founded in 1900, and the

American Civic Association, founded in 1904, of which Charles Mulford Robinson was secretary. These associations organized campaigns to publicize their objectives and promoted some interesting exhibitions, which contributed to making the problems of city administration and urban planning seem more real to the public. These activities may be considered the first manifestations of that project for education in planning, which remained one of the most original initiatives of progressive urbanism.

Although these associations were by and large philanthropic in origin and eminently private in character, they did not limit their work to purely charitable social assistance. Far from being merely passive, they exercised a twofold pressure: on the one hand, by publicizing the gravity of the conditions in which a good part of the population lived and, on the other, by closely pursuing the political powers and urging reforms and provisions that had much in common with the aims of the progressives. Their efforts were explicitly recognized by Ely, who showed that the improvements obtained in the administration of New York City were due in large measure to the activities of organizations such as the State Charities Aid Association, the Charity Organization Society, and the Women's Health Protective Association.[138] The necessary relationship among the improvement of living conditions, projects of urban restructuring, the creation of green spaces and adequate road systems, and the revision of administrative institutions became the prime object of study for urban planners, as demonstrated, for example, by Robinson's writings. The reawakening of a collective civic interest almost appears to have been a more important goal than the actual planning projects themselves. John Ihlder asserted, "What we are aiming at is not a series of public improvements. These are only incidental. What we desire is the creation of a new sense of citizenship, a new and vital interest in the city as our common heritage. If we can secure that the improvements will follow inevitably."[139]

In this idealistic atmosphere, steps were taken in certain specific problem areas, destined, despite their limited scope, to exert considerable influence on American planning theories. Housing for the poor was one of the urgent problems during this period.[140] Philanthropic activities and health investigations—often promoted and financed by the associations cited above—dramatically focused attention on this problem, while books such as Jacob A. Riis's *How the Other Half Lives* (1890) and the nascent realistic fiction attracted the attention of an ever wider public.

With the end of the nineteenth century, the role of philanthropy declined, but not as rapidly as might be supposed. Even if they had lost some of their original characteristics, private citizens' organizations received a strong new impetus in the early years of the twentieth century, and civic associations began to exercise an increasingly important role by integrating their efforts with those of public institutions or even merging with them. This phenomenon reveals the way in which problems related to urban reform became objects of general interest on the part of successively more varied social groups. It was in this atmosphere that urban planning further matured as a discipline through experiences of a progressively more defined and specialized nature that accompanied the slower process of institutional reform. A typical example of this general phenomenon is provided by New York, where some of the most eminent figures of the progressive movement were active, and where one of the most advanced urban laws of the epoch was passed.

In 1894, New York City established the Tenement House Committee. At the very end of the century the committee tackled the problem of the revision of the building code that since the Tenement Law of 1867 had favored the development of the dumb-bell tenement. Among the principal authors of the revision, who had to struggle with Tammany and Mayor Robert A. Van Wyck, were Lawrence Veiller, Robert W. de Forest, and Otto M. Eidlitz, all associated with philanthropic organizations and all destined to play major roles in subsequent years. Veiller was one of the most active supporters of the initiative; in 1899 he guided the Tenement House Committee of the Charity Organization Society in the work of revising the building code and organized the provocative Tenement House Exhibition of 1900. In the same year, supported by Governor Theodore Roosevelt, Veiller fought for the formation of the New York State Tenement House Commission, the proposals of which were adopted in 1901, although not without strong opposition. For many years after 1901 Veiller directed the Tenement House Department, which controlled the application of the new Tenement House Law.[141]

Veiller's work is remembered not only for the transformation it brought about in the role of the civic associations but also because the building regulations adopted in New York during these years, based on the theories he so actively supported, strongly influenced the urban reforms numerous other American cities were preparing to carry out. In 1914 Veiller published *Model Housing Law*, which was substantially critical of the results obtained in the first years of the century. Despite all his merits, however, it appears that Edith Elmer Wood's negative judgment of Veiller's efforts was fully justified. Wood attributed the predominantly "restrictive" character of the various housing laws adopted in the United States during the first decades of the century to Veiller's political position and that of the National Housing Association. In her view, a restrictive regulation could in no way be considered a law for the resolution of the housing problem, which had to be solved, instead, in the terms of a comprehensive legislation on housing; a regulation for the tenement house could produce only limited effects: "Restrictive housing legislation is that form which seeks to prevent the erection of bad houses through the establishment and enforcement of minimum standards of light, air, sanitation, and safety. It may also prevent filth and dilapidation by establishing and enforcing minimum standards of maintenance. The best restrictive legislation is only negative. It will prevent the bad. It will not produce the good."[142]

The New York legislation, in fact, provided no more than a series of controlling regulations. Instead, Wood's criticisms and the view of the housing problem elaborated after 1917 by future members of the Regional Planning Association of America were aimed at a comprehensive reform that would take into account the legislative and institutional aspects of the problem and plan the financing of housing projects.

The same voices that had been raised against the restrictive housing legislation also criticized New York's zoning provisions. The Tenement Law of 1901 and the Zoning Ordinance of 1916 were politically similar. Indeed, the supporters of the zoning law came from the same circles as those who had put through the tenement reforms; this was particularly true of the principal theoretician of zoning, Edward M. Bassett.

The Zoning Ordinance of 1916, although it was another product of restrictive legislation, derived ultimately from the controversies and many studies and investigations on urban congestion. Benjamin C. Marsh—a disciple of Simon Patten, influenced in part by the ideas of Henry George—was particularly concerned with this problem; Marsh was active in the Committee on Congestion of Population and in 1908 organized an exhibition on congestion at the American Museum of Natural History in New York.[143] In 1910, New York Mayor William J. Gaynor charged Marsh with the task of preparing a report on urban congestion; from the results of this investigation stemmed the creation of the Heights of Buildings Commission in 1913 and the Commission on Building Districts and Restrictions in 1914, with Bassett as president.[144]

The zoning law enacted in 1916 established three principal categories of zones in Manhattan: residential districts, commercial districts, and districts with no restriction. The more radical critics of this legislation have at various times pointed out that it was, in reality, far less a remedy for congestion than an incentive for speculation. Werner Hegemann wrote, "In New York the last legal 'limitations' of this time-honored 'individualism' were defined by the 'new' Tenement House Law of 1901, the Zoning Ordinance of 1916, and the Multiple Dwelling Law of 1929. . . . The most unique of these ordinances is the Zoning Resolution of 1916 which defines the different 'zones' or districts in which a New Yorker can build either exclusively business or residential buildings, or—in other 'zones'—indiscriminately anything he wishes."[145]

In an article on the 1916 law, one of its drafters, George B. Ford, explained that it had resulted from some obvious compromises, dictated principally by "the necessity of conserving real estate values." Ford concluded his article by asserting that the zoning ordinance should be considered only "half" of a law that actually aimed at resolving the problem of housing.[146] This somewhat questionable statement only confirms that the efforts of the progressive movement were now increasingly conditioned by a relationship created between the progressives themselves and the more dynamic strata of private enterprise. This convergence of interests came about through the gradual weakening and replacement of the old patterns and alignments of laissez-faire, the philanthropic origins of a good part of urban reformism, and the changed sociopolitical conditions that were beginning to make the chaotic development of the city disadvantageous for the large corporate enterprises in their attempt to "rationalize" speculation and the increment of property values.

It is thus not by chance that the only public efforts in the field of housing that were not merely restrictive were those of "model settlements" for workers or inhabitants of low-income groups, situated, moreover, on the periphery of the large cities. Among the examples that might be cited, the work of the Massachusetts Homestead Commission is particularly interesting and had a certain significance for reform proposals made after 1917. Edith Elmer Wood, writing in 1919, was among the first to draw the attention of planners to the work of this commission by singling out its three principal contributions: the direct public financing of low-cost housing; experimentation with a type of planning that begins from the problem of housing; and educational and propaganda work favoring the diffusion of planning experiments.

When the commission was first formed in 1909, it was animated by concepts that did not differ substantially from those that traditionally inspired such undertakings. The principal function assigned to the commission was to indicate areas to be acquired and eventually put on the market under favorable conditions, with the aim of encouraging the population to move away from the congested areas of the city. It thus operated according to a scheme that went back in general outlook to the Homestead Act of 1862. Moreover, one of the influential members of the commission was Kenyon L. Butterfield, a supporter of the Country Life Movement, and one of the concerns of the MHC was creating agricultural schools. Among the planning projects considered by the commission as models, the experiments made in New Zealand and Australia once again figured prominently.[147] In 1913, however, the MHC was authorized to enlarge the scope of its activity and to experiment with the construction and autonomous management of residential settlements; it was thus transformed into a public planning and financing agency. After proposing a series of projects, among them that for Billerica, between 1916 and 1917, the commission received an appropriation of $50,000 from the state, which it employed in constructing twelve dwellings in Lowell, designed by Arthur C. Comey. In 1919 the activity of the MHC came to an end.[148]

Despite the modesty of its actual accomplishments, the commission's reports for the seven years between 1913 and 1919 are important documents. The work of the MHC went beyond mere assistance; in contrast to the policy pursued by "restrictive" legislation, its program prefigured a planning policy based on direct public financing, on the integration of planning and economic management, and on the study of advanced residential standards. In addition to its important propaganda activity, the work of the commission demonstrated the undeniable improvements resulting from the practice of planning as complementary to the problem of housing.[149]

Plan of Lowell, Massachusetts, indicating
works completed or projected by the
Massachusetts Homestead Commission. The
innermost circle encloses the business district.
The numbers correspond to the MHC's projects; blacked areas indicate completed
works and outlined areas, projects under
consideration.

A one-family house (type 1) designed for
an MHC project in Lowell by Arthur C.
Comey, 1917-18.

Zoning Will Prevent This

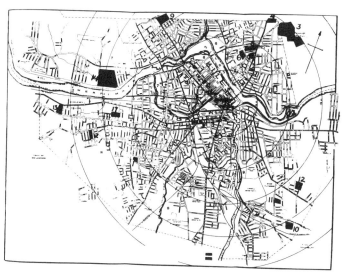

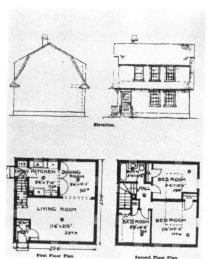

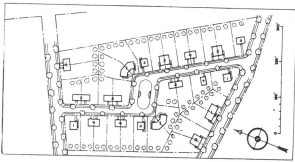

Cartoon that appeared in an Evansville,
Indiana, newspaper in 1924 during a local
campaign for the adoption of zoning legislation. Following the example of New
York, the enactment of such laws was
sought in many American cities.

Plan of the subdivision of a 7-acre plot for
an MHC project in Lowell by Arthur C.
Comey, 1917-18.

Plan of the subdivision of a plot acquired
by the MHC in the area of Parker Street,
Lowell, by Arthur C. Comey, 1917-18.

As already noted, the particular character of the MHC initiative was related to certain foreign projects—particularly the Advances to Workers Acts of 1906 and 1913 and the Workers' Dwelling Acts of 1905, 1906, 1914 in New Zealand—but the commission's activity also reflected some common conceptual components of the progressive planning tradition. This relationship is clear, for instance, in the MHC's resuscitation of the homestead ideal as a solution to congestion, its decentralist views, and the attention it gave to the formal development and social implications of the one-family house. Nevertheless, within the panorama of urban planning during this period, the Massachusetts Homestead Commission remained a substantial anomaly, and it was precisely its most unusual aspect that would attract the attention of the reformers of the 1920s.

European Influences on Urban Planning in the Progressive Era

The discussion and enactment of zoning laws, which extended from New York to numerous other American cities, was influenced in large part by the study of what had recently been done in Europe, above all in Germany.[150] American architects and planners visiting Europe began to take more interest in the application and consequences of building regulations in European cities than in the great Baroque and Renaissance examples of urban planning. In the meantime, the manuals and other writings of the English and, even more, the German urbanists became increasingly well known, judging from the ample space given to such literature in the bibliographies of American publications during the period.

At the Town Planning Conference in London in 1910, America and Europe exchanged experiences. Obviously, this was not the only occasion for such a confrontation, and the ideas of the European theorists had certainly begun to circulate well before that date, but the conference was in any case an exceptional and significant event. In London, Stübben, Eberstadt, Geddes, Howard, Unwin, and Hénard encountered Burnham, Robinson, and Bassett, and the discussion that took place concerned not only theoretical positions but, indeed, actual examples and types of urban planning.

The European manuals contained ideas—reaffirmed in part at the London conference by Stübben—that had been partially carried out in America, particularly in certain City Beautiful projects. This was the case, for instance, of the American planning projects based on a superficially organic vision of urban development, in which the essential purpose of the plan was to coordinate and rationalize—principally by means of the layout of streets—already existing urban subdivisions that remained internally unaffected by the plan except in the extent to which it accelerated the dynamics of the real-estate market. Other examples were American planning projects in which the problem of urban form was considered as the simple product of the restructuring and integration of different functions. These practices and the viewpoint inspiring them were the direct premises to the enactment of restrictive urban legislation. At the London conference, however, it was precisely this concept of planning that was criticized.[151]

For primarily "formal" reasons, Burnham's plans—not street plans, but city plans—were essentially the only alternative offered at the time to the state of things as presented by the Americans at the London conference. Thus except for Burnham's work, Rudolf Eberstadt's ironic warning to the English urbanists against too much admiration for the German street-planning system could have been extended to America: "The admiration for this system came too late . . . at the very moment when we wished to do away with it." The new proposals being made in Germany were, in fact, more in line with the ideas put forward in the United States by the critics of merely restrictive legislation. In London, Eberstadt affirmed, "Especially with regard to the objects of this Conference I should say Germany is the only land where you can study closely the inseparable connection between town planning, street planning, and the basis of social life—that is, housing."[152]

The influence of German legislation is evident in the ample information on the regulations of cities such as Düsseldorf, Frankfurt, and Berlin contained in an official document of the United States Senate, published in 1910 along with the proceedings of the First National Conference on City Planning, held in Washington in 1909. It was not only because of their zoning laws, however, that Germany and England were taken as models by American planners. Rather, it was the Garden City movement that most directly attracted the attention of the progressives and subsequently of the reformers. Among the principal supporters of the garden city in the United States was again Benjamin C. Marsh, who sustained the validity of the works of Ebenezer Howard and his followers, as well as of the German workers' villages. In 1906, with the support of rich financiers, the Garden City Association of America was founded; during the same period American journals began to carry numerous articles about European garden cities.[153] Raymond Unwin and, to a lesser degree, Thomas Adams were the most attentively followed sources of information about experiments and ideas on the other side of the Atlantic.[154]

The success of the garden city in America had various reasons. In the first place, the garden city was in keeping with decentralist theories that received considerable support from the progressives in their fight for a policy capable of resolving the problems of congestion. Second, the garden city was considered an effective model for attracting the financial interest of business enterprises, because of the stable yield it guaranteed, the possibility it offered for enlarging the real-estate market, and the means it provided for removing the labor force from urban unrest. Third, as a new and entirely planned city and a programed formula for its management, the garden city made possible not only a series of economies that permitted the realization of higher residential standards but also the definitive integration of the housing problem and the planning operation. For these reasons the garden city offered an "alternative"—and it was taken up as such—to the results of restrictive legislation. By guaranteeing investment an "equitable" yield but not aggravating congestion, the garden city permitted progressivism and financial power to find still further points of convergence.

One of the first projects undertaken from this joint perspective was the construction of Forest Hills Gardens, New York, financed by the Russell Sage Foundation and designed by Grosvenor Atterbury and Frederick Law Olmsted, Jr. Even if Forest Hills did not fully achieve its objective, it represented an important precedent for similar subsequent initiatives—not the least because of its high building and planning standards.[155] The influence of the garden city was strongest in designs made for small settlements and suburbs. A. P. Melton's mature example of the traditional grid plan in his 1907 design for the town of Gary, Indiana, is clearly an exception when it is compared with the numerous communities of the epoch that were comparable to the European garden suburb and garden city, by this time a constant model in America. In its repetition of uniform urban modules spaced along a continuous connecting strip, however, Gary was one of the most interesting urban designs of the period, despite its traditionalism.[156]

The town of Torrance, California, designed in 1912, was also related to the theories of the garden city—less for the plan by Frederick Law Olmsted, Jr., however, than for the system of control over building development exercised by the Union Tool Company, which entrusted Irving Gill with the architectural coordination of the entire community. Until the war numerous industries undertook projects of this type. Some of the better examples are Kohler Village, Kohler, Wisconsin; Mark, Indiana, planned by Howard Van Doren Shaw; Goodyear Heights, Akron, Ohio, by Warren H. Manning; and the particularly valid design by Morell and Nichols for Morgan Park, Duluth, Minnesota.[157]

Quite different from these examples is the plan by Bertram G. Goodhue for the town of Tyrone, New Mexico. Here the architecture is inspired by the local tradition, while the plan is a curious combination of a symmetrical "monumental" center and a naturalistic dispersion of the surrounding residential settlements. Clarence Stein collaborated with Goodhue in this project.[158]

A typical architect and town planner of the period was John Nolen, student of Simon Patten in Philadelphia, who began his professional activity in 1904-05 and was a major figure in American architecture through the New Deal years; during the 1910s and 1920s he was one of the most successful professional in the country. Despite the obvious contradictions in his work implied by this fact, Nolen's designs and numerous writings exemplify the uncertainties, difficulties, and achievements of the phase of transition from the "enlightened" paternalism of the nineteenth century to the reformism of the twentieth. During his long career, Nolen produced a vast number of works, but within the context of this essay certain aspects of his thought are of even greater interest.

In a book published in 1912, Nolen traced his activity during his earliest professional years, analyzing his projects for Roanoke, San Diego, Montclair, Glen Ridge, Reading, and Madison. In the initial pages and conclusion of this work, he expressed some interesting convictions, not new for the epoch but set forth with particular coherence, on the value of planning. For Nolen, too,

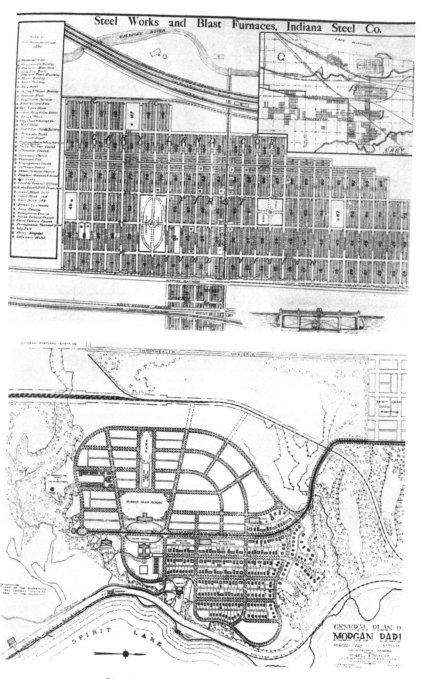

Plan for the industrial town of Gary,
Indiana, by A. P. Melton, 1907.

Plan for the industrial community of Morgan
Park, Duluth, Minnesota, by Morell and
Nichols, 1917.

"aesthetic ends" were a secondary objective, but not in the sense that this conviction was held by someone like Ihlder; rather, Nolen maintained that the modern concept of "beauty" was based on the social utility and functional performance of the results. For Nolen, planning was a "science" that permitted one to know the needs of the urban community and provide for them by creating services.[159]

In his commitment to this theory, Nolen gave shape to principles of urban reform that summarized the experiences traced in the foregoing pages and were among the most advanced of the period. He insisted on the necessity of carrying out large-scale urban surveys and preparing comprehensive urban plans for housing-reform programs. His main objective, however, in pursuit of which he was active in the principal professional associations of the time, was to obtain recognition of an institutional role for planning offices within municipal administrations. Nolen was convinced that the increased importance planning was achieving was only an aspect—and certainly not the least significant—of the fact that "the field of collectivism is being steadily extended and its power increased."[160] This belief led Nolen to assert the need for legislative and administrative reforms that would guarantee municipalities the possibility of obtaining credit, thus acquiring an assured financing that would allow them to compete with private enterprise.[161]

Characteristically, Nolen was particularly impressed in a number of trips to Europe by the legislation adopted in German and Swiss cities and by English progress in housing. The influence of the garden-city tradition is evident in his plans, but the most interesting aspect of Nolen's numerous projects for American cities remains his constant emphasis on the complementary relationship between urban and institutional reform. In an article in 1916, he summed up a conviction that may be considered canonical in the "philosophy" of this epoch: "There are really three parties to every land subdivision: the owner or operator; the prospective user, either as owner or tenant; and the public. Surely it would represent a great advantage if we could come to look upon these three parties as partners in a common enterprise with certain overlapping interests in the proper subdivision and sale of land."[162] To this end, Nolen concluded, it was necessary to create public planning agencies the activity of which, far from harming the land and real-estate market, would surely increase its value.

The eclectic diversity of Nolen's work is striking. In the project for San Diego, for instance, his primary concern was with organizing the accesses to the city visually and functionally; in his design of the water front, he adopted typical City Beautiful solutions, which also appear in the broad diagonal arteries and urban perspectives of his plan for Madison. At Reading, Pennsylvania, on the other hand, one encounters a very different situation, explained by Nolen in the following terms: "It is a mistake to confine city planning to consideration of streets, public buildings, parks and play grounds. A vital feature is the homes for the people."[163] Each project was endowed with some specific characteristic; at

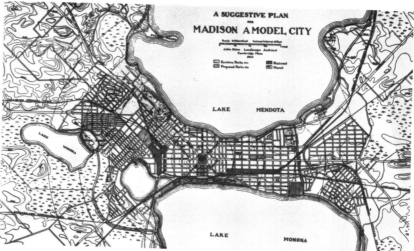

Proposed design for the bay front, San Diego, California, by John Nolen, 1908.

Plan for Madison, Wisconsin, by John Nolen, 1910.

Plan for the industrial village of Kistler, Pennsylvania, John Nolen, 1918.

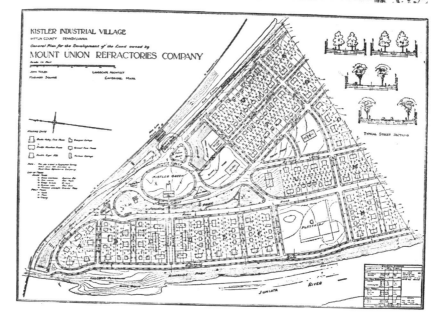

Reading the entire plan is conceived in terms of the "destruction" of the existing grid scheme, while the plan of Kistler, Pennsylvania, is distinguished by a distribution that can be related to the tradition of the romantic suburb. Rather than formal inconsistency, however, this diversity denotes a pragmatic approach. For Nolen, as already observed, planning was not primarily a means to "aesthetic ends" but, rather, an instrument of reform; to the achievement of such a goal, "system, wise planning, public-spirited enterprise" was Nolen's clear and consequential formula.

Nolen's designs may also be considered from a purely formal point of view, but this is not, in my opinion, the only way of judging them. Quite beyond their architectural forms, they are unified plans in which architecture is significant only to the extent that it contributes to underlining the unity and continuity of the urban structure. Nolen's work indeed affirms that planning is not a task of individual and partial interventions but an instrument for elaborating comprehensive urban designs, of which architecture is only a part, and not the most important.[164]

In this context, it is useful to turn briefly to one of Nolen's collaborators, Earle S. Draper. Although Draper's works referred to here were actually produced in the 1920s, they are, nevertheless, closely related to the work discussed in the preceding pages and, indeed, drew their inspiration from the same sources. In the years immediately after the war, Draper was particularly active in North Carolina, South Carolina, and Georgia, where he designed workers' villages for the textile industry, which was enjoying a period of prosperity in the early 1920s. In speaking about these projects Draper explicitly affirmed that his model was the garden city, a relationship that is quite obvious from an examination of one of his better plans, that for the town of Chicopee, Georgia, commissioned by the firm of Johnson and Johnson. Equally interesting is his design for the Calloway Mills settlement at La Grange, Georgia, in regard to which Draper asserted the characteristic progressive theory that an undertaking financed by private capital and made effective by good standards of planning could serve as a model for municipal administrations that still lacked urban legislation and planning agencies.

One of the most interesting aspects of Draper's plans is the attention he gave to the study of planning costs; in his designing of house types, his investigations became a sort of cost-benefit analysis. The villages he built in the South further demonstrate the solid status of the garden-city theory in American planning during the first decades of this century; the importance acquired by this theory takes on particular significance in Draper's case if one considers that during the New Deal he would direct the Land Planning and Housing Division of the Tennessee Valley Authority. In addition to his adherence to the garden-city model, still other aspects of Draper's work are completely in keeping with the type of planning described in these pages. They include his analytic interest in the economic components of planning and housing, his integration of planning and housing in terms of design, and his concept, typical of the Progressive Era,

Plan for Venice, Florida, by John
Nolen, 1926.

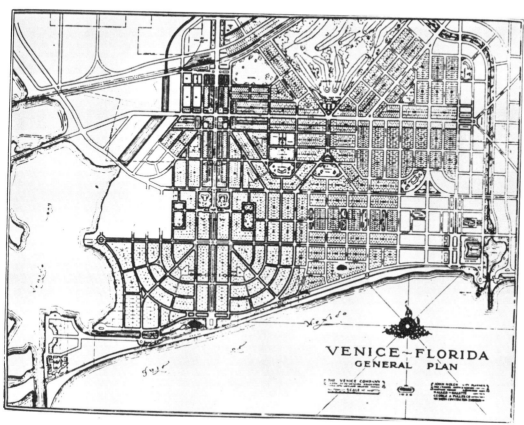

Plan for the industrial town of Chicopee,
Georgia, by Earle S. Draper, 1927.

Plan for the residential settlement of Calloway Mills in the industrial district of La
Grange, Georgia, by Earle S. Draper, about
1927.

of the convertibility of "enlightened" private undertakings and public initiatives.

Draper also provides a forthright statement on the sociopolitical aims animating the creation of garden cities, industrial villages, and residential suburbs for low-income groups: "While it is too early to definitely state that village improvement has had a strong effect in combating bolshevism and minimizing the serious labor difficulties which have attended industrial development in other sections of the country, it is only fair to state that in the opinion of some of the best informed mill men in the South the general improvement work has been a not inconsiderable factor in reducing the labor unrest to the minimum."[165]

The "City Functional" and the Concepts of Progressivism

During the first twenty years of this century, planning considerably improved and refined its techniques. Urban plans became comprehensive projects of urban renewal, supported by laws and regulations that, beginning with the provisions for zoning and housing, became increasingly efficient. In addition, the idea of the garden city proved congenial to the American tradition; taken up as a model for the urban projects of "enlightened" private enterprise, it led to the ever more thorough study of problems regarding location, the economic and financial aspects of urban projects, and standards of planning and housing.[166]

The construction of workers' villages brought with it undeniable improvements in location, services, and housing. These projects were generally privately financed and aimed at attracting business interest in this type of investment. Such projects could guarantee capital a "just" remuneration in the form of a stabilized yield, which would remain essentially unaffected by the fluctuations of the market; this favorable economic aspect was accompanied by the old theory of the stabilizing effect of this type of settlement project on labor relations. Together, these two cardinal concepts formed the principal theme of the progressives' campaign: planning was a useful and remunerative investment, not an unproductive expenditure. Nolen's views were characteristic; in addition to all the other difficulties inherent in the creation of ways to control urban development was the problem of enabling the public institutions to compete with private enterprise. The propaganda for the plan as an investment, attractive to the private investor, could equally well arouse the interest of the municipal administrations.

In this effort, the work of the voluntary organizations was of the greatest importance. In their battle for administrative efficiency—a cause that often brought together progressives, alert businessmen, and planners—civic clubs, commercial clubs, chambers of commerce, and voters' leagues promoted and financed studies, urban plans, and even some actual urban renovations. It was during these years that the idea of a "managerial" city administration, of a municipality run by "pure technicians," took hold. Behind such proposals it is not difficult to sense the desire to "remove" control of the cities from the traditional political forces, from the hands of the political machines. In pursuit of these aims, the principle of seeking direct public approval of urban-reform initiatives was greatly emphasized. Samuel P. Hays has written:

Reformers ... wished not simply to replace bad men with good; they proposed to change the occupational and class origins of decision-makers. Toward this end they sought innovations in the formal machinery of government which could concentrate political power by sharply centralizing the processes of decision-making rather than distribute it through more popular participation in public affairs. According to the liberal view of the Progressive Era, the major political innovations of reform involved the equalization of political power through the primary, the direct election of public officials, and the initiative, referendum, and recall.[167]

A politics of efficiency had to be based on "democratic" reforms that would assure consensus: the technocratic, managerial prospect depended on replacing "participation" with the "politics of consensus." On the administrative side, these changes involved contesting boss rule; on the side of "democracy," however, they signified a substantial victory for the politicoeconomic forces that could benefit from concentrating power and streamlining administration.[168] Concentration of power and apolitical technical management proved to be two sides of the same ideological coin. In supporting the apolitical character of administrative reforms, progressive liberalism split from the reformers who, viewing the situation in almost opposite terms, denounced the liberal institutions as impolitic. Considered within this general context, the social role of the professional town planner is further clarified; between the progressives' fight for efficiency and progressive ideology, planning became the link that reconciled the "values" of the latter with the former.

In the first decade of the twentieth century, architects and planners strengthened their professional associations, or created new ones, in an effort to ensure a continual exchange of experiences and information and to give a social status to the new professional categories. At the same time, publications appeared that gave greater and more detailed attention to planning techniques, statistical studies, and the legislative and administrative aspects of the planning initiatives that were now multiplying throughout America.[169]

In May 1909, the First National Conference on City Planning was held in Washington. The participants at this conference did not limit themselves to mere appraisals of the planning situation in terms of the principal initiatives; rather, they offered the material for a veritable compendium of planning theories. All the themes and issues referred to in the preceding pages were touched on and summarized. Frederick Law Olmsted, Jr., spoke about the European experiments and the example of the German cities. Frederick L. Ford affirmed, "Since 1902 a great number and variety of reports and articles upon city planning have been prepared. . . . If some of the reports now issued had appeared ten years ago they would have been ridiculed as visionary and impracticable. What is the meaning of this great change in public sentiment within seven years? It means a great civic awakening is sweeping this country from the Atlantic to the Pacific and from the Gulf to the Great Lakes." John Nolen, Robert Anderson Pope, and Benjamin C. Marsh reemphasized the economic advantages of planning and its role in resolving congestion; Pope asserted, "City planning through removing the laboring classes from the congested districts promotes industrial efficiency. . . .

Again industrial efficiency is further increased through specially planned transportation facilities, which subordinate the interest of any individual, or group of individuals, to the interests of the whole community. Further, city planning means a great increase in national wealth. It is an economic truism that the industrial economy and efficiency ultimately accrue to the whole people."[170]

Scientific and statistical analyses of urbanized areas were the objects of growing interest during this period and found ready financing. The Russell Sage Foundation, for example, conducted a famous investigation in Pittsburgh, and the "Boston 1915" movement further vitalized that city's strong progressive tradition.[171] A new profession had gained recognition and the discipline was widely taught in the universities. Meanwhile, newspapers and magazines published increasingly frequent reports on the activities of various civic associations and municipal administrations. Journals such as the *American City* dedicated part of their pages to profiles of particularly distinguished public administrators or to information on the latest technological innovations for the improvement of urban services. Photographs of administrators, mayors, firemen, policemen, and ladies of various charitable organizations beside fire trucks, hydrants, street lamps, buses, and ambulances were also a common feature.[172]

In 1917, the town planning committee of the American Institute of Architects published *City Planning Progress in the United States*, which listed in minute detail all urban legislation enacted and planning projects undertaken in American cities with populations of 25,000 or more. In addition to being a reference work, the book was obviously intended as a propaganda instrument, and the publishers took care to inform the reader that the material was in no way protected by copyright. The introduction lists, in almost chronological order, all the steps necessary in organizing a plan, and emphasis is placed on technique rather than content. The final goal of the organizers—the educational campaign, the propaganda that wins consensus—was presented quite precisely as a technique.[173] The primary example was the publicity campaign organized around Burnham's plan for Chicago. The "City Functional" was undoubtedly a more complex project and involved a more mature technical instrumentation than Burnham's grand City Beautiful projects, but it had nevertheless to obtain and create the same interest and an equal consensus—that, indeed, was its aim. Thus planning was being transformed into an instrument of order: the efficient city was above all a model of stability and social equilibrium, and, as Pope maintained, it is a truism that efficiency brings advantages for all—in order to achieve it, all must agree to produce it.

Meanwhile, others had a very clear idea of the most immediate advantages of the efficient, functional city. Opening the Washington conference in 1909, Henry Morgenthau affirmed the necessity of creating parks, gardens, services for crowded areas, and good housing; within fifteen years the whole southern part of Manhattan would be available "for business and commercial purposes and hotels."[174] The work and ideology of planning and the concepts of efficiency of the new post-laissez-faire business enterprise were brought together in a comprehensive project of education about planning. The cities' riches belong to everyone, thus everyone must be responsible for the rational employment of their capital. The myth of the just, equilibrated, efficient city had become technical in character; by continually bringing the great values of American democracy up to date, this myth was now "scientifically" pursuing its political course.

Another result of the Progressive Era was important provisions for safeguarding the nation's natural wealth and stimulating the agricultural economy. Legislation to conserve natural resources corresponded with progressive businessmen and planners' ideals of rationalization of production, while the "return to the land" was another facet of the many-sided controversy over urban congestion. During Theodore Roosevelt's presidency, Gifford Pinchot headed the national Division of Forestry and subsequently the United States Forest Service, created in 1905. In 1909 the National Conservation Association was founded, with Charles W. Eliot as president.

The revival of the homestead tradition also reflected the policy position of a large part of the progressive movement, destined to be overridden, as already noted, by the position of the reformers, among them Thomas J. Walsh, Robert M. La Follette, and George W. Norris. These men, going beyond the primarily "conservationist" policy of the progressives, took on the problem of comprehensive legislation and planning for the utilization of resources. In this field, too, the largely restrictive sectional policy of 1910s progressivism was proving inadequate. In the controversy provoked by the passage of the Water Power Act of 1920, these two positions were clearly defined; numerous aspects of this controversy can elucidate the origins of some of the most important provisions of the New Deal.[175]

From the First World War to the New Deal: The Regional Planning Association of America

The ideals and technical achievements of the urban planning of the Progressive Era were further defined and developed during the First World War. This was made possible by the federal government's adoption of a wartime policy of direct intervention in the economic sphere, which had important consequences for urban planning in terms of the construction of industrial settlements and workers' housing. This policy actually lasted only about twelve months, but in the atmosphere of a "war economy," it seemed, at least briefly, that the reformers' long campaign for active participation by public institutions and for federal financing of building and planning activities had finally succeeded. Garden cities and model villages rose throughout the United States, and architects and planners worked directly for federal agencies. A new way of directing the economy and of working in various fields of production appeared to be evolving.

During this period, the federal government financed the construction of a large number of settlements, mostly for workmen, and many thousands of workers were directly affected by these projects. This activity gave rise to a search for new standards for building and planning and resulted in the definitive formulation of many ideas partially experimented in earlier years. Understanding the transformation of the professional mentality and the technical progress made in building and planning methods as a result of these wartime experiences is extremely important, even from a historical point of view, in placing the activities and accomplishments of the New Deal in a more exact perspective. During the second decade of the century, at the same time as the war emergency experiments were undertaken, urban theories were continually enriched by knowledge of European activities, and, in addition, new information was arriving on the Soviet Union's achievements in economic planning, to which a certain regionalist-oriented component of the Conservation movement was particularly receptive. All these elements were consolidated in the 1920s and formed the theoretical and technical background of what might be termed the "tradition" of the New Deal. The Progressive Era had brought to the fore the need for a wholly new conception of the function and use of public institutions at all levels of government.[176] The activities examined in the following pages were only part of the attempt to give real form to this new conception, to develop theory into policy, and to transform ideas into institutions.

The impulse toward reform of the period between the end of World War I and the 1930s was best interpreted by the Regional Planning Association of America, through both its ideology and its actual work in the field of building and planning. Within the panorama of American culture, this association, formed of private individuals of various professions, stood out by virtue of its intellectual stature and dignity. Its members' ideas were a typical expression of the continuity and consistency of the Yankee cultural tradition. By grounding themselves in this tradition they represented not only the synthesis between the theoretically formulated needs promulgated in the Progressive Era and the hopes and experiences offered by the wartime economic policy but also the actual link between these conceptions and the ultimate synthesis of the New Deal.

The Construction of Workers' Villages during the First World War

When the United States entered the war in April 1917, its production system was in the course of full expansion. American industry was already committed to meeting growing demands and supporting the war effort of the European allies. With the country's direct participation in the conflict, the production flow had to be not merely maintained but, indeed, very sharply stepped up to meet the demands of its own armed forces. The efficient organization of production, the financing of industrial enterprises, and the maintenance of an adequate labor force immediately became central and pressing issues.

In response to the situation, the federal government made a series of provisions and adopted an emergency policy that may be called that of a "war economy." In part, this policy was based on the utilization of the federal government's buying power, which functioned as a price-stabilizing measure and, at the same time, favored the rationalization of production processes and

ensured the provision of services aimed at increasing productivity. The organization of this "piloted" economic system was provided by federal agencies controlling certain fundamental sectors of the economy, such as the War Industries
Board, the Food Administration, Fuel Administration, Railroad Administration,
and Shipping boards, which constituted, in embryonic form, the institutional
structures of a planned economy.[177]

In pursuit of this policy and within this general structure, particular agencies
were organized and charged with creating a large number of workmen's settlements or with providing urban services, according to the requirements of the war
industries. The most important of these agencies were the Division of Transportation and Housing of the Emergency Fleet Corporation (EFC) of the United
States Shipping Board; the United States Housing Corporation (USHC) of the
Department of Labor, directed by Otto M. Eidlitz; and the Ordnance Department. Design work for the new settlements began at the end of 1917, after an
initial federal government grant of $50 million to the United States Shipping
Board in September and the allotment of an equal sum to the Department of
Labor.

In the *Journal of the American Institute of Architects* the federal government
had been strongly urged to make such provisions by a group of architects and
planners gathered around Charles H. Whitaker, all of whom fought for the
creation of federal planning agencies and insisted on the need for government-
financed housing. These were the same voices that had been raised against purely
restrictive urban legislation. Wood, for example, explicitly considered the construction of the "war villages" as overturning of the restrictive outlook. The
articles pressing for such provisions, which appeared more and more frequently
in the journal, were often heated in tone. An editorial published in September
1917, for instance, stated: "At Bridgeport, Connecticut, for example, a new
factory for war purposes is being rushed to completion. It will employ a
thousand operatives. There is at present, as we are informed, not a single house
available for rent in Bridgeport, nor is there any capital available for building.
The Government is, we are told, furnishing money for the new building to
contain the machinery while the housing problem is totally ignored! Could
anything be more shortsighted?"[178]

Whitaker and his group did not limit themselves to denouncing the lack of
government policy on housing, however. The AIA journal also carried an
abundance of accurate information on the efforts of other countries in the area
of wartime construction; the workers' villages built in England, for instance,
were amply covered. Frederick L. Ackerman, sent to England expressly to study
these experiments, published a series of extremely interesting accounts. He
carefully analyzed the legislative aspects of the English projects, their technical
achievements, and their social implications and concluded that only the direct
intervention of the federal government in this sphere of production could assure

procurement of the necessary materials, regularity of consignment, and coordination of design and construction methods; above all, only such intervention could control the inflationary processes of the building industry.[179]

Even with the intervention of the USHC and EFC in the field of low-cost housing, the aims expressed in the journal were realized actually only in part. The direction taken by the government housing policy was largely set by Eidlitz. In reality, these agencies had a double purpose, and their activities were not directed entirely to the problem of dwellings. Only a part of their funds were, in fact, used for the construction of new settlements through federal financing of companies especially created by the industrial enterprises the federal agencies intended to aid in their increasingly difficult task of putting together a sufficient labor force. A large part of the government funds was employed, instead, to improve other services, particularly transportation. Only a fraction of the hundreds of thousands of workers affected by these provisions benefited in terms of new housing.[180]

The aim of the federal intervention was to create conditions of efficiency in relation to production. The operations of the federal agencies enabled industrial enterprises to place the greater part of their investments in production installations by freeing them from the burden of the "social costs" that served to block the dynamics of the labor market. The government's ultimate objective was obviously the overall growth of productive capacity; it was to be achieved not only through industrial expansion but also through a substantial increase in productivity itself. In the context of such a project, the inflated cost of housing presented no small obstacle. Thus the government agencies sought to intervene, first of all, by providing services, largely in the form of adequate transportation; where this plan of action proved impossible or insufficient, they resorted to constructing new settlements, which had the added effect of stimulating a static field of production.[181]

According to the principal supporters of this second type of intervention, its aims were, first, to wrest the land market from the exclusive control of private speculators by exercising an indirect control over prices through the use of public financing; second, to control costs in the building industry—on the one hand, by utilizing the federal agencies' buying power to stabilize prices and, on the other, by imposing standardization in production and in techniques of construction and design; and, third, to define and create new standards for planning and housing. These objectives were partially achieved in the construction of the "war villages," but the projects actually had little direct effect on the future situation in building construction, the real estate market, and planning. In other words, the experience of these twelve months essentially produced only a model, extremely rich in potential but deficient in immediate results.

The abrupt termination of these experiments at the conclusion of the war clearly demonstrated that they had been understood as a specific and completely contingent economic necessity rather than as a general strategy and policy of development; they had been instituted in response to the need to increase productive efficiency rapidly and not as the result of a new conception of industrial growth and the role of public institutions. Immediately after the war these government projects were accused of having promoted a socialist system and a collectivist ideology—a "terrible" accusation indeed.

Whitaker responded to these criticisms in his article "What is a House?"—contained, along with articles by other contributors to the AIA journal, in *The Housing Problem in War and Peace*. He claimed that it made no sense to speak of "socialism" or "paternalism" in regard to such undertakings, since they actually only signified paying a debt to the past by responding to the need for a new way of organizing commerce and industry. Greater productive efficiency, Whitaker and his collaborators asserted, could not be achieved by considering solely the technological problems of industry; rather, industry had to be organized rationally as a comprehensive social system—in other words, as Veblen conceived it. In order to avoid disastrous shortsightedness, furthermore, it was necessary to consider and act on all the factors that determine the cost of labor, since the labor market is not regulated exclusively by its relation with production. This fundamental concept was to reappear, brought up to date and expressed in diverse ways, in most of the writings of those who joined the Regional Planning Association of America after the war and was, in fact, to constitute one of the theoretical bases of their proposals.[182]

More than 120 architects and planners worked on the construction and the "war villages." Among those employed by the EFC Ackerman was chief of the design branch; B. A. Haldeman, chief of town planning; Robert D. Kohn, chief of production; and Henry Wright, assistant for town planning. Among the 61 architects working for the USHC were Arthur C. Comey, Burt L. Fenner as general manager, Herbert S. Hare, Henry V. Hubbard, C. Grant La Farge, and Frederick Law Olmsted, Jr. Many others, including John Nolen and Clarence S. Stein, collaborated closely with these organizations. Of the two agencies, the EFC was concerned with constructions for workers in the shipbuilding industry, and the USHC was similarly occupied with the munitions industry.

When direct federal intervention in the problem of war workers' housing became government policy, two basically different theories were formed concerning the government's role and continued to coexist throughout the war. One believed that the federal projects should be limited to the construction of temporary settlements that could easily be eliminated once the emergency was over; the other felt it necessary that the government finance permanent communities to be used even after the emergency period. The first assumed the intervention to be directed exclusively to resolving problems that arose from a specific and anomalous situation. The second interpreted the government's adoption of this policy as the necessary consequence of a historical evolution, the effects of which had suddenly been brought to the fore by an emergency situation; this evolution demanded not the resolution of contingent problems but, rather, strategic solutions to the structural problems of industrial society, in which the stability of labor relations and productive efficiency depend to no small extent on the policy adopted for housing.

Whitaker, Ackerman, and many others of their group adopted the second viewpoint and spoke explicitly of the need to plan for the continuation of these housing projects even after hostilities ceased. The "war villages" served the immediate purpose of locating the labor force as economically as possible in relation to the productive installations; this general rule, the reformers maintained, should be followed even in normal times. Thus they proposed that, after the emergency, the ownership of the houses be transferred to limited-liability companies or cooperatives that would stimulate the formation of communities based on what Ackerman called the "Own Your Own Home" principle. Occupant ownership was thus the objective to be pursued during the phase of normalization, since it not only guaranteed the formation of real communities but also further reinforced the stability of the labor market.[183] This principle was implicit, moreover, in the choice of models for the "war villages," which in their conception drew heavily on the legislation adopted in Australia and New Zealand and, above all, on the English garden cities, although in this case there were significant differences in the methods of financing the construction of the communities. Ultimately, the "war villages" were yet another expression of the decentralist ideology, which had become by this time a sort of territorial discipline based on the scientific study of the best possible location for settlements and the maximally efficient relationship between factory and dwelling.

The permanent settlements built through the intervention of government agencies reflected, for the most part, a good level of architecture and planning, and a few deserve special mention. John Nolen prepared the plan for Union Park Gardens in Wilmington, Delaware; Electus D. Litchfield, with the collaboration of Pliny Rogers, built one of the most important of these villages, Yorkship in Camden, New Jersey; Kilham and Hopkins worked on the Atlantic Heights project in Portsmouth, New Hampshire; Henry V. Hubbard and Francis Y. Joannes, that in Newport News, Virginia; Bissel and Sons, that in Norfolk, Virginia; Dean and Dean, that in Niagara Falls, New York, and A. H. Spahr, that in Erie, Pennsylvania. The architecture of these communities was, on the whole, completely traditional in form, but the house and apartment types studies, the technical standards employed, and the relationship between dwellings and urban plan were generally interesting. In some cases, the designs were limited to a slight animation of the traditional grid plan, as in Kilham and Hopkins's project for Atlantic Heights, but they were usually more subtle and complex. The plan for Yorkship, for example, rotates around a large, central green area, while other green areas characterize the principal axes of the plan and serve to resolve the more complex intersections of the street system. Clarence W. Brazer's project for the Westinghouse settlement in South Philadelphia is also interesting, since the

Plan for Well Hall, Eltham, Kent, an English workers' village built by the government in 1918 under wartime economic provisions.

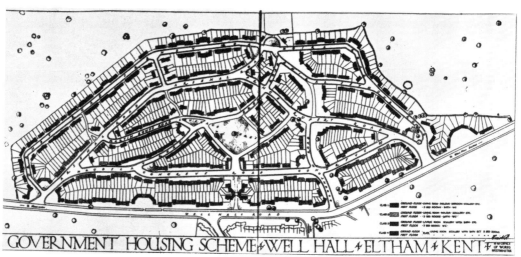

Emergency Fleet Corporation project: preliminary plan for Westinghouse Village, South Philadelphia, by Clarence W. Brazer, 1918-19.

Emergency Fleet Corporation project: plan for Hilton Village, Newport News, Virginia, by Henry V. Hubbard and Francis Y. Joannes, 1918-19.

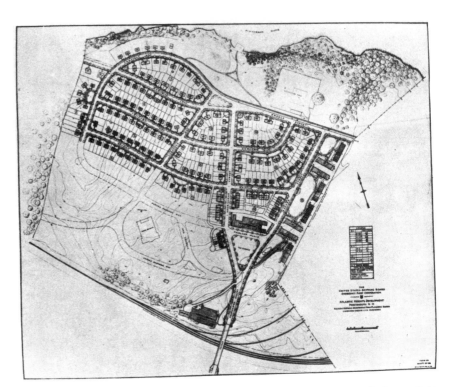

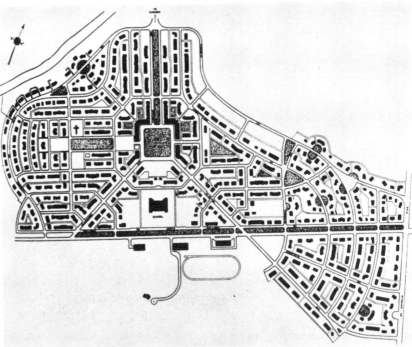

Emergency Fleet Corporation project: plan
for Atlantic Heights, Portsmouth, New
Hampshire, by Kilham and Hopkins,
1918-19.

Emergency Fleet Corporation project: plan
for Yorkship Village, Camden, New Jersey,
by Electus D. Litchfield; Pliny Rogers,
collaborator.

Exterior view of a house type for Atlantic Heights by Kilham and Hopkins.

Exterior view of a house type for Westing-house Village by Clarence W. Brazer.

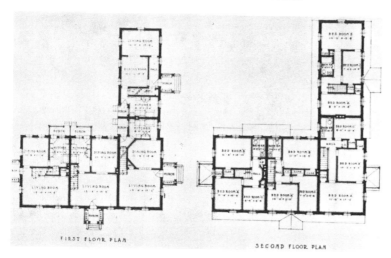

FIRST FLOOR PLAN

SECOND FLOOR PLAN

Plan of a house type for Westinghouse Village by Clarence W. Brazer.

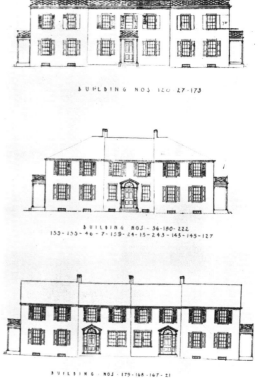

BUILDING NOS 120 27-173

BUILDING NOS 56-180-222
155-135-46-7-159-24-15-243-143-145-127

BUILDING NOS 179-168-167-21

Elevations of various house types for York-ship Village by Electus D. Litchfield.

plan, centered on a strongly geometrical triangular area enlivened at its center by the curvilinear layout of the houses, makes use of culs-de-sac in the row houses on Delaware Street on either side of the principal axis.

The construction of Yorkship may serve as an example of the actual functioning of these initiatives and the typical procedures imposed by Eidlitz. The settlement, which was intended for the workers of the New York Shipbuilding Company in Camden, New Jersey, was located in an area of 225 acres; 90 acres were subdivided into 2,400 lots, on which 907 houses, apartment buildings, stores, and a theater were to be built. The dwelling types were varied; the row-house solution was rejected, and worked out, instead, were twenty-seven house and apartment types that could be adapted in seventy different ways. The average cost of each lot was $450; that of the houses, $2,700. The necessary capital for construction was furnished by the EFC to the Fairview Realty Company, controlled by the New York Shipbuilding Company, at an interest of 5 percent, repayable at the rate of 3 percent a year. The houses could be sold to the occupants, but in its own transactions Fairview Realty was not allowed to charge an interest rate greater than 5 percent. As the statistical analysis demonstrated, this procedure made it possible to keep the per capita cost of land at a tolerable level and restrain speculation.[184]

This procedure was one of the most important achievements of the "war villages," but it was not the only one. At the end of the war, those who campaigned for the continuation of this federal policy repeatedly pointed out that the standards achieved were generally satisfactory, that planning the projects and standardizing construction systems had made possible significant economies, and that the concentration of the design work and procurement had held down increases in production costs. In 1918, the USHC published a handbook entitled *Standards Recommended for Permanent Industrial Housing Developments*, which remains a most important document for understanding the changes brought about by the "war villages" in the way of conceiving the solutions to the problem of low-cost housing.[185]

By the end of the war the activities of the EFC and the USHC had produced the following results: the EFC had spent $12 million on transportation facilities and had granted $70 million in loans for the construction of new settlements and housing, creating 9,185 houses and apartments and providing accommodations for 7,564 single people; the USHC had spent $52 million, contributing to the creation of new houses or apartments for 5,998 families and constructing accommodations for 7,181 single people. Together the various activities of these two agencies had affected 360,000 workers and their families.[186]

After the war, despite the clear opposition in government circles, many campaigned not only for the continuation of this policy but for its expansion. To this end, a further increase in the credit funds and, in some cases, a complete reorganization of the system of financing construction were requested. Greater centralization and coordination of activities through the creation of a federal housing bureau and encouragement for the formation of cooperatives and limited-dividend companies were also sought.[187] Many of these ideas reappeared in the theories of the reformers of the 1920s, and the experiences of the war years eventually proved invaluable during another period of emergency, after 1929 and during the New Deal. Moreover, the "war villages" may be considered an embryonic expression of that mixed economy about which certain reformers would construct an original theory and form new proposals, which would ultimately be put into operation in the 1930s, even if only partially.

The Formation of the Regional Planning Association of America

Charles H. Whitaker was an outstanding figure in the panorama of American architecture and urbanism and was at the center of the most interesting initiatives in this field in the period of the "war economy" and during the years when the Regional Planning Association of America was formed. The collaborators Whitaker had gathered around him on the *Journal of the American Institute of Architects* made up a goodly part of the group that created the RPAA. This association was intensely active during the 1920s and the early 1930s, but its activities came to an end at the beginning of the New Deal. Numerous documents attest to its existence even after 1933, however, as well as to some attempts to revitalize the association; the most serious seems to have been made in 1948.[188]

The RPAA was an informal group of architects, planners, exponents of the Conservation movement, sociologists, and economists founded in New York in 1923. One of the earliest documents related to its formation is a proposal, signed by Clarence S. Stein and dated March 7, 1923, for the creation of a Garden City and Regional Planning Association. At a meeting in the New York office of Robert D. Kohn in April of the same year, with Alexander M. Bing, John L. Bright, Lewis Mumford, Eugene Henry Klaber, Nils Hammarstrand, Benton MacKaye, Sullivan W. Jones, and Stein in attendance, the association was named the Regional Planning Association of America, and its first executive committee was formed. Later in 1923, the association joined the International Garden Cities and Town Planning Federation, on the council of which it was represented by Frederick L. Ackerman.[189]

An initial work program for the association was presented to the executive committee on June 12, 1923, by Mumford, MacKaye, Stuart Chase, and Stein; it set the following tasks for the RPAA: (1) to undertake and support the creation of garden cities, within the terms of a comprehensive plan for the development of the region; (2) to develop relations between its members and English planners and, more specifically, carry out studies in connection with those made by Patrick Geddes at Edinburgh; (3) to prepare territorial analyses and plan projects on a regional scale that would take up and publicize MacKaye's concept of the Appalachian Trail—"the development in mind is that of a series of services"; (4) in collaboration with the Committee on Community Planning of the AIA, of which Stein was secretary, to undertake studies and participate in propaganda activities in favor of regionalism; and (5) to conduct a series of analyses on key regions, including Berkshire County in Massachusetts, the area between Bear Mountain, New York, and Netcong, New Jersey, the anthracite region of Pennsylvania, the Shenandoah Valley in Virginia, and the Tennessee River basin.[190] This program dedicated ample space to explaining the importance of resuming MacKaye's Appalachian Trail project; as noted earlier, MacKaye had discussed this project with Mumford and Stein during a series of meetings at Hudson Guild Farm in 1921, before he published his article on the subject.

The Appalachian Trail was essentially a plan for revitalizing a depressed region, which would be used for agriculture and silviculture and which was at the same time an important natural reserve. MacKaye proposed the creation of a complex of recreational installations that could resolve certain problems of the surrounding urban population and give a boost to the economy and productive activities of the region, thereby encouraging the formation of new settlements. The objective of the project was summed up clearly in a phrase of MacKaye's famous article: "Industry would come to be seen in its true perspective—as a means in life not as an end in itself."[191] In its essence we have already encountered this concept in the thought of the theorists of the "war villages" and it reappeared essentially unchanged in the RPAA's initial program of 1923.

The spirit animating MacKaye's work goes back almost directly to the ideals of the Golden Day; his project was an original synthesis of the nascent regionalism and the transcendentalist "philosophy of nature." These same observations apply to Mumford and numerous other members of the RPAA. It was, however, Mumford and MacKaye who contributed most to directing the association to regionalist studies and the regionalist point of view; they were the real theorists of regionalism, and it was they who furnished the group with its most significant ideological and cultural motivations. It is indeed indicative that just such a plan as the Appalachian Trail can be considered as one of the possible birth certificates of the RPAA. Its members took suggestions and inspiration from this cultural leaven; although they were often engaged in specific studies and concerned with problems of a well-defined scope, in the ten crucial years of collective activity they developed a comprehensive philosophy of planning, in which it is difficult to distinguish individual contributions. This philosophy was ultimately expressed as a comprehensive territorial plan based on the analysis and interdisciplinary study of all the aspects—economic, natural, geographic, ethnic, historical, and so on—that structure the region as an entity.

Within this general frame of reference, several particular problems engaged the attention of the association and were addressed repeatedly in the studies and writings of its members. First and foremost was the need for new housing legislation. In their efforts toward a solution to the housing problem, they brought together experiences derived from the "war villages" and the example of decentralist legislation in New Zealand and Australia within the terms of a continual updating of the garden-city ideology. The use of the term *ideology* of the garden city and not the garden city as a *model* is significant here, because the residential settlements of the RPAA represented an unquestionable advance over the "war villages" and the antecedent English undertakings. This undeniable progress applied to the planning and housing solutions adopted, the unitary character of the projects, the analyses of the design of house and apartment types, and the relationship of the new settlements with the preexisting urban structures.[192] Significant in regard to the RPAA's aims and achievements in this field of endeavor is an unpublished study for a "garden community," prepared by Stein, Wright, and Bing as early as 1923. The proposals contained in this study indicate very clearly the motivations that were to guide the association in the projects of this type it subsequently carried out.[193]

An aspect of the association's work that is interesting and has been little examined was the propagation of its theories, an activity that brought the group into contact with some of the most important figures of modern urbanism. Their most obvious relationship was with the English Garden City movement and its exponents; these contacts were maintained directly through its own members and through British planners close to the RPAA, such as Raymond Unwin and, to a lesser extent, Thomas Adams. Fundamental, however, was the RPAA's relationship with Patrick Geddes. Geddes was presented to the group by Mumford at the Hudson Guild Farm in May 1923, and his influence was particularly decisive for MacKaye and Mumford. The group also had contact with German planners and their work and a much more tenuous relationship with Russian experiments. Whitaker, like Mumford, was in contact with Walter Kurt Behrendt, editor of *Die Form*, who was probably the source of their more direct knowledge of German planning activities, especially Martin Wagner's work. In addition, Ernst May and Wilhelm Schmidt, author of the regional plan for the Ruhr, together with Unwin, Ebenezer Howard, Barry Parker, and many other foreign guests, were present at a meeting held at the Hudson Guild Farm on April 25-26, 1925, following the International City and Regional Planning Conference, which had been held in New York City.[194] Stein and Wright visited England, particularly Letchworth, in 1923 and met with Howard and Unwin. During the years that followed, Wright was in contact with Hugo Häring and Werner Moser, while Stein was interested in the Dutch architectural and urban projects, as several of his articles demonstrate.

The contact with the Soviet Union was much less evident and certainly never direct, aside from a few trips to Russia made by members of the RPAA—one of them by Chase in 1927. These contacts were also generally made slightly later, at the end of the 1920s or in the 1930s, and their influence on the work of the RPAA was slight.[195] More important was the interest with which the group followed the results of Russian planning. It is interesting for ideological reasons, especially in the case of Mumford, to consider the general attitude toward Russia in these circles at a moment in American history when it could certainly not have been easy to maintain an "objective" position in regard to the new socialist state.

Any attempt to analyze the ideological position of a figure such as Mumford would require consideration of a wide range of problems and phenomena and would necessitate delving deep into a crucial historical period in the culture and politics of the United States. The scope of this task is obviously too great for it to be accomplished in this essay, although a few observations will be made here. It is hardly less difficult to clarify the positions of the other members of the RPAA, whose ideologies are so diverse and so composite in character that classification is not easy. Whitaker seems to have been particularly susceptible to Bellamy's influence, and his writings also often reveal analogies with the views of Henry George, while Ackerman was influenced principally by Veblen. Wright, intellectually one of the most lucid members of the association, was more independent, as were Wood and Stein. In an unpublished youthful essay, Stein expressed some of the principal ideals of the Progressive Era. American democracy, he reflected, signified "equality" and "government by the people," principles still unrealized, which the political system did not allow to take concrete form. Stein concluded his brief manuscript with a criticism of the Constitution as "made by men of the past" and, significantly, with a citation from Herbert Croly.[196]

Very generally, the ideology of the RPAA can be said to have stemmed ultimately from Veblen and Dewey; onto this basic line of thought, however, were grafted the resumption of the European regionalist tradition, especially that of France, the influence of Geddes's "sociology," and certain principles of the European decentralist tradition from Kropotkin to Howard. The result was a new synthesis, at once pragmatic and idealistic and animated by a sincere and deeply-rooted dedication to civic reform, derived from the values of the American tradition.

Mumford defended the association's political connections by underlining the fact that the RPAA had never identified itself with any political party. Obviously, however, the members of the RPAA were, in a certain sense, involved politically through their contacts with various public institutions and specific government agencies. In regard to the political world as such, however, they remained detached; they relied on the coherence of their own theories and on the capacity of their ideas to impose themselves, rather than on the possibility of finding direct channels for their implementation. The relationship of the members of the RPAA with New York governor Alfred E. Smith was extremely important, particularly in view of their collaboration on the famous 1926 plan for the region of New York. The members' ties with the governor actually predated the creation of the RPAA. They had been securely established as early as 1919, when the New York State Reconstruction Commission was created and Stein became secretary of its Housing Committee. In 1923, the same year the RPAA was founded, the New York State Commission of Housing and Regional

Planning was created, with Stein as its chairman. The association also maintained relationships with unions and labor-movement organizations, although these are poorly documented. In the Stein archives there does exist, however, an interesting document concerning a housing platform that was submitted to the New York Labor Party, and Chase, Wright, and Stein collaborated with the Workers Education Bureau.[197]

In addition to these specific connections and relationships, the RPAA always acted in the most open manner possible and sought to establish contacts with the greatest possible variety of movements and organizations; it welcomed any possibility of encountering and comparing diverse theories and ideas and of finding new roads to the realization of its ideals. As Roy Lubove has written, "The kernel of the RPAA's program was the cooperation of the social architect and planner in the design of large-scale group and community housing, financed in some measure by low-interest government loans, and directed toward the creation of a regional city. Sunnyside and Radburn were conceived as first steps in this realization."[198]

The following statement by Mumford hardly exhausts the subject of the significance of the RPAA's ideological and historical role, but is a direct testimony of the association's aims and achievements:

We were never in a limited sense a propagandist organization. Our main effort was to collaborate in our thinking and to educate ourselves. We conceived the design of a new housing development at Sunnyside Gardens and a project for a Garden City at Radburn, New Jersey, as experimental efforts to create a better type of urban development and ultimately a new form for the city. What we added to the work done by Howard's followers in England was the concept of the region, not the metropolis, as the focus for urban development.[199]

RPAA Studies and Projects in Building and Planning

In the years immediately following the war, future members of the RPAA made a series of studies and published numerous articles, unquestionably among the most advanced of the epoch, on the problems of housing and planning. In the early 1920s, the *Journal of the American Institute of Architects* continued to provide information on European building and planning activities and on related legislation adopted in foreign countries. At the same time, the journal dedicated space to the most advanced technical research of American architects and urbanists.

In 1923 Edith Elmer Wood published *Housing Progress in Western Europe*, a synthesis of the studies and projects carried out during the war and the years immediately preceding it. The best parts of Wood's work are those dedicated to the study of the English housing policies, while the parts dealing with other European countries are more superficial. Her principal subject is the various forms of public intervention in building construction carried out in Europe. The model indicated as the most suited for adoption in the United States, however, is that of the garden city, conceived as the nucleus of a comprehensive project of territorial development, which must be accompanied by a credit policy offering special concessions and tax exemptions for building initiatives.[200]

In more direct reference to the American situation, some of the hypotheses deducible from this study had been aired earlier in a three-way debate among Wood, Ackerman, and John J. Murphy, published in 1920 in a volume entitled *The Housing Famine. How to End it.* Some particular differences in outlook among the three are more significant than similarity of their viewpoints. Unlike Murphy, Wood and Ackerman pointed out that the desperate situation presented by the housing problem indicated not a general crisis in this field of production but a crisis in a single specific sector, that of low-cost housing for lower-income groups. This attitude is particularly significant not only for its obvious ideological implications but also as an indication of an unusually thorough and analytic examination of the housing problem. From this debate emerges yet another notable difference of position, this time between Ackerman and Wood, two future members of the RPAA. Ackerman criticized the credit policy suggested by Wood as a way of revitalizing the building industry. In view of these criticisms, Lubove's statement that the members of the RPAA sought housing reform facilitated by low-interest government loans appears to be too great a generalization; it is true on the whole, but not absolutely so. The measures Ackerman recommended, for example, were decidedly more drastic; they included not only a "technocratic" reform in the management of planning and building problems but also assumed, in Veblenian terms, a comprehensive restructuring of the relations of production, which is, of course, something that goes far beyond the question of a type of credit policy.

Ackerman's position was thus much more radical than Wood's. In his view, once the problems of the building industry are seen to differ depending on the class for which its products are destined, it is clear that the crisis can be solved only by a comprehensive process of the redistribution of wealth; for the evils of urbanization and congestion the only valid remedy is a new way—a structural way—of conceiving industrial development. Congestion, Ackerman repeatedly stated, is the direct consequence of economic and productive concentration.[201] This principle makes clear his frequent warnings to planners not to limit themselves to studying the "effects" but to search out the "causes" of the urban crisis. Taking up a concept that had led Mumford to reject attempts at resuscitating Henry George's theories, Ackerman criticized the view of those who saw a possible solution to the crisis in transferring the greater part of the tax burden onto land in the hope of stimulating the construction industry. Similarly, he criticized those who interpreted the housing problem as the result largely of a lack of available capital and saw its solution primarily in terms of financing and credit policies; this was, at least in part, Wood's view when she proposed using postal savings as a source of credit funds for building initiatives. Ackerman also actively supported the idea of encouraging occupant ownership in housing, but in this he was not alone in the early 1920s and among the members of the RPAA.[202]

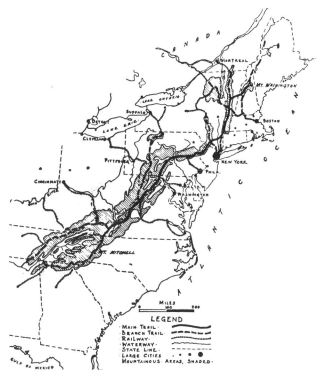

Suggested location for the Appalachian Trail (from Benton MacKaye, "An Appalachian Trail," *Journal of the American Institute of Architects,* October, 1921).

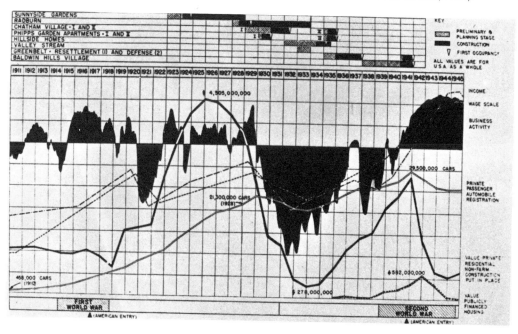

Graph of the principal undertakings by members of the Regional Planning Association of America, planned and constructed between 1923 and 1941, superimposed on a graph indicating the general economic trends of this period.

Some of the theories outlined here also figure in the interesting report made in 1920 by the New York State Reconstruction Commission's Housing Committee, of which Stein was secretary. At first glance, the proposals contained in this document may seem similar to those pleaded for during the war; the report, in fact, recommends the establishment of a centralized planning institution, the formation of planning boards in all communities in the state with more than 10,000 inhabitants, and the creation of a credit system for construction. Many of the ideas and proposals found in the report, however, were completely new; among these were the specification of the physical and social dimensions of projects; the importance of the global vision—house, industry, transportation—as a guide for planning; the identification of the problem of low-cost building as the principal object of housing reform; and, finally the clear-cut position in favor of financing through special credit facilities and low-interest loans, a proposal that, unlike indiscriminate tax exemption, would make the means of financing a matter of policy, serving also as a control measure.[203] In Lubove's words,

The Committee's analysis of the housing problem and the conclusions reached differed sharply from the typical housing survey of the Progressive Era. The prewar survey tended to focus upon sanitary and social pathology of the slums, supplemented by recommendations for code enactment and enforcement; but in 1919-1920 minimum standards legislation to control commercial builders had no relevance to the existing situation, and Stein's Committee directed its attention instead to means by which to increase the supply and reduce the cost of housing.[204]

Despite the support of Governor Smith, the proposals contained in this report were not put into operation. The trend of the proposals would be taken up, however, within a much reduced context, by the City Housing Corporation, a limited-dividend company financed by the New York contractor Alexander M. Bing, a member of the RPAA.

The essential aims of the City Housing Corporation were expressed in the "Preliminary Study of a Proposed Garden Community," prepared by Bing, Stein, and Wright in 1923, to which reference has already been made. The basic idea of a limited-dividend company was not new; it had had a long tradition that began in England and was taken up again in the Progressive Era. It would be wrong, however, to attribute philanthropic or public-assistance aims to the City Housing Corporation, as some contemporary observers did. The Corporation's objective was principally to demonstrate that it was possible to reconcile and integrate the efforts of private financiers—or, better still, cooperatives—with the active intervention of public financing in the field of housing. In a booklet entitled *Homes and Good Citizenship*, distributed by the City Housing Corporation, its aims were set forth clearly:

1) develop better plans and methods for housing construction and demonstrate the advantages deriving from land purchases and housing construction conducted as large scale operations;

2) develop building types specifically adapted to low-cost housing;

3) demonstrate to the low-income buyer that he can own a first class house at

the same price he now pays to rent a second class one;

4) encourage and develop forms of cooperative home ownership;

5) demonstrate the value of large green spaces in the price of homes and convince entreprenuers and contractors that it is possible to provide such spaces without undermining the economic soundness of the housing venture;

6) convince the public of its social obligation to make it possible for citizens of restricted means to live in decent houses. [205]

From the theoretical point of view the ideas were hardly new; they can indeed be traced back to the economic tradition, extending from Proudhon to Sax, which Engels liquidated once and for all. On the basis of these premises the City Housing Corporation undertook the construction of a live model of urban planning, the housing development of Sunnyside in the borough of Queens, near Manhattan, an enterprise that won much praise but attracted few material contributions. [206] The designers of the project were Stein, Wright, and Ackerman, and the principles that guided their work were the cumulative result of the various theories discussed so far. The land acquired for this project was in an area across the East River where land was still available at low cost. The location of Sunnyside negatively affected its urban plan because of the preexisting grid layout of the area; thus situated, however, the settlement acquired an added significance from the contrast it presented with the surrounding residential blocks built by the Metropolitan Life Insurance Company. [207]

The 1,202 family units were constructed between 1924 and 1928, in Stein's words, "as a continuous large-scale operation." Although it indicated the realization of the theories developed in the preceding years, this method of construction was not the outstanding feature of Sunnyside. What really distinguished this residential development, separated from the surrounding grid layout, was the creation of "open spaces for natural green" within the various individual dwelling complexes, communal garden areas cut off from the urban scene, which served greatly to stimulate the collective life of the community. Another prominent feature of Sunnyside was the design of the house and apartment types. These were worked out with the aim of holding down production costs as much as possible without lowering building standards and living comfort, an aim achieved through the group planning of the dwellings, the judicious choice of construction techniques, and the standardization of technical installations. The effect of the depression eventually blighted the initial success of this model project; menaced with foreclosure, the settlement's property owners' association attacked the City Housing Corporation, from whom they sought postponement or reduction of the mortgage payments. "The irony of the situation," wrote Stein, "was that the City Housing Corporation had stimulated and helped community organization, and those living in Sunnyside had thus become accustomed to forming their own organizations." [208]

Early in 1928 the City Housing Corporation undertook the creation of another model settlement, which remains the most important product of the RPAA: Radburn, New Jersey, "the town for the motor age." Radburn, planned

MODERATELY PRICED

ONE and TWO FAMILY HOUSES and
CO-OPERATIVE GARDEN APARTMENTS

NOW READY AT

Sunnyside

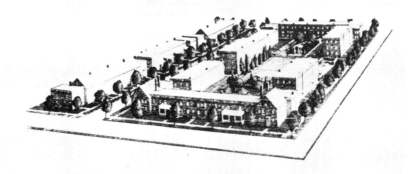

The New Garden Homes of Queens

CAROLIN STREET near QUEENS BOULEVARD
At BLISS STREET SUBWAY STATION

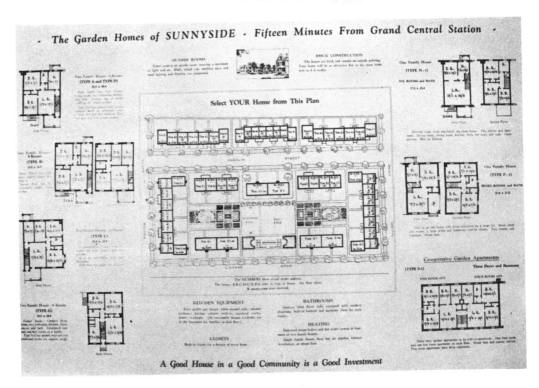

Illustrated brochure describing the residential settlement of Sunnyside, New York, design by Clarence S. Stein and Henry Wright, with the collaboration of Frederick L. Ackerman, and constructed in 1924-28.

by the same designers as Sunnyside, further developed the principles of the earlier undertaking, but on a much more ambitious scale. Indeed, Sunnyside was still only an urban section, while Radburn, conceived for 25,000 inhabitants, was a town.

The development of the site on which Radburn was to rise was in no way conditioned by preexisting settlements, as had been the case at Sunnyside; thus Stein and Wright had a free hand in the creation of the plan of Radburn, which was one of the most important products of contemporary American planning. In fact, Radburn's major merits have traditionally been identified in just this plan, based on a strict separation of the road systems through the creation of through-roads that do not interfere with the life of the residential complexes, which are served by a secondary road system, further articulated by the culs-de-sac of each of the residential complexes, or superblocks, as their architects termed them. This scheme made it possible for each superblock, composed of diverse building types, to enclose a continuous interior park, the greenery of which forms the core of each complex.

The sources for this scheme are many, including the garden cities of Howard's followers, Clarence Perry's concept of the "neighborhood unit," and some prewar garden suburbs. The real model for Radburn, however, was Olmsted's plan for Central Park; Stein himself compared Olmsted's separated traffic scheme to the Radburn road structure.[209] The significance of Radburn, however, does not end here. At various times both Wright and Stein emphasized the progress made in the design of the dwellings in comparison with those of Sunnyside. What is most striking, however, is not the intrinsic quality of these designs but the fact that at Radburn the building types are simply the architectural aspect of the urban plan. There is no break between the two scales. Considered in this light, the street layout acquires a more complex significance and the resumption of Olmsted's scheme is seen to be inspired by something more than an ideal; far from being merely a brilliant resuscitation of a cultural heritage, the choice of this model made possible the use of solutions that guaranteed continuity between urban plan and architectural exigencies.

A brief publication that is useful in understanding this point is Wright's sixteen-page paper, written in 1929 and published the next year as *Some Principles Relating to the Economics of Land Subdivision;* in my opinion this is one of the most important studies to have come out of the RPAA. The paper consists of a comparative analysis of various schemes of land subdivision, with the aim of demonstrating the economic efficiency of solutions that make it possible to enlarge the perimeter of ground areas toward the street without increasing the dimensions of either the street system or the construction areas—a model that develops a tendency found in certain studies of the English school, Unwin's, in particular. Such an hypothesis, which Wright illustrates only briefly with Radburn, cannot hold up, however, unless the street structure is ordered "hierarchically" and, above all, unless the building types adopted are quantified

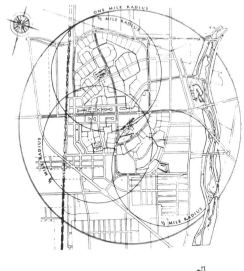

Plan for Radburn, New Jersey, designed by
Clarence S. Stein and Henry Wright, with
the collaboration of Frederick L. Ackerman,
Andrew J. Thomas, and James Renwick
Thomson, and constructed in 1928-33.

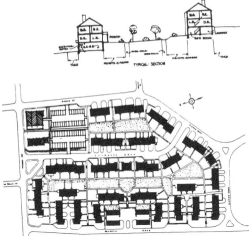

General plan for Radburn, New Jersey, indicating the neighborhoods laid out with half-
mile radii.

Partial plan for Chatham Village, Pittsburgh,
designed by Clarence S. Stein and Henry
Wright and constructed in 1930-32.

in relation to the same range of economic variables considered for the complex as a whole. A few marginal aspects of Wright's study are not completely clear, and it is limited to the consideration of a reduced number of variables, since its immediate aim is to demonstrate the rationality and economic "feasibility" of settlements provided with ample internal green spaces that result from the use of certain residential types. Despite these limitations, Wright's study remains the best explanation of the Olmsted-inspired plan of Radburn.[210]

With what has been said so far in mind, it is interesting to turn briefly to the architecture of Sunnyside and Radburn. The "indifference" of the RPAA architects to the study of form on a strictly architectural scale can be somewhat perplexing to those used to identifying modern architecture with the white facades of the European rationalist architects. The architecture of the RPAA is significant for the house and apartment types devised and the urban standards it realized, rather than for its formal expression. This architecture is the product of construction, and the function it expresses is that of standards, construction methods, and the rationalization of services; here "form" must be sought in the organic fusion of plan and dwelling, in social considerations, and in the open spaces of natural greenery, rather than in "facades."

What stood behind this "architecture without architecture" was not the artistic avant-garde of the Modern movement but the "American tradition" of Concord and Olmsted. The New England towns and Central Park, like Radburn, were without "architecture," and yet they were the complete products of an architectural culture. Far from being an autonomous provincial expression, the architecture of the RPAA assumed a concept of form that had its origins in a complex tradition, in which the architectural language was completely secondary in comparison to the form that unity, as such, expressed.

With the crash of 1929, the City Housing Corporation suffered a definitive collapse, even though Radburn, unlike Sunnyside, had attracted substantial financial support and not mere praise for its merit.[211] The "Radburn idea," in fact, was destined to have a certain following and proved to be one of the more important models created by American urban planning.[212]

During the 1930s Stein and Wright carried out other projects, which further refined the theories tried out at Sunnyside and Radburn. In Pittsburgh, beginning in 1930, they built the first nucleus—128 row houses—of Chatham Village. In its plan, this settlement took up once again the scheme of separated road systems, but the project also marked the end of the ideal of occupant ownership that had been pursued by the City Housing Corporation. Also in 1930 and again, as in the case of Chatham Village, for a private company, Stein built a complex of 6-story apartment houses, destined for low-income tenants. It was built on land originally acquired by the City Housing Corporation for the development of Sunnyside but subsequently purchased by the Society of Phipps Houses. In the Phipps Garden Apartments, Stein made experimental use of the results of a series of studies on apartment-house planning that had been carried out in the preceding years and developed by Wright, in particular. Thus, although this complex is based on the intense utilization of the ground, it is difficult to interpret the apartment plans and the types of the apartment blocks themselves as simply taking up ideas on the garden apartment elaborated during the period by various architects; they are, instead, a development of concepts already present in the earlier settlements designed by Stein and others of the group.

From a strictly architectural point of view, the Phipps Garden Apartments and the Hillside Homes—another residential complex of multi-storied apartment houses built by Stein in 1934-35 in the Bronx and financed for 85 percent by a federal loan—are the most interesting examples of Stein's work, although as urban projects they lack the innovative quality of the Radburn plan. They, too, are "closed" complexes, animated toward the court by the emerging volumes of the facades that result from the use of T-shaped elements in the solution of the plan. This is a severe and polemical urban architecture that makes no compromise with its surroundings, but it is also an architecture that stands up to a comparison with some fundamental European works, such as the Vienna Höfe or certain urban quarters designed by the Dutch architects.[213]

The best summary of these projects is found in various passages of Henry Wright's *Rehousing Urban America*, published in 1935. This volume systematically presents all the principles elaborated by the RPAA on the problem of housing, including the selection of projects to be undertaken, the distinction between renovation of a blighted area and slum clearance, the prevention of slums, and the analysis of building types as the factor determining the economic efficiency of the venture. Wright also dedicated part of his book to new building techniques and to an analysis of the most recent European work, particularly that of German architects and planners.[214]

Wright continually states that reducing construction costs depends on all the factors that have been discussed here, but he does not fail to demonstrate that these "technical" achievements lose their efficacy unless they are accompanied by a building policy capable of making them work—in other words, by a revision of the systems of financing and credit. In graphic form, this complementarity can be studied in the diagrams illustrating a booklet published by the Workers Education Bureau in 1927, in the compilation of which Stein and Wright collaborated.[215]

The views expressed by the RPAA did not go entirely unheeded, as demonstrated by the New York State Housing Law passed in 1926. The New York State Commission of Housing and Regional Planning had intended this law to sanction the establishment of a State Housing Board and a State Housing Bank; as passed, however, the law authorized the first of these agencies but not the second. Thus, although the 1926 law represented a certain measure of progress over the 1920 legislation, it was still conditioned by it. Once again the provisions for financing did not reflect a new credit policy—as both the RPAA and the commission maintained was necessary—but merely codified "passive" systems of tax exemption for housing initiatives that met certain minimal requirements.[216]

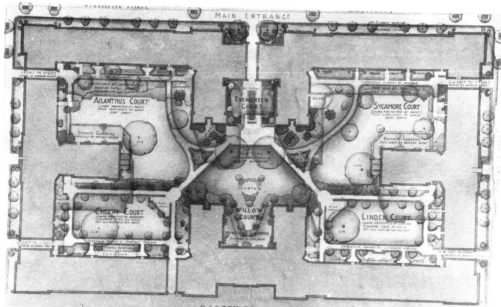

General plan for the garden courts,
Phipps Garden Apartments, New York,
designed by Clarence S. Stein and constructed in 1930.

Aerial view, Phipps Garden Apartments.

View from inside the courts, Phipps Garden Apartments.

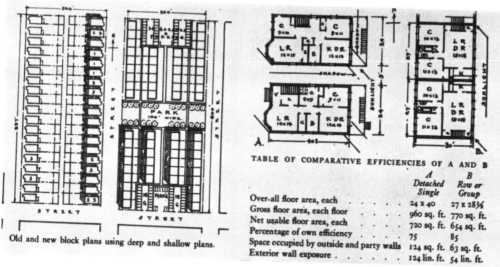

TABLE OF COMPARATIVE EFFICIENCIES OF A AND B

	A Detached Single	B Row or Group
Over-all floor area, each	24 x 40	27 x 28½
Gross floor area, each floor	960 sq. ft.	770 sq. ft.
Net usable floor area, each	720 sq. ft.	654 sq. ft.
Percentage of own efficiency	75	85
Space occupied by outside and party walls	124 sq. ft.	63 sq. ft.
Exterior wall exposure	124 lin. ft.	54 lin. ft.

Old and new block plans using deep and shallow plans.

Comparison of lot plans to green spaces and comparison of efficiencies of house types by Henry Wright, about 1935.

Experimental studies for open-stair apartment plans by Henry Wright, about 1935.

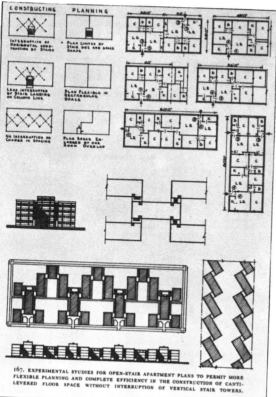

167. EXPERIMENTAL STUDIES FOR OPEN-STAIR APARTMENT PLANS TO PERMIT MORE FLEXIBLE PLANNING AND COMPLETE EFFICIENCY IN THE CONSTRUCTION OF CANTI-LEVERED FLOOR SPACE WITHOUT INTERRUPTION OF VERTICAL STAIR TOWERS.

THE CONSTRUCTION DOLLAR:

Shows where the CENTS WHICH MAKE UP EACH DOLLAR OF ORIGINAL CONSTRUCTION COST go to in various types of buildings in different parts of the country.

Highest Class Fireproof 15-story N.Y. Type Apartment on land $6,000 per front foot. Rents $100 to $150 per room per month.

Small Frame 4-room House and lot. Improvements not complete. Brooklyn, N.Y. Selling price, $5,400.

5-story Non-fireproof Walk-up on land $600 per front foot. Rents $16 to $22 per room per month.

5-room Bungalow on 35 foot lot. Improvements not complete. Detroit, Mich. Selling price, $7,200.

6-room Brick Row House, Philadelphia, Pa. Selling price, $7,000
Lot 14 ft. x 40 ft.

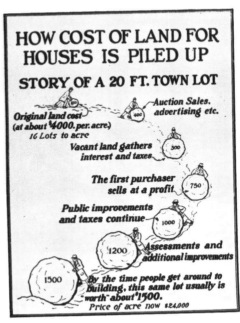

HOW COST OF LAND FOR HOUSES IS PILED UP

STORY OF A 20 FT. TOWN LOT

Original land cost (at about $4000 per acre) 16 Lots to acre

Auction Sales, advertising etc.

Vacant land gathers interest and taxes

The first purchaser sells at a profit.

Public improvements and taxes continue

Assessments and additional improvements

By the time people get around to building, this same lot usually is "worth" about $1500.

Price of acre now $24,000

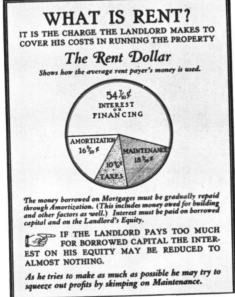

WHAT IS RENT?

IT IS THE CHARGE THE LANDLORD MAKES TO COVER HIS COSTS IN RUNNING THE PROPERTY

The Rent Dollar

Shows how the average rent payer's money is used.

The money borrowed on Mortgages must be gradually repaid through Amortization. (This includes money owed for building and other factors as well.) Interest must be paid on borrowed capital and on the Landlord's Equity.

☞ IF THE LANDLORD PAYS TOO MUCH FOR BORROWED CAPITAL THE INTEREST ON HIS EQUITY MAY BE REDUCED TO ALMOST NOTHING.

As he tries to make as much as possible he may try to squeeze out profits by skimping on Maintenance.

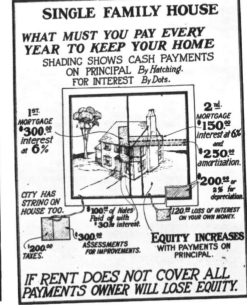

SINGLE FAMILY HOUSE

WHAT MUST YOU PAY EVERY YEAR TO KEEP YOUR HOME

SHADING SHOWS CASH PAYMENTS ON PRINCIPAL *By Hatching.*
FOR INTEREST *By Dots.*

EQUITY INCREASES WITH PAYMENTS ON PRINCIPAL.

IF RENT DOES NOT COVER ALL PAYMENTS OWNER WILL LOSE EQUITY.

Diagrams explaining the economic factors
of housing in relation to construction, land
costs, rents, and home ownership (from
Arthur C. Holden, *Primer of Housing*,
Workers Education Bureau, New York,
1927).

Six years later, in the midst of a dramatic historical juncture, the ideas of which the RPAA and the New York State Commission had become the interpreters were taken under consideration at a conference called by President Herbert Hoover in Washington to discuss the shape of a new housing policy. In the volume that summarizes the results of this conference a few pages are dedicated to the experiments at Radburn and Sunnyside, and include also some questionable observations. It is not for their criticism, however, that these pages are important but, rather, for their testimony to the way in which the ideas of the City Housing Corporation ultimately became a significant and integral part of the concerns of American urbanism. Indeed, the whole volume—which is important, in any case, for the perspective it affords on the policies that were to be put into operation by the New Deal—ultimately centers, if not on the RPAA's experiments, certainly on the subjects to which this association had dedicated its attention and efforts.[217]

At the Washington conference, the "specialized" way in which the housing problem was examined, aspect by aspect, technique by technique, marked a further step toward a definitive change from the general and generic approach of the Progressive Era. In Washington in 1932, housing and planning, as "technologies," were dealt with from the common perspective of "policy," and their unification had a far more solid, structural basis than the Progressive Era's idealistic affirmations of good will.

To all these changes the RPAA made a fundamental contribution. Without the bridge it threw over what Mumford has called the general planning and building folly of the 1920s, even the undertakings of the New Deal would probably have been different; the efforts of this association surely inspired not only the program of construction of the greenbelt towns but also various aspects of the "philosophy" of the Tennessee Valley Authority.

A "Plan" for New York, 1923-1926

One of the most important urban studies carried out in the United States is constituted by the reports of the New York State Reconstruction Commission issued between 1919 and 1923 and, in particular, the reports of the New York State Commission of Housing and Regional Planning that appeared between 1923 and 1926. These documents, submitted to Governor Smith, contain the results of analytic investigations and a great quantity of statistical material concerning not only New York City but also the entire surrounding region. In addition to Stein and Wright, the whole membership of the RPAA made a determinant contribution to this work and provided its theoretical guidelines and analytic insights. In 1926 this long collaboration concluded with the Commission of Housing and Regional Planning's report of February containing the legislative proposal described in the preceding pages and with its report dated May 7, a document that collected, analyzed, and elaborated data that made up what might be termed the rudiments of a "comprehensive plan" for an operation on regional scale.[218]

A more exact description is provided by the report itself, which stated, "Two years ago the Commission of Housing and Regional Planning began this preliminary study of the relation of the resources of the State to its economic history. . . . This report is not a plan. It is a collection of analyses of some small part of the final data that will serve as a basis of future planning."[219] Anyone who expects to find the description of an actual project in this document will be disappointed. The analysis of the historical development of the state of New York is illustrated with a series of diagrams that summarize the revelant statistical information, with the aim of indicating a possible range of "tendencies" of development. In addition, this study brings together the principal productive and socioeconomic factors of territorial growth. In place of the traditional, anarchic growth, the report offers an explicit model of planned development for the region, based on the most efficient utilization of new technological resources, including the progressive replacement of steam power with electricity, the transformation of the road system, and the expansion of public and private transportation. In regard to urban polarization, congestion, and productive activity, all these factors imply a different situation; indeed, they end by directly opposing the existing one.

Thus efficient and economical utilization of technology implies a policy of decentralization; congestion is ultimately an obstacle to the comprehensive development of resources.[220] This conclusion results in part from the data collected on trends in the land market. The commission's analyses, in fact, demonstrate that when land prices increase faster than the population, a policy of decentralization is vital and, at the same time, functions as a stimulus to the creation and development of yet other technological means. These concepts are considered in the context of another problem treated in the report, that of the policy to be followed in utilizing natural energy resources.

This problem gives rise to two major issues: first, the function and use of electrical energy in a program for the decentralization of production and, second, the regulation of the use of hydroelectric power. These were not new concerns and had been the center of debate for some time; in the commission's report, however, they are approached in the context of a "tradition" that, through the RPAA and regionalist concepts, would ultimately unite the Conservation movement with the Tennessee Valley Authority.[221] In the report, these arguments are viewed in terms of objective factors and are expressed in statistical tables, charts, and projective diagrams. Ultimately, it appears, the sole aim of this "comprehensive plan" is to demonstrate its own necessity—it is not a plan, but a discourse on a plan and for a plan.

Despite the complexity of the problems involved, the report is animated by a substantially "optimistic" spirit: the "insoluble" problems of the pyramiding city can find a solution; technology has the power; it is up to man to decide on its use. The report states:

The problem therefore arises whether these activities shall be related to a general plan or shall be controlled only by the most proximate considerations. The uncoordinated economic planning that has characterized our past development neglects imponderable social values. A business man can only remotely concern himself with the conditions of life of his workers. . . . The aim of the State should be clearly to improve the conditions of life rather than to promote opportunities for profit. Obviously there is need of a plan to which at least activities of the State shall conform. The action of the State will strongly influence some private developments. At this point the effective control of the State ends.[222]

The historical road traced in this essay might end here, since the commission's report represents one of the most mature and definitive expressions of the ideology of planning that I have sought to reconstruct as a typical product of progressive thought. Actually, however, it is just the beginning of a new "story." This "plan," which has numerous points of contact with the theory of a mixed economy supported by certain members of the RPAA, contains a model and a wealth of insights that would cease to be the exclusive concern of an idealistic group of intellectuals before many years had passed and would become part of the far more complex ideology of the New Deal.

The "plan" of the Commission of Housing and Regional Planning has attracted little attention from critics and historians, who have concentrated instead on another "regional" plan for New York—that elaborated at essentially the same time by a large group of urbanists financed by the Russell Sage Foundation. Unlike the New York State Commission, the Committee on the Regional Plan of New York and Its Environs began in 1922 to prepare an actual project for New York. Under the direction of Thomas Adams, many American architects were employed in this enterprise; among them were Frederick Law Olmsted, Jr., and Hugh Ferriss, the fashionable draftsman of the time, as well as numerous exponents of "progressive planning," such as Edward M. Bassett and Robert W. de Forest.[223] This plan, supported by a notable publicity campaign, undertook to interpret and conform as well as possible to the aims of the organization that assured its funding.[224]

Although Adams's work and publications in the period immediately following the war were related, from a theoretical point of view, to the pursuits of the RPAA, and in spite of the sporadic contacts that took place between the association and the foundation, the two plans for New York prepared in the 1920s differ substantially and reflect the essentially different positions of Adams and the RPAA. Although he judged the Russell Sage Foundation plan with excessive harshness, Mumford rightly demonstrated it to be both compromising and conditioned by a basically rigid and shortsighted conception of the problem, precisely the conception the RPAA and the Commission of Housing and Regional Planning had attempted to overcome.[225]

There is, indeed, a fundamental difference between the two studies, which amounts to nothing less than two essentially different ways of understanding regional planning as a means and envisaging its ends. The research of the Russell Sage Foundation added little to the results of the New York State Commission's

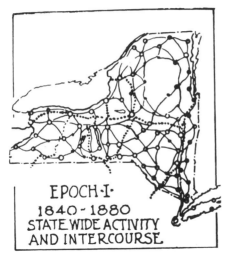

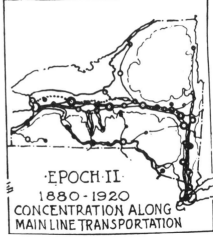

EPOCH·I·
1840-1880
STATE WIDE ACTIVITY
AND INTERCOURSE

·EPOCH·II·
1880-1920
CONCENTRATION ALONG
MAIN LINE TRANSPORTATION

Diagrams of three epochs of development in New York State (from *Report of the Commission of Housing and Regional Planning to Governor Alfred E. Smith*, May 7, 1926).

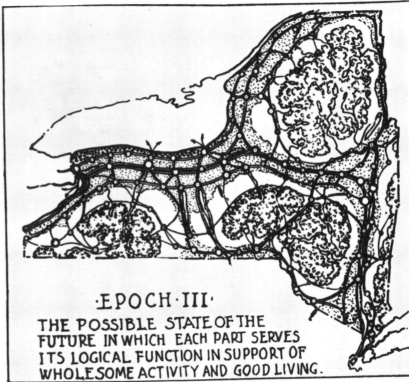

·EPOCH·III·
THE POSSIBLE STATE OF THE FUTURE IN WHICH EACH PART SERVES ITS LOGICAL FUNCTION IN SUPPORT OF WHOLESOME ACTIVITY AND GOOD LIVING.

Scheme of land uses in the New York region (from *Report of the Commission of Housing and Regional Planning to Governor Alfred E. Smith*, May 7, 1926).

FOREST RESERVE & WATER SUPPLY   DAIRYING & GRAZING   GARDENING·MANUFACTURING·ORCHARDS
HIGHLANDS · UPLAND PLATEAU · FERTILE PLAIN · LAKE

Proposals for the Russell Sage Foundation's
Regional Plan of New York and Its Environs:

Aerial view of southern Manhattan
showing the elevated waterfront boulevard
proposed by Nelson P. Lewis, 1921.

Plan for elevated boulevards in Manhattan,
1923.

Plan for regional highway routes, 1928.

studies. The extensive work performed by Adams's group produced a series of hypothetical projects that aimed, at most, at restructuring some portion of the existing urban reality. The commission's 1926 report, on the contrary, was the premise to a project that in itself represented a new way of understanding the comprehensive development of the region. Beyond its statistical conclusions, the report provides a glimpse of a plan for a city-region, not a design for a city in the region. The Russell Sage project resulted from a completely different conception of the uses and aims of planning—as Ackerman often asserted, it is not enough to analyze the phenomena; the task is to transform their causes.

The essential arguments of the 1926 report can most readily be gathered from a special issue of *Survey Graphic* that appeared a year earlier, on May 1, 1925. The issue is composed entirely of articles by RPAA members and is a source of paramount importance for understanding the significance of the regionalist theories pursued by the association. All the typical arguments are presented, from the theory of the community of controlled size to the hypothesis of the garden city as a regional urban entity, and include Ackerman's sharp criticism of those who confuse development with concentration and congestion as well as Wright's warning against considering the problem of housing in the limited terms of the rehabilitation of slums.[226]

This number of *Survey Graphic* contains four major articles, by Mumford, Stein, Chase, and Robert B. Bruère. Mumford provides the context in which all the other contributions find their place. His lead article delineates the basic theories of a project of development that goes beyond "conservationist" concepts and decrees the end of the paleotechnic era: the "fourth migration" will be founded on the "technological revolution." New means of transportation, particularly the automobile, are the vehicles of a new historical movement toward urban decongestion that sets in motion the formation of new market areas and implies the end of static relations of production; new means of communication make urban polarization obsolete; new energy sources free the choice of location for productive activities from the dictates of a passed era: "It remains for regional planning to develop all these factors at once, as part of the technique of the fourth migration."[227]

The "great city" as "the sum of all our possible aspirations," Stein affirms, is only a dream. The dynamics of its development are tainted; as the product of an inflated system, "the dinosaur city" is the very contradiction of well-being.[228] Chase demonstrates that the unbalanced territorial distribution of industry and the waste it creates can be eliminated by transportation systems structured according to production needs and by the planned and rational use of resources. "But more important than the elimination of such wastes, are the savings to be made through decentralization of population. Henry Ford has discovered that highly standardized, highly subdivided industry need no longer become concentrated in large plants with all the inconveniences of transportation and housing that hamper such community arrangements."[229] According to the theory

Projects of the United States Resettlement
Administration, Suburban Resettlement
Division:

Plan for Greenbelt Town, Maryland, by
D. D. Ellington, R. J. Wadsworth, H. Walker,
1935-37.

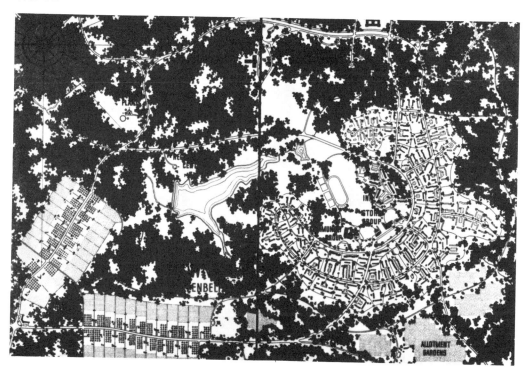

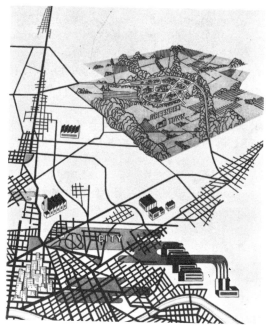

Diagram of the relationship of Greenbelt
Town, Maryland, to the preexisting urban
settlements.

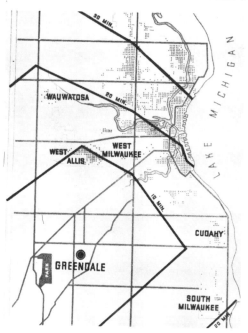

Map indicating the location of Greendale
Town, Wisconsin, in relation to the pre-
existing urban settlements, prepared by
J. Crane, E. Peets, H. H. Bentley, W. G.
Thomas, 1935-37.

elaborated by Bruère, systems of energy distribution are the fundamental structures of a new territorial distribution of settlements, and he attempts to demonstrate that the management of "giant power" can ensure comprehensive control over development.[230]

Benton MacKaye's contribution to this issue of *Survey Graphic* is the most old-fashioned of the series. In the spirit of an old sage developed through the trials of nature, MacKaye treats generically the analyses that demonstrate the need to eliminate bottlenecks in the flow of materials, products, and merchandise between settlements of different "geo-economic" types, and asserts forcefully that "to chart the framework for real *living* and not existence merely, is another fundamental of the new exploration."[231]

Rather than in an *Auflösung der Städte*, the ideology of the RPAA consists in a "technological myth," created from a meticulous survey of the disasters caused by the laissez-faire system of urban management and the conjunction of these analyses with the theories of Geddes and Veblen. The city-region is, in fact, the synthesis of a world that has in technique and technology its own equilibrating reason, one that contains fundamentally sound premises that must be given the means to express themselves. The dream of the RPAA inherited from Whitman was "the place where the great city stands," the hope in a world capable of finding values, strengthening others, and creating yet new ones, and of redistributing "lost gifts" to man. Nothing like this fundamentally optimistic view of technology, this argument with the congestion of the great city, or this faith in the true and equitable teachings of nature, leads back with more direct conviction to the very core of the tradition founded during the Golden Day.

The regionalism of the RPAA was the synthesis of the tradition of reforming the American city that has been the subject of this essay. Just as Radburn summarized the tradition that led from the rural cemeteries, through the "regionalism" of Olmsted, to the naturalistic suburb and the "war villages," the RPAA's decentralist theories were the fruit of experience gathered from the company towns and industrial settlements. The ideals of home ownership and the cooperative organization of communities originated in a part of nineteenth-century reformist ideology; they were reinforced by Ely's criticism of the "Bismarckian" organization of Pullman and represented the definitive relinquishment of any faith in the capacity of the profit system to produce by itself the means of overcoming its internal contradiction. It was, of course, this same relinquishment of faith that gave rise to the agitation for a plan and for the revision of the role of government institutions, which formed the kernel of progressivism's campaign for reform.

Conclusion

After the historic 1925 issue of *Survey Graphic*, the regionalism of the RPAA made still further progress. The association held an important meeting on the subject in 1930, and one of its last official acts, before the long parenthesis of the New Deal, was the organization of a Round Table on Regionalism, held in

July 1931 at the Institute of Public Affairs of the University of Virginia. Significantly enough, the major address was delivered by Franklin D. Roosevelt.[232]

Although this essay ends at the opening of the New Deal, the New Deal is necessary to its conclusion. As Rexford G. Tugwell has written, the most significant part of New Deal politics is to be found not in the immediate results of its emergency provisions but in the indications contained in them of a strategy fittingly adapted to the possibility of constructing a system that could ward off a catastrophic repetition of the depression.[233] The extent to which this possibliity was realized is obviously a matter that exceeds the scope of this essay; directly pertinent, however, are both the emphasis Tugwell places on the New Deal as the era that definitively rejected a passive or merely compensatory conception of politics and his attempt to trace the theoretical tradition that lay at the base of the overturning of this view. In this way the New Deal is seen as the resolution in political terms of a tradition that had expressed itself in terms of values rather than politics.[234]

It is thus that the Regional Planning Association of America has appeared to me the conclusive episode in this story. The RPAA represented the final search for a reconciliation between the world of ethics and the world that was becoming technical, but a reconciliation uncontaminated by the terms of politics. This utopia was its most original contribution as well as its impassable limit, and in its striving toward such a goal the RPAA interpreted the perennial attempt of the bourgeois spirit to substitute ethics for politics. This attempt was expressed in the construction of a "world of values," on the basis of which, fortified by an aristocratic intellectual heritage, the RPAA pursued a metahistorical and atemporal synthesis, in which the succession of eras was resolved in a continual evolution—in Geddes's terms as well as Whitman's—toward a "perfectly equilibrated" utopia. Thus is explained the RPAA's conditional adherence to the New Deal: when politics took the upper hand over ethics agreement was no longer possible.[235]

The principal theoretician of the RPAA is Lewis Mumford. His work transforms the subjects treated here into a complex ideological construct and gives them a definitive theoretical dignity. A great deal has been written about Mumford's work, and inevitably so, since he has passed through all the principal events in American culture since World War I. He has been described as a socialist, and certainly he has often been close to socialists and communists.[236] He has also been spoken of as sympathizing with fascism, and, just as certainly, he has fought against fascism.[237] He has been termed a theoretician of nostalgic medieval and romantic myths and of antiurban culture. Critics have variously stressed Spengler's or Veblen's influence on Mumford, his relationship with Geddes, or the superficiality of his approach to the economic and structural problems of the events he has treated.[238]

Some of these criticisms grasp a partial truth; all find a pretext in the thousands of pages Mumford has published. Few have understood, however, as did Van Wyck Brooks, that Mumford's work cannot be dissected, that he is a comprehensive problem of American culture.[239] Constantly present in Mumford is a conviction Geddes also held: history expresses its evolution in forms; these forms are not the romantically synthetic attributes of a work of intellect, however, but the images of civilization; they represent its ultimate value and provide its classification. Thus Mumford does not write history in the strict sense of the term, in the same way that he does not write books on sociology or architectural criticism. Instead, he wanders through history in search of a phoenix that rises again, stronger than history itself, bearing the secret of the perennial "continuity of values." In this sense, Mumford's work cannot be judged by ordinary standards; either one rejects it as useless or one reads it as an attempt outside of history to remind men that "to take advantage of our experience and our social heritage and to help in creating this new idolum is not the smallest adventure our generation may know. It is more imaginative than the dreams of the transcendentalists, more practical than the work of the pragmatists, more drastic than the criticism of the old social revolutionists, and more deeply cultural than all our early attempts to possess the simulacra of culture. It is nothing less than the effort to conceive a new world."[240]

Mumford's "new world" ends by coinciding with a certain myth that, with faith in an unending youth, continues to be perpetuated in the United States. By tirelessly resuscitating the "original values" of the American gentry, nourishing the myth, Mumford has dignified the bourgeois world of America and alleviated the inferiority complex stamped on the plaster facades of Chicago's White City. This myth has before it only two alternatives, however: to pass rapidly into the archives of history or to perpetuate itself as ideology, violating with the very confirmation of its survival all historical and political logic.

Mumford has taught that every epoch is a form. If forms have received a great deal of attention in this essay, it is because, in the progressive urban planning of America, forms are often ultimately identified with that atemporal "world of values" I have wished to examine critically. The particular historical path pursued here has, in fact, made it possible to analyze how the transition from the maximally elaborated form of romantic landscape to the technological absence of form took place on the basis—and it is this that Mumford has codified—of essentially unchanged motivations. On the one hand, this fact demonstrates the blanket applicability of the myth and its ideology; on the other, it proves the neutrality of form in the history I have traced, where the function of form is apparently reduced to the perpetuation of pure values.

All these phenomena reveal an intrinsically defensive disposition and a perennial state of insecurity. This common characteristic of the culture makes it possible to apply, even to the ingenuous and dramatic, fascinating and banal

"My God, Ed! The whole damned thing's been declared unconstitutional!"

Cartoon by Robert Day that appeared in
the *New Yorker*, June 8, 1935, after the
Supreme Court found the provisions of the
National Recovery Act unconstitutional.

world of the American intellectual, an expression much less literary and optimistic than those used by Mumford to construct the attractive myth of the Golden Day—indeed, one full of desperate solitude if applied to the America of today. Walter Benjamin wrote these words almost as if to foretell an arduous destiny: "the road of the intellectual to the radical criticism of the social order is the longest, just as that of the proletariat is the shortest."

Notes

1

Herbert Croly, *The Promise of American Life* (1909; reprint ed., Dutton, New York, 1963), p. 3.

2

Lewis Mumford, *Herman Melville: A Study on His Life and Vision* (Harcourt, Brace, New York, 1929), pp. 187, 189, 190.

3

Ibid., p. 193

4

Vernon L. Parrington, *Main Currents in American Thought,* 3 vols. (Harcourt, Brace, New York, 1927-1930), vol. 2, pp. 405-406.

5

F. O. Matthiessen, *American Renaissance* (Oxford University Press, New York, 1941).

6

John Coolidge, *Mill and Mansion* (Russell and Russell, New York, 1967), pp. 9-17, demonstrates that the industrial revolution began in America in New England. Nobumichi Hiraide, in "The New England Town and the Beginning of American Capitalist Democracy," *American Journal of Economics and Sociology* 20, Oct. 1961, p. 534, has written: "Not the industry of the old type, but the rural industry which developed from the town was necessary for the development of American capitalism. Just so, not the transatlantic markets monopolized by big merchants, but the local markets, with the transactions among farmers and craftsmen, direct producers and consumers.... That which was the basis for the spontaneous development of capitalism in America and arranged promptly for the conditions which made the development possible was the free land ownership originated from the town. This is the economic significance of the town system in New England as a starting point of American modern society." On the early New England community, see Kenneth A. Lockridge, *A New England Town. The First Hundred Years* (Norton, New York, 1970). Two works that have contributed decisively to creating the concept of the New England community are Van Wyck Brooks, *The Flowering of New England, 1815-1865* (Dutton, New York, 1936), and Lewis Mumford, *Sticks and Stones. A Study of American Architecture and Civilization* (1924; reprint ed., Dover, New York, 1955).

7

Parrington, *Main Currents* 2, p. 389.

8

Ibid. 2, pp. 388, 399-400.

9

Journals of Ralph Waldo Emerson, 1820-1872 (Houghton Mifflin, Boston, 1909-1914), vol. 6, p. 355.

10

Walt Whitman, *Democratic Vistas,* 1871; see Mark Van Doren, ed., *The Portable Walt Whitman* (Viking, New York, 1945), p. 399.

11

Quoted in John L. Hancock, "Planners in the Changing American City, 1900-1940," *Journal of the American Institute of Planners* 33, Sept. 1967, p. 295.

12

Lewis Mumford, "A Backward Glance," in idem, ed., *Roots of Contemporary American Architecture* (Dover, New York, 1972), p. 5. In the same essay Mumford states, "The first architectural writings on this tradition antedate any new building forms: the architects spelt the new ideals out in words long before they learned the art of translating them into sticks and stones and steel. The new possibilities that had first disclosed themselves in America were first plumbed by the writers of the Golden Day, by Emerson, Hawthorne and Thoreau, by Whitman and Melville" (p. 4). For a more complete analysis, see Lewis Mumford, *The Golden Day. A Study in American Literature and Culture* (Boni and Liveright, New York, 1926).

13

Henry David Thoreau, *Walden or, Life in the Woods* (1854; Modern Library ed., New York, 1950), p. 46.

14

Christopher Tunnard and Henry Hope Reed, *American Skyline: The Growth and Form of Our Cities and Towns* (Houghton Mifflin, Boston, 1955), p. 86.

15.

On utopian communities, see also Giorgio Ciucci "The City in Agrarian Ideology and Frank Lloyd Wright: Origins and Development of Broadacres," this volume.

16

The *Manifesto of the Communist Party* contains the first embryonic criticisms of the utopian tradition, criticisms that were subsequently corrupted by Engels and thoroughly reelaborated in Marx's later writings. For a valid historical reconstruction of the position of scientific socialism in regard to utopia, see Massimo Cacciari, "Utopia e socialismo," *Contropiano* 3, Sept.-Dec. 1970. The classic contributions to the criticism of utopia remain those of the German sociologists, Martin Buber, Karl Mannheim, and the early school of Frankfurt, and, in other ways, that of Joseph Alois Schumpeter. Antiurbanism has been analyzed as a component of European thought, with scant results in regard to utopia, in Carl E. Schorske, "The Idea of City in European Throught: Voltaire to Spengler," in Oscar Handlin and John Burchard, eds., *The Historian and the City* (MIT Press and Harvard University Press, Cambridge, Mass., 1963), pp. 95-114.

17

Lewis Mumford , "Origins of the American Mind," *The American Mercury* 8, July 1926, p. 354. The literature on the utopian communities of America is vast; works readily available for consultation are Mark Halloway, *Heavens on Earth* (Dover, New York, 1966), a classic history of the subject; Charles Nordhoff, *The Communistic Societies of the United States* (1875; reprint ed., Dover, New York, 1966); John Noyes, *History of American Socialism* (1870; reprint ed., Dover, New York, 1966); William A. Hinds, *American Communities and Cooperative Colonies* (Kerr, Chicago, 1908); Albert Fried, ed., *Socialism in America from the Shakers to the Third International* (Doubleday, New York, 1970), which contains important documents. See also Morris Hillquit, *History of Socialism in the United States* (Dover, New York, 1971); Arthur E. Morgan, *Nowhere Was Somewhere: How History Makes Utopias and Utopias Make History* (University of North Carolina Press, Chapel Hill, 1946); Lewis Mumford, *The Story of Utopias* (1922; reprint ed., Viking, New York, 1962); Donald Drew Egbert and Stow Persons, eds., *Socialism and American Life* (Princeton University Press, Princeton, 1952). On particular groups and communities see Lindsay Swift, *Brook Farm, Its Members, Scholars and Visitors* (Macmillan, New York, 1900), which contains an important bibliography; George B. Lockwood, *The New Harmony Movement* (Appleton, New York, 1905); Karl J. R. Arndt, *George Rapp's Harmony Society, 1785-1847* (University of Pennsylvania Press, Philadelphia, 1965). On the specific issue of the utopian communities and town planning, see John W. Reps, "Cities of Zion: The Quest for Utopia," in idem, *Town Planning in Frontier America* (Princeton University Press, Princeton, 1971); William J. Murtagh, *Moravian Architecture and Town Planning* (University of North Carolina Press, Chapel Hill, 1967); Martin Meyerson, "Utopian Tradition and the Planning of Cities," *Daedalus* 90, winter 1961; Richard T. Ely, "Amana: A Study of Religious Communism," *Harper's Monthly* 105, Oct. 1902; David Riesman, "Some Observations on Community Plans and Utopia," *Yale Law Journal* 57, Dec. 1947, which treats the entire utopian production of the United States in general terms. Among the most recent studies are the new edition of Arthur E. Bestor, *Backwoods Utopias* (University of Pennsylvania Press, Philadelphia, 1971); Liselotte and Oswald M. Ungers, *Kommunen in der Neuen Welt, 1740-1971* (Kiepenheuer & Witsch, Cologne, 1972); Dolores Hayden, *Seven American Utopias* (MIT Press, Cambridge, Mass., 1976).

18

For the quotations from the *Encyclopedia Britannica* and Joel Barlow, see Michael Kraus, "America and the Utopian Ideal in the Eighteenth Century," *Mississippi Valley Historical Review* 22, Mar. 1936, pp. 497-500. See also Mumford, *Sticks and Stones*, pp. 13-31.

19

Brook Farm, founded in 1841 by John Ripley, a former Unitarian minister, was a transcendentalist-inspired community that sought to integrate intellectual activity with manual work and the cultivation of about 160 acres of land. In 1844, after it took the name Brook Farm Phalanx, Emerson and Thoreau broke away. The Brook Farm Phalanx employed all its resources in building a phalanstery that was destroyed by fire on the very day of its inauguration. By 1846 the life of the community had essentially ended.

20

On Etzler's work see W. H. G. Armytage, "John A. Etzler, an American Utopist," *American Journal of Economics and Sociology* 16, Oct. 1956.

21

On Mormon town planning, in addition to the works already cited and the studies of John W. Reps, see Lowry Nelson, *The Mormon Village: A Pattern and Technique of Land Settlement* (University of Utah Press, Salt Lake City, 1952); Charles L. Sellers, "Early Mormon Community Planning," *Journal of the American Institute of Planners* 28, Feb. 1962.

22

After describing the plan of the community, John W. Reps, *The Making of Urban America* (Princeton University, Princeton, 1965), p. 456, states, "Zoar remains as a reminder of what utopian America was like a century or so ago." On the Separatists, see Catherine R. Dobbs, *Freedom's Will: The Society of the Separatists of Zoar* (William Frederick Press, New York, 1947).

23

See Norman T. Newton, "Early American Background," in idem, *Design on the Land. The Development of Landscape Architecture* (Harvard University Press, Belknap Press, Cambridge, Mass., 1971), pp. 246-266.

24

The projects in Boston are discussed in Charles W. Eliot, *Charles Eliot, Landscape Architect* (Houghton Mifflin, Boston, 1902), p. 240. See also idem, "A List of Books on Landscape Gardening Held to Have Influenced the Beginnings of Modern Gardening, 1625 to 1834," *Garden and Forest* 1, Apr. 18, 1888.

25

Vincent Scully, *American Architecture and Urbanism* (Thames and Hudson, London, 1969), p. 89. The sources of this attitude go back even farther than Jeffersonian physiocracy. See Reps, *Town Planning in Frontier America*, pp. 425-426. On the Horticultural Society, see Albert E. Benson, *History of the Massachusetts Horticultural Society* (Massachusetts Horticultural Society, Boston, 1929); Robert Manning, *History of the Massachusetts Horticultural Society* (Massachusetts Horticultural Society, Boston, 1880). On the rural cemeteries, see Andrew J. Downing, "Public Cemeteries and Public Gardens," *Horticulturalist*, July 1849, also contained in idem, *Rural Essays* (Leavitt, New York, 1869); for a brief general discussion of the phenomenon, see Reps, "Cemeteries, Parks and Suburbs: Picturesque Planning in the Romantic Style," in idem, *Making of Urban America*. On Mount Auburn Cemetery, see Cornelia Walter, *Mount Auburn Illustrated*, Rural Cemeteries of America Series (Martin, New York, 1847). On Greenwood Cemetery in Brooklyn, see Nehemiah Cleveland, *Greenwood Cemetery. A History of the Institution from 1838 to 1864* (Anderson and Archer, New York, 1866); idem, *Greenwood Illustrated*, Rural Cemeteries of America Series (Martin, New York, 1847). For a brief, interesting reference to the phenomenon, see Albert Fein, "The American City: The Ideal and the Real," in Edgar Kaufmann, Jr., ed., *The Rise of an American Architecture* (Pall Mall Press, London and New York, 1970), pp. 81-83.

26

See Daniel Aaron, *Men of Good Hope* (Oxford University Press, New York, 1969), p. 40 and the chapter on Theodore Parker.

27

Reps, *Making of Urban America*, p. 330.

28

Wayne Andrews, *Architecture, Ambition and Americans. A Social History of American Architecture* (Free Press of Glencoe, New York, 1964), pp. 103-104. On the historical styles discussed here, see Thomas E. Tallmadge, "The Greek Revival," in idem, *The Story of*

Architecture in America (Norton, New York, 1936); Tunnard and Reed, "The Romantic Era," in idem, *American Skyline;* John Burchard and Albert Bush-Brown, *The Architecture of America. A Social and Cultural History* (Little, Brown, Boston, 1961), especially the first sections. Particularly important are some chapters in James Marston Fitch, *American Building, the Historical Forces that Shaped It* (Houghton Mifflin, Boston, 1966); Talbot Hamlin, *Greek Revival Architecture in America* (Oxford University Press, New York, 1944). For an overall view, see William H. Pierson, Jr., *American Buildings and Their Architects. The Colonial and Neoclassical Styles* (Doubleday, New York, 1970).

29
Karl Marx, *The Eighteenth Brumaire of Louis Bonaparte,* 1852; see "Excerpts from the Eighteenth Brumaire of Louis Bonaparte," in Karl Marx and Friedrich Engels, *Basic Writings on Politics and Philosophy,* Lewis S. Feuer, ed. (Doubleday, New York, 1959).

30
Quoted in Fitch, *American Building,* pp. 72-73. Particularly interesting for an understanding of Latrobe as a representative figure of the bourgeois architect is his 1806 letter to Robert Mills, published in Talbot Hamlin, *Benjamin Henry Latrobe* (Oxford University Press, New York, 1955), pp. 538ff.

31
On Moller's influence, see Don Gifford, ed., *The Literature of Architecture. The Evolution of Architectural Theory and Practice in Nineteenth Century America* (Dutton, New York, 1966), pp. 32-33. On the period as a whole, see James Early, *Romanticism and American Architecture* (Barnes, New York, 1965).

32
On Davis, see Roger H. Newton, *Town and Davis Architects* (Columbia University Press, New York, 1942): Wayne Andrews, "Alexander Jackson Davis," *Architectural Review* 109, May 1951. On Llewellyn Park, see Christopher Tunnard, *The City of Man* (Scribner's Sons, New York, 1953), pp. 183ff.

33
On these principles, see the material from Andrew J. Downing, *Architecture of Country Houses, Including Designs for Cottages, Farm-Houses, and Villas, with Remarks on Interiors, Furniture, and the best Modes of Warming and Ventilating* (New York, 1850), included in idem, *Rural Eassays,* and in Gifford, *Literature of Architecture,* pp. 199ff.

34
See Fein, "American City," p. 75.

35
Downing, "Public Cemeteries and Public Parks."

36
Fein, "American City," p. 74. On the Mall design, see John W. Reps, "Downing and the Washington Mall," *Landscape* 16, Spring 1967.

37
Leo Marx, *The Machine in the Garden: Technology and the Pastoral Ideal in America* (Galaxy Books, New York, 1967), p. 11; see also Roderick Nash, "The American Cult of the Primitive," *American Quarterly* 18, June 1966. On Downing, see W. G. Jackson, "First Interpreter of American Beauty: A. J. Downing and the Planned Landscape," *Landscape* 1, Winter 1952; Sarah Lewis Pattee, "Andrew Jackson Downing and His Influence on Landscape Architecture in America," *Landscape Architecture* 19, Jan. 1929; "The Debt of America to A. J. Downing," *Garden and Forest* 8, May 29, 1895. Various interesting ideas are also found in the following works by Vincent Scully: "American Villas. Inventiveness in American Suburbs from Downing to Wright," *Architectural Review* 115, Mar. 1954; "Romantic Rationalism and the Expression of Structure in Wood: Downing, Wheeler, Gardner and the 'Stick Style,'" *Art Bulletin,* June 1953; "American Houses: Thomas Jefferson to Frank Lloyd Wright," in Kaufmann, *Rise of An American Architecture.*

38
On the origins of the concept of the public park, see Newton, *Design on the Land,* p. 267. Mumford speaks of the importance of the European experiments in *Sticks and Stones,* pp. 94-95. For the activity of William Cullen Bryant, the best source is his own *Letters of a*

Traveller, or Notes on Things Seen in Europe and America (Putnam, New York, 1850); but
see also Curtis J. Johnson, *Politics and a Belly-Full: The Journalistic Career of William
Cullen Bryant, Civil War Editor of the "New York Evening Post"* (Vintage, New York,
1962). On London, "a utilitarian model" see Fein, "American City," pp. 83-84; on Paxton,
see George F. Chadwick, *The Works of Sir Joseph Paxton, 1803-1865* (Architectural Press,
London, 1961), pp. 44-71; on Gourlay's work see Fletcher Steele, "Robert Fleming Gourlay,
City Planner," *Landscape Architecture* 6, Oct. 1915; on the formation of a landscape
culture in general, see George F. Chadwick, *The Park and the Town. Public Landscape in the
19th and 20th Centuries* (Praeger, New York, 1966).

39

On these aspects of Olmsted's life, see Laura Wood Roper's three important articles:
"Frederick Law Olmsted in the 'Literary Republic,'" *Mississippi Valley Historical Review*
39, Dec. 1952; "Mr. Law and Putnam's Monthly Magazine: A Note on a Phase in the Career
of Frederick Law Olmsted," *American Literature* 84, Mar. 1954; "Frederick Law Olmsted
and the Western Free-Soil Movement," *American Historical Review* 56, Oct. 1950. Olmsted's book *Walks and Talks of an American Farmer in England* has recently been republished (University of Michigan Press, Ann Arbor, 1967). His writings on the South have been
collected in Arthur M. Schlesinger, ed., *The Cotton Kingdom: A Traveller's Observations on
Cotton and Slavery in the American Slave States* (Knopf, New York, 1953), and have been
discussed by Broadus Mitchell, *Frederick Law Olmsted: A Critic of the Old South* (John
Hopkins University Press, Baltimore, 1924). The classic text for the study of Olmsted's
work is Frederick Law Olmsted, Jr., and Theodore Kimball Hubbard, eds., *Frederick Law
Olmsted: Landscape Architect*, 2 vols. (Putnam's Sons, New York, 1924); taking its place
beside it is Laura Wood Roper's recent *Biography of Frederick Law Olmsted* (John
Hopkins University Press, Baltimore, 1973). The following are good anthologies of his
writings, with useful introductions: Albert Fein, ed., *Landscape into Cityscape. Frederick
Law Olmsted's Plans for Greater New York City* (Cornell University Press, Ithaca, 1968); S.
B. Sutton, ed., *Civilizing American Cities. A Selection of Frederick Law Olmsted's Writings
on City Landscape*, (M.I.T. Press, Cambridge, Mass., 1971). The best historical analyses,
other than those provided by Roper, are those by Fein; in addition to Fein's "American
City," see "Frederick Law Olmsted," *Town and Country Planning* 31, Dec. 1963; "Parks in
a Democratic Society," *Landscape Architecture* 55, Oct. 1965; and *Frederick Law Olmsted
and the American Environmental Tradition* (Braziller, New York, 1972). See also Julius Gy.
Fabos, Gordon T. Milde, V. Michael Weinmayr, *Frederick Law Olmsted, Sr. Founder of
Landscape Architecture in America* (University of Massachusetts Press, Amherst, 1968).
Some of the more recent literature on Olmsted has been reviewed by Jan R. Stewart in
Journal of the Society of Architectural Historians 30, Dec. 1971; see also idem, "Parks,
Progressivism and Planning," *Landscape Architecture* 58, Apr. 1968.

40

See Newton, *Design on the Land*, p. 273; Seymour Mandelbaum, *Boss Tweed's New York*
(Wiley, New York, 1965), pp. 70-75; Alexander B. Callow, *The Tweed Ring* (Oxford
University Press, New York, 1966).

41

Lewis Mumford, *The Brown Decades. A Study of the Arts in America, 1865-1895* (1931;
reprint ed., Dover, New York, 1971), p. 40.

42

See Frederick Law Olmsted and Calvert Vaux, *Description of a Plan for the Improvement of
Central Park: "Greensward"* (New York, 1858), reprinted in Fein, *Landscape into City-
scape*, pp. 64-88, especially pp. 65-68. Very useful for an understanding of Olmsted's
convictions and as an aid to biographical study is Charles C. McLaughlin, "Selected Letters
of Frederick Law Olmsted" (Ph.D. diss. Harvard University, 1960). The statement about
Radburn, which is Mumford's, is confirmed by Clarence S. Stein, *Toward New Towns for
America* (Reinhold, New York, 1957), p. 44.

43

See Fein, *Landscape into Cityscape*, pp. 71-74. Something of Olmsted's "protofunction-
alist" attitude is revealed in his description of the yachts he saw in Portsmouth harbor. The

English boats were beautiful, he commented, "in an arbitrary manner, . . . without regard to the primary beauty of utility" (Olmsted, *Walks and Talks*, pp. 289-295). The concept expressed here by Olmsted was quite similar to that of Horatio Greenough, another attentive observer of ship forms.

44

Frederick Law Olmsted, "A Fragment of Autobiography," in Fein, *Landscape into City-scape*, p. 52.

45

This attitude is clear from Olmsted's objections to certain modifications made in the plan of Central Park; in fact, he strongly opposed any attempt to disrupt the relationship established between the park and the city. See New York City Department of Public Parks, *Second Annual Report of the Board of Commissioners of the Department of Public Parks for the Year Ending May 1, 1871 (Bryant, New York, 1871)*. On Olmsted's interest in education, see Henry Hope Reed and Sophia Duckworth, *Central Park. A History and a Guide* (Potter, New York, 1967); Clay Lancaster, "Central Park 1851-1951," *Magazine of Art* 44, Apr. 1951. Also interesting are the articles by Vaux's collaborator Samuel Parsons, Jr.; see Parsons, "Interesting Facts in Regard to the Development of Central Park," in American Society of Landscape Architects, *Transactions, 1899-1908* (Horace McFarland, Harrisburg, 1908), and Samuel Parsons, Jr., and W. R. O'Donovan, "Art of Landscape Gardening in Central Park," *Outlook* 84, Sept. 1906.

46

See Frederick Law Olmsted, *Public Parks and the Enlargement of Towns* (American Social Science Association, Riverside Press, Cambridge, Mass., 1870), reprinted in Sutton, *Civilizing American Cities*, pp. 79, 83.

47

See Fein, *Frederick Law Olmsted*, p. 33.

48

Olmsted, Vaux and Company, *Preliminary Report upon the Proposed Suburban Villages at Riverside, near Chicago*, (Sutton, Brownes, New York, 1868), reprinted in Sutton, *Civilizing American Cities*, p. 295. On this concept, see Fabos, Milde, Weinmayr, *Frederick Law Olmsted*, pp. 47-56. On Riverside, see "Riverside Illinois. A Residential Neighborhood Designed over Sixty Years Ago. Selected from the Papers of Frederick Law Olmsted, Senior," *Landscape Architecture* 21, July 1931; Howard K. Menhinick, "Riverside Sixty Years Later," ibid. 22, Jan. 1932.

49

Frederick Law Olmsted, *Seventh Annual Report of the Board of Commissioners of the Department of Parks for the City of Boston for the Year 1881*, City Document no. 16 (Boston, 1882), reprinted in Sutton, *Civilizing American Cities*, p. 227. On the Boston park system, see Sylvester Baxter, *Boston Park Guide* (Small, Maynard, Boston, 1898); idem, "The Boston Metropolitan Park Movement," *Garden and Forest* 5, Feb. 10, 1892; idem, "Baltimore Municipal Art Conference," *Municipal Affairs* 3, Dec. 1899; Boston Metropolitan Park Commission, *A History and Description of the Boston Metropolitan Parks* (Wright and Potter, Boston, 1900); Frederick Law Olmsted, Jr., "The Metropolitan Park System of Boston," in American Society of Landscape Architects, *Transactions, 1899-1908;* John Charles Olmsted, "The Boston Park System," ibid.; Clarence Pullen, "The Boston Park and Parkways System," *Harper's Weekly* 34, Sept. 27, 1890; Andrew Wright Crawford, "The Development of Park Systems in American Cities," *Annals of the American Academy of Political and Social Science* 25, Mar. 1905. On the urban development of Boston, see Walter Muir Whitehill, *Boston. A Topographical History* (Harvard University Press, Cambridge, Mass., 1975).

50

Robert M. Copeland, *The Most Beautiful City in America. Essay and Plan for the Improvement of the City of Boston* (Lex and Shepard, Boston, 1872), p. 10.

51

Fein, *Frederick Law Olmsted*, pp. 60-61. On Boston as the center of reform, see the fundamentally important book by Arthur Mann, *Yankee Reformers in the Urban Age.*

Social Reform in Boston, 1880-1900 (Harper Torchbook, New York, 1966), especially the chapters dedicated to the Protestant movement (pp. 73-101), the cultural avant-garde (pp. 145-174), and Bellamy's influence (pp. 153-159). On urban and institutional transformations in Boston during this period, in addition to the works cited in note 49, see Sam B. Warner, Jr., *Streetcar Suburbs. The Process of Growth in Boston, 1870-1900* (Atheneum, New York, 1971). On Bellamy see Parrington, *Main Currents;* Morgan, *Nowhere Was Somewhere;* Aaron, *Men of Good Hope,* pp. 94-132; John H. Franklin, "Edward Bellamy and the Nationalist Movement," *New England Quarterly* 11, Dec. 1938; Edward Bellamy, "How I Came to Write *Looking Backward,*" *Nationalist* 1, May 1889. On the utopian literature of the late nineteenth century in general, see Allyn B. Forbes, "The Literary Quest for Utopia, 1880-1900," *Social Forces* 6, Dec. 1927.

52

See Henry-Russell Hitchcock, *The Architecture of H. H. Richardson and His Times* (MIT Press, Cambridge, Mass., 1966), especially pp. 213-214; Mariana Griswold Van Rensselaer (Mrs. Schuyler Van Rensselaer), *Henry Hobson Richardson and His Work* (1888; reprint ed., Dover, New York, 1969), which contains some interesting quotations from the Richardson-Olmsted correspondence.

53

In 1888 Jacob Weidenmann published a book entitled *Modern Cemeteries,* but his most important work was *Beautiful Country Houses. A Handbook of Landscape Gardening* (Judd, New York, 1870).

54

Boston Metropolitan Park Commission, *Report 1919,* (Boston, 1919), p. 19.

55

Eliot, *Charles Eliot,* p. 375. Sylvester Baxter's statement appeared in "Thirty Years of Greater Boston's Metropolitan Park System, *Boston Transcript,* Sept. 29, 1923; see also Newton, *Design on the Land,* pp. 333-335; Sylvester Baxter, "A Monumental Work of Landscape Architecture: The Metropolitan Park System of Boston," *Architectural Record* 25, June 1909.

56

Robert M. Copeland and H. W. S. Cleveland, *A Few Words on the Central Park* (Boston, 1859); H. W. S. Cleveland, *The Public Grounds of Chicago: How to Give Them Character and Expression* (Lakey, Chicago, 1869); idem, *Landscape Architecture as Applied to the Wants of the West* (1873; reprint ed., University of Pittsburgh Press, Pittsburgh, 1965). An important article for the study of Cleveland's work is Theodora Kimball Hubbard, "H. W. S. Cleveland, an American Pioneer in Landscape Architecture and City Planning," *Landscape Architecture* 20, Jan. 1930.

57

See H. W. S. Cleveland, "Suggestions for a System of Parks and Parkways for the City of Minneapolis," in Board of Park Commissioners of the City of Minneapolis, *First Annual Report for the Year Ending March 13th, 1884.* p. 6.

58

See H. W. S. Cleveland, *The Aesthetic Development of the United Cities of St. Paul and Minneapolis* (Minneapolis Society of Fine Arts, Minneapolis, 1888): idem, *The Park System of St. Paul and Minneapolis* (Smyth, Saint Paul, 1887).

59

Montgomery Schuyler, "Last Words About the World's Fair," *Architectural Record* 3, Jan.-Mar. 1894, reprinted in William H. Jordy and Ralph Coe, eds., *American Architecture and Other Writings by Montgomery Schuyler* (Atheneum, New York, 1964), p. 282. For other significant judgments of the fair, see Thomas Adams, *Outline of Town and City Planning* (Russell Sage Foundation, New York, 1935), pp. 167-173; Mumford, *Sticks and Stones,* pp. 127-135; Fitch, *American Building,* pp. 210-213. Notable is the exceptional critical viewpoint of Hegemann, strongly adverse not only to the fair but also to the Chicago school, to the Park Commission's plan was Washington, to Mumford, and to Charles H. Whitaker's *Story of Architecture. From Ramses to Rockefeller;* see Werner Hegemann, *City Planning Housing* (Architectural Book Publishing, New York, 1936), vol. 2, pp. 343-394. On

Olmsted's role in the fair, see Frederick Law Olmsted, "The Landscape Architecture of the World's Columbian Exposition," *Proceedings of the Twenty-seventh Annual Convention of the American Institute of Architects and World Congress of Architects* (Inland Architectural Press, Chicago, 1893). For a general perspective, see Mel Scott, *American City Planning Since 1890* (University of California Press, Berkeley and Los Angeles, 1969), pp. 43ff. On the White City, see Mario Manieri-Elia, "Toward an 'Imperial City': Daniel H. Burnham and the City Beautiful Movement," this volume. I have expressed some ideas on this subject elsewhere; see Francesco Dal Co, "Louis Henry Sullivan: la qualità nell'epoca della metropoli. Appunti su 'Autobiografia di un'idea,'" *Rassegna dell'Istituto di Architettura e Urbanistica* 7, Apr. 1971.

60

Quoted in John W. Reps, *Monumental Washington. The Planning and Development of the Capital Center* (Princeton University Press, Princeton, 1967), p. 109.

61

Hegemann, *City Planning Housing 2,* pp. 387-394.

62

Reps, *Monumental Washington,* p. 198.

63

William H. Wilson, *The City Beautiful Movement in Kansas City* (University of Missouri Press, Columbia, 1964), p. 48. Wilson's is the most complete work on this subject and is useful for the study of the movement in general.

64

Ibid., p. 49. On Kansas City, see also Henry C. Haskell, Jr., and Richard B. Flower, *City of the Future. A Narrative History of Kansas City, 1850-1950* (Glenn, Kansas City, 1950); William H. Wilson, "Beginning of the Park and Boulevard Movement in Frontier Kansas City," *Missouri Historical Review* 56, Apr. 1962; Henry Schott, "A City's Fight for Beauty," *The World's Work* 11, Feb. 1906; George B. Ford, "The Park System of Kansas City, Missouri," *Architectural Record* 40, Dec. 1916; C. R. Ashbee, "Kansas City, Missouri: The Influence of a Park System," *Town Planning Review* 6, Apr. 1916; H. van Buren Magonigle, "In Memoriam, George Edward Kessler," *Journal of the American Institute of Architects* 12, Mar. 1924.

65

See Wilson, *The City Beautiful Movement in Kansas City,* p. 52. The most important document for understanding the conception of the plan is *Report of the Board of Park and Boulevard Commissioners of Kansas City, Mo., Embracing Recommendations for the Establishment of a Park and Boulevard System for Kansas City. Resolution of October 12, 1893* (Hudson-Kimberly, Kansas City, 1893). Also valuable is George E. Kessler, "Kansas City Park System and Its Effect on the City Plan," *Proceedings of the Ninth National Conference on City Planning*, Kansas City, May 7-9, 1917. For a discussion of the economic implications of the plan, see idem, "Actual Distribution of the Cost of Kansas City Parks and Boulevards," *Proceedings of the Fifth National Conference on City Planning*, Chicago, May 5-7, 1913; William Buchholz, "Acquirement of Kansas City Park and Boulevard System and Its Effect on Real Estate Values," *Proceedings of the Ninth National Conference on City Planning*, Kansas City, May 7-9, 1917.

66

Charles Mulford Robinson, *Modern Civic Art, or the City Made Beautiful* (Putnam's Sons, New York and London, 1903), p. 28. In the last few pages I have been referring to the City Beautiful movement as a whole, singling out the aspects of it that are related to ideas and practices of "progressive urbanism." From this point of view, Kessler's work is, in my opinion, extremely important. Here, obviously, I am treating phenomena merely in terms of tendencies, but the task that remains is clarifying and defining the very concept of City Beautiful, as Manieri-Elia has done in regard to the work of Daniel H. Burnham in the opening essay of this volume.

67

A classical source for the issues treated in this chapter is Charles R. Van Hise, *The*

Conservation of Natural Resources in the United States (Macmillan, New York, 1922). More recent and complete studies include Samuel P. Hays, *Conservation and the Gospel of Efficiency. The Progressive Conservation Movement* (Harvard University Press, Cambridge, Mass., 1959); Frank E. Smith, *The Politics of Conservation* (Random House, New York, 1966).

68

See Samuel Eliot Morison and Henry Steel Commager, *The Growth of the American Republic* (Oxford University Press, New York, 1962), vol. 2, pp. 134-135.

69

See Walter Prescott Webb, *The Great Plains* (1931; reprint ed. Blaisdell Publishing Co., Waltham, Mass, 1959), pp. 419-422. Powell's report of 1878 has recently been republished; see John W. Powell, *Report on the Lands of the Arid Region of the United States, with a More Detailed Account of the Lands of Utah*, ed. Wallace Stegner (Harvard University Press, Cambridge, Mass., 1962).

70

Quoted in Webb, *The Great Plains*, p. 356.

71

Ibid., p. 355. An interesting collection of Powell's writings is George Crossette, ed., *Selected Prose of John Wesley Powell* (Godine, Boston, 1970). On Powell's work, see also William C. Darrah, *Powell of the Colorado* (Princeton University Press, Princeton, 1951); Wallace Stegner, *Beyond the Hundredth Meridian* (Houghton Mifflin, Boston, 1954); John V. Terrell, *The Man who Rediscovered America* (Weybright and Talley, New York, 1969).

72

See Lewis Mumford, *The Culture of Cities* (1938; reprint ed., Harcourt Brace Jovanovich, New York, 1970), p. 302.

73

Elwood Mead, "Irrigation Legislation," *Outlook* 72, Apr. 12, 1902; idem, *Irrigation Institutions* (Macmillan, New York, 1909).

74

Report of the Commission on Land Colonization and Rural Credits of the State of California (Sacramento, Nov. 29, 1916), quoted in Roy Lubove, *The Urban Community. Housing and Planning in the Progressive Era* (Prentice-Hall, Englewood Cliffs, N.J., 1967), p. 31.

75

See U.S., Congress, House, Committee on Labor, *Hearing on the Crosser Colonization Bill*, Dec. 15-20, 1916 (Government Printing Office, Washington, D.C.); Elwood Mead, *Summary of Soldier Settlements in English-Speaking Countries* (U. S., Department of the Interior, Washington, D.C., 1918). On MacKaye's use of the same examples, see Benton MacKaye, *Employment and Natural Resources* (U.S., Department of Labor, Washington, D.C., 1919), especially pp. 107-109.

76

For the influence of Marsh's study on the exponents of regionalism, see Mumford, *Brown Decades*, pp. 32-35; Lewis Mumford, "The Theory and Practice of Regionalism," *Sociological Review* 20, Jan. 1928, p. 21; Patrick Geddes and Victor Bradford, "Rural and Urban Thought: A Contribution to the Theory of Progress and Decay," ibid. 21, Jan. 1929, p. 6; Marshall Stalley, ed., *Patrick Geddes: Spokesman for Man and the Environment* (Rutgers University Press, New Brunswick, N.J., 1972), pp. 312ff.

77

H. W. S. Cleveland was particularly concerned with the problem of forests; the original edition of his *Landscape Architecture as Applied to the Wants of the West* included an essay on "Forest Planting on the Great Plains," and in 1886 he published *The Culture and Management of Our Native Forests*. For a brief, interesting document on the Conservation movement, see also William Letwin, ed., *A Documentary History of American Economic Policy Since 1789* (Norton, New York, 1972), pp. 275ff.

78

The information on the origin of the Applachian Trail project is taken from an unpublished typescript by Benton MacKaye, "Some Early A[ppalachian] T[rail] History," probably from 1956, in the Clarence S. Stein archives in New York. On the history of the Appalachian Trail, see Benton MacKaye, "An Appalachian Trail: A Project in Regional Planning," *Journal of the American Institute of Architects* 9, Oct. 1921; idem, "The Applachian Trail: Guide to the Story of Nature," *Scientific Monthly* 34, Apr. 1932. For biographical data on MacKaye, see Lewis Mumford's introduction to Benton MacKaye, *The New Exploration* (University of Illinois Press, Urbana, 1962). On the history and purposes of the Appalachian Mountain Club, see Charles E. Fay, "The Appalachian Mountain Club," *Annals of the American Academy of Political and Social Science* 35, Jan.-June 1910.

79

"[MacKaye] was the first educated forester, who helped President Roosevelt organize the first Governors Conference in 1908—the first time that the President of the U.S. ever invited the Governors to the White House. They went back to their capitals and created state conservation agencies, which fell into disuse after the first world war" (Charles S. Ascher to Francesco Dal Co, March 25, 1973).

80

MacKaye, *Employment and Natural Resources*, p. 10.

81

Ibid., p. 12.

82

Ibid., pp. 22-23.

83

Ibid., p. 29.

84

On the working units, see ibid., pp. 81-82, 133ff.

85

MacKaye, *New Exploration*, p. 148.

86

The two essays referred to are "The Significance of the Frontier in American History," delivered as a lecture in 1893 and published in the *American Historical Association, Annual Report for 1893*, (Washington, D.C., 1894), and "Social Forces in American History," *American Historical Review* 16, Jan. 1911, both reprinted in Frederick Jackson Turner, *Frontier and Section* (Prentice-Hall, Englewood Cliffs, N.J., 1961).

87

Arthur M. Schlesinger, *Paths to the Present* (Macmillan, New York, 1949), p. 233.

88

On the relationship between industrial development and urbanization, see Blake McKelvey, *The Urbanization of America, 1860-1915* (Rutgers University Press, New Brunswick, N.J., 1963), p. 45. For the statistical data, see Adna Ferrin Weber, *Growth of Cities in the Nineteenth Century. A Study in Statistics* (1899; reprint ed., Cornell University Press, Ithaca, 1963), pp. 20-40. On the impact of the Civil War on the process of industrialization see Ralph Andreano, *The Economic Impact of the American Civil War* (Schenkman, Cambridge, Mass., 1962), The relationship between the growth of industrial production and the number of wage earners is treated in Victor S. Clark, *History of Manufactures in the United States* (McGraw-Hill, New York, 1929); Clark states, "In 1860 the product of our manufacturing industries was valued at less than $2,000,000,000 and our factories and work shops employed about 1,300,000 wage earners. In 1914, the last year for which we have a comparable dollar, the product had multiplied by more than twelve and exceeded $24,000,000,000, while the number of wage earners had increased over fivefold, to slightly above 7,000,000" (vol. 3, p. 351).

89

Shigeto Tsuru, "The Economic Significance of Cities," in Handlin and Burchard, *Historian and the City*, p. 49. For a discussion of Tsuru's theory, see Alexander Gerschenkron, "City Economics. Then and Now," ibid., pp. 56-62.

90

The city's role as the necessary basis for the increase of productive specialization and as the fundamental socioeconomic structure for the development of inventions and innovations has been discussed many times, in general as well as in reference to American history; sufficient reference for the period covered here is the interesting analysis by Allan R. Pred, *The Spatial Dynamics of U.S. Urban-Industrial Growth, 1800-1914. Interpretive and Theoretical Essays* (MIT Press, Cambridge, Mass., 1966); see, especially, "Industrial Inventions, Industrial Innovations: Some Locational Relationships with Urban Growth" and the discussion of the tables on pp. 106-108. See also Robert Higgs, "Cities and Yankee Ingenuity, 1810-1920," in Kenneth J. Jackson and Stanley K. Schultz, eds., *Cities in American History* (Knopf, New York, 1972), pp. 16-18; Higgs asserts the parallel progress and development of urbanization and inventions. For a general treatment of the subject, see Richard L. Meier, "The Organization of Technological Innovation in Urban Environments," in Handlin and Burchard, *Historian and the City*, pp. 74-83; idem, *A Communication Theory of Urban Growth* (MIT Press and Harvard University Press, Cambridge, Mass., 1966).

91

Simon Kuznets, *National Income: A Summary of Findings* (National Bureau of Economic Research, New York, 1946). The literature on economic cycles in 1873-1914 is vast; a few of the more interesting analyses are G. H. Moore, *Statistical Indicators of Cyclical Revivals and Recessions* (National Bureau of Economic Research, New York, 1950), which maintains that in 1873-1914 the phases of expansion were only six months longer than the phases of recession; Wesley Mitchell, *Business Cycles: Problem and Its Setting* (National Bureau of Economic Research, New York, 1927), which demonstrates that the relationship of periods of prosperity to periods of depression in 1894-1914 was reduced to a ratio of 2:1, in comparison with the 9:1 ratio of the years between 1865 and 1896. For a schematic summary, see the table in Paul A. Baran and Paul M. Sweezy, *Monopoly Capital. An Essay on the American Economic and Social Order* (Modern Reader Paperbacks, New York and London, 1968), p. 229. On wages, a basic document is U.S., Department of Labor, Bureau of Labor Statistics, *History of Wages in the United States, 1860-1890*, Bulletin no. 499 (Government Printing Office, Washington, D.C., Oct. 1929). See also Albert Rees, *Real Wages in Manufacturing, 1890-1914* (Princeton University Press, Princeton, 1961). A good summary table of real wages is contained in August C. Bolino, "American Socialism's Flood and Ebb: The Rise and Decline of the Socialist Party in America, 1901-1912," *American Journal of Economics and Sociology* 82, no. 2, 1963.

92

Baran and Sweezy, *Monopoly Capital*, p. 227.

93

On this period, see ibid., chap. 8, where the authors state that "the years after 1907 were characterized by mounting surplus absorption difficulties and the kind of 'creeping stagnation' with which we have become familiar in the later 1950's and early 1960's. . . . If the First World War had not come along, the decade 1910-1920 would have gone down in United States history as an extraordinarily depressed one" (p. 234). On building construction trends, see Willford I. King, "Building National Prices," *Architectural Record* 49, Jan. 1921; idem, "The Building Prospect I, II, III," ibid., Apr., May, June 1921; idem, "The Business Outlook for 1923," ibid. 53, Jan. 1923.

94

In the 1870s the first attempts were made at federal regulation of the railroads; one of the most notable efforts in this direction was that of the Granger movement. In 1887 the Interstate Commerce Act was passed; this first "progressive" victory over the trusts was later perfected with the Sherman Antitrust Act of 1890 and the formation of the Federal Trade Commission in 1914. See the chapters entitled "Regulation of Railroads" and "Antitrust Policy," in Letwin, *American Economic Policy*, pp. 157-246.

95

Along with the history of unionism, that of the political parties of the labor movement should also be considered; as it cannot be addressed in the space of this essay, the reader is referred to Mark Karson, *American Labor Unions and Politics, 1900-1918* (Southern Illinois

University Press, Carbondale, 1958); M. Hillquit, *History of Socialism;* David Shannon, *The Socialist Party of America. A History* (Macmillan, New York, 1955); Fried, *Socialism in America;* John R. Commons, *History of the Labor Movement* (Kelley, New York, 1949); Egbert and Persons, *Socialism and American Life;* Ira Knipis, *The American Socialist Movement, 1897-1912* (Greenwood Press, New York, 1968); Daniel Bell, *Marxian Socialism in the United States* (Princeton University Press, Princeton, 1967); Christopher Lasch's important *Agony of the American Left* (Random House, New York, 1969); Theodore Draper, *The Roots of American Communism* (Viking Press, New York, 1957); Werner Sombart's classic "Study of the Historical Development and Evolution of the American Proletariat," *International Socialist Review* 6, nos. 3, 5, 6, 1905. An important bibliographical source is Walter Goldwater, "Radical Periodicals in America, 1890-1950. A Bibliography with Brief Notes," *Yale University Library Gazette* 34, no. 4, 1963; in addition, *Labor History*, published by the Temiment Institute of New York, regularly offers bibliographical information.

96
The principal sources for the history of American unionism are David Saposs, *Left Wing Unionism* (International Publishers, New York, 1926); Philip S. Foner, *History of the Labor Movement in the United States*, 4 vols. (International Publishers, New York, 1964); Selig Perlam, *History of Trade Unionism in the United States* (Macmillan, New York, 1959); Samuel Gompers, *Seventy Years of Life and Labor*, 2 vols. (Dutton, New York, 1925); Philip Taft, *The A. F. of L. in the Time of Gompers* (Octagon Books, New York, 1970); Eugene V. Debs, *Life, Writings and Speeches* (Kerr, Chicago, 1908); Maurice F. Neufeld, *A Bibliography of Labor Union History* (Cornell University Press, Ithaca, 1954).

97
On the Industrial Workers of the World, see Foner, *History of the Labor Movement.* Interesting information is also available in Charles A. Madison, *American Labor Leaders*, and in the writings by some of the principal figures of the IWW; see Elizabeth Gurley Flynn's *Sabotage* and *I Speak My Own Piece;* Emma Goldman's *Living My Life;* William D. Haywood's *Bill Haywood's Book.* Patrick Renshaw's pleasantly written *Wobblies, The Story of Syndacalism in the United States* (Doubleday, Anchor Books, New York, 1967), ends thus: "In James Jones' novel *From Here to Eternity* one of the characters discusses his experiences in the IWW. 'It was their vision that made them great,' he says. 'And it was their belief which made them powerful. And sing! You never heard anybody sing the way those guys sang! Nobody sings like that unless it's for a religion!' This faith in the possibility of a better society must remain their justification—and their epitaph." This is the literary conclusion, not mine.

98
Sidney Fine, *Laissez Faire and the General-Welfare State. A Study of Conflict in American Thought, 1865-1901* (University of Michigan Press, Ann Arbor, 1964), p. 351; see also the entire chapter "In Quest of Reform."

99
On the origins of American sociology, see the first parts of Roscoe C. and Gisella J. Hinkle, *The Development of Modern Sociology* (Random House, New York, 1954). On certain characteristics of the Chicago school, see Guido Martinotti's introduction to *Citta e analisi sociologica* (Marsilio, Padua, 1968); Alessandro Pizzorno's introduction to the Italian translation of Robert E. Park, Ernest W. Burgess, Roderick D. McKenzie, *The City* (University of Chicago Press, Chicago, 1925), published in Italy by Comunita, Milan, 1967. On the importance of the Chicago school of sociology for regionalist theories, see John Friedmann, "The Concept of Planning Region. The Evolution of an Idea in the United States," in John Friedmann and William Alonso, eds., *Regional Development and Planning* (M.I.T. Press, Cambridge, Mass., 1964), pp. 507-514.

100
On the history of muckraking, see C. C. Regier, *The Era of the Muckrakers* (North Carolina University Press, Chapel Hill, 1932); Louis Filler, *The Muckrakers*, (Pennsylvania State University Press, University Park, 1976). On the position of the muckrakers, Ray Stannard Baker commented, "We 'muckraked' not because we hated our world but because we loved

it. We were not hopeless, we were not cynical, we were not bitter" (quoted in Richard Hofstadter, *The Age of Reform. From Bryan to F. D. R.* [Knopf, New York, 1955], p. 195). On the origin of the word *muckraker*, attributed to Theodore Roosevelt, see Richard Hofstadter, ed. *The Progressive Movement, 1900-1915* (Prentice-Hall, Englewood Cliffs, N.H., 1963), pp. 18-19.

101

On the influence of the urban problem on literature, see Robert H. Walker, "The Poet and the Rise of the City," in Alexander B. Callow, Jr., ed., *American Urban History. An Interpretive Reader with Commentaries* (Oxford University Press, New York, 1969), pp. 363-373.

102

David M. Chalmers, *The Social and Polical Ideas of the Muckrakers* (Citadel Press, New York, 1964), pp. 115-116.

103

Quoted in ibid., pp. 12-13.

104

Immediately afterward, Roosevelt added, "Again, I do not have any sympathy with the reformer who says he does not care for dividends." See Theodore Roosevelt, *The New Nationalism* (Prentice-Hall, Englewood Cliffs, N.J., 1961), pp. 36-37.

105

See Arthur S. Link, *Woodrow Wilson and the Progressive Era, 1910-1917* (Harper Torchbooks, New York, 1963), pp. 54-80.

106

See Richard Hofstadter, *The American Political Tradition and the Men Who Made It* (Knopf, New York, 1948), chaps. 9, 10. On the consequences of Wilson's politics, see Link, *Woodrow Wilson;* William Appleman Williams, *The Contours of American History* (World, Cleveland and New York, 1961), pp. 390-412. On the relationship between progressivism and new forms of business enterprise the literature is vast; a few brief references are Robert H. Wiebe, *Businessmen and Reform* (Harvard University Press, Cambridge, Mass., 1962); Gabriel Kolko, *The Triumph of Conservatism* (Free Press of Glencoe, New York, 1963); Christopher Lasch, *The New Radicalism in America, 1889-1963* (Knopf, New York, 1965); James Weinstein, *The Corporate Ideal and the Liberal State, 1900-1918* (Beacon Press, Boston, 1968). On the position of the left, see the repeated references in Max Eastman's editorials entitled "Knowledge and Revolution" in the *Masses,* issued from 1911 to 1917; Charles T. Hallinan, "Roosevelt and the Third Party," ibid. 4, Aug. 1912. See also Francesco Dal Co, preface to Annachiara Danieli, *L'Opposizione Culturale in America. L'età progressista e "The Masses"* (Feltrinelli, Milan, 1975).

107

For the two quotations from Roosevelt see Roosevelt, *New Nationalism,* p. 39; Hofstadter, *American Political Tradition,* p. 229. On the Roosevelt-Croly relationship, see the essay by William E. Leuchtenburg, "Theodore Roosevelt's 'The New Nationalism,' " which forms the preface to Roosevelt's *New Nationalism.*

108

Hofstadter, *American Political Tradition,* p. 252.

109

Walt Whitman, *Democratic Vistas,* 1871; see Van Doren, *Portable Walt Whitman,* pp. 427-428.

110

On the history of Paterson, see Charles Shriner, *Four Periods of Paterson History* (Lont and Overcamp, Paterson, N.J., 1919); William Nelson, *History of Paterson and Its Environs* (Lewis Historical Publishing, New York, 1920).

111

On Lowell, see the enormously useful, classic study by Coolidge, *Mill and Mansion,* to which the reader is referred for all further bibliographical information. On the relationship between urbanization and economic development in this early period of the nineteenth century, see also Pred, *U.S. Urban-Industrial Growth,* pp. 152ff.

112

Coolidge, *Mill and Mansion*, p. 22.

113

Francis Cabot Lowell founded the Boston Manufacturing Company in Waltham, Massachusetts, with capital of $400,000. At his death in 1817, the enterprise was carried on by Nathan Appleton and Patrick Tracy Jackson, who made Kirk Boott director. In 1822 a new site was acquired on the Merrimack River, and the Merrimack Manufacturing Company was created to supplant the Boston Manufacturing Company. In the same year, Boott prepared a plan for the new town of Lowell. The industrial plant consisted of 5 mill units laid out to economize water frontage; the plan also included the construction of dwellings for the employees, for which Boott even prescribed the materials to be used.

114

See ibid., pp. 26-27; on the growth of the population and the trend in land values in Lowell, see the graphs, pp. 142, 143.

115

According to Coolidge the five social classes of Lowell were, at the top of the pyramid, the executives of the company; (the stockholders did not live in the community); next, the skilled workers; third, the actual labor force of the factory, composed for the most part of unmarried farm girls; fourth, the occasional laborers engaged in the canal work and building construction; and, beside these four groups, the inhabitants not directly employed by the company. The dwellings the Merrimack Manufacturing Company built for its employees were physically separated from the residences of the other inhabitants of the town, who lived to the other side of the main street and were not subject to the company's regulations. See ibid., pp. 33-35.

116

Ibid., pp. 73-74.

117

See ibid., p. 109. On the organization of work in Lowell, see also Bernard A. Weisburger, "The Working Ladies of Lowell," *American Heritage* 12, Feb. 1961.

118

See Reps, *Making of Urban America*, pp. 417-420.

119

On the history of Cairo, see John W. Reps, "Great Expectations and Hard Times: The Planning of Cairo, Illinois," *Journal of the Society of Architectural Historians* 16, Dec. 1957. On the general phenomena of urbanization discussed here, see Graham R. Taylor, *Satellite Cities: A Study of Industrial Suburbs* (Appleton, New York, 1915); E. R. L. Gould, "The Housing of the Working People," in *Eighth Special Report of the Commission of Labor*, ed. Carroll D. Wright, Commissioner of Labor (Government Printing Office, Washington, D.C., 1895); Grosvenor Atterbury, "Model Towns in America," *Scribner's Magazine* 52, July 1912; Arthur C. Comey and Max S. Wehrly, "Planned Communities," in U.S., National Resources Committee, Urbanism Committee, *Supplementary Report*, pt. 1, vol. 2, *Urban Planning and Land Policies* (Government Printing Office, Washington, D.C., 1939).

120

For the story of George Pullman's enterprises, see Joseph Husband, *The Story of the Pullman Car* (A. C. McClory, Chicago, 1917); Steward H. Holbrook, *The Story of American Railroads* (Crown, New York, 1947); Almont Linsey, *The Pullman Strike* (University of Chicago Press, Chicago, 1967), chap. 2. Also interesting is the pamphlet *The Story of Pullman*, distributed by Pullman's Palace Car Company at the Transportation Building of the Columbian Exposition in 1893.

121

In my opinion, the most complete work on the town of Pullman is Stanley Buder, *Pullman: An Experiment in Industrial Order and Community Planning, 1880-1930* (Oxford University Press, New York, 1970). On the aspects of George Pullman's personality mentioned here, see pp. 38-45. On the history of the town of Pullman, see also Linsey, *Pullman Strike*, chap. 3, 4; Duale Doty, *The Town of Pullman* (Struhsacher, Pullman, 1893); Robert Lillibridge, "Pullman: Town Development in the Era of Eclecticism," *Journal of the Society of Architectural Historians* 12, Oct. 1953; William T. W. Morgan, "The Pullman Experiment in Review," *Journal of the American Institute of Planners* 20, Winter 1954; Irving Pond, "America's First Planned Industrial Town," *Illinois Society of Architects Monthly Bulletin*, June-July 1934; George C. Nimmons, "Modern Industrial Plants I," *Architectural Record* 44, Nov. 1918. On the more specifically social aspects of the town, see the basic essay by Richard T. Ely, "Pullman: A Social Study," *Harper's Monthly* 70, Feb. 1885; Charles H. Eaton, "Pullman Paternalism," *American Journal of Politics* 5, 1894, pp. 571-579; Thomas B. Grant, "Pullman and Its Lessons," ibid., pp. 190-204; Edwin L. Shuey, "A Model Factory Town," *Municipal Affairs* 3 no. 1, 1899; Francesco Dal Co, "Città modello e controllo sociale," *Quaderni storici* 9, Sept.-Dec. 1974.

122

Buder, *Pullman: An Experiment*, p. 35.

123

Ely, "Pullman: A Social Study," see also Shuey, "Model Factory Town," p. 145.

124

According to the table drawn up by Buder, the population of Pullman grew from 4 in 1881 to 8,603 inhabitants on July 28, 1885; see *Pullman: An Experiment*, p. 89.

125

The quotation is from Ely, "Pullman: A Social Study," p. 464, where the author criticizes the policy of not conceding proprietorship of the houses to the workers. On the system of rents in Pullman, see Buder, *Pullman: An Experiment*, p. 90 table.

126

See Linsey, *Pullman Strike*, pp. 90-105. Tables summarizing the trends in salaries and employment in Pullman in 1893 and 1894 appear in Buder, *Pullman: An Experiment*, pp. 163-167.

127

On the dimensions of the strike, see Linsey, *Pullman Strike*, pp. 239ff. On the role of the American Railway Union and the consequences of the strike for it, see Foner, *History of the Labor Movement*, 2:261-278. Contemporary accounts are numerous; the best known are William Carwardine, *The Pullman Strike* (Kerr, Chicago, 1894); Edgar A. Bancroft, *The Chicago Strike of 1894* (Gunthrop Warren, Chicago, 1895). The basic works on the federal intervention are Grover Cleveland, *The Government in the Chicago Strike of 1894* (Princeton University Press, Princeton, 1913); and the extremely important document prepared by the United States Strike Commission, *United States Commission's Report on the Chicago Strike of June-July 1894*, Senate Executive Document no. 7, 53rd Cong., 3rd Sess. (Government Printing Office, Washington, D.C., 1895). See also Harvey Wise, "The Pullman Strike: A Study in Industrial Warfare," *Journal of the Illinois State Historical Society* 32, Sept. 1939.

128

U. S. Strike Commission, *Report*, pp. xxxvff.

129

Ely, "Pullman: A Social Study," p. 465. See also Sanford Cohen, "Conservatism, Radicalism and Unionism," *American Journal of Economics and Sociology* 16, Jan. 1957, a general article, in which Pullman is not directly mentioned.

130

Henry George died in New York on October 29, 1897. In the course of his life he had many different occupations, including ship-boy, printer, miner, and journalist; George had connections with the principal political movements of the epoch and himself undertook a political career; he was also in contact with many exponents of the progressive movement and with numerous labor leaders. See Anna George De Mille, *Henry George, Citizen of the World* (North Carolina University Press, Chapel Hill, 1950); Henry George, Jr., *The Life of Henry George* (Doubleday, Doran, Garden City, N.Y., 1930); Charles A. Baker, *Henry George* (Oxford University Press, New York, 1955); Steven B. Cord, *Henry George: Dreamer or Realist?* (University of Pennsylvania Press, Philadelphia, 1965); Aaron, *Men of*

Good Hope, pp. 55-91. On George's relations with Britain, see Elwood P. Lawrence, *Henry George in the British Isles* (Michigan University Press, East Lansing, 1957); Bernard Newton, "The Impact of Henry George on British Economists," *American Journal of Economics and Sociology* 30, Apr., July 1971.

131
On the single tax as a land tax, see Aaron, *Men of Good Hope*, p.71. On the "nationalization" of land, see Steven Cord, "A New Look at Henry George," *American Journal of Economics and Sociology* 27, Oct. 1968, especially pp. 397-398. On the concept of property, as well as on other aspects of George's thought, see the interesting account of the debate between Henry George and Serge Schevitch in New York on October 25, 1887, with Samuel Gompers as moderator, "Henry George versus Serge Schevitch. Single Tax versus Socialism," in Fried, *Socialism in America*, pp. 234-243. For a general perspective on George's ideas within the history of economic thought, see the fine discussion in Mark Blaug, *Economic Theory in Retrospect*, rev. ed. (Irwin, Homewood, Ill., 1968), pp. 88-89; see also Paul Samuelson, "Economists and the History of Ideas," *American Economic Review* 52, Mar. 1962.

132.
M. Blaug, *Economic Theory in Retrospect*, p. 89.

133.
The quotation is from "Henry George versus Serge Schevitch," p. 239. On George's "system of values," see Aurele A. Durocher, "Social Ideas of Henry George," *American Journal of Economics and Sociology* 20, Oct. 1961. For a general reconstruction of the economic theories found in George's work, see C. B. Fillebrown, *The Principles of Natural Taxation*, (C. C. McClurg, Chicago, 1917). On the diffusion of his ideas, see Aaron, *Men of Good Hope*; A. N. Young, *The Single Tax Movement in the United States* (Princeton University Press, Princeton, 1916). For some instances in which George's theories were taken up again, see F. G. Garrison, "Single Tax and the War Problem," *Masses* 8, Aug. 1916; Louis E. Post, "Real Estate Men and the Single Tax," *American City* 7, Aug. 1912; Charles T. Root, "Not a Single Tax!" ibid. 9, July 1913; Byron W. Holt, "The Single Tax Applied to Cities ," *Municipal Affairs* 3, June 1899. A brief but important work is Henry George, "A Single Tax Upon Land," *Century Magazine* 40, July 1890. See also the discussion of George in Ciucci, "City in Agrarian Ideology," this volume.

134
Mumford, *Story of Utopias*, p. 161. On Bellamy, see above the references in n51.

135
Riesman, "Some Observations," pp. 192ff. See also Elizabeth Sadler, "One Book's Influence. Edward Bellamy, *Looking Backward*," *New England Quarterly* 17, Dec. 1944; Aaron, *Men of Good Hope*, pp. 92-132; Parrington, *Main Currents*, 3, pp. 302-315.

136
See William C. Frederick, "Was Veblen Right about the Future of Business Enterprise?," *American Journal of Economics and Sociology* 24, July 1965, p. 239; Helen P. Liebel, "Thorstein Veblen's Positive Synthesis," ibid., April 1965, pp. 203-204. On Veblen's work, see Joseph Dorfman, *Thorstein Veblen and His America* (Gollancz, New York, 1934); L. E. Traywick, *Parallelism in the Economic Ideas of Karl Marx and Thorstein Veblen* (University of Illinois Press, Urbana, 1942); Rexford G. Tugwell, "Veblen and *Business Enterprise*," *New Republic* 98, 29 Mar. 1939.

137
Blaug, *Economic Theory in Retrospect*, pp. 679-680. See also Forest G. Hill, "Veblen, Berle and the Modern Corporation," *American Journal of Economics and Sociology* 26, July 1967, pp. 280-283. Extremely important for an understanding of Veblen's influence, as well as that of Simon Patten and the new economic science created in America during the Progressive Era, is Rexford G. Tugwell, "The New Deal: The Progressive Tradition," *Western Political Quarterly* 3, Sept. 1950, especially pp. 403-414.

138
See Richard T. Ely, *The Coming City* (Crowell, New York, 1902), pp. 101-107; Roy Lubove, "The New York Association for Improving the Conditions of the Poor: The Formative Years," *New York Historical Society Quarterly* 43, July 1959.

139

John Ihlder, "The Development of Civic Spirit," *Proceedings of the National Municipal League of Cincinnati Conference for Good City Government*, 1909, p. 432. On the results of the City Beautiful movement, as the term is used here, see Frederick Law Olmsted, Jr., "The Limits of City Beautification," *American City* 2, May 1910; "The City Beautiful: the Ideal to Aim at," ibid.; Scott, *American City Planning*, pp. 65ff; Roy Lubove, "Housing Reform and City Planning in Progressive America," in *Cities in American History*, ed. Jackson and Schultz, p. 345.

140

See Robert W. de Forest and Lawrence Veiller, *The Tenement House Problem. Including the Report of the New York State Tenement House Commission of 1900*, 2 vols. (New York, 1903); Edith Elmer Wood, *The Housing of the Unskilled Wage Earner. America's Next Problem* (Macmillan, New York, 1919), pp. 31-45.

141

To my knowledge the most fully documented study on Veiller's work is Roy Lubove, "Lawrence Veiller and the New York State Tenement House Commission of 1900," *Mississippi Valley Historical Review* 47, Mar. 1971. On the philanthropic organizations, see Marvin E. Gettleman, "Charities and Social Classes in the United States, 1874-1900." *American Journal of Economics and Sociology* 22, Apr., July 1963. On these issues and others, see the special issue of the *Survey* 25, Mar. 25, 1911, dedicated to "Congestion of Population. Symposium on the Report of the New York Commission." Theodore Roosevelt expressed progressive ideas on the issue of philanthropy in "Reform Through Social Work," *McClure's Magazine* 16, Mar. 1901. On the New York tenement-house exhibition of 1900, see Jacob A. Riis, "The Tenement House Exhibit," *Harper's Weekly* 44, Feb. 3, 1900.

142

Edith Elmer Wood, "What is a House? VI: Constructive Legislation and Its Lesson for the United States," *Journal of the American Institute of Architects* 6, Feb. 1918, p. 58. For Wood's criticism of Veiller, see *Housing of the Unskilled Wage Earner*, pp. 60-80. On Veiller's own position, see Lawrence Veiller, "The Housing Problem in American Cities," *Annals of the American Academy of Political and Social Science* 25, Jan.-June 1905; idem, *Model Housing Law* (Russell Sage Foundation, New York, 1914); idem, *Housing Reform: A Handbook for Practical Use in American Cities* (Russell Sage Foundation, New York, 1919).

143

On Benjamin C. Marsh's activity, see Scott, *American City Planning*, pp. 84ff. Marsh's most interesting work is *An Introduction to City Planning: Democracy's Challenge to the American City* (Marsh, New York, 1909); see also idem, *Lobbyist for the People: A Record of Fifty Years* (Public Affairs Press, Washington, D.C., 1953); idem, "City planning in Justice to the Working Population," *Charities and The Commons* 19, Feb. 1, 1908.

144

On New York zoning, see Wood, *Housing of the Unskilled Wage Earner*, pp. 231-232; Scott, *American City Planning*, pp. 153ff.; George B. Ford, "How New York City Now Controls the Development of Private Property," *City Plan* 2, Oct. 1916. On Bassett's work, see Edward M. Bassett, "Zoning Practice in the New York Region," in *Regional Plan of New York and Its Environs: A Form of State Enabling Act for Zoning* (New York, 1924); idem, *The Board of Appeals in Zoning* (National Municipal League, New York, 1922). Fundamental for the study of this problem is U.S. Department of Commerce, Advisory Committee on Zoning, *Zoning Primer* (Government Printing Office, Washington, D.C., 1922); the Advisory Committee included, in addition to Bassett, I. B. Hiett, J. Ilder, M. Knowles, N. P. Lewis, J. H. McFarland, F. L. Olmsted, Jr., and L. Veiller.

145

Hegemann, *City Planning Housing* 1, p. 163. On zoning in relation to the problem of congestion, see George B. Ford, "City Planning and Congestion," in the special issue of the *Survey* 25, Mar. 25, 1911. In addition to the criticisms made by Wood and Hegemann, see Henry Wright, *Rehousing Urban America* (Columbia University Press, New York, 1935), pp. 69-70. On the "philosophy" of zoning, see Lawson Purdy, "Zoning of Cities," *Proceedings of the Sixth National Conference on Housing*, Chicago, October 15-17, 1917.

146
See Ford, "How New York City Now Controls," in which the author states: "Constantly the Commission wanted to be more drastic than they were, but they restrained themselves as they felt it was far more important to plan a law which would be likely to be upheld by the courts rather than to secure all they felt desirable with the possibility of the whole law being declared unconstitutional. . . . Another thing which the Commission kept continually in mind was the necessity of conserving real estate values" (p. 6).

147
For the examples of foriegn legislation considered by the Massachusetts Homestead Commission see MHC, *Second Annual Report* (Wright and Potter, Boston, 1915), appendix 3. On the MHC's agricultural activities, see idem, *Third Annual Report* (Wright and Potter, Boston, 1915), pp. 9ff. On its propaganda activities, see idem, *Sixth Annual Report* (Wright and Potter, Boston, 1918), pp. 18ff; idem, *Seventh Annual Report* (Wright and Potter, Boston, 1920), pp. 8ff. In addition to the evaluation made in 1919 by Wood, *Housing of the Unskilled Wage Earner*, pp. 209-221, the most important contribution to the study of the MHC is contained in Roy Lubove, *Community Planning in the 1920's: The Contribution of the Regional Planning Association of America* (University of Pittsburgh Press, Pittsburgh, 1963), pp. 5-15.

148
The MHC, already formed in 1909, was actually instituted by law in 1911. Its members were C. Gettemy, chairman, H. Sterling, secretary, K. L. Butterfield, A. C. Comey, W. D. Foster, C. A. Parker, A. L. Thorndike, G. C. Whipple, and E. W. White. The most important documents on the creation of the MHC and its aims are MHC 688, *Bill for the Creation of the Homestead Commission* (Wright and Potter Boston, 1910); MHC 198, *Adverse Report of the Homestead Commission* (Wright and Potter, Boston, 1919); MHC 258, *Favorable Report of Minority of the Homestead Commission* (Wright and Potter, Boston, 1919); Massachusetts Bureau of Statistics, *Homesteads for Workingmen*, Labor bulletin, no. 88 (Wright and Potter, Boston, 1912); MHC 1615, *Report of the Metropolitan Plan Commission* (Wright and Potter, Boston, 1912); MHC, *What City Plan Means*, bulletin no. 1 (Wright and Potter, Boston, 1913); *Teaching Agriculture to Families as a Relief for Unemployment and Congestion of Population*, bulletin no. 3 (Wright and Potter, Boston, 1915). See also Charles Gettemy, "The New Massachusetts Legislation Regulating Municipal Indebtedness," *National Municipal Review* 3, Oct. 1914; Walter H. Kilham, "Housing by the Commonwealth of Massachusetts," *Journal of the American Institute of Architects* 4, Mar. 1918.

149
On the relationship between planning and housing, see MHC, *Seventh Annual Report*, pp. 22-23. In an interview in May 1972, Lewis Mumford maintained that the influence of the MHC on subsequent planning activity in America was slight, while Roy Lubove, in an interview during the same period, spoke of the MHC as primarily a symbol and considered the termination of this experiment a consequence of the radical character of the commission. In my opinion the most accurate evaluation remains Wood's, cited above.

150
On the progress of zoning and the extension of the application of this type of legislation, see George B. Ford, *Building Zones. A Handbook with Special Reference to Their Application in New York City under the Zone Resolution of July 25th, 1916* (Lawyers Mortgage Company, New York, 1917); Theodora Kimball Hubbard and Henry V. Hubbard, *Our Cities To-day and To-morrow. A survey of Planning and Zoning Progress in the United States* (Harvard University Press, Cambridge, Mass., 1929), appendix 2; Gordon Witnall, "History of Zoning," *Annals of the American Academy of Political and Social Science* 155, May 1931.

151
On the practice followed in America, see the chapters entitled "Zoning" and "Major Street Plans and Traffic Relief" in Hubbard and Hubbard, *Our Cities*. The writings of the German urbanists are amply cited in the bibliography of John Nolen, ed., *City Planning. A Series of Papers Presenting the Essential Elements of a City Plan* (Appleton, New York, 1917). On

the circulation of the knowledge of European experiments in America, see Frederic C. Howe, "A Way Toward the Model City," *World's Work* 21, Dec. 1910. Also significant was the participation of Hénard—*in absentia*—at the 1906 convention of American architects; see Eugène Hénard, "The Artistic Development of Paris," *Proceedings of the Thirty-ninth Annual Convention of the American Institute of Architects*, 1906. The importance of German planning was explicitly recognized in Frank Koester, "American City Planning, I," *American Architect* 102, Oct. 23, 1912, pp. 144-145, and in Cornelius Gurlitt, "German City Planning," *Architectural Record* 24, Aug., Nov. 1908. From 1910 on, the journal *American City* was a major source of information about European undertakings.

152
Rudolf Eberstadt, "Town Planning in Germany: The Greater Berlin Competition," in Royal Institute of British Architects, *Town Planning Conference, London, 10-15 October 1910. Transactions* (London, 1911), pp. 314, 320.

153
It should be recalled that the garden cities and German industrial villages were amply represented at the London conference in 1910. On British and European undertakings contemporary American journals offered full documentation, of which a few examples are Frank Chouteau Brown, "A German 'Garden City' Suburb Designed by George Metzendorf," *Architectural Review* 4, Apr. 1916; Elsa Rehmann, "Margarethenhöhe bie Essen," *Architectural Record* 36, Oct. 1914; J. K. Klaber, "The Garden City of Hellerau," ibid. 35, Feb. 1914; Edward E. Pratt, "The Garden Cities in Europe," *American City* 7, Dec. 1912; Thomas Adams, "Planning for Civic Betterment in Town and Country," ibid. 15, July 1916; John Ihlder, "Financing English Housing," ibid. 12, Oct. 1915; Lawrence Veiller, "Are Our Great Cities Menaced? The Garden City as a Way Out," *Architectural Record* 51, Feb. 1922.

154
On Unwin's importance in this regard, see Frederic J. Osborne, *Green-belt Cities* (Schocken Books, New York, 1971), pp. 38-39. Among Raymond Unwin's writings published in America are "Improvement of Towns," *Craftsman* 8, Dec. 1901, and "The Relation of Land Values and Town Planning," *Annals of the American Academy of Political and Social Science* 51, Jan. 1914. Among Adams's writings see Thomas Adams, "Need for a Constructive Policy in Regard to Town Planning," *City Plan* 1, June 1915; idem, "Planning for Civic Betterment."

155
See Scott, *American City Planning*, pp. 88ff.; Samuel Howe, "Forest Hills Gardens," *American Architect* 102, Oct. 30, 1912; "Forest Hills Gardens," *American City* 4, Mar. 1911; Atterbury, "Model Towns in America"; and, especially, Giorgio Ciucci, "Qualità contro disgregazione urbana. Forest Hills Gardens," *Casabella*, no. 426, 1977.

156
On Gary, see Reps, *Making of Urban America*, pp. 427ff.; Henry B. Fuller, "An Industrial Utopia: Building Gary, Indiana, to Order," *Harper's Weekly* 51, Oct. 12, 1907; John K. Mumford, "This land of Opportunity: Gary the City that Rose from a Sandy Waste," ibid. 52, July 4, 1908.

157
A few of the works on these and similar undertakings are George D. McCarthy, "Morgan Park. A New Type of Industrial Community," *America City* 14, Feb. 1916; "Morgan Park. An Industrial Suburb for the Minnesota Steel Company," *American Architect* 113, June 1918; L. L. Smith, "The Industrial Garden City of Kohler, Wisconsin," *American Landscape Architect* 3, Sept. 1930; Ralph F. Warner, "The Town of Mark, Indiana. A Manufacturer's Housing Enterprise," *Architectural Review* 6, Nov. 1918; idem, "Allwood. An American 'Garden Village' near Passaic, N.J.," ibid., Feb. 1918; A. T. Luce, "Kincaid, Illinois. Model Mining Town," *American City* 13, July 1915; George H. Miller, "Fairfield. A Town with a Purpose," ibid. 9, Sept. 1913; Charles C. May, "Indian Hill. The Industrial Village at Worcester, Massachusetts," *Architectural Record* 41, Jan. 1917. Articles of a general character on this type of undertaking include Robert L. Davidson, "A Check List of the Principal Housing Developments in the United States," ibid. 5, Apr. 1917; MHC, *Second*

Annual Report, p. 30 and the following table; Lawrence Veiller, "Industrial Housing Developments in America, I, III, and IV," *Architectural Record* 43, Mar., May, and June 1918; John Nolen, "American Small Towns," *Town Planning Review* 16, July 1934; idem, "Industrial Village Communities in the United States," *Garden Cities and Town Planning* 11, Jan 1921; Warren H. Manning, "A Step Toward Solving the Industrial Housing Problem," *American City* 12, Apr. 1915.

158
On Tyrone, see Bertram G. Goodhue, "The New Mining Community of Tyrone, N.M., *Architectural Review* 6, Apr. 1918; Clarence S. Stein to M. A. Mikkelsen, July 3, 1918 (5-page typecript), Clarence S. Stein archives, New York.

159
See John Nolen, *Replanning Small Cities* (Huebsch, New York, 1912), p. 5. The best contributions to the study of Nolen are John L. Hancock, "John Nolen, The Background of a Pioneer Planner," *Journal of the American Institute of Planners* 36, Nov. 1960; and his far more comprehensive *John Nolen and the American Planning Movement: A History of Culture Change and Community Response. 1900-1940* (University of Pennsylvania Press, Philadelphia, 1964).

160
See Nolen, *Replanning Small Cities*, p. 156. On this aspect of Nolen's thought, see idem, *New Towns for Old. Achievements in Civic Improvement in Some American Small Towns and Neighborhoods* (Marshall Jones, Boston, 1927), pp. 146ff.; Hancock, *John Nolen*, pp. 3, 235-236.

161
See Nolen, *Replanning Small Cities*, pp. 158ff.

162
Idem, "Real Estate and City Planning," *City Plan* 2, Apr. 1916, pp. 5-8.

163
Idem, *Replanning Small Cities*, p. 111.

164
A brief bibliography of Nolen's writings can be found in Hancock, "John Nolen, Pioneer Planner"; a complete list is provided in idem, *John Nolen. A Bibliographic Record of Achievement* (Cornell University, Ithaca, 1976).

165
Earle S. Draper, "Activity in Southern Mill Village Development," *Textile World Journal*, Feb. 7, 1920. Analagous considerations are found in idem, "Southern Mill Village Development," ibid., Feb. 4, 1922; idem, "Mill Village Development," ibid., Feb. 9, 1924; idem, "Southern Textile Village Planning," *Landscape Architecture* 18, Oct. 1927; idem, "Proposed City Planning Improvements for an Industrial Section of La Grange," *American City* 42, June 1930.

166
On these aspects of garden-city planning, see Raymond Unwin, "Planning for the Expansion of Cities," (Lecture given at Columbia University, January 7, 1937), reprinted in Walter L. Creese, ed., *The Legacy of Raymond Unwin: A Human Pattern for Planning* (MIT Press, Cambridge, Mass., 1967), pp. 193ff.; Dugald MacFayden, *Sir Ebenezer Howard and the Town Planning Movement* (MIT Press, Cambridge, Mass., 1970), pp. 699ff.

167
Samuel P. Hays, "The Politics of Reform in Municipal Government in the Progressive Era," in Callow, *American Urban History*, p. 429.

168
On urban reform and boss rule, the bibliography is enormous, and only a few works are listed here. Roy Lubove, *Twentieth Century Pittsburgh*, (Wiley, New York, 1969), is particularly useful; see also Jack Tager, *The Intellectual as Urban Reformer. Brand Whitlock and the Progressive Movement* (Press of Case Western Reserve University, Cleveland, 1968); Melvin C. Holli, *Reform in Detroit: Hazen S. Pingree and Urban Politics* (Oxford University Press, New York, 1969); Sam B. Warner, Jr., *The Private City: Philadelphia in Three Periods of Its Growth* (University of Pennsylvania Press, Philadelphia, 1968). Several anthologies are

also useful. See Oliver P. Williams and Charles Press, eds., *Democracy in Urban America. Readings on Government and Politics* (Rand McNally, Chicago, 1970), which is particularly rich in material; Anselm L. Strauss, ed., *The American City. A Sourcebook of Urban Imagery* (Penguin Press, London, 1968). Specifically on boss rule and machine politics, see Alexander B. Callow, *The Tweed Ring* (Oxford University Press, New York, 1966); Mandelbaum, *Boss Tweed's New York*; Gustavus Myers, *The History of Tammany Hall* (Dover, New York, 1971); Mosei Ostrogorski, "The Politician and the Machine," in Callow, *American Urban History*; Zane L. Miller, "Boss Cox's Cincinnati. A Study in Urbanization and Politics, 1880-1914," *Journal of American History* 54, Mar. 1968. For bibliographical references on the "managerial" trend in urban reformism, see Hays, "Politics of Reform."
169

See Scott, *American City Planning*, pp. 41-42 and the chapter "Science and the City Functional." A few of the works published during this period are Theodora Kimball, *Classified Selected List of References on City Planning* (National Conference on City Planning, Boston, 1915); Robinson, *Modern Civic Art*; Veiller, *Housing Reform*; Flavel Shurtleff and Frederick Law Olmsted, Jr., *Carrying Out the City Plan* (Russell Sage Foundation, New York, 1914); Nelson P. Lewis, *The Planning of the Modern City* (Wiley, New York, 1916); Carol Aronovici, *The Social Survey* (Harper Press, Philadelphia, 1916); Frederick Law Olmsted, Jr., "The Basic Principles of City Planning," *American City* 3, Aug. 1910; John Nolen, "City Making," ibid. 1, Sept. 1909. For more detailed information, see the *Proceedings* of the National Conferences on City Planning and the National Conferences on Housing.
170

The statements by Ford and Pope are quoted from *Proceedings of the First National Conference on City Planning*, Washington, May 21-22, 1909, included in U.S., Congress, Senate, *City Planning: Hearing before the Committee on the District of Columbia, United States Senate*, Document no. 422, (Government Printing Office, Washington, D.C., 1910), pp. 71-77 (hereafter cited as *City Planning: Hearing*), which also contains a document supplying information on European urban legislation.
171

On the "Boston 1915" movement, see Scott, *American City Planning*, pp. 110-117; on the Pittsburgh survey (1907-08), see Lubove, *Twentieth Century Pittsburgh*, pp. 6ff.
172

The principal publications summarizing the reform activities of this period are "List of American City Planning Reports," *American City* 11, Dec. 1914; John Nolen, "Twenty Years of City Planning," *National Municipal Review* 16, June 1927; Hubbard and Hubbard, *Our Cities*; the most important and fully documented work remains, George B. Ford, ed., *City Planning Progress in the United States* (American Institute of Architects, Washington, D.C., 1917). On the legislative aspects, see Charles Mulford Robinson, "City Planning Legislation," in Nolen, *City Planning. A Series of Papers*.
173

See Ford, *City Planning Progress*; Hubbard and Hubbard, "Educating the Public to Support City Planning," in idem, *Our Cities*. See also Charles F. Taylor, "The March of Democracy in Municipalities," *National Municipal Review* 2, Feb. 1913; idem, "Municipal Initiative, Referendum and Recall in Practice," ibid. 3, Oct. 1914; Frederick Law Olmsted, Jr., "How to Organize a City Planning Campaign," *American City* 9, Oct. 1913.
174

Henry Morgenthau, "A National Constructive Program for City Planning," in *City Planning: Hearing*, p. 60.
175

See Irving Mark, "The Homestead Ideal and Conservation of Public Domain," *American Journal of Economics and Sociology* 22, Apr. 1963; Philip P. Wells, "Our Federal Power Policy," *Survey Graphic* 51, Mar. 1, 1924.
176

Antonio Negri has written, "1849-1870; 1870-1917: these seem to be the periods within which one can find the only adequate basis for a preliminary work of conceptualization on the theory of the contemporary state" ("La teoria capitalistica dello stato nel '29: John M. Keynes," *Contropiano*, no. 1968, p. 3). Although in certain respects Negri's essay, since reprinted in various places, no longer seems to me as pertinent and up to date as when it first appeared, it was nevertheless this work that first stimulated my own studies in this area.

177
An excellent article on this period is George Soule, "Chaos or Control?" reprinted in Richard Polenberg, ed., *Radicalism and Reform in the New Deal* (Addison-Wesley, Reading, Mass., 1972).

178
"The War—The Machine—The Man!" *Journal of the American Institute of Architects* 5, Sept. 1917, p. 421. On the activities of the federal agencies, see "Government War Housing," *Architectural Record* 6, May–June 1918, and 7, July–Oct. 1918; "A Brief Record of Progress in the Government's War Housing Program," *Journal of the American Institute of Architects* 6, Sept. 1918; "War Housing in the United States," *Housing Betterment* 8, Feb. 1919. For complete lists of the designers employed by the EFC and USHC, see *Journal of the American Institute of Architects* 7, Jan.-Feb. 1919. The basic sources are Frederick L. Ackerman, ed., *Housing the Shipbuilders* (U.S., Shipping Board, Passenger Transportation and Housing Division, Emergency Fleet Corporation, Philadelphia, 1920); George B. Ford, ed., *Report of the United States Housing Corporation, 1* (U.S., Department of Labor, Washington, D.C., 1920); Henry V. Hubbard, ed., *Report of the United States Housing Corporation* (U.S., Department of Labor, Washington, D.C., 1919). See also Charles H. Whitaker, "Housing as a War Problem," *Proceedings of the Sixth National Conference on Housing*, Chicago, October 15-17, 1917. On Wood's position, see Wood, *Housing of the Unskilled Wage Earner*, pp. 234ff. A synthesis of these arguments is found in Roy Lubove, "Homes and 'A Few Well Placed Fruit Trees': An Object Lesson in Federal Housing," *Social Research* 27, Winter 1960; see also idem, *Community Planning in the 1920's*, chap. 2.

179
See Frederick L. Ackerman, "The State as Absolute Agent of Control in War," *Journal of the American Institute of Architects* 5, Nov. 1917, especially p. 562. The necessity of government intervention to control building costs was maintained by John Ihlder, "Government Aid to Housing in War-Time—and After," ibid., Oct. 1917. For articles containing information on the English undertakings, see Frederick L. Ackerman, "The Significance of England's Program of Building Workmen's Houses," ibid., Nov. 1917; Ewart G. Culpin, "The Remarkable Application of Town-Planning Principles to the War-Time Necessities of England," ibid., Apr. 1917; "Government Housing Scheme. Well Hall, Eltham, Kent," ibid., Sept. 1917; "An Industrial Town Built by the British Government, Eastriggs," ibid., Oct. 1917; graphic and photographic documentation is contained in successive numbers of the *Journal of the American Institute of Architects*. Basic for the study of this period is a collection of articles from the journal, Charles H. Whitaker, Frederick L. Ackerman, Richard S. Childs, Edith Elmer Wood, *The Housing Problem in War and Peace* (Journal of the American Institute of Architects, Washington, D.C., 1918). See also Frederick L. Ackerman, "War-Time Housing—England's Most Urgent Civic Lesson for America," *American City* 18, Feb. 1918.

180
See Otto M. Eidlitz, "Housing Munition Workers," *American City* 18, June 1918; Lubove, "Homes," pp. 475-476; Miles L. Colean, *Housing for Defense: A Review of the Rule of Housing in Relation to America's Defense and a Program for Action* (Twentieth Century Fund, New York, 1940), which summarizes the initiatives of the federal agencies. See also Bernard M. Baruch, "The War Industries Board," *Journal of the American Institute of Architects* 6, Sept. 1918; "War Industries Board," ibid., Oct. 1918.

181
See Charles H. Whitaker, "War and the Building Industry," *Journal of the American Institute of Architects* 6 Aug. 1918, p. 375; "Quantity House Production Methods, Construction Branch, Emergency Fleet Corporation," *American Architect* 115, Mar. 5, 12, 1919, which

also offer an insight into the working methods of the EFC. On the USHC's methods of design, see the interesting unpublished document, U.S., Department of Labor, Bureau of Industrial Housing and Transportation, Design Branch, "General Instructions to Committee of Designers," May 24, 1918 (12-page typescript), Avery Library, Columbia University. Sylvester Baxter, "The Government's Housing Activities," *Architectural Record* 44, Dec. 1918, p. 561, underlines the advantages deriving from federal intervention in housing and states that the principal problem such intervention must resolve is that of turnover. The importance of establishing control over the real-estate market was discussed frequently by Whitaker; see especially his "What is a House?" in Whitaker et al., *Housing Problem in War and Peace*.

182

For Whitaker's response to the accusation of "socialism," see Whitaker et al., *Housing Problem in War and Peace*, p. 7. On the housing problem as a component of labor costs, see Ackerman, in ibid., p. 44; Childs, in ibid., p. 55. See also Frederick L. Ackerman, "Houses and Ships," *American City* 19, Aug. 1918; idem, "The Real Meaning of the Housing Problem," *Journal of the American Institute of Architects* 6, May 1918, especially p. 231; Whitaker, "War and the Building Industry."

183

Numerous works on this subject have already been cited; see also the very interesting, unpublished document, "War-Time Housing. The Immediate Need, Report of the Committee on City Planning of the City Club of New York," dated January 25, 1918 and signed by Clarence S. Stein. This 14-page typescript, in the Stein archives in New York, ends with the following summary: "We must have housing to win the war. Such housing must be permanent. . . . Such housing must be financed by the government which must accept a certain war loss, but should not waste by building badly. The character of such housing must be based on the social and physical needs of the workers and not on their wages. Such housing must be made a related part of the industrial life of the community" (p. 13).

184

On the problem of speculation, see Lubove, "Homes," pp. 472–473. The bibliography on the federal agencies' project is extensive; along with the works already cited, see Karl B. Lohmann, "The Gains in Town Planning from the Building of Emergency Towns," *American City* 20, May 1919; Alfred C. Bossom, "Homes for War Time Workers," *Architectural Record* 44, Sept. 1918; Robert H. Moulton, "Housing for Women War Workers," ibid., Nov. 1918; "The United States Housing Corporation Project no. 59 at Bath, Maine," ibid. 45, Jan. 1919; William E. Groben, "Union Park Gardens. A Model Garden Suburb for Shipworkers at Wilmington, Del.," ibid.; Sylvester Baxter, "The Government's Housing at Bridgeport," ibid., Feb. 1919; William C. Tucker, "The Plumbing Standards for the Housing Projects of the Emergency Fleet Corporation," ibid. 46, July 1919; Ralph F. Warner, "Yorkship. A New Town for the Emergency Fleet Corporation, near Camden, N.J.," *Architectural Review* 6, June 1918; M. S. Franklin, "Union Park Gardens, Wilmington, Del. A Government Housing Project for Shipworkers," ibid. 7, Sept. 1918; "A Housing Development at Watertown, N.Y., for the United States Housing Corporation," ibid., Dec. 1918; Ralph F. Warner, "Muscle Shoals. A New Industrial Town in Alabama," ibid. 8, Jan. 1919; "Development for the United States Housing Corporation at Quincy, Mass.," ibid; "The Town of Perry Point, Md. A Development by the Ordnance Department," ibid., Feb. 1919; "Development for the United States Housing Corporation at Waterbury, Conn.," ibid. 9, Dec. 1919; Richard H. Dana, Jr., "The Group House. Its Advantages and Possibilities," ibid. 10, Feb. 1920; Richard S. Childs, "The First War Emergency Government Towns for Shipyard Workers," *Journal of the American Institute of Architects* 6, May 1918; Henry V. Hubbard and Francis Y. Joannes, "The First War Emergency Government Towns. Hilton, Virginia" ibid. 6, July 1918; "The First War Emergency Government Towns. Atlantic Heights," ibid., Sept. 1918; "The First War Emergency Government Towns. Groton, Connecticut," ibid., Nov. 1918; "Westinghouse Village at South Philadelphia, Pa.," *American Architect* 115, Feb. 12, 1919. More general and retrospective are Frederick L. Ackerman, "An Appraisal of War Housing," *Pencil Points* 21, Sept. 1940; Talbot F. Hamlin, "Architects and the Defense," ibid.

185

U.S. Department of Labor, United States Housing Corporation, *Standards Recommended for Permanent Industrial Housing Developments* (Government Printing Office, Washington, D.C., May 1918). For two important articles on the standards adopted in the government-financed communities, see Lawrence Veiller, "Industrial Housing Developments in America, II. The Government's Standards for War Housing," *Architectural Record* 43, Apr. 1918; "The Report of the United States Housing Corporation," *American Architect* 116, Sept. 24, 1919.

186

See Colean, *Housing for Defense*, pp. 12ff.; Lubove, "Homes," p. 476.

187

On the discussions that led to the termination of these experiments, see Lubove, "Homes," pp. 482ff.; Charles H. Whitaker, "The Senate and the United States Housing Corporation," *Journal of the American Institute of Architects* 8, Mar. 1920. The most important official documents on the subject are U.S. Congress, Senate Committee on Public Buildings and Grounds, *Senate Reports*, no. 620, 65th Cong., 3rd sess. (Government Printing Office, Washington, D.C., 1919); U.S. Congress, House Committee on Public Buildings and Grounds, *House Reports*, no. 181, 66th Cong., 1st sess. (Government Printing Office, Washington, D.C., 1919). Many voices were raised in favor of continuing the policy of federal intervention; see, for example, George Gove, "Community Values in Government Housing," *American City* 22, Jan. 1920, but see primarily Clarence S. Stein, "Housing and Reconstruction," *Journal of the American Institute of Architects* 6, Oct. 1918, especially pp. 471-472; Frederick L. Ackerman, "American Reconstruction Problems. National Planning," ibid., Nov. 1918, especially p. 509; Charles H. Whitaker, "Post-War Committee. Preliminary Conclusions," ibid. 7, Sept. 1919. Finally, the following articles are indispensible: Frederick L. Ackerman, "Nation Planning," *National Municipal Review* 7, Jan. 1919; Richard S. Childs, "What Will Become of the Government Housing?" ibid.; Ernest Cawcroft, "The Present and Future Government of War-Created Communities," ibid.

188

In his introduction to Stein's *Toward New Towns*, p. 15, Lewis Mumford says that the activity of the RPAA lasted ten years (1923-1933). This is also the interpretation of Lubove, whose *Community Planning in the 1920's* is the most complete study available on the RPAA. Various documents subsequent to 1933 exist, however; in particular, a serious attempt was made in 1948 to revitalize the association. See the circular sent by Clarence S. Stein to the members of the RPAA, "Proposed Relationship of the RPAA with the New Towns Committees," dated June 25, 1948, and "A Program for the Regional Planning Association of America," drawn up by Stein and dated March 18, 1948, both in the Stein archives, New York. The most interesting documents, also in the Stein archives, are the minutes of the meetings held during that year and the 5-page typescript by Lewis Mumford, "The Regional Planning Association of America: Past and Future," dated September 6, 1948, in which Mumford states that from 1933 to 1948 the association was inactive, the main work of its members being the film *The City*. Mumford attributes this inactivity to the association's practical success; its members were dispersed during this period to carry out actual planning projects—MacKaye with the TVA, Wright with the Resettlement Administration, Catherine Bauer with various housing agencies, Stein as planner and consultant for various projects, including Hillside Housing, Greenbelt, and Baldwin Hills Village, Ackerman working for the Public Works Administration and the New York City Housing Authority, and Kohn heading the PWA housing division.

189

"Proposed Garden City and Regional Planning Association," signed by Clarence S. Stein and dated March 7, 1923, in the Stein archives, New York, where the minutes of the meeting held in Kohn's New York office, dated April 20, 1923, can also be found. The first executive committee was formed of seven members; Alexander M. Bing, John I. Bright, Benton MacKaye, and Clarence S. Stein were elected president, first and second vice presidents, and secretary, respectively. According to another document in the Stein archives, the members were F. L. Ackerman, F. Bigger, A. M. Bing, R. Van Nest Black, J. I. Bright,

L. Brownlow, R. B. Bruère, S. Chase, N. Hammarstrand, T. Johnson, S. W. Jones, E. H. Klaber, R. D. Kohn, B. MacKaye, L. Mumford, C. S. Stein, C. H. Whitaker, E. E. Wood, H. Wright; added in November 1931 were C. Aronovici, T. Augur, C. W. Ervin, C. M. Ford, J. Gaus, W. R. Greeley, E. T. Hartmann, and H. A. Reynolds. Not included in these lists is Catherine Bauer, who joined the association in 1930 and became the executive secretary, according to a letter from Lewis Mumford to me, October 14, 1971. Benton MacKaye, "The RPAA Era. A Reminiscence," an undated typescript in the Stein archives, also lists among the founders of the RPAA Art Young, a brilliant cartoonist for the more militant leftist magazines.

190

The program drawn up by Mumford, MacKaye, Chase, and Stein consists of a 7-page typescript, in the Stein archives.

191

MacKaye, "An Appalachian Trail," p. 327. For more on the Appalachian Trail, in addition to the references given above in n78, see MacKaye, *New Exploration*, p. 200ff.; idem, "Appalachian Power. Servant or Master?" *Survey Graphic* 51, Mar 1, 1924. On the relationship of this "philosophy" with "outdoor culture," see the interesting study by Peter J. Schmitt, *Back to Nature. The Arcadian Myth in Urban America* (Oxford University Press, New York, 1969), pp. 177ff; on its relationship with regionalism in particular, see pp. 182-184. On the development of MacKaye's idea, see Hugh B. Johnson, "The Appalachian Trail and Beyond," *Journal of the American Institute of Architects* 56, Oct. 1971. For the history of the Appalachian Trail, see also the entries in MacKaye's unpublished diary for July 21, 1921, and November 4, 25, 26, 1923 (Stein archives, New York). The Hudson Guild Farm in Netcong, New Jersey, was created by the Ethical Culture Society to serve as a vacation place for the population of Chelsea, on New York's West Side, between 23rd and 33rd streets. It could also accommodate groups such as the RPAA for brief visits. Clarence S. Stein was for some years president of the Committee of Hudson Guild, a post held later by his sister, Gertrude Stein.

192

In "The Influence of Letchworth in America," a 2-page typescript, dated June 22, 1953, in the Stein archives, New York, Clarence S. Stein states that it was the idea of the garden city, and not the garden cities built in England, that influenced American architects. He also speaks of à trip he made to England with Henry Wright at the time when work was beginning on Sunnyside and of meeting there with Unwin and Howard; Stein declares that he was more impressed with Hampstead than Letchworth, of which he criticizes various aspects.

193

See A. M. Bing, H. Wright, C. S. Stein, "Preliminary Study of a Proposed Garden Community, in the New York City Region," 38-page typescript, 1923, in Avery Library, Columbia University. As the preface states, its aim was to create an operative model demonstrating the validity of a policy for abolishing city slums through the construction of decentralized settlements. The document is also interesting for its brief analysis of the principal "model communities" built in the United States (pp. 25ff).

194

On the regional plan for the Ruhr, see Wilhelm Schmidt, *Die Tätigkeit des Siedlungsverbandes Ruhrkohlenbezirk* (Essen, 1926). In a letter to me dated December 23, 1972, Lewis Mumford draws attention to two meetings of the members of the RPAA at Hudson Guild Farm, in May 1923 and April 1925. At the second meeting, in addition to the members of the RPAA, the following foreign guests were present: W. Schmidt, E. May, J. Brix, R. Heiligenthal, R. Unwin, B. Parker, E. Howard, A. Bruggeman, de Rutte, Bassompierre, W. Chapman, C. B. Purdom, A. J. Hodell, and A. Keppler. MacKaye also emphasized the importance of this meeting in "RPAA Era," in which he calls Geddes "the Christopher Columbus of regional planning." For a brief documentation of the relationship between Mumford and Geddes, see Francesco Dal Co, "Dalla 'Progressive Era' al New Deal. La questione di Muscle Shoals," *Casabella*, no. 425, May 1977.

195

In a letter to me dated April 30, 1973, Stuart Chase described his trip to Russia in the summer of 1927 with what was termed "the First American Trade Union Delegation," comprising, in addition to five union men led by Albert F. Coyle, George Counts of Columbia University, Jerome Davis of Yale University, Paul Douglas, Arthur Fisher, and Rexford Tugwell, all of Columbia University, Charleston Washburne, and Chase himself. His letter concludes, "We made various investigations and trips over a period of two months, and interviewed Stalin for six hours in the Kremlin. As a result, we wrote a book which I helped to edit, published by the John Day Company in New York, entitled *Soviet Russia in the Second Decade.* Our findings were both plus and minus, with a minimum of ideology. For myself, I could not agree with Lincoln Steffens, who said at the time in Moscow, 'I have seen the future at work.' Stalin really scared me!" In an interview in May 1972, Mumford affirmed the importance of the Russian experiments, stating that, although they did not represent a model for the RPAA, they were followed with particular interest around 1925. Clarence S. Stein made numerous trips to Europe and even to Russia; Henry Wright, in addition to visiting England with Stein, probably visited Germany in 1933 and came into contact with Mies van der Rohe in Berlin.

196

Clarence S. Stein, "An Inditement fo American Democracy," 7-page manuscript, dated February 14, 1914, Stein archives, New York. For the ideological positions of Whitaker and Ackerman, I have relied on Mumford's judgment, confirmed in Lubove, *Community Planning in the 1920's,* p. 42, and Henry S. Churchill, "Henry Wright: 1878-1936," *Journal of the American Institute of Planners* 26, 1960, p. 293.

197

See "Memorandum on a Housing Platform. Submitted to the New York Labor Party by the Special Problem Committee," 9-page typescript, Stein archives, New York; this document is unsigned and undated but is in any case from the 1920s.

198

Lubove, *Community Planning in the 1920's,* p. 47. On the social role of the architect as conceived by one of the most important members of the RPAA, see Frederick L. Ackerman, "The Architect's Part in the World's Work," *Architectural Record* 37, Feb. 1915.

199

Mumford to Dal Co, October 14, 1971.

200

See Edith Elmer Wood, *Housing Progress in Western Europe* (Dutton, New York, 1923), pp. 4-5, 22; on p. 187, Wood attempts to deflate the notion that American workers enjoy a higher standard of living than European workers. For further information on Foreign legislation and experiments, see Thomas Adams, "The Need of Town-Planning Legislation and Procedure for Control of Land as a Factor in House-Building Development," *Journal of the American Institute of Architects* 6, Feb. 1918; A. G. Waller, "Town-Planning in New Zealand," ibid., Dec. 1918; Nils Hammarstrand, "Planning in Australia," ibid.7, Jan. 1919; Frederick L. Ackerman, "The Housing Question in Other Countries," ibid., May 1919; Stephen H. Child, "House and Town Planning in Holland," *American City* 26, Feb. 1922; Edith Elmer Wood, "The Cité-Jardins of Lyons and Rheims," ibid. 28, March 1923; these are obviously only the most important references. Significant within this context are Adams's contributions to American journals during the period just preceding the one considered here; see Thomas Adams, "Housing and Town Planning in Canada," *American City* 12, Apr. 1915; idem, "Progress in Town Planning and Civic Improvement in Canada," ibid. 14, Jan. 1916; idem, "Planning for Civic Betterment in Town and Country," ibid. 21, July 1919. For Clarence S. Stein's contribution in this area, see his "Amsterdam Old and New," *Journal of the American Institute of Architects* 10, Oct. 1922.

201

See John J. Murphy, Edith Elmer Wood, Frederick L. Ackerman, *The Housing Famine. How to End It* (Dutton, New York, 1920), pp. 213-215, 242ff.; Ackerman states, "For if it were possible through subvention (which I deny) to overcome the discrepancy, our whole system of loan credit and investment for profit would go by the boards. Financial business may exist and continue only by creating and maintaining a discrepancy. The result of maintaining this discrepancy is financial profit; hence the concentration of wealth in the hands of individuals; hence, as I have shown, the concentration of industry; hence of population. Our problem (congestion, slums, shortage) resolves itself into that of setting events in motion toward the redistribution of wealth" (p. 245).

202

See ibid., p. 223; Lewis Mumford, "Attacking the Housing Problem on Three Fronts," *Nation* 109, Sept. 6, 1919.

203

See State of New York, Message from the Governor, *Report of the Reconstruction Commission on the Housing Situation*, Legislative document no. 78 (Lyon, Albany, 1920). Some of these concepts had already been expressed by certain members of the RPAA; see, in particular, Henry Wright, "The Interrelation of Housing and Transit," *American City* 10, Jan. 1914.

204

Lubove, *Community Planning in the 1920's*, p. 34.

205

City Housing Corporation, *Good Homes and Good Citizenship* (n.d.), p. 7. On Bing's position, see Alexander M. Bing, "Can We Have Garden Cities in America?," *Survey Graphic* 54, May 1, 1925; idem, "Minimum Costs for Low-Rental Apartments, *Journal of Land and Public Utility Economics* 5, May 1929; idem, "The British Building Guild," *Survey Graphic* 47, Oct. 29, 1921. An interesting recognition of the validity of the City Housing Corporation's idea appeared in the *Evening World*, Oct. 17, 1924.

206

Interesting in this regard is the contact between the City Housing Corporation and the group of urbanists working on the plan of New York for the Russell Sage Foundation. A memorandum by J. M. Glenn, member of the Russell Sage Committee on the Regional Plan of New York and Its Environs, relates to two letters, dated October 22 and 27, 1924 from Alexander M. Bing to Thomas Adams, director of the Russell Sage plan, which concern the City Housing Corporations's request that the foundation underwrite a certain number of shares for the amount of $150,000. Glenn's memorandum followed a report by Adams, dated November 25, 1924, on the aims of the City Housing Corporation; along with a generally positive evaluation of the corporation's proposals, Adams expressed serious doubts about the possibility of the corporation's actually realizing its cooperative aims. Adams concluded by suggesting that the foundation contribute to the corporation with symbolic financing: "The Russell Sage Foundation might, as a token of its interest in improved housing conditions, contribute a nominal sum of say $10,000 to the capital stock of the Corporation, but should point out that it is unable to do more at the present stage of the operations of the Corporation, but may be glad to *consider* the question of subscribing a further amount when the Corporation is prepared to enter upon the proposed project of building a garden village or garden city." The documents are in the Collection of Regional History and University Archives, Cornell University, Regional Planners Association Papers, 2688, ser. 3, box 15.

207

Obviously the location of Sunnyside was guided not by any polemical intention but more simply by the possibilities of the land market. When, however, Lewis Mumford notes that the blocks built by the Metropolitan Life Insurance Company occupy from 55 percent to 90 percent of their land, while the buildings of Sunnyside cover only 28 percent, the polemical intent is clear. See "Houses—Sunnyside Up," *Nation* 120, Feb. 4, 1925, p. 115.

208

Stein, *Toward New Towns*, p. 34. This book is naturally the fundamental work for any study of the RPAA's works, but on Sunnyside some articles are also interesting, see Alexander M. Bing, "Sunnyside Gardens: A Successful Experiment in Good Housing at Moderate Price," *National Municipal Review* 15, June 1926; Clarence S. Stein, "A New Venture in Housing," *American City* 32, Mar. 1925; interview with Alexander M. Bing, "New York's First Satellite Town," *National Municipal Review* 18, Mar. 1928.

209
See Stein, *Toward New Towns*, pp. 44-47, figs. 23-25; Lewis Mumford, *The Urban Prospect* (1956; reprint ed., Harcourt Brace and World, New York, 1968), pp. 56ff.

210
See Henry Wright, *Some Principles Relating to the Economics of Land Subdivision*, paper no. 1 (American City Planning Institute, New York, 1930). In addition to Wright's paper the publication contains an interesting debate on the author's proposals, with H. M. Lewis, M. W. Weir, J. Ihlder, L. Purdy, R. Van Nest Black, G. B. Ford, E. P. Goodrich, R. Whitten, G. H. Herrold, and G. H. Gray participating.

211
In a letter to me, dated March 25, 1973, Charles S. Asher, legal consultant to the City Housing Corporation, wrote, "Mr. Bing was the Maecenas of Radburn. He invested heavily of his own funds and persuaded his other rich friends to do so. Mr. J. D. Rockefeller Jr. invested 3,000,000. He was the active president of the Company. He wanted to cease building skyscrapers with his brother, Leo, and do something socially useful. He was president of the American Ethical Union, a humanist federation of societies in many U.S. cities, also in London and Vienna."

212
On Radburn, in addition to works already cited, see City Housing Corporation, *Radburn. Protective Restrictions and Administration* (New York, 1929); Charles S. Asher, "Government by Contract in Radburn," in C. Woodbury and A. Coleman, eds., *Urban Redevelopment: Problems and Practices* (University of Chicago Press, Chicago, 1953); National Resources Committee, *Supplementary Report of the Urbanism Committee*, vol. 2, *Urban Planning and Land Policies* (Government Printing Office, Washington, D.C., 1939), pp. 97ff.; Henry S. Churchill, *The City Is the People* (Norton, New York, 1962), pp. 77ff.; Henry Wright, "The Radburn Plan," *National Real Estate Journal* 30, Sept. 30, 1929; Henry M. Propper, "A New Town Planned for the Motor Age," *American City* 38, Feb. 1928; idem, "Construction Work Now Under Way on the 'Town for the Motor Age,'" ibid. 39, Oct. 1928; idem, "Social Activities in the Town for the Motor Age," *National Municipal Review* 19 Nov. 1930; Charles S. Asher, "The Extra-Municipal Administration for Radburn," ibid. 18, July 1929. Further bibliographical information can be found in Stein, *Toward New Towns*. Although it is more general, Lewis Mumford's "Mass Production and the Modern House," *Architectural Record* 67, Feb. 1930, is important in this context. On the influence of the "Radburn idea" see Clarence S. Stein, "The Radburn Idea" (Address given at the awarding of the Sir Ebenezer Howard Medal, March 28, 1960), 14-page typescript, March 17, 1960, in the Stein archives, New York.

213
On Chatham Village and Hillside Homes, see Stein, *Toward New Towns*, especially the bibliography on pp. 376-377. The best documented article on the Phipps Garden Apartments is Isadore Rosenfield, "Phipps Garden Apartments," *Architectural Forum* 56, Feb. 1932. See also Charles F. Lewis, "A Moderate Rental Housing Project in Pittsburgh," *Architectural Record* 70, Oct. 1931; "Buhl Foundation Builds a Second Unit of Chatham Village," *American City* 50, Sept. 1935; "Hillside Group Housing," *Architectural Record* 72, Oct. 1932. On the multi-story apartment house and apartment complexes, see Henry Wright, "The Modern Apartment House," *Architectural Record* 65, Mar. 1929; idem, "The Apartment House. A Review and a Forecast," ibid. 69, Mar. 1931; idem, "How Can Apartment Facilities Be Provided for the Lower-Income Groups?," ibid. 71, Mar. 1932. On the subsequent construction activities at Hillside by members of the RPAA, the reader is referred to Stein's book. It is important, however, to record the project for Queensbridge, New York—in which Stein did not participate directly—as it took up many of the principles noted here; complete information on this project can be found in an unpublished document, "Summary Report of the Housing Development for Queensbridge Dwellings," dated October 16, 1933, prepared by the Housing Study Guild, in the Collection of Regional History and University Archives, Cornell University, Henry S. Churchill Papers, 2347, box 3, folder 3-21. The report was drawn up by Aronovici, Zimmerman, Herrick, Dumper,

Gerscovici, Cobb, Meyer, Haines, Lescaze, Churchill, Lowenthal, and Baum; Henry Wright collaborated in designing the project.

214

See Henry Wright, *Rehousing Urban America* (Columbia University Press, New York, 1935); on the RPAA projects, see pp. 37-48; on European work, pp. 86-96. This important book takes up ideas from many of Wright's previously published articles, including those that appeared in *Architecture* in 1933. The most interesting part of the book follows Chapter 10; for related material, see Henry Wright: "What Does the Architect Know About Small House Costs?" *Architectural Record* 70, Dec. 1931; idem, "The Architect and Small House Costs," ibid. 72, Dec. 1932; idem, "The Cost of Housing," *Architectural Forum* 56, Mar. 1932.

215

See Arthur C. Holden, *Primer of Housing* (Workers Education Bureau Press, New York, 1927).

216

See State of New York, *Report of the Commission of Housing and Regional Planning for Permanent Housing Relief*, Legislative document no. 66, February 1926, (Lyon, Albany, 1926), p. 51, appendix A. For a synthesis of the arguments treated here, see Lubove, *Community Planning in the 1920's*, pp. 73ff.

217

See John M. Gries and James Ford, *Slums, Large-Scale Housing and Decentralization* (The President's Conference on Home Building and Home Ownership, The National Capital Press, Washington, D.C., 1932).

218

The most important report of the New York State Reconstruction Commission is that of 1920, cited in n203. The New York State Commission of Housing and Regional Planning was originally made up of C. S. Stein, chairman, S. W. Jones, state architect, L. Grossman, commissioner of highways, B. L. Shientag, industrial commissioner, O. Cabana, G. Grove, E. Sachs Barr, M. Chamberlain, and E. A. Winslow; its composition changed over the years. Its reports made between 1923 and 1925 are basic sources of information on the urban situation in New York; they contain statistical data of major importance in constructing a picture of the population's living conditions, and they keep the building situation and the trend of the housing and land markets under continual surveillance. Of the three reports made in 1926, the first, dated January 11, contains an analysis by Donald H. Davenport of the effect of population movement and congestion on public expenditures in New York; the second, submitted in February, is cited in note 216. The third report is the one specifically mentioned here and in the following pages; see State of New York, *Report of the Commission on Housing and Regional Planning to Governor Alfred E. Smith*, May 7, 1926 (Lyon, Albany, 1926, hereafter cited as State of New York, *Report to the Governor*). For a brief summary of the commission's activities, see Clarence S. Stein, "The New York State Regional Plan," *City Planning*, July 1, 1925.

219

State of New York, *Report to the Governor*, p. 11.

220

See ibid., pp. 49-52.

221

See Lewis Mumford's introduction to Stein, *Toward New Towns*, p. 15.

222

State of New York, *Report to the Governor*, pp. 64-65.

223

The Committee on the Regional Plan of New York and Its Environs was initially composed of C. D. Norton, chairman, R. W. de Forest, F. A. Delano, J. H. Finley, J. M. Glenn, H. James, G. McAneny, D. W. Morrow, F. L. Polk, F. B. Pratt, and L. Purdy; N. P. Lewis was director of the engineering division; the advisory committee was made up of B. F. Cresson, Jr., J. Downer, F. L. Olmsted, Jr., M. R. Sherred, D. L. Turner, and G. C. Whipple. T. Adams was general director of plans and surveys.

224
On the publicity campaign organized around the plan, see the complete list of initiatives in the Collection of Regional History and University Archives, Cornell University, Regional Planners Association Papers, 2688, ser. 3, box 10, folder 117. A document that officially clarifies the relationship between the plan itself and the aims of the Russell Sage Foundation is a reserved communication from Thomas Adams to John M. Glenn entitled "Scope and Aims of the Russell Sage Foundation and Their Relation to the Plan of New York and Its Environs," dated March 25, 1924, in the Collection of Regional History and University Archives, Cornell University, Regional Planners Association Papers, 2688, ser. 3, box 11.

225
See Lewis Mumford, "The Plan of New York," *New Republic* 71, June 15 and 22, 1932. In a letter to me dated April 15, 1973, Mumford states: "Until Thomas Adams committed himself to the Russell Sage project, we felt very close to him, because of his affiliation with Ebenezer Howard and his later work in Canada. But though we recognized the excellent work of Clarence Perry on Neighborhood Planning, done under Adams, and included Perry in later meetings, Adams took our intellectual opposition to his basic ideas as a personal affront and for a time even his son Frederick Adams felt hurt by our criticism. The fact is that our basic premises were essentially incompatible: he favored metropolitan concentration, we stood for the regional reorganization of urban communities, with the intent to limit further growth of center, while putting metropolitan facilities on a regional basis for an ever larger population." Mumford was not, of course, the only one to criticize the Russell Sage Foundation plan, and it is interesting to note the difference in positions even among those directly connected with it. John Nolen, for instance, in a letter to Thomas Adams, dated March 24, 1928, criticized section 3 of the general plan in these terms: "The present plans seem to me eminently sound and conservative in character, and probably represent as much as can be wisely recommended at this time. On the other hand, New York will probably outgrow them, and still larger schemes will be brought forth for consideration in the future. Satellite communities—industrial, agricultural and mixed—is a subject to consider by itself at some later day." Also interesting is the important 21-page typewritten report by Frederick Law Olmsted, Jr., dated December 10, 1923 and sent to Adams, entitled "An Attempt to Reach Some Fundamentals." Both documents are in the Collection of Regional History and University Archives, Cornell University, Regional Planners Association Papers, 2688, ser. 3, box 1 and box 11, folder 154.

226
In addition to the articles that will be mentioned specifically, *Survey Graphic* 54, May 1, 1925, contains Frederick L. Ackerman, "Our Stake in Congestion"; Lewis Mumford, "Regions—to Live In"; Alfred E. Smith, "Seeing a State Whole" (the graphic material from this article reappeared in the commission's May 7, 1926 report); Henry Wright, "The Road to Good Houses"; C. B. Purdom, "New Towns for Old"; Alexander M. Bing, "Can We Have Garden Cities in America?"; Joseph K. Hart, "Two-Generation Communities." See also Dal Co, "Dalla 'Progressive Era' al New Deal." Material from this issue of *Survey Graphic* has recently been reprinted in the interesting volume edited by Carl Sussman, *Planning the Fourth Migration* (M.I.T. Press, Cambridge, Mass., 1976).

227
Lewis Mumford, "The Fourth Migration," *Survey Graphic* 54, May 1, 1925, p. 133.

228
Clarence S. Stein, "Dinosaur Cities," ibid., pp. 137-138.

229
Stuart Chase, "Coals to Newcastle," ibid., p. 146.

230
Robert B. Bruère, "Giant Power—Region Builder," ibid.

231
Benton MacKaye, "The New Exploration: Charting the Industrial Wilderness," ibid., p. 157.

232
The program of the 1930 meeting included the following presentations: Lewis Mumford, "An Outline of the Need for Regionalism"; W. R. Greeley, "Ten-Year Program for New

England"; Russell Van Nest Black, "Ten-Year Program for Pennsylvania"; Henry Wright, "The New York State Regional Plan"; Stuart Chase, "The Russian Plan and What We can Learn from It"; see RPAA minutes, October 17-19, 1930, Stein archives, New York. On the Round Table at the University of Virginia, see Sussman, *Planning the Fourth Migration*, pp. 197-217.

233

See Rexford G. Tugwell, "The New Deal in Retrospect," *Western Political Quarterly* 1, Dec. 1948, p. 380.

234

See Rexford G. Tugwell, "The New Deal: The Progressive Tradition," ibid. 3, Sept. 1950.

235

I am presently preparing a study on the participation of the members of the RPAA in the New Deal; some information is available on this subject in Stein, *Toward New Towns*, including Mumford's introduction; Churchill, *City is the People;* Alfred Mayer, *Greenbelt Towns Revisited* (National Association of Housing, New York, 1968). Very important is Churchill's unpublished typescript on the greenbelt towns, in the Collection of Regional History and University Archives, Cornell University, Henry S. Churchill Papers, 2347, box 2, folder 5.

236

See Daniel Aaron, *Writers on the Left* (Hearst Corporation, New York, 1965).

237

Fascism, which represents the corruption and destruction of values, is precisely the opposite of what Mumford's work wished to reconstruct. See Lewis Mumford, "The Corruption of Liberalism," *New Republic* 102, Apr. 29, 1940; idem, *Faith for Living* (Harcourt, Brace, New York, 1940).

238

Mumford is considered "antiurban" by White and White, *Intellectual versus the City*. One of the most bewildering judgments of Mumford, and, by extension, of the RPAA, is found in Jane Jacobs, *The Death and Life of Great American Cities* (Random House, New York, 1961), pp. 19-21. For some interesting criticisms of Mumford, see F. B., "Current Criticism of 'the State,'" *Sociological Review* 40, Autumn 1919; Howard Mumford Jones, "Metropolis and Utopia," *North American Review* 246, Autumn 1938, which contains some just observations on regionalist thought; Albert J. Nock, "The Amazing Liberal Mind," *American Mercury* 44, Aug. 1938, on Mumford's "political" positions; J. B. Coates, "Inspiration is not Enough," *Fortnightly*, Feb. 1953, pp. 112-118, which contains a strained parallel between Mumford and Mannheim; Meyer Shapiro, "Looking Forward to Looking Backward," *Partisan Review* 5, July 1938, a criticism from the Marxist point of view and the best attempt to demonstrate Mumford's apolitical character.

239

See Van Wyck Brooks, "Lewis Mumford: American Prophet," *Harper's Monthly* 204, June 1952. A more thorough exposition of my own judgment can be found in Francesco Dal Co, "La forza della tradizione," introductory essay to the Italian translation of Mumford's *Brown Decades* (Marsilio, Venice, 1977).

240

Mumford, *Golden Day*, pp. 282-283.

GIORGIO CIUCCI

The City in Agrarian Ideology
and Frank Lloyd Wright:
Origins and Development of Broadacres

Is not a man better than a town?
—Emerson

Introduction

In 1894, in the midst of an economic crisis that shook America and its whole
system severely, a book appeared that had great and immediate success, William
Dean Howells's *A Traveler from Altruria*. Howells's work is a consistent and
subtle condemnation of accumulation, exploitation, the traditional classes,
monopolies, and, ultimately, the city, the tangible expression of the capitalist
system. In contrast to all this, the author describes a country where cooperation,
altruism, and rationality reign supreme. This utopian but nevertheless realizable
country is Altruria, the perfected example of a new natural order that will
supplant accumulation, monopolies, and all other problems and evils arising
from industrialism.

One of Altruria's inhabitants explains its social organization to a citizen of
Ameriky. After an attack on cities as they used to be in Altruria before the
advent of the commonwealth—cities "which increased and fattened upon the
country, and fed their cancerous life with fresh infusions of its blood"—the
Altrurian recounts how they rapidly fell into ruins and how "their sites are still
so pestilential, after the lapse of centuries, that travelers are publicly guarded
against them." The Altrurian continues:

A part of one of the less malarial of the old cities, however, is maintained by the
commonwealth in the form of its prosperity, and it is studied by antiquarians for the
instruction, and by moralists for the admonition it affords. A section of a street is exposed,
and you see the foundations of the houses; you see the filthy drains that belched into the
common sewers, trapped and retrapped to keep the poison gases down; you see the sewers
that rolled their loathsome tides under the streets, amidst a tangle of gas pipes, steam pipes,
water pipes, telegraph wires, electric lighting wires, electric motor wires and grip-cables; all
without a plan, but make-shifts, expedients, devices, to repair and evade the fundamental
mistake of having any such cities at all.
There are now no cities in Altruria, in your meaning, but there are capitals, one for each
of the Regions of our country, and one for the whole commonwealth. . . . But as the
capitals are the centers of all the arts, which we consider the chief of our public affairs, they
are oftenest frequented by poets, actors, painters, sculptors, musicians and architects. We
regard all artists, who are in a sort creators, as the human type which is likest the divine, and
we try to conform our whole industrial life to the artistic temperament. Even in the labors
of the field and shop, which are obligatory upon all, we study the inspirations of this

temperament, and in the voluntary pursuits we allow it full control. Each, in these, follows his fancy as to what he shall do, and when he shall do it, or whether he shall do anything at all. In the capitals are the universities, theaters, galleries, museums, cathedrals, laboratories and conservatories, and the appliances of every art and science, as well as the administration buildings; and beauty as well as use is studied in every edifice. . . . All transportation in the capitals, whether for pleasure or business, is by electricity, and swift electrical expresses connect the capital of each region with the villages which radiate from it to the cardinal points.

The villages are mainly inhabited by those who prefer a rural life; they are farming villages: but in Altruria it can hardly be said that one man is more a farmer than another. . . . The home is the very heart of the Altrurian system. . . . Now a man is born and lives and dies among his own kindred, and the sweet sense of neighborhood, of brotherhood, which blessed the golden age of the first Christian republic is ours again. . . .

The machines that were once the workman's enemies and masters are now their friends and servants. . . . The farm work, as well as the mill work and the shop work, is done by companies of workers; and there is nothing of that loneliness in our woods and fields which, I understand, is the cause of so much insanity among you.[1]

In 1935—forty years after this attack on urban society, which for Howells was the blatant expression of the grave contradictions of the capitalist system—at Rockefeller Center in New York, Frank Lloyd Wright exhibited a project for a decentralized community that recalls in many respects Howells's description of Altruria. Broadacre City, which Wright proposed as a model for the decentralized occupancy of the land, was situated in Usonia, the future America, and expressed "a new integrity bound to scatter servile imitation, to take away all urban stricture and depravity first from the regional field and then—as is the case with all inadvertent health—absorb and regenerate the tissue poisoned by cancerous overgrowth."[2] Thus Wright's ideal community, too, came into being as a condemnation of the city, a "fibrous tumor" that is nothing else than an "avaricious aggregation which cruel ambition has built" and wherein "lurk the ambitions and frustrations of the human being urbanized out of scale with its own body. . . . Incongruous mantrap of monstrous dimensions! Enormity devouring manhood, confusing personality by frustration of individuality! Is this not Anti-Christ? The Moloch that knows no God but *more*?"[3]

Like Howells, Wright demonstrated the ethical, Protestant will to attain salvation by combatting the forces of evil, forever identified in money, the annulment of man, and exploitation, all brought together in and represented by the city. This reproof was generated by the rejection of the existing world, which led to the search for a different world, the establishment of which required the conquest of a new territory. The Shaker colonies, Rappite communities, Amana villages, and Oneida colony had affirmed with religious certainty the idea of creating a different social organization within a self-sufficient community. This was a goal the Mormons achieved in the desert, not merely in terms of an isolated model but, in the Salt Lake City experiment, on a new and broader scale. The ideas of the distribution of land to all, of artisan work and work in small industries integrated with that of agriculture, of autonomous and responsible government, and of technology applied to the land became common points of reference in the evolution of the American agrarian ideology, right down to the subsistence homestead program of the New Deal.[4]

In *The Living City* Wright expressed the same belief in the salvation of the individual through the rejection of society and the creation of a community life. In Wright's city, too, modern technology is employed on a new scale and for new ends; by overcoming distance it tends to annul limitations imposed by space, and it also makes the industrial machine a servant of man. These are, in fact, the primary conditions for the realization of a new way of life, which, in Wright's view, also demanded other changes: a different direction and management of public affairs, which would come under the influence of artists, particularly architects; a centralization of community functions, such as zoos, botanical gardens, art museums, libraries, and theaters; and a decentralization of the population, integrated into rural life, the only natural life.

Thus the same concepts that were an integral part of Altruria are found again in Usonia. In the forty years separating one from the other, opposition to the city on the part of the American intellectuals evolved in stages and was expressed on different levels.[5] The novelist and the architect bring into focus two fundamental stages of American antiurban thought, which actually evolved along two different lines. On the one hand, the regionalists sought a response to the evils typical of the city and the society responsible for them; on the other, an agrarian ideology developed, which saw in the city—above all, in the cities of the East—the reason for the decline of the frontier ideal of life. Despite their many similar aims and tendencies, regionalists and agrarians soon proved mutually antagonistic. Although their concepts and ideologies developed on the basis of ideas that were frequently identical—they submitted to the same influences, drew on the same sources, and made the same analyses of the city—they were to differ in the ultimate, conclusive phase, that is, in their political and social proposals.

The inhabitant of Altruria describes the new Promised Land, and the citizen of Broadacres recognizes the new frontier in Usonia. The former represents a turning point; the latter, the end of the antiurban ideology as it had been developed from the concepts of Jefferson and elaborated through the ideas of the anarchists and the utopian socialists from Kropotkin to William Morris. At this point the ideological and political concepts of Howells and Wright diverge, and the utopian socialism of the one clashes with the democratic individualism of the other. Despite the fact that their final products, proposals for a new social organization, coincide in many respects, Wright was never to pass from Spencerian evolutionism to a knowledge of Marx, while in Howells's case this passage would take place within the space of a generation. The teachings of William Morris, filtered through the pages of the *Studio* and *News from Nowhere*, were to offer Wright a means of clarifying the significance of the return to the land and to a prebourgeois society. For Howells, Morris was to be the means to a knowledge of Marxist thought.

In time, these two trends came to represent two distinctly different positions regarding city and country: that of progressive, liberal thought, open to the ideas of a communist society, and that of conservative and generically democratic thought, dedicated to the refounding of a community that exalts the values of the individual. In the almost half-century separating Howells's utopian socialism from Wright's anarchic individualism, antiurban thought continued to evolve. What I wish to examine here generally is the development of the agrarian ideology in regard to the city, its evolution at the end of the nineteenth century, and its rekindling in the years between 1920 and 1930, and, more specifically, the connections, largely indirect, between agrarian conceptions and Wright's works and theories. Wright is considered here, with broad approximation, as the conclusion of this particular line of nonurban thought, as the one who attempted to give a physical image to the formulations of the agrarian intellectuals and, more generally, to that current of American thought that constantly reacts to the city with anguish.

The mythical world of the pioneer and the entire culture of the American Renaissance, the ideal of the "wilderness," of the purity of country life, and of the strength of individualism and democracy in the Jeffersonian sense, were all concepts developed by antiurban thought in its own particular manner. There are, indeed, points of contact between these concepts and those that gave birth to city planning, but the use of the concepts differed in the two cases by virtue of a different interpretation of the past, as well as by the different context in which they were taken up. The protagonist of *A Traveler from Altruria* and Wright's Usonian draw their common origin from Thomas Jefferson, from the founders of the religious communities of the Shakers, Rappites, and Moravians, and from the creators of Brook Farm and the inhabitants of New Harmony; they were flanked by the protagonists of the eighty or more utopian novels published in America at the end of the nineteenth century. Later, Ralph Borsodi, Baker Brownell, and the Southern Agrarians would be united against the city and centralizing industrial society; all would be devoted to the recovery of nature and a return to the land, to the idealization of the uncorrupted world of the frontier, and to the "agrarian order" as the only possibility for civilization.[6] The city, symbol of evil and negation of the traditional values, was abandoned for nature. Nature would henceforth be the only term of reference needed. Social relationships would be conceived solely as natural relationships.

The Agrarian World and the Myth of the Frontier

In 1890 the superintendent of the Census announced that there no longer existed a frontier line in the United States, as the entire territory had been conquered. While, on the one hand, the end of the frontier arrested the great colonizing process that had prompted both private enterprise and the national government to send masses of workers to the West, on the other, it gave rise to the myth of the frontier, which would make its official entry into American history just a few years later.

The need to create a federal organization for the colonization of the West had first been felt immediately after the Civil War and was regularly taken up again during each economic depression. The programs and proposals concerned the granting of land to soldiers and to unemployed Eastern workers. As early as 1862, the Homestead Act had favored Union veterans. In 1877 a bill was submitted to Congress that aimed at resolving the problem of the unemployed, whose numbers had rapidly risen after the depression of 1873, through the creation of colonies administered by the Public Land Office. In 1885 the Senate Committee on Education and Labor proposed that colonization be organized by the federal government: "Colonization has always been the natural relief of overcrowded centers. In this way surplus labor has gone back to the soil."[7] Fred X. Heissinger, a landscape and garden engineer from New York City and a member of this same committee, appealed to the states and the federal government to cooperate in establishing colonies for immigrants and laborers in the South and West. Heissinger's idea was "to form a company or an association to find land, establish model farms, finance purchases, secure clear deeds, and provide farm machinery."[8] The rural crisis had already begun, however, and such proposals remained on paper; they were to come to the fore again after World War I and, in broader form, after the crash of 1929. The time span of development of the truly American ideology of the myth of the frontier extended, in fact, from the late nineteenth century into the 1930s.

In Chicago in 1893, in the atmosphere of the Columbian Exposition, which celebrated the urban and industrial future of America, Frederick Jackson Turner delivered a famous lecture, "The Significance of the Frontier in American History." Before the congress of the American Historical Association, Turner stated that the first period of American history had ended, a period that represented a continual "return to primitive conditions on a continually advancing frontier line." "American social development had been continually beginning over again on the frontier. This perennial rebirth, this fluidity of American life, this expansion westward with its new opportunities, its continual touch with the simplicity of primitive society, furnish the forces dominating American character. The true point of view in the history of this nation is not the Atlantic coast, it is the Great West."[9] Walden had finally found its historian, for by now it had a new culture behind it, a culture of its own.

Much has been said and written about Turner's views, which, moreover, he later modified. What remains firmly fixed, however, is his attack on the school of historians contaminated by European "germs," on immigration, and on the capitalist world of the Eastern cities.[10] Turner's thesis, with its affirmation of the freedom from institutional control that the frontier signified for the individual, gave life to and "nourished an agrarian philosophy and agrarian myth that purported to set forth the character and destinies of the nation. . . . Agrarian theory encouraged men to ignore the industrial revolution altogether, or to regard it as an unfortunate and anomalous violation of the natural order of things."[11] Paradoxically, it was in a society bent on exalting the world of the city and the new capitalist accumulation that Turner created his historical synthesis of agrarian virtue as opposed to urban corruption. This was a concept handed down unchanged from Thoreau and the transcendentalists to Wright and others after him; in its descent it embraced the Jeffersonian concept of democracy, the Populism of the late nineteenth century, the New Deal, and, ultimately, the "new conservativism" of the 1960s.[12]

Turner's pronouncements marked the beginning of a new and different idealization of the West. At the same time, however, his views were the natural expressions of the current of thought that fought against the desperate situation of the farmers, on whom the weight of the system's recurrent depressions fell, and that found in agriculture and the West the matrix of the American character. Indeed, Turner became the spokesman for the progressive populism that interpreted in political terms the deterioration of the farmers' economic conditions and the parallel phenomenon of the increasingly marked exclusion of representatives of the agrarian world from positions of power. His was the voice of a Protestant, agricultural America aligned against industrialization and against the city, where the masses of Catholics and Jews of the "new immigration" were concentrated. The intellectual and political movements tied to this vein of thought gave credit to the analysis of the situation made some years earlier by Henry George; they saw in laissez-faire the only bulwark against the power of the monopolies and the urban centers.

When George published *Progress and Poverty* in 1879, he dedicated it "to those who, seeing the vice and misery that spring from the unequal distribution of wealth and privilege, feel the possibility of a higher social state and would strive for its attainment." There were indeed many who felt this possibility and were willing to fight for it, if we are to believe George's son, according to whom two million copies of *Progress and Poverty* were sold in the twenty-five years following its appearance.[13]

In his book, George undertook an analysis of the causes of the industrial depressions that had begun to plague the country. The serious economic difficulties of 1873 culminated in the real crisis of 1876-78, which gave rise to disorders throughout the country, from New York to San Francisco. Crisis and disorder reinforced the strength of the conservatives in the 1878 elections and procured widespread favor for the policies of laissez-faire.[14] Threats to the property right and its abuses brought forth a confused response from the American middle class, one cast in terms of the ideal of liberty and the myth of personal achievement. Henry George was the interpreter of this widely diffused sentiment, which he supported with an economic theory: "What I have done in this book, if I have correctly solved the great problem I have sought to investigate, is, to unite the truth perceived by the school of Smith and Ricardo to the truth perceived by the school of Proudhon and LaSalle; to show that *laissez faire* (in its full true meaning) opens the way to the noble dream of socialism; to identify social law with moral law."[15]

Rather than depending on the "necessarily destructive methods" and "necessarily tyrannical organization" of the labor unions, George aimed to salvage democracy through the values of liberty, supported by the classical concept of the equality of rights: "The equal right of all men to use the land is as clear as their equal right to breathe the air—it is a right proclaimed by the fact of their existence."[16] George affirmed that the basic rights of man predate any evolution, because the basis of all human laws is the divine law; divine law reigns supreme over all and is expressed through nature; it exists above and before all human laws, which must conform to this higher law.

George coupled this hypothesis with an appeal to the Constitution and the Bill of Rights, two moral laws that lead necessarily, once they are recognized by all men, to a different economic and social right and to a new political configuration—individual and social well-being become reality. The solution to the social crisis consisted, therefore, in the return to free competition, ethical principles, and social justice, in brief, to eighteenth-century laissez-faire. The natural consequence of such a political and social viewpoint was the condemnation of land ownership, seen as unnatural and contrary to divine law. To parcel out the land in many small properties was not sufficient. The evils stemming from the private ownership of land had to be abolished through a tax, the single tax, that would do away with the unjust increment of land values and leave the greater value he has created through his own labor to the man who works the land. The spirit of the pioneer who freely conquers and freely works his own soil was thus given a first theoretical formulation. In George's agrarian proposal, labor and capital were reunited without conflict. The image of a society based on the distributive principle was given a rationalization, which opened the way to the redemption of rural life.

The success of George's book reflected both the economic depression that had descended on the farmer and the end of the West as an adventure. Intellectuals discovered that the miserable conditions of rural life were determined by the politics of the big cities. Hamlin Garland's *Main-Travelled Roads* and *Prairie Folks*[17] described a marvelous but desolate West, rich but exploited by the rest of the country, its inhabitants left to bitter and heart-rending poverty. The demand for social justice was the logical consequence of such a situation, and the farmers' cause assumed the tone of social protest. For many, George became a master, and from his analysis stemmed the rebukes of the city and the government of the East.

The clash between the rural world of the West and South, the political and intellectual position of which was expressed in the Populist movement, and the urban world of the nascent corporations, which drew its strength from the unionized workers and the new entrepreneurs, came with the 1896 elections. The campaign of the Republican candidate, William McKinley, was managed by

Marcus Hanna, who has been defined the first modern businessman. The Democratic contender, William Jennings Bryan of Nebraska, succeeded in giving
concrete expression to the agrarian protests by means of a forceful and pene-
trating attack on the Eastern industrialists and the New York financiers. In the
name of laissez-faire, Bryan lashed out against the big cities, the cause of the
farmers' curtailed liberty.

By the thousands, the farmers of Kansas and Nebraska had been led to
abandon their lands and move to the cities, but Bryan declared, "Burn down
your cities and leave our farms, and your cities will spring up again as if by
magic, but destroy our farms, and the grass will grow in the streets of every city
in the country."[18] Although the election results were close, Bryan's defeat was a
severe blow to the hopes of the agrarians and farmers and marked the decline of
the agrarian movement. Their political program was shattered; what remained
were the voices of the masters and the world of dreams.

On the farms, the grass was growing higher, while the city populations
increased ever more rapidly. In Chicago, the city that had seemed to represent a
compromise between the industrial East and the agricultural West, the number
of inhabitants rose from 112,172 in 1860 to 1,698,575 in 1900; in 1910, it
reached 2,185,283.[19] The big cities were the determining factor in the defeat of
Bryan's program. They also provide the key to the interpretation of American
development: "The city, no less than the frontier, has been a major factor in
American civilization."[20]

The reality of the American situation in these years was thus the very opposite
of Turner's heroic and romantic concept of the frontier. Between 1860 and
1900, for every inhabitant that went to or returned to the farm, twenty went to
the city. To the unsatisfied rural population, the city represented a safety
valve.[21] As Arthur M. Schlesinger stated, "In America in the eighties urbanization for the first time became a controlling factor in national life. Just as the
plantation was the typical product of the *antebellum* Southern system and the
small farm of the Northern agricultural order, so the city was the supreme
achievement of the new industrialism."[22] Furthermore, the West can actually be
demonstrated to have been more conservative than the East. The idea Turner
nourished of a frontier peopled by liberal, independent, freedom-loving men is
far from the true picture of the conquest of the West: "If initially there were
certain 'liberal' impulses, the wealthier land speculators and town builders soon
took control of the political parties of the frontier and gave them a generally
conservative tone."[23] The post-Turnerian analysis of the frontier has revealed its
myth to be only a myth, and even the European immigrants who went to the
West later were conservative: "For every liberal [who emigrated to the West]
there were ten conservatives.... They emigrated, in fact, because they were
conservatives—conservatives being those that have something to conserve. They
wanted to conserve their religion, or their property, or their standing in
society."[24]

Nevertheless, the concept of the land as a factor of social stability and democracy, which stemmed from Jefferson and was reaffirmed by Turner, and which had inspired the Homestead Act and the official proposals mentioned above, was to accompany the course of agrarian ideology from the late nineteenth century down to the New Deal and beyond. In 1940 the committee appointed by the secretary of agriculture, Claude R. Wickard, and representing all the federal agencies concerned with agriculture reached a conclusion that was a compendium of agrarian thought: "The U.S. Department of Agriculture believes that the welfare of agriculture and of the Nation will be promoted by an agricultural land tenure pattern characterized by efficient family-size owner-operated farms, and one of the continuing major objectives of the Department will be the establishment and maintenance of such farms as the predominating operating farm unit in the United States."[25] Thus, after a century and a half, the Jeffersonian model was reproposed in its identical form and described as a "continuing major objective." In 1940, however, many agrarian intellectuals were decidedly opposed to the government, which they considered a centralizing organization contrary to the concepts of decentralization and distributism. These views will be discussed later in this essay, also in relation to Wright's position.

The myth of the frontier was thus intimately connected with the Jeffersonian idea of agriculture as the principal source not only of well-being but, above all, of human virtue and those characteristics most congenial to popular self-government. In this Jeffersonian vein, Howells and many other writers and thinkers concerned themselves with the plight of the farmers of the frontier, directing their attention more to the sociological than to the economic aspects of the problem. For Jefferson, democracy had been the supreme good and agriculture, the economic instrument for attaining that good; agriculture had signified the small farm and individualism, the small proprietors, the "cultivators of the earth," whom Jefferson termed "the most valuable citizens": "I think our governments will remain virtuous for many centuries as long as they are chiefly agricultural; and this will be as long as there shall be vacant land in any part of America. When they get piled upon one another in large cities, as in Europe, they will become corrupt as in Europe."[26]

The frontier was the symbol of free land to be conquered and thus also of democracy. The frontier was America "the garden of the world," dear to Jefferson. When the country discovered there was no more free land, however, at the same time as the myth of the frontier developed, credit was given to theories, enunciated as early as 1870, that saw enormous possibilities in the transformation of the desert, the "new garden." Many decades later, Frank Lloyd Wright would take upon himself the task of giving physical form to the desert-garden.

**Between Transcendentalism
and Urban Sociology**

The crisis of the rural areas and the growth of the cities at the end of the nineteenth century were paralleled by a change in the comparative value of agricultural and urban land. The progressive impoverishment of the farm lands, accelerated by the sieges of drought and bad weather that struck the United States in 1880 and the years following caused a devaluation of agricultural land and a reduction in the income of rural families. In 1880 it could still be said that country and city land values were largely equal; by 1890 the value of agricultural land had decreased to half that of urban real estate. Similarly, in 1890, the average wealth of rural families was fixed at $3,250, while that of urban families at more than $9,000. This situation was further aggravated by a decrease in the selling price of farm products that was particularly marked in the period between 1880 and 1890 and was made doubly onerous by increased interest rates on mortgages and debts contracted by the farmers.[27]

As already noted, the new "consciousness of capital" and the discovery of its implications for urban life resulted in many intellectuals taking a stand against the urban phenomenon and corruption of the city. The city was undergoing a radical transformation. Becoming industrial, it was gathering to it, increasingly rapidly, the native American population in flight from the rural areas, as well as the new immigrants from abroad. The traditional agrarian world, once the basis of the American economy, was in serious crisis. Jefferson had identified the city with the European city, which represented a danger, a model that, if not rejected, would corrupt the values then forming in America. The intellectuals of the late nineteenth century no longer viewed the city as a threat but as an evil that had already contaminated the healthy part of the nation. They did not, however, limit their reactions to an indiscriminate attack on the urban world, not did their antipathy stem exclusively from a view of the city as "inferior to the wilderness." Writers as diverse as William Dean Howells, Henry Adams, Henry James, John Dewey, and George Santayana deplored the stereotyped life of the city but went decidedly beyond the transcendentalist concepts that saw nature as the only remedy for the brutality of industrial civilization. In the view of these men, the city impeded human contacts and relationships because it was primitive and barbaric, but it was nevertheless in the city, the city still not sufficiently civilized, that one had to act.[28] Morton and Lucia White have commented on this phenomenon:

For a variety of reasons Chicago became the most conspicuous locale of this new way of looking at the city. It was the home of a great university, which had opened its doors in the nineties and which became a center of urban sociology and, it might be said, of urban philosophy. One can understand, therefore, why William James looked to Dewey and other Chicago intellectuals as his friends, and why they regarded him as their spiritual leader. For Chicago at the turn of the century was the home of James's pupil, Robert Park, his worshipper, Jane Addams, and his disciple, John Dewey.[29]

Among those working within the city in the name of civilization during these years was Frank Lloyd Wright. Even if he was not intensely involved, Wright was living in the same circles, in the same intellectual atmosphere. After his rupture

Frank Lloyd Wright's home on Forest Avenue in the Chicago suburb of Oak Park, as it appeared when the building was completed in 1889.

Jane Addams's Hull House, Chicago. The University of Illinois's Chicago Circle Campus was later built on this site, with the front of Hull House left standing.

with "liebermeister" Louis Sullivan in 1893, Jane Addams's Hull House and the intellectuals who gathered there became one of Wright's two poles of cultural reference in Chicago.[30] The other was Steinway Hall, where, in 1896, a group formed around the studio of Dwight Perkins that included, in addition to Perkins, Robert C. Spencer, Jr., Myron Hunt, and Wright himself. Gradually expanded to the number of eighteen, the group had its common point of reference and model in Louis Sullivan. The "Eighteen," who formed the Prairie school aimed to apply to the house the same "organic" principles Sullivan had applied to the buildings of the city.[31]

Thus, in Wright, the lessons of Sullivan, permeated with transcendentalism and the spirit of Concord, were superimposed with one of the most advanced expressions of American culture of the moment. In order to understand Wright's evolution and his later adherence to the agrarian position, it is necessary to bear in mind this double allegiance, this suspension between the mythical world of the pioneer, dear to the transcendentalists, and the daily reality of work in Chicago. Wright lived in direct contact with the main figures of the city's intellectual life. The lectures he gave at Hull House were a real contribution to the development of ideas concerning the necessity of working to "civilize" urban life. But his position in regard to this intellectual environment was always uncertain; he could neither adhere to it fully nor detach himself from it completely, and he oscillated between the atmosphere of Oak Park, where he lived with his family, and the city, which he reached each day by rail.

Wright's contribution as an architect to the community studies undertaken by those associated with Hull House—in other words, by the nascent urban sociology of Dewey and Robert Park—was limited to the problem of the house. Largely an urban culture by this time, America idealized the arcadian myth, and Wright, too, participated in this idealization. Related to the city in both its origins and its character, the arcadian myth supplanted the traditional agrarianism of the preceding years. It actually took shape within the passage from the casual, chaotic urban society to the community inserted within a larger, organized context, and the ideas and concepts of town planning that were being developed at this time in England became a specific point of reference.

In 1900, on a lecture tour in the United States, Patrick Geddes spent several weeks in Chicago as Jane Addams's guest at Hull House, making contact with the intellectual circles of the city. Nevertheless, no understanding was established between Geddes and Wright. The meeting with Geddes did have an influence on Walter Burley Griffin, however, the architect who entered Wright's studio the following year. Griffin, the only member of his studio from whom Wright sought criticism and advice,[32] took an immediate interest in the English planning experiments. Wright himself remained detached from the problems of urban planning and closed within the sphere of concerns of a life of organized relationships, of a community, such as that of Oak Park.

The only place Wright found to apply the teachings of his "liebermeister" was beyond the urban limits, in the Chicago suburbs; in other words, in the concentration point of the contradiction between the reality of the city and the dream of regaining a rural existence. At first, the suburb was a place that served the newly arrived rural population as a buffer against the impact of the city; later, the suburb became the refuge for the urbanized population. In 1888 Wright established his own residence in a suburb, while continuing to work in the Loop, and for a time he maintained an equilibrium between his aspirations toward a rural life and the world of business. The suburb, Robert Park's "subcommunity," became the ideal place to live and the model for a type of urban development that offered a compromise between the city and the still rough and brutal frontier.[33]

The words of Andrew Jackson Downing were still valid for Wright at the time he chose to live in Oak Park: "So long as men are forced to dwell in log huts and follow the hunter's life, we must not be surprised at lynch laws and the use of the bowie knife. But when smiling lawns and tasteful cottages begin to embellish a country, we know that order and culture are established."[34] Downing's "smiling lawns and tasteful cottages" were those of Newport, Rhode Island, but they were also to embellish Oak Park and the nearby communities of River Forest, Riverside, and Evanston, the Chicago suburbs in which Wright was to build some of the most beautiful houses of his early period.[35]

In this world, at once urban and rural, in this "middle landscape,"[36] Wright lived an apparently tranquil existence for over twenty years, united with his family and in friendship with his neighbors. He seems to have adapted readily to a principle enunciated by Henry George: "Substitute for the tenement house, homes surrounded by gardens, and . . . settle agricultural districts before people [are] driven far from neighbors to look for land. The people of the cities . . . thus get more of the pure air and sunshine of the country, the people of the country more of the economies and social life of the city."[37]

For Wright, at this time, such a view did not yet signify a radical transformation of the relationship between city and country but merely a passive acceptance of suburbia. He developed no theory around this position but merely filled the building lots that real-estate speculation prepared by dividing up the land. Unconcerned with constructing a theory of the city, he devoted himself to his own professional activity and the commissions this involved, whatever they might be. Essentially, Wright allowed himself to drift along in the stream of a tranquil and traditional family life, situated at the margin of urban concentration. He was a sympathizer of the theorists and supporters of suburbia, for whom, as Adna Ferrin Weber wrote, the "rise of the suburbs" was the "solid basis of a hope that the evils of city life, so far as they result from overcrowding, may be in large part removed."[38]

Bird's-eye view of Oak Park from the north-
west in 1873, sixteen years before Wright
built his own residence there. To the right
are the lots on which would rise Unity
Church and fifteen of the prairie houses
built in the area between 1889 and 1913.

Corner of Lake Street and Marion Street
in the center of Oak Park in 1884. In the
above figure these two streets meet in the
area immediately behind the railroad station.

The new city that would result from suburbanization rather than urbanization would be "the hope of democracy." This was the title of Frederic C. Howe's book, published in 1905, which asserted the importance of favoring communities of small houses outside the city: "For the open fields about the city are inviting occupancy, and there the homes of the future will surely be. The city proper will not remain the permanent home of the people. Population must be dispersed. The great cities of Australia are spread out into the suburbs in a splendid way. For miles about are broad roads, with small houses, gardens, and an opportunity for touch with the freer, sweeter life which the country offers."[39] Certainly the reference to a country still largely unsettled was not merely casual on the part of a man such as Howe, for whom the frontier, in Turner's conception, signified the consolidation of democracy. With Howe, the proposals for colonization organized and directed by the federal government returned to the fore, even if the frontier no longer meant only the West but now extended far beyond the Pacific coast.

A model of ideal life did not interest Wright, however, who remained closed in his world of Oak Park, where he attempted a personal synthesis of the contrast between city and country. Such a synthesis was to be applied a few years later on a very different scale by one of the group of Steinway Hall. The competition for the new Australian capital, entered and won by Walter Burley Griffin, would offer Wright's respected collaborator the opportunity of verifying the possibility of a convergence between the concept of the city as an official, representative organism and the house as conceived by the Prairie school, enriched by the ideas of Geddes.

In order not to upset the precarious equilibrium he had achieved in Oak Park, Wright did not involve himself with theories of the city. For him, the city was a complex of separate edifices: the residence on one hand, the commercial building on the other. The two elements, conceived on Sullivan's model, differed and contrasted with no logical relationship.

In Chicago, the recognized position Wright duly achieved was that of an architect who worked within the "community" to give new form to the house, not of one who intervened in the form of the city. The ambiance of Wright's life was what Park was in 1921 to label a "subcommunity," one of the "natural areas" of the city: "The urban community turns out to be a mosaic of minor communities, many of them strikingly different one from another, but all more or less typical."[40] According to Park, almost all cities have these "natural areas," which can be the business center, the residential areas, the industrial districts, satellite cities, slums, or immigrant colonies. They are "natural" because, far more than the result of planning, they are the result of an ecological process that influences the ordered distribution of population and of functions in relation to the city. Oak Park was one of these "subcommunities," and it was here that Wright sought to establish those human relationships the city could not offer; the "subcommunity" was the only valid answer to a complete and associated life.

Unlike Wright, his clients were not in contact with the cultural circles of the city, and they became the occasion for verifying and imposing a different model of life. According to Leonard K. Eaton, the people for whom Wright built houses were not interested in books and had never read Henry George or Edward Bellamy, much less Frank Norris or Theodore Dreiser; Wright's clients "read the daily newspaper, some of the mass circulation magazines of the period, an occasional novel or two, and that is about all."[41] Nevertheless, his clients were not just ordinary people; they were members of the upper-middle class, businessmen, and generally self-made. Certainly there was no contact between these clients, who were thoroughly attached to the real world of the city, and the supporters of the single tax or the dreamers of *The Valley of Democracy*.[42] The intellectual world that was so remote from them desired to understand them, however; they became the model for the study of the developing leisure class that Thorstein Veblen was conducting at just this time at the University of Chicago.

The sociological characteristics that Veblen identified and effectively criticized belonged not only to the groups with whom Wright was associated in Oak Park but, leaving aside the cultural expression of his works, also to Wright himself. Like Wright, his clients recognized the importance of the "natural": "The latter-day upper-class canons of taste do not so consistently insist on an unremitting demonstration of expensiveness and a strict exclusion of the appearance of thrift. So, a predilection for the rustic and the 'natural' in parks and grounds."[43] The Oak Park group, like the larger group defined by Veblen, liked to participate in ostensibly disinterested, public-spirited organizations and movements, which "served ... to keep them in mind of their superior status by pointing the contrast between themselves and the lower-lying humanity in whom the work of amelioration is to be wrought."[44] William Winslow, one of Wright's first clients, enjoyed printing his own deluxe editions, in the composition of one of which Wright himself participated in 1897.[45] Winslow's taste in books was thus typical of Veblen's leisure class, whose "conscious ground of preference [was] an intrinsic excellence imputed to the costlier ... article."[46] Within this class, what distinguished one from the other, though not always, was the varying expression of their basic cultural development.

Wright found himself between two worlds, that of Hull House and all it implied, and that of the clan that included his clients, who were often his neighbors and to whom he tried to attune himself. Both were attached to the city, one criticizing it in order to improve it, the other drawing from it its own well-being—those who wanted to transform the city and those who were actually transforming it. Between the life of the city with all its cultural implications and that of suburbia as an expression of human contacts, Wright sought a higher synthesis, but between the intellectual society and the clan of family life there neither was nor could be any relationship.

To understand Broadacres, it is necessary to go back to these precedents—not, however, to reconstruct the consistency and unity of Wright's life experience but, rather, to reveal as spurious exactly the consistency that many critics, along with Wright himself, have affirmed.[47] Broadacres was an attempt to bring together an entire life experience in a single general vision, to overcome the contradiction between the world of the clan and the reality of the clan, between the human relationships and what is hidden behind them. Broadacres overcame the essentially urban arcadian myth and proposed the return to the life of the farmer, where life and culture are not yet separate, to the world of the frontier conceived as an autonomous culture, to a prebourgeois world and thus one not corrupted by capitalist development. Whitman had lucidly cried, "Do I contradict myself? / Very well I contradict myself / (I am large, I contain multitudes)." Wright, while he recognized Whitman as a precedent, wished to propose nothing other than the absence of contradiction. In this sense, Broadacres was neither utopian nor real but simply outside its time. Born late, it was the answer to the urban-development problems of the late nineteenth and early twentieth century, as Wright had experienced them.

The untimeliness Wright showed in respect to the events that marked the beginning of a change from laissez-faire to monopoly, also characterized the later development of his thought. Wright's later thinking was indeed representative of the ultimate expressions of democratic agrarianism in the moment in which they rejected the social and economic implications of the transformation of American society. With time, the positive and progressive aspects of the defense of laissez-faire against the monopolies were transformed into negative and reactionary positions; the attack on monopoly became an attack on government intervention, seen as a source of danger to individual liberty. The criticism of Edward Bellamy's "collectivist" society and the Nationalist movement, expressed by Henry George in the name of liberty and personal individuality, can be taken as an historical precedent to the Southern Agrarians' criticism of the National Industrial Recovery Act of 1933.[48] In the Agrarians' view, the economic and political planning necessary to administer such a law could only lead to the "political, moral, and intellectual slavery of the individual."[49] In opposition to the idea of large scale industrialization and the centralization of political and economic management, invoked once again was the return to a wide diffusion of the property right.

Broadacres came into being and developed side by side with the formation and definition of such viewpoints; against monopolistic capitalism and as an answer to programs leading to "the slavery of the individual," Wright proposed a return to the land, to nature, to the small proprietor, and to the world of the frontier. The frontier, and thus Turner's thesis of the frontier as a source of values, were concepts taken up by Wright only in about 1930. For Wright, as for Turner, "democracy was not born from the dreams of theoreticians, nor was it brought to America aboard the *Susan Constant* or the *Mayflower*. Rather, it emerged from the American forest, completely free of any contaminating contact with the Old World."[50]

At the end of the nineteenth century, however, the enthusiastic acceptance that the theory of the frontier found among the Populists had, instead, been resolved for Wright in the space of Oak Park and in a position that wavered between the "organic" principles derived from Sullivan and the sociological criticism of the way of life encountered at Hull House. In 1898, when, with the Spanish-American War, the United States emerged from its traditional isolationism, Wright was still absorbed by the idea of the community. The frontier as a "human conquest," as an "ideal of liberty and democracy," had become expansionist politics directed to the conquest of new markets; under the presidency of Woodrow Wilson, an adherent of Turner's theories, it would lead the country to intervene in the First World War.[51] Only much later was Wright to find in the uncorrupted West—or rather, in the only part of the West still uncorrupted: the desert—the possibility of a new form of life born from nature. Only then would he undertake the recovery of the wilderness, understood as the matrix of American culture that remains vital and creative far from the city, as the place that gives continuity and vigor to the myth of the frontier and its "values."[52]

The Recovery of Individuality

Henry George's ideas on the need for cities to grow organically, which were to influence more than one generation of city planners, had not yet been assimilated by Wright during the period of his life passed between Oak Park and the Loop. Only much later did he accept George's thesis and attempt to rationalize the anti-individual chaos of the city, proposing Broadacres, a plan for the organic growth of suburban America, as a model solution. Wright's adhesion to Geroge's ideas was never to be complete, however. Passing from the arcadian myth to the agrarian proposal, Wright found it difficult to reconcile the single-tax theory with the conception of private property as the fullest expression of individuality.

Around the turn of the century, urbanization began to undermine the utopian dream of a society without cities and people looked to Henry George with the ardent interest of those who discover that poverty is the consequence of the increment of real estate values and that a different organization of human life can be created by combatting the mechanisms of this phenomenon within the formative processes of the city. After the flood of utopian novels, came the efforts to confront the reality of the city directly. The formation of a school of sociology that analyzed the city and the interest in Geddes's urban theories were two manifestations of this new, direct approach to the urban problem.

Between 1895 and 1902, no fewer than twenty-five articles devoted to the city appeared in the *American Journal of Sociology*. At the same time, the cooperative and homestead experiments conducted in New Zealand attracted interest, European urban theories and projects were studied, and cooperative planning found supporters. Between 1907 and 1917, more than a hundred American cities undertook planning projects. From these few facts alone, it is clear that in the early years of the twentieth century the urban problem assumed a national dimension.[53]

Wright had sought a synthesis between the life of the city and that of the suburbs, but he could not accept a compromise, and he realized that his existential equilibrium was about to collapse. Living between the boundless prairie of the West, mythical territory of the American pioneer, and the city, still far from the suburbs but rapidly expanding, Wright decided deliberately to overturn this balance before the city crushed his individuality. On what might appear a sudden impulse, but was actually the logical consequence of his determination to renounce completely the choice he had made twenty years earlier under very different conditions, Wright fled not only from Oak Park but also from his family. At a single stroke he freed himself of all responsibilities and assumed other, enormous ones.[54]

Oak Park had grown from 4,000 inhabitants in 1890 to 18,000 in 1910; in Daniel H. Burnham's 1909 plan for Chicago, it was within the great arc designed as the limit of the city. Oak Park had been overtaken by the city, indeed, had become city, and the myth of a house in the country but near the city, of the select and close-knit clan, and of a free and independent life now collided with urban reality. Wright's rejection of the physical and social setting, however, necessarily meant abandoning his wife and six children as well and resolving the situation with a striking and dramatic gesture; his flight to Europe with the wife of a client and neighbor expressed his desire for a definitive break with everything.

When Wright returned from Europe, his first reaction was to abandon the city, too, and take refuge in a new "home," Taliesin, the residence-studio that he built in Wisconsin, near the places of his childhood and his relatives, which recalled his own origins close to the land. Renouncing the city was necessary if he was to begin again from zero, but it did not yet signify the rejection of the city in its totality; the city was evil, but in it the "organic spirit" could still survive.

Wright's conception of the city was not that of the bitter place of struggle and violence that George Bellows was painting and Upton Sinclair and the muck-rakers denouncing. Rather, the image of the city Wright was fighting against seems still to have been that created by the Columbian Exposition in 1893, the "white cloud" that appeared on the horizon overshadowing the natural environment, and by which "art is tortured, twisted, choked, mangled, beaten, bruised, torn."[55] The advent of the corrupt culture of New York in the genuine Chicago had marked the beginning of the end for Sullivan. It was this image that Wright now had clearly before his eyes, and his rejection of Chicago was perhaps the

View facing west on Madison Street from
Oak Park Avenue, Oak Park, 1903.

Unemployed men in front of the Oak Park
Bank, June 1933. By the 1930s, this out-
lying, upper-middle-class Chicago suburb
had changed character and become part of
the city itself.

rejection of a similar end for himself. The city he believed he could dominate had become for Wright, as it had for Sullivan, the "City of Indifference," the "City of Contrasts": "Cast your eye over the sumptuous beauty, the color, the spread, the open-far horizon of Lake Michigan, and then turn to this ugliness and horror on its shore. On a Sunday, if the wind be from the Lake, there comes into view as a revelation the pellucid, the delicately beautiful atmosphere with which Nature canopies man here. On a Monday morning behold how he pollutes it with his mental outpourings, his moral murk!"[56]

Once the organic message had failed, even in the sphere of the urban residence, the only salvation was in constructing a refuge that contained in itself the spirit of Jefferson's Monticello, Thoreau's Walden, Emerson's Concord, and Whitman's wilderness. The concepts of the American Renaissance in themselves, however, were not sufficient to recreate a lost environment. New sources, new references, new experiences were needed.[57]

The European sojourn meant a great deal to Wright; it restored his faith in himself and allowed him to discover an entirely constructed nature, that of Italy. But Europe also signified classicism, and for Wright, who twenty years earlier had rejected Burnham's offer to send him to study at the Ecole des Beaux Arts, classicism meant the Columbian Exposition, New York, and more generally, the "imperial city." Europe could therefore not be adopted as a precedent or a point of reference. And, at this moment, not even the contemporary European experiments in town planning interested him.

Thus when the Town Planning Conference opened in London in 1910, Wright, who was then living between Italy and Germany, was not present. Beginning again from zero did not mean redirecting his interests and experiments but, rather, going back to the origins of his own individuality, probing the ego. Wright deserted the London conference, where the planning achievements of America (Burnham with his plans for Chicago and Washington) confronted those of England (the garden cities of Howard and Geddes) and Germany (Stübben and Eberstadt presenting the great plans for Berlin and other German cities).[58] Wright's field of interest, however, left him no alternative to the rejection of the city.

From the Villino Belvedere, his residence in Fiesole, he went to Berlin to prepare for publication a portfolio illustrating his entire architectural production.[59] He also went to Darmstadt to meet Joseph M. Olbrich but arrived after he had died. He corresponded with Charles R. Ashbee, whom he had met in Chicago in 1900, but never succeeded in arranging a meeting.[60] Thus Wright lived isolated from the world, granting his distracted attention to only a few particular architectural experiments. His visit was to prove very important for European architecture (Mies's judgement is enough to confirm this), but it had little importance in the evolution of the American master's own thought or work.

Wright's original, even if limited, interest in urban problems, shown by his participation in the activities of Hull House and his presence in the Steinway Hall group, had now completely fallen away. The experiments and theories of Patrick Geddes and Ebenezer Howard had no value for him. Indeed, even earlier, Wright had taken no interest in Geddes's neotechnical order or Howard's garden city, the city of the industrial era that expressed that order. Then, however, his lack of interest had merely demonstrated the different position of one who had definitively accepted the suburb of Oak Park and recognized in the suburban residence the possibility of creating an ideal life in harmony with nature, even within the city. Now, however, the failure of his Oak Park experience implied the outright rejection of the Letchworth model.

The search for Wright's lost individuality lead far away from the cooperatively organized society proposed by Howard, based in part on the theories—but above all on the "values"—of Bellamy. The anarchic aspect of Wright's exclusive individualism, which implied acceptance of the Jeffersonian dictum "that government is best that governs least" could not but reject Bellamy's "industrial army" and the "Great Trust" that commanded it. Howard's attempt to begin the transition from the competitive system to the cooperative commonwealth, "on a very much smaller scale" than that hypothesized by Bellamy, was evidently viewed by Wright, correctly, as nothing more than a particular expression of Bellamy's Great Trust.[61]

At this time, even the idea of advanced technology as the sole means of creating a different society formed no vital part of Wright's thought. This theme was common to all the utopian proposals of the late nineteenth century and adhered to later by the Southern Agrarians in their proposals for the renewal of the South. Wright was to embrace this idea only in the late 1920s, however, just as it was only then that he developed any sympathy with distributist concepts, which were being defined in England while Wright was in Europe. Hilaire Belloc's manifesto for an agrarian society, published in 1911, eventually became a point of reference for Wright, as well as for the Southern Agrarians. Together with G. K. Chesterton, founder of the journal of the Distributist League, the G. K. Weekly, Belloc adopted as a model the agrarian society of the late Middle Ages, a culture based on the wide distribution of productive property, particularly land.

Belloc, whose writings would appear in 1937 in the Southern Agrarians' journal, the American Review, maintained that the principle of property is normal and necessary to man; like Jefferson, he believed that the lack of property leads man to slavery: man aspires to possess to the extent that he is free, and he desires to be free to the extent that he can achieve his own ends and conform to his own nature. Focusing on the property right, the Distributists asserted that the "common man is served by our intention . . . while the contrary efforts of Capitalism and Communism (which is Capitalism's twin brother) disserve him."[62]

The appropriation of Belloc's theories by the agrarian intellectuals was thus natural, and the search for a middle road between the two extremes of capitalism and communism was likewise to animate the development of Wright's thought. The return to a rural world of small-property owners was not seized on exclusively as a solution to the economic crisis; it was also seen as the salvation of a class that, with industrialization and the awakening class-conciousness of the proletariat, was witnessing the destruction of the very values from which it drew its strength. As an alternative to the proletariat, the "mob" that Wright disdained, as well as to the great accumulation of wealth in the hands of a few, was offered the ideal of an integral, classless, prebourgeois society.[63] The festive gatherings in late medieval Italian costume that were to take place some decades later in the Wisconsin countryside, promoted by Wright, represented this ideal, classless but hierarchical, agrarian society.

For the moment, however, Wright was interested in neither distributism nor Turner's sectionalism and still less in nascent regionalism. He had chosen to be an architect, and this, it seems, is what he wished to remain. His decision was clearly indicated by the portfolio of his works that he himself edited in Europe, which was published by Wasmuth in Berlin in 1910 and republished in the following year, in a reduced format, with a preface by Ashbee.[64] In this publication all Wright's works, from the first houses designed in 1893 to the last projects prepared before his flight from Oak Park, are presented as a continuous architectural development. It is indeed an exceptional documentation of his work, and it stimulated an enormous response in Europe, becoming an undisputed reference for many subsequent experiments there.

At the very end of this portfolio, however, Wright presented a project that seems to indicate a desire to open a different perspective on his entire production. The Como Orchards Summer Colony, "designed to give accommodation to a group of university men owning adjoining orchards and wishing to live near in summertime,"[65] appears as a new departure, involving the organization of a space that is not limited to a single building lot. The project is, in fact, quite separate from the rest of the work presented in this portfolio. Although the architecture of the buildings is Wrightian in style, the general layout, organized on a central axis, seems influenced by the work of a landscape architect. Wright prepared the preliminary design in April 1909, five months before his departure for Europe, but the project was completed only after his flight from Oak Park.[66] For reasons that remain unclear, the architect chosen by Wright to take over his studio in his absence was Herman V. von Holst, son of a German historian settled in Chicago.[67] Work on the Como Orchards project had been left uncompleted, and von Holst put the preparation of the working drawings in the hands of Marion Mahony, Wright's faithful and efficient collaborator, who was then executing the major part of the drawings for the German publication.[68] In

Taliesin, Spring Green, Wisconsin, the residence Frank Lloyd Wright first built for
himself in 1911, shown in its present form,
as reconstructed after it was destroyed by
fire in 1925.

A festive gathering in late medieval costume
at Taliesin; in the left foreground, Iovanna
Wright, daughter of Frank Lloyd and
Olgivanna, is carrying gifts to her parents,
seated at the table.

Wright's absence, von Holst and Mahony made use of the assistance not only of William E. Drummond but also of Wright's one-time collaborator, Walter Burley Griffin, who was particularly interested in landscape.[69]

The layout of the Como Orchards Summer Colony, which is an attempt to combine a general organizational plan of classical derivation with the architecture of the prairie houses, reflects, directly or indirectly, Griffin's influence.[70] The inclusion of this project in a publication dedicated expressly to the work of a single architect brings to mind the often severe judgments passed on the master by Mahony and Drummond.[71] The outbursts of individuals obviously oppressed by Wright's leadership apart, however, what is of interest here is the significance of such a conclusion to the portfolio. The utopian community immersed in an orchard in the mountains of Montana, which appears in the final pages of the German publication, in fact, represents Wright's first response to the crisis that had overwhelmed him. The Como Orchards project was proposed to Wright in 1908, when his tranquil existence in the midst of the Oak Park clan was already shaken and thus just before his break with this world. It is an idealization of communal life, inspired by a bygone type of existence, possible only far from the city in the midst of nature. As the final product of Wright's Oak Park period, the communal complex signified the only possible conclusion to his own work and his own existence.

Part of the project was to be actually executed, but not by Wright. The two collaborators, Mahony and Drummond, followed through the construction of a dozen cabins, as well as the clubhouse situated on the central axis.[72] Wright's absence, however, does not detract from the fact that Como Orchards represented the model of a new type of life, which was the genesis of Taliesin. The complex was created for people who were in daily contact through their work and life within the university and who chose to live together even in the summer. That the complex was also a form of speculation was a consideration Wright simply put aside; for him Como Orchards was a place to live in the summertime, exactly as Taliesin East was to be many years later.

In 1913, just a few years after his return from Europe, Wright participated unofficially in a competition for the design of a typical residential section on the outskirts of Chicago.[73] Wright's proposal made use of residential units grouped in fours, a solution adopted in an earlier proposal, which he had published in 1901 as "A Home in a Prairie Town."[74] These units, repeated many times as two-story houses, as well as in the form of "better-class houses," occupy two-thirds of the area and make up nine-tenths of the residential units of the entire settlement; despite this fact, however, they accommodate fewer than half of the inhabitants. The other buildings, houses for workers' families and apartments grouped in complexes for single men and others, separated from them, for single women, are located along the two outer sides of the settlement, far from the better-class homes.

Plan for the Como Orchards Summer
Colony, Darby, Montana, prepared by
Frank Lloyd Wright's studio in 1909 for
a group at the University of Chicago.

Plan by Walter Burley Griffin for the Trier
Center Neighborhood at Winnetka, Illinois,
1911.

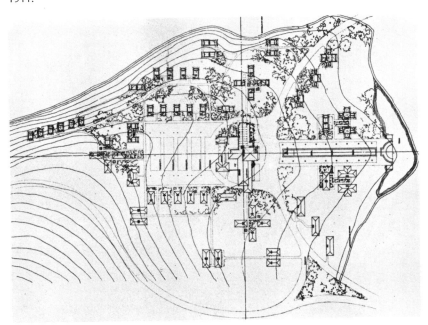

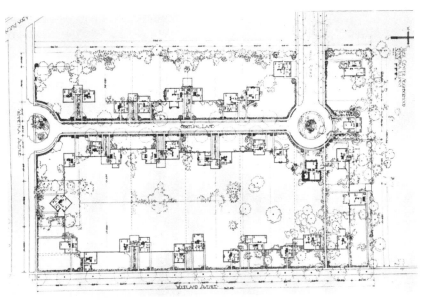

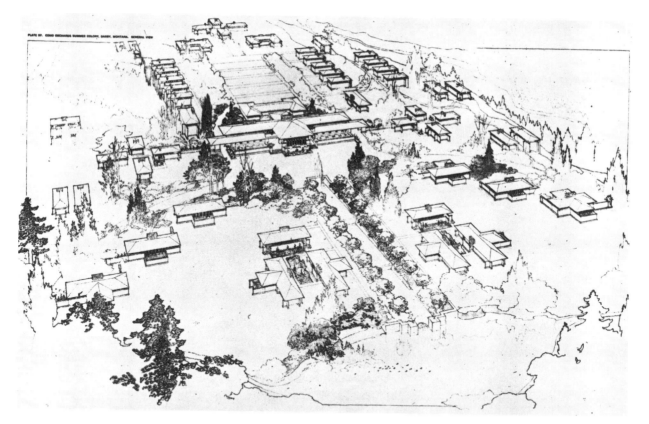

Bird's-eye view of the project for Como Orchards Summer Colony, Darby, Montana, prepared by Frank Lloyd Wright's studio in 1909.

The clubhouse at the center of the Como Orchards Summer Colony, constructed under the supervision of Marion Mahony and William E. Drummond between 1909 and 1910.

Although he was designing for a supposedly interclass situation, Wright passively accepted the conventions of a division based on the prerogatives of class and a distinction of the sexes. The teachings of Geddes, who in his lectures in America also spoke of the sexes and the emancipation of women, continued to be rejected by Wright, despite the fact that after 1909 his own personal life was marked by the rejection of conventions. The general layout of the project clearly reflects the class distinctions; a filter of greenery and civic installations directly at the disposition of the "better-class" residential area separates it from the commercial area and that of the other classes. The latter never penetrate the interior of the site; their life takes place, instead, in contact with the main street, which is set apart from the residences of the more well-to-do class. A system of streets and intersections within the site directs and separates the traffic of the various sectors, which thus remain isolated from one another. The square lot at the edge of the city was here accepted in its traditional structure, divided in a grid of small lots and organized as distinct communities, with a precise division of functions based on the presence of different classes. Wright's approach was a "technical" one, as his report on the project also indicates. He did not attempt to change the social organization of the settlement but merely aimed at resolving, at least for the "better class," the problem of the noise and dust of the city streets.

It is interesting to compare Wright's project with the winning designs, particularly that of the city planner Arthur C. Comey of Cambridge, Massachusetts, who the following year would design Billerica Garden Suburb in Massachusetts, and in 1923 would work out a model of spatial organization for an entire metropolitan area.[75] Within a small compass, Comey's solution anticipated the scheme of a diagrammatic system of arteries extended, in varying scale, over the whole territory. In his design, the unity of the square lot is broken by a diagonal organization, along which the principal services and civic installations are situated, while the residential construction is uniformly distributed, without class distinction, over the whole area. Rejecting the idea of resolving the problem of the city in terms of the treatment of a single square lot, Comey interpreted the residential settlement as part of a more general spatial organization. For Wright, on the contrary, the problem was one of creating a number of communities that were largely autonomous but still integrated as a unit. Thus, while at Como Orchards, the clan of university professors was grouped around a common meeting place, in the proposal for a typical residential section on the outskirts of Chicago, the various social groups were divided by the civic installations, which provided a meeting place but also served to separate the various areas or communities.

Taliesin, built in 1911 and thus after Como Orchards and before the preparation of the project for Chicago, complements these two undertakings according to a precise scale of values: on one level, the urban settlement, which must reconcile the autonomy of the individual and the distinction of social class with the integration of the community and its various income groups; on yet another level, the provincial colony, where it is still possible to reconstruct the optimal model of a select and unified clan; finally, above all else, Taliesin, the unique object, the highest degree of selection.

Twenty years later, Broadacres was to be created from a fusion of these projects. The "better class houses" became the homes and small farms situated at the center of Broadacres, while the houses of the new upper class were to be indicated as "luxurious homes" or as "Taliesin (equivalent)." Thus Taliesin always represented the highest level of Wright's individualist concepts. In 1932 he himself recounted in his autobiography the sentiment that had animated him twenty years earlier when building Taliesin I:

[It had to] be a natural home, not natural as caves and log-cabins were natural, but native in spirit and the making. . . . It was still a very young faith that undertook to build that house. It was the same faith, though, that plants twigs for orchards, vineslips for vineyards, and small whips to become beneficent shade trees. And it planted them all about! I saw the hill-crown back of the house as one mass of apple trees in bloom, perfume drifting down the Valley, later the boughs bending to the ground with red and yellow and white spheres that make the apple tree no less beautiful than the orange tree.

Wright wrote at length about his vision of this new home in nature. It was to be not only a home but also "an architect's workshop, a dwelling as well, for the young workers who would come to assist. And . . . a farm cottage for the farm help. The place was to be self-sustaining if not self-sufficient, and with its domain of two hundred acres was to be shelter, food, clothes and even entertainment within itself. It had to be its own light-plant, fuelyard, transportation and water system."[76] Taliesin was the still personal model of an autonomous settlement situated within nature and an agrarian world: a place outside the world, far from the city he had so clamorously rejected but which, in fact, still existed and in which he continued to build. A return to his childhood, to Grandfather and Grandmother, "something splendid in themselves," to myths, and to a prebourgeois society. At Taliesin Hilaire Belloc's manifesto was applied in America.

Wright's concepts of autonomy and self-sufficiency stemmed from the agrarian and individualist tradition of America. Considered in relation to similar late nineteenth-century conceptions, Taliesin was a belated expression. At the same time, it anticipated the "agrarian myth" that developed at the end of the second decade of our own century from the writings of Belloc, the rediscovery of Turner, and the hypothesis of an integral life. Departing from the experience of Taliesin and these latter antiurban trends, Wright would arrive at the same conclusions reached, just a bit earlier than Broadacres, by other intellectual groups, first among whom were the Southern Agrarians and members of the National Catholic Rural Life Conference.[77] In the years immediately following 1910, city and country still coexisted as two opposing parties. With time, however, the agrarian myth of the land as the principal factor of development

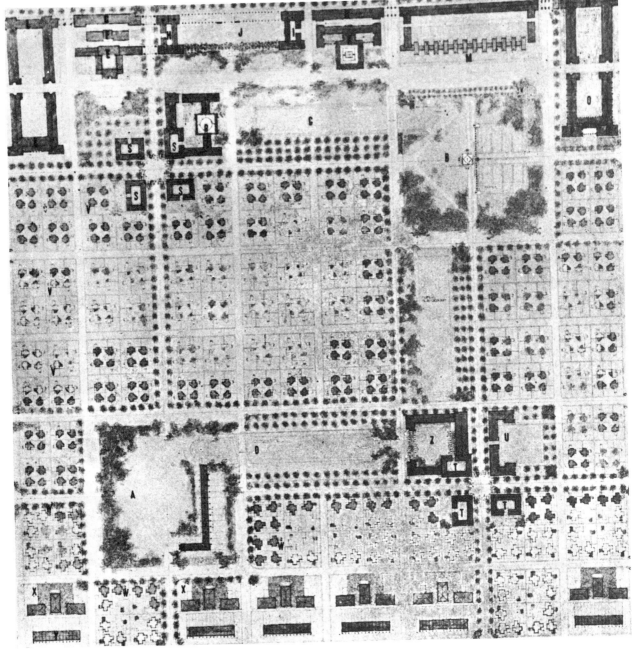

Plan of Frank Lloyd Wright's unofficial entry in the 1913 competition for the development of a typical residential section on the outskirts of Chicago. *A*, park for children and adults, zoological gardens; *B*, park for young people, bandstand, refectory, athletic field; *C*, lagoon for aquatic sports; *D*, lagoon for skating and swimming; *E*, theater; *F*, heating, lighting, and garbage-reduction plant; fire department; *G*, stores, with three- and four-room apartments above; *H*, gymnasium; *I*, natatorium; *J*, produce market; *K*, universal temple of worship, nonsectarian; *L*, apartment building; *M*, workmen's semidetached dwellings; *N*, four- and five-room apartments; *O*, stores with arcade; *P*, post office; *Q*, bank; *R*, branch library, art galleries, museum, and moving picture building; *S*, two- and three-room apartments for women; *U*, public school; *V*, seven-and eight-room houses; better class; *W*, two-flat buildings; *X*, two-family houses; *Y*, workmen's house groups; *Z*, domestic- science group, kindergarten.

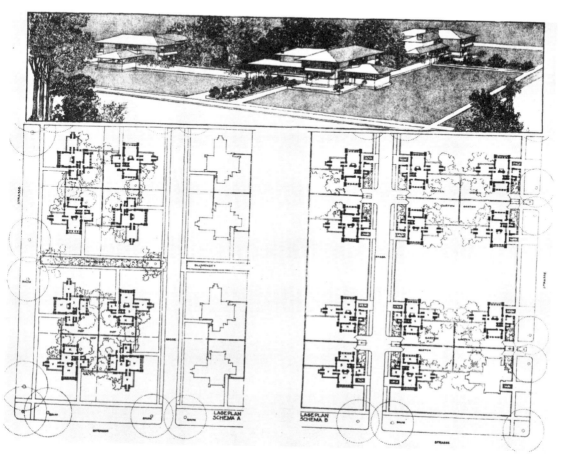

"A Home in a Prairie Town," proposal by
Frank Lloyd Wright for the subdivision of
a lot in four residential units, published in
the *Ladies' Home Journal* in 1901, and reproposed in his project for the 1913
competition.

General plan of Arthur C. Comey's entry
in the 1913 competition for the development of a typical residential section on
the outskirts of Chicago, which won second
prize.

was accepted by many Americans as the only valid premise, the conclusion of which was the disappearance of the city and with it of the evils of society. The relationship between cause and effect was paradoxically overturned.

The Rejection of the City

Wright did not assume a real and critical interest in urban problems before 1920. His work in the city up to that time reveals a basic indifference to the question of urban organization. He passively accepted the distinction between a residential suburb and a commercial center, with a space between the two occupied by apartment houses and industries.

Fervidly pursuing his interest in the suburban residence, it was in this field that he acquired fame throughout the Midwest in the early years of the century. Nevertheless, Wright had a certain number of opportunities for work in the urban center and the gray area immediately surrounding it. In 1894 he designed an amazing office building for the American Luxfer Prism Company, an edifice intended for the Chicago Loop, which strikingly turned a nude wall on the city. In contrast to the exceptional achievement of the Luxfer project, however, the design he prepared in 1900 for the Abraham Lincoln Center was essentially traditional in conception and clearly demonstrated a lack of consistent interest and development in the field of commercial building and urban construction in general. The same marked inconsistency is apparent between the outstanding originality of the Larkin Building in Buffalo, built in 1904, and the quite ordinary E-Z Polish factory built in Chicago in 1905, or the modest City National Bank and Hotel in Mason City, Iowa, built in 1909.

A similar disparity is evident even in his urban housing designs. The Waller and Francis Apartments in Chicago, designed in 1895, were projects resolved in terms of elegant detail. The Francisco Terrace Apartments, however, designed for the same city in the same year, was a notable edifice built about a court, and the Lexington Terraces, designed in 1901, presented a remarkable complex of two large blocks, each enclosing a court and each laid out with a double row of apartments facing on either the court or the street.

The relative value of the individual designs apart, all these buildings passively accepted the lots prescribed for them; even if they were sometimes closed off from the surrounding environment by high or blind walls, they did not in any way oppose their urban ambiance. Very often, in fact, they adapted to the surrounding constructions, from which they were distinguished only by their quality, which Wright's enormous architectural capacity never failed to express. Meanwhile, in the single residences Wright was constructing throughout the Midwest, this same capacity was developing in terms of the architect's ever-growing sympathy for a close-knit, patriarchal way of life.

Even after his flight from Oak Park, Wright's approach to the city remained substantially unchanged. His designs for buildings to be inserted into the network of urban streets drew upon models already tried out. The Press Building, designed for San Francisco in 1912 and partially redesigned in 1920, was a skyscraper that quite pointedly recalled works by Sullivan. The basic elements of the composition were indeed drawn from the "master's" repertory: a high ground floor, an undifferentiated fenestrated body, and a crowning element; next to this skyscraper, a similar but lower building, which in the original design projected forward toward the street but in the 1920 version was, instead, set back from the street and elaborated with a broad arched entranceway that recalled, in simplified form, the entrance of Sullivan's Stock Exchange. In Milwaukee in 1916, Wright built the Richards Houses and Apartments and the Munkwitz Apartments; there, too, he demonstrated the same strictly professional attitude by passively inserting his works in their assigned lots.

This basic indifference and strictly professional approach indicate not only Wright's rejection of the urban problem as it was being formulated in just these years but also his acritical acceptance of and adaptation to the laws of urban speculation. Evident once again is the contradiction rending the architect's existence—the dualism of his urban-antiurban position. The city is evil; yet the "liebermeister" had been willing to participate in the urban process, and the activities of Hull House were also devoted to this end. For Wright, the city remained a divided, double entity; even after he had abandoned the suburbs for the country, he found himself continually confronted by its two contrasting and complementary faces.

The urban world thus remained suspended between the positive and the negative, on a par with the world of the machine. Indeed, a fine thread of reasoning connects Wright's thoughts on the machine with the development of his ideas on the city. The lecture he gave at Hull House in 1901 on "The Art and Craft of the Machine" reveals the same contrasting sentiments: "We are at last face to face with the machine—the modern Sphinx—whose riddle the artist must solve if he would that art live.... Art [is] now mortally sickened by the machine ... [but] the machine is the creature and not the creator of this iniquity ... the machine has noble possibilities unwillingly forced to degradation in the name of the artistic." Thus it is not the machine as such that degrades man but the use man makes of the machine. In the same lecture, Wright added, "Be gently lifted at nightfall to the top of a great down-town office building, and you may see how in the image of material man, at once *his glory and menace*, is this thing we call a city."[78] At this point there come to mind Sullivan's words on the "pellucid ... atmosphere" of Lake Michigan that "man pollutes ... with his mental outpourings, his moral murk."

Seventeen years later, in 1918, in a lecture given at the Chicago Women's Aid, Wright once again spoke about the double, positive and negative face of the city: "Chicago is ... a despair and a great hope. A despair, not so much because ... cruel and crude as because 'culture' has been stuck upon its surface as a businessman's expedient or thoughtlessly bought by the rich as luxury." It is a "great hope" because all that is vital, indigenous, and genuine still exists in

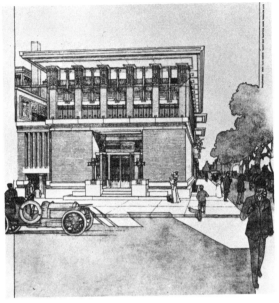

Larkin Company Administration Building, Buffalo, New York, built by Frank Lloyd Wright in 1904 and destroyed in 1950.

Design by Frank Lloyd Wright for the City National Bank and Hotel, Mason City, Iowa, 1909; the construction of the building was completed in 1910.

Design by Frank Lloyd Wright for the
Francis Apartments, Chicago, built in 1895
for the Terre Haute Trust Company of
Indiana.

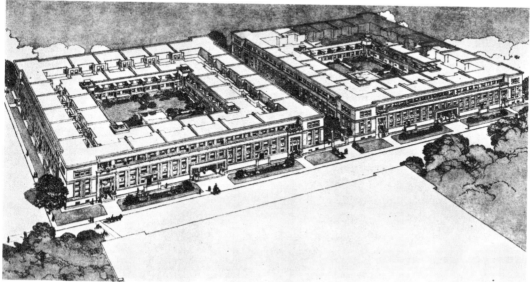

Design by Frank Lloyd Wright for the
Lexington Terraces at Chicago's South
Side, a project begun in 1901 for
Edward Waller, Jr.

Chicago. Chicago is the "big town" of cultural forces, the center of significant movements and significant figures in the fields of "architecture, music, literature, the theatre, education, and recreation." "Chicago is the only great city that is America-conscious, that has a sense of destiny; American. The case for American originality is at stake here. Chicago must find culture from *within* or all America is reduced to a colony of Europe; we of Chicago are her only hope."[79]

Wright spoke of "we of Chicago," although by 1918 he had not lived in the city for over nine years. He made this appeal to Thoreau's autochthonous culture—here transferred, astonishingly enough to the city—after listing the names of those who produced culture in the city. Jane Addams and Thorstein Veblen, John Dewey and Vachel Lindsay, as well as Carl Sandburg and Edgar Lee Masters, almost all of Wright's own generation, were actually, however, figures in revolt against Emersonian optimism. By means of a contrasting pessimism, they were all attempting to make explicit "the resentment welling up in the American heart at the loss of the older freedom and individual dignity."[80]

Wright registered these cultural expressions, which can hardly be defined as antiurban, and he accepted, in part, the naturalistic realism of many members of the Chicago intelligentsia, who were animated by a free and creative individualism and by the spirit of protest. Actually, however, these cultural sources, as well as others assimilated subsequently, were to serve him fifteen years later in generating his conception of Broadacres. They were, in fact, only part of the eclectic collage found even in his architectural works in the period following his return from Europe. In his 1918 lecture, the comparison of positive Chicago and negative New York—which went back in time a quarter-century to the East-West antagonism lived by Sullivan and momentarily resolved in the Columbian Exposition—demonstrates Wright's belief in the idea that the city is evil not in itself but, rather in its use. At this point the contradiction in Wright's position is clear; he admits the existence of an American urban culture in Chicago but has nevertheless abandoned the city because it is there that culture is destroyed.

What Wright was expressing in 1918 was essentially the vital struggle of a man laboriously seeking a solution to a severe crisis of values. In comparison with other protagonists of American architecture, Wright was late in succumbing to this crisis. Having taken refuge in the neutral field of the domestic residence for the upper-middle class, he had warded off the crisis that eventually overcame him all the more violently. He did not arrive at a different attitude toward the city until 1920. Even after this date, however, his approach was far from clear-cut or single-minded. In 1921, just when Wright designed his first real skyscraper, he also began "a direct continuous study"[81] that took preliminary form in two unpublished attacks on the city, "In Bondage" and "The Usonian City," and reached a first conclusion in 1932 in his book *The Disappearing City.*[82] Thus, curiously, Wright produced his most decisively urban designs at the same time as he defined his unequivocal opposition to the urban phenomenon in its totality.

In the period following his return from Japan, when Wright was on the West Coast, intent upon constructing a series of houses completely different in character from the prairie houses, he began work on an office building for A. M. Johnson, president of the National Life Insurance Company of Chicago. The task Wright set himself in this project was to apply to a vertical edifice the idea, developed earlier in other works, of a supporting structure concentrated in a central nucleus. The lot on which the building was to rise, in Water Tower Square near the present site of the John Hancock Center, was approximately 300 by 100 feet, with the longer side facing south. Working on this project, as Wright himself recounted in his autobiography, he "discovered" standardization and its application on a large scale—"the kind of standardization in building that gave us the motor car." On the exterior, his edifice would be seen as surfaces of "opalescent, iridescent copper-bound glass."[83]

Only in 1924 did Wright's idea take shape in a preliminary design that was a fascinating attempt finally to assert himself in the big city that had so often rejected his architecture. The city for which the project was conceived was not yet the "vast prison with glass fronts," in which the skyscraper "is no exalted order of merit" but, rather, "conspicuous proof of the cultural lag and a fine example of our conspicuous waste."[84] For Wright in 1924, the city was still the Chicago of 1918, comprised of negative elements but also of cultural potential. And it was precisely from the man who had faced the city with this spirit that Wright sought approval and support:

I had the good fortune to explain the scheme in detail and show the developed preliminary drawings to liebermeister Louis H. Sullivan shortly before he died. Gratefully I remember— and proudly too—he said: "I had faith that it would come. It is a work of great art. I knew what I was talking about all those years—you see? I could never have done this building myself, but I believe that but for me, you could never have done it." I know I should never have reached it, but for what he was and what he himself did. This design is dedicated to him.[85]

Thus Wright not only felt himself to be the direct descendent of Sullivan but even asserted that the pupil had surpassed the master. The National Life Insurance skyscraper was a fantastic and anticipatory vision of a new city, an enormous step forward in respect to the old city that can be glimpsed around it in Wright's drawings. It was to remain, however, only an exceptional expression of the architect's "wish" for a city—a wish that was to prompt Wright on many occasions to respond to urban commissions with designs bespeaking a fantastic, futuristic vision of a complex, concentrated city.

During the same period in which he wrote "In Bondage" and "The Usonian City," Wright designed still other urban buildings. They included a "steel cathedral embracing minor cathedrals," an incredible, utopian space to accommodate a gathering of a million people, as well as a design of a skyline for Chicago, intended as a counterproposal to the skyscrapers of New York and to the city divided according to the grid of real-estate speculation.[86] The design of the "cathedral" would reappear later in the Broadacres model and was taken up

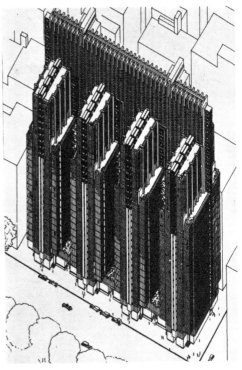

Design by Frank Lloyd Wright for the Press
Building, San Francisco, a project begun in
1912, shown here in the variant design of
1920.

Design for a skyscraper by Frank Lloyd
Wright, prepared for the National Life Insurance Company of Chicago, between
1920 and 1925.

again as late as 1954 in the Beth Sholom Synagogue in Philadelphia. Meanwhile, a series of events and experiences stirred Wright's personal life, leading him always closer to the definitive abandonment of any urban illusion and reinforcing, instead, his never-quelled antagonism toward the city that destroys the individual, expressed in the two essays cited above.

This concatenation of events marking this transitional period is once again described by Wright himself, even if his interpretation of their significance be somewhat distorted. On August 15, 1914, a "ghastly tragedy" struck Wright's life. While Wright was in Chicago overseeing the final phase of construction of the Midway Gardens, Taliesin was burned to the ground by a servant from Barbados, who, in a fit of madness, also killed Mamah Cheney, the ex-wife of the Oak Park neighbor and client, who had accompanied Wright to Europe. Shortly thereafter, in circumstances recounted in his biography, Wright met Miriam Noel, a "brilliant, sophisticated" woman, "Parisian by adoption and preference," whom he took with him to Japan, where the Imperial Hotel was under construction.

Together with the Midway Gardens, the Imperial Hotel marked the high point of Wright's eclecticism and constant search for a wider range of cultural references. His interest was now directed to worlds of the past, and he drew on the cultures of the Maya, Japan and the American Indians for their positive, joyous qualities. The fascination of tradition led Wright to experiment with the most diverse architectural expressions during this period. Not following a continuous, patient line of research but, instead, constantly seeking renewed inspiration through new incentives—literary and ideological as well as visual—he readily adapted a continuously changing figurative vocabulary to various models.

Finally, Wright felt the need for a complete change even in his relationship with Miriam Noel. The union between the man who never ceased to feel his tie with an autonomous and independent American culture and the refined and brilliant woman for whom Paris was the unique pole of reference was not destined to last. The fire that destroyed Taliesin for the second time in 1925 seems once again to have burned Wright's past. Shortly before he had met Olgivanna, a woman born in Montenegro, which "like Wales . . . was a mountainous little country whose people were never conquered." She "had grown up in a patriarchal family in an official society with a mind and will of her own," and, according to Wright, she descended from a "people not unlike my own Welsh forbears . . . her upbringing had much in common with my own."[87]

His recent past was thus blotted out, and he returned to his origins. At the age of fifty-eight he was about to refound his own existence, but at just that moment Wright, Taliesin, and his private life became the objects of a violent attack on the part of the scandal-mongering press. Within a short time he was forced to leave his home and new family and "to roam the streets of New York alone." "It was then I began to write. I tried to write some impressions of the big city. 'In Bondage' was one. 'The Usonian City' another; later to begin this work [the autobiography]."[88]

This experience cut short any relationship whatsoever with the city. What had to be reconstructed was home and family—the first, as a refuge from the city and its more brutal expressions: the lawyers, the press, and the police; the second, as a refuge from the "mob" and from any form of artificial intercourse. The idea of the community-clan, so clamorously cast aside in 1909, was thus slowly regenerated, but in a new form; family and cultural environment were now differently integrated. The contradictions that had led to Wright's flight from Oak Park were thus negated, and the rejection of the urban reality that had given rise to them now resolved positively his past history, which could henceforth be presented as a single, solidly consistent life experience.

Taliesin III represented the recovery of an entire American past, enriched with elements of other cultures. It was the cornerstone of Broadacres, the symbol of a reacquired unity that made it possible to reconstruct, a posteriori, a fictive continuity that cancels all contradiction, which is indeed the significance of both the autobiography and Broadacres. The autobiography was the testimony of a life not lived in vain; as such, it was necessarily a constant point of reference, even if a distorted one, for all who wished to understand its author's life experience; it was also, however, an affirmation of that experience as one single, uninterrupted course. Similarly, Broadacres was the formal definition of a space that contained part of the past and all of the future of Wright's architecture, a place in which his designs were no longer isolated but, rather, inserted into a total system that justified their existence. In the totality of Broadacres, Wright's works were no longer designs for a single client with whom he had found an "elective affinity" but projects for a society that had in itself the values of the American frontier, rebaptized "Usonia."

Behind Broadacres, however, there lay not merely Wright's personal experience but also decades of agrarian thought and antiurban concepts. In both form and meaning, Broadacres was derived from ideas that, between 1910 and 1930, animated the trends and movements that favored a return to the land and to nature. Wright formalized the Broadacres proposal at the time when this rejection of urban civilization appeared feasible not only on the theoretical level but also, ideally, on the economic and political level. The model he proposed represented a synthesis of the utopias of the late nineteenth century and the more concrete proposals of the 1920s and 1930s. Up to 1910, Wright held a unique, avant-garde position in the field of architecture but was completely divorced from urban problems. Only after 1930 did he seek to assert himself in this field too. In doing so, however, he replaced his one-time lack of interest with a complete rejection of the scientific urban planning that had been developing in just those years. Broadacres was, and remains, the formal expression of one man's personal antiurban conceptions, even if Wright sought broader structural references in objective reality to support his individual, subjective vision of an idyllic and "democratic" society.

The Rebirth of the Agrarian World

In The United States during the second decade of this century, many factors contributed to kindle interest in new types of agricultural development, connected with new concepts of land use and new proposals for a "return to the land." Projects inspired by such perspectives gained favor even in government circles, where the back-to-nature movement reflected the enthusiasm that George E. Mowry has defined as a perverting "social nostalgia . . . convenient politically for America's ruling economic classes to foster the rural virtues."[89] This alliance of individualist Jeffersonian agrarianism with expanded governmental responsibility was perhaps best represented by Franklin K. Lane, the secretary of the interior. In the years immediately following World War I, Lane found it possible to put his ideas into action by means of a program he himself proposed to President Wilson for the soldiers returning from Europe. In place of the distribution of land that had been usual in such programs as long as the frontier existed, the proposal for the veterans now foresaw a new type of colonization, with a planned development and the offer of a secure, communal life. For Lane, looking ahead meant concentrating on agriculture; the "spirit of democracy," he wrote, "does not thrive where men live without hope of land ownership. There is something peculiarly subtle in the feeling that a bit of the soil is one's own. It makes for a stronger, higher citizenship. It gives birth to loyalties that are essential to national life and to a healthy home life."[90] This program was not, however, limited to a simple return to the land and nature. In order to achieve these ideal results, Lane felt it necessary to integrate rural life with the advantages of the city.

The controversy that arose in the same years over the use of national parks and the opening of them to automobile traffic offered Lane a still wider range of action. In 1916 the national parks came under the control of a branch of the Department of the Interior, the first concern of which was to adapt the parks to the urban visitor, their principal user. The parks became the other face of the city, places unthinkable without the city and without the desire for the "wilderness." The parks could not be touched by any form of economic development but had to be "kept accessible by any means practicable." According to Lane, it was necessary to extend "the splendid cooperation developed during the last three years among chambers of commerce, tourist bureaus, and automobile-highway associations for the purpose of spreading information about our national parks and facilitating their use and enjoyment."[91] A road network became the logical complement of nature, making it accessible. Nature was now seen as a national heritage to be placed at the disposal of the inhabitant of the city, just as, for Turner, the frontier had been the outlet offered the oppressed city worker who desired to escape the shackles of organized society.

Lane's position and that of the movements for a return to the country and nature, viewed as complementary to the city, found parallel expression in Wright's contemporary attitude toward Chicago as a "positive" city possessing a genuine American culture and in his decision to live isolated in nature while continuing to travel in the states of America and on the roads of the world. On the whole, the ideas of Lane and Wright were an appeal to nature that did not exclude the city, or at least not the type of city that provided an impulse for the development of American culture. At the same time, this enthusiasm for nature and a life in nature favored individuality, the "wilderness," and, in general, the ideal of life, shared by many American intellectuals, that had been defined by Turner in 1893. It is certainly not without significance that in 1921, when Turner's work was published for the first time in a complete and definitive form, the urban population of America had just reached 51.2 percent of the total population.[92] Thus the moment that witnessed the diminution of the rural population from a majority to a minority also witnessed the rebirth of agrarian America's protest against industrialization and the city. Just as Turner's concept of the frontier had been enthusiastically embraced in the period of the Populist revolt, it was now taken up by the agrarian movements.

Wright lived in full the contradiction of the moment, the twofold aspect of American life. On one side were the cities, increasingly confirming their role in the nation's life while remaining "strongholds of the new plutocracy"; against them, between 1903 and 1917, the intellectuals lashed out with critical realism, fired by the dream of a democratic renascence of the East.[93] On the other was the country, the small provincial places of the South and West, where the "true" American spirit, uncontaminated by contact with the Old World, was still conserved. Jack London's individualism and the agrarian dream of Meredith Nicholson's *Valley of Democracy* proclaimed a single ideal of life. For Wright, as for the popular novelist David Graham Phillips, if a man remained in the city too long he inevitably lost that quality that made him American; to find "a real American, a man or a woman who looks as if he or she would do something honest and valuable," one had to go west.[94]

Toward the end of the second decade of the century, Wright took up the position of the thinkers who a quarter of a century earlier, had vehemently accused the city of depriving native America not only of its morality, but also of its talent for creative work and its sense of beauty. Hostility toward the city became also hostility toward the European immigrants, who now began to enter political life and the world of business, as well as that of organized crime.[95] Urban life lost all attraction, and its place was filled by an ideal rural model that acquired progressively greater definition in the course of the 1920s.

One of the first concrete proposals to be put forward after Lane's program was that of a private citizen, aiming during these years at the presidency. Henry Ford interpreted the preoccupations and needs of a broad stratum of America and sought to reconcile them with his own interests. His program for the development of the region of Muscle Shoals on the Tennessee River in Alabama became a point of reference for the subsequent development of agrarian thought.

The first phase of the Muscle Shoals story ended in February 1921 with a Senate debate on the utilization of the nitrate deposits in this zone and the

Dorothea Lange, *The Road West*, New Mexico, 1938.

Design for the possible development of Muscle Shoals on the Tennessee River in Alabama, prepared by the *Scientific American* in 1922 on the basis of Henry Ford's ideas for the construction of a 75-mile long city.

water power of the Tennessee River—and thus on the development of one of the poorest areas of the South.[96] The discussion ran aground, however, because of the large Southern companies' lack of interest in the project. The secretary of war, Edward Weeks, could do no more than register the impossibility of developing this region according to any of the standard procedures for such interventions. The second phase of the story began in July of the same year. What was in question this time, however, was no longer the government's program but Henry Ford's. This new proposal, according to Ford and his followers, was a nonprofit program, conceived solely in the interest of the farmers and of national well-being. His scheme foresaw the production of low-cost fertilizer and the utilization of surplus productive power for the production of commodities such as aluminum, textiles, and steel and the construction of auto parts. The government was to complete the second dam and construct a third dam. Ford was to take a hundred-year lease on all these installations, providing at his own expense the nitrate plants (from which his profit would be limited to 8 percent), the electric power plants, and the hook-up with a plant already existing in Gorgas, Alabama.

Ford's proposals won him enormous popularity in the Southern states. As Donald Davidson, one of the major poets among the Southern Agrarians, was later to write, Ford's program appeared to offer Southern business and industry a concrete possibility of competing with the North.[97] Moreover, Ford saw this development as a counterproposal to the urban confusion usual in the North. Muscle Shoals was to be a very extended settlement, larger than Detroit but designed as a linear city seventy-five miles long, immersed in greenery for the protection of the health and the social well-being of the workers and their families. Backed by the prestigious Ford name, the idea of a city that could eliminate the defects and dangers of the traditional city was lauded by the American press, for whom the project also represented a recovery of the agrarian myth. According to the *New York Times*, the "benefits of rural or near-rural life would not be entirely lost" in this project, with its groups of small cities and small communities. "A City All Main Street," wrote the *Literary Digest*, publishing an article from the Chicago journal *Engineering and Contracting*, which recognized the positive qualities of a linear city conceived in terms of the parallel layout of settlements and transportation routes, according to a scheme that made it possible for everyone to live in easy reach of his place of work. In conclusion, the *Literary Digest* concurred on the importance of the project and its contribution to the future of city planning.[98]

But Ford's proposal, which had the promotional support of Thomas A. Edison, was bitterly opposed in the sixty-seventh Congress by George W. Norris, who was to be one of the promoters of the Tennessee Valley Authority during the presidency of Franklin D. Roosevelt. Norris revealed the self-interested aspect of Ford's proposition; the government would pay for the installations of

Muscle Shoals, which would then produce, in addition to fertilizer, automobiles and other products. Norris predicted that Ford would create a city that would make New York look like a country village.[99] In the course of the 1920s, the problem of Muscle Shoals, and thus the problem of the development of sources of energy in general, was hotly debated in Congress and throughout the country as a whole.

Ford's urban project was never actually designed but only described. The city he proposed was directly related to Arturo Soria y Mata's linear city and took up the idea of a community of houses and small pieces of land—each family with its own acre of ground—organized linearly and dispersed in nature.[100] In its growth, the city was to be self-sufficient, and the houses were to be constructed with materials produced in series by the Ford industries. Thus Ford's proposal for Muscle Shoals implied the formation of a new relationship between government and private enterprise. It was, however, also part of a policy of industrial decentralization aimed at a greater control over the working force and offered the double advantage of a control over salaries that also actually favored the sale of consumer goods. In fact, the worker would be bound to his job through the possession of land, which he had to cultivate and from which he had to draw a part of his sustenance. While on the one hand, this unreimbursed, obligatory self-sufficiency signified a reduction in the worker's objective remuneration, on the other, it reduced his living expenses, thus automatically favoring the sale of consumer products. The great "synthesis" of agriculture and industry expressed in Ford's *Today and Tomorrow*, published in 1926, became an integral part of the policies adopted in opposition to the urban worker.

Ten years after his proposal for Muscle Shoals, in the midst of the depression, Ford insisted on a similar program. He foresaw the creation of 50,000 little gardens in the area of Detroit and announced that, beginning in 1932, no employee in Iron Mountain, Michigan, could keep his job unless he cultivated a garden to provide a part of his food. According to Ford, "the man too lazy to work in a garden during his leisure time does not deserve a job."[101]

Like Donald Davidson, Wright applauded Ford's program for Muscle Shoals, without, however, taking account of those eminently unaltruistic aspects immediately seized upon by Senator Norris. In a lecture in 1930 Wright commented,

Ford is a man from whom the future had a right to expect something beside sentimentality. He is a man of common sense. He is a man that really has contributed a good deal to our country. He has successful ideas. His proposition for Muscle Shoals was one of the best things that I have heard of as a solution of the excess machine increment. . . . What to do with the man at the machine? Ford's proposal was for the decentralization of industry. If he could get Muscle Shoals he was going to have lots of little factories. He was going to give every man a few acres of ground of his own. In the summer the men would work on the ground. In the winter they would go to work with their machines in the factory, the machines in the factory giving such facility that they need only work at the machines 5 or 6 months of each year.[102]

This same theme, which was eventually to be applied to Broadacres, was taken up in the course of Wright's famous lectures at Princeton, also delivered in 1930. Wright again referred to Ford's program, citing it in concluding an attack on concentration:

Only when the city becomes purely and simply utilitarian will it have the order that is beauty and the simplicity which the machine, in competent hands, may very well render as human benefit. . . .

This, *the only possible ideal machine*, seen as a *city*, will be invaded at ten o'clock, abandoned at four, for three days a week. The other four days of the week will be devoted to the more or less joyful matter of living elsewhere under conditions natural to man. The dividing lines between town and country are even now gradually disappearing as conditions are reversing themselves. The country absorbs the life of the city as the city shrinks to the utilitarian purpose that now alone justifies its existence. Even that concentration for utilitarian purposes we have just admitted may be first to go, as the result of impending decentralization of industry. It will soon become unnecessary to concentrate in masses for any purpose whatsoever. The individual unit, in more sympathetic grouping on the ground, will grow stronger in the hard-earned freedom gained at first by that element of the city not prostitute to the machine. Henry Ford stated this idea in his plan for the development of Muscle Shoals.

Even the small town is too large. It will gradually merge into the general nonurban development. Ruralism as distinguished from urbanism is American, and truly democratic.[103]

Electrification was Ford's objective for the entire region of Muscle Shoals, just as it was the objective of those desiring to abandon the city and create models of democratic life in the country, or as it was for Patrick Geddes, who considered electricity the "magic wand" that would emancipate the woman in society and thus society itself.[104] "The future in the hand of electricity" was a constantly recurring theme during the 1920s for those who aimed at a regeneration of rural life and the creation of new conditions for the farmer.[105] A few years later, Wright was to develop Broadacres on the basis of this same concept. His pursuit paralleled that of the Southern Agrarians, the intellectual movement that attempted a regeneration of the South after the crisis of 1929, the effects of which on rural areas, already sorely tried by the downward trend of the agricultural market in the preceding years, were disastrous.

Now that technology offered new, unlimited possibilities, the rebirth of the rural areas finally appeared feasible, and a new agrarian and populist feeling took hold in America. The era of Sinclair Lewis's *Main Street* had passed, and Ford's "City All Main Street" was now showing the way to a fusion between traditional, antiurban agrarianism and Thoreau's "nativism." Prohibition and the Ku Klux Klan were two immediately visible expressions of the conflict between city and country and evidenced the forebodings and the ethnic tensions underlying American life, at times demonstrating violently the widespread "aversion . . . to the immigrant drinking masses, to the pleasures and amenities of city life, and to the well-to-do classes and cultivated men."[106]

Although crude and ingenuous, the appeal the Ku Klux Klan made to the "uncultured" was an appeal to a natural, and thus American, condition, a

The first Ford automobile workshop.

Dorothea Lange, *Tractored Out*, Childress
County, Texas, 1938.

concept long since elaborated in a very different form and at a very different level by Thoreau. In a speech delivered in 1926, the Klan's Imperial Wizard and Emperor, Hiram Wesley Evans, declared, "We are a movement of plain people, very weak in the matter of culture, intellectual support, and trained leadership. We are demanding . . . a return of power into the hands of the everyday, not highly cultured, not overly intellectualized, but entirely unspoiled and not de-Americanized, average citizen of the old stock."[107]

Nativist and agrarian antiurbanism received a strong new impetus at the 1924 Democratic National Convention and again during the presidential campaign of 1928. In both instances the presidential candidacy of Alfred E. Smith, product of the New York City political machine, descendant of Catholic immigrants, and a "wet," gave rise to a heated battle, in which the opposing forces were aligned according to the schematic division between Protestant-prohibitionist-rural and Catholic-antiprohibitionist-urban groups. These were indeed the issues held to be decisive for the destiny of America. After the Democrats' defeat in the 1928 elections, a Midwestern newspaper editorialized, "America is not yet dominated by its great cities. Control of its destinies still remains in the smaller communities and rural regions, with their traditional conservatism and solid virtues. . . . Main Street is still the principal thoroughfare of the nation."[108] Actually, however, as Richard Hofstadter has emphasized, Republican control of the cities was swept away by the Democratic candidacy of Al Smith, who opened the way to Roosevelt and made it possible for him "to surmount the old dualism, so troublesome to the Progressives, between the political ethos of the urban machine and that of nativist Protestant America."[109]

The mentality that had formed during the 1920s, which this editorial eloquently expressed, did, however, provide fertile ground for entirely unique, subjective, and personal renunciations of the city, which in this atmosphere gained widespread approval. In the last of his six lectures at Princeton in 1930, Wright foresaw a different distribution of food and supplies, which, although he did not refer to it specifically, obviously drew on Ralph Borsodi's Suffern experiment: "Cities are great mouths, New York the greatest mouth in the world. With generally perfect distribution of food and supplies over the entire area of the countryside, one of the vital elements helping to build the city has left us forever, to spread out on the soil from which it came: local products finding a short haul direct, where an expensive long haul and then back again was once necessary. Within easy distance of any man's dwelling will be everything needed in the category of foodstuffs or supplies which the city itself can now supply."[110]

Wright's own experiences, his taking refuge definitively at Taliesin, the discovery of the desert, the formation of a close-knit, self-sufficient community isolated from the rest of the world—all of which will be examined further on—cannot be fully understood without taking into account similar flights and evasions attempted by others. Among these, Borsodi was specifically referred to in *Architecture and Modern Life*, published by Wright and Baker Brownell in 1937.[111] Borsodi's renunciation of New York, the city where he lived and worked, was complete. The strikes, the protests, the rising prices and soaring rents, which transformed the American cities in 1920 and the following years, were the circumstances that prompted him to leave. On an eight-acre farm two hours by train from New York City, Borsodi isolated himself and organized a self-sufficient life based on cultivating the land and producing his own instruments for living and working. This one-family establishment tended to grow, and a short time later Borsodi founded Suffern, a small, completely self-sufficient town with home-style production of all its food, textiles, and clothing and its own working of woods and metals. Suffern was an attempt to carry out the idea of an integrated life leading to a thorough reorganization of society, an ideal of decentralization where the family once again became the center of associated life. Animating this initiative, as Borsodi himself affirmed, was the spirit of the American pioneer, except that the traditional Bible was here replaced by Emerson's "Self-Reliance."

Directly related to the distributism of Belloc and Chesterton, Borsodi's idea was a condemnation of the entire system of the factory and industry, as his 1929 book, *This Ugly Civilization*, makes explicit. This work, along with Borsodi's *Flight from the City*, published in 1933, in which he elaborated his ideas of communal life into a constructive program, enjoyed wide distribution in America. Wright, like the Southern Agrarians, referred directly to Ralph Borsodi, and the viewpoints of all coincided in opposing industrialization in favor of an ideal life obtainable through the return to the land and to home production.[112] This view was particularly strong among the Southern Agrarians. Formed at Vanderbilt University in Nashville, Tennessee, their movement assumed a specifically agrarian character about 1928, when their political and social outlook became clearly defined.[113] In the face of the poverty of the South, which had felt the full force of the agricultural depression of the 1920s, the Southern Agrarians condemned the Northern "progressive" spirit that scorned the "conservative" South, and in this very conservatism they found the virtues and values the North had long since lost. They looked to the past, indeed as far back as the late Middle Ages, which represented the world of art, learning, and morality,[114] but also to Puritan New England and the antebellum South,[115] two worlds not yet divided by different forms of economy.

By the time this group of Southern writers sent *I'll Take My Stand* to press in 1930, their position was unequivocal. Northern industrialism transported to the South would ruin even this region; the encouragement of an agricultural economy based on the small, privately owned farm was the only way to preserve the healthy Southern life. The South, like the West, was still the nation's great hope; by joining their forces against the business-ridden, industrialized East, a society based upon individualism and on proprietorship extended to the great majority of the population appeared a realizable goal. The crisis of 1929 reinforced the vision of an ideal society favoring ownership of the means of production and thus necessarily free and prosperous. Large-scale industrialization, concentrating ownership of the means of production in the hands of a few, created an insecure and completely subjugated proletariat, while class-consciousness and the bitter economic and social conflicts transformed the middle class into salaried slaves. For Allen Tate, Marxism was not sufficiently revolutionary, since it aimed to overcome capitalism with a capitalism of the left. According to the Southern Agrarians, capitalism could be overcome solely by the diffusion of private property. This was the teaching of the Jeffersonian tradition, the very basis of America; the solution to the crisis of American civilization was the return to American culture.[116] Spengler had arrived in the New World.

The Southern Agrarians viewed Borsodi's experiment within the more general context of an agrarian economy and the return to a rural culture. Donald Davidson, for instance, did not consider the victory of the city decisive, nor did he view the tendency toward national unity under the aegis of the North as in any way definitively established.[117] Even if Borsodi's views did not completely coincide with the movement's ideology, he was nevertheless among the limited number of collaborators of the Southern Agrarians' journal, the *American Review;* the others included Allen Tate, John Crowe Ransom, Frank L. Owsley, Donald Davidson, and Hilaire Belloc, whose distributist theory the Agrarians wholly accepted. In 1936 Borsodi wrote in the *American Review* that a society wishing to achieve prosperity and well-being had to apply agrarian and distributist principles, and the population had to consist essentially of families living in the country and working their own farm. The right to land ownership, conceived in Henry George's terms as a gift of nature, gave every family the possibility of acquiring land and establishing a farm.[118] For Borsodi, as for Wright, the concept of a wider distribution of productive property stemmed from the belief that property is necessary to man if he is not to become a slave.

The analysis of the decentralists, who included also the supporters of the National Catholic Rural Life Conference, began from the premise that the intensive growth of industries and cities after the Civil War had divided American society into opposing factions. Aligned on the one side were the enthusiasts of economic centralization, concentrated in the Eastern cities that had ties with Europe and were dominated by Republican politics. On the other side were the farmers and the small businessmen of the South and Midwest, generally aligned with the Democrats, "the party of rural America, of the farmer, the shopkeeper, the artisan." In order to face this situation, the agrarian movements proposed an alliance between South and West, since the desire of both was "to defend home, stability of life, the practice of leisure, and the natural enemy of both [was] the insidious industrial city."[119]

The decentralist movements accepted technology and aimed, in particular, at the replacement of steam power with electricity, a change that would make feasible the development of small factories and home-style industries and, by facilitating communication, would also tend to integrate the rural areas with national life. The decentralists also sought the large-scale introduction of the automobile, which would make it possible to abandon the city and spread out over the territory. Roosevelt's victory in the elections of 1932 was encouraging for the decentralists, who considered him sympathetic to their economic views, an opponent of Wall Street, and a supporter of rural America. [120] Only later, especially after Roosevelt's great centralizing programs were under way, did the decentralists change their view of his administration. In the early 1930s, however, many points of the Democratic program coincided with the position of those who favored a return to the land and to nature.

Between Nature and Technology

In the late 1920s, the idea that American could outlive her fame only by plotting a new destiny became a certainty for Wright; in place of the chronic depression that plagued the rural areas while the cities continued their impetuous growth, a democracy had to be created that would be based on agriculture, the small proprietor, and the decentralization of industry. As has been indicated, this was hardly an isolated position but, instead, part of a widespread movement inspiring highly personal initiatives as well as government programs. Even if a great part of America was by sentiment close to the tradition of the frontier and the farmer, however, it was nevertheless during the second decade of the century that the movement of farmers to the cities reached increasingly vast dimensions; rural immigrants totaled from 400,000 to over a million each year. In face of this urban onslaught, to believe in the absolute necessity of configuring a different and decidedly antiurban life pattern and of reorganizing the entire national economy on an agricultural basis was no more than an evasion. With the crash of 1929, similar evasions became tantamount to total indifference; the tremendously urgent problems posed by the depression could surely not be solved by the proposal of any single individual.

As already noted, Wright was still living in two worlds in the early 1920s, the urban and the rural, and only subsequently did he form the different vision of a life in nature to be achieved through technology. The theory he had expounded in 1901 about the capacity of the machine in the hands of man to create a more beautiful world was modified in the late 1920s; he then began to see the possibilities offered by the machine to create a new spatial organization as making feasible the creation of a new world. In Wright's view, this "new world" would be born from the union of nature, the only historical precedent of the independent, native American culture, with technology, the power enabling an undifferentiated occupation of physical space and making possible a new epic conquest of the frontier.

After ten years of searching for inspiration among the primitive and historical traditions of the Japanese and Maya cultures, the American Indians, and the Middle Ages, Wright arrived at the simple and elating discovery that the only true precedent was the purest American nature—the desert. In 1927, in order to design the winter resort of San Marcos, Wright set up an outpost of his Spring Green community in the Arizona desert, where he and his group were fired by the spirit of the pioneer who occupies a desolate territory and turns it into a cheerful garden. Writing of this experience in his autobiography, Wright declared, "A human gaiety in the Desert is underway."

The commercial speculation that lay at the base of this enterprise did not interest Wright, who saw only the possibility of constructing a new world according to his own vision. Just as, a few years earlier, Florida had attracted large numbers of people fascinated with the possibility of enriching themselves by transforming a swampy region into an eternal springtime haven, the Arizona experiment mixed commercial speculation with a sense of recovering nature. What had been done in Florida would be attempted in the Western desert. "The time indeed was coming when the annual flight to the South would be as regular and impressive as the migration of the Canada Goose."[121]

Wright, too, followed this migratory route, and his dream of the conquest of nature became a reality. To design the resort complex of San Marcos in the Desert, Wright and his collaborators built an encampment on the model of the old Western forts, composed of living quarters, a work area, and communal spaces. Ocotillo Camp came into being as a place to design and live a new adventure as a group, isolated and independent, just as Borsodi had wished to be in his experiment. At the center of the encampment, almost like an altar, was a place to gather and confirm the united intent of this communal undertaking. Wright could now recompose the fragments of his own past into a unified experience, pioneering, new and untried. He could begin again, but not from zero. His past life had also to acquire full significance, as it could only by situating it within the general context of a return to nature, the great and all-embracing Mother. It was from this point that Wright was to launch his flight toward Usonia, leaving behind the contaminated and corrupted world of the city.

Here in this wonderland an architect and his helpers are actually working away to build a simple camp, a camp we shall call it. A human inhabitant of unmitigated wilderness of quotidian change—unchangeably changing Change. For our purpose we need fifteen cabins in all. Since all will be temporary we will call them ephemera. And you will soon see them like a group of gigantic butterflies with scarlet wing spots, conforming gracefully to the crown of the outcropping of black splintered rock gently uprising from the desert floor.[122]

The basic layout of Ocotillo Camp consisted of a few fundamental directional axes around which the spaces and constructions could be organized with great liberty. The temporary buildings were of wood covered with canvas to give protection from the sun and permit the circulation of air. Figuratively, they were a precedent for the solution adopted in 1938 at Taliesin West, the winter residence Wright was to build in the Arizona desert, to which every year at the first snowfall he would migrate like a bird, together with the whole clan of Taliesin East.

Ocotillo Camp was the seed from which developed the idea of the city that Wright was to synthesize some years later in Broadacres. Created as a place to carry out a design project, Ocotillo became a visible expression of the back-to-nature concept that occupied the thoughts and aims of so many in these years. A community in the making, Ocotillo was a training ground independent of official educational practices, a place with its own laws, not governed by conventions, and a place of work far from the city. In reality, the society created there was also extraneous to America, but for Wright Ocotillo became the first point of land conquered for America, the first settlement of Usonia, the future promised land he felt was already present in the American spirit. Ocotillo was the point of no return.

To evaluate fully the significance of Ocotillo as a turning point in Wright's thought, it is necessary to retrace the events of his personal life, so intimately interwoven with his thoughts about the city and the ideal of community life. The years before the great crash were years of torment for Wright. He was harassed by ever-mounting debts, without work, no longer with any assistants and far from Taliesin; all seemed to proceed on the worst possible course. Under these circumstances, the proposal to build a winter resort in Arizona, a short distance from Phoenix and near the Mormon town of Mesa, offered not only the hope of emerging from a difficult situation but also the possibility of working far from the Eastern cities, in an uncontaminated, pioneer territory.

In his autobiography Wright significantly placed the Arizona and Ocotillo Camp experience between a plea for Usonia and an attack on New York. [123] His train of thought, running from the mythical promised land to the desert to be built on and back to the "man-eating skyscrapers," reveals the role this comparison played in developing his concept of "the new city [that] will be nowhere, yet everywhere. Broadacre City." From that time on there was to be no more contamination by the "significant insignificance" the city expresses, no more acceptance of urban culture. Condemnation of the city was to be continuous and unrelenting; the image of the city became a place where children no longer play in the street, a place to rent a room for the night or eat a solitary meal in a cafeteria. These firmly held views did not, however, preclude Wright's maintaining a permanent residence at the Plaza Hotel in New York as late as the 1950s.

His renunciation of the city was more an intellectual act than the expression of heartfelt hatred. Condemning the city and constructing a new world were the only possibilities for giving significance to the whole of his past life; they represented the recovery of this life and the annulment of its contradictions. Broadacres was part of the resuscitation of rural America that was then being carried out by American culture, and as the formalization of a "genuinely American" response to the great crisis, it even appeared to have a place within the perspectives of the New Deal. Actually, however, it was only the response of a single individual attempting to cancel out all contradictions, regardless of

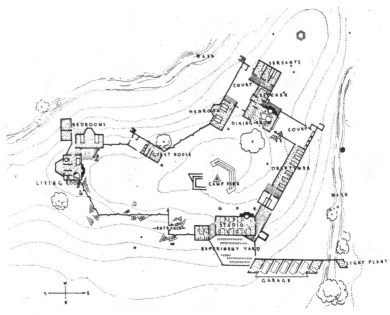

Plan of Ocotillo Camp at Salt Range, near
Chandler, Arizona, built by Frank Lloyd
Wright as a place to carry out the design of
the residential complex of San Marcos in the
Desert, commissioned by Alexander Chandler
in 1927.

Ocotillo Camp, photographed from outside
its enclosure.

Ocotillo Camp, interior of one of the cabins.

San Marcos in the Desert, view from the principal entrance of the residential complex, designed by Frank Lloyd Wright at Ocotillo Camp beginning in 1927.

Taliesin West, Frank Lloyd Wright's winter residence in the Arizona desert at Maricopa Mesa, built in 1938.

whether the equilibrium Wright felt capable of achieving with his proposed model found space in an America seeking to plot a new development.

Wright's proposal stemmed from the conviction that an America unmarked by the nonculture of urban life still existed. Arizona and the whole region of the Southwest became the place to put into operation the recovery of an uncorrupted nature. One has only to leaf through the pages of the *Southwest Review* to find the elements that fascinated Wright: the color and the light of the desert, the perfume of the flowers, the broad spaces, and the great silence unbroken by the sound of the machine.[124] This was the new world to be constructed. This was a place that could give birth to the synthesis of divine and human intervention: "I am writing this on the Phoenix plain of Arizona" in 1928. "The ruddy granite mountain-heaps, grown 'old,' are decomposing and sliding down layer upon layer to further compose the soil of the plain. Granite in various stages of decay, sand, silt and gravel make the floor of the world here. Buildings could grow right up out of the 'ground' were this 'soil,' before it is too far 'rotted,' cemented in proper proportions and beaten into flasks or boxes—a few steel strands dropped in for reinforcement."[125] The architect, who was to be invested with the very highest authority in Broadacres, is here envisaged as the lone man before God, the natural creator of eternal values. Broadacres was to be the physical form of this new world born from the desert; it was to be the realization of Usonia.

Wright's rediscovery in the desert of the mythical land of the pioneer, of the American epic, and even of the direct derivation of the organic principle from the thought of the American Renaissance led him to attempt to recover the American culture of the frontier. Before this experience he had felt himself to be, and was considered, an architect above what was taking place in the world; afterward, although he remained outside of any direct intervention, he felt dedicated to the construction of a different world.

The protests that arose in the rural areas during the 1920s, the crisis of agriculture that transformed the American economic and social system, and the crisis of the traditional family brought about by urbanization and its accompanying social transformation, together with his own personal crisis, contributed very largely to forming Wright's vision of a solution to the state into which America had fallen. Even before 1929, he himself lived in a general crisis, with disastrous repercussions for Taliesin and the ideal model of community life, disrupting his own existence and that of his new family; instead, in the desert Wright once again found his identity and a place to work without restrictions.

When even the Ocotillo project was interrupted by the crash of 1929, his break with the rest of the world became definitive. Wright viewed his personal vicissitudes as well as the events of October on Wall Street as disasters that stemmed from a single cause: a mistaken economic system that had its most clamorous, violent, and deleterious expression in the large cities. It was the source of the system of laws that had forced him to pass several days in jail, of the system of the scandal-mongering press that had made him and his personal life the objects of public scorn, of the system of credit that had threatened to close Taliesin (saved only by his wealthy friends), and, indeed, of the city itself, which had excluded him and deprived him of work. Broadacres was created as the negation of all these adverse forces. Its new laws were to be based on the Jeffersonian dictum "that government is best that governs least." A different system of mass media would make possible a more correct analysis of reality than that of the urban gossip columns. A new system of credit and exchange, based on the work of the individual, would offer equal opportunities to all.

The condemnation of industrialism developed into an attack on science as it was used and applied. Like the Southern Agrarians, Wright believed that the industrial city destroyed art and religion and that democracy was a farce when it was not operative in the economic institutions. The ideas expressed in Broadacres were the same as those professed by the agrarian intellectuals: education should once again be conservative and selective; progress signified man's effort to triumph over the forces of nature; the decentralization of industry, the return to the land, and the recovery of the past were the means of obtaining an integral society, which had to be based on the private ownership of the means of production. As Jefferson had affirmed, the man without property was not free. The return to agriculture as "a way of life" and the family were the two fundamentals of this integral society.

The publication of the 1930 Census included an analysis of the data on population and living conditions, and, responding to the need for the formation of a standard of living index, furnished analyses of rural housing and the possibility of access to electricity, running water, the telephone, radio, and automobile. In reconsidering these data, the journal *Rural Sociology* pointed out that such an index must take account of the interrelationship of all these elements and that the sum of the interrelations among them could be considered a measure of their representativeness.[126] The specific problems raised by the agrarian groups and by individual enterprises such as Borsodi's and Wright's were registered by the government, at least in part, and were actually taken up in a number of governmental programs. What so radically separated the viewpoints of the "traditionalist" intellectuals from those of the government, however, was the very issue of the government's role in the agricultural and industrial reorganization of the country.

The Tennessee Valley Authority experiment, created in 1933, marked a significant change from utopian hypotheses to real possibilities and became the touchstone for all similar interventions. Certainly, at least at first, neither the Southern Agrarians nor Wright took a negative view of the TVA experiment, which offered regions like Alabama and Tennessee hope for coordinated and integrated development of small industries and agriculture at a high level.[127] The use of electricity favored both decentralization and communications, making it possible to combat the chaotic concentration of the city as well as the desolate isolation of the country. Self-sufficient energy production also meant the possibility of independence from the concentrated financial and industrial power of the East and thus the possibility of programing a type of territorial development completely different from that dictated by large-scale industrialization. According to the Southern Agrarians, small industries' capital would not be governed by New York, and profits could be reinvested in the South. The "region," which Howard Odum had identified on the sociological level, influencing the Nashville intellectuals, seemed on the verge of taking form as an economic entity.

Among the Southern intellectuals, however, a dissenting voice was raised by Donald Davidson. Although not wholly unfavorable to it at first, Davidson began in the mid-1930s to express a decidedly negative opinion of the TVA, which he considered "an irresponsible projection of a planned, functional society into the midst of one of the most thoroughly democratic parts of the United States." This government intervention was not only harmful in itself but would also do nothing to foster decentralization or increase Southern-owned industry. On the contrary, according to Davidson, the TVA would open the region to "a rush of Northern industry . . . land speculators and homesteaders." It was merely "another Yankee raid into Southern territory," and its ultimate aims were alien to the rural South. For Davidson, the Tennessee Valley Authority completely repudiated the regionalist hypothesis.[128]

Nevertheless the TVA remained a point of reference for the movements and individuals intent on revitalizing the rural areas. Even for Wright, the TVA could express the future of America and, above all, could give credibility to the proposal he himself was formulating. In *Architecture and Modern Life*, published in 1937, this view of the TVA emerges very clearly, even if it was formed a posteriori and stated indirectly. The book contains essays by Wright and Baker Brownell, but each author declares his agreement with what the other has written. In one of his essays Brownell speaks about a visit to the dam at Norris in the mountains of Tennessee. The town, named for the stalwart adversary of Henry Ford and his Muscle Shoals project, had been built for the workers on the dam and accommodated 1,700 people, whose dwellings were sparsely distributed around a civic center that included a large auditorium, a library, and a place to exhibit handicrafts. In Brownell's words, "It is clear after several days about the dam and its vicinity that the TVA all in all is building more than a dam. It is building a civilization. The visitor there is looking into the next century."[129] For Brownell, the dam was the expression of the new power the structure of American society had to assume, a power founded, as Jonathan Daniels "discovered,"[130] on a tradition predating the American Constitution, the tradition of the first colonies. Created from practical necessity and built as a place to live, the town of Norris went back to the tradition of Puritan New England, which Allen Tate recognized as the only valid precedent and model for American society. In Norris the idea of Ocotillo Camp had its official counterpart.

Sponsored by Arthur E. Morgan, a devoted admirer of Edward Bellamy and member of the Tennessee Valley Authority,[131] Norris came into being as an experiment in the construction of a new society. It proclaimed the necessity of returning to nature and the land, but in a new form and with a different organization of life. This village, situated near the dam that produced energy for the countryside and for industry, became an ideological symbol for a great many of Roosevelt's collaborators. As a concrete, functioning enterprise, it also tended to obliterate schematic divisions and won the cooperation and support of progressives and conservatives alike.

Norris was indeed a project that could bring forth unanimous agreement with the solution to the problem of creating a better standard of living as it was formulated by Milburn L. Wilson, director of the Division of Subsistence Homesteads, the agency that put into operation the Roosevelt administrations's first land-use program. In Wilson's view the answer to this problem was precisely the decentralization of industries and the development of a new type of industrial settlement, which the machine now made possible.[132] In 1933, when Ralph Borsodi was granted a loan from the Division of Subsistence Homesteads for a project in Dayton, Ohio, the "agrarian flight" and "emphasis on self-sufficiency" seemed to have won the day. In Borsodi's project, the farmers were to construct their own homes, produce crops sufficient for their own families on small plots of ground, participate in group undertakings, share the pasture land, and also, during a certain period, work at jobs in Dayton. A modified form of single tax was to regulate the farm rents.[133]

It was during this period of programs for a reorganization of land use, of government housing developments, and of provisions favoring the farmer that Wright began to work on his Broadacres project, which he intended as a model for development that would offer a valid solution to the problems of urban and rural America. When the drawings and model of Broadacres were exhibited at Rockefeller Center in 1935, however, Wright's position was clearly revealed as that of an intellectual completely immersed in the conservative dreams of the agrarians and closed to the progressive hopes of the New Deal.

In 1940 the journal *Free America*, established the previous year on the initiative of Herbert Agar and Allen Tate, published a brief essay on Wright by Frederick Gutheim, in which the convergence of Wright's conceptions and those of the Southern Agrarians was openly proclaimed. Wright was recognized as a prophet of decentralization and *The Disappearing City* and Broadacres, as proposals for development modeled on the type of life realized at Taliesin. In Gutheim's words, "The Taliesin Fellowship has been living the life of Broadacre City, the life the model of Broadacre City implies but cannot itself show. . . . [Taking place at Taliesin], perhaps better than anywhere else in the world, is a realistic and convincing experiment in breaking down the conventional town-country barriers." And Gutheim emphasized that it was in the image of the balanced existence achieved at Taliesin that Wright "has patiently explained by words and examples that we must create an integrated life if our civilization is to be fulfilled."[134]

Broadacres

Like Taliesin, Broadacres was created outside the current institutional structure of America. As a result of the vicissitudes of his personal life, Wright's outlook in the early 1930s was closer than ever to the spirit of Thoreau, except that Thoreau's anarchism, the result of the translation of transcendentalist individualism into political terms, was transformed by Wright into a proposal for new and different institutions. The concept of moral law as the fundamental law, superior to statutes and constitutions, which lay at the base of Thoreau's "Civil Disobedience," made sense to Wright only in terms of new institutions. While Thoreau had affirmed the right to follow the dictates of one's own judgment without restrictions and to break the laws of society whenever they proved inferior to such dictates, Wright proposed new social laws; they, too, however, were based on subjective judgment. In the Broadacres program, for instance, banks, which had been responsible for Wright's precarious situation in the late 1920s, had to become disinterested institutions and their architectural forms, modest and simple; universities "should not be large but be qualified and qualifying. Why not somewhat like the old monastic institutions?" The courts of law, where Wright had appeared as a defendant, would be "greatly reduced by the simplification of a true people's government" in Broadacres.[135]

Broadacres was, in fact, a proposal for a place in which man could live a life based on the Jeffersonian concept of self-government. Attenuating Thoreau's "extremism," which had modified the Jeffersonian maxim to the point of declaring, "That government is best which governs not at all," Wright affirmed his own anarchic individualism by proclaiming the necessity of rejecting life in the capitalist city and regaining man's innate "natural" condition. Uncontaminated, wild nature, which for Thoreau could be understood and enjoyed only by isolating oneself from the world in a hut in the midst of the woods, was now to be recaptured by means of the most advanced technology. It was no longer the inhabitant of the city who would seek the reason for his own existence in nature, as Thoreau had advocated or as Wright had done in first taking refuge at Taliesin in 1911; now it was the inhabitant of the country, the man who lived in nature, who would extract from the city the undeniable advantages it offered. This was the great difference in Wright's position in the 1930s from that held at the time he had founded Taliesin.

Wright had always remained outside the official management of the city, had never served on commissions dealing with urban problems or participated in movements for civic betterment. As noted earlier, the development of city planning in the 1910s had had no interest for Wright, who was completely dedicated to his position as an architect of homes for the upper-middle-class American. Instead, Broadacres was generated from the consideration of problems involved in an industrial and technological restructuring of the rural areas and, even if it was utopian, was intended as a solution to the delicate problem of developing the agrarian world in relation to that of industry. Although Broadacres had no relation whatsoever to the projects for a new territorial organization that were under study in America in the 1930s, it was nevertheless a typical expression of the post-1929 atmosphere, which gave rise to a proliferation of programs for restructuring rural areas and creating new, self-sufficient communities. Wright, however, disregarded the scientific attempt of the regionalists to achieve a new scale of operation by treating the complex problems of costs, transport, zoning, and park programs as a whole, just as he disregarded the attempt to integrate planning with the rationalization of building production that government intervention now offered in this field. These were developments ignored by Wright, who remained totally absorbed in the vision of a "new urban era" that would come about through man's good will.

Although Broadacres was a step backward in comparison not only with regionalist efforts but even with earlier concepts, it cannot be said that Wright did not sense the new terms of the problem. The fact is that while Broadacres could only have been conceived at this moment of intense concern with the relations between rural life and industry, with model establishments for living and working, and with regional development, it was nevertheless actually identifiable with the "section," in Turner's sense of the term, an entity separate from the rest of the country. Even if Wright believed his proposal overcame and went beyond sectionalism and regionalism, Broadacres and Usonia remained isolated, autonomous, and individualistically closed within a single cultural perspective, which was that of Wright himself; surrounding them was an indifferent territory, regulated and controlled by extraneous laws.

Despite the new scale of Wright's proposal, it was completely unrelated to any real program of economic and social research and stemmed instead from a subjective hypothesis formulated solely on an intuition. Based on this intuition, formed over a period of time from various sources and previously made analyses, Broadacres was imbued with concepts and ideas directly suggestive of parallel experiments. Thus Broadacres appears to converge with the policies of the New Deal, the back-to-the-land movement, the TVA, soil-conservation programs, and decentralization. Actually, however, Wright's views on the problem of restructuring agriculture were wholly divorced from any consideration of a more general solution to the economic crisis. For Wright, all endeavor was still concentrated on the search for a balance suitable to a prebourgeois society, in which agriculture represented the absolutely fundamental element of the economic and social structure. His position coincided in this respect with that of the Southern Agrarians, but not with their regionalism; with the movement of the painters of the American scene, but not with their critical realism; with the self-sufficient communities of Borsodi, but not with Borsodi's involvement with the Division of Subsistence Homesteads.

General plan of Norris, Tennessee, begun in
1934 as part of the development program
of the Tennessee Valley Authority.

Norris, Tennessee, residential area.

Norris, Tennessee, civic center with the
school in the background.

Illustration by Ernest Born for an article by
Frank Lloyd Wright in the *American
Architect*, May 1932.

Frank Lloyd Wright's original design for
Broadacres.

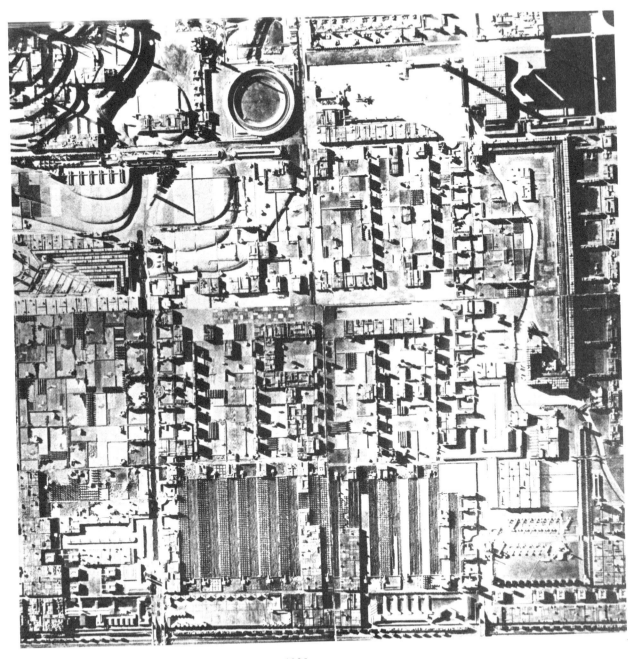

Model of Broadacres, exhibited in 1935 at
Rockefeller Center, New York; the area
represented is 4 square miles.

In Broadacres, what Wright ultimately proposed was quality for all. During his Oak Park years, and to a certain extent even in those that followed, Wright had held the opinion that the city, urban life, and the world of business excluded quality, which could be attained only within the family and the clan, who counterbalanced the brutality of the city. The two worlds could coexist; they were complementary and, indeed, appeared inseparable, but when the city's "lack of quality" overtook the world of the family and clan, coexistence was no longer possible. Completely shaken by this event in his own life, Wright began the search, first in Europe and then wherever he was, for a new quality that would make possible his own existence as an artist. As discussed earlier, it was the desert that offered the possibility of recovering values and opened a perspective on a new life, a life that rose from the world of nature, the only reality unchangeable in its continuous changing.

Broadacres was not only a proposal of quality; more important, it was a demonstration of quality, expressed in the opposite of urban largeness: small homes, small industries, small schools, a small university, small laboratories, and small farms. General decentralization had to be accompanied by architectural reintegration, however; thus "architecture would necessarily again become the natural backbone (and architects the broad essential leaders) of such cultural endeavor."[136] In this way, Wright fully restored the image of himself that urban America had so thoroughly shaken and had long since relegated to the sidelines. He could no longer be the architect of the American home, once the life in that home had been completely subordinated to an industrial social structure that was opposed to the institution of the family as the basis of prosperity.

Wright's book written with Brownell quotes the address given by O. E. Baker at the conference on integral society. After stating that only the preservation of the rural home and family and the rural institutions could preserve the prosperity of democratic American agriculture, Baker concluded, "It is becoming clear that the land is the foundation of the family, and that the family is the foundation of the democratic state."[137] At this point Wright's identification with the agrarian world was complete; it was made possible by the technical means the Southern Agrarians also recognized as the only hope for the renascence of the agricultural South.

For Wright, three principle inventions made Broadacres possible: the automobile, and thus the general mobility of the individual; electrical intercommunication, and thus the end of traditional rural isolation; and, finally, standardized machine-shop production, bringing together machine invention with scientific discovery. He believed these inventions had extracted too high a price from America, however, because three inherent rights of man had been overlooked in the course of their development:

1. His social right to a direct medium of exchange in place of gold as a commodity: some form of social credit.

2. His social right to his place on the ground as he has had it in the sun and air: land to be held only by use and improvements.

3. His social right to the ideas by which and for which he lives: public ownership of invention and scientific discoveries that concern the life of the people.[138]

Broadacres was the complete expression of these three assumptions, which contain the essence of Wright's entire thought on social organization. George R. Collins has carefully examined these three "rights" and identified their sources:[139] C. H. Douglas's social credit,[140] Henry George's right to land ownership, and the publicity of discoveries asserted by Edward Bellamy. As always, Wright accepted ideas from any source so long as they could contribute to reinforcing the vision of an agrarian society structured on political and social systems that opposed those of the city and favored minimal forms of government. Thus, although Bellamy had based his own model of society on the regimentation of work and the government of the Great Trust, Wright could still draw upon him for some particular aspect of his thought. Wright's most direct source, however, was Henry George, whose influence and ideas can be continually discerned in Broadacres.

Wright's "countrywide, countryside city" depended directly on concepts contained in *Progress and Poverty:* the use of electricity ("All the currents of the time run to concentration. To resist it successfully we must throttle steam and discharge electricity from human service");[141] the right to land ("The equal right of all men to the use of land is as clear as their equal right to breathe the air—it is a right proclaimed by the fact of their existence");[142] the integration of city and country, apart from the single tax, which Wright rejected ("The people of the cities would thus get more of the pure air and sunshine of the country, the people of the country more of the economies and social life of the city");[143] the annulment of government and laws ("Society would thus approach the ideal of Jeffersonian democracy, the promised land of Herbert Spencer, the abolition of government");[144] and the opportunity for all to be "capitalists" ("The more equal diffusion of wealth would unite capitalist and laborer in the same person").[145] These and many other of George's ideas are encountered in Broadacres and, indeed, form its basic ideology.

For Wright, the form of Broadacres reflected the function it had to serve: "Form and function are one in Broadacres." The model he prepared with the help of his student-apprentices, who flocked to the old master after the founding of the Taliesin Fellowship in September 1932,[146] represented four square miles of a typical countryside development that summarized all the architect's proposals for a new social organization.[147] The model was conceived for 1,400 families, with an average of five or more members per family, and thus for more than 7,000 inhabitants.[148] Created for conditions in a temperate zone, it was adaptable with a few changes to northern or southern climates. The basic elements of the plan were services and civic installations, including the parks; transportation, with a differentiated traffic system; and dwellings, which also

STUDENTS AT TALIESIN WORK WITH MATERIALS AND BUILDERS' TOOLS

1 Conference with representative of steel industry.

2 Model of Broadacre City in the making.

3 Student at work on model.

4 Clearing a site for construction.

5 Out of a rut.

6 Student burning lime.

7 Sawing lumber.

EDUCATION OF THE ARCHITECT • SCHOOLS

Members of the Taliesin Fellowship engaged in various activities at Taliesin, Spring Green, Wisconsin, 1933-36.

Grant Wood, *Dinner for Threshers* (detail),
1933 (Whitney Museum of American Art,
New York).

Weekly festive gathering of the Taliesin
Fellowship for music and discussion on
Sunday evening in the living room of
Taliesin, Spring Green, Wisconsin, November
1936.

John Steuart Curry, *Baptism in Kansas*, 1928
(Whitney Museum of American Art, New
York).

Taliesin Fellowship student-apprentices
around the model-in-progress of Broadacres.

included the laboratories and workshops. Thus industry was directly connected with the home, and only a limited area was dedicated exclusively to small industries.

Regardless of the fact that Wright configured the site occupied by the settlement as a square, the structure of Broadacres goes back to the linear city. The direct line of descent from the linear city of Soria y Mata—who became a staunch supporter of Henry George at the end of the nineteenth century—to Ford's city at Muscle Shoals was continued in Wright's Broadacres.[149] Even Wright's scheme is, in fact, based on a principal road axis, to which all the automobile services and the industries are connected, and from which a secondary road network accommodates the dwellings, services, and civic functions. Wright's linear city could, however, be extended over the territory in any direction by the introduction of a new means of transport, the helicopter, or aerotor as Wright called it, which does not require a markedly directional structure; only the ground traffic, automobiles and monorail, must maintain a precise directionality, to which the organization of the whole is invariably related.

Parallel to this principal artery is a strip of vineyards and orchards, bounded at one end by a large parking lot and at the other by a commercial complex. This filter strip separates the noisier and more "urban" part of Broadacres from the residences. The residential area occupied the broad center strip of the model, and within it the dwellings are sparsely distributed around the school, which thus becomes the focal point of the composition. Situated in the strip beyond and parallel to this residential area are the county seat, with a large lake in front of it, the sporting clubs, the professional offices, and the stadium; farther along this same strip are located the aquarium, zoo, arboretum, and the scientific and agricultural research building. These latter points are situated at the foot of a hill on which rise the more elaborate dwellings: the "luxurious dwelling (House on the Mesa)," "Taliesin (equivalent)," and "luxurious homes." These are the terms Wright himself used to describe these residences, which were obviously destined for those at the apex of the "broad-based pyramid" that for Wright represented the "true capitalist system."[150]

In Broadacres, houses are no longer classified according to the number of rooms but according to the number of cars the family owns, so that the dwellings are distinguished as one-car, two-car, three-car, or five-car houses. The automobile becomes the measure of individual liberty and indicates the make up of the family unit. Indeed, it was the cardinal element in the physical and spatial organization of Broadacres, a fact that reflected the unprecedented development in the use of the motor car in these very years; the 5,360,000 cars produced in 1929 was a level that would not, in fact, be surpassed until 1953.

The continual mixture of reality and utopia, of the acceptance of the facts as given and proposals for the future, is the prime characteristic of Broadacres. On the one hand, it embraces many of the utopian ideas of the nineteenth century; on the other, this proposal foreshadows the endless development of the American suburbs, themselves real linear cities organized along the roads leading out from the cities. The plan of Broadacres shows once again the grid of streets that characterized the first Jeffersonian towns, such as Jeffersonville, or the towns of the frontier, particularly those of the Mormons.[151] In Wright's town, however, the grid has been transformed by the overriding desire to channel its unlimited expansion along principal directional routes. The result is a representation at the same time of both the immense American territory to be occupied in all directions and the directionality of a principal artery that, according to the scheme of a linear city, theoretically connects the points of concentrated activity.

Within this scheme, which rationalizes the teritory and makes it real and ready for use, Wright could insert his past projects. The context organized in this way justified their existence. As part of Broadacres, they become, in fact, no longer projects for individual patrons but works created for a society that has behind it all the "values" of the American frontier. What Broadacres was intended to signify was the existence in the America of the 1930s of a *real* possibility, given the means available, of organizing society in a different way. When reintegrated with healthy and uncorrupted nature, American life would reacquire the old spirit of the pioneer, of the man who, living a life of complete individualism, could only be healthy and uncorrupted. The nature of man was such; centralization, concentration, the city destroyed his innate, genuine values.

The spirit that animated the Ocotillo Camp was no longer employed to create a resort for millionaires from the desert wilderness but, instead, to invent a proposal for rescuing Wright's own experience as an artist from failure. In Broadacres, Thoreau and Emerson, Whitman and Carlyle, Lane and Belloc, Borsodi and the Southern Agrarians were all brought together in a mythical place where the "mob" is eliminated: "Spirit only can control it. Spirit is a science mobocracy does not know."[152] Broadacres was Wright's declaration that there was no break with the past, not even with his own past. His "countrywide, countryside city" was valid precisely because it demonstrated this continuity. Writing his autobiography and contemporaneously developing his proposal for Broadacres was Wright's way of affirming that his own life experience was the logical outcome of a century of American culture. Thus backed by the implicit validity of assumptions elaborated over time, all the contradictions of that experience were cancelled out; the autobiography was the irrefutable demonstration that Broadacres was formed over time in a wholly positive process.

Taliesin, inserted in Broadacres, was no longer the center of an isolated world but, instead, the leading house of the city. Next to it on the Broadacres plan is the House on the Mesa, the luxurious dwelling of the ideal Usonian. Unlike the Robie House or Taliesin, the House on the Mesa was conceived not as a

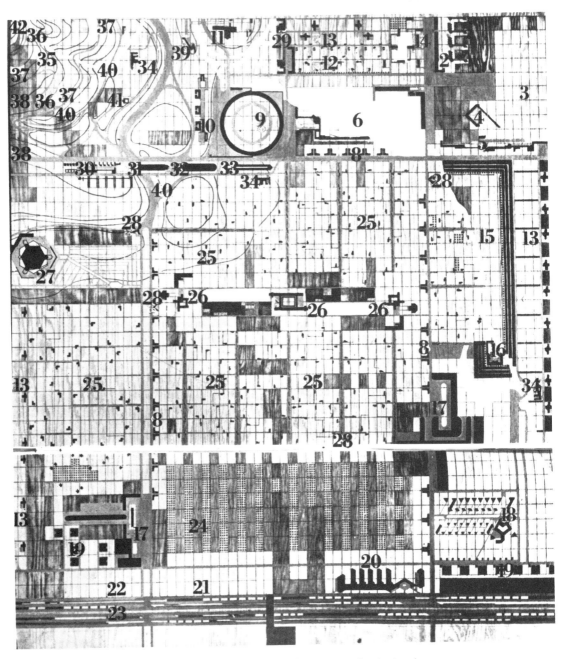

Plan of Broadacres. (1) county seat—administration; (2) aerotor—post port and administration; (3) polo; (4) baseball; (5) clubs; (6) lake
and stream; (7) crafts and county architect;
(8) professionals; (9) stadium; (10), hotel;
(11) sanitarium; (12) small industry; (13)
small farm units; (14) small apartments;
(15) interior park; (16) music garden;
(17) merchandising; (18) automobile inn;
(19) little factories and dwellings above;
(20) factory assembly; (21) aerotor service;
(22) aerotor factory; (23) main arterial;
(24) vineyards and orchards; (25) homes;
(26) schools; (27) temple, columbarium,
and cemetery; (28) neighborhood guest
houses; (30) scientific and agricultural research; (31) arboretum; (32) zoo; (33),
aquarium; (34) luxurious dwelling (House
on the Mesa); (35) Taliesin (equivalent);
(36) luxurious homes; (37) water supply;
(38) forest cabins; (39) country club;
(40) apartment houses; (41) small school
for small children; (42) automobile objective.

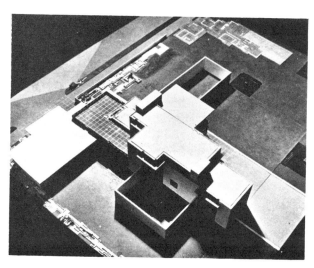

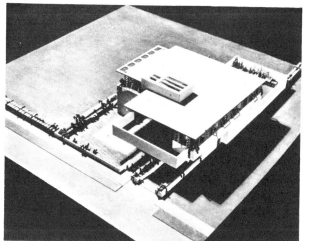

Model of the three-car house at Broadacres.

Model of the two-car house at Broadacres.

grottolike refuge from the world but as a space open on nature, the new nature created by the architect-demigod. With its broad expanses of glass and its interiors free on any weighty historical reminiscences, this prototype of the Usonian houses was actually the exact opposite of the prairie houses. Their difference did not mean that they could not coexist, however. Indeed, they had to coexist, because Wright had to introduce his past into Broadacres if it was to assume the significance of a total experience.

Along with Taliesin and the House on the Mesa, many designs produced in the years of greatest crisis for Wright are also included in Broadacres, where they serve to demonstrate the positive quality of that crisis. These were the projects elaborated by Wright in the period after 1923-24 when he did not succeed in building anything. Reflecting on this period in 1930, Wright wrote, "The last actual work on plans was done at Taliesin in 1923-24 nearly seven years ago. I am hungry for work, not honors. Some further work on the cantilever glass and metal skyscraper for Mr. Johnson of the National Insurance Company, and a study for the automobile objective for Gordon Strong, these seem to have ended my active period of work."[153] Preceding as it does the account of the Ocotillo Camp undertaking, this passage demonstrates that Ocotillo signified a new beginning. In Broadacres, however, even this negative period could be recuperated and affirmed as something quite other than inactive and unproductive. Thus the Nakoma Country Club, designed in 1924, the Planetarium at Sugar Loaf Mountain, designed in 1925 for Gordon Strong, and the Steel Cathedral, designed in 1926, appear in Broadacres, as do the San Marcos Water Garden Tourist Camp and the Standardized Village Service Station, both from 1928, the St. Mark's Tower from 1929, which would actually be built as the Price Tower in 1953, the apartment house designed for Elizabeth Nobel in 1929, the Capital Journal, designed for George Putnam in 1931, which became the basis of the design for the Johnson Wax Building built five years later, a skyscraper designed for Chicago in 1931, identifiable with the Broadacres administration building, the Davidson Farm from 1932, and a theater that derives from another project of this same year.[154]

Of all these buildings, the most indicative of the effort Wright made to reconstruct his whole artistic career as a unitary process in time is the St. Mark's Tower. It is also the work that best reveals the complex contradictions involved in such an effort. The tower had originally been designed for St. Mark's Park along Second Avenue, between 11th and 12th streets, in New York. Later it was isolated from the urban context and inserted in the Broadacres plan, where it became one of the cardinal elements of the formal and spatial organization; the skyscraper became possible only if inserted in an unlimited, boundless territory.

Thus Wright recomposed his own life experience and emerged from the impasse he had reached after his flight from Oak Park. The invention of Broadacres furnished the different context in which his projects, extraneous to America, became integral parts of Usonia. Wright's idea of dispersing his projects over the countryside became the authentic expression of his own particular thinking and of agrarian thought in general. As Lewis Mumford has written,

This dream of total dispersion, which would carry further the spontaneous disruption of the city that is now going on everywhere, may be only the logical expression of a dominant trait in Wright's architecture: ideally, each building of his must stand alone, free from the support of other buildings, in a completely natural setting. If you put all his structures together in a city, the result would be an aesthetic jungle of dissident, competing buildings; far from lending themselves to contrapuntal treatment, they are all solo performances. [155]

The 1940 proposal for the Crystal Heights Hotel, which projected a series of St. Mark's Towers placed next to each other, is the very image of this "aesthetic jungle." [156] Designed for the residential area of Washington beyond the limits of L'Enfant's plan, Wright's project was intended as a response to the official architecture of the Mall, a proposal for the least urban of American cities. Actually, it was a striking demonstration of the absolute singularity and individuality of his unique architectural "objects." In 1953, Wright had the opportunity to build the St. Mark's Tower, which was renamed the Price Tower, after its patron. It rose not in New York but in Bartlesville, Oklahoma, where it became the symbol of a "new conquest" possible only in America's provinces. [157]

The Broadacres program of providing an acre for every man and integrating work in the fields with work in small industries led back to Ford's idea for Muscle Shoals. In a review of *Architecture and Modern Life* in the *Partisan Review* in 1938, Meyer Shapiro noted this relationship: "The deurbanizing of life, the fusion of city and country on a high productive level, is an ideal shared by socialists and anarchists. But when presented as in Wright's books as an immediate solution of the crisis, it takes on another sense. It is the plan of Ford and Swope, a scheme of permanent subsistence farming with a corvée of worksharing in the distant mill, of scattered national company villages under a reduced living standard." [158] What Wright's ideal community proposed was the transformation of the middle class, "the real subject of his anxiety," into conservative farmers, with the aim of recovering their "human integrity."

This primeval integrity still existed in Spengler's "centers of landscape," the "meeting-points of rural life-interests" precedent to the cities. Like Spengler, Wright saw in the "earthboundness" of the farmer the means of escaping the social disintegration of the city. The farmer who works his own land, Spengler's "man [who] himself becomes plant," and for whom "the earth becomes Mother Earth," submits to the laws of nature, following her rhythm and slow transformations, and his dwelling, "itself plant, thrusts its roots deep into its 'own' soil." [159] Such an integral life was still feasible in the United States South and West, in those areas not yet corrupted by "modern civilization," where it was still possible to found a new way of life and development based on traditional American culture. Broadacres became the model of a new ideal community,

Model of Broadacres exhibited in the living room of Taliesin. In the background is a model of the cantilevered St. Mark's Tower, which was inserted into Broadacres, forming one of its focal points and emphasizing the idea of decentralization.

Model of St. Mark's Tower, designed by
Frank Lloyd Wright in 1929 for the East
Village, New York, and later inserted into
Broadacres.

Price Tower, built by Frank Lloyd Wright
in Bartlesville, Oklahoma, in 1953-56, on
the model of the St. Mark's Tower.

which contained the whole past, present, and future of both Wright and America. In three or four generations, Wright predicted, the cities would be abandoned, for the people would be completely won over by this new way of life.

General decentralization would be made possible through electricity and new technological innovations; architectural reintegration would be provided by the architect. As Shapiro observed, "The social imagination of Wright should not be classed with that of the great Utopians whom he seems to resemble."[160] In fact, Broadacres was not a utopia, not an organic construction of a new society; rather, it was the organization in a formal key of a series of contributions and conceptions recovered for the purpose of reforming civilization by means of a new architecture. At the same time it provided a general context into which to insert the salient points of the architect's own experience. As Shapiro rightly concluded, however, "Even under more prosperous conditions, the great mass of architects have no chance for original artistic creation; they are salaried workers submerged in a capitalist office, with little possibility of self-development."[161]

It was precisely this dependent relationship that Wright refused. He had to be and to remain free and individual; his clients had to submit to his vision of life. It is characteristic that Wright's one and only professional relationship with a government agency failed, even if not through his own fault.[162] The architect, the unique creator of Broadacres, not only made his world concrete by means of a new architecture, but even conjured up its tomorrow; the helicopters that resemble flying saucers, the automobiles of a new design that dart along multilevel roads, and the ultrarapid monorails essentially already existed, but in Wright's drawings they become symbols of the future. In Wright's view, man was still the slave of the machine, but it was nevertheless technology that would grant him the maximum individual liberty by making possible the unlimited occupation of the territory. The tradition of the West and the myth of the nomadic pioneer were revived and brought up to date in Broadacre City.

For many today, Wright represents the image of the architect in its original artistic totality. The unswerving, unitary character of his life experience as architect and the absence of any contradictions, both fictive qualities, are coupled with his authentic inventive individuality and raised up as a model. In the struggle against the general "crisis" of the discipline, Wright has become a symbol, and his example appears to be the only one offering a way out. The concept of the architect as "the broad essential leader" signifies the artist-technician capable of designing an architectural masterpiece and planning the territory as well.

Wright's territory was outside of time, however, and his buildings, the focal points from which life radiates, have become lost in the immense American suburb. The houses, the cantilevered towers, and the service stations were the three elements that formed the nodal points of the Broadacres road network, and the House on the Mesa, designed in 1931, the St. Mark's Tower, designed in

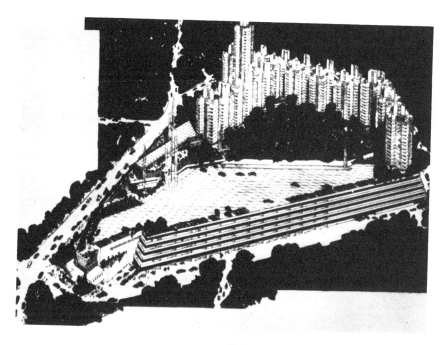

Design by Frank Lloyd Wright for the
Crystal Heights Hotel, including stores and
a theater, to be situated between Connecticut and Florida avenues in Washington,
D.C., 1940.

Drawings for Broadacres. Huge traffic arteries running through the countryside, electric automobiles, and helicopters resembling flying saucers enrich the rural scene, indicating a new spatial organization of life and human settlements.

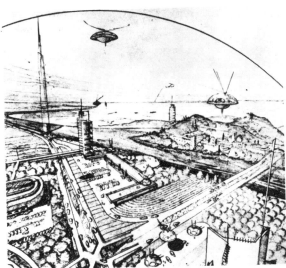

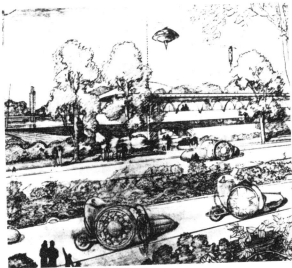

Dorothea Lang, *Crossroads Store,*
Alabama, 1937.

Design by Frank Lloyd Wright for a
standardized village service station, 1928.

Service station built by Frank Lloyd
Wright in Cloquet, Minnesota, 1958.

Frank Lloyd Wright's funeral at Taliesin,
Spring Green, Wisconsin, April 1959.

1929, and the Standardized Village Service Station, designed in 1928 were all actually built in later years. The America that accepted these and other masterpieces, however, had become a place in which Wright's "quality" and the values on which it was based were absorbed and transformed.

The frontier and the technological future, nature and science, were to be stripped of the quality with which Wright endowed this twofold conception; Wright's ideal city would be realized only in the grotesque and preposterous form of Disneyland and Disney World. Not merely the realm of Mickey Mouse and his friends, nor only for children, Disneyland has become a place where the great public finds its realm. Today Broadacres is proposed again by critics as an alternative to urban chaos and thus to the consequent loss of values and traditional roles; Disneyland, with its popular appeal to the American dream, succeeds in fusing the values of tradition with the future of the country and transforms the "lack of quality" it expresses into a "new quality."[163]

Notes

1

William Dean Howells, *A Traveler from Altruria* (1894, reprint ed., Hill and Wang, New York, 1957), pp. 187-195.

2

Frank Lloyd Wright, *The Living City* (Horizon Press, New York, 1958), p. 110.

3

Ibid., pp. 59-60.

4

See Paul K. Conkin, *Tomorrow a New World: The New Deal Community Program* (American Historical Association, Cornell University Press, Ithaca, 1959), pt. 1.

5

On the attitude of the American intellectual toward the city see Morton and Lucia White, *The Intellectual versus the City: From Thomas Jefferson to Frank Lloyd Wright* (Harvard University Press and MIT Press, Cambridge, Mass., 1962). See also Leo Marx's criticism of the Whites' book in "Pastoral Ideals and City Troubles," *Journal of General Education* 20, no. 4, Jan. 1969, p. 270.

6

For a thorough analysis of the return to nature and the arcadian myth in American thought, see Peter J. Schmitt, *Back to Nature. The Arcadian Myth in Urban America* (Oxford University Press, New York, 1969). See also Henry Nash Smith, *Virgin Land: The American West as Symbol and Myth* (1950; reprint ed., Harvard University Press, Cambridge, Mass., 1970); Leo Marx, *The Machine in the Garden: Technology and the Pastoral Ideal in America* (Galaxy Books, New York, 1967).

7

The Reverend Heber Newton, in U.S. Congress, Senate, Committee on Education and Labor, *Investigation of the Relations between Labor and Capital*, 48th Cong. (Government Printing Office, Washington, D.C., 1885), p. 575; quoted in Conkin, *Tomorrow a New World*, p. 16.

8

Conkin, *Tomorrow a New World*.

9

Frederick Jackson Turner, *The Frontier in American History* (Holt, New York, 1921), pp. 2-3. Turner's 1893 lecture, originally published in the *American Historical Association, Annual Report for 1893* (Washington, D.C., 1894), became the first chapter of this book, which brings together the author's most important essays written between 1893 and 1918.

10

See Mauro Calamandrei, "Il pensiero storiografico di F. J. Turner," introduction to the Italian translation of Turner's book, *La frontiera nella storia americana* (Il Mulino, Bologna, 1967).

11

Smith, *Virgin Land*, p. 259.

12

See Daniel J. Elazar, *Cities of the Prairies. The Metropolitan Frontier and American Politics* (Basic Books, New York, 1970), p. 45.

13

Henry George, Jr., introduction to *Progress and Poverty*, 25th anniversary ed. (Doubleday, Page, Garden City, N.Y.), pp. vii-x.

14

For a discussion of the situation, see William Appleman Williams, *The Contours of American History* (World, Cleveland and New York, 1961), pp. 313-317.

15

George, *Progress and Poverty*, p. xv.

16

Ibid., p. 336.

17

These volumes are collections of stories written by Garland beginning in about 1883; Parrington considered them "the first authentic expression and protest of an agrarian

America then being submerged by the industrial revolution." The first edition of *Main-Travelled Roads* contained an introduction by Howells. See Vernon L. Parrington, *Main Currents in American Thought*, 3 vols. (Harcourt Brace and World, New York, 1930), 3:294-297, 391-392.

18

Quoted in Richard Hofstadter, *The Age of Reform. From Bryan to F. D. R.* (Knopf, New York, 1955), p. 35; see also Williams, *Contours of American History, pp. 334-336.*

19

In 1860 Chicago was one of the six American cities with a population between 100,000 and 250,000. The same year the urban population of the United States made up 19.8 percent of the total population and was distributed in 392 cities, of which 93 had more than 10,000 inhabitants. By 1900 the urban population had grown to 39.7 percent of the total population and was distributed in 1,737 cities, of which 440 had more than 10,000 inhabitants. In 1910 the urban population had risen to 45.7 percent of the total, distributed in 2,262 cities, 597 of which had more than 10,000 inhabitants. The data are from Elazar, *Cities of the Prairies*, table 1-1.

20

Arthur M. Schlesinger, *Paths to the Present* (Macmillan, New York, 1949), p. 233.

21

See W. Stull Holt, "Some Consequences of the Urban Movement on American History," *Pacific Historical Review* 22, Nov. 1953, pp. 337-351.

22

Arthur M. Schlesinger, *The Rise of the City, 1878-1898* (Macmillan, New York, 1933), p. 79.

23

Page Smith, *As a City upon the Hill. The Town in American History* (1966; reprint ed., M.I.T. Press, Cambridge, Mass., 1973), p. 113.

24

Marcus L. Hansen, "Remarks," in Dixon Ryan Fox, ed., *Sources of Culture in the Middle West* (Appleton-Century, New York and London, 1934), pp. 103-110; quoted in Smith, *City upon the Hill*, p. 113.

25

Quoted in A. Whitney Griswold, "The Agrarian Democracy of Thomas Jefferson," *American Political Science Review* 40, no. 4, Aug. 1946, pp. 657-681.

26

Jefferson to James Madison, December 20, 1787, quoted in Griswold, "Agrarian Democracy," p. 668.

27

The data are from Arthur M. Schlesinger, *The Rise of Modern America, 1865-1951*, 4th ed. (Macmillan, New York, 1951), p. 146.

28

See Morton White, "Two Stages in the Critique of the American City," in Oscar Handlin and John Burchard, eds., *The Historian and the City* (MIT Press and Harvard University Press, Cambridge, Mass., 1963), pp. 84-94.

29

Morton and Lucia White, "The American Intellectual versus the American City," *Daedalus*, Winter 1961, p. 175. The article is a concise version of the authors' book cited in n5.

30

Hull House, established at the end of the nineteenth century, was directed by Jane Addams and dedicated to cultural activities and social-welfare work. Built in the neo-Tudor style by the Pond brothers, it was intended to be a modern version of a medieval monastery and comprised a drama workshop, handicraft rooms, eating facilities open to the poor, and dormitories for the staff of social workers. Allen Pond, one of the two architects, said of Hull House, "In our unevangelical, scientific, industrial age, [it] is the legitimate sociological successor of the evangelizing and teaching and working monastic establishment of the earlier and middle Christian centuries. The monastic quadrangle, with its combination of refectories, assembly rooms, libraries, shop and individual bedrooms, is the analogue of the settlement building today" (quoted in Mark L. Peisch, *The Chicago School of Architecture* [Random House, New York, 1965], p. 68). For the history of Hull House, see Jane Addams, *Forty Years at Hull House* (New York, 1935).

31

On Steinway Hall, see H. Allen Brooks, "Steinway Hall, Architects and Dreams," *Journal of the Society of Architectural Historians* 22, no. 3, Oct. 1963, pp. 171-175. On the Prairie school, see idem, *The Prairie School* (University of Toronto Press, Toronto and Buffalo, 1972; Norton, New York, 1976).

32

This fact was reported in 1966 in an interview by Barry Byrne, who was a draftsman in Wright's studio from 1903 to 1908; quoted in Robert E. McCoy, "Rock Crest / Rock Glen: Prairie School Planning in Iowa," *Prairie School Review* 5, no. 3, 1968, p. 15, n79.

33

See Scott Donaldson, "City and Country: Marriage Proposals," *American Quarterly* 20, Fall 1968, pp. 547-566.

34

Quoted in John Burchard and Albert Bush-Brown, *The Architecture of America. A Social and Cultural History* (Atlantic-Little, Brown, Boston, 1961), p. 101.

35

See Everett Chamberlin, "Types of Suburbs," in *Chicago and its Suburbs* (Hugerfold, Chicago, 1874), pp. 407-416. In speaking of the formation of the suburbs of Parkside, Lake Forest, Riverside, Park Rise, and Mount Forest, Chamberlain emphasized the "natural" quality of the sites chosen. See also Harold M. Mayer and Richard C. Wade, *Chicago: Growth of a Metropolis* (University of Chicago Press, Chicago, 1969).

36

Marx, *Machine in the Garden.*

37

George, *Progress and Poverty*, p. 449.

38

Adna Ferrin Weber, *The Growth of the Cities in the Nineteenth Century. A Study in Statistics* (1899; reprint ed., Cornell University Press, Ithaca, 1963), p. 475.

39

Frederic C. Howe, *The City: The Hope of Democracy* (Scribner's Sons, New York, 1905), p. 204.

40

Quoted in Park Dixon Goist, "City and 'Community': The Urban Theory of Robert Park," *American Quarterly* 23, spring 1972, p. 53. On Park's analysis of the community, see Robert E. Park, Ernest W. Burgess, and Roderick D. McKenzie, *The City* (University of Chicago Press, Chicago, 1925).

41

Leonard K. Eaton, *Two Chicago Architects and Their Clients. Frank Lloyd Wright and Howard Van Doren Shaw* (M.I.T. Press, Cambridge, Mass., 1969), p. 33. For a sociological portrait of the middle-class family of Chicago in the years of Wright's professional formation, see Richard Sennett, *Families Against the City. Middle-Class Homes of Industrial Chicago, 1872-1890.* (Harvard University Press, Cambridge, Mass., 1970).

42

This is the title of the book of essays by Meredith Nicholson (Scribner's Sons, New York, 1918), in which the towns and villages of the Middle West are places of well-being uncorrupted by wealth and the inhabitants typical middle-class Americans who base their life on friendship and solidarity. The spirit of equality that unites them is founded on the evaluation of individuals according to their innate qualities.

43

Thorstein Veblen, *The Theory of the Leisure Class* (1899; reprint ed., Random House, Modern Library New York, 1934), p. 103.

44

Ibid., p. 253.

45

Between 1896 and 1897, Winslow printed William C. Gannett and Frank Lloyd Wright's *House Beautiful* (Auvergne Press, River Forest, Ill.; facsimile ed., Prairie School Review Press, Park Forest, Ill., 1963).

46

Veblen, *Theory of the Leisure Class*, p. 122.

47

In recent years Broadacres and Wright's whole production have been reconsidered. Among the most interesting critical contributions are George R. Collins, "Broadacre City: Wright's Utopia Reconsidered," in *Four Great Makers of Modern Architecture* (symposium held at Columbia University, March-May 1961; Da Capo Press, New York, 1970); Norris Kelly Smith, *Frank Lloyd Wright. A Study in Architectural Content* (Prentice-Hall, Englewood Cliffs, N.J., 1966); Robert C. Twombly, *Frank Lloyd Wright. An Interpretive Biography* (Harper & Row, New York, 1973). Among the many books and articles published since Wright's death, see, in addition to those cited in other notes, especially Vincent Scully, "The Heritage of Wright," *Zodiac*, no. 8, 1961, pp. 8-13; Finis Farr, "Frank Lloyd Wright: Defiant Genius," *Saturday Evening Post*, Jan. 7, 14, 21, 28, and Feb. 4, 1961; Peter Blake, *Frank Lloyd Wright* (Penguin Books, Harmonsworth, Middlesex, 1963); Edgar Kaufmann, Jr., "Frank Lloyd Wright's Years of Modernism, 1925-1935," *Journal of the Society of Architectural Historians* 24, no. 1, 1965, pp. 31-33; Henry-Russell Hitchcock, "Frank Lloyd Wright 1867-1967," *Zodiac*, no. 17, 1967, pp. 6-10; Martin Engel, "Frank Lloyd Wright and Cubism: A Study in Ambiguity," *American Quarterly* 19, no. 1, Spring 1967, pp. 24-38; Norris K. Smith, "Frank Lloyd Wright and the Problem of Historical Perspective," *Journal of the Society of Architectural Historians* 26, no. 4, Dec. 1967, pp. 234-237; Rayner Banham, "The Wilderness Years of Frank Lloyd Wright," *Journal of the Royal Institute of British Architects* 76, no. 12, Dec. 1969, pp. 512-518; Edward Frank, "Filosofia organica, architettura organica e Frank Lloyd Wright," *L'architettura cronache e storia* 15, no. 169, Nov. 1969, pp. 426-486; Bruno Zevi, "Frank Lloyd Wright domani," ibid., p. 423; Edgar Kaufmann, Jr., "Frank Lloyd Wright: The Eleventh Decade," *Architectural Forum* 130, no. 5, June 1969, pp. 173-183; Martin Pawley, *Frank Lloyd Wright. Public Buildings* (Thames and Hudson, London, 1970); Giorgio Ciucci, "Frank Lloyd Wright, 1909-1938: dalla crisi al mito," *Angelus Novus*, no. 21, 1971, pp. 85-117; Jonathan Barnett, "Rethinking Wright," *Architectural Forum* 136, no. 5, June 1972, pp. 42-47; William Allin Storrer, *The Architecture of Frank Lloyd Wright. A Complete Catalogue* (M.I.T. Press, Cambridge, Mass., 1974); John Sergeant, *Frank Lloyd Wright's Usonian Houses. The Case for Organic Architecture* (Whitney Library of Design, New York, 1976). The interest in Wright is also witnessed by the reprinting of many of his own writings and of earlier books concerning him, by the special issue of *Historic Preservation*, Apr.-Sept. 1969, dedicated to the Pope-Leighy House, and by the numerous exhibitions, among them the one held in Naples in December 1976 and January 1977, dedicated to Wright's designs from 1887 to 1959.

48

See Arthur E. Morgan, *Edward Bellamy* (Columbia University Press, New York, 1944), pp. 392-393. Although Wright derived some of his opinions from Bellamy, he was against the type of society Bellamy imagined. Bellamy was for centralization, the "beautiful" city, a simple house but a "splendid" public life, and the government of the Great Trust. Wright, on the contrary, was for decentralization, the annulment of the city, a life that expressed itself completely within the home, and minimal government. The absence of private property envisaged by Bellamy was diametrically opposed to Wright's concept of a wide diffusion of the property right.

49

On the position of the Southern Agrarians toward the policies of the New Deal, see Edward Shapiro, "Decentralist Intellectuals and the New Deal," *Journal of American History* 58, no. 4, Mar. 1972, pp. 938-957; idem, "The Southern Agrarians and the Tennessee Valley Authority," *American Quarterly* 22, Winter 1970, pp. 791-806.

50

Calamandrei, "Il pensiero storiografico di F. J. Turner," p. xvii.

51

In the period when Turner was still developing his ideas, Wilson had already accepted his thesis on the significance of the frontier. Wilson viewed the crisis of 1890 as a result of the closing of the frontier and believed that a new expansion would be a "natural and wholesome impulse." See Williams, *Contours of American History*, p. 411. See also, Richard Hofstadter, *The American Political Tradition and the Men Who Made It* (Knopf, New York, 1948), chap. 10.

52

White and White, *Intellectual versus the City*, especially chaps. 3, 12.

53

For an ample discussion of the birth and development of urban planning in the United States see Francesco Dal Co, "From Parks to the Region: Progressive Ideology and the Reform of the American City," this volume.

54

On the Oak Park period, see Grant Carpenter Manson, *Frank Lloyd Wright to 1910. The First Golden Age* (Reinhold, New York, 1958).

55

For the quotations, see Louis H. Sullivan, *Autobiography of an Idea* (1924; reprint ed., Dover, New York, 1956), p. 314; idem, *Kindergarten Chats (Revised 1918) and Other Writings* (George Wittenborn, New York, 1947), p. 107.

56

Sullivan, *Kindergarten Chats*, p. 110.

57

George R. Collins has listed the sources of Wright's ideas for Broadacres: "In the course of lecturing and writing about his plan, Wright openly and generously acknowledged his debt to more than thirty individuals. To list some whom he mentioned: The Arabian Nights, The Bahaist writings, Edward Bellamy, William Blake, Ralph Borsodi, John Brown, Samuel Butler, Thomas Carlyle, C. H. Douglas, Ralph Waldo Emerson, Henry George, Silvio Gesell, Johann Wolfgang von Goethe, Heraclitus, Thomas Jefferson, Jesus Christ, Lao-tse, Abraham Lincoln, Giuseppe Mazzini, George Meredith, Thomas Paine, Paracelsus, John Ruskin, Percy Bysshe Shelley, Louis Sullivan, Henry David Thoreau, Leo Tolstoi, Jules Verne, Victor Hugo, George Washington, Walt Whitman. They are all, indeed, present (and more besides) in an orgy of literary eclecticism" ("Broadacre City," p. 68). Wright prepared this "orgy of eclecticism" in the years immediately following his flight to Europe. Actually, he already knew some of these authors, not only the transcendentalists but also, for instance, Carlyle. In 1908, in his essay "In the Cause of Architecture," Wright recalled how in 1894 he had formed a series of propositions on architecture with a phrase of Carlyle's before him: "The ideal is within thyself, thy condition is but the stuff thou art to shape that same ideal out of"; see Frank Lloyd Wright, *On Architecture. Selected Writings 1894-1940*, ed. Frederick Gutheim (Duell, Sloan and Pearce, New York, 1941), p. 32. Ruskin, along with William Morris, is also frequently cited in Wright's earliest writings.

58

On the London conference, see Royal Institute of British Architects, *Town Planning Conference, London, 10-15 October 1910. Transactions* (London, 1911); Giorgio Piccinato, *La costruzione dell'urbanistica. Germania 1870-1914* (Officina, Rome, 1974). See also chapter 8 of Manieri-Elia, "Toward an 'Imperial City': Daniel H. Burnham and the City Beautiful Movement," this volume.

59

The portfolio, *Ausgeführte Bauten und Entwürfe von Frank Lloyd Wright* (Wasmuth, Berlin, 1910) contains an introduction by Wright; see also the new American edition, with a foreword by William Wesley Peters, *Buildings, Plans and Designs of Frank Lloyd Wright* (Horizon Press, New York, 1963).

60

See Alan Crawford, "Ten Letters from Frank Lloyd Wright to Charles R. Ashbee," *Architectural History, Journal of the Society of Architectural Historians of Great Britain* 13, 1970, pp. 64-73.

61

Bellamy was actually opposed to the isolated cooperative colony. In the *New Nation*, May 2, 1891, he wrote: "It is very evident that nationalists are not, as a rule, believers in co-operative colonies as the most effective means of spreading faith. The reason for this is that a colony is economically at a great advantage, as it is only part of a vast competitive system" (p. 232). See Stanley Buder, "Ebenezer Howard: The Genesis of a Town Planning Movement," *Journal of the American Institute of Planners* 35, no. 6, Nov. 1969, pp. 392, 397, n3.

62

Letter from Hilaire Belloc in response to a letter from Bernard Shaw, *American Review* 8, no. 3, Jan, 1937, pp. 314-320.

63

Precedents for such a position can be found in Henry George, who identified two dangerous classes, the too rich and the too poor. Similarly, the Populists spoke of the "upper and lower scum" of society, and Howells affirmed that inventions, art, and culture in America came neither from the "uppermost" nor from the "lowermost" classes but from the middle-class man. As George E. Mowry has stated, "In the first decades of the twentieth century the progressive never questioned where ability and righteousness resided. Nor was he uncertain of the sources of the nation's evils. 'From above,' one wrote, 'come the problems of predatory wealth.... From below come the problems of poverty and pig-headed and brutish criminality'"; see *The Era of Theodore Roosevelt and the Birth of Modern America, 1900-1912* (Harper and Row, New York, 1958), p. 103.

64

The first edition is cited in n59. The second, reduced edition, with a preface by Charles R. Ashbee, appeared with the same title in 1911 and it, too, was published in Berlin by Wasmuth; the new American edition, with a foreword by Edgar Kaufman, Jr., is entitled *Frank Lloyd Wright, the Early Work* (Horizon Press, New York, 1968).

65

From the caption of plate 97 of the 1910 Wasmuth edition.

66

Manson, *Frank Lloyd Wright to 1910*, p. 207.

67

According to Brooks, Wright probably chose von Holst because he had his office in Steinway Hall; see *Prairie School*, p. 86. Manson notes that Marion Mahony, Wright's most faithful collaborator, had worked for a certain period in von Holst's studio but does not consider this a real reason for Wright's choice; see *Frank Lloyd Wright to 1910*, p. 212. Some other, more direct relationship between Wright and von Holst, such as the belief in theosophy, cannot be excluded. Indeed, a large part of Wright's cultural and philosophical sources coincide with those of the theosophists. Among the names most frequently cited in the American theosophical journal the *Theosophical Path*, which first appeared in 1911, are those of Buddha, Jesus Christ, Lao-tse, Confucius, Carlyle, Goethe, Whitman, Longfellow, Paracelsus, and Bellamy, all found in the writings of Wright. On Griffin's and Geddes's relations with the theosophists, see Manieri-Elia, "Toward an 'Imperial City,'" this volume, n215-217.

68

Manson, *Frank Lloyd Wright to 1910*, p. 213.

69

Ibid., p. 217; McCoy, "Rock Crest/Rock Glen," p. 15.

70

Griffin's town designs from the same period show the same combination of planning and architectural aspects; Trier Center Neighborhood at Winnetka, Illinois, and Ridge Quad-rangles in Chicago, for instance, both designed in 1911, are similar to Como Orchards and very different from Wright's 1913 design for a typical residential section on the outskirts of Chicago. See James Birrell, *Walter Burley Griffin* (University of Queensland Press, St. Lucia, Brisbane, 1964), pp. 57-62.

71
See, for example, Suzanne Ganschinietz, "William Drummond," *Prairie School Review* 6, nos. 1, 2, 1969. The manuscript by Marion Mahony, "The Magic of America" (Burnham Library, Chicago Art Institute), also contains some rather unflattering criticisms of Wright.

72
Ganschinietz, "William Drummond," no. 2, p. 12.

73
See Alfred B. Yeomans, ed., *City Residential Land Development. Competitive Plans for Subdividing a Typical Quarter Section of Land in the Outskirts of Chicago* (University of Chicago Press, Chicago, 1916), pp. 37-47, reprinted in *Western Architect* 25, no. 1, Jan. 1917, pp. 6-8 and plates. See also Robert C. Twombly, "Undoing the City: Frank Lloyd Wright's Planned Communities," *American Quarterly* 24, no. 4, Oct. 1972, pp. 538-549.

74
Frank Lloyd Wright, "A Home in a Prairie Town," *Ladies' Home Journal* 18, Feb. 1901.

75
See Arthur C. Comey, "Regional Planning Theory: A Reply to the British Challenge," *Landscape Architecture* 8, Jan. 1923, pp. 81-96; published in book form, with the same title, by C. E. Nash, Augusta, Me., 1923. Comey conceived of a road system forming a triangular network of regional and local traffic axes; at the intersections of the principal axes the commercial centers are situated; from these nodal points the industrial zones develop linearly along the transport arteries; distributed within the primary road network are the residential areas, served by a secondary road network. Broad agricultural areas and green spaces separate the diverse linear elements. The model of life Comey had in mind was a rational version of the American residential suburb. See Collins, "Broadacre City," pp. 60, 63, where Comey's ideas are related to the Broadacres scheme; Thomas A. Reiner, *The Place of the Ideal Community in Urban Planning* (Trustees of the University of Pennsylvania, 1963). On Comey's work with the Massachusetts Homestead Commission, see Dal Co, "From Parks to the Region," this volume.

76
Frank Lloyd Wright, *An Autobiography* (Duell, Sloan and Pearce, New York, 1943), pp. 168-169.

77
On the Southern Agrarians and their relations with the National Catholic Rural Life Conference, see the essays by Shapiro cited in n49; see also John L. Stewart, *The Burden of Time. The Fugitives and Agrarians* (Princeton University Press, Princeton, 1965), pp. 180ff.; Conkin, *Tomorrow a New World*, pp. 14-15, 25.

78
Frank Lloyd Wright, *Writings and Buildings*, ed. Edgar Kaufmann and Ben Raeburn (World, Cleveland and New York, 1960), pp. 55-73.

79
Wright, *On Architecture*, pp. 85-97.

80
Parrington, *Main Currents* 3, p. 319.

81
See Wright, *Living City*, p. 245.

82
These two essays probably became "The Tyranny of the Skyscraper" and "The City," two of the six lectures given at Princeton University in 1930. *The Disappearing City* was reissued in 1945 as *When Democracy Builds;* it was later completely rewritten and published in 1958 as *The Living City.*

83
Wright, *Autobiography*, pp. 254-259.

84

Wright, *Living City*, pp. 58-59.

85

Wright, *Autobiography*, p. 259.

86

See Henry-Russell Hitchcock, *In the Nature of Materials, 1887-1941. The Buildings of Frank Lloyd Wright* (Duell, Sloan and Pearce, New York, 1942), p. 82; Arthur Drexler, *The Drawings of Frank Lloyd Wright* (Bramhall House, New York, 1972), plates 114, 115, 273.

87

Wright, *Autobiography*, p. 275.

88

Ibid., p. 276.

89

George E. Mowry, *The Urban Nation, 1920-1960* (Hill and Wang, New York, 1965), p. 2.

90

Franklin K. Lane, in U.S. Department of the Interior, *Annual Report for the Fiscal Year Ending June 30, 1918* (Government Printing Office, Washington, D.C., 1919), p. 11, quoted in Conkin, *Tomorrow a New World*, p. 51.

91

Franklin K. Lane, in U.S. Department of the Interior, *Annual Report*, p. 112, quoted in Schmitt, *Back to Nature*, p. 162.

92

Twenty-six percent of the total population lived in 68 centers of more than 100,000 inhabitants; 16.5 percent, in 684 centers of 10,000 to 100,000 inhabitants. See Elazar, *Cities of the Prairies*.

93

See Parrington, *Main Currents* 3, p. 405.

94

See David Graham Phillips, *Golden Fleece. The American Adventures of a Golden Hunting Earl* (McClure, New York, 1903), pp. 57-58.

95

See Daniel Bell, "Crime as an American Way of Life: A Queer Ladder of Social Mobility," in Alexander B. Callow, Jr., ed., *American Urban History. An Interpretive Reader with Commentaries* (Oxford University Press, New York, 1969), pp. 274-291.

96

On the origins of the Tennessee Valley Authority, see Preston J. Hubbard, *Origins of the TVA. The Muscle Shoals Controversy, 1920-1932* (Vanderbilt University Press, Nashville, Tenn., 1961), especially chaps. 1-4.

97

Donald Davidson, *The Tennessee*, 2 vols. (Rinehart, New York, 1946-1948), vol. 2, p. 184, cited in Hubbard, *Origins of the TVA*, p. 40.

98

On the city of Muscle Shoals, projected but never actually designed, see "A City All Main Street," *Literary Digest* 73, Apr. 8, 1922, pp. 72-74; Littel McClung, "The Seventy-five Mile City," *Scientific American* 127, Sept. 1922, pp. 156-157, 213-214; *New York Times*, Jan. 12, 1922.

99

Hubbard, *Origins of the TVA*, chaps. 3-5.

100

See George R. Collins, "Lo sviluppo della pianificazione lineare," introduction to Arturo Soria y Mata, *La città lineare* (Il Saggiatore, Milan, 1968), especially pp. 63-64. See also idem, "Linear Planning throughout the World," *Journal of the Society of Architectural Historians* 18, no. 3, 1959, pp. 74-93.

101

Quoted in Conkin, *Tomorrow a New World*, p. 29.

102

Frank Lloyd Wright, lecture given in Chicago in 1930 to the National Terra Cotta Society, in idem, *On Architecture*, p. 144.

103

Frank Lloyd Wright, "Modern Architecture. 6: The City," in idem, *The Future of Architecture* (Horizon Press, New York, 1953), p. 175.

104

Patrick Geddes, *Cities in Evolution* (Williams and Norgate, London, 1915), p. 129.

105

In the United States, as elsewhere, electricity was taken up as a revolutionary movement. See, in particular, Paul Hutchinson, "Revolution by Electricity. The Significance of the Tennessee Valley Experiment," *Scribner's Magazine*, Oct., 1934.

106

Hofstadter, *Age of Reform*, p. 288.

107

Quoted in ibid., p. 294.

108

Quoted in Francis E. Rourke, "Urbanism and American Democracy," in Callow, *American Urban History*, p. 378.

109

Hofstadter, *Age of Reform*, p. 300.

110

Wright, "Modern Architecture 6: The City," p. 177.

111

Baker Brownell and Frank Lloyd Wright, *Architecture and Modern Life* (Harper and Brothers, New York, 1937), pp. 177-179.

112

In 1933, reviewing the second edition of *The Ugly Civilization*, Donald Davidson considered Borsodi's work within the broader context of an agrarian economy but warned that it was possible for the Suffern experiment to develop in a direction contrary to agrarian life in the Jeffersonian acceptance of the term; see Donald Davidson, "Agrarianism for Commuters," *American Review* 1, no. 2, May 1933, pp. 238-242. On the relationship between Wright's ideas and those of Borsodi, see Paul and Percival Goodman, *Communitas. Means of Livelihood and Ways of Life* (Vintage Books, New York, 1960), pp. 88-93.

113

See Stewart, *Burden of Time*, especially chap. 3, "Toward Agrarianism."

114

Ibid., p. 321.

115

Ibid., p. 354.

116.

See Patrick F. Quinn, "Agrarianism and the Jeffersonian Philosophy," *Review of Politics* 2, Jan. 1940, pp. 87-104.

117

Donald Davidson, review of Arthur M. Schlesinger, *The Rise of the City, 1878-1898*, in *American Review* 1, no. 1, Apr. 1933, pp. 100-104.

118

Ralph Borsodi, "Land Tenure," *American Review* 7, no. 5. Oct. 1936, pp. 556-563.

119

Quoted in E. Shapiro, "Decentralist Intellectuals and the New Deal," p. 941.

120

Roosevelt's agrarian ideas developed principally while he was governor of New York. In the first years of the century he had already begun to apply scientific methods of cultivation and soil conservation on his own estate of Hyde Park. In 1920 Roosevelt maintained that it was possible to keep the people in the country by employing them at intervals in local

industry. As governor of New York, he worked for the decentralization of industry and for a new equilibrium between city and country through facilitating transportation and communication. Rural electrification, roads, reforestation, and new local industries were integral parts of a broader program of rural planning. The principal result of Roosevelt's land-use policies was the establishment of the National Planning Board in 1933; its first task was the preparation of a report on land and water resources. See National Planning Board, Federal Emergency Administration of Public Works, *Final Report—1933-34* (Government Printing Office, Washington, D.C., 1934), which states, "Country and rural planning is relatively underdeveloped thus far, but will unquestionably be forced to the front in the near future, as such problems as land use and educational facilities become more urgent, and as subsistence homesteads and organizations such as the Tennessee Valley Authority become more familiar" (p. 24). With time the NPB extended its concern to urban problems and technological development (1937), the national economic structure (1938-1940), scientific studies of the population (1937-42), regional planning (1942), and many other fields. See Arthur M. Schlesinger, Jr., *The Age of Roosevelt: The Coming of the New Deal*, (Houghton Mifflin, Boston, 1957); Charles E. Merriam, "The National Resources Planning Board. A Chapter in American Planning Experience," *American Political Science Review* 38, no. 6, Dec. 1944, pp. 1075-1088.
121

John Kenneth Galbraith, *The Great Crash* (Houghton Mifflin, Boston, 1954; Penguin, Harmondsworth, Middlesex, 1961), p. 32.
122

Wright, *Autobiography*, p. 310. See also Olgivanna Lloyd Wright, *Frank Lloyd Wright, His Life, His Work, His Words* (Horizon Press, New York), pp. 102-109.
123

Wright, *Autobiography*, pp. 304-317.
124

"Points of View," *Southwest Review* 14, Summer 1929, pp. 474-494.
125

Frank Lloyd Wright, "In the Cause of Architecture, VII: The Meaning of Materials—Concrete," *Architectural Record* 64, no. 2, Aug. 1928, p. 99.
126

Walter C. McKain, Jr., "The Concept of Plane of Living and the Construction of a Plane of Living Index," *Rural Sociology* 4, no. 3, Sept. 1939, pp. 337-343.
127

See, in particular, E. Shapiro, "Southern Agrarians and the Tennessee Valley Authority."
128

Ibid., pp. 803-804.
129

Brownell and Wright, *Architecture and Modern Life*, p. 67.
130

Jonathan Daniels, *A Southerner Discovers the South* (Macmillan, New York, 1943); With a touch of irony, Daniels recounts how Arthur E. Morgan and his wife, both opposed to alcohol and tobacco, tried to prevent the sale of beer in Norris; the vote taken among the "selected" workers who lived in the town, however, favored selling beer.
131

In his critical monograph, *Edward Bellamy*, Morgan defined the author of *Looking Backward* as a "rebel against the city" (pp. 94-96) and cited the following declaration from Bellamy's unpublished papers: "The only thing I can't understand is that . . . any . . . man with a soul can be satisfied to live in a city of brick and stone instead of in a country of hills, forests and brooks." This attitude was shared by Wright, who, however, could not accept the organization of work envisaged in *Looking Backward*. See also n48.
132

See Milburn L. Wilson, *Farm Relief and Allotment Plan* (University of Minnesota, Minneapolis, 1933), p. 50. Wilson was particularly inspired by the high standard of living in the

Mormon communities and the example they offered directly influenced the work of the federal agency Wilson directed.

133

See Ralph Borsodi, "Dayton, Ohio, Makes Social History," *Nation* 136, 1933, pp. 447-448. Borsodi's was the first project approved by the Division of Subsistence Homesteads. The second was Arthurdale, West Virginia, in which Eleanor Roosevelt took a direct interest. The first group of prefabricated houses was built in a few months, but after a year and a half only 125 dwellings had been completed. Despite the numerous criticisms of this experiment, Arthurdale was the most publicized of the subsistence homestead communities. For a brief assessment of the subsistence homestead program, see Conkin, *Tomorrow a New World*, pp. 237-255. By the middle of 1935, 20 self-sufficient communities were in existence and another 40 had been approved; 6,500 people had been accommodated.

134

Frederick Gutheim, "Frank Lloyd Wright: Prophet of Decentralization," *Free America. A Magazine to Promote Independence* 5, no. 4, Apr. 1941, pp. 8-10.

135

Wright, *Living City*, pt. 4, pp. 181-216.

136

Ibid., p. 215.

137

Brownell and Wright, *Architecture and Modern Life*, pp. 254-260. A book by O. E. Baker, Ralph Borsodi, and Milburn L. Wilson, *Agriculture in Modern Life* (Harper and Brothers, New York, 1939), sustained many theses similar to those of Brownell and Wright's book. In addition to the similarity of the title, which paraphrases *Architecture and Modern Life*, the two publications are curiously similar in their structure, with individual contributions and a final discussion among the authors, who agree very largely with each other.

138

Frank Lloyd Wright, "Broadacre City: A New Community Plan," *Architectural Record* 77, no. 4, Apr. 1935, pp. 244-245.

139

Collins, "Broadacre City," p. 57.

140

See C. H. Douglas, *Economic Democracy* (Palmer, London, 1921).

141

George, *Progress and Poverty*, p. 325.

142

Ibid., p. 336.

143

Ibid., p. 449.

144

Ibid., p. 453.

145

Ibid., p. 466.

146

The Taliesin Fellowship, a school, professional studio, and farm, was essentially a learning workshop. Norris Kelly Smith has traced the source of inspiration of the fellowship to King Arthur's Round Table as presented in Tennyson's retelling of the Arthurian tales. Smith notes that Wright himself said, "Taliesin, a Druid, was a member of King Arthur's Round Table." The community spirit of the fellowship was imbued with the traditions of the frontier and its myth, which were being illustrated during the same period by the regionalist painter, as exemplified in works such as John Steuart Curry's *Baptism in Kansas* or Grant Wood's *Dinner for Threshers*. The first quarters of the Taliesin Fellowship were in the Hillside Home School, which had been built by Wright for his aunts Nell and Jane Lloyd-Jones in 1902, on part of the same land where he later built his own residence. Today the Taliesin Fellowship has become the Taliesin Associated Architects. See *The Taliesin Fellowship* (Spring Green, Wis., 1933); N. K. Smith, *Frank Lloyd Wright*, pp. 119-120.

147

The model of Broadacres was executed in Arizona beginning in the winter of 1932-33. The project was initially financed by Edgar J. Kaufmann at the suggestion of his son, the future architectural historian, who was then working with Wright. In 1936 Kaufmann commissioned Falling Water, the house of the "typical Usonian."

148

See Seymour Stillmann, "Comparing Wright and Le Corbusier," *Journal of the American Institute of Architects*, Apr.-May 1948, pp. 171-178, 226-233. Stillmann compared the number of inhabitants of Broadacres with that of other "utopian" proposals.

149

See also Collins, "Lo sviluppo della pianificazione lineare."

150

See Wright, *Autobiography*, p. 325.

151

See John W. Reps, *The Making of Urban America* (Princeton University Press, Princeton, 1965).

152

Frank Lloyd Wright, *Genius and Mobocracy* (Duell, Sloan and Pearce, New York, 1949), p. 13.

153

Wright, *Autobiography*, p. 303.

154

See Hitchcock, *Nature of Materials*, p. 87; Drexler, *Drawings of Frank Lloyd Wright*, plates 134-136.

155

Lewis Mumford, *From the Ground Up* (Harcourt Brace Jovanovich, New York, 1970), p. 87. The quotation is from the essay "A Phoenix Too Infrequent," originally published in the *New Yorker* in 1953.

156

See Hitchcock, *Nature of Materials*, p. 101, figs. 411-413.

157

See "The Price Tower," in William A. Coles and Henry Hope Reed, eds., *Architecture in America: A Battle of Styles* (Appleton-Century Crofts, New York, 1961), pp. 354-384.

158

Meyer Shapiro, "Architect's Utopia," *Partisan Review* 4, Mar. 1938, p. 42.

159

See Oswald Spengler, *The Decline of the West*, 2 vols. (Knopf, New York, 1926-1928), especially vol. 2, chap. 4.

160

M. Shapiro, "Architect's Utopia," p. 45.

161

Ibid., p. 47

162

See Talbot Wegg, "Frank Lloyd Wright versus the USA," *Journal of the American Institute of Architects* 103, no. 2, Feb. 1970, pp. 48-52. In 1940 a number of architects (Gropius, the two Saarinens, Kahn, Stein, Neutra, Wurster, Stubbins, and Wright) were invited by Clark Foreman of the Division of Defense Housing to design one hundred workmen's houses for Pittsfield, Massachusetts, and were granted the maximum freedom. Bureaucratic difficulties blocked Wright's design, a fact that convinced him of the impossibility of Washington's ever entrusting a project to a "free" individual like him.

163

On the interpretation of Disneyland as a monument to this "new quality," see Charles W. Moore, "You Have To Pay for the Public Life," *Perspecta* 9/10, 1963, pp. 57-97. On Walt Disney World, see Peter Blake, "Walt Disney World," *Architectural Forum* 136, no. 5, June 1972, pp. 24-41; Giorgio Ciucci, "Walt Disney World," *Architecture Mouvement Continuité*, no. 35. Dec. 1974, pp. 42-51.

MANFREDO TAFURI

The Disenchanted Mountain:
The Skyscraper and the City

Introduction

... Jimmy Herf came out of the Pulitzer Building. He stood beside a pile of pink
newspapers on the curb, taking deep breaths, looking up the glistening shaft of the
Woolworth. It was a sunny day, the sky was a robin's egg blue. He turned north and began
to walk uptown. As he got away from it the Woolworth pulled out like a telescope. He
walked north through the city of shiny windows, through the city of scrambled alphabets,
through the city of gilt letter signs.

Spring rich in gluten ... Chockful of golden richness, delight in every bite, *the daddy of
them all*, spring rich in gluten. Nobody can buy better bread than PRINCE ALBERT.
Wrought steel, monel, copper, nickel, wrought iron. *All the world loves natural beauty.*
LOVE'S BARGAIN that suit at Gumpel's best value in town. Keep that schoolgirl com-
plexion. ... JOE KISS, starting, lighting, ignition and generators.

This is the way John Dos Passos begins the chapter entitled "Skyscraper" in
Manhattan Transfer, published in 1925. In the "city of scrambled alphabets"
and kitsch publicity—"*All the world loves natural beauty*"—Cass Gilbert's Woolworth Building is seen as a magical event. In the literary context, its telescopic
mass provides an interceding image between the absolute unnaturalness of the
"city of gilt letter signs" and the disenchanted nostalgia for a "spring rich in
gluten."

Thus the skyscraper is perceived as an element of mediation, a structure that
does not wholly identify with the reasons for its own existence, an entity that
remains aloof from the city. The Neogothic structure of the Woolworth Building
soaring upward in successive stages before the broad, open space of City Hall
Park was an explicit response to the skyscraper as developed by the Chicago
school. In Chicago an attempt had been made to achieve visual and dimensional
control of the skyscraper, an organism that, by its very nature, defies all rules of
proportion; in New York, the ascending lines of force of this organism of
potentially infinite development, were given free reign; the isolation of the
Woolworth Building is in perfect accord with this concept.

This was an old controversy, however, and Cass Gilbert's work, far from
initiating it, actually concluded it. At the end of World War I, the experiments
and acclaimed models of George B. Post, Harvey Ellis, Louis Sullivan, Daniel H.
Burnham, and Gilbert no longer held up in face of the increasingly explosive

problems of the urban structure they conditioned. The skyscraper as an "event," as an "anarchic individual" that, by projecting its image into the commercial center of the city, creates an unstable equilibrium between the independence of the single corporation and the organization of collective capital, no longer appeared to be a completely suitable structure. The control of this "anarchic individual," in the absence of the necessary institutional means, became an obsessive problem. In the early 1920s, the Woolworth Building, which captured Dos Passos's imagination, could still serve as a model, but the reasons justifying its creation belonged to a bygone epoch.

The *Chicago Tribune* Competition

In 1922, when, with great fanfare, the management of the *Chicago Tribune* opened the famous competition for a new administration building for "the world's largest daily newspaper," the crisis of the skyscraper became strikingly evident. Significantly, the official program of instructions distributed to the entrants was wholly concerned with formal eloquence, while structural aspects were completely ignored. Thus beginning this examination of the business centers of the American cities with an analysis of the *Chicago Tribune* competition has a deliberate provocative intent. Moreover, since this argument must necessarily be presented in terms of key events, the competition of 1922 makes it possible to examine not only the unresolved crisis already mentioned, but also the relations between European and American architectural culture.

The history of the American skyscraper, from the first empiric application of the elevator to tall commercial edifices—such as the Jayne Granite Building in Philadelphia (1849-52), designed by William L. Johnston or the Equitable Life Insurance Company Building in New York (1868-70), designed by Gilman, Kendall and Post—to the types established around 1890 by George B. Post or Bruce Price, is, in fact, the history of a close relationship among technological innovations, structural innovations, and innovations in the design of the architectonic organism. Despite their disagreements, both Winston Weisman and J. Carson Webster make clear the thoroughly structural nature of the process of development of the skyscraper up to the impasse of the 1920s.[1]

This impasse was manifest by a break with the interrelationship of the creative factors that had previously characterized the development of the skyscraper. Between about 1900 and 1920, the tried models by now became canonical and the repertory fixed, construction in the large commercial centers left a series of problems unresolved. What had been, between 1850 and 1890, a continual development rich in results now became a process of involution.

In the first place, the intimate relationship that had existed between technological innovation and developments in the architectonic organism was sundered. By this time the rigid organization of the building industry and its division in infinite numbers of small firms contradicted the very nature of the skyscraper and gave rise to evasions and hybrid concessions to the ideology of the "Cathedrals of Business" on the part of the designers. In other words, architects resorted to a formal language that could adequately publicize and exalt the concentration of capital the skyscraper expressed, but they ignored the scientific study of its economic efficiency or technological possibilities.

Second, the single building operations within the city, as speculative ventures, entered into conflict with the growing need for control over the urban center as a structurally functional whole. In the face of the problem of ensuring the efficiency of the central business district in terms of integrated functions, the exaltation of the "individuality" of the skyscraper in downtown Manhattan, already dramatically congested, was an anachronism. The corporations, still incapable of conceiving the city as a comprehensive service of development, in spite of their power, were also incapable of organizing the physical structures of the business center as a single coordinated entity.

The triumph of eclecticism was the consequence of these unresolved problems, the expression of their passive acceptance. The completely uninhibited and pragmatic character of American eclecticism, however, actually had its origins in a tradition inaugurated with the Virginia Capitol, for which, in 1786, with Clérisseau's help, Jefferson adopted the model of the Maison Carrée of Nîmes. Jefferson's intention was clear; the building had first and foremost to convey a composite significance—the sacredness of the lay temple, with its references to the Roman Republican virtues. Thus the capitol was a "ready made" in need of only a few functional adaptations. In this case, the values and meanings under-lying its forms were accepted as a system of conventions; as such, they were interpreted as something stable and immutable.[2]

For Post, Corbett, or Cass Gilbert, just as for Jefferson and Latrobe, the European models had the character of a convention. The value they expressed changed—Republican virtues for Jefferson, the austere elementariness of Greek democracy for Latrobe, Gothic sacredness for Gilbert's "Cathedrals of Commerce," which exalted business enterprise—but the architects' indifference to the stylistic material remained identical. In the skyscrapers of the 1910s it is as if the architectural process were quite explicitly split in two; the effort at formal design was reduced to a minimum in order to allow maximal concentration on function and structure. Cass Gilbert's Woolworth Building (1911-13) is an illuminating example of this phenomenon.[3]

This primacy of structure and subordination of style was perfectly understood by Montgomery Schuyler in his famous article on the evolution of the sky-scraper published in *Scribner's Magazine* in 1909.[4] Schuyler investigated the same subject further in 1913, in an article in which he discussed the Woolworth Building, Ernest Flagg's Singer Building (1906-08), and the Metropolitan Tower of Napoleon Le Brun and Sons (1905-09), leaving aside almost all consideration of their formal aspects.[5] This critical practice was the result of a lucid distinc-tion. On the one hand, there were the products of construction, such as skyscrapers, destined to a "distracted use" within the dynamics of the metropolis and valid for their contribution to the formation of the complex

View of City Hall Square, New York, about
1883. At left, City Hall, begun by Joseph-
Francois Mangin and finished by John Mc-
Comb, Jr. (1802-1812). The building to
the right with the tower is the Tribune
Building by Richard Morris Hunt (1873-75),
at the extreme right, the Potter Building.
The Municipal Building by McKim, Mead
and White, completed in 1908, does not
yet appear.

Jayne Granite Building, Philadelphia, by
William L. Johnston, 1849-52.

Havermeyer Building, New York, by
George B. Post, 1891-92.

Design for the Odd Fellows Temple, Chicago,
by Adler and Sullivan, 1891.

Woolworth Building, overlooking City Hall Park, New York, by Cass Gilbert, 1911-13.

structure of the business centers; on the other, the architectural objects, such as Richardson's buildings, which Schuyler analyzed with minute attention to their stylistic expression—in other words, works separate from the "working city" in which style could gain full autonomy.[6]

What is of interest here is that this particular line of criticism persisted in America up to the early 1920s. In 1921, in an article illustrated by Hugh Ferriss, C. Matlack Price stated explicitly that "to be able to see a building without seeing its stylistic rendering is to see architecture."[7] Praising the Woolworth Building and Helmle and Corbett's Bush Building, Price continued, "From the point of design, the Gothic manner affords a peculiarly happy solution for the problem of terminating the tall building, as is admirably evidenced in the top of the Bush Building. This is probably one of the finest silhouettes of all the tall buildings of New York."[8]

This is exactly the opposite of the formalist point of view. Asserting the primacy of the organism over formal expression, Schuyler and Price assigned a secondary, instrumental value to architectural style, an attitude directly anti-thetical to the ideological value attributed to the new, nonfigurative language by the European avant-garde in these same years. In a certain sense, a continual de-idealization of architecture was taking place in the United States. By emphasizing the purely conventional character of the use of "styles," American eclecticism of 1910-20 liquidated the organic conception of architecture; thus it fell into line with the concepts of organic architecture's bitter rival, the City Beautiful.

It was just when this process had reached its zenith that the crisis of the skyscraper and its consequent urban significance were made evident by the *Chicago Tribune* competition. Led by Robert McCormick, director of the great Chicago newspaper, the competition for the new building was actually part of a program to develop the northern area of the city, beyond the Chicago River, which had been an objective ever since the early years of the century.[9] Significantly, however, despite this urban dimension of the *Chicago Tribune's* initiative, the program of the competition insisted on the aim of creating "the most beautiful and distinctive office building in the world" and exempted the entrants not only from any consideration of the relationship between the new edifice and the urban system but even from any adequate technological controls. The skyscraper of the world's largest newspaper, an organization intimately connected with the tumultuous development of the city of Chicago, had to be "an inspiration to [its own] workers as well as a model for generations of newspaper publishers."[10]

The theme of "civic beauty" served to make attractive a speculative venture of vast proportions. In 1902, the *Chicago Tribune* had constructed its own 8-story building between Madison and Dearborn streets; after seventeen years, however, the congestion of the old business district and the newspaper's organizational needs advised a move to an area outside the Loop. The development of North

Michigan Avenue, which had also received a strong impulse from Burnham's plan, clearly indicated the best direction for the first decentralization initiatives. McCormick himself recognized this to be the most favorable area for a program aimed at overcoming the anarchic proliferation of building projects by co-ordinating the efforts of single proprietors with those of the municipal administration.[11] In 1919, immediately after the completion of the artery, McCormick purchased the property at 431-439 North Michigan Avenue; by 1920 the bare functional block of the new Tribune Plant by Jarvis Hunt had already been constructed on the lot. The new skyscraper would therefore be situated between the Tribune Plant and the boulevard. The site of the Tribune's future administration building was certainly in an enviable location. Situated as a crucial nodal point of Michigan Avenue, the site offered the possibility of constructing an edifice that would become a point of reference of urban scale and thus also accentuate the *Chicago Tribune's* pioneering effort in the development of an area destined to become the necessary complement to the Loop.[12]

In spite of all this forethought, the organization of the competition seems to have been completely improvised. Ten American architects, among them Benjamin Wistar Morris, Bertram G. Goodhue, Howells and Hood, and Holabird and Roche, were expressly invited to participate, with expenses to be reimbursed fixed at $2,000. The original closing date was November 1, 1922, later extended by a month. The program for the competition, prepared by Howard L. Cheney, the *Tribune's* advisory architect, was exceedingly general. The entrants had to present only two plans (a ground plan and a typical floor plan), plus elevations and one perspective drawing of their projects. The only functional consideration stipulated was that the designers should consider that, of the projected 400-foot building, only the lower floors were to be occupied by the *Chicago Tribune*; the upper floors would be leased to commercial firms. As already noted, nothing was requested in terms of technological considerations; indeed pure scenography was encouraged. The competition and its program met with enthusiasm among American architects, especially those invited to participate. And the jury, which was scarcely representative of the current trends in American architecture, was quick to arrive at a decision.[13]

The verdict was announced on December 3, 1922: the first prize of $50,000 went to Howells and Hood; the second, of $20,000, to Eliel Saarinen; and the third, of $10,000, to Holabird and Roche.[14] The publicity campaign did not end with the closing of the competition, however. Instead, it became an occasion for sensitizing the American public to the problems of architecture. Since June 1922 the *Sunday Tribune* had been publishing articles dedicated to the architecture of all periods and this continued through January 1923. At the closing of the competition, 155 of the 263 perspective drawings submitted in the competition were sent to twenty-seven American cities in an exhibit organized and financed by the *Chicago Tribune*.[15]

The massive participation by American architects—145 entries—affords a comprehensive view of the architectural situation in the United States in the 1920s. The entire range of eclectic propositions appeared in a competition pervaded by the most absolute cynicism. The more or less literal Gothicism of Helmle and Corbett, of Paul Hermann, or of the design by Louis Bourgeois, Francis Dunlap and Charles L. Morgan was equivalent to the vacuous classicism of Benjamin Wistar Morris or Frank Fort, while Alfred Fellheimer and Steward Wagner's effort, or Paul Gerhardt's, to create "significant forms" led to pyramidally developed designs and the use of Egyptian imagery.[16] The irony of the anthropomorphic designs presented by some cartoonists was thus not unjustified. The assortment of projects all too obviously bent on achieving some impossible qualitative distinction reflected the crisis of the skyscraper itself.

Among the American entries, however, were three projects that represented, each in its own way, the ultimate response of the Chicago School to the problem of the skyscraper—the designs submitted by Walter Burley Griffin, William E. Drummond, and Lippincott and Billson. In other words, by two former collaborators of Frank Lloyd Wright and by an architect closely linked to the same line of descent (Roy Lippincott was Griffin's brother-in-law and collaborated in Griffin's Australian projects).

Griffin's proposal, prepared in his Melbourne studio during a period of professional crisis and stasis, was the architect's last attempt to reassert himself in the American scene.[17] The design pursues certain tendencies of his Australian work, including his experiments in the use of materials, which he carried out very successfully in his complex at Castelcrag, begun in 1921. But it also continues the expressionistic overwroughtness, based on the fracturing or multiplication of forms and on a new eclecticism that he had adopted in the Chinese Club (1915) and Newman College (1916) in Melbourne and was to use again in the Melbourne Capitol Theater (1924) and the City Council Incinerator at Sidney (1934-35), as well as in his work in India. Griffin's skyscraper for the Chicago competition fits perfectly into this line of development. The monumentality of the lower block and the insistent display of the supporting structures of the stepped towers contrasts with the fractured treatment of the crowns of the towers and the window elements inserted like precious independent objects. In this design Griffin, indeed, appears obsessed by purely graphic definition, as if he wished with this ostentatious multiplication to contest the very unity of the skyscraper.[18] It would seem that in his *Chicago Tribune* project and the work of his last years Griffin was expressing a personal stylistic crisis; such self-criticism, however, was foreign to the current concerns of urban America. Although Griffin's design was undoubtedly poorly understood by the jury, an interpretation of the skyscraper as an exceptional object in which to inscribe autobiographical notations was also quite outside the scope of the competition. Lippincott and Billson's proposal, which attempts to endow a

Design by Holabird and Roche for the
Chicago Tribune competition, 1922 (third
prize).

Design by Alfred Fellheimer and Steward
Wagner for the *Chicago Tribune* competition, 1922 (honorable mention).

Design by Frank Herding and W. W.
Boyd, Jr., for the *Chicago Tribune* competition, 1922.

Design by Walter Burley Griffin for the
Chicago Tribune competition, 1922.

Design by William E. Drummond for the
Chicago Tribune competition, 1922.

Design by Lippincott and Billson for the
Chicago Tribune competition, 1922 (honorable mention).

conventional organism with qualitative distinction by means of a geometric play in the vaguely Gothic-inspired terminal structures, managed to win an honorable mention.

Drummond's project, in contrast, is something of a shock and should perhaps be considered as the expression of an ironic attitude rather than a serious proposal.[19] Grafted onto a uniform block of fifteen stories, which, according to the canons of the Chicago school, frankly reveals its structure, are two independent volumes with a jumble of decorative elements that reach an absurd rhetorical climax in the terminal tower. In a display of classical imagery worthy of the set of some early film spectacular in the style of Pastrone or Griffith, a sort of enormous baldaquin composed of porticoes and exedras rises amidst gigantic tripods. At this point Drummond's polemical attitude toward the rhetoric solicited by the competition's sponsor becomes explicit. The architect's irony, however, is also a cover for his complete abdication. What is surprising in the attitudes of Griffin and Drummond is that both ignore completely Wright's hypotheses on the tall building—the cohesion of the Steinway Hall group had been sundered for some time.

The overall dreariness of the American participation in the *Tribune* competition stemmed directly from the absence of any consideration of the urban role of the skyscraper, such as that attributed to it later by Le Corbusier.[20] The American architects no longer produced "events" on the metropolitan scale but, instead, labored to give formal stability to architectural objects the intrinsic laws of which were ignored. The iron-clad laws dominating the architectural profession and the construction market prohibited the necessary jump in scale from the individual object to the control of a complex structure like the commercial centers. This problem was confronted only in the limited terms of zoning proposals, and the pragmatic outlook reigning within the profession inhibited even the most advanced architects from proposing projects that called for anything more than restructuring the traffic system.

The absurdity of the *Chicago Tribune* conpetition lay in the desire to give stability to the concept of the skyscraper as an "object" by conferring upon it institutional sanctity, in other words, in the wish to exalt and consecrate the very autonomy that would now of necessity have been contested, if the goal had been, instead, to open up new perspectives. By imposing a symbolic mask that could result only in hybrid solutions, the 1922 competition can be seen, historically, to have marked a turning point in the conception of the skyscraper, at least on a theoretical level.

Only one of the symbolic themes treated in the competition is noteworthy: the skyscraper in the form of a column. Commentators on Adolf Loos's famous design in the form of a Doric column have often failed to note, in addition to the Austrian architect's exploit, two other proposals, by American architects, that adopt an analogous theme. In Matthew L. Freeman's design, a stumpy Doric column rises above a block that terminates in triangular pediments; Paul

Satirical design by the *Chicago Tribune*
cartoonist Frank King for the *Chicago
Tribune* competition, 1922.

Design by Adolf Loos for the *Chicago
Tribune* competition, 1922.

Design by Paul Gerhardt for the *Chicago
Tribune* competition, 1922.

Gerhardt of Chicago presented a design close to Loos's, except that the Doric is replaced by an Egyptian column.[21] These proposals would later be described as indicating the appearance of a prophetic pop spirit; in the case of Loos, at least, it has been suggested that his intention was ironic, his gigantic inhabited column being a mere mockery of eclecticism.

Loos's own article on his design, however, contains not a trace of irony.[22] Actually, all the contradictions of his position are present in his column. America, seen and praised by Loos in the 1890s, was a nation of two faces; one showed that it knew how to absorb and make a supratemporal use, on a gigantic scale, of the European conceptions of order and form—the America of the Columbian Exposition—while the other uninhibitedly adhered to the laws of everyday life. Loos was to demonstrate his admiration for Sullivan's attempt at a synthesis of these two opposites,[23] but his own theories pointedly reproduced this schism: on the one hand, architecture, the utensil of a middle class so rich in qualities that in its daily life it had no need to keep its own values continually before its eyes; on the other, art, the "reflecting on values," which was possible only in the pauses the universe of work concedes to comtemplation.[24]

The Loos of years preceding the *finis Austriae* was not the Loos of the years following the war. In 1922, in full view of the Chicago Loop, he wished deliberately to "reflect on values"; in an obsessive search for nonephemeral forms, he wished to compromise the very symbol of order—and in its most authentically classical version—by using it in an everyday manner. The estrangement of the column became an allegory of urban estrangement. In his article, Loose explicitly referred to the formal alienation of the Metropolitan Building and the Woolworth Building.[25] At the same time he spoke of the sensational effect created by the contrast between the cubic block and the fluted shaft of the column of polished black granite as the only one possible for spectators of an epoch "disillusioned like our own."[26]

It would be possible to comment at great length on this Loosian ambiguity and play of equilibrium between the call to a supratemporal continuity of value and the gigantic enlargement of a fragment as a way of imposing its presence on the distracted metropolitan public. In fact, Loos seems in 1922 to have lost the clarity that characterized his prewar conceptions. His column is not symbolic; it is only a polemical declaration against the metropolis seen as the universe of change. A single column extracted from the context of its order is not, strictly speaking, an allegory; rather, it is a phantasm. As the paradoxical specter of an order outside of time, Loos's column is gigantically enlarged in a final effort to communicate an appeal to the perennial endurance of values. Like the giants of Kandinsky's *Der gelbe Klang*, however, Loos's gigantic phantasm succeeds in signifying nothing more than its own pathetic will to exist—pathetic, because it is declared in the face of the metropolis, in the face of the universe of change where values are eclipsed, the "aura" falls away, and the column and the desire to communicate absolutes become tragically outdated and unreal. The mute silence of Loos's column was the result of a utopian interpretation of the "new order" of industrial civilization, made by an intellectual who was constant in his attempt to find an ideal synthesis within the dramatically fragmented reality in which he lived.

But what was the model for this column? Was it not, perhaps, that tripartite form adopted habitually, from about 1880 on, in the skyscrapers of Post, Sullivan, and Holabird and Roche? Post's Havermeyer Building in New York (1891-92), Adler and Sullivan's Union Trust Building in Saint Louis (1892-93), Holabird and Roche's Marquette Building (1893-94), and the Broadway-Chambers Building by Cass Gilbert (1899-1900) all seek a dimensional control of the "object" skyscraper according to a three-part division of basement level (base), principal homogeneous structure (shaft), and crowning (capital). Such a transposition resolved the need to domesticate and possess completely the compositional elements derived from Beaux-Arts teachings in the terms of American pragmatism.[27] The program implicitly assumed in order to arrive at such a solution was made explicit in Loos's project of 1922, just how consciously we do not know, but so emphatically that no further comment on the theme was possible.

Although the two American architects were certainly far from Loos's intellectualism, the proposals submitted by Freeman and Gerhardt may also be explained in light of these considerations. Both endowed the skyscraper with a very particular expression, extraneous to the Loop and ostentatiously monumental. Their intent was obviously to create an allusion to the desire for stability of forms and institutions, a pause in the continuity of the "metropolis without quality." It was Loos himself who had recognized in 1910 that such a pause can be identified only with the superfluous or with death.

The projects of the German and Austrian architects in general pose different problems and concern the subject of this essay only indirectly. Nevertheless, they are extremely interesting from the point of view of the relations between American and European architectural culture in the 1920s. Apart from the isolated case of Loos, these projects clearly reflect the dichotomy within the architectural avant-garde of central Europe. In fact, in their projects for the *Chicago Tribune* competition, the German architects simply continued the development of their own ideas regarding the high-rise office building, a current concern in postwar Germany. This concern was not limited to the competition for the Berlin skyscrapers on Friedrichstrasse or Kemperplaz, but also included Adolf Behne's and Max Berg's studies of the relationship between the housing shortage and the possibility of restructuring the old centers by concentrating the work area in a few strategic points, thereby freeing a great quantity of space in the very heart of the city for dwellings. In this regard Berg's proposals, published in 1920 in *Stadtbaukunst*, are exemplary.[28] The adhesion to their own particular problems and concerns, however, limited even the most advanced projects presented by the German group, who were otherwise differentiated among themselves.

On the one hand, the projects of Walter Gropius and Adolf Meyer, of Max Taut, and of Ludwig Hilberseimer already tended, even if ambiguously, to a silent *Neue Sachlichkeit*. On the other were the projects of Thilo Schoder, Walther Fischer, Gerhard Schroeder, Max Ronneburger, and Clemens Holzmeister—in other words, of architects who chose the path of a moderate Expressionism. This second group was less interested in making a contribution to the form of the American city than in experimenting, on a grand scale, a tendency common to all radical cultural circles of Weimar Germany. It is hardly by chance that projects such as those by Fischer, Holzmeister, Peter Birkenholz, and Schoder all presented, in more or less rarefied terms, designs of Gothic inspiration. Similarly Gothicizing, but with an evident irony, was Bruno Taut's pyramidal structure with its concrete ribs converging at the apex.[29]

The particular stylistic differences among such projects may easily be left aside. What counts is that they all seem to have been conceived as a response to the problem raised by Bruno Taut himself in his *Stadtkrone*.[30] Indeed, they are apparently proportioned not to the scale of the American metropolis but, rather, to that of the small or medium-sized German city. The problem these architects really posed themselves was that of the symbolic *communal* building, the exalted epic expression of the longed-for reconciliation of the individual with the collectivity through a "new sanctity" introduced by art.

This was the theme of the early works of Adolf Behne, of the second generation of Expressionism, and of the *Aktivismus* movement; the reference to the Gothic was in keeping with the effort to reestablish an ethnically defined "community" through architecture. Unsurprisingly, then, the Chicago projects of Schoder, Schroeder, or Birkenholz fell perfectly in line with the designs elaborated for tall buildings in Magdeburg, Breslau, and Berlin. In 1923 Behne remarked that Bruno Taut's project for the *Tribune* competition, like that of Scharoun, "once taken as a model . . . would transform the city of Chicago into a negro village."[31] Just a few years earlier, however, Behne himself had praised the reconciliatory virtues of a primordial artistic expression as the new religion of communities that were no longer alienated. The paradox of projects like Bruno Taut's or Holzmeister's is that they chose the most eminently urban building type as the vehicle for expressing an essentially antiurban ideology.

This was indeed their objective; the skyscraper was considered in terms of the precapitalist village bell tower; thus it was sufficiently full of symbolic values to serve as a point of reference for a "community of individuals." In 1924, commenting on the results of the Chicago competition, Gerhard Wohler described this conception very clearly:

The German skyscraper is assigned a definite role within the urban context: it is the expression of forces concentrated in a single point, and thus its value lies not in itself but in its relation to the comprehensive image of the city. What is revitalized here is the medieval idea of the cathedral. The function of the cathedral, which dominates the urban image with its mass and is the symbol of metaphysical aspiration and spiritual comportment, was to be assumed by the skyscraper, its translation in modern terms, since in a certain sense the skyscraper represents the exaltation of work.[32]

In other words, the skyscraper is the "cathedral of work." In this light, the "Expressionist" skyscrapers of the Chicago competition may quite logically be seen as the other face of the ideology that inspired the *Siedlung*, or German industrial village. Both represented an attempt to counter the reality of the metropolis with the regressive utopia of the village. This was still the opposition of the *Gemeinschaft* to the *Gesellschaft*, of the organic community to the impersonal organized society, that had been treated explicitly and conclusively by Ferdinand Tönnies in the late nineteenth century.[33]

Compared with such regressive responses, the projects of Gropius and Meyer, Max Taut, and Hilberseimer offered far more up-to-date solutions. In Gropius's project Giulio Carlo Argan has perceived "the skyscraper as a symbolic form, image of the spatial infiniteness in which we are enabled to live by virtue of an architecture that has completely absorbed the means, procedures, and very rhythm of industrial production."[34] Indeed, Gropius's skyscraper is, strictly speaking, a "symbolic form," an image of the structures on which the productive universe is based, which rejects any specific reference and asserts its own autonomy as an image. Only in this way is it possible to explain the network of sculptural intersections created from the structural frame—the latter an explicit reference to the models of William Le Baron Jenney and Holabird and Roche—and the gratuitous horizontal caesuras that connect the volumes with the surrounding space in this design. It is precisely by means of this open play of intersections relating building and space, however, that Gropius, too, manages to avoid rather than interpret the logic of the skyscraper itself. In fact, while the organism prescribed by the competition is absolutely neutral, the staggering of the two volumes and the syncopated dislocation of the balconies are articulations that make every attempt to restore a communicative dimension to this structure, in itself indifferent and completely inarticulate. It is the indifference of the skyscraper that Gropius understands as the ultimate reality and that, in spite of everything, he tries to defy.

This conception and resolution of the problem can be explained by the particular position of the *Chicago Tribune* design within Gropius's development. In 1922, the same year that witnessed the opening in Berlin of the first exhibit of Soviet art in Germany, as well as the year of the provocative meeting of the avant-garde at Weimar,[35] Gropius left behind—in his designs for the Kallenbach house, the municipal theater in Jena, and the Chicago skyscraper project—the prophetic and populist romanticism that had pervaded his architecture in the period from 1918 to 1921.[36] Nevertheless a certain relationship still existed between the Chicago skyscraper and the earlier Sommerfeld house. According to Gropius himself, the wood of the Sommerfeld house alluded to the primordial dwelling, the refuge of the primitive community—wood as the "material of the people." The 1922 skyscraper proclaimed, instead, that the moment had arrived for an integrated community of builders to create their own "cathedral of work"; through the development of the semantic potential of the technological

Design by Walter Fischer for the *Chicago Tribune* competition, 1922.

Design by Max Ronneburger for the *Chicago Tribune* competition, 1922.

Design by Gerhard Schroeder for the *Chicago Tribune* competition, 1922.

  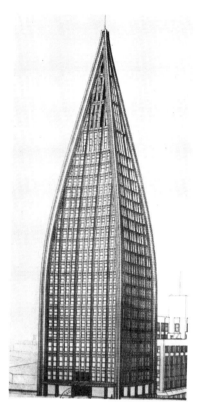

Design by Clemens Holzmeister for the
Chicago Tribune competition, 1922.

Design by Stahler and Horn for the *Chicago
Tribune* competition, 1922.

Design by Bruno Taut, with the collaboration of W. Günther and K. Schutz, for the
Chicago Tribune competition, 1922.

Design by Adolf Meyer and Walter Gropius
for the *Chicago Tribune* competition, 1922.

Design by Max Taut for the *Chicago Tribune*
competition, 1922.

Design by Ludwig Hilberseimer for the
Chicago Tribune competition, 1922.

image itself, the skyscraper communicates its message to the "new order," inviting it to give shape to the hopes of European radicalism.

In the work of Max Taut, too, the *Chicago Tribune* competition marked a turning point. In general, in fact, the avant-garde architects of Weimar Germany participated in the competition exactly because it offered the chance to try out, in a metropolitan project of the highest order, new and radically different hypotheses from those inspired by the late romantic and populist conceptions to which the German intellectuals of the "opposition" had previously clung. Polemical self-criticism is much more evident in Max Taut's project than in that of Gropius. Taut's design, like Gropius's, is based on a staggering of volumes, introduced in homage to a principle of deliberate asymmetry; both designs were clearly influenced by the "dynamic equilibriums" of international Constructivism, launched at Weimar and Düsseldorf in the same year, by Lissitsky and Van Doesburg as imperative to the attainment of a synthesis of the avant-garde movements.[37] As in the case of Gropius, Taut's denuded volumes are articulated in an effort to communicate their own programmatic essentialness. In place of Gropius's gratuitously added forms, Taut's skyscraper presents continuous vertical divisions to which even the entrance conforms, while the surfaces, scanned by their pure structure, are tenuously articulated by the slight projection of the glass boxes that accent the angles and the face of the terminal tower.

Gropius's and Taut's projects can be compared with those entered in the 1923 competition for the Palace of the People in Moscow and that opened in 1924 for the Leningradskaja Pravda, also in Moscow. I do not wish to undertake a discussion in this essay of the frequently noted analogies between Gropius's project and the Vesnin brothers' design submitted in the Moscow competition of 1923.[38] What is of immediate interest for this analysis is the similar communicative intent of these projects. In their Chicago skyscrapers, Gropius, to a great extent, and Taut, to a lesser, undertook to create a symbolic object on a metropolitan scale—the edifice of a great daily newspaper as the universe of information. The task the Vesnin brothers set themselves was comparable, except that they were far beyond Gropius's ambiguity and unhesitatingly declared the absolute priority of the allegorical value of their *machine à communiquer*.

In the Chicago competition, in comparison to the projects of Gropius and Taut, that of Ludwig Hilberseimer annuls the communicative capacity of architecture.[39] Hilberseimer's design, not included in the official publication of the competition,[40] is actually the logical conclusion of a process begun with Gropius's project and further pursued in Taut's. His skyscraper is totally free of any desire to communicate; like the contemporary works of Mies Van Der Rohe, it is reduced to a pure sign, the "deathly silence" of which it thoroughly accepts. Hilberseimer's project reflects the situation of the avant-garde movements of Berlin, strongly influenced by the polemical anti-Expressionist and anti-Dadaist propaganda of Lissitsky and Moholy-Nagy. Speaking of his project for the 1922 competition, Hilberseimer himself cited the critical position of the magazine G—in other words, of the most radical of the Elementarist publications.[41]

The historical significance of the three projects here analyzed is, indeed, paradigmatic. From Gropius's design to Hilberseimer's, they offer a synchronous demonstration of the entire course of the avant-garde movements; from Gropius's attempt to endow the pure articulation of signs with semantic value, through the mediation of Max Taut's project, this line of development ultimately produces an hallucinatory emptiness. It is also significant that all this took place in a project for a skyscraper. The evolution represented by these three designs actually prefigures the historical development that was to take place between the McGraw-Hill Building and Lever House.

Very different from the purity of conception characterizing the two inter-related tendencies of this particular group of German architects is the generic Mendelsohnian inspiration of Scharoun's design or of the design submitted anonymously but known to have been the work of Alfons Anker and the Luckhardt brothers.[42] The German entries also included some ironic projects, such as Ludwig Koloch's or the design by Heinrich Mossdorf, Hans Hahn, and Bruno Busch, in which the skyscraper is terminated in the form of an Indian with his tomahawk raised in the air, a contradictory allusion to Chicago as the city symbolic of the pioneers. The irony expressed in such proposals, however, merely reveals a fundamental uncertainty.

A greater homogeneity of expression characterizes the Dutch entries in the competition, but here, too, except perhaps for B. Bijovet and J. Duiker's skyscraper, the projects presented were essentially extraneous to the specific problems of the American city. Aside from D. F. Slothouwer's and D. Roosen-burg's very confused designs, projects such as those of Meischke and Schmidt, of A. van Baalen, or of D. A. van Zanten are all intent on synthesizing formal expressions drawn from either the works of the Wendingen group or the experiments of the Dutch avant-garde, in an effort to place maximum emphasis on the unique and unrepeatable character of the skyscraper. For example, in van Baalen's design, the best of these projects, a pure sphere rises above a massive block, articulated by bow windows and by relieved surfaces in the manner of Wijdeweld; the symbolic sphere is an element found also in the project by the German W. Funke, but in van Baalen's case it was adopted for its character as an hermetically provocative, autonomous geometric object.

In other words, the Dutch entrants were deeply involved in a particular architectural development in their own country, then in its conclusive stages, and were not open to experimentation divorced from purely formal concerns. Significantly, however, the real protagonists of that development in Holland—again excepting Bijovet and Duiker—did not take part in the Chicago competition. Bijovet and Duiker, on the other hand, produced a skyscraper project that, unlike Griffin's or Drummond's, makes use of Wright's formal expression. A tower emphasized by angle piers and projecting horizontal planes is inserted between the two arms of a fifteen-story structure, marked by similar projecting planes and extended to connect with the preexisting structure behind. Contrasting with this schematic geometry is the complex interplay of volumetric forms that animates the basement level, where a series of progressively more projecting elements culminates in the aggressive jut of the two publicity signs that directly relate the building to the space of the street. The prominent overhang of the terminal elements of the two arms flanking the tower—inspired by the cornices of Wright's Press Building for San Francisco—relate them to the geometric puzzle of the basement level. In contact with the street forms take on a marked animation; in the upper levels characterization is provided by the undifferentiated superimposition of planes. Ultimately this design reveals an outlook similar to the other Dutch entries; rather than a methodological proposal, Bijovet and Duiker's project is an interpretation, "made in Holland," of purely formal problems presented by the American city. Even their rendering of Wright's language is too literary to be convincing.

Closer to the line of development of Max Taut's or Hilberseimer's project was that by the Danish architect Karl Lönberg-Holm, not included in the official publication of the competition. In Lönberg-Holm's design, the vertical accents of the central block are forcibly inserted within the horizontal stratification of the wings, with an elementary logic not unlike that of Neo-Plasticism. The Danish architect's project would perhaps be recalled later by Raymond Hood in his design for the McGraw-Hill Building.[43]

The projects of the European architects of the Modern movement thus anticipated, in one way or another, the formal language of the skyscraper in the 1930s. Not one of them was capable, however, of dealing with the fundamental problems that had brought about the crisis of the skyscraper. These architects obviously considered the United States the place to test the hypotheses of the avant-garde movements, and any consideration outside this range of problems was purely secondary. The truth of the matter is that, without exception, the Eruopean participants were incapable of adequately adapting their own contrasting interests to the solution of the real problems hidden behind the ambiguously formulated requests of the *Chicago Tribune*.[44] To the false American certainties, the Europeans, avant-garde and regressive alike, could respond at this moment only with confused and conflicting uncertainties; in these projects America as seen from Europe appears far more a literary myth than an objective reality.

The outcome of the competition was in all probability known from the start. With the choice of Howells and Hood's design, certainly motivated at least in part by chauvinistic considerations,[45] the jury only confirmed the dominant trend in American architecture. Undeniably, however, the winning project was one of the most notable of the Neogothic designs submitted precisely because the stylistic concerns were completely secondary.[46] The octagon of the Tribune

Design by Hentze and Richter for the
Chicago Tribune competition, 1922.

Design by Heinrich Mossdorf, Hans Hahn,
and Bruno Busch for the *Chicago Tribune*
competition, 1922.

Design by Hans and Wassili Luckhardt and
Alfons Anker for the *Chicago Tribune*
competition, 1922.

Design by A. van Baalen for the *Chicago Tribune* competition, 1922.

Design by D. A. van Zanten for the *Chicago Tribune* competition, 1922.

Design by B. Bijovet and J. Duiker for the *Chicago Tribune* competition, 1922.

Design by Marcello Piacentini for the *Chicago Tribune* competition, 1922.

Design by Einar Sjostrom and Jarl Eklund for the *Chicago Tribune* competition, 1922.

The Chicago Tribune Building by John Mead Howells and Raymond Hood, 1922-24.

Design of the facade of the Chicago Tribune Building on Michigan Avenue, showing the projected enlargement, prepared by John Mead Howells and Raymond Hood.

Design by Eliel Saarinen for the *Chicago Tribune* competition, 1922 (second prize).

Ground plan of the Chicago Tribune Building, including the projected enlargement, by John Mead Howells and Raymond Hood.

Tower, scanned by the rhythm of the pilasters and vertical struts that dissolve its volumetric consistency, is endowed at the entrance level and in the development of its terminal structure with forms of a literary Gothicism completely extraneous to the organism of the skyscraper. If, on the one hand, the Tribune Tower was a prelude to the purified verticalism of Howells and Hood's Daily News Building, on the other, it reflected, still more than the Woolworth or Bush Buildings had done, the detached pragmatism of the American professionals in regard to what they considered the "added value" of stylistic form.

When the Tribune Tower is considered in light of the structural and technological aspects of its construction, style is seen to be, strictly speaking, no more than an added value. The study of the construction problems was entrusted to Frank E. Brown and Henry Jackson Burt, men directly involved in the technological innovations of building construction in Chicago, and to the technical office of Holabird and Roche; many of the solutions devised are remarkably interesting. Not only was intelligent use made of the existing underground transportation system in order to free Michigan Avenue of excavation work and storage of construction materials, but a notable solution was adopted for the wind-bracing, which was provided by a system of diagonal structures coinciding with the window frame. The originality of the composite structure in iron, cement, and masonry, however, remains completely independent of the architectural organism.[47]

Howells and Hood's skyscraper very clearly marked the end of the Neogothic mythology and indicated a new direction that was to be followed until the early 1930s, when a new system of formal conventions—that of the International style—would provide American architectural practice with the possibility of reconciling structure and form. In 1922, however, the experiments of the European avant-garde were considered insufficient to satisfy the qualitative aspirations of the *Chicago Tribune*. The projects of the radical German architects, with their invocation of the "silence of the sign," the formal contrivances of the Dutch participants, and the worn-out Expressionist formulas were all incapable of indicating the "system of certainties" that America was searching for. To such a request these designs responded with the uncertainty of an expression still in the phase of laborious definition. Nor did the results of the competition—publicized with exhibitions in many American universities and cultural institutions—have any interest for European culture.

It is symptomatic that an acute and competent observer like Werner Hegemann had few words for the architectural aspects of the question when he published the *Chicago Tribune* projects in *Wasmuths Monatshefte*. Instead, Hegemann took advantage of the occasion to discuss the subject of comprehensive control over business centers and focused his attention on the Regional Plan of New York and Its Environs in relation to planning in German cities.[48] In his article Hegemann was concerned with solutions and proposals for the complete restructuring of urban centers. Recalling solutions he himself had studied in 1913, he published the schemes proposed in about 1923 by Harvey

Wiley Corbett for the separation of different types of traffic in the heart of New York by means of a system of streets and sidewalks on two levels and advocated a more restricted and exceptional use of the skyscraper office building. Gerhard Wohler, in his comments on the Chicago competition, expressed a position very similar to Hegemann's. Wohler emphasized the conflict between individual large-scale undertakings and the problem of traffic congestion, for which he cast blame less on private enterprise than on municipal administrations that failed to plan efficient systems of coordination and radical renewal.[49] Essentially, Hegemann and Wohler criticized the chaotic insufficiency of the means of growth and control that the Chicago competition made so evident. Instead of the call to a new quality, which contradicted the very premises of American development, Hegemann raised the unresolved problem of indirect control over the commercial and financial metropolis, considered as a unit, as a *structure*. This was a problem that Eliel Saarinen, who won second prize in the competition, was to confront immediately after his first trip to the United States.

This is a connection between Saarinen's *Chicago Tribune* design and his subsequent proposals for projects in Chicago and Detroit that must here be made clear. The Finnish architect's skyscraper for the 1922 competition actually presented no essential innovation in the building type. Rather, what so impressed the jury and the American critics was the unity of the organism, characterized by the skillful composition of volumes rising one from the other in a "telescopic" ascent.[50] Like Howells and Hood's design, Saarinen's negates the consistency of the walls, but by means of a far more articulated use of the vertical structures. Completely new, however, is the composition based on a veritable metamorphosis of forms. In the passage from one volume to another, for instance, the vertical rhythm becomes denser, at times even through the use of statuary, so that the points of juncture are softened in the gradual continuity of rising forms.

Thus Saarinen offered the Americans a model of the skyscraper in which the setback structure is balanced by a continuous and modular development of the volumetric articulation. The organic quality of his design was to be interpreted as the victory of architecture over the artificiality of the metropolis. As the model of an "enchanted mountain," it would inspire Ralph Walker's Barclay-Vesey Building in New York, Albert Kahn's Maccabees and Fisher buildings in Detroit, and Charles Z. Klauder's project for the new University of Pittsburgh (significantly called the "Cathedral of Learning"), as well as the Bell Telephone Building in Cleveland by Mills, Rhines, Bellmann and Nordhoff. Indeed, for some years Saarinen's severe romanticism encouraged the demand for idealistic masks, with which business men and corporations felt it necessary to cover the harsh reality of the financial and speculative ventures connected with urban concentration and the development of commercial construction. In 1927 Richard Neutra commented on just this tendency to exhibition of romantic forms, implicitly contrasting such abstract idealism with the complexity and novelty of a semantically neutral organism such as Holabird and Roche's Palmer House.[51]

In any case, it is interesting to examine the reasons behind Sullivan's well-known eulogy of Saarinen's project and his condemnation—actually not too severe, however—of the design by Howells and Hood.[52] First of all, Sullivan did not criticize but, rather, praised the program of the competition and described the desire "to erect the most beautiful and distinctive office building in the world" as "inspiring" and "magnanimous."[53] It was from this point of view that Sullivan saw in Saarinen's skyscraper the act of a "Master of Ideas," the romantic adventure of a "Free Spirit" that attacks and overcomes the anonymity of the metropolis:

Qualifying as it does in every technical regard, and conforming to the mandatory items of the official program of instructions, it goes freely in advance, and, with the steel frame as a thesis, displays a high science of design such as the world up to this day had neither known nor surmised. In its single solidarity of concentrated intention, there is revealed a logic of a new order, the logic of living things; and this inexorable logic of life is most graciously accepted and set forth in fluency of form. Rising from the earth in suspirations as of the earth and as of the universal genius of man, it ascends and ascends in beauty lofty and serene to the full height limit of the Chicago building ordinance, until its lovely crest seems at one with the sky.[54]

For Sullivan, the mind of man had here succeeded in expressing itself in designing an object in which gigantic size was not antithetical to the organic ideal; Saarinen's skyscraper rose from the ground as the synthesis of individual will with nature.[55]

In Saarinen's design, Sullivan probably saw realized an intention he himself had not completely expressed, except in the "minor" works of his late period. Indeed, with Saarinen's skyscraper, far more than with those of Sullivan, organic logic enters the city. What counts still more, however, is that it makes its entrance by emphasizing structural values and not by means of a refined dichotomy between organism and purely added elements, which had reached its high point in the Schlesinger and Mayer Department Store. In interpreting Saarinen's project as a "mountain" Sullivan thus saw correctly. Its "telescopic" structure, the metamorphosis of forms that takes place before the eyes of the spectator, and its heroic "primitivism"—an aspect much emphasized by Creese[56]—appeared to Sullivan the means most suited to achieving the utopian synthesis between city and nature; the mountain is unquestionably the only natural form in keeping with "the city where fierce men and women pour forth," as Whitman sang. And certainly such concepts were not extraneous to Saarinen's project. It is interesting, however, by delving further into his design to see just what aspects of it escaped the aging Sullivan.

In an article in the *Western Architect* in 1923, Saarinen stated that up to that time he had not taken an interest in developments in American commercial structures.[57] Despite this assertion, however, his study of Richardson's architecture is evident in at least three works of his Finnish period—the Pohjola

Insurance Building in Helsinki (1901), the Joensun town hall (1912-13), and the Helsinki bank (1920), today next to Aalto's Rautatalo.[58] Moreover, Saarinen was to make use of this source immediately after his move to the United States, in his work at Cranbrook Academy in Bloomfield Hills, Michigan, both in the general conception of the complex and in the School for Boys. In both the Helsinki bank and the Cranbrook School for Boys, what interested Saarinen in Richardson's style was the organic quality of his forms and their reciprocal dependence. Furthermore, Saarinen's own repeated declarations of allegiance to an architecture conceived "in the nature of materials" seem to confirm Sullivan's interpretation of the Finnish architect as the heir of the organic tradition of American architecture.[59] To evaluate correctly this view of Saarinen, however, other factors must be borne in mind. Above his drawing table at Hvitträsk, Saarinen is known to have kept a photo of the facade of Sullivan's Transportation Building.[60] According to Albert Christ-Janer, however, Saarinen was attracted by what he considered the "qualities of rebellion" implicit in the decorative tour de force of the portal of the Transportation Building more than by its specific formal solution.[61] In any case, from the very beginning of his activity as urbanist, Saarinen's line of thinking was certainly completely different from that of the so-called Chicago school.

In the 1923 article mentioned above, Saarinen seems to have wished to explain his *Chicago Tribune* project further by implicitly criticizing the basic premises of the competition. His interpretation of the skyscraper is, in fact, exactly the opposite of the whole American experience in the matter of the skyscraper: not a structure materializing the concept of laissez-faire, and thus not an image of the competition among the great commercial concentrations but an element capable of exercising a formal control over the urban complex as a whole.[62] The proposal Saarinen made in this brief work seems, indeed, to have had no precedent in America, except the summary image accompanying Sullivan's article on the use of setback skyscrapers published in the *Graphic* in 1891. As Donald Hoffman—who rediscovered this article, which had long escaped the attention of scholars—has pointed out, Sullivan's concern, like Adler's, was wholly to find a building type capable of compensating public and private interests.[63] As Adler's article of 1892 makes clear, their considerations of the problem, which departed from recognizing and deploring the public loss incurred by the indiscriminate proliferation of skyscrapers, actually tended to safeguard and boost the economic value of the tall office building.[64]

In other words, the illustration that accompanies Sullivan's article was in no way intended as a model for a coordinated urban project, as is also quite clear from the deliberately wide variety of styles indicated in these setback skyscrapers. Sullivan's study was ultimately only a plea for the methodical application of experiments made in Chicago—by Le Baron Jenny in the Manhattan Building of 1889-91 and by Adler and Sullivan themselves in the Shiller Building of 1891-92—and given complete formal expression in Sullivan's 1891 design for

Theoretical design by Louis Sullivan for a
city of setback skyscrapers (drawing en-
graved by H. von Hofsten, *Graphic* 5,
December 19, 1891).

the Odd Fellows Temple, the setback skyscraper that reveals the distance between the concerns of the 1880s and those of Saarinen. A sort of didactic demonstration of the advantages of the setback skyscraper, Sullivan's Temple, like Saarinen's *Chicago Tribune* project, tends to a metamorphic development of the volumes. The formal technique adopted, however, is typically additive; the forms are not born from one another but merely juxtaposed. In this sense, Saarinen's design realized something not completely expressed by Sullivan. As a formal structure, Saarinen's skyscraper is, in fact, much closer to the Woolworth Building and to the towers of the eclectic New York architects than to the models of the Chicago school. In no way does Saarinen attempt to delimit or to "close" the image of the skyscraper, as the tripartite scheme elaborated by Post and developed by Sullivan, Root's traditional solutions, or the Reliance Building typically tried to do.

Saarinen's project tends to present itself as no more than an element of a whole that is dominated by multiplicity, change, and velocity and to project, in architecture, these typical conditions of the metropolis. This attitude also demonstrates concerns and concepts foreign to the Sullivan tradition. In my opinion the only line of research comparable to Saarinen's in the 1920s was that pursued in Vienna in 1922-23 by Peter Behrens and Alexander Popp on the *Grossstadt* dominated and controlled by the setback skyscraper. In order to evaluate Saarinen's contribution to American urbanism adequately, it is necessary to analyze some of the projects he prepared between 1923 and 1925 and to compare them with his earlier experience as an urban planner. In light of these analyses, the design for the competition of 1922 can assume a new significance.

Eliel Saarinen and the Coordinated Skyscraper Complex: The Chicago Lakefront and Detroit Riverfront Projects

In 1923, on his own initiative, Saarinen prepared a complete project for the development of the Chicago lakefront between Grant Park and Michigan Avenue, which was given great prominence in the *American Architect*.[65] It was obviously a promotional enterprise, but it also exemplified the ideas expressed in a still nebulous form in Saarinen's article published earlier that year in the *Western Architect*. The initiative constituted a development of Saarinen's *Chicago Tribune* project on the basis of certain urban concepts with which he had experimented earlier in his plans for Munksnäs-Haga (1901-15), Canberra (1912), Reval (1911-13), and Helsinki (1917-18).[66]

These four plans, in fact, reveal a common basic conception. What dominates all of them is a compactness of structure. At Reval and Helsinki, this compactness results from a respect for the continuity between the new urban structures and the preexisting urban organisms. In the plans for Munksnäs-Haga and Canberra, variations on the elementary geometric schemes are expedients adapted in order to apply Camillo Sitte's teachings in the characterization of the principal centers of the city. In Saarinen's urban plans these primary centers have two outstanding fundamental characteristics. First, any simplistically natural component is excluded (thus contemporary German and English trends are criticized), and there is a marked emphasis on the continuous and compact ordering of constructed forms. The fragmented and decentralized structure of the Helsinki plan results from the geological formation of the site, and the peripheral construction of the suburb of Munksnäs-Haga is offered as an alternative, and a clearly secondary one, to the construction of the central area of the settlement. The second characteristic is the skillful use of the traffic system as a consolidating element of the urban structure. Especially in the plan for Helsinki, Saarinen was among the avant-garde in his attempt to control this fundamental component of the modern metropolis.[67]

These two salient characteristics were at the center of discussion in two encounters of fundamental importance for the history of modern urbanism: the Town Planning Conference held in London in 1910, where Burnham's City Beautiful was confronted with the garden-city theory and the experiments of the German urbanists, and the conference on traffic organized in 1914 by the Deutscher Werkbund.[68] The plans of Saarinen's Finnish period seem, in fact, to represent something of a synthesis of the emphasis on formal structure of the German tradition of planning, the particular means offered by Sitte's teachings, the principles of decentralization drawn from Howard, and an avant-garde interest in the new significance of traffic within the metropolis, which once again connects Saarinen's interests with those of Behrens.[69]

The same ideas and conceptions, applied on a different scale and with different means, were at the base of Saarinen's project for the Chicago lakefront. His proposal took up an idea from the Burnham and Bennett plan, which had never been carried out: the creation, in connection with the development of Grant Park, of a monumental park boulevard running from Congress Street to the northern district of the city. Saarinen, however, endowed this project with a significant functional aspect that had not been part of the Burnham plan. He located his development in just the area of the lakeshore where it would be possible to create a center that would have direct effects within the Chicago Loop. In this area of Grant Park, between 23rd Street and the Chicago River, Saarinen's project called for the creation of a linearly extended monumental complex, which would also include extensive underground parking facilities at the service of the entire business district of the city.

On various occasions, Saarinen himself emphatically praised Burnham's plan for Chicago, criticizing it only for its failure to take account of the urban possibilities inherent in the skyscraper. Thus Saarinen's lakefront project attempted to graft onto the basic indications of Burnham's plan qualities Burnham himself had intuitively recognized in the creation of the Flatiron Building in New York. In this sense, however, Saarinen's project was also a response to the limited and shortsighted conditions imposed by the *Chicago Tribune* competition. The Chicago lakefront project was therefore presented as the resuscitation of one of the outstanding features of Burnham's plan for Chicago; in describing the genesis of his idea, Saarinen had words of sincere admiration for the City Beautiful concept.[70] In the 1909 plan for Chicago he quite evidently recognized the same relationship between coordinating principles and the ideal of order that had guided his own previous experiences as urban planner. For Saarinen the urban concepts of Sitte, Stübben, and Burnham were complementary, but Saarinen was also sensitive to the greater scale of the American metropolis. He interpreted the phenomenon of commercial concentration in particular areas as part of the dynamics of the American city and thus as a reality not to be questioned and in which one could interfere only to rationalize its internal relationships. In such a rationalizing effort, Saarinen's principal concerns were, first, the relation between points of primary importance and traffic and, second, the coordination of private initiatives. In this sense, it is significant that in considering the possibility of expanding the Chicago Loop Saarinen took account of the northern sector of the city along North Michigan Avenue, beyond the Chicago River, precisely the area in which the new *Chicago Tribune* building was being erected. Thus the lakefront development was actually a continuation of the project he had submitted in the competition of 1922. Now, however, he introduced a scale unusual in American urban planning for its complexity. Saarinen's proposal did not involve long-term comprehensive planning and was thus, properly speaking, an urban-design project, the plan of an individual sector, architecturally defined and inducing notable effects in the general structure of the Loop.

In fact, by starting with an analysis of the dynamics of traffic in the heart of the Chicago business district, Saarinen conceived as an integral part of his project an enormous, well-equipped, four-level parking area beneath Grant Park, traversed by Grant Boulevard, running like a central artery between the project's two extremes, Grant Plaza to the north and the projected Chicago Tower to the south.[71] In the strip that extended for two miles between these extremes, Saarinen structured his development project, conceived as a grand monumental complex and automobile terminal. On Grant Plaza, in immediate contact with the underground street traffic installations and the underground railroad station, he located the skyscraper of the Grant Hotel and the new concert hall. Their separate placement on the plaza and their diverse heights make these two buildings points of reference marking the two axes of Grant Boulevard and Madison Street. Grant Park, freed of the traffic of Grant and Tower boulevards, both passing at a depressed level in this stretch and crossed by one-way bridges for local traffic, becomes an urban promenade, where the flow of traffic has been reduced to a "spectacle." The second skyscraper, the Chicago Tower, closes this *enfilade* at its southern end.

The electrification of the Illinois Central Railroad line was indispensible to Saarinen's plan, since it would permit the Illinois Central station to be placed underground, immediately below the Grant Hotel, thereby freeing the park of railroad traffic. The surrounding area, thus increased in value, would then be available for residences and places of business. From this viewpoint, Saarinen's

Proposal by Eliel Saarinen for the Chicago
lakefront, plan for the development of Grant
Park and the area north of the Chicago
River, 1923.

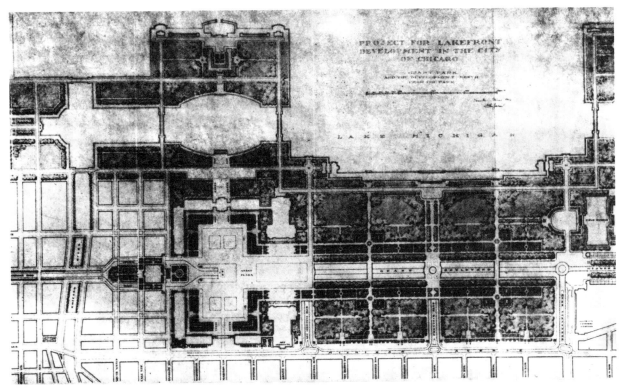

Proposal by Eliel Saarinen for the Chicago
lakefront, view of the entrance colonnade
on Michigan Avenue, 1923.

Proposal by Eliel Saarinen for the Chicago
lakefront, view of Grant Boulevard, with
the Chicago Tower in the distance, 1923.

Proposal by Eliel Saarinen for the Chicago
lakefront, cross sections of the central
fountain and automobile terminal, 1923.

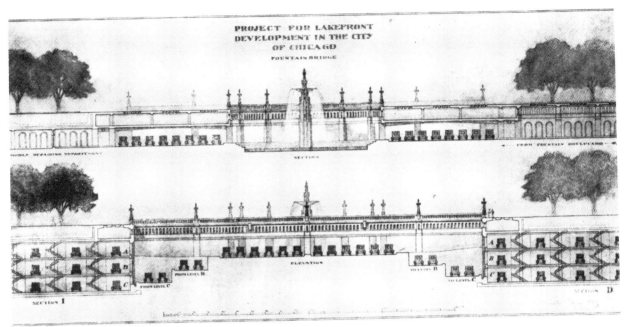

Proposal by Eliel Saarinen for the Chicago
lakefront, view of Grant Hotel and Grant
Plaza, 1923.

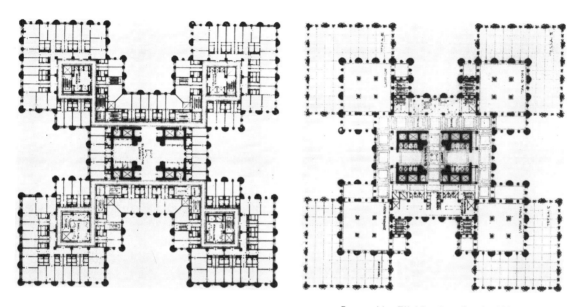

Proposal by Eliel Saarinen for the Chicago
lakefront, Grant Hotel, typical floor plan
and plan of the main public floor, 1923.

project was completely in keeping with the City Beautiful tradition. Michigan Avenue was conceived as a high-level commercial promenade; Tower Boulevard, between the museum and the Chicago Tower, was to be constructed with continuous porticos for deluxe shops; a colonnade would serve as a filter between Grant Plaza and the city. The architect himself cited the Louvre and the Place de la Concorde as his models.[72]

Conceived as a monumental center, as a "monument to Chicago," Saarinen's lakefront was a sort of enormous "terminal," not only for automobile and rail traffic but also, figuratively, in respect to the dynamics of the city. By connecting the high-density construction of this two projected skyscrapers with large open spaces, rapid traffic systems characterized as an "urban spectacle," and the greenery of Grant Park, Saarinen, in fact, proposed making a different use of construction concentration. At the same time, however, precisely because of its particular functional characteristics, his lakefront project was not really a generally applicable model for the development of the business center. Saarinen advanced the theory of coupling high-concentration construction and open spaces but conceived it as an "exception" to the Loop. Rather than part of the commercial city, Saarinen's lakefront was a place from which to contemplate it. The architect himself spoke of the view of the city to be enjoyed from the top of his hotel, which was to be situated directly above the underground station:

I wish to see Chicago advance along the lines I have emphasized in my project. I do not mean thereby the architectonic style in which I have clothed the plan, for it is individual, but the architectonic grouping of the masses as a framing for the whole in order to form an harmonic rhythm of city views around Grant Park.

And I see a stranger arrive in Chicago. From Central Station he makes his easy way by elevator to the hotel above. From its garden terraces a beautiful panorama greets his eye. To the West and North he sees the growing metropolis and above it farther to the North the green park girdle along the length of the shore. Below him Grant Plaza expands Southward in majestic repose, surrounded by flower beds and public buildings in harmonic monumentality; farther away verdant Grant Park and in the distant South, Chicago Tower's monumental pinnacle flashing in the sun high above the city's smoke and dust. To the Eastward, Lake Michigan spreads its wide expanse in green and violet, fading toward the horizon.

And he finds Chicago—in the heart of America—a beautiful city.[73]

By now it should be quite clear that Saarinen's proposal contained two contradictory hypotheses. On the one hand, through his analysis of the skyscraper he had come to realize a close relationship between urban form and the renewal of skyscraper design, and on the basis of this relationship his project was aimed at control over the comprehensive form of the city by acting on only one sector of it. It is evident that Saarinen's resumption of the formal values of the City Beautiful, which he enriched with a new formal proposal based on the rationalized use of an exceptional element represented by the skyscraper, is completely coherent with this aspect of his project.[74] On the other hand, however, it was just the exceptional character Saarinen granted the skyscraper that prevented him from making it the basis of an authentically innovative urban planning proposal.

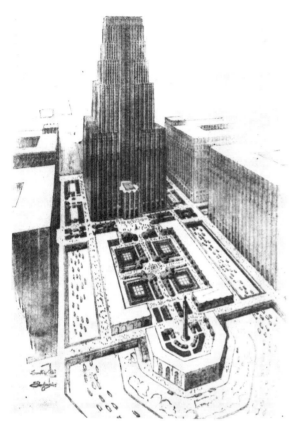

Proposal by Eliel Saarinen for the Chicago
lakefront, view of Grant Hotel and Grant
Plaza, from above, 1923.

Proposal by Eliel Saarinen for the Chicago
lakefront, view of the Chicago Tower.

Criticizing, as Saarinen did, the irrational proliferation of skyscrapers in the business centers of American cities could have led to formulating a project for the planned reorganization of the building industry. Such a project would have involved determining to what extent a building type that presupposes a strong concentration of invested capital could act as a stimulus for technological innovations and thus affect productive cycles connected with the building industry. To pursue such a line of research, however, it would have been necessary to liberate the skyscraper from its iron-bound relationship with real-estate speculation. The insertion of the skyscraper, as a very distinctive element of a highly concentrated commercial center, into a new economic cycle would have been something of a utopian project, but at least would have corresponded to real problems. Saarinen's proposal liberated the skyscraper from contradictory mechanisms of speculation, but only in formal terms. What he offered was the image of a possible liberation, the conditions for which were not analyzed by the architect, who at this point arrested his efforts.

In other words, Saarinen deliberately kept his architectural proposal on an ideological level. To achieve the desired control over urban form by means of planning and designing in terms of a coordinated project Saarinen relied on nothing more than the power of his proposal's formal values to convince the community. His intuition of a new complex scale of intervention was not accompanied by the elaboration of a realistic plan of investment. In Saarinen's view, just as, slightly later, in that of Thomas Adams, the proposals of the urban designer could not and must not assume a coercive character; instead, they were to be put into operation by agencies and individuals prompted to respond to the proposed urban project solely by its inherent powers of persuasion.[75] Such an outlook is reflected even more clearly than in his Chicago lakefront proposal in Saarinen's Detroit riverfront proposal, prepared in 1924 during his stay at the University of Michigan, where he had been invited by Emil Lorch.[76]

In the Detroit plan, too, traffic was a primary consideration. And once again Saarinen brought together parking facilities serving the entire business district, an underground station, and a complex of buildings of essentially prestigious function, including a Memorial Hall, a building for exhibitions, an auditorium, and a skyscraper facing the river. As in Chicago, he extrapolated the skyscraper from its natural context and use; as a "memorial to the *genius loci*" the skyscraper once again became a monument. (In Saarinen's reelaboration of this 1924 project in 1947, it is interesting that the monumental accent disappears in favor of an emphasis on installations of a social nature, which dominate the large open space).[77]

In comparison with his Chicago lakefront proposal, Saarinen's Detroit project is not only much less elaborated but also much more open to formalistic concessions. The pioneering aspects of the new dimension of his design are seriously limited by the evident compromise between a proposal on the metropolitan scale and the somewhat superfluous character of the project itself. In this sense, it is significant that the Detroit skyscraper is much closer than those designed for Chicago to the towers Saarinen introduced as formal accents in his urban plans of the 1910s—for example, the town hall of Reval and the parliament buildings of Canberra or Helsinki—or to the skyscraper in the form of a fantastically represented mountain in a 1908 drawing by Saarinen, which foreshadows the images of Hugh Ferriss.[78] The isolated Detroit skyscraper is essentially a return to the project for the *Chicago Tribune* competition, and it is also similar to the unexecuted project for the Burton Memorial at Ann Arbor, designed by Saarinen in 1925 at the request of the students of the University of Michigan.[79]

This similarity is not, however, indicative of a casual regression. As was already evident in his 1922 skyscraper design, the "eloquence" of Saarinen's "enchanted mountains" derived in great part from their conception as spectators of the urban scene. This, indeed, was the role explicitly reserved for the two high buildings of the Chicago lakefront; the enchantment of the skyscraper was assured by its extraneousness to the commercial center.

In my view it was not merely the chance occasions of work that led Saarinen to abandon his researches on the level of urban design after 1925 and to embrace the late romantic, communal ideas of George G. Booth with great conviction.[80] In the Chicago lakefront project, the tradition of civic art in Sitte's terms was resolved in an urban-design proposal that was new in its complexity and scale; in the Cranbrook campus, this tradition was isolated in an anachronistic nostalgia for the bygone values of the extraurban world of the craftsman.[81]

The Regional Plan of New York and Its Environs and the Problem of Congestion

The concept of planning the city center as an integrated system and the close association of multifunctional skyscrapers, railroad stations and parking facilities, and open spaces adapted to civic use was proposed by Saarinen at a moment when American urbanism was suffering serious defeats. The Finnish architect's plans were, in fact, in a certain sense, in keeping with progressive ideas of civic improvement. Slightly later, in 1927, Richard Neutra, like Saarinen, was prompted to delineate projects of a sectorial nature that nevertheless affected the entire metropolitan area.[82] The European architects obviously felt strongly the need for comprehensive control over the dynamics of the city, a goal that proved immediately antithetical, however, to the laws of urban growth and to the organization of the construction industry in America. In any case, the European architects clearly viewed the skyscraper very differently from their American colleagues.

In 1922, Perret designed his utopian urban structure of isolated skyscrapers and Le Corbusier exhibited his "city for three million inhabitants," followed in 1924 by Lissitsky and Stam's project for a ring of skyscrapers around the center of Moscow. Indeed, the European avant-garde demonstrated an almost mythical faith in a building type they had still not tried out directly and just when Americans were discovering the economic disadvantages of tall buildings and a critical analysis of the skyscraper was revealing its technological contradictions.

The New York zoning law, enacted in 1916, and that of Chicago, enacted 1923, exercised only minimal controls over the use of urban space and lacked any provisions for public investment. Such laws could hardly encourage the unified, coordinated type of undertaking proposed by Saarinen; they merely regulated the current practice of isolated building projects in the business centers dominated by the corporations. Instead, it was in the context of attempts at regional planning between 1920 and 1930 that new utopian conceptions of control over urban concentration were delineated. The Regional Plan of New York and Its Environs, promoted by the Russell Sage Foundation and directed by Thomas Adams, is a particularly significant example, since it represents an extreme compromise between regional planning and the "philosophy" of zoning. Prepared in the years immediately preceding the crash of 1929 and covering the entire range of urban problems brought to the fore in the 1920s, this plan is a major episode in the process considered here.

The year 1929 clearly marked a turning point in the history of the cities in the United States. Paradoxically, the last large building projects were undertaken in the heart of Manhattan and Philadelphia just at the time of the great crash—Rockefeller Center, the Philadelphia Saving Fund Society Building, and the Empire State Building were built between 1929 and the early 1930s on the basis of earlier investments and took advantage of the favorable economic conditions for construction brought about by the depression. At the same time, however, the American metropolises with their internal imbalances began to undergo a radical transformation, which was brought about precisely by the effects of the anticyclical economic measures that were gradually put into operation. This transformation was due less to any degree of public control over high-level capital investment than to a shift of interest from the city as a place of autonomous production and a source of capital accumulation to the region as a coordinated whole. The control of relations between production and consumption became the new utopia; the housing problem and the question of energy sources sprang to center stage as areas in which to test the anticyclical effectiveness of government interventions.

It would be possible to analyze at length the encounters and clashes between the progressive American intelligentsia—with the Regional Planning Association of America in the front ranks—and the empirical economic planning of the New Deal. It is more significant, however, to point out that precisely during the crucial years of the depression, while federal measures were concentrated on restraining unemployment (8,000,000 were unemployed in 1931 and 13,000,000 in 1932, according to the official statistics), initiatives in regional economic planning were put into operation; they were certainly still confined to the limbo of general ideology but were nevertheless supported by federal and local governments.

In 1932, while still governor of New York, Franklin D. Roosevelt recalled a meeting with Charles Dyer Norton that had taken place in 1909 and declared his interest in "not the mere planning of a single city but in the larger aspects of planning," adding that "perhaps the day is not far distant when planning will become a part of the national policy of this country."[83] For Roosevelt, this goal meant pressing for the actual institutionalization of planning, in other words, for control over the relations between investments and consumption, determined within a spatial dimension most suitable to its realization—the dimension of the region, defined in terms of its integrated functions.

Roosevelt's reference to Norton's studies was not merely casual. It was on the basis of his research that, beginning in 1923, Thomas Adams directed the elaboration of a regional plan for the New York City region. Thus the initiatives of Norton, of Alfred White, and of Robert W. de Forest were continued in the work of Adams and the Committee on the Regional Plan of New York and Its Environs, of which Norton was chairman from 1921 until his death in 1923.[84] In exactly the same year as Adams began research for the Regional Plan of New York, the Regional Planning Association of America was founded. A history of the movement for regional planning in the United States could demonstrate that Adams's plan for New York, which became the object of great controversy in 1932, constituted both a moment of crisis in the regionalist ideology and a wasted opportunity for carrying out a general study on the restructuring of the economic cycles of the building industry and the rebuilding of the metropolitan centers.

The Englishman Thomas Adams, much respected for his earlier work in Canada, had been a supporter of regional integration, of control of natural resources and sources of energy, and of control over real estate speculation. In 1926 he was able to describe publicly a preliminary draft of the Regional Plan of New York. The ample funds at the committee's disposal made possible extensive exploration of the geophysical, economic, and urban features of the five hundred communities in the 5,528 square miles of Greater New York (roughly the area that had been defined years before by Norton).

The plan was envisaged on the scale of 20,000,000 inhabitants, which calculations indicated would be the population of the New York City region within thirty or forty years. As a guide to development, the plan was limited to general and preliminary provisions, elastic in time; the development of the details was left to the local communities. The first phase of the study confirmed the strict complementarity between the metropolitan regions of New York and New Jersey, recognized by earlier investigators. The principle of complementarity of regional structures was at the base of Adams's hypotheses. Indeed, the 1926 preliminary plan already projected the creation of a system of transportation routes connecting Long Island and New Jersey, on the one hand, and the Bronx and Queens, on the other, without directly involving the area of Manhattan. On the basis of economic analyses made by Robert M. Haig, which revealed a tendency toward decentralization of commercial enterprises away from Manhattan to the suburbs of Brooklyn, the Bronx, and Queens, Adams proposed a

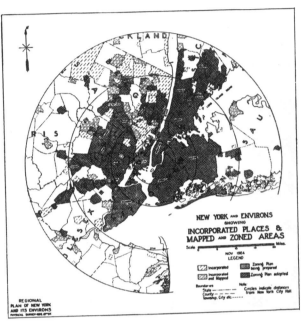

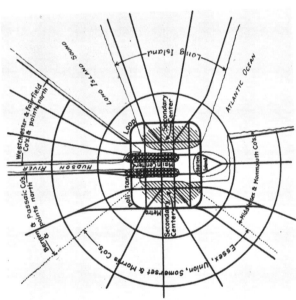

Regional Plan of New York and Its Environs,
map indicating the zoning legislation situation of the various parts of the New York
City region in November 1924.

Regional Plan of New York and Its Environs,
diagram of regional functions and relative
transportation systems.

network of minor commercial centers and satellite communities. The reduction in commuting to and from Manhattan was thus presented as a means of safeguarding the "vital pulse of the region." Shorter distances between residences and places of work were part of an attempt to touch off a process of reequilibration through a more controlled use of space, restrictions on the right to its use, and new regulations for the use of space within the city center.

Apart from his vagueness about ways of implementing the plan, Adams seems up to this point to have agreed with the guiding principles of the Regional Planning Association of America. This agreement was only apparent, however. Rather than opposing the "philosophy" of zoning, which was then revealing its inefficiency as a means of indirect control, Adams's conception of the region as the unitary entity of the undertaking left it intact;[85] in the case of New York the regionalist concept was conditioned from the very beginning by the weight of the already existing concentration. Meanwhile, however, with the elaboration of the plan of the Philadelphia Tri-State District, the formation of the Chicago Regional Planning Association, and similar initiatives in Los Angeles, the United States appeared pervaded by a genuine enthusiasm for regional planning.[86] The limitations of Adams's plan were immediately noted by Lewis Mumford and were to become but ever more evident during the depression years, when the completed plan lay unexecuted.

Under the impulse given to the ideal of planning by Governor Franklin D. Roosevelt, in the last of the many publications on the Regional Plan of New York and Its Environs, *The Building of the City*, issued in 1931, Adams presented its building programs in perspective images. This was far more than a mere academic exercise; through these visualizations Adams pointedly intended to "educate" the citizenry to the plan. In his view, "the highest art of city building" is that produced out of "the desires and impulses of a free people": "If the future of the city is to be developed in greater perfection it will be because of the public demand. What that demand will be will depend on the education, guidance and inspiration given by those who, by reason of knowledge and understanding are given the power to lead." Thus there could be no imperative plan, no coercion. Instead, a regional plan would be put into operation spontaneously by citizens conscious of the necessity for self-government: "We can only hope that education will develop foresight, that the greatness of the need will develop a passion for improvement, and that both things will lead to unity of action so that the New York-New Jersey metropolitan region shall achieve unique distinction among great city-regions for the order and true economy, the balance and true dignity of its buildings."[87]

Realism and abstraction are strangely mixed in these assertions. Adams was so concerned not to interfere in any way with existing rights and institutions that he rejected even the possibility of public intervention in low-cost housing. In keeping with this fundamental principle, he placed all his hopes in an "education to the plan" that would somehow, miraculously, overcome all the merciless

economic laws of capitalism in cyclical phase. His invocations of good will had
something of an Enlightenment air about them and ring false in the tragic years
of the depression and the manifest impotence of the Hoover administration.

The ideology inherent in the Regional Plan of New York is incomprehensible,
however, unless it is seen in relation to the urban principles of its sponsor, the
Russell Sage Foundation. Both Adams and the Russell Sage Foundation were, in
fact, perfect interpreters of the concept of slum clearance in its dual aims of
philanthropy and real estate speculation. Both Henry Wright and Lewis Mumford were to attack severely the practice that considers the housing question in
terms of slum clearance; for them, the real problem was that of creating systems
that would make the formation of slums impossible. On the contrary, however,
philanthropically inclined American capitalism quite logically welcomed occasions for investment in slum clearance. The project for the Lower East Side of
Manhattan, which I shall examine shortly, was a significant example.

In accord with this outlook, Adams and the Russell Sage Foundation supported a type of control left to the purely "restrictive" zoning legislation.
Edward M. Bassett, legal director of the Regional Plan, had been one of the
principal authors of the New York zoning ordinance in 1916. Bassett, Nelson P.
Lewis, executive engineer of the Regional Plan, and Frederick Law Olmsted, Jr.,
who was also involved in Adams's project, all three members of the Advisory
Committee on Zoning of the United States Department of Commerce, were
among the authors of a document used extensively by the staff of the Regional
Plan—A Zoning Primer, published in 1922 by the Department of Commerce. In
addition, Bassett, Lewis, Olmsted, and most of the members of the depart-
mental Advisory Committee were supporters of the Housing Reform movement.

Their concept of the housing problem was thus the complete opposite of that
of the Regional Planning Association of America. The zoning they defended
tended not only to confirm and increase real estate values in the urban area but
also to stimulate the dynamics of the building market in congested zones, giving
rise to an inflationary process. The zoning of Bassett and Adams was to be
attacked as an instrument of speculation by Wood, Whitaker, and Hegemann.[88]
Although the limitations of the 1916 zoning law were criticized in the Russell
Sage Foundation plan for New York, the revisions of this law the plan called for
could not in any way overcome its inherent characteristics. What I have called
the "Enlightenment" character of Adams's ideology may be better understood
in the light of these considerations.

In any case, as part of the effort to arouse a spontaneous civic consciousness
for the betterment of the urban environment, the plan was set forth in The
Building of the City in terms of images visualizing the future New York. To the
same end, Adams's book also offered studies of the massing of commercial
edifices according to new building regulations, research on transportation
systems and services, proposals for civic centers in Brooklyn and Newark, for

settlements, and for a host of undertakings within Manhattan, including the architectural development of the waterfronts.

In analyzing Adams's proposals, Mel Scott has observed quite accurately that many of the designs prepared for the occasion demonstrate the survival of the taste of the City Beautiful.[89] This was not the only anachronistic aspect of the plan, however. Despite the regional extent of the provisions, Adams's New York is completely turned in on itself. It has merit only as a balanced composition of commercial and residential structures; the principle of decentralization is taken up purely as a means of effecting urban decongestion, not in terms of the region as a new productive entity. Adams spoke of the region as a unit, but only to indicate variously proportioned areas of land destined for public or private use and to prescribe a policy of acquisition on the part of the communities. Nor did the principle of decentralization contradict intense concentration of construction in his view. Adams, in fact, seems to have tended toward the idea of a *ville radieuse;* for certain precisely delimited zones he accepted a construction based on skyscrapers of unlimited height, provided services, open areas, transportation systems, and parking facilities could be dimensioned according to adequate standards.[90]

The most ambiguous aspect of the Regional Plan of New York, however, is precisely its response to the problem of congestion. The Regional Survey's statistical analysis of the distribution of building bulk in central-city areas constituted, in effect, a demonstration of the economic disadvantages of high-concentration construction. In 1931 Adams summarized the results of the Regional Survey as follows:

1) The density of building that is economically sound is that which can be maintained without excessive cost for locomotion in all its forms. The question of what bulk pays best in relation to a given cost of land, or what height is made possible by invention of new methods of building construction are of secondary importance. To ascertain what is an ideal degree of concentration of building, we have first to discover what is the degree of concentration that can be most efficiently and economically served by railroads, transit lines and streets. Anything which exceeds that degree of concentration is excessive from an economic point of view. One of the greatest needs in New York City and the surrounding Region is to follow the making of the Regional Plan with the preparation of a carefully worked out estimate of the extent to which means of locomotion can be provided, in the future, to supply the needs of any given degree and character of concentration of building and population. What is required is a full and continuous investigation and a carefully prepared analysis by public authorities of the relation between transportation, transit and traffic, and different degrees of building density and different kinds of building uses. The making of this estimate would involve large expenditures and a continuous process of inquiry over a period of years by each of the more populous cities in the Region.
2) The physical characteristics of the New York region do not afford a sufficient excuse for excessive concentration in any of its parts, for instance in Manhattan, because in the first place it is probably more economical to overcome these obstructions by the erection of bridges and tunnels than to overcome the defects of congestion, and in the second place there is adequate land space to provide for all urban growth without overcrowding any part.
3) The forces that will continue to make New York grow will be the continued effectiveness of its transportation facilities to serve industrial and residential functions and the attainment of a better balanced distribution of these facilities and functions.

ARCHITECTURAL STUDY OF TYPE OF DEVELOPMENT SUGGESTED ALONG A RAISED EAST WATERFRONT SECTION FROM E 32ND TO E 40TH STREETS (OLD LONG ISLAND FERRY AND TOWER HOUSES)

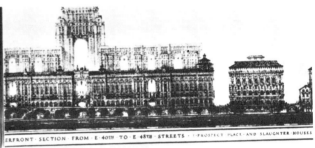

ARCHITECTURAL STUDY OF TYPE OF DEVELOPMENT SUGGESTED ALONG A RAISED EAST WATERFRONT SECTION FROM E 40TH TO E 48TH STREETS (PROSPECT PLACE AND SLAUGHTER HOUSES)

ARCHITECTURAL STUDY OF TYPE OF DEVELOPMENT SUGGESTED ALONG A RAISED EAST WATERFRONT SECTION FROM E 48TH TO E 56TH STREETS (BEEKMAN PLACE TO SUTTON PLACE)

ARCHITECTURAL STUDY OF TYPE OF DEVELOPMENT SUGGESTED ALONG A RAISED EAST WATERFRONT SECTION FROM E 79TH TO E 87TH STREETS (VICINITY OF CARL SCHURZ PARK)

Regional Plan of New York and Its Environs,
proposal for the architectural development
of the East River waterfront between 32nd
and 87th streets, visualized in drawings by
Francis S. Swales.

4) The degree of light and access to outer air that is necessary in buildings for health is also economically desirable, as it is one of the best means of maintaining property values.[91]

Adams's four points agree perfectly with the conclusions of a study on the skyscraper by Frederick A. Delano, published in 1926 in the *American City*, as well as with the first investigations of the Committee on the Regional Plan of New York; both recognized a close relationship between periods of crisis in the development of the rapid-transit systems and moments in which a reform of the building code regulating building heights and construction density appeared urgent.[92] Moreover, the Regional Survey agreed with a study made by the Building Owners and Managers Association of New York in indicating a surplus of office space in the area of Manhattan.[93] For a total of 291 buildings, the investigation showed that 2,000,000 square feet were unrented in 97 buildings in the Grand Central area; 800,000 square feet, in the downtown financial district; and 500,000, in the plaza district between 50th and 62nd streets. Despite this situation, 3,500,000 square feet of office space were in the course of construction and would be ready for rental in 1931. Thus the proportion of unrented space was 5 percent in the downtown area, 10.9 percent in the City Hall district, 11.8 percent in the Grand Central area, and 25.4 percent in the area of the Plaza.

The conclusions drawn from these studies all indicated the necessity of applying the principle of a "reasonable speculation," through limitations on building heights, requirements for space between constructions, new regulations for the massing of buildings, and criteria for dimensional limitations on construction devised in relation to the transportation systems.[94] Thus the city center continued to be considered an agglomeration of lots, for which the collectivity could demand no more than the good will of private individuals and firms in limiting possible profits in order to attain a still greater yield over a longer period of time. Quite beyond the weakness of the regulations proposed, the collectivity remained without defenses. In Adams's words,

Improvement in the central area depends mainly on the voluntary action of owners of property and on their initiative in obtaining collaboration from the city in reducing densities.

There are only two definite directions in which improvement can be obtained in the central areas. One is by amending the zoning law so as to obtain the maximum restriction that the owners will approve in reducing heights and areas of occupancy; and the other by carrying out elaborate physical improvements in the areas of highest density, such as the widening of streets or the building of streets and sidewalks on two levels. [italics added][95]

With this statement Adams took a stand against the proposals for a special tax on high buildings, as well as against the ideas of Raymond Hood, who, making himself the spokesman of the New York speculators, argued against the practicality of this combination of new regulations with a hypothetical collaboration between private concerns and public powers; Hood proposed, instead, a simple ratio of 12 to 1 between constructed areas and surrounding streets. Writing in 1929 in the *Nation's Business*, the organ of the National Chamber of Commerce, Hood offered a model of center-city concentration that was in a certain way prophetic.[96] The type of skyscraper he proposed was actually a "City under a Single Roof." His construction would occupy three blocks, with the possibility of being extended into the surrounding area. The ground level would be left for traffic and parking; the second through the tenth floors, allotted to storage space, stores, theaters, and so on; the eleventh through the twenty-fifth, office space; the twenty-sixth through the thirty-fifth, clubs, restaurants, and hotels; the uppermost floors would be reserved for residential apartments. Place of work, residence, and recreation facilities were thus united in a single structure, which Hood hailed as a panacea for metropolitan ills that would eliminate commuting and congestion and offer enviable social services and urban standards.

The building with which Hood exemplified his proposal was a cross-plan skyscraper, the arms formed by blocks lower than the central core; with different functional characteristics, it revived Adler and Sullivan's 1881 design for the Odd Fellows Temple. What is of greater interest, however, is the centralization of residence and place of work in a single structure. This was an anticipation of the super-skyscrapers of the 1960s and 1970s, but with one difference—Hood theorized an almost complete reconstruction of Manhattan on the basis of his model, to be carried out within about twenty years. This hypertrophic concentration, which would eliminate not only the phenomenon of commuting but also, paradoxically, the drama of congestion, was valid only if New York could be transformed into a *ville radieuse.* Farther on I shall discuss how Hood intended to extend his utopia over the entire grid of New York; what is important at this point is that Hood's article and proposal were a blatant contradiction of any idea of decentralization.

Adams's declarations on improving the center-city areas certainly make no concessions to the commercial center as a functional unity. The new standards and regulations proposed in the Regional Plan of New York were limited to assuring that skyscrapers would be surrounded by ample spaces for public use and by low buildings, with the more general aim of creating a series of "nerve centers," or nodal points, of composite function (industry, business, residence, educational and recreational facilities).[97] The comprehensive model that emerges from the plan is an organization of such centers in a network dominated by Mahnattan, the primary "nerve center." The desired urban equilibrium was thus obtained through a series of cautious compromises between the confirmation of centralization and the organization of a massive decentralization.[98] "It is probable," wrote Adams, "that the Utopia of the perfect 'garden city' will influence future urban growth in the New York region at least as much as the Utopia of the perfect 'skyscraper city' and that the expansion of the city-region will evolve along lines that will show an attempt, at least, to embrace the best features of both."[99] With this statement Adams admitted the impracticability of any single model for such a complex structure, and recognized, in his own way, that the proposition of a city of any single tendency was a utopian one.

A unitary character was sought, however, in the treatment of individual portions of the plan, particularly the city center, where the skyscraper was envisaged, as in E. Maxwell Fry's drawings of the future skyline of Manhattan, as the informing element of programmatically coordinated rebuilding projects. [100] The proposals for downtown Manhattan concentrated, in fact, on a few eminently architectonic complexes (such as City Hall Square, Battery Park, and the waterfronts) and on introducing a multileveled traffic system with elevated walkways and arcades for pedestrians, which recalled Corbett's studies made for such a project. [101] It is essentially only in this last proposal that the plan offered anything like a comprehensive restructuring of the city center, and even this was merely a rationalization in minimal terms of the existing situation.

Perhaps the most complete image of the new organization envisaged for the subcentral areas is provided by the project for the renewal of the Lower East Side of Manhattan. The starting point for an economic revitalization of the degraded area extending from 14th Street south to the Manhattan Bridge and inland from the East River to Third Avenue and the Bowery was to be the creation of a parkway between Chrystie and Forsyth streets. The plan for this area also foresaw the development of middle-class dwellings and low-cost housing, along with various social facilities, services, and a system of streets and sidewalks on two levels, and assumed the continuous development of a series of isolated commercial skyscrapers to either side of the projected Chrystie-Forsyth Parkway. [102] In this specific project, as in many of the plan's other general suggestions, it is possible to recognize a premise and stimulus to projects actually undertaken later on. On the Lower East Side, Peter Cooper Village and Stuyvesant Town, in their dreariness, still bear witness to attempts at a renewal of this area. Similarly, in many other districts of New York the Regional Plan inspired building projects or the construction of transportation facilities on a small and a large scale. [103] The perspective drawings by Cass Gilbert, Hugh Ferriss, E. Maxwell Fry, Harvey Wiley Corbett, and Francis S. Swales, which presented visualizations of the plan's architectural proposals, had therefore the same value as the elaborate drawings with which Burnham's plan for Chicago had been presented to the public.

Once the general criteria for the undertaking were established, city planning could revert to the techniques of the City Beautiful, even if the architectural language was now different and open to choice. The City Beautiful presentation in itself is far less significant, however, than the attempt to demonstrate that the superurban fantasies of Fry or Ferriss could take their place as part of the ideology and hypotheses of the Russell Sage Foundation undertaking; for the Regional Plan of New York and Its Environs, there was no contradiction between Radburn and Rockefeller Center. It is on this very point that Mumford based his criticism of the plan. [104] For him, Adams's plan, despite its projected garden cities and its regional extent, merely confirmed the chaotic methods that normally governed urban growth. Indeed, in Mumford's view, the Russell Sage

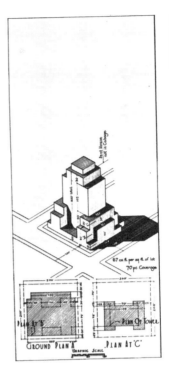
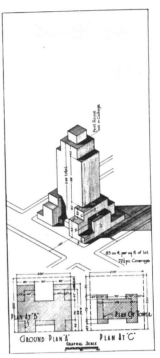
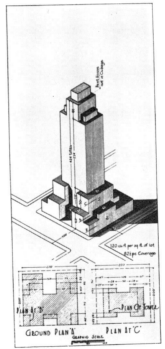
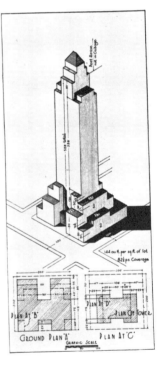

Regional Plan of New York and Its Environs,
recommended regulations for the massing
and heights of buildings in the business
centers of areas of various size and location:
upper left, close suburban or intermediate
areas (smaller communities); *upper right*,
close suburban or intermediate areas (larger
communities); *lower left*, subcentral areas
(in New York City and in the largest of the
surrounding cities); *lower right*, central
areas (New York City).

Regional Plan of New York and Its Environs, drawings of past, present, and future skylines by E. Maxwell Fry: *above*, skyline of medieval Antwerp; *center*, New York's artificial mountain range in the 1920s; *below*, the future city of towers.

Regional Plan of New York and Its Environs, proposals made by Harvey Wiley Corbett about 1923 for a separated traffic system in Manhattan.

Regional Plan of New York and Its Environs, plan of the Lower East Side, showing the parks and street widenings proposed as part of the project of revitalization of this area.

Regional Plan of New York and Its Environs, view of the proposed Chrystie-Forsyth Parkway, part of the project of revitalization of the Lower East Side, as visualized by E. Maxwell Fry.

Proposal by George B. Ford for an apartment house complex of setback skyscrapers in New York City, indicated in the Regional Plan as an example of urban reorganization.

Regional Plan of New York and Its Environs, portion of the tower city of the future visualized in a drawing by E. Maxwell Fry.

plan favored metropolitan concentration. Writing in 1932, Mumford noted that
Adams foresaw an intensive concentration even in suburban areas; the fact that
it would be subject to regulations only confirmed the basic acceptance of the
idea of centralization. Furthermore, Mumford considered the very definition of
the region of New York as presented by Adams to be "a purely arbitrary
concept, based upon future possibilities of transportation and past facts of city
growth."[105]

According to Mumford, Adams's plan was based on one fundamental principle—that the city continue to be developed according to the rules that had
governed its growth up to that time. The plan, a scheme to be carried out
roughly within the next thirty-five years, was projected into the future, but its
outlook was that of the immediate tomorrow. Mumford concluded that the
Regional Plan of New York and Its Environs "was conceived . . . in terms which
would meet the interests and prejudices of the existing financial rulers . . . and
its aim from the beginning was as much welfare and amenity as could be
obtained without altering any of the political or business institutions which have
made the city precisely what it is."[106] In this view Mumford was resolute.
Genuine regional planning could not be based on the existing institutions; its
principal task was the reform of the institutions and the creation of means of
control over the dynamics of the territory. Institutional reform was the premise
for regional planning.[107]

Adams responded to this vehement attack in the pages of the *New Republic*,
which had carried Mumford's articles, and his line of defense was characteristic:
"I would rather have the evils that go with freedom than have a perfect physical
order achieved at the price of freedom." He defined Mumford "an esthete-
sociologist, who has a religion that is based on high ideals but is unworkable."
Emphasizing that the urban control demanded by Mumford required the direct
action of a "despotic government," Adams implicitly accused his adversary of
collectivism.[108] Mumford's criticisms, like those expressed earlier by Edith
Elmer Wood, touched on concepts in the field of regional planning that the
Regional Planning Association of America would attempt to promote within the
politics of the New Deal, primarily public intervention as a regulating factor in
the economy of the building industry and as an incentive to the technological
renewal of construction methods. In its indecisiveness and ambiguity the
Regional Plan of New York was unable to contribute to fulfilling such needs
even in the circumscribed field of the structures of the commercial center.
Despite the vagueness of its aspirations, the principle of an "equilibrated centralization" might have led to the formulation of hypotheses for control over the
sector of the building industry involved in high-concentration construction, in
terms of a rationalization of production and a dynamics in keeping with the
commercial city. The abstractly "democratic" tone of Adams's proposals, however, was poorly adapted to set off innovative processes in the urban economy of
the country. In this sense, the Regional Plan of New York and Its Environs was
tied to the past; its outlook was confined within the limits of the 1920s.

This limitation does not mean, however, that no reverberations of the plan were felt beyond its specific content. On the contrary, between 1928 and 1930, in the wake of the interest the plan aroused, the subject of the destiny of Manhattan and the chaotic conditions that prevented it from functioning as a general service in the direction of the nation's economy came strikingly to the fore in the form of proposals for a comprehensive control of its physical structure. Even if ingenuously formulated, the problem of the coordinated restructuring of the major business center of the United States was finally posed, and the proliferation of individual initiatives was recognized as contrary to the essential unity of its function. The projects of Ferriss and Hood, which I shall discuss briefly, may be considered the first acknowledgment of the need to make the city center function as a unified structure in the service of collective capital.

Hugh Ferriss: Ode to the Skyscraper

It is impossible to ignore the relationship between Thomas Adams's proposals for Manhattan and Hugh Ferriss's *Metropolis of Tomorrow*. In this volume, published in 1929, the former draftsman of Cass Gilbert, Corbett, and Hood translated the images suggested by the rebuilding programs of the Regional Plan of New York into the vision of a late romantic utopia.[109]

Ferriss's role in the development of a "poetic of the skyscraper" is generally exaggerated. Even Vincent Scully has seen in Ferriss's designs a stimulus for the interpretation of the building regulations of New York's 1916 zoning law in a decidedly expressionistic key.[110] According to Scully's interpretation, the vision of the metropolis Ferriss offered is a translation into urban terms of the overwhelming wilderness of the Grand Canyon; the city of skyscrapers appears as a new, indomitable nature, extraordinary and alarming in its stupefying potential. Undeniably, in his graphic rendering of such works as the Waldorf-Astoria Office Building by Shreve, Lamb and Harmon or the Chanin Building by Sloan and Robertson, Ferriss tended to present the architectural language of the new skyscrapers of New York or other American cities as a savage primitivism. Similarly, in attempting to derive a formal optimum of massing from the regulations of the New York zoning ordinance, Ferriss seized on the pregnant expressivity of the high-rise complex evoked by continually setback profiles.[111] In his own words, however, for the designer, this represented merely "the rough shapes with which he must deal . . . the crude clay of the future city."[112] Ferriss considered this primitivism only a phase, one rich in a potential that had to be unleashed and, of necessity, given an organization.[113]

From this point of view, the designs of his "imaginary metropolis" are symptomatic as well as disappointing. While Ferriss's images certainly give full reign to the concept of the skyscraper expressed by Saarinen in his *Chicago Tribune* design, the plan of Ferriss's city, dominated by a triangle at the vertices of which are situated the Business Center, Art Center, and Science Center, is no more than an updated version of the classic precapitalist utopia, in this case one with a theosophical flavor. The circle inscribed with two intersecting triangles, which connect the buildings of the city center and the central avenues of the street network that radiates from this center, has an explicit symbolic significance. What Ferriss presents with prophetic import and overlaid with humanistic finality is actually nothing more than a typical "regressive utopia," an ingenuous attempt to reintegrate the universe of "values" in the city dominated by the "flux of the monetary current."[114]

The historical significance of the designs of this able conjurer of images lies in their poetic celebration of the skyscraper. The skyscraper is "sung" by Ferriss in an attempt to restore an "enchantment" to what could by this time be only a "disenchanted mountain." In this sense Ferriss was Saarinen's only follower in the 1920s, and with reason; only as a purely literary image could the skyscraper any longer assume an "aura." The results of the *Chicago Tribune* competition had made this quite clear.

Nevertheless, between 1920 and 1930 not only all the architectural journals but also other publications were frequently illustrated with drawings by Ferriss; the general public could identify urbanized America with his exalted images of skyscrapers. Significantly, Ferriss worked for the Russell Sage Foundation and the Regional Plan of New York. His alluring visions of the city of the future served as propaganda for the type of control offered by zoning and the concept of "regulated speculation." William H. Jordy has written:

In extending the contemporary Gothic esthetic toward the Metropolis of Tomorrow, Ferriss depended on a composite of contrary influences: on Le Corbusier's "radiant cities" of widely spaced skyscrapers, but as modified by New York density and Beaux-Arts composition and symbolism. The entire population of this imaginary metropolis seems to have lived a glamorously decadent penthouse existence replete with martinis and costume balls, as though the milieu of *The Great Gatsby* had been transported from East and West Egg to Manhattan. Social considerations, except as they affected the limousine set, were nil.[115]

Ferriss's images conveyed the idea of an adventurous, epic construction of the city by mythic, superhuman forces. During the depression years, this interpretation of the dynamics of the city, in which Ferriss uninhibitedly mixed Futurist suggestions with Beaux-Arts tradition, appeared hopelessly anachronistic. Similarly anachronistic was his utopian proposal for a reconciliation of these constructive forces with a wholly pre-Enlightenment concept of the entity *man*. The anguished atmosphere of his drawings belonged to a bygone world; anguish in the face of a potential revealed as uncontrollable by the individual could by this time take form only as a stylistic mannerism, or at best as nostalgia.

Yet this process reflects exactly what took place in the construction of the great metropolitan centers of America in the years between 1920 and 1930. The introduction of zoning in New York did not give rise to any structural reconsiderations. The setback skyscraper—exactly as advocated by Adler and Sullivan—entered the panorama of the American city as an "individual". Although indifferent to problems of true quality, in keeping with the pragmatic tradition, this individual was carefully outfitted with suitable ceremonial dress. The models could vary; indeed; the years from 1923 to 1932—from Saarinen's interpretation

Third of four solutions studied for setback skyscrapers (from Hugh Ferriss, *The Metropolis of Tomorrow*, 1929).

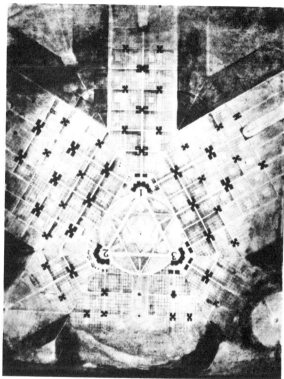

Plan for the center of the "imaginary metropolis" (from Hugh Ferriss, *The Metropolis of Tomorrow*, 1929).

View of the business center of the "imaginary metropolis" (from Hugh Ferriss, *The Metropolis of Tomorrow*, 1929).

of the skyscraper to the exhibition of the International style at the Museum of Modern Art in New York[116]—were characterized by a proliferation of formal themes and linguistic references, which were generally divorced from structural problems and would largely be put aside in the early 1930s. From this point of view, the two decorative styles that invaded the American skyscraper during this period were only apparently contradictory. The decorations of a vaguely Mayan flavor (the vagueness of the cultural reference was essential to its pragmatic use) and those inspired by Art Deco, merely corresponded to two different but equally ideal pursuits. The former, relating the metropolis to the native and primordial cultures of pre-Columbian America, sought to assert the "new primitivism" of the developing commercial city; the latter, by adopting stereotyped forms of a purely decorative and unrhetorical nature, attempted an alignment with bourgeois European taste and its more moderate figurative tendencies.[117]

A rapid review of the activity of a typical professional, such as Raymond Hood, between 1922 and 1931 may serve to clarify this situation.[118]

Raymond Hood: From the Tribune Tower to "Manhattan 1950"

In 1924, while the Chicago Tribune Building was on its way to completion, Hood's American Radiator Building rose in New York City, a tower overlooking Bryant Park and perceptible as an isolated object. In this work the rarefied Gothicism of the Tribune Tower disappeared in favor of a structure that diminishes in a series of setbacks, accelerated in their succession toward the top and emphasized by the stone pinnacles that contrast with the homogeneous wall surfaces of black brick. If the form of the terminal structures and the corners of the edifice cut at 45-degree angles still recall the Chicago skyscraper, in the over-all form of the American Radiator Building it is not difficult to detect Saarinen's influence.

It is simply impossible, however, to expect any linguistic consistency whatsoever from Hood. While a subdued Neogothic reappears in his Bethany Union Church in Chicago (1926), in his design for the Central Methodist Episcopal Church in Columbus, Ohio, and in the Masonic Temple and Scottish Rite Cathedral in Scranton, Pennsylvania (1929), suggestions from the Perpendicular Gothic are enriched by notable innovations in the design of the organism. In these same years a superficial adherence to Loos's purism is demonstrated in Hood's National Radiator Building in London (1928), an austere structure in polished black granite against which the Baroque-like ornamentation of bronze and multicolored vitreous enamels of the entrance, show windows, and terminal decoration make a striking contrast.[119] Just two years later, however, in the Beaux-Arts Apartments in New York (1930), carried out in collaboration with Murchinson, Godley and Fouilhoux, Hood adopted a stylistic expression wavering between the International style and the influence of Art Deco and an organism vaguely suggestive of the architecture of Michel Roux-Spitz. When called upon to design the McCormick Mausoleum in Rockford, Illinois, in 1927, however, Hood had not hesitated to produce a sort of dolmen naturalistically

60 Wall Tower, New York, view of a model
of a vaguely Mayan-inspired skyscraper
placed above one of its entrances, building
designed by Clinton and Russell, Holton
and George, 1930-32.

carved from the local rock, with a primitivism evocative of Richardson. In this case, the explanation for the stylistic turnabout is simple: the McCormick Mausoleum was intended to celebrate the return to nature of a giant of business enterprise, and a romantic treatment was thus required.[120]

Hood's attitude was far from being simply a remarkable open-mindedness; instead, his versatility conformed to a precise professional calculation—between architecture and capitalistic development there must be not merely an alliance, but a close collaboration. In Hood's view, the architect had to be capable of assuming responsibility not only for the economy of his building in itself but also the long-term commercial operations that would take place there, the formal aspects of which are charged to his care by his client. In a statement quoted by Arthur T. North, Hood affirmed:

The success of a building is measured by the degree of satisfaction to its occupants in its use, by its economic soundness and its acceptability to the public, all of which are contingent upon the adequacy of the plan. While there are similarities common to the plans for all types of urban buildings, they are individually conditioned by the limitations of the plot; by building ordinance requirements; by cost of land and building construction, taxes, overhead charges, available funds and other items. The architect demonstrates his professional ability by correctly correlating all of these factors in the production of a successful building.[121]

Certainly Hood's professional ability in this sense was remarkable, as one of his former assistants recently recalled.[122] The range of his economic considerations did not exceed the limits of the individual undertaking, however. One would search in vain in Hood's writings for any concrete analysis of the building industry as such. He was therefore the ideal architect for the great private patrons of the 1920s and 1930s.

Writing in 1932 on the design work for Rockefeller Center, then in progress, Hood defined the approach of this building operation as one of "cost and return." Although he knew this to be an idea "unpalatable to some architects"— the reference to Frank Lloyd Wright and the "architectural left" led by Mumford was quite explicit—he was nevertheless convinced that "being obliged to make a project stand on its own financial feet and to submit its details and materials to a constant critical analysis leads to honesty and integrity of design."[123]

It was with the same outlook that Hood produced the two works with which he made his most outstanding contribution to the linguistic development of the skyscraper: the Daily News (1930), jointly with Howells, and McGraw Hill (1931) buildings in New York. Once again, no cultural hypotheses need be advanced on the geneses of these buildings. Like Hood's previous works, they came into being from the exigency of creating architectonic structures that in themselves functioned as publicity.[124] In the Daily News Building, this end was achieved by the uninterrupted vertical thrust of the white piers, further enhanced by the contrast of the spandrel panels of black and dark red brick laid in an interlaced pattern. It could be obtained equally well, however, by the elements of a vaguely Mendelsohnian flavor that form the crowning and articulate the wall at ground level of the McGraw-Hill Building, completely faced with rectangular blocks of glazed blue-green terracotta.[125]

Both skyscrapers were to rise on 42nd Street, and thus in an area that had still not been subjected to high-concentration construction at the time they were built. Like the Chanin Building and the Chrysler Building, both near the Daily News, they were pioneering enterprises, and Hood's adoption of new stylistic expressions drawn from diverse European sources was in keeping with the avant-garde role his buildings were to assume within the dynamics of the city. This function can even explain, in part, why Hood chose two completely different treatments for the exterior surfaces of these buildings, the two most advanced in the years around 1930 and not only in New York.

The stark verticality of the Daily News Building has aptly been described as a "modern projection of the norm for Beaux-Arts Gothic."[126] Such an emphatic underlining of a structure that is, in reality, reduced to slender steel supports has no justification other than as a purely formal choice, however. The horizontal bands of windows of the McGraw-Hill Building, in contrast, make it evident that the exterior wall is dissolved in an enveloping vitreous surface. To achieve this effect, however, Hood had to mask the supporting piers and resorted to the use of color as an expedient; the piers that interrupt the continuous bands of windows are covered in metal painted dark greenblue, which picks up the color of the window shades.

Earlier, I indicated Lönberg-Holm's design for the *Chicago Tribune* competition as a possible source for the McGraw-Hill Building. Another source, however, is perhaps more direct—the blocks projecting from the great slab in the design eleborated by Frank Lloyd Wright, between 1920 and 1925, for the offices of the National Life Insurance Company of Chicago. Because Hood extracted this element from its context and ignored the formal interrelationships of Wright's structure, the borrowing is quite easily disguised; it is nevertheless explicit in the crowning element and the strong vertical accent given the centrally placed service shaft. Thus the models of the avant-garde served with great distinction to support the publicity operation.

In the panorama of Manhattan, both the Daily News and the McGraw-Hill buildings, in fact, assumed a progressive role; they very pointedly attempted, two years before the New York exhibition of the International style, to establish a real relationship with the formal expressions of the European avant-garde. In the foreword to his small monograph on Hood's work, Arthur T. North offered a truly amazing explanation of Hood's eclecticism, but one that might well be read as a defense, by extension, of the whole of American architecture at the beginning of the 1930s. North wrote, "Constant change is an attribute of life. Buildings are an indispensable element of life, and architecture, therefore, to perform its true function, must change constantly.... Such a

Design by Raymond Hood for the Central
Methodist Episcopal Church, Columbus, Ohio.

McCormick Mausoleum, Rockford, Illinois, by
Raymond Hood, 1927.

Daily News Building, New York, view from
below and detail of the entranceway, by
Raymond Hood with John Mead Howells,
1930.

McGraw-Hill Building, New York, by
Raymond Hood, 1931.

concept of architecture precludes the practice of adapting architectural precedents when they are inherently unfit. Into such an architectural period we are now entering."[127] The same idea was expressed by Hood himself, who asserted: "The contemporary concept of architecture precludes the evolution of an American 'style.' A style is developed by copying and repetition, both destructive to creation and maximum usefulness, which is essential to building."[128] In the absurdity of its paradox this statement sounds like a kitsch distortion of the exaltation of contradiction offered by Whitman in his "Song of Myself."[129]

In the ultimate analysis, what Hood's work as a whole really proclaimed was the necessity of ensuring the self-publicizing character of the single architectural object within the uncertain and mutable structure of the commercial metropolis. Certainly, the law of change was essential for an architect like Hood. It is, however, equally certain that his work was in no way based on an abstract or idealistic concept of change—a concept basic to the vitalist currents of the European avant-garde—but, rather, on a wholly realistic and commercial consideration of its usefulness. In the early 1930s, the purified architectural expressions imported from Europe, adopted on the grand scale of the Manhattan skyscraper, afforded a communicative potential greater than that of even the Chrysler Building or the Empire State Building. In the composite metropolis in continual mutation, still dominated by the exuberant vitalism of the Art Deco skyscrapers, the clamorous insertion of an avant-garde object produced a shock as no other formal language could. This intensification of visual stimuli served the self-proclaiming, publicity function of the architecture of the commercial metropolis so effectively that architects were disposed to forego unleashing the potential implicit in the structure of the skyscraper.

In Hood's McGraw-Hill Building or Howe and Lescaze's Philadelphia Saving Fund Society skyscraper, the renewal of formal expression was carried out in organisms that added nothing to the formulas established by George B. Post or Cass Gilbert. In the face of the utopias visualized by Thomas Adams, the unsatisfied demands of the Regional Planning Association of America, and the stereotyped building practice of commercial and financial capital in the early 1930s, the American metropolises—incapable of any radical renewal despite the chaos and inadequacy of their existing structures—were outliving their own fame. It may be surprising, then, that among Hood's projects between 1929 and 1931 was a scheme for the development of the entire island of Manhattan.[130]

The drawings and photomontage with which Hood presented his "Manhattan 1950" project have much in common with the images of Hugh Ferriss's *Metropolis of Tomorrow*. Although their interpretations differ, both responded to the problem of restructuring the downtown and the heart of the commercial center of New York. The pyramidal profiles of Ferriss's skyscrapers, tunneled through by the flow of motorized and pedestrian traffic on different levels and connected by low structures that weld the gigantic isolated vertical complexes into a whole, are found again in Hood's scheme. There, too, the traffic system is organically related to the skyscraper complexes. Moreover, both Ferriss and Hood foresaw the connection of Manhattan with the areas across the Hudson and East rivers by means of bridges, the supports of which are skyscrapers between which rows of apartment houses are suspended above the water. Formally, of course, their designs differ. Ferriss's bridges, which in reality only interpreted the model of residential bridges Hood had designed as early as 1924, are conceived as double catenaries, between which the traffic passes. Hood, in contrast, develops his bridges in a progressive series of structures according to the principle adopted in the design of setback skyscrapers.

At the base of such proposals was the stimulus afforded by the programs of the Regional Plan of New York and Its Environs. Ferriss translated that plan into the utopian terms of his "metropolis as a humanistic machine," while Hood was concerned, instead, with giving a realistic appearance to a program that had already received Mumford's severe criticism. Nevertheless, Hood's proposal actually contained more than one element antithetical to the directives of the Regional Plan. While Adams's plan called for transportation systems between the subcenters of the region that would not involve the area of Manhattan, Hood's system of bridges not only confirmed but exalted to the maximum the concept of centralization and intense concentration in Manhattan. In a certain sense, Hood's project was a response to the proposals of regional decentralization from the point of view of massive financial and industrial capital; the principle of pure speculation was pitted against attempts at rationalization on a regional scale. In Hood's project, however, although lower Manhattan was still the area of maximum construction concentration, a series of business centers, in the form of pyramidal clusters of skyscrapers, were to be distributed with a certain regularity throughout Manhattan. This concession to the principle of "reasonable speculation" was offset, however, by the introduction of "speculation on space," offered by twenty-four residential bridges capable of housing 3,000,000 persons.

It would be useless to examine the value of Hood's proposal from a strictly functional point of view; it was not intended to furnish solutions. His aim, rather, was to offer an ideal image of the metropolis; in keeping with the order of the day in conceptions of the reorganization of urban centers, his visualization took on the aspect of a systematized mountain chain. Furthermore, Hood's clusters of skyscrapers are used in a way that contradicts the principles of speculation and implies comprehensive control over the urban form, something the very organization of the real estate economy could not but radically reject. Thus, even if Hood's realism excludes any solutions based on a literal application of the principle of the *ville radieuse* to Manhattan, his project was utopian; it may also be considered, at least theoretically, as closing the utopian chapter of American urbanism.

While satisfying vain and abstract cultural aspirations with the elaboration of this schematic plan for "Manhattan 1950," contemporaneously, Hood was involved as a practicing architect in the planning and design of Rockefeller Center, the most significant urban undertaking in New York in the 1930s.

Photomontage of the "Manhattan 1950"
project, a proposal by Raymond Hood for
the restructuring of Manhattan with multiblock, multifunctional skyscrapers and
residential bridges, 1929.

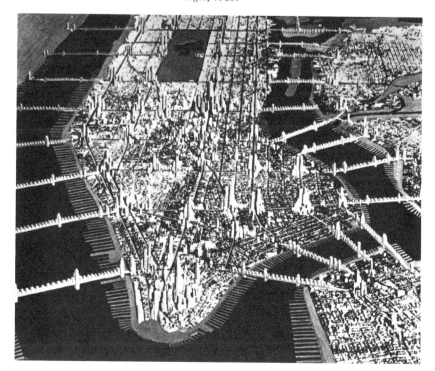

Design for a residential bridge by Hugh Ferriss, after a proposal made by Raymond Hood about 1924.

Design by Raymond Hood of the residential bridges of his "Manhattan 1950" project, 1929.

**The Creation of
Rockefeller Center**

In Rockefeller Center (1931-1940), the anticipatory ideas of Saarinen, the programs of the Regional Plan of New York, Ferriss's images, and Hood's various pursuits were finally brought into synthesis. This statement is true in spite of the fact that Rockefeller Center was completely divorced from any regionalist conception and that it thoroughly ignored any urban considerations beyond the three midtown lots on which the complex was to rise. It was, in fact, a selective synthesis, the significance of which lies precisely in its choices and rejections. From Saarinen's Chicago lakefront, Rockefeller Center drew only its amplified scale and the coordinated unity of a skyscraper complex related to an open space provided with services for the public. From the recently developed taste for the International style, it accepted volumetric purity, without, however, renouncing the enrichments of Art Deco. From Adams's images of the new Manhattan, it extracted the concept of a contained and rational concentration, an oasis of order. Moreover, all the concepts accepted were stripped of any utopian character; Rockefeller Center in no way contested the established institutions or the current dynamics of the city. Indeed, it took its place in Manhattan as an island of "equilibrated speculation" and emphasized in every way its character as a closed and circumscribed intervention, which nevertheless purported to serve as a model.

The history of the project illuminates its outlook.[131] The beginnings of the initiative go back to 1926-27, when the Metropolitan Opera Company decided to creat a new cultural center by constructing an opera house in conjunction with an office-studio building on 57th Street between Eighth and Ninth avenues. In the summer of 1927, Benjamin Wistar Morris, the architect who had been entrusted with the project in collaboration with Joseph Urban, made a trip to Europe; there he studied not only the outstanding opera houses but also urban complexes such as Place de la Concorde, Place Vendôme, and Saint Peter's Square. It was a grand tour in the authentic City Beautiful tradition. In this case, however, it produced quite unforeseen effects. Morris returned from Europe convinced that the construction of a prestigious cultural edifice in the heart of Manhattan had to be accompanied by the creation of an open square, not only because of the contribution it could make to a new "Civic Art" but, even more, because of the speculative advantages it could offer.

In the project prepared by Morris in December 1927, the conventionally designed building of the Metropolitan Opera and Century Theater faces on an open, landscaped square, but architecture and square are not yet coordinated.[132] In Morris's subsequent project, however, prepared in May 1928 for a new site between Fifth and Sixth avenues and 48th and 51st streets, three constructed volumes are continuously connected by bridges passing over the streets and by elevated promenades that run along the buildings and on which are situated stores and restaurants.

The site of this new project, which had been indicated to the Metropolitan Opera Company by the real estate agency of William A. White and Sons, was the

Proposal for the new Metropolitan Opera
House complex, prepared by Benjamin
Wistar Morris in May 1928.

Proposal for the new Metropolitan Opera
House complex, prepared by Benjamin
Wistar Morris for the competition of May
1929.

property of Columbia University; unlike the sites previously considered, it seemed ideal for such a development, not only because of its proximity to the theater and shopping areas but also because of its easy access. Obviously, however, various levels of speculation were involved in such an operation, and the Metropolitan Opera Company apparently found itself in a losing position due to the difficulty—not resolved by Morris—of offsetting the high cost of building the Opera House with structures that could ensure a high level of profit. In the meantime, however, a new protagonist, who was to overturn the plans completely, appeared on the scene.

On May 21, 1928, Morris's proposal was presented at a dinner at the Metropolitan Club; in attendance was Ivy Lee, representing John D. Rockefeller, Jr., who would be impressed by the project's economic potential. The gathering had been organized by R. Fulton Cutting with the aim of finding adequate financial support for the project. In presenting his proposal, Morris carefully emphasized the great financial benefit it promised in comparison with the usual speculative venture, precisely because of its open space and the particular organization of the "plaza."[133]

In December 1928, with Rockefeller's support, the Metropolitan Square Corporation was formed to develop the new site belonging to Columbia University, a lease for which was signed in January 1929. According to its stipulations, the Metropolitan Square Corporation would pay $3,300,000 a year for twenty-one years, with the possibility of three consecutive renewals of the same contract. At the termination of this period, the land and buildings would become the property of Columbia University.

In September 1928, just before the formation of the Metropolitan Square Corporation, Rockefeller had sought the advice of the Todd, Robertson and Todd Engineering Corporation on the speculative possibilities of the site. The corporation, in turn, engaged the architects L. Andrew Reinhard and Henry Hofmeister to draw up a plan for the site.[134] When, however, the Metropolitan Square Corporation nominated an architects' advisory board on February 20, 1929, these still little-known architects were not among its members. The eclectically chosen board included William T. Aldrich, Cross and Cross, Benjamin Wistar Morris, York and Sawyer, S. H. Bennett, Cass Gilbert, Charles A. Platt, Harvey Wiley Corbett, M. B. Medary, and John Russell Pope. From this moment until the end of the year, there apparently existed more of a competition than a collaboration between Rockefeller and the Metropolitan Opera Company. Indeed, it is not impossible that Rockefeller was preparing to supplant the Metropolitan Opera Company, or at least strongly to influence their initiative, even before the Wall Street panic of October 1929.

In May 1929, certain architects on the advisory board were invited to participate in a competition for the design of Metropolitan Square; significantly the "plaza" was included among the mandatory items in the program. Among the schemes presented, Corbett's was one of the most interesting, mainly because the architect had the opportunity of a concrete project in which to develop the proposals he had advanced several years earlier for the rational separation of traffic in Manhattan, proposals that had won the praises of Werner Hegemann.[135] Corbett's design consists of a U-shaped layout with a large plaza opening on Fifth Avenue, from which a graded walkway leads up to the elevated entrance of the centrally situated Opera House; an elevated promenade bordering all four sides of the Opera House gives access, also by the use of bridges, to the seven peripheral buildings of the complex and allows crosstown traffic to pass freely on 49th and 50th streets.

The first phase of planning was interrupted in December 1929 when, in the wake of the great crash, the Metropolitan Opera Company saw fit to abandon the development. Despite what he would later describe as the absolute uncertainty of its financial outcome, Rockefeller decided to take on the enterprise alone.[136] At this point, the role of the firm of Todd, Robertson and Todd became decisive for the outcome of the project. On October 1, 1929, a contract had been signed placing the Metropolitan Square Corporation under the managerial control of the two firms of Todd, Robertson and Todd and Todd and Brown, Incorporated. On October 28, 1929, Reinhard and Hofmeister were appointed architects of the project, with Morris, Hood, and Corbett as consultants. In November, Todd, Robertson and Todd officially began their scientific study of the economic aspects of the project.

Rockefeller had to take account of the unfavorable conditions weighing on the enterprise. The effects of speculation had called forth the sum of $3,300,000 for the annual lease on three lots from which Columbia University had previously drawn only $300,000 a year from the rents on the existing houses, restaurants, and offices. Moreover, the Chrysler Building and the Empire State Building were adding another million square feet of office space to an already surfeited market, while the depression was making the inability to pay rents an increasingly widespread phenomenon.[137]

Also significant was the fact that Rockefeller's new, commercial building program, which would replace the cultural center promoted by the Metropolitan Opera Company, would be located peripherally in respect to the zone of commercial development of Manhattan at the time, the northernmost point of which had been reached by the Empire State and Chrysler buildings. Located still farther north, Rockefeller Center pushed this development almost to the limit of Central Park. Thus it had the advantages of uncompromised accessibility and a position peculiarly adapted to an initiative of unusually large scale and deliberately exceptional character.

Although it helped to determine Rockefeller's decision, the support guaranteed the project by O.D. Young and David Sarnoff of the Radio Corporation of America, by M. H. Aylesworth of the National Broadcasting Company, and by Samuel L. Rothafel of the Roxy Theater was still not sufficient. In order to avoid a disastrous outcome for the enterprise, the rule of immediately procuring future tenants had to be respected. Hugh Robertson was called on to accomplish this task and made every possible use of the means offered by Rockefeller's financial organization, up to the very limits of legality, to achieve his aim. As many of the companies interested in installing their offices in the future buildings of Rockefeller Center were bound by their present leases for varying numbers of years, Robertson undertook to liquidate their leases with funds allocated by Rockefeller for the purpose and considered as long-term investments.[138]

This procedure, possible only for an industrial giant of Rockefeller's caliber, and many other financial facilitations conceded as incentive were applied in an operation of vast scale, which had dramatic effects on the Manhattan real-estate market. Writing in 1938, Frederick Lewis Allen, one of the severest critics of the Rockefeller Center project, observed:

> If the construction contracts being let for the building were saving the construction companies and reducing unemployment, on the other hand the inexorable drive of the Rockefeller renting office appeared to be ruining the real-estate business. August Hecksher filed suit for ten million dollars, claiming unfair competition, and many building-owners who did not file suit turned purple in the face at the mere thought of Messrs. Rockefeller and Todd. But the tenants came in, until at last the stampede was on.[139]

In a situation of continual bankruptcy, which considerably reduced the number of commercial firms in New York, the operation Rockefeller had put in motion gave rise to serious imbalances that accentuated the already severe state of panic reigning in the real-estate business. In this sense, Rockefeller Center was an explicit response to the utopian concept of an urban equilibrium proposed during the same period by the Regional Plan of New York. Indeed, the project made clear just how and to what extent the economic forces in question intended to manage the destiny of the city.

Even the diligence of Rockefeller's renting office, however, was not sufficient to guarantee the enterprise a profitable yield. It was immediately clear to Rockefeller that an undertaking of such magnitude required the scientific organization of its planning and execution, so that the entire range of economic variables might be thoroughly absorbed and integrated in the planning and design itself. The complex staff, installed on the twenty-fifth and twenty-sixth floors of the Graybar Building, was organized in a precisely coordinated system. The Metropolitan Square Corporation, the president of which was Arthur Woods, was responsible for the comprehensive control of the undertaking. The actual management of the enterprise was in the hands of the firms of Todd, Roberton and Todd and Todd and Brown. Specifically, Todd and Brown managed the execution of the buildings and controlled the daily and monthly expenses, as well as the financial budget allotted monthly by the Metropolitan Square Company to the three general contractors.[140] Even the system of financing differed from common practice. The three general contractors— Hegeman-Harris, John Lowry, and Barr, Irons and Lane—did not anticipate capital. Rather, on the basis of a detailed estimate, they submitted monthly requisitions for the necessary financing from the Metropolitan Square Corporation. With this system, capital had to be borrowed only once, and thus the whole operation benefited from a reduction of interest charges.[141]

The rational organization of the work extended to the selection of the contractors, the choice of materials, the tabulation of the design and construction operations, and the arrangement of production and time schedules.[142] In a series of articles published in the *Architectural Forum* in 1932, the designers themselves emphasized the originality of the working method and the productive results of a collaboration among groups of specialists by means of periodic conferences.[143] Webster B. Todd affirmed that only in an undertaking on a vast scale was it really possible to take advantage of technological innovations.[144] The major innovation, however, also stimulated by the unusual scale of the Rockefeller Center development, was precisely the rational organization and minute planning of the design and execution at all levels. Rockefeller Center demonstrated how a large-scale undertaking coordinated as a unit could immediately give rise to a new organization of the building economy. Planning and design became scientific and supraindividual in a concrete way, quite beyond any "ideology of the anonymous." It would be left to the "allied arts" to exalt the "human" and social aspects of the undertaking.[145] Within such an organization, the role of the architect was not only precise but also clearly delimited.

At the conclusion of a meeting on November 1, 1929, and thus before the withdrawal of the Metropolitan Opera Company, John R. Todd gave the architects a preliminary program summarized in four points:

1) Fifth Avenue frontage in both blocks developed with shopping type buildings having two buildings in each block.
2) High office buildings to be placed on the westerly end of each of the north and south blocks.
3) An additional tall office building to be designed for the easterly end of the southerly block.
4) Centre portion of north-south blocks would be net leased to department stores; new streets to be cut through giving full frontage on all sides of the department stores.[146]

A plan drawn up by Reinhard and Hofmeister and dated November 25, 1929, illustrated the managers' intentions. With the Metropolitan Opera Company's abandonment of the project in December 1929, however, a new structural scheme was needed to take account of the laws of maximum utilization of the land. The change is quite clear when Morris's design prepared for the competition of May 1929, in which the central space in front of the Opera House is conceived as a sort of agora bordered by four skyscrapers, is compared with the scheme designated as G_3, prepared by Reinhard and Hofmeister with the agreement of Rockefeller himself and dated January 8, 1930.

Winston Weisman's studies have demonstrated that scheme G_3 was crucial for the history of the planning of Rockefeller Center.[147] It seems even more significant, however, that the elementary ensemble of scheme G_3—four slab

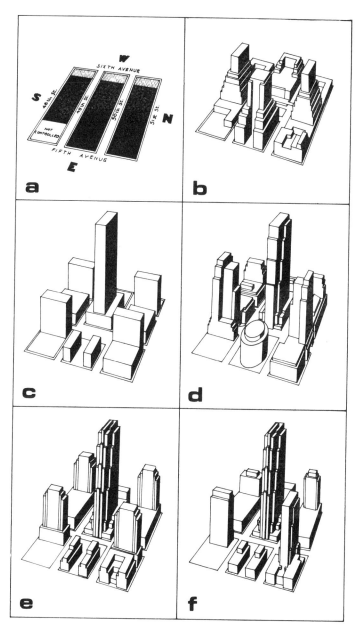

Schematic history of the planning of Rocke-feller Center, New York: *a*, site leased by Columbia University, 1929; *b*, scheme proposed by Benjamin Wistar Morris for this site in May, 1928; *c*, scheme G_3 by Reinhard and Hofmeister, January 1930; *d*, scheme H_1 by Associated Architects, May 1930; *e*, 1933 scheme by Associated Architects; *f*, solution adopted in 1935.

skyscrapers parallel with Fifth Avenue, situated approximately in the four corners of the area, and a higher slab at the center, perpendicular to the avenue, with lower connecting structures—does not differ much from the plan of November 1929; this similarity would seem to confirm my hypothesis that Rockefeller had an alternative plan in mind even before the Metropolitan Opera Company withdrew. In any case, scheme G_3 marked the end of the competition that had existed up to this time among the architects of the advisory board. Offering as it did a rational exploitation of the building code, ample surrounding space isolating each building, coordination of the various blocks, and satisfactory relations among traffic system, construction, and plaza, this general scheme was immediately accepted by what would henceforth be the studio of the Associated Architects: Reinhard and Hofmeister; Corbett, Harrison and MacMurray; Hood, Godley and Fofor Fouilhoux.[148]

The architectural planning and the studies of the economic possibilities of the complex went on side by side. Scheme G_3 was examined element by element in terms of the commercial attraction to be expected from each part. In response to the request of the Chase National Bank, a new scheme, designated as H_1, was worked out in May 1930. On Fifth Avenue, in the area just in front of the plaza and central skyscraper, two alternative structures of unusual form were proposed, one elliptical, the other pyramidal. The elliptical structure won out, and, in the official publication of 1931, Radio City appears enriched by the contrast between the slab of the RCA Building and the oval tower of the Chase National Bank. Reinhard explicitly defined this elliptical building as a "recognizable marker," a means of attracting the public into the complex.[149] Once the negotiations with the Chase National Bank failed, however, the bombastic oval tower was eliminated. Corbett and Hood, however, insisted on introducing unusual forms at the center of the complex to attract public attention, and various schemes based on effect-producing combinations of elementary geometric forms were, in fact, worked out beginning in July 1930.[150] These were purely graphic exercises, however, and were marked by uncertainty and ingenuousness that derived from the absence of any syntactic code; they demonstrate nothing more than the desire to endow an economically exceptional undertaking with unusual forms.

At this point, the managerial group again intervened in the planning and this time with decisive effect. The design of the complex had to take into account Hugh Robertson's idea of attracting the interest of foreign countries in the development. This aim was realized by introducing a series of four rectangular blocks laid out perpendicularly to Fifth Avenue, two occupying the central space formerly intended for the elliptical structure of the Chase National Bank and two at the northeastern angle of the site. In scheme D of October 1932, a promenade leading to the Sunken Plaza appears between the two centrally placed foreign buildings, the Maison Française and the British Empire Building. With the content of the project schematically established, it remained for the architects to supply the specific solutions, which had also to coincide with the well-defined social physiognomy with which the colossal undertaking began to be presented to the public. In this sense, the comparison of Rockefeller Center with the great architectural monuments of the past, made in the pamphlet published by the public-relations department of the Metropolitan Square Corporation, was more than mere rhetoric:

The Taj Mahal lies in solitary grandeur on the shimmering bank of the Jumna River. Rockefeller Center will stand in the midstream rush of New York. The Taj is like an oasis in the jungle, its whiteness tense against the gloomy greenness of the forest. Rockefeller Center will be a beautiful entity in the swirling life of a great metropolis—its cool heights standing out against an agitated man-made skyline. And yet the two, far apart in site and surroundings, are akin in the spirit. The Taj, in tribute to pure beauty, was designed as a temple, a shrine. Rockefeller Center, conceived in the same spirit of aesthetic devotion, is designed to satisfy, in pattern and in service, the many-sided spirit of our civilization. By solving its own varied problems, by bringing beauty and business into closer companionship, it promises a significant contribution to the city planning of an unfolding future. [151]

Significantly, it was only after the organization of the complex had been established through the study of the economic possibilities of the various alternative solutions that the architectural question as such came into play—and even then, only to the extent that architecture was capable of demonstrating its usefulness as publicity. In this regard, the design phase between 1930 and 1933, concerned with the creation of a system of gardens on the roofs of the British Empire Building, the Maison Française, and the lower levels of the RCA and International buildings, is particularly interesting. Reinhard has stated that the idea of roof gardens connected in a continuous system by means of stairs and bridges was first proposed by Hood, who presented his idea in 1930 at one of the regular meetings of the architects and the managerial group in the Graybar Building. [152]

It is indicative that the meeting had been called to study new ways of attracting future tenants. In outfitting the roofs of the lower constructions of Rockefeller Center with a system of gardens on different levels, greatly varied and carefully planned in regard to their natural layout and the services they would afford—restaurants, tea gardens, spaces for outdoor exhibitions, and so on—Hood's intention was to endow the complex with the only type of landscape possible for an eminently unnatural architectonic structure. Significantly, after the publication of the Associated Architects' design for the hanging gardens, New York newspapers spoke of Rockefeller Center as a modern version of the gardens of Babylon. [153]

As it appeared in the designs of 1931-32, this "New Babylon" was intended for two types of spectators: first, the public, who would actively use the terraces as an urban park, and, second, the employees of the skyscrapers, who would passively enjoy the natural spectacle below them from the enviable position of their place of work. According to Hood, it was precisely the spectacular effect of this landscape project that offered possibilities for higher profits. In yet another

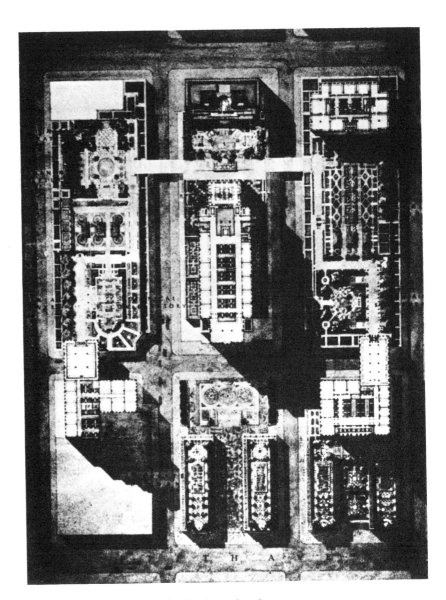

Rockefeller Center, plan for the roof gardens
and bridges connecting the blocks of the
complex, design by Associated Architects,
1932; rendering by John Wenrich.

Rockefeller Center, view of the roof gardens
on the lower blocks of the complex, with
the bridges over 49th and 50th streets, by
Associated Architects, 1932.

way, however, it would appeal to the collective imagination and accentuate the attractiveness of Rockefeller's operation as a contribution to the general urban scene. In the Associated Architects' 1932 design, the Roof Gardens, presented in precise and highly elaborated drawings, connected the lower blocks of the complex in a continuous artificial park, complete with bridges passing over 49th and 50th streets. It was the first time that a commercial development had deliberately and ostentatiously presented itself as a civic attraction for the entire community. Rockefeller Center, indeed, seemed intent on integrating speculative aims, new conditions for work in the commercial city, and open spaces for leisure and recreation into a single, gigantic financial and publicity operation— and all in the blackest years of the depression.

Between 1932 and 1933, while the form of the hanging gardens was still under discussion, five buildings of the complex were completed and immediately rented at a rate of $2 per square foot. Thousands of workmen had been employed in their construction and thus advantage had been taken of the low cost of labor in this period of depression, but by just the opposite reasoning a "progressive" social connotation was attributed to the enterprise. More than all else, however, Rockefeller Center seemed a symbol of the capitalist will and duty to succeed, a lively image of the spirit of economic revival, a promise of the continuity of America's urban "adventure." In December 1939, at the ceremony celebrating the completion of the complex, Thomas A. Murray emphasized that during the depression Rockefeller had employed 75,000 construction workers.[154] (In the principal biography of John D. Rockefeller, Jr., the total number of people employed in the design and execution of the entire project is reported to have been 225,000.)[155] In a radio broadcast when work on the center was just beginning, Rockefeller was exalted for "his challenge to the depression, his gallant defiance of the dark spirit of hard times, his expression of faith in the future of America."[156]

Rockefeller presented himself as the spokesman of a democratic capitalism, a Maecenas concerned with social problems. Beginning in about 1926, he involved himself in the restoration of historic Williamsburg, and in 1927, prompted by his wife's interest, he was part of the group that founded the Museum of Modern Art. He was also concerned with projects for national parks in Wyoming, Maine, and New Jersey, supported the construction of The Cloisters, and financed the Radburn undertaking with three million dollars.[157] The Rockefeller Center development was a sort of contradictory companion piece to the project for Palisades Interstate Park in the New York-New Jersey region. In fact, Rockefeller apparently operated on two planes: one tending to put into effect some partial programs on the vaster territorial scale indicated in the Regional Plan of New York and Its Environs; the other, completely governed by business reality. Even in his center, however, he tended to fuse these two planes to a certain extent by integrating services and recreational facilities on a metropolitan scale with building speculation, thus continually underscoring his own personal role in the country's economic revival under the New Deal.

Diverting an enormous sum of industrial capital into construction—$125 million, according to the official data—and thus into a field of production favored by the economic crisis, Rockefeller demonstrated that he knew how to "use" the depression wisely. He was also adept at presenting periodically the evolution of his project, which was followed attentively not only by the specialized journals but also by magazines and newspapers. For many Rockefeller's undertaking reflected the American hope in the capacity of an enterprising capitalism, solicitous of the welfare of the community, to overcome the crisis.[158] It was just this presentation of the project, however, that was to provoke severely polemical criticism. Writing in *Harper's Magazine* in 1932, Frederick Lewis Allen accused Rockefeller Center of wanting to be much more a place of mass amusement than an authentic cultural center, while letters to the *Herald Tribune* and the *New York Times* denounced the project as a purely speculative venture devoid of any real social motivation.[159]

The same line of criticism was directed against the enterprise in 1933 by M. R. Werner in the pages of the *Atlantic Monthly*. After citing Ortega y Gasset's *Revolt of the Masses* and describing at length the shows offered at the Roxy, Werner concluded by inveighing against Rockefeller for having allowed himself to be drawn along by the taste and demands of the masses, to whom his Center offered colossal mediocrity.[160] Allen's romantic anticapitalism, and also that of Mumford, who attacked Rockefeller Center in his articles in the *New Yorker*,[161] was transformed in Werner's tirade into an openly reactionary position.

In comparison with such criticisms, the response made to Allen by Merle Crowell, director of the public-relations department of Rockefeller Center, was at least more coherent. Crowell made it known that no a priori program for Radio City existed. The characteristic functions of the center were left to be determined by its future tenants, including a radio station, an opera company, foreign consulates, insurance companies, and large stores. Rockefeller Center was not conceived as a cultural Olympus, but, rather, as a "sincere attempt to incorporate art into business" by introducing a high aesthetic standard into the daily use the mass public would make of the complex.[162] Crowell's article also presented the proposal for the Roof Gardens, which was described as a model for similar future undertakings in the city, and made known the design for the covered arcade between the two lower buildings on Fifth Avenue, conceived as a monumental passageway to the office building complex, for which, significantly, Giuseppe Mengoni's Galleria in Milan was cited as a source of inspiration.[163]

The balance between the purely speculative venture and the social physiognomy of the undertaking was thus delicate; especially in the atmosphere of the depression, with construction activity practically blocked, it played an important part in the realization of the enterprise. In keeping with the weight given the social aspect, the plaza became an element of primary importance in the design proposals from 1930 on. Plaza and roof gardens were obviously complementary and constituted an attempt to give form to a new type of urban landscape, thus demonstrating that high-concentration construction did not exclude the search for a new, more complete and self-sufficient image of the city. It is difficult, however, to compare the Associated Architects' proposal with the projects of the European avant-garde, which surely played a role in the conception of "the first landscaped skyscraper," as Weisman has labeled Rockefeller Center. Le Corbusier's *ville radieuse* or the cities of setback skyscrapers envisaged by Behrens or Sauvage also brought nature into a completely artificial environment of high concentration, but Rockefeller Center was quite different, since it was not a residential structure and its relationship with the community was in no way utopian.

The changes in the initial building program resulted from a careful calculation of foreseeable profits. In 1933 it was decided to eliminate the bridges over 49th and 50th streets, thus excluding the idea of a continuity of the elevated levels. In 1935 an increase was called for in the projected volume of the International Building, which in the earlier projects had formed a pendant to the skyscraper on the opposite side, but which now had to be rotated, disrupting the symmetry of the complex. Later on, the low structures along the sides of the complex were replaced by the skyscrapers of the Associated Press and Eastern Air Lines.[164]

The process was elementary; the incorporated nature of the "New Babylon" was replaced by a progressive increase in density and height and a characterization of the complex obtained by exclusively architectural means. It was the consistent application of this process that promoted and justified the anomalous 90-degree rotation of the International Building, and not, as Giedion was to interpret the interrelationships of the buildings, the result of any calculated consideration of the effects such an anomaly would produce on the perception of the complex as a whole.[165] The method of design followed in the formal definition of the RCA Building is, in this sense, symptomatic. This building was already indicated in scheme G_3 as the dominant structure of the complex. Hood explained the design of its organism as resulting from a central core containing the elevator shafts and service facilities and a scientific study of the spatial distribution and proportions offering maximum uniform light and air to all parts of the building.[166] Once the technological structure and the relation with the semi-independent block of the National Broadcasting Company Studios were established,[167] so too was the building's geometric shape—"the Slab" that so impressed public and critics alike and was destined to constitute a lasting model. Even the staggered setbacks that articulate its volume and accentuate its slenderness resulted from functional considerations of elevator shafts and the principle of uniform lighting.

At this point, the only unresolved feature of the building was its walls. By what only seems paradoxical in a project so thoroughly controlled by functional and economic considerations, the architects found themselves at this juncture in the role of simple designers. Various studies were made of the fenestration; a design of vertical development, similar to that finally adopted, was offered along with designs for horizontal organizations according to groupings or a regular grid.[168] The same problem was faced at almost the same time by Howe and Lescaze in designing the Philadelphia Saving Fund Society Building.[169] The design problems of the Philadelphia skyscraper, however, were worked out in the terms of the practical needs of the client and the architects' conscious attempts to find a new formal expression for the tall building, while the architects of Rockefeller Center appear to have been completely indifferent about the various designs they themselves had elaborated. Reinhard explicitly stated that the various models for the walls were designed as a selection for all possible tastes. Indeed, as Jordy has acutely noted, the unitary character of the design of Rockefeller Center is due in large part to the collaboration of architects who did not belong to the avant-garde and were therefore quite unidealistically disposed to compromise.[170]

It is interesting, however, that the final choice for the surfaces of the RCA Building followed not the example of the most innovative of Hood's contemporary works, the McGraw-Hill Building, but, rather, that of his Daily News Building. Although the choice may have been influenced by functional considerations—the greater flexibility in the modules for the offices, the vertical solution of flattened piers is undoubtedly the one that affords the greatest sense of volumetric compactness. It seems, indeed, as if the Associated Architects wanted to endow the overall structure of Rockefeller Center with a bare essentialness. From the models that were published from time to time, it appears that the RCA Building was established almost in its final form in the first months of 1932.[171] The uninterrupted verticality of its wall surface was adapted to enrichment in its lower levels with Art Deco ornament without the essentialness of its volumetric purity being challenged.

The plaza, however, still remained the dominant feature of the complex, and it was to this that the managerial group now turned its attention. As early as 1931, the plaza below street level and a shopping area opening onto it had become fundamental elements for the thorough exploitation of the commercial idea Morris had outlined in 1927, still with cultural pretensions. The problem became that of facilitating public access to this lower level. A first proposal called for an underground bus terminal and garage that would compel the commuter employees of the complex to enter the commercial area when they arrived and departed. It was also necessary, however, to attract the general public along Fifth Avenue. To ths end, in 1931, the Associated Architects presented a first scheme for the Sunken Plaza, in which an oval space dominated by a monumental fountan was enriched with scenographic effects provided by elaborate mosaic pavements, flowers, greenery, and even statuary. The still vaguely Beaux-Arts decor of the plaza was thus made to serve as an element of attraction for the public. All attention was concentrated on ways of inducing the public to enter the shopping area. The task of the architects became the study of the stairs from the street level to the plaza, which had to be designed in such a way that once the public had descended them it would be obliged to enter the shopping

Rockefeller Center, cross section looking west at the stage of design reached in the late 1930s: G, partially underground garage; TA, trucking area; T, tunnel from 50th Street; P, plaza; C, underground pedestrian concourse; 1, United States Rubber Building; 2, Center Theater; 3, Eastern Airlines Building; 4, RCA Building; 5, RKO Building; 6, Associated Press Building.

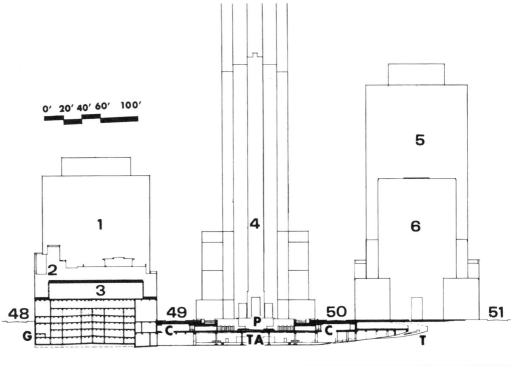

Rockefeller Center, RCA Building: *below,* plans of ground floor and typical office floor of the thirty-sixth to fortieth stories; *above,* comparison of the usable space at the level of the thirty-sixth to fortieth floors in the RCA Building and in a rectangular slab structure without setbacks.

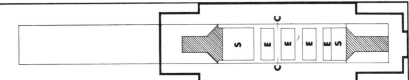

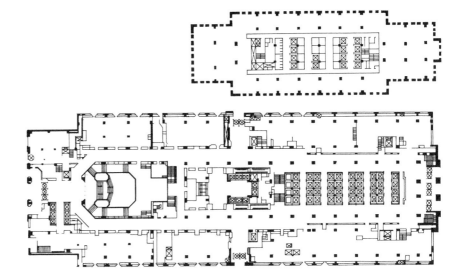

Rockefeller Center, model of the complex
at the stage of design reached in the mid-
1930s, seen in a lateral view from 51st
Street.

The Rockefeller Center model seen in a rear
view from Sixth Avenue.

Oval design for the Sunken Plaza, Rockefeller Center, by Associated Architects,
1931.

Rectangular design for the Sunken Plaza,
Rockefeller Center, by Associated Architects,
1932.

area. In the 1932 project, however, the Sunken Plaza lost the academic character and Neo-Baroque curvature of the schemes of the preceding year. In keeping with the formal purfication carried out in the design of the skyscrapers, even the plaza acquired a greater essentialness. Inserted within a system of pedestrian walkways and regularized in rectangular form, it was now scanned by a structural module echoing the RCA Building; the fountain—the only rhetorical element allowed to remain, for its obvious value as an unusual attraction—was placed against the wall opposite the entrance stairs.

With this project the Sunken Plaza assumed nearly its final form, although, as is well known, it was to change in function. In place of the shopping area, it now serves as an outdoor restaurant in the summer and as an ice-skating rink in the winter. Thus the plaza accentuated its own originality, becoming the animating spirit of the complex and notably increasing its economic possibilities. The change in function came about in 1936 and was not the result of any decision by the architects. The fact is that the subway station under the center was opened only in 1940, and the creation of the skating rink—serving a sport that in the America of the 1930s was still very much reserved for the upper classes—was intended to correct economic predictions that had proved erroneous. Even aside from certain critics' romantic enthusiasm for the layout of the promenade and plaza,[172] the pedestrian entrance opening on Fifth Avenue, flanked by the two international edifices that frame the RCA Building in a direct perspective and further commented on by the succession of water basins disposed along the central axis, forms a worthy introduction to the surreal spectacle of the skating rink (or summer restaurant), submerged in an ordered forest of skyscrapers. The urban surrealness is readily allied with the detached composure of the architectural definition. Indeed, the deliberately restrained and ordered style of the architecture accentuates this festive *mise en scène* of the plaza, in which the public of midtown Manhattan participates daily.

The plaza thus became quite literally a pulsating urban center, a point of magnetic attraction for the public, with a drawing power analogous to that of the two theaters of the complex (Radio City Music Hall and Center Theater, the latter demolished to make way for the Eastern Air Lines Building).[173] Nevertheless, the closed character of the plaza and the lack of any connection between Rockefeller Center and Sixth Avenue has been criticized, and not wholly without reason.[174] In my opinion, however, in analyzing the complex as a whole, it is more important to consider a project that was never carried out, which involved the relationship of Rockefeller Center with the surrounding urban area.

In 1936, the same year the decision about the function of the plaza became effective, an area on 53rd Street was acquired for the new edifice of the Museum of Modern Art, built in 1939 by Stone and Goodwin. Rockefeller was personally interested in this initiative, and Wallace Harrison, as he himself confirmed in a recent interview,[175] became involved as architect in a new undertaking closely related to that of Rockefeller Center. The project consisted of grafting a second plaza onto the center, one situated between the Museum of Modern Art and the Associated Press Building, which closes the side of Rockefeller Center along 51st Street, and flanked by the projected buildings of the Columbia Broadcasting System and of what was to become the Solomon R. Guggenheim Museum, the latter opening on Sixth Avenue.

Because of the resistence of one of the property owners affected by the new operation and, perhaps, as Jordy suggests, because of Rockefeller's weariness, the project never materialized.[176] Thus connected with Rockefeller Center the new plaza would have created a cultural center in the heart of the new commercial area of Manhattan and anticipated the operation carried out later with Lincoln Center. Moreover, this extension of Rockefeller's enterprise would have offered a precise indication of its possible developments in space and time. The two plazas—the first in the heart of a commercial complex, the second in the center of a specialized cultural complex—would have broken the isolation of Rockefeller Center. It would also have asserted to the utmost the absolute autonomy of the great corporations in determining the use of the urban land. The concentration of construction for commercial use created by Rockefeller in a zone still peripheral to the most intensely developed areas of the 1920s, would have been complemented by a cultural and exclusively social center that the radical criticism of the time advocated as an alternative to Rockefeller Center. Business and culture would have been allied within the metropolitan structure and on a scale adapted to it.

Although this initiative was not carried out, traces of the concept remain in and around the center—certainly in Rockefeller Plaza itself and in the roof gardens of the lower buildings of the complex, even though they represent only a fraction of the program envisaged by Hood. Its traces are also apparent, however, in the outdoor sculpture garden of the Museum of Modern Art, designed by Philip Johnson. In contrast, the construction of Carson and Lundin's Esso Building on 51st Street facing the Associated Press Building, in 1946-47, definitively closed the possibility of a rational connection of Rockefeller Center with the surrounding area.[177] The spaces within Rockefeller Center are thus autonomous, and the reciprocal connection between them and the various parts of the complex accentuate its character as an undertaking closed within itself and served by an efficient subway system that assures its shopping area the steady daily influx of large numbers of people, to whom are added the 26,000 people employed within the center.

Paradoxically, for an undertaking so strongly characterized as a speculative venture, the public success of Rockefeller Center surpassed its economic success.[178] In the new complex of fourteen buildings dominated by the RCA Building and comprising two theaters, the NBC studios, shopping areas, an observatory, museums and exhibits, foreign consulates, night clubs, restaurants,

Aerial view of Rockefeller Center and the adjacent area, about 1960: *extreme right*, the Esso Building by Carson and Lundin (1946-47); *top right*, the Time-Life Building by Harrison and Abramovitz (1957-59).

These were the first two in the numerous series of isolated skyscraper projects in the area around Rockefeller Center.

hanging gardens, and offices, favorable and opposition critics agreed in seeing a promise for the large-scale renewal of American cities.

The similarities between two such opposing judgments as those of Sigfried Giedion and Frederick Lewis Allen are significant. After describing Rockefeller Center both as the first urban undertaking in the heart of a great commercial city to be conceived as a coordinated unit and as a response on a grand scale to the historical avant-garde, Giedion concluded his analysis with the following statement:

What really needs to be changed is the entire structure of the City. The parkway and Rockefeller Center are only small beginnings, isolated new growths in the immense body of New York, like the young branches of a tree. But it must not be forgotten that tiny new branches properly grafted can change the whole inner structure of a plant. Rockefeller Center is simply in advance of its period in the urban scale. What must change is not the Center but New York itself. The city must adopt the new scale which is identical with that of its bridges and parkways. Only then will the civic center stand amidst greenery. Until then it will stand as a reminder that the structure of the city must be transformed, not in the interest of single individuals but for the sake of the community as a whole.[179]

For Giedion, therefore, Rockefeller Center was a "model." Yet even Allen, at the end of a vehemently critical article published in 1938, in which he defined the center as "the very citadel of artificiality" and interpreted it as the image of a super-corporation that exploits the inhuman concentration of the metropolis for its own speculative ends, asserted that the wasted opportunity of Rockefeller Center nevertheless constituted a "half-promise" for the future of the city. In the layout of the Plaza and in the technological efficiency of the installations seen on guided tours of the RCA Building, the middle-class tourist found a "Paradise Regained." He can also become conscious, however, Allen concluded, that what represents an increase in urban congestion in Rockefeller Center could be utilized in the future in the conquest of humane standards of light, green spaces, and services in a renewed community.[180]

From City to Megalopolis: Pittsburgh's Golden Triangle and Urban Planning as a "Negligible Discipline"

Rockefeller Center thus represented the final result of the general debate on the structure of the American city. In response to attempts at comprehensive control of the urban organism, it demonstrated that the only type of undertaking with any real possibility of influencing urban dynamics was one limited in scale and wholly in keeping with the existing, traditional laws of urban growth. As has been described, Rockefeller Center came into being on the basis of an analytic study of its economic possibilities. In this enterprise speculation assumed not a mere guise of social beneficence, but the aspect of a real public benefit; it ventured to proclaim that the collectivity was enriched to the extent that the interest on the capital investment increased for the private speculator. Indeed, if Rockefeller Center contained any ideological residue, it was in this attempt to celebrate the reconciliation of the trusts and the collectivity on an urban scale.

In other words, the realism that characterized the creation of Rockefeller Center—to the point of cynicism—marked the end of any utopian ideal of comprehensive public control over the urban structure. Rockefeller Center represented, instead, a victory for the zoning law; the neutrality of this type of legislation was in this case matched by a perfect understanding of its full possibilities. At the same time, however, Rockefeller Center marked the definitive eclipse of the "skyscraper as an individual." Presenting itself as "a city within a city," it had no need to create shock effects, as did the McGraw-Hill, Daily News, or Chrysler buildings. In Radio City, spectacular effects were reserved for the directly commercial spaces—the promenade, the skating rink, and the roof gardens. Although the vertical thrust of the RCA Building, underscored by the ascending rhythm of its staggered setbacks, served as its culminating mountain crest, the complex as a whole was created under the sign of a formal disenchantment that reaches its high point in the almost Loosian purism of the lower buildings on Fifth Avenue, reminiscent of Hood's design for the Polish National Alliance Building or his National Radiator Building in London. The face remains, however, that during the depression years the public followed the planning and construction of Rockefeller Center as a final urban "adventure" and as a promise for the future. The same was true in the case of Philadelphia, where the Philadelphia Saving Fund Society Building also took advantage of the favorable situation for construction that the depression created.

The fact that Rockefeller Center respected in full the elementary outlines of the New York grid was fundamental. To influence concretely the urban structure, proposals for comprehensive restructurings, such as those of Moses King, Corbett, Ferriss, or Adams, were superfluous and ultimately inadequate; it was enough to interpret with sufficient boldness the possibilities offered by the existing city. Rockefeller Center also offered a response to the ideas advanced by Saarinen in the early 1920s. The principle of a rational organization of the constituent elements of the city—local traffic, pedestrian traffic, underground transportation, parking, commercial areas, skyscrapers, leisure and recreation— was accepted in full. On the contrary, a dominantly civic and public characterization could not be accepted for the new urban structures, thus the specific, unrepeatable character of Saarinen's Chicago lakefront and Detroit riverfront projects was rejected. Rockefeller Center, indeed, presented itself as a model that could be repeated on the same or lesser scale. For this reason it can be viewed as one of the pyramidal clusters of skyscrapers proposed as part of Hood's "Manhattan 1950" project. Seen in this way, as one of the mountain chains Hood inserted sporadically into the New York grid, it demonstrates the enormous possibilities for exploitation that existed in the perpetually changing magnetic field represented by the city's grid plan of 1811. In fact, Rockefeller Center brought forth an immediate response from Manhattan's indifferent grid; the functions and level of concentration of the surrounding zone were completely overturned, thus provoking a series of initiatives that substantially changed the character of the area. Nor is the immediacy of this impact lessened by the fact that, because of the depression and the interim of the Second World War, it was for the most part made manifest only later.

Diversely, Rockefeller Center as a model for restructuring the city in terms of its elementary variables was taken up only after the war, in projects of varying size. If the plaza element was distorted and reduced to a simple free space in the Lever House or the Seagram Building, the lesson of Rockefeller Center, especially in its criteria of economic organization, was absorbed and followed in Philadelphia's Penn Center, Pittsburgh's Golden Triangle, and the Civic Center in Chicago.[181]

The revision of the New York zoning law advocated in 1956 by Frank Fogarty as an incentive for the creation of free spaces for social use at the foot of skyscrapers became a reality in the early 1960s. The area of Manhattan in the general vicinity of Rockefeller Center was soon saturated with curtain-walled masses taking advantage of the height conceded in exchange for areas of space left free. The separate, individual character of the projects, the lack of controls, and the absence of any provisions for their rational integration into the urban structure, however, have meant that an increase in yield and profits has been granted for a disordered and improvised succession of miniscule plazas, which affect the urban organism neither functionally nor formally with the intensity achieved in Rockefeller Center. In face of the proliferation of skyscrapers along Sixth Avenue, Rockefeller Center remains a paradoxical model. Amidst the glass-encased volumes of the Equitable Life Insurance, Exxon, and Celanese buildings, the new McGraw-Hill Building, the Hilton, and the CBS Building, along with the patina of its exterior surfaces and the restrained tone of its formal definition, Rockefeller Center has maintained its unity. It has not succeeded, however, in transmitting this quality to the building enterprises that today surround it.

In a polemical article published in 1965 in the *Architectural Forum*, Peter Blake specifically accused the authorities who have allowed the development of the Avenue of the Americas to reach its present state of disorder and irrationality. In contrasting this development with Rockefeller Center, however, Blake seems to have overlooked completely the fact that, for the Rockefeller model to be operative in such a development, the possibility of a succession of investments comparable to that of Rockefeller's must be present, as must the economic conditions that stimulate such gigantic concentrations of capital in commercial building enterprises.[182] Raymond Hood's "Manhattan 1950" project assumed the possibility of just such an intensity of investment, constant over a long period, as well as the coordination of minor investments in concentrated nuclei; for this reason Hood's project was a utopia. Beyond such considerations, Blake's criticism remains in the limbo of observations on civic art: "Where the old Rockefeller Center grouped its buildings to create a variety of streets, malls, and a single landscaped, sunken plaza, the new Sixth Avenue is

Aerial view of midtown Manhattan in the
1960s, with the profile of the RCA Building
of Rockefeller Center rising in the right
center ground (photo by L. B. Schlivek).

a chaotic agglomeration of piazzas, piazzettas, piazzettinas, arcades and 'courts.' Where the motto of the Beaux Arts period was 'when in doubt, do a boulevard,' the motto of some of today's architects seems to be 'when in doubt, do a plaza.' "[183]

This is not the scale on which the American city most fully reveals its internal crisis, however. Paradoxically, the impossibility of planning the American city is demonstrated not only by the episode of Rockefeller Center but also by the urban-renewal projects of the Kennedy and post-Kennedy eras. These recent gigantic operations of reconcentration have been conditioned by the ponderous reality of profits and yield. It is indicative that after inspiring the development of the area north of 42nd Street between Park and Sixth Avenues, thus giving rise to a center alternative to the downtown, the Rockefellers undertook a directly contradictory operation in the late 1950s with the construction of the Chase Manhattan Building in the vicinity of Wall Street. The Chase Manhattan Building, the World Trade Center, and the various recent proposals for Battery Park constitute a continuous chain of initiatives that all tend toward a reconcentration of functions in the most congested area of New York. At best, they aim at a localization of integrated functions—residence, place of work, and a high level of services—as in the proposal for Battery Park City by Harrison and Abramovitz, Philip Johnson and John Burgess, and Conklin and Rossant. Emphasizing the waste and inefficiency of daily commuting, such projects take a clear stand against the classic concept of decentralized functions.[184]

In the proposal for Battery Park City, as well as in the megastructure designed by Paul Rudolph for the Graphic Arts Center, this tendency toward reconcentration is pushed to the extreme by exploiting the possibility of expanding on the water. The process is completely analogous to that of the residential bridges of Hood's "Manhattan 1950" project, prepared in 1929. Both Battery Park City and the Graphic Arts Center, despite the diversity of their conceptions, create residential structures in immediate contact with the downtown and indirectly affect its specific organization and the economic interests concentrated there. It is necessary now, however, to examine a case that appears to contradict the observations on such phenomena made so far—the urban renewal of Pittsburgh and its central business district in the Golden Triangle.

Unlike Rockefeller Center, the revitalization of the central business district of Pittsburgh was largely controlled by the public authority working closely with the local economic forces and was undertaken within a regional perspective. What Roy Lubove has defined as the "Pittsburgh Renaissance" may therefore serve as an example of collaboration among private capital, public authority, various planning agencies, political parties, and public opinion, in direct contrast to the complete disregard of regional planning initiatives, a governmental policy of laissez-faire, and the gigantic undertaking of a private and individual economic force observed in New York.[185]

At this point it is necessary to return to the situation in the 1920s when, under the pressure of a grave crisis in the urban economy, a private planning organization was formed in Pittsburgh, as in other major cities in the United States. The Citizens Committee on City Planning was organized by a group of Pittsburgh industrialists who recognized the phenomena compromising the interests of private and collective capital, as well as those of the community. The most prominent technician of the organization was Frederick Bigger, founding member of the Regional Planning Association of America and organizer of the Pittsburgh group, who from 1922 on was also a member of the City Planning Commission and was to serve as its director from 1934 to 1954. Bigger was thus the first link between the city's group of "enlightened" capitalists and a public planning organization. Moreover, his conception of planning coupled social idealism with maximum efficiency, and he fought for a centralized control based on analyses and scientific techniques of intervention on the physical environment. Even if only ideologically, Bigger's work was a first step toward the centralization of planning initiatives, and thus his position was radically different from that of Adams's.

The Citizens Committee on City Planning published two studies in 1920 and 1921 (*Pittsburgh Playgrounds* and *Major Street Plan*) and four others in 1923, treating all aspects of urban and residential standards, urban services, and the problem of transportation. An obvious conflict existed, however, between the Citizens Committee, which had come to represent the interests of the public, and the governmental agencies, which were subject to pressure from individual economic and political interests. The City Planning Commission, in fact, concentrated its attention almost exclusively on preparing a zoning ordinance, based on that of New York. Amidst great controversy and in the face of organized opposition, the law was approved in 1923. Even the limits on building heights and the zoning provisions themselves—all thoroughly conservative measures— were attacked as undermining the city's economic progress. The Pittsburgh Real Estate Board declared that such restrictions "serve no good purpose and . . . retard the city's growth and prosperity."[186] According to the Board of Trade, the peculiar topographic formation of the central business district of Pittsburgh made the indiscriminate proliferation of skyscrapers necessary. And the *Pittsburgh Realtor* served as the polemical spokesman of T. A. Watkins, one of the city's principal contractors.[187] Indeed, it seemed that an unbridgeable gap had opened between the interests of productive capital and those of real estate speculation.

The zoning law, in any case, very quickly proved to be completely inefficient, largely because of the lack of any coordination among the initiatives of the various communities of the region. It became clear that the problem could be adequately confronted only by the establishment of a unified authority. In 1923 the Commission to Study Municipal Consolidation proposed the creation of a federation of municipalities. Between 1926 and 1928 the provision was approved by the state legislature and electorate. It had become evident that any decision regarding the city had to take account of its inevitable repercussions in the region. In the meantime, the problems presented by the great increase of motor traffic, the disastrous location of the railroad lines within the city, and the inefficiency of the urban and regional road systems became problems of fundamental importance. The Chamber of Commerce expressed alarm and presented the city's situation in the gloomiest of terms. Their reaction gave a new impetus to the initiatives of the Citizens Committee on City Planning, significantly rebaptized the Pittsburgh Regional Planning Association. In 1939 this association summoned Robert Moses to draw up a plan for a new traffic system.[188] Moses focused his attention on the situation in the Golden Triangle, located between the central business district and the confluence of the Allegheny and Monongahela rivers, and concluded that the renewal of the urban economy depended essentially on the revitalization of this area.

Along with the removal of the railroad lines that so chaotically encumbered this area, Moses's plan called for the creation of a new system of highways to serve as the basis for the structural reorganization of the business center. The relocation of the Pennsylvania Railroad was thus intended as the first step toward a complete renewal of the city. His scheme called for the construction of Duquesne Way along the Allegheny River and a parkway along the Monongahela, as well as the creation of a large park on the tip of the Golden Triangle. These proposals immediately aroused criticism, but they were eventually to form a part of the projects carried out after the war.[189]

The influence of Moses's report was decisive in still another sense. Also in 1939, the Golden Triangle Division of the Chamber of Commerce was formed under the influence of Richard K. Mellon, who had recently assumed the direction of Mellon and Sons, one of the most important capitalist concentrations of Pittsburgh. Mellon would from now on be the leader of a group of young businessmen who were intent on collaborating with the public authorities to resolve the city's increasingly critical situation. The economic renewal of the community was thus taken in hand by a capitalist group capable of making the weight of their decisions felt with a far greater force than the group that had instituted the Citizens Committee on City Planning. The objective of the Golden Triangle Division was quite clear: "crystallize citizen effort behind a movement to stop depreciation of real estate values within the Golden Triangle by making it a better place in which to work and transact business."[190]

Mellon's initiatives would be forced to a standstill in the war years, but in the immediate postwar period the need for a solution to the problems that had been left suspended came to the fore with still greater urgency. One of the major economic centers of the United States, Pittsburgh was among the cities least equipped to carry out its specific functions. Covered with smog, regularly flooded, immobilized by a chaotic traffic, its malfunctioning threatened the

breakdown of all the commercial and economic activities that had Pittsburgh as
their center. The response to this situation came once again from the capitalist
group whose interests were damaged by such complete inefficiency. In 1943,
Richard K. Mellon organized a meeting of selected businessmen to discuss the
future of Pittsburgh. The result was the formation of the Allegheny Conference
on Community Development, in which a decisive role was played by Wallace
Richards, director of the Pittsburgh Regional Planning Association since 1937.

Various circumstances make the activity of the Allegheny Conference on
Community Development unique in the United States. Mayor David Lawrence
and the city council collaborated with it, as did the whole political organization
dominated by the Democrats. Actually, however, the new planning initiatives
won support of Democrats and Republicans, businessmen and technicians alike,
as well as the approval of the state authorities. Pittsburgh was therefore in the
vanguard in making use of all possible provisions for urban renewal. This enabled
the Allegheny Conference to work out practicable plans with realistic cost
estimates, to institute studies, to organize public consensus through the press,
and to present itself as the interpreter of the general interests of the community.
Following Moses's view of the problem, the Allegheny Conference recognized
that the renewal of the city was the fundamental premise for the revitalization
of the regional economy. Accordingly, along with projects for flood control and
the purification of the atmosphere, plans were prepared for Point Park and the
Golden Triangle. Thus was begun the renewal of the central business district, an
enterprise in which the Allegheny Conference on Community Development, the
Pittsburgh Regional Planning Association, and Governor Edward Martin collaborated. Meanwhile, under the influence of Mayor Lawrence and stimulated by
the effects of the fire that destroyed the Wabash Railroad facilities in the area of
the Point in 1946, the Urban Redevelopment Authority was formed [191]

Thus consolidated, the planning organizations were enabled in 1946 to
proceed gradually with the acquisition of the property necessary for the creation
of Point Park and the renewal of the Golden Triangle. The Urban Redevelopment Authority negotiated a contract for financing with the Equitable Life
Insurance Company, which involved no federal aid. In 1950 the plan for
Gateway Center and Point Park, initially an area of 59 acres, could be put into
operation. The experience was, indeed, exceptional for a planning project in the
United States, since the Equitable Life Insurance Company, which guaranteed
long-term leases for 60 percent of the new offices to be created by the renewal
program, insisted that its investment be based on an economic plan resulting
from the combined power of the local government and the large industries.
Collective capital and its political instruments could thus be recognized as a
single operative entity in the renewal of Pittsburgh. Westinghouse, Jones and
Laughlin, Pittsburgh Plate Glass, and six others among the city's most important
firms signed twenty-year contracts for the new offices in the Golden Triangle.
Between 1952 and 1953, the three cruciform steel towers of Gateway Center, 20

to 24 stories high, were completed. To these were added the State Office Building (1957), the Bell Telephone Building (1958), an underground garage for 750 cars (1959), the Hilton Hotel (1959), a 22-story skyscraper (1960), the IBM Building (1963), and the Gateway Tower Apartments (1964).

The Golden Triangle complex did not, however, constitute a model island. It was in direct contact with the new Point State Park at the tip of the peninsula and was connected with the rest of the city and the region by a new system of roads that followed approximately Moses's plan. The Fort Pitt Bridge, the new Fort Duquesne Bridge, Duquesne Boulevard along the Allegheny, and the Penn Lincoln Parkway along the Monongahela formed the basic structures of a new regional network of rapid connections between the city and the region. At the same time, the Crosstown and Bigelow boulevards, also forseen in the 1939 plan, ensured crosstown connection tangent to the new Civic Arena, Chatham Center, and Duquesne University.[192] The result was a comprehensive restructuring, concentrated in a number of different programs. Along William Penn Place, to the north of the Golden Triangle and at the very center of the commercial city, rises the complex formed by Harrison and Abramovitz's Alcoa Building and the Mellon Bank-United States Steel Building, separated by the green space of Mellon Square Park. The skyscraper of the Mellon family, major figures in the urban-renewal projects, dominates the city's skyline and celebrates the merits of the Mellons by its very dimensions and location. After Rockefeller's example, the space of the park ensures the complex not only greater financial yield but also social recognition.

An urban renewal on this scale could not have been controlled by the local capitalist groups, but the work of the Urban Redevelopment Authority was nonetheless carried out in strict conformity with concrete programs for expanding and revitalizing the large industrial and commercial firms. The inclusion within the Golden Triangle of a large number of luxury apartments is highly significant, since it not only permitted the municipality to increase the real-property tax revenue—an incentive in many urban-renewal programs in the United States—but also assured an automatic selection of the inhabitants of the central business district.

Like the project for Battery Park City, the new downtown Pittsburgh included residential structures—reserved, however, for the clients of the Hilton Hotel and the managers who could afford to live in Gateway Center, Allegheny Center, and the luxury apartments of Lower Hill. Thus the renewal of Pittsburgh—animated by Bigger's social ideology, the efforts of the citizenry and the democratic press, and a collective capital concerned with the destiny of the community—was revealed at its completion to be a wholly uncompromising instrument of class. The project was denounced from the architectural and urban design viewpoint for the absolute lack of formal coordination among the buildings, the absence of architectural images, and the unifunctionality of the new Golden Triangle;[193] the suggestions for improving these conditions made by the Pittsburgh Regional

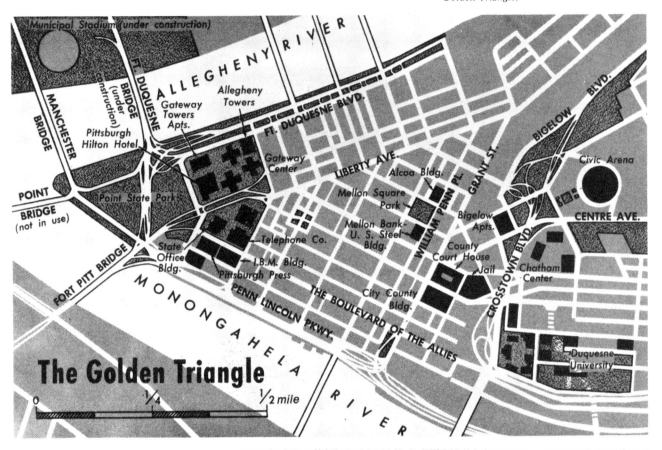

Urban renewal in Pittsburgh, plan of the Golden Triangle.

Municipal Stadium (under construction)

MANCHESTER BRIDGE

POINT BRIDGE (not in use)

FT. DUQUESNE BRIDGE (under construction)

ALLEGHENY RIVER

Gateway Towers Apts.

Allegheny Towers

FT. DUQUESNE BLVD.

Pittsburgh Hilton Hotel

Gateway Center

LIBERTY AVE.

Alcoa Bldg.

BIGELOW BLVD.

Civic Arena

Point State Park

Mellon Square Park

Mellon Bank-U. S. Steel Bldg.

WILLIAM PENN PL.

GRANT ST.

Bigelow Apts.

CENTRE AVE.

FORT PITT BRIDGE

State Office Bldg.

Telephone Co.

I.B.M. Bldg.

Pittsburgh Press

County Court House

Jail

CROSSTOWN BLVD.

Chatham Center

PENN LINCOLN PKWY.

THE BOULEVARD OF THE ALLIES

City County Bldg.

MONONGAHELA RIVER

The Golden Triangle

Duquesne University

0   1/4   1/2 mile

Urban renewal in Pittsburgh, aerial view of the Golden Triangle in 1965, with Point State Park and Gateway Center in the foreground.

Planning Association, however, might serve as a pleasant cosmetic, but they could not change the substance of the gigantic undertaking. The renewal of Pittsburgh, carried out through the coordination of various agencies and on the basis of a series of programs defined over a period of time, did not have the formal unity of Rockefeller Center. Rather, within the existing American institutions, it followed the laws of growth dictated by the best possible compromise among the myriad counterbalanced and interrelated forces of the "great society." If Rockefeller Center represented the most complete "disenchanted mountain" of the 1930s, renovated Pittsburgh was the maximum example of the "disenchanted city" of the 1960s. The capitalist city no longer hid its face beneath a romantic mask; no Mendelsohn would ever again photograph Pittsburgh as a mysterious forest;[194] no Saarinen or Ferriss would be moved to "sing" its force. The "city without quality" created itself in Pittsburgh as the direct expression of the forces that actually manage it.

In the 1960s, the protests of the black population and the inhabitants of the slums against the various urban processes induced by the operations described here made it clear that the urban crisis had only been moved to other areas and that, ultimately, the price of renewal was to be paid by the lower classes.[195] It is useful at this point to recall that in 1947, on the suggestion of Edgar J. Kaufmann, who was interested in the city's revitalization, Frank Lloyd Wright presented his own imaginative proposal for the Golden Triangle and Point Park. Wright's design consists of a huge circular structure to which a skyscraper is attached, the whole to serve as office complex and garage and offer various public services on a roof garden; suspended over the water is a second, low circular structure. This was one of Wright's most fascinating urban projects but also one of his most absolutely antiurban. Once again, Wright was the bearer of a "truth" that transcended the mechanisms of development of the almighty dollar. His fascinating image nevertheless presupposed the massive intervention in Pittsburgh of a single economic force functioning as an absolute power—exactly the opposite of the policy actually pursued by the Urban Redevelopment Authority and the Pittsburgh Regional Planning Association. The ultimate significance of this comparison, however, lies in the fact that, whether the renewal project was accomplished as it actually was or Wright's fascinating design had been executed, the economic reality of the "Pittsburgh Renaissance" for the masses destined to submit to its effects would in no way have been different.

The case of Pittsburgh is certainly unique, but the analysis might be extended to the renewal of Philadelphia or to the processes at work in Chicago in order to demonstrate the continuity in time and space of the economic policy that governs the relations between the renewal of city centers and the comprehensive processes of development. The still-unclarified reality underlying these tendencies (even leaving aside the determining factors of real estate speculation) is that at the level of economic organization achieved in the Atlantic region of

Frank Lloyd Wright's project for a Community Center, Point Park, Pittsburgh, 1947.

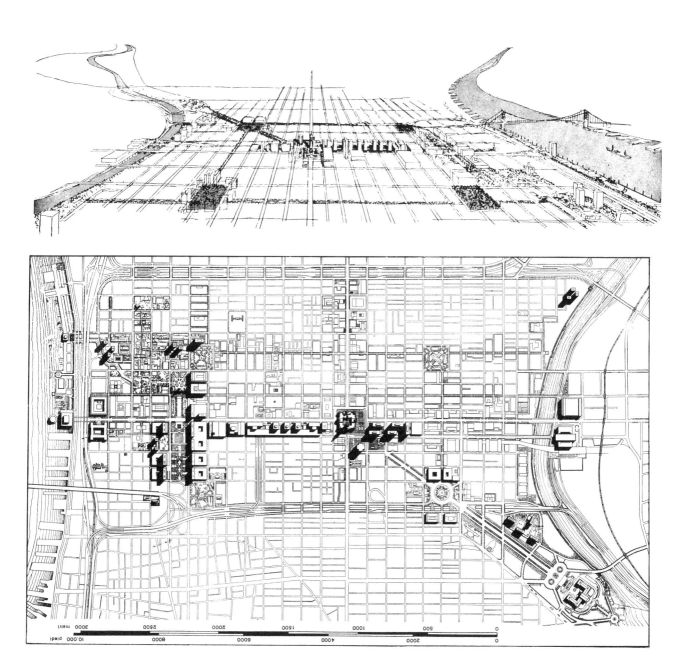

Philadelphia City Planning Commission,
bird's-eye view and plan of the renewal project for the city center, 1960.

Urban renewal in Philadelphia, Society Hill
project, at the stage reached in the early 1960s,
plan by I. M. Pei and Associates.

the United States, it not only is impossible to plan the commercial centers or single sections of the city but, moreover, has little importance for the general efficiency of the system.

A case in point is the proposal for Manhattan contained in the recent regional plan of New York, developed by the City Planning Commission and published in 1969. In addition to accepting, more or less passively, programs already in an advanced stage of preparation, such as that for Battery Park City, the major undertaking called for in this plan is a radical restructuring of the street system of midtown Manhattan according to a project prepared by the Regional Plan Association.[196] This project calls for the complete and systematic adoption of a differentiated traffic network, but this updated version of the proposal advanced by Corbett in the early 1920s is much more an abstract exercise in urban design than a practical proposal for the reform of the urban economy.

It is thus indeed possible to admire parts of the 1969 plan, for instance, the creation of axes of greenery on multiple levels along the present 48th and 53rd streets.[197] The reality of the matter, however, is that this plan is destined to remain no more than a proposal, an ineffective invocation of a renewed equilibrium between public intervention and private decisions about investments. Unless the near future proves me wrong, the congenital vice of American urbanism, already present in the ideology of the City Beautiful, that is, the vice of institutionalizing the unessential role of proposals representing a basic principle, is present once again in this plan. In view of the growing complexity of the economic phenomena in play, such proposals cannot but remain inoperative. Today more than ever, the projects elaborated by public or private planning agencies are part of an urban-planning tradition that the current economic processes may tranquilly consider a "negligible discipline."

The recent history of American cities, particularly of the Atlantic Megalopolis, as Jean Gottmann had called it, seems, in fact, to confirm the "necessity," for the present stage of capitalist development, of the ambiguities Mumford deplored in Adams's plan for New York. The business centers, productive areas, residential zones, and industrial structures of the Atlantic Coast certainly by now constitute a "system." Yet almost nothing of regionalism or Keynesian economics has entered into the capitalist management of this region and its building industry.[198] The ambiguity between decentralization and concentration is therefore not a prerogative of the Regional Plan of New York and Its Environs; no exclusive hypothesis holds up in a self-regulating system without plans. A decentralization of residence and plants is coupled with an increased concentration of administrative offices and a tendency toward residential reconcentration. Representing these two latter trends, the World Trade Center and what will be Battery Park City quite naturally present themselves as closely integrated operations.

City Planning Commission of New York, plan of 1969, model of proposals for Lower Manhattan.

City Planning Commission of New York, plan of 1969, proposal for the East River waterfront, Lower Manhattan.

City Planning Commission of New York, plan of 1969, proposal for Battery Park City.

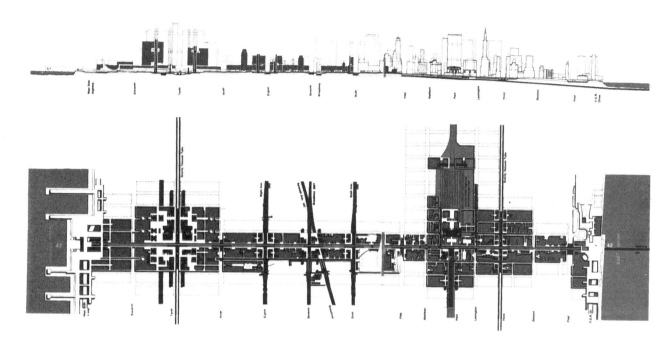

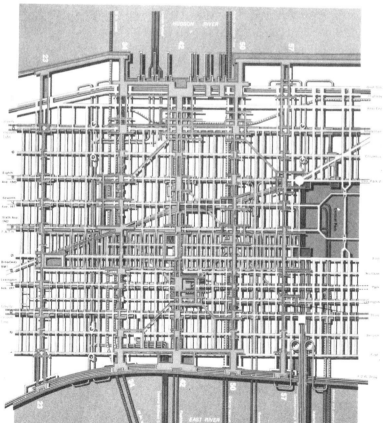

City Planning Commission of New York,
plan of 1969, project prepared by Regional
Plan Association for the restructuring of
the street network of Manhattan, cross section
and plan of proposal for 42nd Street.

City Planning Commission of New York,
plan of 1969, project prepared by Regional
Plan Association for the restructuring of
the street network of Manhattan, diagram
of projected multilevel traffic system.

Thus the model of Rockefeller Center, of the multiblock skyscraper, in which American urbanism placed such hope in the period between 1940 and 1950, has not constituted a new departure on which to base a progressive restructuring of the city. It has contributed, however, to making clear the antiutopian significance of any project on an urban scale. In this sense, projects such as Battery Park City or the Embarcadero Center in San Francisco[199] may be considered the most authentic heirs of Rockefeller Center's lesson: the urbanized territory rejects any utopia, and thus all attempts to restore lost enchantment to an urban "adventure," which now reflects only the necessary imbalances of capitalist development, must be relegated to the "museums on a community scale" that the Battery and Embarcadero enterprises represent.

At this point, however, a paradoxical phenomenon intruded the urban scene. Corresponding to the failure of the multiblock skyscraper was the introduction in the American city in the 1960s of the super-skyscraper, such as New York's World Trade Center or the John Hancock and Sears buildings in Chicago. Neither technological revision nor urban-planning logic underlies these undertakings. On the contrary, an accurate technological criticism can demonstrate the absolute lack of logic in the crisscross structures of the John Hancock Building or the overblown dimensions of the World Trade Center. The two surreal towers marking the tip of Manhattan or the truncated pyramid of Chicago's super-skyscraper are only inflated, empty signs, intent on communicating nothing beside their own surreal presence.

Everything can be sacrificed to the metaphysics of quantity they incarnate: economy of general conception, technological logic, and urban-planning logic as well. The John Hancock Building and the World Trade Center seem to wish to represent—on a new scale—what was achieved in 1902 with the Flatiron Building, in 1913 with the Woolworth Building, and in 1931 with the Empire State Building—the creation of a skyscraper as a unique event, multiplied in height to achieve, by itself, the formal control of the urban skyline, the skyscraper intent on dominating, through its own dimensions, the unnatural forest of the metropolis.

The Flatiron enunciated with all the means at its disposal its own profound faith in the laws and tendencies of urban growth; the Woolworth soared upward according to a telescopic logic that corresponded to its situation in the urban scene; and the Empire State could justify its height by the pioneering function it served in midtown Manhattan. At least until the 1940s, in spite of polemic criticism from progressive circles, the popular imagination could still sense an integration between skyscraper and metropolis. It was not without reason that the directors of the film *King Kong* killed their ape on the top of the Empire State Building: technological civilization conquers the irrational sentimentality of the "noble savage."[200]

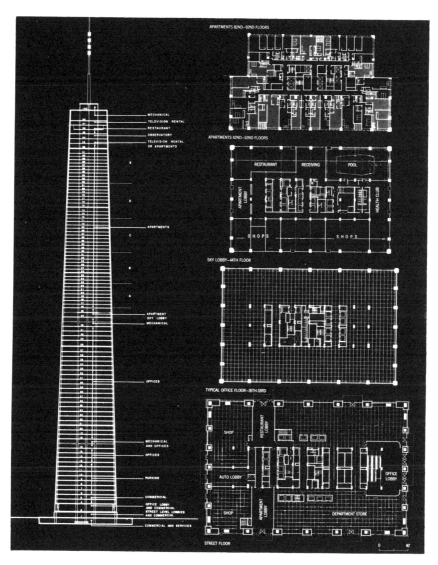

John Hancock Building, Chicago, 1082
feet high; diagram of elevation and floor
plans at various levels, by Skidmore, Owings
and Merrill; Bruce Graham, architect;
Fazlur Khan and H. Srinivasa Iyengar,
engineers.

John Hancock Building, Chicago, completed
in 1968 (photo by Ezra Stoller).

With the World Trade Center, the John Hancock Building, and the other super-skyscrapers designed for Chicago and San Francisco, however, the relationship between skyscraper and city has been definitively broken. Frank Lloyd Wright's mile-high skyscraper had an internal logic. Condensing in itself an entire city, it was coherently placed in the ideal prairie of Usonia. The new super-skyscrapers, however, are not in the desert; they are within the city even if they refuse to take part in it. Far more than Rockefeller Center, they are cities within cities. In the John Hancock Building, for instance, people can live, work, and participate in social life without ever leaving the gigantic antiurban machine.

This, indeed, is the real substance of these inventions, in spite of their intended aim of serving as eloquent symbols of the metropolis and its dynamics. It is not emerging urban masses that erupt on the skylines of Manhattan, Chicago, and other American metropolises but, rather, antiurban paradoxes, artificial technological "miracles." Here the laws of urban growth in the American city are overturned. The insertion of such structures in the two-dimensional grid of the city tends to negate the city itself in a desperate effort to escape its irrationalities. With the John Hancock Building and the World Trade Center, as already noted, skyscrapers again became exceptional events that enclose the paradox of the metropolis within themselves. But these are events that, through their presuming to attain the value of a totality, reveal a desperation shared by intellectuals and businessmen alike—the desperation of one who sees himself impotent to control, with his antiquated instruments, the enigmatic course of the indomitable White Whale.

Notes

1

See especially Winston Weisman, "New York and the Problem of the First Skyscraper," *Journal of the Society of Architectural Historians* 12, no. 1, 1953, pp. 13-21; idem, "A New View of Skyscraper History," in Edgar Kaufmann, Jr., ed., *The Rise of an American Architecture* (Pall Mall Press, London-New York, 1970), pp. 115-160; J. Carson Webster, "The Skyscraper: Logical and Historical Considerations," *Journal of the Society of Architectural Historians* 18, no. 4, 1959, pp. 126-139. This is not the place to take up the controversy between Weisman and Webster, which primarily concerns the criteria for classifying building types and the bases of comparison. It is interesting, however, to note that both authors' analyses are based on a structural criterion. It is not possible to give a complete bibliography on the history of the skyscraper here; among the significant contributions, in addition to the works cited above, are Claude Bragdon, "The Skyscraper," *Architectural Record* 21, Dec. 1909, pp. 84-96; Francisco Mujica, *History of the Skyscraper* (Archeology and Architecture Press, New York, 1930); Carl W. Condit, *The Chicago School of Architecture* (University of Chicago Press, Chicago, 1964). The following articles by Montgomery Schuyler are indispensable: "The Skyscraper Up-to-Date," *Architectural Record* 8, Jan.-Mar. 1899, pp. 230-257; "The Skyscraper Problem," *Scribner's Magazine* 34, Aug. 1903, pp. 253-256; "The Evolution of the Skyscraper," ibid. 46, Sept. 1909, pp. 257-271; these articles are now available in William H. Jordy and Ralph Coe, eds., *American Architecture and Other Writings by Montgomery Schuyler* (Atheneum, New York, 1964). See also *L'architecture d'aujourd'hui*, no. 178, 1975; *Archithese*, nos. 17, 18, 20, 1976, all special issues devoted to this subject. On the relation between the development of the skyscraper and economic cycles, see Heinz Ronner, "Skyscraper: à propos Oekonomie," *Archithese*, no. 18, 1976, pp. 44-49 and 55. The special issue of *Casabella*, no. 418, 1976, dedicated to the "Triumph and Failure of the Skyscraper," is very general in its treatment of the topic.

2

See Fiske Kimball, *Thomas Jefferson Architect* (1916; reprint ed. with introduction by Fr. Doveton Nichols, Da Capo Press, New York, 1968); Thomas W. Waterman, "Thomas Jefferson. His Early Works in Architecture," *Gazette des Beaux Arts* 24, no. 918, 1943, pp. 89-106; idem, "French Influence on Early American Architecture," ibid. 38, no. 942, 1945, pp. 87-112; James S. Ackerman, "Il presidente Jefferson e il palladianesimo americano," *Bolletino del Centro Studi A. Palladio* 6, Pt. 2, 1964, pp. 39-48. See also Manfredo Tafuri, *Architecture and Utopia. Design and Capitalist Development* (MIT Press, Cambridge, Mass., 1976), pp. 25-34; this is a translation of *Progetto e Utopia* (Laterza, Bari, 1973).

3

See Montgomery Schuyler, *The Woolworth Building* (New York 1913), reprinted in Jordy and Coe, *American Architecture;* idem, "The Towers of Manhattan and Notes on the Woolworth Building," *Architectural Record* 33, Feb. 1913, pp. 99-122. See also Gunvald Aus, "Engineering Design of the Woolworth Building, *American Architect* 103, no. 1944, 1913, pp. 157-170; Edwin A. Cochran, *The Cathedral of Commerce* (Broadway Park Place Co., New York, 1916). The disastrous effects of the Woolworth Building on traffic congestion in Manhattan were brought out in a lucid article by Raymond Unwin, "Higher Building in Relation to Town Planning," *Journal of the Royal Institute of British Architects* 31, no. 5, 1924, pp. 125-140. On the story of the inauguration of the Woolworth Building and the controversy the building provoked, see Rosemarie Bletter, "King Kong en Arcadie. Le gratte-ciel américain apprivoisé," *Archithese*, no. 20, 1976, especially pp. 28-30.

4

Schuyler, "Evolution of the Skyscraper."

5

Schuyler, "Towers of Manhattan."

6

See the Schuyler articles collected in the chapter "The Richardsonian Interlude," in Jordy and Coe, *American Architecture*, pp. 81-174.

7

C. Matlack Price, "The Trend of Architectural Thought in America," *Century Magazine* 102, no. 5, 1921, p. 710.

8

Ibid., p. 712. American literature of the 1920s on the skyscraper, however, oscillated between deploring the effects of congestion provoked by tall buildings and interpretations in a scenographic key. See, for example, Herbert Croly, "New York's Skyscrapers," *Architectural Record* 61, no. 4, 1927, pp. 374-375; idem, "The Scenic Function of the Skyscraper," ibid. 63, no. 1, 1928, pp. 77-78. But see Kenenth M. Murchison, "The Spires of Gotham," *Architectural Forum* 52, no. 6, 1930, pp. 786, 878; see also the defense of free speculation by Paul Robertson, president of the National Association of Building Owners and Managers, in "The Skyscraper Office Building," ibid., pp. 879-880.

9

In McCormick's own words: "In 1904 or '05, Carter Harrison appointed a committee of aldermen to work in conjunction with a similar committee of the South Park Board to devise means of widening Michigan Avenue. Henry Foreman was chairman of this committee and I was secretary. At that time Mr. Lawson favored a plan for a tunnel from Randolph Street and Michigan Boulevard to some place on the north side (I believe preferably the present outer drive). Another plan suggested was double-decking Michigan Avenue originally to connect with Rush Street at Ohio. Our committee had two other members, Ernest Graham and Jarvis Hunt. Jarvis Hunt, in my presence, made the first suggestion of the present boulevard although he advocated a still wider boulevard than the one we have. Our committee recommended the improvement substantially as it has been built, but Mayor Dunne's board of local improvement was hostile. The project was later taken up by the Chicago Plan Commission." See *The International Competition for a New Administration Building for the Chicago Tribune MCMXXII* (Chicago Tribune, Chicago, 1923) pp. 3-4n.

10

Ibid., p. 1. In this official publication of the competition, containing reproductions of the perspective drawings of all the entries, the newspapers's contribution to the development of the city was carefully pointed out. According to the information it furnishes, the *Chicago Tribune* employed 13,000 people in 1922 and had a daily circulation of 4,000,000 copies.

11

Ibid., p. 3.

12

Ibid., p. 4. In 1921 the Michigan Avenue Bridge was built, breaking the barrier between the Loop and the area beyond the Chicago River; in 1919-21, Graham, Anderson, Probst and White built the Wrigley Building at 400 North Michigan Avenue.

13

The competition was opened on June 10, 1922, and the jury was composed of Alfred Granger of the American Institute of Architects, Joseph M. Patterson and Robert McCormick, directors of the *Chicago Tribune*, Edward S. Beck and Holmes Onderdonk, also of the *Chicago Tribune*. The jury was assisted by an advisory committee composed of B. M. Winston, chairman, Dorsey Crowe, E. I. Frankhauser, Sheldon Clark, Harvey A. Wheeler, and Joy Morton, who together represented the Chicago City Council, the Chicago Plan Commission, and the North Central Association. Thus the principal decision-making and consultative agencies of the city collaborated with the private initiative in the final verdict. On November 23, 1922, the jury was already able to indicate as prize-worthy a preliminary group of twelve designs, among which were those of Howells and Hood and Holabird and Roche. Saarinen's design arrived on November 29 and so impressed the jury that they decided to include it among the prize-worthy entries. On December 3, 1922, the final decision was announced: "Never before has the 'quality of beauty' been recognized as of commercial value by an American business corporation, and yet all the greatest architecture of the past has been based upon beauty as its fundamental essential. . . . Let us hope that the results of The Tribune Competition may impress this essential upon the mind of American business so emphatically that the whole aspect of our American cities may be permanently influenced thereby. One gratifying result of this world competition has been to establish the superiority of American design" (*International Competition*, p. 44). See also the editorial published in the *Chicago Tribune*, on December 3, 1922. On the competition, see, in addition to the works cited in subsequent notes, Frank Schulze, "Chicago Architecture between the Two Wars," in Oswald Grabe, Peter C. Pran, Frank Schulze, *100 Years of Architecture in Chicago* (O'Hara, Chicago, 1976), pp. 41-43.

14

In 1922, the firm of William Holabird and Martin Roche included, in addition to the titular members, John A. Holabird, William's son, John W. Root, Jr., and Edward A. Renwick.

15

In addition to the 145 designs presented by American entrants, foreign proposals were submitted as follows: Australia, 1 (that of Griffin); Austria, 5 (plus Loos's, which was sent from Paris); Belgium, 2; Canada, 4; Cuba, 2; Denmark, 2; England, 4; Finland, 2; France, 6; Germany, 8; Holland, 11; Hungary, 4; Italy, 11; Luxembourg, 1; Mexico, 1; New Zealand, 1 (that of Lippincott and Billson); Norway, 3; Scotland, 3; Serbia, 1; Spain, 2; Switzerland, 6. There were 8 anonymous entries, among which that of the Luckhardt brothers. The absence of such figures as Le Corbusier, Mies van der Rohe, and Behrens—that is, of architects who were involved at the time with large-scale urban problems of theoretical dimensions exceeding the limits imposed by the competition—is significant. On Italian participation in the competition and the relationship of Italy to America in the matter of the skyscraper, see Giorgio Muratore, "Métamorphose d'un mythe: 1922-1943. Le gratte-ciel américain et ses reflets sur la culture architecturale italienne," *Archithese*, no. 18, 1976, pp. 28-36.

16

Even outstanding firms of the Chicago school, such as Holabird and Roche or Schmidt, Garden and Martin, were careful not to stray from the reigning stylistic eclecticism; the mandatory qualitative distinction was sought in a montage of formal references drawn from the most varied European and non-European repertories. Within the general barrage of banality, a few of the designs submitted, including those by Bertram G. Goodhue or George F. Schreiber, or the design by Ralph Thomas Walker and McKenzie, Voorhees and Gamelin, Associated, stand out for their synthetic treatment of volumes, while the proposal submitted by Frank Herding and W. W. Boyd, Jr., shows the influence of German Expressionist experiments on the faceted modelling of volumes.

17

See James Birrel, *Walter Burley Griffin* (University of Queensland Press, St. Lucia, Brisbane, 1964), pp. 157ff.

18

Griffin's design pursued a concept not unlike that of the entry by Albert J. Rousseau of Ann Arbor, Michigan, which won an honorable mention.

19

Condit, *Chicago School*, p. 209n46.

20

See Le Corbusier, *Quand les cathédrales étaient blanches* (Paris, 1937).

21

There exists no thorough critical analysis of Loos's design, but see Ludwig Münz, *Adolf Loos* (Il Balcone, Milan, 1956); Ludwig Münz and Gustave Künstler, *Das Architekt Adolf Loos* (Schroll Verlag, Vienna-Munich, 1964); Mihaly Kubinsky, *Adolf Loos* (Henschelverlag, Berlin, 1970); Herman Czech and Wolfgang Mistelbauer, *Das Looshaus* (Löcker und Wögenstein Verlag, Vienna, 1976). On the relationship between Loos and American architecture, see Roland L. Schachel, "Adolf Loos, Amerika und die Antike," *Alte und Moderne Kunst* 15, no. 113, 1970, pp. 6-10; Leonard K. Eaton, *American Architecture Comes of Age. European Reaction to H. H. Richardson and Louis Sullivan* (MIT Press, Cambridge, Mass. 1972), especially the chapter "Adolf Loos and the Viennese Image of America," pp. 109-142. See also Massimo Cacciari, "Loos/Wein," in Francesco Amendolagine and Massimo Cacciari, *OIKOS. Da Loos a Wittgenstein* (Officina, Rome, 1975).

22

Adolf Loos, "Die *Chicago Tribune* Column," *Zeitschrift des Österr. Ingenieur- und Architekten-Vereines* 75, no. 3-4, 1923, reprinted in Heinrich Kulka, *Adolf Loos, das Werk des Architekten* (Schroll Verlag, Vienna, 1931). I myself advanced the hypothesis of an ironic intention in Loos's column skyscraper in Manfredo Tafuri, *Teorie e storia dell'-architettura* (1968; rev. ed., Laterza, Bari, 1976), p. 97.

23

Loos's appreciation of Sullivan's work is witnessed by his intention of opening a school in Paris in the direction of which the old master would have a part. See Ester McCoy, "Letters from Louis Sullivan to R. M. Schindler," *Journal of the Society of Architectural Historians* 20, no. 4, 1961, pp. 179-184.

24

I refer here to the distinction between art and architecture made by Loos in his 1910 lecture "Architektur," published in *Trotzdem* and reprinted in *Sämtliche Schriften Adolf Loos* (Harold Verlag, Vienna-Munich, 1962), 1: 302ff.

25

Loos, *"Chicago Tribune* Column."

26

Ibid.

27

According to Montgomery Schuyler, the first example of this type of tripartite skyscraper was George B. Post's Union Trust Building in New York (1889-90), a work of evident Richardsonian inspiration; see Schuyler, "Skyscraper Up-to-Date." Weisman traces the origins of this type to an earlier work by Post, the Produce Exchange in New York (1881-84), which constituted a precedent for Richardson's own Marshall Field Warehouse, and to Post's Havermeyer Building in New York, in which the architect created a highly successful organism, also notable for its height. Particular note should be taken of the exceptional quality of Post's activity in general and of his role as inventor of structural models for the skyscraper. See Winston Weisman, "The Commercial Architecture of George B. Post," *Journal of the Society of Architectural Historians* 31, no. 3, pp. 176-203.

28

Max Berg, "Der Bau von Geschäftshochhäusern in Breslau zur Linderung der Wohnungsnot," *Stadtbaukunst*, nos. 7, 8, 1920, pp. 99-104, 116-118. At the time Berg was the city architect of Breslau; like Hegemann later, he conceived of a completely different use of skyscrapers, relating them to the nodal points of the urban center. Despite the difference in scale, his proposals for tall commercial buildings concentrated on the Lessing Platz, near the Cathedral, and on the Schweidnitzer Stadtgraben in Breslau are somewhat reminiscent of Peter Behrens's ideas for the center of Berlin, published in 1913 in the *Berliner Morgenpost*. Compare also the Poelziglike Expressionism of Berg's designs with the designs for the *Chicago Tribune* skyscraper presented by the "moderate" wing of the German participants in the competition. Interestingly, a plan similar to Berg's for Breslau was prepared in the 1920s, at the request of the Prussian Academy of Architecture, by Bruno Möhring, whose aim was to rationalize functions in the commercial center of Berlin and to control speculation. See J. Schultz, "Hochhäuser and City-Gedanke in Deutschland 1920 bis 1923," *Deutsche Architektur*, no. 12, 1964, p. 750; Donatella Calabi, preface to Werner Hegemann, *La Berlino di Pietra* (Mazzotta, Milan, 1975), p. iv, Italian translation of *Das steinerne Berlin* (1930).

29

It was common practice in Weimar Germany to endow commercial centers with late-romantic architectural imagery. Among the German architects related in some way to Expressionism, there existed a subtle polemic with the "impersonal" American city. It is quite clear, for example, in the exaltation of an "antiurban" vitalism that characterizes Adolf Rading's "Stadt, Form, Architekt," *Die Form*, no. 1, 1925, now available in *Die Form. Stimme des deutschen Werkbundes 1925-34* (Bertelsmann Fachverlag, Berlin, 1969), pp. 115-121. The most remarkable manifestations of this tendency arose in the competition for a commercial skyscraper in Cologne, promoted by Konrad Adenauer, the mayor of the city, at the suggestion of Fritz Schumacher; its results were criticized with caustic irony in an anonymous article, possibly by Werner Hegemann, entitled "Kolner Hochhaus-Carneval," *Wasmuths Monatschefte für Baukunst*, no. 3, 1926, pp. 91-127. On Bruno Taut's design for the Chicago competition, see Kurt Junghanns, *Bruno Taut, 1880-1938* (Deutsche

Bauakademie und Henschelverlag, East Berlin, 1970). On American-German relations in regard to the skyscraper, see Walter Kurt Behrendt, "Skyscrapers in Germany," *Journal of the American Institute of Architects* 11, no. 9, 1923, pp. 365-370; Cervin Robinson and Rosemarie Haag Bletter, *Skyscraper Style. Art Deco New York* (Oxford University Press, New York, 1975); Manfredo Tafuri, "La dialectique de l'absurde. Europe-USA: les avatars de l'idéologie du gratte-ciel," *L'architecture d'aujourd'hui*, no. 178, 1975, pp. 1-19; Schultz "Hochhäuser und City-Gedanke." See also Wolfgang Pehnt, *Expressionist Architecture* (Thames and Hudson, London, 1973).

30

See Bruno Taut, *Die Stadtkrone* (Verlag E. Diederichs, Jena, 1919).

31

Adolf Behne, *Der moderne Zweckbau* (Munich, 1926), actually written in 1923. See also idem, "De Duitsche Torenhuis Bouw," *Wendingen*, no. 3, 1923, pp. 15-17.

32

Gerhard Wohler, "Das Hochhaus in Wettbewerb der 'Chicago Tribune'," *Deutsche Bauzeitung* 108, no. 54, 1924, pp. 315-320, and no. 57, pp. 345-351.

33

See Ferdinand Tönnies, *Gemeinschaft und Gesellschaft* (O. R. Reislad, Leipzig, 1887). On this concept, see also Massimo Cacciari, *Metropolis* (Officina, Rome, 1973).

34

Giulio Carlo Argan, *Walter Gropius e la Bauhaus* (1951; reprint ed., Einaudi, Turin, 1970), p. 100.

35

See Manfredo Tafuri, "URSS-Berlin, 1922; du populisme à l'Internationale constructiviste," *VH 101*, nos. 7-8, 1972, pp. 53-87.

36

Recent studies on Gropius's earliest activity have shed light not only on the continuity of his development but also on new motives animating his work after 1921-22; they have thus done away with the idea of a Gropius completely consistent in his production from the Fagus Factory to the Bauhaus at Dessau. See especially Wolfgang Pehnt, "Gropius the Romantic," *Art Bulletin* 53, no. 3, 1971, pp. 379-392; Marcel Franciscono, *Walter Gropius and the Creation of the Bauhaus in Weimar. The Ideals and Artistic Theories of Its Founding Years* (University of Illinois Press, Urbana, 1971); H. Klotz, "Materialen zu einer Gropius-Monographie," *Architectura*, no. 2, 1971; Pehnt, *Expressionist Architecture*, pp. 107ff.

37

See *De Stijl* 5, no. 4, 1922.

38

It has become common practice to compare Gropius and Meyer's design for the *Chicago Tribune* competition with that of the Vesnin brothers for the Palace of the People in Moscow, despite the lack of any complete analysis of the two projects and their different sources. See, for example, Michel Ragon, "La Révolution architecturale en URSS de 1922 à 1932," *Cimaise*, nos. 85-86, 1968, pp. 46ff.; counter to all historical evidence, Ragon considers Gropius's 1922 design dependent on that of the Vesnin brothers of 1922-23. The comparison is more objective in A. Cinjakov, "Brat'ya Vesniny," *Architektura SSSR*, no. 3, 1967, pp. 41-54; for the English translation of this article, "The Vesnin Brothers," see O. A. Shvidkovsky, *Building in the USSR 1917-1932* (Praeger, New York, 1971), especially pp. 49-50.

39

See Ludwig Hilberseimer, "Das Hochhaus," *G*, no. 2, 1932. See also idem, *Berliner Architektur der 20er Jahre* (Neue Bauhausbucher, Florian Kupferberg, Mainz and Berlin, 1967), p. 51.

40

Many projects prepared in Europe for the Chicago competition were never submitted because of lateness or other accidental reasons. A German project not entered—very interesting for its prophetic decorative design—is in the private archive of Professor Tilman Buddensieg, who very courteously brought it to my attention, in Berlin.

41

Hilberseimer, "Das Hochhaus."

42

See Gustave Adolf Platz, *Die Baukunst der neusten Zeit* (Propyläen Verlag, Berlin, 1927), p. 443, which contains a photo of a model of Hans and Wassili Luckhardt and Alfons Anker's project.

43

See Behne, *Der moderne Zweckbau;* Vincent Scully, *American Architecture and Urbanism* (Thames and Hudson, London, 1969), p. 151.

44

Italy was amply represented. Among the eleven entrants were the Romans Giuseppe Boni and Vittorio Pino, who presented eclectic designs; Saverio Dioguardi of Bari, the Neapolitan Arturo Tricomi, who prepared a curiously puristic design; and Marcello Piacentini, with a banal academic offering. See Muratore, "Métamorphose d'un mythe." Equally negative judgments can be pronounced on the projects divorced from any trend, such as that by Hentze and Richter of Hamburg, who presented a montage of cylindrical volumes obviously inspired by Richardson, or that of the Finns Einar Sjostrom and Jarl Eklund, who grafted Neogothic modulations onto an emphatically vertical pyramidal structure that vaguely evoke the aura of a Nordic saga. Among the few French entries, that of J. Batteux of Rennes is not without a certain distinction.

45

This bias was quite obvious to contemporary observers. In addition to Sullivan's explicit accusation, see Wohler, "Das Hochhaus"; Don Gifford, ed., *The Literature of Architecture. The Evolution of Architectural Theory and Practice in Nineteenth Century America* (Dutton, New York, 1966), pp. 624-631.

46

Both John Mead Howells (born 1869) and Raymond Mathewson Hood (born 1881) were graduates of the Massachusetts Institute of Technology and attended the Ecole des Beaux Arts in Paris. Hood worked first for the firm of Cram, Goodhue and Ferguson in Boston, taking up their Neogothic style, and then for Palmer Hornbostel and Jones in New York. Finally, in 1914, he established himself independently, together with Rayne Adams. Hood's Mori Restaurant in New York (1924) was a soberly classical work, while in the St. Vincent de Paul Asylum in Tarrytown, New York, designed in 1924 in collaboration with Jacques André Fouilhoux, he was inspired by seventeenth-century French models. On Hood's early work, see Francis S. Swales, "Draftmanship and Architecture as Exemplified by the Work of Raymond Hood," *Pencil Points,* May 1928, pp. 259-269. Hood's notable stylistic adaptability served greatly to further his professional career and even permitted him, after 1929, to take up enthusiastically the canons of the International style. The work of the firm of J. M. Howells and R. Hood Associated included the Chicago Tribune Tower and the unexecuted project for its enlargement of the apartment house at 3 East 84th Street and the Daily News Building in New York City, and the Joseph M. Patterson house at Ossining, New York (1930). In this last work, the firm's final tribute to the European avant-garde, the articulated aggregations of pure volumes are further elaborated by an abstract use of color See Arthur Tappan North, ed., *Raymond Hood* (McGraw-Hill, Whittlesey House, New York 1931). While it is true that in his early work Hood applied his Beaux-Art training in interpreting the Neogothic, this influence remained for him essentially an abstract composi tional concept. In this regard it is indicative that the sphere in the atrium of his Daily News Building can be found in a monumental design he executed in 1920; there, however, it still had the character of an Enlightenment memento. See "Raymond Mathewson Hood," *Architectural Forum* 62, no. 2, 1935, pp. 126-133, which contains a good deal of bio graphical material and presents illustrations of little-known works. The invitation to enter the *Chicago Tribune* competition was originally directed only to Howells, who did not wish to participate alone and therefore sought Hood's collaboration. See ibid., p. 130. For further bibliography, see n118.

47

It is interesting to note the different views of Howells and Hood's design on the part of American and European critics. Tallmadge, and later, Solon, treated the winning project as a purely formal object, while Neutra minutely analyzed its technological characteristics and emphisized the contradictions between the technological innovations and the architectural design. See Thomas E. Tallmadge, "A Critique of the *Chicago Tribune* Building Competition," *Western Architect* 32, no. 1, 1923, pp. 7-8, in which the Howells and Hood proposal is praised but declared artificial and inferior to the designs of Goodhue and Rebori; Leon V. Solon, "The Evolution of an Architectural Design, 1. The *Tribune* Building Tower, Chicago," *Architectural Record* 59, no. 3, 1926, pp. 215-225, in which drawings related to the whole course of development of Howells and Hood's design are published; Richard Neutra, "Die ältesten Hochhäuser und der jüngste Turm," *Die Baugilde*, no. 21, 1924. On the construction of the Tribune Tower, see the detailed description in Carl W. Condit, *Chicago 1910-29, Building, Planning and Urban Technology* (University of Chicago Press, Chicago, 1973), pp. 112-114 and the relevant notes.

48
Werner Hegemann, "Das Hochhaus als Quelle von Verkehrschwierigkeiten," reprinted in *Amerikanische Architektur und Stadtbaukunst* (Ernst Wasmuth, Berlin, 1925), pp. 44-54.

49
See Wohler, "Das Hochhaus."

50
American criticism was unanimous in its eulogy of Saarinen's *Chicago Tribune* design. Leaving aside for the moment Louis Sullivan's judgment, the unconditional approval of Pond and Tallmadge was echoed by Tilghman, while Swartwout was the only one to point out the ridiculousness of Sullivan's statement, taken up by Pond, about the "splendid interpretation of the spirit of the American people" in the Finnish architect's design. See Irving K. Pond, "Eliel Saarinen and His Work. A Word of Appreciation and Greeting," the *Western Architect* 32, no. 7, 1923, pp. 75-77; Tallmadge, "Critique of the *Chicago Tribune* Building Competition"; Egerton Swartwout, "Review of Recent Architectural Magazines," *American Architect* 123, no. 2422, 1923, pp. 574-578, especially p. 575. See also the editorial *"Chicago Tribune* Building," *Architecture* 47, no. 3, 1923, pp. 87-88. Among the comments on the competition, the most enthusiastic response to Saarinen's entry was Tallmadge's:

In his extraordinary conception, Architecture, long bound with the chains of precedent and bent double with the load of commercial expediency, bursts its bonds and stands up as a man. It is as though some Titanic seed, planted deep in the earth, had suddenly sprung from the mould into the light in a shimmering bloom of stone and steel. It's the best design since Amiens! ... The design in general consists of a pyramidal and telescopic mass, with strongly marked vertical elements and with the surface slightly enriched with ornament and carved figures. The extraordinary sense of exaltation, in my opinion, is obtained not so much by the vertical elements as by the entire absence of the usual horizontal lids or clamps known as cornices, for without these heavy prison bars the building escapes, as it were, in joyous freedom into the sky. (p. 7)

On the value of verticalism as a means of formal control over the urban scale, compare Tallmadge's description with Saarinen's own words in regard to New York City; see Eliel Saarinen, "A New Architectural Language for America," *Western Architect* 32, no. 2, 1923, p. 13. See also n62 of this essay. For a stylistic analysis of Saarinen's project see Walter L. Creese, "Saarinen's *Tribune* Design," *Journal of the Society of Architectural Historians* 6, nos. 3-4, 1947, pp. 1-5, in which the project is seen as the logical development of Sullivan's work on the skyscraper and is related in its formal language to Olbrich.

51
Richard Neutra, *Wie baut Amerika?* (Julius Hoffman Verlag, Stuttgart, 1927); see pp. 24ff. for an analysis of the Palmer House and pp. 75ff. on the significance of what Neutra calls the "impersonal romanticism" of American architecture, which he considers a sort of mass reaction to the environment created by a technological universe in the course of development.

52
Louis H. Sullivan, "The *Chicago Tribune* Competition," *Architectural Record* 53, no. 2, Feb. 1923, pp. 151-157, reprinted in Maurice English, *The Testament of Stone. Themes of Idealism and Indignation from the Writings of Louis Sullivan* (Northwestern University Press, Evanston, Ill., 1963), pp. 63-70.

53

Sullivan, "*Chicago Tribune* Competition," p. 152.

54

Ibid., p. 153.

55

It is interesting that in praising Howells and Hood's project Alfred Granger, the only architect on the jury for the competition, adapted a reasoning very close to that used by Sullivan in regard to Saarinen's design. Granger wrote,

Springing from solid foundations which satisfy the eye it soars upward growing lighter and more graceful as it mounts until it flowers at the top with all the grace and beauty of the Gothic spires of the old world; and yet it is not Gothic, neither is it Romanesque, although the round arch is used wherever an arch is needed. Many have asked me to name its style, but I could not answer because it is not of any of the established styles. Because it has *Style*, it is of our day and our land, a land of aspiration and idealism in spite of the coarse materialism which surrounds us and at times engulfs us. . . . But the main point to be emphasized, the quality which makes it a work of architecture is, as I said, *beauty*. But to be really beautiful it must tell the *truth*, must have beauty of function as well as beauty of line. The men who designed the Tribune Tower did not attempt simply to cover their steel frames with fine material finely cut. They used only stone, but the stone is so handled in scale that it could never be imagined as being self supporting and independent of the steel behind it. The steel is covered as is the skeleton of the human body but, while the covering, like the flesh and muscles, satisfies the eye, the frame always makes its presence felt through the covering.

See Alfred Granger, "The Tribune Tower as a Work of Architecture," *Western Architect* 34, no. 11, 1925, p. 112.

56

Creese, "Saarinen's *Tribune* Design," pp. 2ff.

57

Saarinen, "New Architectural Language."

58

The town hall of Joensun was built by Saarinen in 1912-13, following a competition he won in 1909; see "Eliel Saarinen: Examples of Work in Finland," *American Architect* 124, no. 2429, 1923; Pond, "Eliel Saarinen and His Work," p. 77. The Helsinki bank is, strangely, missing from the catalogue of Saarinen's work compiled by Albert Christ-Janer but is correctly included in Calzolari's more summary catalogue; see Vittoria Calzolari, "Eliel Saarinen architetto finlandese," *Casabella continuità*, no. 211, 1956, pp. 25ff. The influence of Richardson and Sullivan on Scandinavian architecture has been studied by Leonard K. Eaton, who demonstrates that their influence reached far beyond the single case of Saarinen; see "Richardson and Sullivan in Scandinavia," *Progressive Architecture* 47, no. 3, 1966, pp. 168-171. The subject has been further pursued by Tselos, who recognizes Richardsonian elements in the Finnish pavilion at the Paris International Exposition of 1900, designed by Saarinen, Gesellius, and Lindgren; see Dimitri Tselos, "Richardson's Influence on European Architecture," *Journal of the Society of Architectural Historians* 29, no. 2, 1970, especially p. 160. See also Eaton, *American Architecture Comes of Age.*

59

See Albert Christ-Janer, *Eliel Saarinen*, introduced by Alvar Aalto (University of Chicago Press, Chicago, 1948), p. 9.

60

Ibid., p. 10.

61

Ibid.

62

Like all his other theoretical works on urban planning, Saarinen's article is dominated by a search for elements making it possible to maintain a formal unity in the city. For him the skyscraper was a means of achieving this objective, provided the current conception of the skyscraper as an individual entity was relinquished. This, as I shall point out, only apparently contradicts the formal qualities of his *Chicago Tribune* project. This passage, in which Saarinen seeks a formal unity for Manhattan, is typical: "I procured a photograph of New York City, showing a forest of skyscrapers with the greatest imaginable variation in height and width, placed a sheet of tracing paper over it and drew faithfully the same conglomeration of buildings, using, however, an exclusively vertical style of architecture. I believe that the picture obtained by this means, on the whole is the logical city picture for the American large cities, and discloses the rules that ought to be promulgated in the creation of an American art of city building" ("New Architectural Language," p. 13).

63

Louis H. Sullivan, "The High-Building Question," *Graphic* 5, Dec. 19, 1891, p. 405, reprinted in Donald Hoffmann, "The Setback Skyscraper City of 1891: An Unknown Essay of Louis H. Sullivan," *Journal of the Society of Architectural Historians* 29, no. 2, 1970, pp. 181-187.

64

Dankmar Adler, "Light in Tall Office Buildings," *Engineering Magazine* 4, 1892; on this article see Hoffman, "Setback Skyscraper City," pp. 182-183.

65

Eliel Saarinen, "Project for Lakefront Development of the City of Chicago," *American Architect* 124, no. 2434, 1923, pp. 487-514; an editorial comment appears on p. 515. See also *Architekten* 4, no. 2, 1924, pp. 15-28; Christ-Janer, *Eliel Saarinen*, pp. 51ff. Saarinen probably chose Michigan Avenue for his project because it had been among the most popular in Chicago since the years immediately preceding the war. On November 3, 1914, at the time of the local elections, a referendum on proceeding with this portion of the Burnham and Bennett plan at a total cost of $3,800,000 was held, with 80,000 votes in favor of the project; see the article by Walter D. Moody, managing director of the Chicago Plan Commission, "Creating a World-Famous Street," *American City* 11, no. 6, 1914, pp. 453-455. Furthermore, as Mario Manieri-Elia points out in "Toward an 'Imperial City': Daniel H. Burnham and the City Beautiful Movement," this volume, many of the undertakings called for in the plan of 1909 were put into operation only in the 1920s; thus Saarinen's proposal met with ready interest on the part of the public.

66

Saarinen's plan for the settlement of Munksnäs-Haga near Helsinki was commissioned by Julius Tallberg, an "enlightened" businessman interested in creating an integrated community of exceptional quality. With Tallberg and Leo Lerche, Saarinen made a trip to study Stockholm, Copenhagen, Hamburg, Karlsruhe, and Munich. See Eliel Saarinen, *Munksnäs-Haga* (Lilius and Hertzberg, Helsinki, 1915); Gustav Strengell, *Stadtplanskonst* (Lilius and Hertzberg, Helsinki, 1915); *Der Städtebau* 17, nos. 3-4, 1920, pp. 21-27. On the plan for Reval, see "Stadtplanung für Reval," ibid. 18, nos. 5-6, 1921, pp. 45-56. On the plan for Canberra, see Councilor Wernekke, "Der Wettbewerb um einen Bebauungsplan für die Bundeshauptstadt von Australien," ibid. 10, nos. 7-8, pp. 73-77, 86-89; Christ-Janer, *Eliel Saarinen*, pp. 44-46; Mark L. Peish, *The Chicago School of Architecture* (Phaidon, London, 1964; Random House, New York, 1965), pp. 115-116. On the plan for Helsinki, see Jung Bertel, *Suur-Helsinki* (Lilius and Hertzberg, Helsinki, 1918); *Der Städtebau* 18, nos. 3-4, 1920, pp. 21-27; Giorgio Piccinato and Manfredo Tafuri, "Helsinki," *Urbanistica*, no. 33, 1961, pp. 88ff.

67

In 1914, at the conference on traffic organized by the Deutscher Werkbund, Osthaus praised Saarinen's station in Helsinki as the best European example of its kind. See Karl Ernst Osthaus, "Der Banhof," in *Der Verkher, Jahrbuch des deutschen Werkbundes* (Eugen Diederichs, Jena, 1914), p. 41.

68

See Royal Institute of British Architects, *Town Planning Conference, London, 10-15 October 1910. Transactions* (London, 1911); *Der Verkher*.

69

Saarinen made the acquaintance of Behrens in Düsseldorf in 1907, and Behrens's influence is clearly recognizable in his design for the Expositions Building in Helsinki (published in *Moderne Bauformen* 8, no. 8, 1909, pp. 343-344) and in the Winter house at Ladoga, both designed in 1908. Most important, however, is the affinity between their research on building types and on the relationship between the metropolis and the new conditions of its perception and use dictated by urban and extraurban traffic. On this topic, see the basic article by Peter Behrens, "Einfluss von Zeit und Raumausnutzung auf moderne Formentwicklung," in *Der Verkher*, pp. 7-10; the ideas expressed here on the problem of urban communications and on the preception of the city were taken up again by Behrens in "Zeitloses and Zeitbewegtes," (Address given at the opening of the exhibition "10 Jahre von Peter Behrens"), *Österreische Kunst*, 1932, pp. 5ff.

70

Saarinen wrote,

This possibility of making Chicago a city beautiful on a truly grand scale was most strikingly visualized by Mr. Burnham in the city plan he worked out about fifteen years ago. It is a splendid and grandiose project and ought to be adopted in its entirety as a foundation for a rational recreation of Chicago. Before I came to Chicago, or even had a thought of ever coming to the United States, I was, as a town builder, professionally familiar with Chicago's official city plan. I had also studied the afore-mentioned improvement project in all its details. The heart of Mr. Burnham's plan was the laying out of Grant Park and in connection with it a broad monumental park boulevard running West at Congress Street. Upon my arrival in Chicago I expected to see Grant Park ready and the boulevard partly finished, or at least in the process of being built. But Grant Park lay untouched and the monumental boulevard seemed to have been forgotten. The Burnham dream seemed in large part, perhaps altogether, to have met the same fate that overtakes most beautiful dreams in these days. Their realization is delayed until it is too late; or else their magnificence and beauty are so overwhelming that one loses faith in them. The proposed boulevard is an attractive idea and the city's beauty would have been much enhanced had it materialized. However, it was probably found to be too costly. ("Project for Lakefront Development," p. 487)

See also Eliel Saarinen, *The City, Its Growth, Its Decay, Its Future* (Reinhold, New York, 1943), which documents the evolution of Saarinen's thinking in regard to the historical development of American urban planning.

71

Saarinen carefully calculated the costs of the various installations related to his proposal. The project actually depended directly on the hypothesis of placing the Illinois Central station underground in order to permit the intensive utilization of the entire terrain, comprising 2,700,000 square feet. For the underground parking area Saarinen calculated a total construction cost of $60 million, with an annual interest of 5 percent ($3 million) on the municipality's capital investment, to which another $3 million was added for the salaries of the employees, fixed expenses, and other costs. These annual expenses were to be covered by the income from the parking facilities, while the car owners would benefit from the lowered cost of parking it offered. Saarinen wrote, "We see the curious phenomenon that, the more rational and commodious our provisions for automobile traffic are, the greater becomes use for the terminal, and the more profitable the enterprise. In other words, the more monumentally our city plan is arranged, the better becomes the financial result, for the practical and aesthetic here go hand in hand" ("Project for Lakefront Development," p. 506). Promoting his project in terms of its coordinated unity, Saarinen thus tried to demonstrate that his new concepts of urban design were ultimately based on a new way of conceiving the urban economy.

72

Ibid., pp. 504-505.

73

Ibid., p. 514.

74

It should be noted that Saarinen's use of telescopic forms in the *Chicago Tribune* design did not serve the same purpose as it did in the two skyscrapers of the lakefront project. In the *Tribune* design the formal elaboration had an end in itself, the pure image of the American city; in the lakefront project formal elaboration served to relate, at a great distance, the two dominant objects of the complex, making the unity of the whole immediately perceptible. The concept of city building as comprehensive control of the dynamics of the urban scene frequently recurs in Saarinen's writing during this period. See Eliel Saarinen, "Architecture and City Planning," *City Planning* 1, no. 3, 1925, pp. 143ff.; idem, "My Point of View of Our Contemporary Architecture" (Address given at the American Institute of

Architects' convention in San Antonio, Texas, April 1931), included in *The Saarinen Door* (Cranbrook Academy of Art, 1963, pp. 56-60); and an interview with Saarinen by Roger Wade Sherman, "The Art of City Building," *American Architect* 147, no. 2638, 1935, pp. 13-20.

75
In the interview with Sherman, Saarinen is quoted as saying, "When all architects work as a body toward this end, they will become leaders in the development of cities and in the control of an organic coherence. With public confidence as an aid they will be able to control even the activities of parasitical speculators who, under the guise of architecture, spread bad taste and confusion over the country. Thus, architects become the educators of the public and the designers of the cities. And therein exists the spirit of an adequate city-planning control." See Sherman, "Art of City Building," p. 20.

76
Emil Lorch had played a rather important role in the early years of the century within the milieu of the Chicago Architectural Club, furthering with his lectures the cause of "pure form" and influencing even Frank Lloyd Wright. See H. Allen Brooks, "Steinway Hall, Architects and Dreams," *Journal of the Society of Architectural Historians* 22, no. 3, 1963, pp. 171-175; idem, *The Prairie School. Frank Lloyd Wright and His Midwest Contemporaries* (University of Toronto Press, Toronto, 1972). On the Detroit riverfront development, see *Memorial Hall: a Report Made by the Detroit City Council* (Detroit, 1924); Saarinen, "Architecture and City Planning"; *American Architect* 129, no. 2495, 1926, pp. 481-482. On Saarinen's activity in the United States, see also Mario Manieri-Elia, "Trois architectes européen en Amérique: Eliel Saarinen, Mendolsohn, Neutra," *Archithese*, no. 17, 1976, pp. 15-22.

77
See Christ-Janer, *Eliel Saarinen*, pp. 125-126.

78
Ibid., p. 49.

79
Ibid., p. 135; Creese, "Saarinen's *Tribune* Design," p. 3.

80
George G. Booth, publisher of the *Detroit News*, was the founder of Cranbrook Academy of Art, for which he created a teaching program for craftsmen that was in some ways not unlike that of the earliest Bauhaus of Weimar. The academy was to be built near the suburb of Bloomfield Hills, Michigan, the development of which Booth had promoted in 1904 as a residential area. See Christ-Janer, *Eliel Saarinen*, pp. 63ff.; Sharon Lee Ryder, "Saarinen's Atelier," *Progressive Architecture*, no. 7, 1974, pp. 70-75.

81
The relationship between Saarinen's urban theories and the teachings of Sitte has been emphasized by Collins and Collins; certainly Saarinen's three-dimensional vision of the city and his conception of it as a single organism are completely within the tradition begun by Sitte. See George R. Collins and Christiane Crasemann Collins, *Camillo Sitte and the Birth of Modern City Planning* (Phaidon Press, London; Random House, New York, 1965), pp. 91-92.

82
Neutra, *Wie baut Amerika?*

83
Franklin Delano Roosevelt, "Growing Up by Plan," *Survey* 67, Feb. 1, 1932, p. 483.

84
See Mel Scott, *American City Planning since 1890* (University of California Press, Berkeley and Los Angeles, 1969), pp. 287ff. On the role played by Adams in American urbanism during these years, see Francesco Dal Co, "From Parks to the Region: Progressive Ideology and the Reform of the American City," this volume. The Committee on the Regional Plan of New York and Its Environs was composed of Frederic A. Delano, chairman from 1923 on (in place of Charles Dyer Norton), Robert W. de Forest, John H. Finley, John M. Glenn,

Henry James, George McAneny, Dwight W. Morrow, Frank L. Polk, Frederic B. Pratt, and Lawson Purdy. The general organization of this enterprise, in which Adams's official position was that of general director of plans and surveys, is described in Thomas Adams, *Planning the New York Region. An Outline of the Organization, Scope and Progress of the Regional Plan, with a Summary of Studies made up to September 1926* (Regional Plan of New York and Its Environs, New York, 1927), pp. 9-13. See also Blake McKelvey, *The Emergence of Metropolitan America (1915-1966)* (Rutgers University Press, New Brunswick, N.J., 1968), pp. 45ff.; Antonio Monroy, "Piani e progetti per Manhattan," *Lotus*, no. 7, 1970. On Charles Dyer Norton, member of the Commercial Club of Chicago and major figure in the initiative for Burnham's plan for Chicago, see Harvey A. Kantor, "Charles Dyer Norton and the Origins of the Regional Plan of New York," *Journal of the American Institute of Planners* 39, no. 1, 1973, pp. 35-42.

85

Indicative of the inefficiency of zoning legislation was the case of Chicago, where, after thirteen years, the zoning law of 1923 had undergone 13,000 changes or, as they were considered by some, violations; see Scott, *American City Planning*, p. 196. On zoning in New York and America in general and its economic motivations, see Franco Mancuso, "Lo zoning: il controllo del suolo urbano per la mediazione dei conflitti socioeconomici. L'esperienza di New York," in Pierluigi Crosta, Marino Folin, Donatella Calabi, Franco Mancuso, and Stefania Potenzo, *L'urbanistica del riformismo, U.S.A. 1890-1940* (Mazzotta, Milan, 1975), pp. 85-145, which includes an ample bibliography in the notes.

86

See Scott, *American City Planning*, pp. 210-213.

87

Thomas Adams, *The Building of the City*, vol. 2 of *Regional Plan of New York and Its Environs* (Regional Plan of New York and Its Environs, New York, 1931), pp. 25-26, 588.

88

See Edith Elmer Wood, "Restrictive Legislation in the United States," in idem, *The Housing of the Unskilled Wage Earner. America's Next Problem* (Macmillan, New York, 1919), pp. 60-90; Charles Harris Whitaker, "The General Problem of Land Control," in idem, *The Joke about Housing* (Marshall Jones, Boston, 1920), pp. 113-155; Werner Hegemann, *City Planning Housing* (Architectural Book Publishing, New York, 1936-1938), 1:29, 160-178. Hegemann explicitly considered the New York zoning legislation a law for uncontrolled speculation. For a defense of the law, by one of its drafters, see George B. Ford, "How New York City Now Controls the Development of Private Property," *City Plan* 2, no. 3, 1916.

89

Scott, *American City Planning*, p. 289.

90

Adams, *Building of the City*, p. 92.

91

Ibid., p. 160. See also *Regional Survey of New York and Its Environs* (Regional Plan of New York and Its Environs, New York, 1927-1931), 6: 87-121.

92

See Frederic A. Delano, "Skyscrapers," *American City* 34, Jan. 1926. See also Adams, *Planning the New York Region*, pp. 74-75, where Adams states:

That there is a connection between periods of crisis in the rapid transit developments of New York and periods of reform in building heights and densities, appears to be indicated by the fact that the first Heights of Buildings Commission was appointed immediately after long discussion of an expensive program of rapid transit expansion. In an interview with Mr. Edward Bassett in 1907 it was stated that the schemes for new subways would involve a cost of about $300,000,000, and it was suggested that buildings should be restricted in height so as to reduce the necessity for such vast expenditures on transit. It would seem to be likely that New York is entering upon a period when history will repeat itself. The cost of development of rapid transit lines as now proposed, and of others necessary to meet the needs of the immediate future, will bring about increased demands for removing the causes which operate to impose this heavy burden on the community.

93

See *Journal of the Real Estate Board of New York*, Aug. 1930; Adams, *Building of the City*, p. 163.

94

Ibid., pp. 181ff. The examples Adams used to illustrate and confirm the theses expounded are interesting; the principle of the setback in highrise buildings is illustrated with a scheme studied by George B. Ford for an apartment-house complex in New York City, while the "splendid isolation" of the Empire State Building serves as an example of the convergence of private and collective interests; see pp. 184, 186.

95

Ibid., p. 184.

96

Raymond Hood, "A City under a Single Roof," *Nation's Business*, Nov. 1929. See Adams, *Building of the City*, pp. 188-190.

97

Ibid., pp. 339ff.

98

Significantly, Adams cites in support of this view the authoritative opinion of Cass Gilbert, who spoke in favor of decentralization, on January 16, 1931, when he received an award from the Society of Arts and Sciences; see ibid., pp. 346-347.

99

Ibid., p. 108.

100

In indicating a model of a skyscraper for the future reorganization of the city, Adams enthusiastically cited the Woolworth Building in its position overlooking City Hall Park (ibid., pp. 109-112) and published three of Hugh Ferriss's renderings of a proposed scheme for Rockefeller Center by Corbett, Harrison and MacMurray (pp. 112, 113, 115). Among the many ingenuous aspects of Adams's report, his continual reference to the business centers "of the future" in terms of the image of medieval cities bristling with pinnacles is particularly irritating.

101

Ibid., pp. 411-415; see also ibid., pp. 306-313.

102

Ibid. pp. 393ff. The proposals for this district were formulated in cooperation with the East Side Chamber of Commerce and its architectural consultants, John Taylor Boyd, Jr., and Holden, McLaughlin and Associates.

103

See Christopher Tunnard and Henry Hope Reed, *American Skyline* (Mentor Books, New York, 1956), pp. 170ff.; Allan J. Nevins and J. A. Krout, eds., *The Greater City: New York, 1898-1948* (Columbia University Press, New York, 1948).

104

See Lewis Mumford, "The Plan of New York," *New Republic* 71, June 15 and 22, 1932, pp. 121-126, 146-154.

105

Ibid., p. 123. Mumford had attacked Adams's plan earlier, when comparing it very unfavorably with the plan of the New York State Commission of Housing and Regional Planning, begun in 1923. See Lewis Mumford, "Realities vs. Dreams," *Journal of the American Institute of Architects* 13, no. 6, 1925, pp. 198-199; on the New York State Commission plan, see Dal Co, "From Parks to the Region," this volume.

106

Mumford, "Plan of New York," p. 152.

107

Ibid., p. 151.

108

Thomas Adams, "A Communication: In Defense of the Regional Plan," *New Republic* 71, July 6, 1932, pp. 207-210.

109

Hugh Ferriss, *The Metropolis of Tomorrow* (Ives Washburn, New York, 1929), brings together the author's ideas and designs elaborated during the 1920's; see, for example, idem, "Cubes and Pyramids," *Baukunst* 2, no. 1, 1926, pp. 4-18, in which Ferriss expounds his ideas on the possibilities offered by the New York zoning law. Ferriss received his architectural degree from Washington University in Saint Louis in 1911 and worked for three years as a draftsman for Cass Gilbert. With the outbreak of the war, he entered the service of the Committee on Public Information in Washington, D.C., which engaged him in publicizing the work of industries and organizations involved in the war effort. See Frank Chouteau Brown, "The Work of Hugh Ferriss," *Architectural Review* 7, no. 2, 1918, pp. 21-25. Ferriss subsequently opened his own studio in New York, where he specialized in architectural renderings and worked for such figures in American architecture as Goodhue, Gilbert, Corbett, and Hood; in fact, his clients included more than a hundred architectural firms in more than twenty-five cities. Thus, in his own designs, Ferriss was able to offer graphic syntheses of the most advanced ideas of the time. From 1923 on, Ferriss worked as an independent architect for the Committee on the Regional Plan of New York and Its Environs, a fact that explains the affinity between his *Metropolis of Tomorrow* and the studies on the new urban regulations contained in the Regional Plan of New York. See also "Examples from the Recent Work of Hugh Ferriss," *Creative Art* 9, no. 2, 1931, pp. 154-159.

110

See Scully, *American Architecture and Urbanism*. Speaking of Saarinen's *Chicago Tribune* design, Scully states that its formula was immediately taken up in New York:

Hugh Ferriss used it as his model in studying the massing possibilities of the new zoning laws. His stupefying drawings show buildings emerging from mountains, really more Mayan than Gothic in the visual weight of their profiled step-backs. Ferriss' drawings were a kind of recrudescence of romanticism's 'sublime' here in its terminal stages: man small, the environment overwhelming; it was the Grand Canyon, in fact, now shaping the myths of New York and of the Metropolis of the Future no less than those of the Anasazi. . . . The Barclay-Vesey Building of the late 1920's sums it up: Saarinen, Ferriss, mountain mass, and edging the surfaces, a kind of flattened jazz-modern decoration which had swept the board at the Exposition des Arts Décoratifs in Paris, of 1925. ((pp. 152-153).

111

See Ferriss, *Metropolis of Tomorrow*, pp. 72ff.

112

Ibid., p. 82. The four solutions for setback skyscrapers designed by Ferriss (ibid., pp. 72-81) make use of studies carried out by Corbett on the basis of the 1916 New York zoning law; see Harvey Wiley Corbett, "Zoning and the Envelope of the Building," *Pencil Points* 6, no. 3, 1923, pp. 15-18; idem, "The Influence of Zoning on New York's Skyline," *American Architect* 1923, no. 2410, 1923, pp. 1-4.

113

Ferriss, *Metropolis of Tomorrow*, pp. 109ff.

114

Ibid., pp. 138-140. See also Thomas Reiner, *The Place of the Ideal Community in Urban Planning* (University of Pennsylvania Press, Philadelphia, 1963), pp. 57-60. Ferriss's regressive humanism is fully expressed in his late theoretical writings; see Hugh Ferriss, "Technology and Vision," *Journal of the American Institute of Architects* 18, no. 2, 1952, pp. 60-64; idem, "The Impact of Science and Materialism on Art Today," ibid. 22, no. 1, 1954, pp. 3-7; idem, "Time for an Artistic Revival in Architectural Design," ibid. 23, no. 2, 1955, pp. 51-57.

115

William H. Jordy, *American Buildings and Their Architects*, Vol. 4: *The Impact of European Modernism in the Mid-Twentieth Century* (Doubleday, Garden City, N.Y., 1972), p. 65.

116

See Henry-Russell Hitchcock and Philip Johnson, *The International Style: Architecture since 1922* (Norton, New York, 1932; new ed., 1966). The influence of the Museum of

Modern Art exhibition is a question requiring a special investigation, which has not been carried out to my knowledge. But see Hitchcock's retrospective preface to the 1966 edition of *International Style*.

117

Actually, the call to autochthonous sources and the stylistic inflections of Art Deco were two sides of the same coin. The New York architect Alfred C. Bossom explicitly compared the 230-foot-high temple of Tikal in Guatemala, which he called "the original American skyscraper," with his own project for a 35-story setback skyscraper. See Alfred C. Bossom, *Building to the Skies: The Romance of the Skyscraper* (Studio Limited, London, and Studio Publications, New York, 1934). The influence of exotic styles, particularly those of primitive Mexico, on Art Deco in the United States has been treated by Bevis Hillier, *The World of Art Deco*, Exhibition Catalogue of the Minneapolis Institute of Art (Studio Vista, London, 1971), pp. 26ff; but see also idem, *Art Deco of the Twenties and Thirties* (Studio Vista, London, 1968; Dutton, New York, 1968). In *World of Art Deco*, Hillier cites Claude Bragdon, *The Frozen Fountain* (Arno, New York, 1932; reprint ed. 1970). In his book, Bragdon, initially a poster artist influenced by the graphic style of Beardsley and later one of the architects of Grand Central Station, reviewed all the sources of Art Deco and ultimately interpreted the urban landscape dominated by skyscrapers as a vision of gigantic fountains jetting in the megalopolis; his specific example was the Chrysler Building. On the influence of Art Deco on the American skyscraper, see Robinson and Bletter, *Skyscraper Style*; Don Vlack, *Art Deco Architecture in New York, 1920-1940* (Harper and Row, New York, 1974); Manfredo Tafuri, " 'Neu-Babylon': das New York der Zwanzigerjahre und die Suche nach dem Amerikanismus," *Archithese*, no. 20, 1976, pp. 12-24, 51. On Art Deco, see also Giulia Veronesi, *Stile 1925* (Vallecchi, Florence, 1967); Giovanna Massobrio and Paolo Portoghesi, *Album degli Anni Venti* (Laterza, Rome-Bari, 1976), which contains observations on the American skyscraper between 1923 and 1935.

118

Despite its exceptional quality and indicativeness for the history of American architecture, Hood's work has still not been studied with the attention it deserves. In addition to the small monograph volume edited by North, Hood has been treated by Zevi, Burchard and Bush-Brown, and Scully, but only within the context of general historical studies. See North, *Raymond Hood*; John Burchard and Albert Bush-Brown, *The Architecture of America. A Social and Cultural History* (Atlantic-Little, Brown, Boston, 1961), pp. 358-362; Bruno Zevi, *Storia dell'architettura moderna* (Einaudi, Turin, 1950), pp. 490-493. See also Walter H. Kilham, Jr., "The Way of an Architect with a Client," *Journal of the American Institute of Architects* 58, Sept. 1972, pp. 23-26; John A. Kouwenhoven, *Made in America* (Doubleday, Garden City, N.Y., 1948), pp. 250-252. The recent monograph by Walter H. Kilham, Jr., *Raymond Hood, Architect: Form through Function in the American Skyscraper* (Architectural Book Publishing, New York, 1973), contains much useful information but also errors and presents an ahistorical interpretation of the architect's work. See the review of Kilham's book by Carl W. Condit, *Journal of the Society of Architectural Historians* 33, no. 3, 1974, pp. 270-271; see also that by Robert A. M. Stern, "Raymond Hood," *Progressive Architecture*, no. 7, 1974, pp. 110-114.

119

Hood adopted a similar purism in the 1928 apartment house at 3 East 84th Street, New York, where the stark simplicity of the pilasters (their strong vertical accent was a prelude to the Daily News Building) is underscored by the spandrel panels decorated with geometric motifs of vaguely Mayan inspiration; see North, *Raymond Hood*, pp. 52-54.

120

Hood also adopted the romantic Richardsonian expression, which was used in the case of the McCormick Mausoleum to exalt the primordial forces of the work of business enterprise, in his design for the library of Sauda in Norway, also of 1927. In this case, however, a simplified version of Richardson's formal language was suggested not only by the purpose of the building but also by its Nordic location. In addition, it may be noted that when Hood built a house for himself in Stamford, Connecticut, he quite uninhibitedly adopted the concept of the Country House. See the unsigned article, "Raymond Mathewson Hood," cited in n46.

121

See North, *Raymond Hood*, p. 9.

122

See Kilham, "Way of an Architect."

123

Raymond Hood, "The Design of Rockefeller City," *Architectural Forum* 56, no. 1, 1932, pp. 1-7.

124

In Hood's own words:

The incorporation of publicity features in a building is frequently an item for consideration. This feature as an element of modern architecture was first notably incorporated in the Woolworth Building, and with success. The introduction of this element influenced the design of the Chicago Tribune Tower and the American Radiator Building. The lobby of the Daily News Building with its geographical and meteorological exhibits is frankly an appeal to the interest of its readers and the public, justified by the continued interest displayed. The hanging gardens as a feature of the Rockefeller Metropolitan Center on account of their magnitude will have a greater appeal to the public. This feature, when possessing intrinsic merit, is consonant with and is a legitimate attribute of good architecture. It stimulates public interest and admiration, is accepted as a genuine contribution to architecture, enhances the value of the property and is profitable to the owner in the same manner as are other forms of legitimate advertising. (North, *Raymond Hood*, p. 11).

125

The Daily News Building was the work of the firm of Howells and Hood; the McGraw-Hill Building and the Rex Cole Show Rooms in Flushing and Bay Ridge (both 1931) were by the firm of Hood, Godley and Fouilhoux, which later collaborated in the design of Rockefeller Center. The story of the designing of the Daily News Building is recounted in Kilham, *Raymond Hood, Architect*. On the history of the McGraw-Hill Building, see James D. Morgan, "A Tale of Two Towers," *Architecture Plus* 1, no. 9, Oct. 1973, pp. 42-53, 82-83, in which Hood's building is compared with the new McGraw-Hill Building on the Avenue of the Americas. Morgan's article contains an interesting bibliography on the reaction to Hood's skyscraper and also an unused plan by Hood for the layout of the individual offices, with a remarkable solution for the division of the inner office and outer secretary-receptionist space.

126

Jordy, *American Buildings and Their Architects*, 4:64.

127

North, *Raymond Hood*, p. 3.

128

Ibid., pp. 15-16.

129

The liveliness of which North speaks, as expressed by the Jazz Modern style of the period has been analyzed in Arnold Lehman, "New York Skyscrapers: The Jazz Modern Neo-American Beautilitarian Style," *Metropolitan Museum of Art Bulletin* 29, no. 8, 1971, pp. 363-370; and in the evocation of a ball at the Astor in 1931—attended by Raymond Hood, William Van Alen, Harvey Wiley Corbett, and others disguised as skyscrapers—in Rem Koolhaas, "The Architect's Ball—A Vignette, 1931," *Oppositions*, no. 3, 1974, pp. 92-96.

130

See North, *Raymond Hood*, pp. 86-87. See also "Three Visions of New York," *Creative Art* 9, no. 2, 1931, pp. 160-161, which criticized the project as a passive acceptance of the mechanism of concentration. Hood's 1929 project took up an earlier one, from 1924, which had involved only the residential bridges. According to his scheme for multifunctional skyscrapers, mentioned in an earlier section, Hood's 1929 project advanced the hypothesis of direct communication between residence and place of work, with the thirty-sixth to forty-fifth floors of his skyscrapers destined for the residences of their employees. Hood's proposal and other American utopian proposals—such as that made in 1928 by Charles Morgan of Burnham and Company, which projected residential bridges for Chicago—have been analyzed in Cervin Robinson, "Wie wird man ein erfolgleicher Visionär?" *Archithese*, no. 18, 1976, pp. 5-12. Interestingly, for the speculator A. A. Ainsworth, also in 1929, Hood designed the resort town of Arcady, which was to have been built within 16,000 acres of virgin forest on the Atlantic coast near Myrtle Beach, South Carolina. Far from being conceived as a garden suburb, the principal building, a sort of hotel intended for a deluxe clientele, was designed as a setback skyscraper; Arcadia was here contaminated by the persistence of the superurban mythology. On the town of Arcady, see Bletter, "King Kong en Arcadie," pp. 32-34. Bletter cites the privately published pamphlet by Raymond Hood, *Arcady, A National Playground Where the Leaders of Contemporary Life May Sustain Their Capacity for Work by Bringing to Its Utmost the Art of Rest and Recreation* (New York, 1929).

131

The most comprehensive history of the planning and design of Rockefeller Center is still Winston Weisman, "The Way of the Price Mechanism: The Rockefeller Centre," *Architectural Review* 108, no. 648, 1950, pp. 399-406, based entirely on documents in the Rockefeller archives. Weisman has since returned to the subject dedicating articles to particular aspects of the problem; they will be cited in the course of this section. Recent assessments of the influence of Rockefeller Center are contained in Weisman, "New View of Skyscraper History." See also the photographic guide by Samuel Chamberlain, *Rockefeller Center*, 2nd ed. (Hastings House, New York, 1956); David Loth, *The City within a City: The Romance of Rockefeller Center* (Morrow, New York, 1966). For the most complete critical analysis, after Weisman's, see Jordy, *American Buildings and Their Architects* 4, pp. 1-85.

132

The area for which Morris designed the Metropolitan Opera House in 1927 was not the site originally considered but an area between 63rd Street and Broadway. On this first phase of the project, Weisman has brought together documentation from Morris's own archives and from those of Rockefeller; see Winston Weisman, "Who Designed Rockefeller Center?" *Journal of the Society of Architectural Historians* 10, no. 1, 1951, pp. 11-17, in which Morris's role is carefully defined. The role played by Joseph Urban is still unclear; he seems to have been Morris's associate. A former student of the Wiener Akademie, Urban, who was born in Vienna in 1872 and died in New York in 1933, is a particularly interesting figure for the study of relations between European and American culture during the period. Urban was curator of the department of furniture at the Metropolitan Museum of Art from 1918 until his death and was in close contact with Raymond Hood; see the unsigned article "Raymond Mathewson Hood," cited in n46. Judging from the design he entered in the competition for the Palace of the Soviet in Moscow, he appears to have been the precursor of the International style. Robinson and Bletter, *Skyscraper Style*, sheds some light on Urban's activities; through his initiative the New York branch of the Wiener Werkstätte was founded, and he was the designer of three buildings in New York—Ziegfeld Theater (1926-27), the International Magazine Building (1927-28), and the puristic New School for Social Research (1929-1930). Urban's work indeed merits a thorough investigation. On Morris's role in the conception of the plaza of Rockefeller Center, see Winston Weisman, "The First Landscaped Skyscraper," *Journal of the Society of Architectural Historians* 18, no. 2, 1959, pp. 54-59.

133

Morris himself explained, "The whole thing stands or falls on the amount of increased revenue obtainable due to the creation of an open square" (from Morris's notes for the exposition of his project at the Metropolitan Club dinner, quoted in Weisman, "First Landscaped Skyscraper," p. 55).

134

L. Andrew Reinhard and Henry Hofmeister had earlier collaborated with Todd, Robertson and Todd on the construction of the Graybar Building, where the planning and design of the Rockefeller Center project was to be carried out. The scheme they presented, dated September 1928, is perfectly symmetrical in respect to the axis of the Opera House and Opera Plaza, opposite to which, on the east side, a 25-story office building is situated; on either side of the plaza are two hotels of 35 and 37 stories; flanking the Opera House, two apartment buildings. See Weisman, "Who Designed Rockefeller Center?" p. 13, fig. 4. Shortly thereafter, they drew up another scheme, dated September 18, 1928, which is very similar to the first but gives greater importance to the plaza.

135

See Hegemann, "Das Hochhaus." Harvey Wiley Corbett (1873-1954) was one of the most interesting of the American professionals educated at the Ecole des Beaux Arts. Together with MacMurray, he designed the Bush Terminal Office Building in New York, Bush House in London, and the Holy Innocents Church in Brooklyn. Corbett collaborated with Hood not only on Rockefeller Center but also on the Century of Progress Exhibition held in 1933 in Chicago. Corbett's contribution to Rockefeller Center was important in the preliminary stage of the design, but his interest in the project waned during its execution. It will be recalled that the scheme for Metropolitan Square by Corbett, Harrison and MacMurray was rendered by Hugh Ferriss and used as an example of urban reorganization by Adams in *Building of the City*, p. 112ff; see n100. Moreover, Corbett was a member of the board of directors of the Regional Plan Association from 1935 on.

136

Rockefeller later recalled:

Thus it came about that with the depression underway and the values falling rapidly, I found myself committed to Columbia for a long-term lease, wholly without the support of the enterprise by which and around which the whole development had been planned. Moreover, the general financial situation was so steadily getting worse that there was no possibility of subletting unimproved, as contemplated, any portion of the area. . . . There were only two courses open to me. One, to abandon the entire development. The other, to go forward with it in the definite knowledge that I myself would have to build and finance it alone without the immense impetus that the new opera house would have given and with no escape from the fact that under the changed conditions it would be necessary to improve all the land in order to lease it, thus involving immense capital outlays never contemplated. I chose the latter course.

See John D. Rockefeller, Jr. (Address delivered at the opening of the Gymnasium, Rockefeller Center, September 30, 1939) in Raymond B. Fosdick, *John D. Rockefeller, Jr. A Portrait* (Harper & Brothers, New York, 1956), p. 264.

137

See M. R. Werner, "Radio City: From Real Estate to Art," *Atlantic Monthly* 151, no. 4, 1933, pp. 468-476; "Rockefeller Center, Red or Black? A Phenomenon of Exploitation," *Architectural Forum* 61, 1934, pp. 292-298; Fosdick, *John D. Rockefeller, Jr.*, p. 265.

138

The location of the tenants and the various uses for which parts of the center were destined are visualized in the scheme published in "Rockefeller Center, Red or Black?" pp. 294-295.

139

Frederick Lewis Allen, "Look at Rockefeller Center," *Harper's Monthly* 177, Oct. 1938, pp. 506-513.

140

See L. Andrew Reinhard, "Organization for Cooperation," *Architectural Forum* 56, no. 1, 1932, pp. 77-80; Wallace K. Harrison, "Drafting Room Practice," ibid., pp. 81-84; Ernest L. Smith, "The Story of Rockefeller Center, VIII. Supervising Construction and Controlling Costs," ibid., no. 5, 1932, pp. 497-500. The following scheme, from Reinhard's article, explains the staff organization of the Rockefeller Center project:

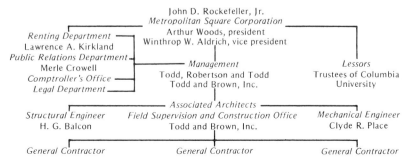

While the role of the firm of Todd, Robertson and Todd was exclusively organizational, the firm of Todd and Brown, Inc., oversaw and organized the execution of the project. In addition to daily reports on work progress and relative expenses, Todd and Brown published a monthly financial report on each building of the complex. Thus the Metropolitan Square Corporation was able to follow closely and examine in detail the economic trend of the undertaking. On the organization of the designers, see Winston Weisman, "Group Practice," *Architectural Review* 114, no. 681, 1953, pp. 145-151; Weisman expresses a highly positive judgment on this sort of bureaucratized teamwork. But see the completely opposite opinion expressed by Henry-Russell Hitchcock, "The Architecture of Bureaucracy and the Architecture of Genius," ibid. 101, no. 601, 1947, pp. 3-6.

141

See Smith, "Story of Rockefeller Center."

142

See Reinhard, "Organization for Cooperation"; Smith, "Story of Rockefeller Center."

143

See Reinhard, "Organization for Cooperation"; Harrison, "Drafting Room Practice."

144

Webster B. Todd, "Testing Men and Materials for Rockefeller Center," *Architectural Forum* 56, no. 2, 1932, pp. 199-204; particularly interesting is the description of the method followed in selecting the three general contractors, who were chosen on the basis of a very detailed questionaire among eleven firms invited to submit bids.

145

See Eugene Clute, "The Story of Rockefeller Center, X. The Allied Arts." ibid. 57, no. 4, 1932, pp. 353-358. See also the bibliography in Jordy, *American Buildings and Their Architects* 4, p. 431n43. The history of the decoration of the complex goes beyond the scope of this essay but is nevertheless of great interest, both for its indication of artistic trends in America of the 1930s and for the controversy that arose over Diego Rivera's inclusion of Lenin in his fresco in the RCA Building.

146

See Weisman, "Way of the Price Mechanism," p. 401.

147

See ibid.; idem, "Who Designed Rockefeller Center?"

148

At various times Reinhard supplied precise lists of the groups of designers and the changes that eventually took place in them; see letter *Architectural Record* 102, no. 2, Aug. 1947, p. 20; letter *Architectural Forum* 88, no. 2, Feb. 1948, pp. 26 and 30. According to Reinhard, the contract signed on July 1, 1930, with the Associated Architects was annulled on June 1, 1935, following Hood's death and Godley's withdrawal. The authorship of the various buildings is as follows:

——RCA Building, RKO Building, Music Hall, Center Theater, Maison Française and British Empire Building, International Building: Reinhard and Hofmeister; Corbett, Harrison and MacMurray; Hood and Fouilhoux.
——Time-Life Building, Associated Press Building: Reinhard and Hofmeister; Corbett and MacMurray; Wallace K. Harrison; Jacques André Fouilhoux.
——Eastern Air Lines Building, Center Garage, United States Rubber Building: Reinhard and Hofmeister; Wallace K. Harrison; Jacques André Fouilhoux.
In an interview recorded by Jordy, Wallace K. Harrison recalled that among the designers who collaborated on the center were Edward Stone, Earl Ladenfeld, George Pawley, and John Walquist; see Jordy, *American Buildings and Their Architects*, 4:56.

149

L. Andrew Reinhard, "What is the Rockefeller Radio City?" *Architectural Record* 69, no. 4, 1931, pp. 277-281.

150

See Hood, "Design of Rockefeller City"; Weisman, "Way of the Price Mechanism," p. 404; Kilham, *Raymond Hood, Architect*.

151

Quoted in Werner, "Radio City," p. 468.

152

See Weisman, "First Landscaped Skyscraper"; *Architectural Forum* 56, no. 1, 1932, pp. 8-12, which includes a first design for the roof gardens; Merle Crowell, "The Story of Rockefeller Center, VII. The Question Answered," ibid., no. 5, 1932, pp. 425-430. See also the interview with L. Andrew Reinhard by Benjamin F. Betts, "Gardens on the Roofs of Radio City," *American Architect* 140, no. 2601, 1931, pp. 34-35, 74, 76; speaking of the roof gardens in terms of the unity they would impart to the complex, Reinhard cited the urban theories of Le Corbusier. In an interview by Jordy, Wallace K. Harrison also attributed the idea of the roof gardens to Hood; see Jordy, *American Buildings and Their Architects* 4, p. 429n20. See also Harvey Wiley Corbett, "Raymond Mathewson Hood, 1881-1934," *Architectural Forum* 61, no. 9, 1934, p. 15; Kilham, *Raymond Hood, Architect.*

153

Weisman, "First Landscaped Skyscraper," p. 59. The image of New York as the "New Babylon" and references to the Tower of Babel were very frequent, however, in American architectural writing in the early part of this century. A reconstruction of Solomon's temple was published in 1925 by Helmle and Corbett, and even Benjamin Wistar Morris's 1929 design for the Metropolitan Square Company has been seen as containing biblical symbolism. See Tafuri, " 'Neu-Babylon' "; Werner Oechslin, "Skyscraper und Amerikanismus. Mythos zwischen Europa und Amerika," *Archithese*, no. 20, 1976, pp. 4-11.

154

Thomas A. Murray, in *The Last Rivet* (Columbia University Press, New York, 1939).

155

See Fosdick, *John D. Rockefeller, Jr.*, p. 266.

156

Ibid., p. 271.

157

Ibid., especially pp. 272-301, 302ff., 327. See also Dal Co, "From Parks to the Region," this volume, n211.

158

See Reinhard, "What is the Rockefeller Radio City?"; Henry H. Dean, "A New Idea in City Rebuilding," *American Architect* 139, no. 2594, 1931, pp. 33-35, 114; Thomas C. Cochran, "The City's Business," in Nevins and Krout, *Greater City*, pp. 166-168.

159

Frederick Lewis Allen, "Radio City—Culture Center?" *Harper's Magazine* 170, Apr. 1932, pp. 534-545. The controversy took on heated tones in 1931 with a series of indignant letters to the *Herald Tribune*; after an anonymous letter defended the project, Percival Goodman, in a letter published April 8, attacked Rockefeller Center as a speculation. See also H. L. Brooks's article following an interview with the architects, *New York Times*, Apr. 5, 1931, and the editorial "A Modern Teapot Tempest. The Functionalist Design for Radio City Has Aroused Public Indignation in New York," *Pencil Points* 12, May 1931, p. 61. The changes made in the project after this controversy were undoubtedly part of an effort to show that speculation and social values need not be contradictory. Among the most cutting critics was Walter Lippmann, who called the Roxy a "pedestal for a peanut," while the *New York Times* of April 3, 1931 (two days before the article by Brooks), termed the project a monstrous architectural aberration. In addition, the undertaking was ridiculed in a popular musical review, *As Thousands Cheer*, which played on Broadway for about a year. In terms of publicity, however, there is no doubt that this controversy favored Rockefeller's project. In 1933, in any case, the criticism slackened; the producer of *As Thousands Cheer* decided to suppress the satirical sketch on the Rockefellers, and John H. Finley, editor in chief of the *New York Times*, wrote a letter of appreciation to Rockefeller on December 4, 1933. By this time the project was asserting itself as a winning economic reality. Late in 1933, John D. Rockefeller, Jr., installed his own offices at the top of the RCA Building.

160

Werner, "Radio City," pp. 475-476.

161

Lewis Mumford, "Mr. Rockefeller's Center," *New Yorker*, Dec. 23, 1933. Mumford resumed his criticism of Rockefeller Center in various later articles in the *New Yorker*, now collected in *From the Ground Up* (Harcourt Brace, New York, 1956).

162

Crowell, "Story of Rockefeller Center."

163

Ibid., p. 430.

164

In the years after 1936, this process turned in on itself. The managers and architects, faced with demands for more office space than projected in the preliminary schemes, were forced to alter the formal equilibrium of the design substantially. For the Associated Press Building, the only possible solution was to upset completely the unitary character of the low block on the north side by constructing a 16-story tower structure, finished in 1938, that infelicitously breaks the volumetric continuity on 51st Street. Analogously, just a bit later, the Eastern Air Lines Building rose as a 16-story slab in the south block; at its base a 2-story shopping space was introduced to offset the cost of the 6-story garage adjoining the building. In 1940 the last skyscraper of Rockefeller Center, the United States Rubber Company Building at the south-west corner of the site, was finished. See Weisman, "Way of the Price Mechanism," pp. 403-404.

165

See Sigfried Giedion, *Space, Time and Architecture* (1941; 3rd. rev. ed., Harvard University Press, Cambridge, Mass, 1954), pp. 752-753.

166

Hood, "Design of Rockefeller City."

167

See O. B. Hanson, "The Story of Rockefeller Center, IX. The Plan and Construction of the National Broadcasting Company Studios," *Architectural Forum* 57, no. 2, 1932, pp. 153-160.

168

Dean, "New Idea in City Rebuilding," pp. 34-35.

169

See William H. Jordy, "PSFS: Its Development and Its Significance in Modern Architecture," *Journal of the Society of Architectural Historians* 21, no. 2, 1962, pp. 47-83; Robert A. M. Stern, "PSFS: Beaux Arts Theory and Rational Expressionism," ibid., pp. 84–102. But see also Jordy, "The American Acceptance of the International Style: George Howe & William Lescaze's Philadelphia Saving Fund Society Building," in idem, *American Buildings and Their Architects* 4, pp. 87ff., where Jordy develops the ideas of his earlier article. See also the chapter dedicated to the PSFS Building in Robert A. M. Stern, *George Howe. Toward a Modern American Architecture* (Yale University Press, New Haven, 1975).

170

See Jordy, *American Buildings and Their Architects* 4, pp. 58ff.

171

See Hood, "Design of Rockefeller City"; Winston Weisman, "Slab Buildings," *Architectural Review* 111, no. 662, 1952, pp. 119-123.

172

See, for example, Jerzy W. Soltan's address at the Harvard Urban Design Conference, quoted in Douglas Haskell, "Unity and Harmony at Rockefeller Center," *Architectural Forum* 124, no. 1, 1966, pp. 42-47; Jordy, *American Buildings and Their Architects* 4, p. 21. Soltan spoke of the skaters in the Sunken Plaza as "Hansel and Gretel skaters in the skyscraper forest," in a surreal and fantastic vision. On the decoration of Rockefeller Center and the 1974 restoration, see David Morton, "Chromatic Relief, Rockefeller Center," *Progressive Architecture* 74, no. 7, July 1974, pp. 60–63.

173

Radio City Music Hall is a particularly important structure in Rockefeller Center, not the least for the controversy it aroused. See Henry Hofmeister, "The Story of Rockefeller Center, V. The International Music Hall," *Architectural Forum* 56, no. 4, 1932, pp. 355-360; Douglas Haskell, "Roxy's Advantage over God," *Nation*, Jan. 4, 1933; Jordy, *American Buildings and Their Architects* 4, pp. 78ff. See also Rem Koolhass, "Roxy, Noah un die Radio City Music Hall," *Archithese*, no. 18, 1976, pp. 37-43.

174

See Jordy, *American Buildings and Their Architects* 4, p. 22.

175

Ibid. 4, pp. 23, 429n8.

176

Ibid. 4, p. 23.

177

The Esso Building and the subsequent Time-Life Building by Harrison and Abramovitz (1957-59), on Sixth Avenue just beyond the RKO Building, are the first elements in a series of isolated undertakings that demonstrate not only the consequences of the closed form of Rockefeller Center but also its ultimate significance for the law of growth of the urban structure. Indeed, Rockefeller's enterprise was an indication that a growth in terms of a series of self-contained islands independent of any broader plan is the only form of growth possible with the means of control and financing typical of the American cities. On the recent developments on the Avenue of the Americas, opposite Rockefeller Center, see Tafuri, "La dialectique de l'absurde." On the building policy of New York during the Lindsay administration, particularly in regard to the skyscraper, see Stephen Zoll, "Super-ville: New York—Aspects of Very High Bulk," *Massachusetts Review* 14, no. 3, 1973; Brian Brace Taylor, "Self-Service Skyline," *L'architecture d'aujourd'hui*, no. 186, 1976, pp. 42-46.

178

See Frank Fogarty, "The Earning Power of Plazas," *Architectural Forum* 108, no. 1, 1958, pp. 106-109, 168, which summarizes the results of an investigation conducted by the *Architectural Forum* on the actual yield of skyscraper-plaza complexes; the principal examples chosen, other than Rockefeller Center, were Gateway Center in Pittsburgh, Penn Center in Philadelphia, and Denver's Mile High Center. The investigation seems to demonstrate that such undertakings are not wholly successful as economic ventures; the yield on the capital investments ranged from only 4 percent to 6 percent. Fogarty concludes that in order to encourage complexes comprising landscaping and open spaces the cities must offer an incentive—following the example of Chicago, where concessions are made on the limitation of building heights for edifices planned with green spaces and open squares. The incentive system recommended by Fogarty serves, in essence, to raise the yield of speculative investments in exchange for urban improvements of an individual and limited scope, free of controls. In regard to Rockefeller Center, the investigation calculated a gross income of $27 million ($5 per square foot) in 1959 and total annual expenditures of $20 million ($8.4 million general expenses, $5.3 million taxes, $3.8 million ground rent to Columbia University, plus depreciation). The 6 percent yield was calculated on the basis of the initial investment, which was officially calculated at $125 million. The $100,000 annual expense for the maintenance of the plaza is covered by the entrance fees to the skating rink and the charge for guided tours. An article published in 1934 listed the following paid and foreseen costs of the Rockefeller Center project: ground, $30 million; RCA Building, $45 million; RKO Building and Music Hall, $8 million; British Building, $1.5 million; Maison Française, $1.5 million; Center Theater, $4 million; other office buildings, $15 million; streets, underground levels, parking facilities, etc., $5 million; other expenses and buildings in the designing stage, $25 million; total, $135 million. See "Rockefeller Center, Red or Black?" Detailed data on the 38-story International Building, in which the selective cooling system was tried out, were published in "International Building, Rockefeller Center, New York," *Architectural Forum* 63, no. 5, 1935, pp. 456-468.

179
Sigfried Giedion, *Space, Time and Architecture*, pp. 756-757.
180
Allen, "Look at Rockefeller Center." Despite the basic thesis of his book, even Wayne Andrews could not help praising Rockefeller Center as an urban-planning project; see *Architecture, Ambition and Americans. A Social History of American Architecture* (Free Press of Glencoe, New York, 1964). As for Weisman, he expressed the following judgment in 1950: "Fourteen buildings of various sizes and shapes tied together with a dollar sign. This was architecture based on the laws of economics not on the canons of proportion—a twentieth century architecture growing out of the soil of contemporary civilization developing its own aesthetic as it progressed. Culturally Rockefeller Centre is as typical of our era as the Gothic cathedrals were of late medieval times or the Baths of Caracalla of the Roman era; it is certainly as much prized by the nation that built it" ("Way of the Price Mechanism," p. 404). Among the more recent judgments, which, in opposition to contrary practices that are still current, praise Rockefeller Center for its free spaces and conception as a coordinated unit, that expressed in Haskell, "Unity and Harmony at Rockefeller Center," is significant.
181
On these projects in general, see Fogarty, "Earning Power of Plazas." On Pittsburgh's Golden Triangle, see Roy Lubove, *Twentieth Century Pittsburgh, Government, Business and Environmental Change* (Wiley, New York, 1969), pp. 119ff. On Penn Center and the renewal of Market East in Philadelphia, see Philip Herrera, "Philadelphia: How Far Can Renewal Go?" *Architectural Forum* 121, no. 2, 1964, pp. 181-184.
182
Peter Blake, "Slaughter on Sixth Avenue," *Architectural Forum* 122, no. 3, 1965, pp. 13-19; but see also Jordy, *American Buildings and Their Architects*, pp. 25-27.
183
Blake, "Slaughter on Sixth Avenue," p. 15.
184
See Governor Nelson A. Rockefeller's February 1, 1966, message, in which he stated:
Because space is at a premium in Manhattan, replacement usually requires displacement. To make room for progress, people's lives are uprooted and beauty is often bulldozed. To make a place for the necessary, the desirable is often dismantled. Now the opportunity exists to add to Manhattan's distinctive locales without making any such sacrifices. The development of Battery Park City adjoining the new World Trade Center presents an opportunity unique for Manhattan: the creation, literally from the ground up, of a large-scale, imaginatively planned community comprising residential, business, light industry, and recreational facilities. Not one family would be displaced and yet new homes would be provided for 13,982 families. Utilizing present engineering knowledge, a landfill operation would enlarge lower Manhattan on the West side of the island. This would create new living and working space adjacent to significant transformations already in progress or being planned. Battery Park City would also represent a new departure in urban renewal. Private enterprise would be supported by public cooperation rather than by public funds (except for the financing of middle- and low-income housing, through the New York State Housing Finance Agency). Instead, the city would allow State-sponsored private development of obsolete, city-owned facilities—with the result that the city would ultimately get a net annual increase of real property tax revenue of close to $18,000,000. Battery Park City would be unique, not only as an example of urban planning, but also as a model of State and local initiatives underwritten by private financing.
See "A Message from Governor Nelson A. Rockefeller," in *Battery Park City. New Living Space for New York* (New York, n. d.). See also Wallace K. Harrison, "A Proposal to Governor Rockefeller," ibid., pp. 2-3, in which the need to arrest the tendency toward residential decentralization is stressed and Battery Park City is presented as an integrated project—with variously priced dwellings, offices, schools, services, work, and parking facilities—in immediate contact with the downtown. On the first plans for Battery Park City, see *Architectural Record* 145, June 1969, pp. 145-150; Tafuri, "La dialectique de

l'absurde," which includes a bibliography relative to the controversies of the early 1970s; "Einer Stadt in der Stadt," *Bauen + Wohnen*, no. 5, 1974, pp. 201-205. On the economic aspects of the World Trade Center, see Mario Manieri-Elia, *L'architettura contemporanea negli USA*, 2nd ed. (Cappelli, Bologna, 1976), pp. 85-88. The current processes of urban renewal have been harshly criticized by Scully, *American Architecture and Urbanism*, pp. 245ff. See also Martin Anderson, *The Federal Bulldozer* (M.I.T. Press, Cambridge, Mass., 1964). Given the breadth of the problems involved in urban renewal, which require adequate analysis, I can barely touch on the subject here, but I intend to treat it on another occasion.

185

My analysis of urban renewal in Pittsburgh is based on the documentation contained in Lubove, *Twentieth Century Pittsburgh*.

186

Ibid., p. 95.

187

Pittsburgh Realtor, June 26, 1923, p. 3; ibid., July 17, 1923, p. 5. See Lubove, *Twentieth Century Pittsburgh*, p. 95n27.

188

Robert Moses, *Arterial Plan for Pittsburgh. Prepared for the Pittsburgh Regional Planning Association* (November 1939).

189

I refer to Point Park, Point Redevelopment, Duquesne Way, Penn Lincoln Parkway, the renewal of the slum area of Lower Hill, and Crosstown Boulevard. Park Martin, engineer of the County Planning Commission, observed that seven of the nine projects in Moses's plan were already anticipated in the commission's 1936 plan. The director of the commission deplored the expenditure of $50,000 for a plan that had already been worked out three years earlier, while Frederick Bigger claimed that he himself had proposed the same ideas. In any case, in 1940 the City and County Planning Commissions, the Chamber of Commerce, and the Pittsburgh Regional Planning Commission gave precedence to the construction of Duquesne Way, to be followed by Crosstown Boulevard. See Lubove, *Twentieth Century Pittsburgh*, pp. 104-105.

190

"Report of Chamber Divisions: Golden Triangle Division," *Greater Pittsburgh*, no. 21, Feb. 1940, p. 11.

191

The Wabash railroad facilities had been bought by the Pennsylvania and West Virginia railroads. The urban renewal project could actually get under way only after the passing of the 1945 Housing and Redevelopment Law of the State of Pennsylvania, which permitted municipalities to form special authorities for the acquisition and renewal of areas indicated by the city-planning commissions, and after the enactment of the 1945 and 1947 laws which permitted insurance companies to invest in urban renewal.

192

On the controversies that arose over the Lower Hill project and over the construction of the retractable roof of the Civic Arena, see Lubove, *Twentieth Century Pittsburgh*, pp. 130-132.

193

Lubove records: "In the late 1960's a group of Pittsburgh architects and artists published a 'manifesto' expressing their determination to no longer silently watch 'our city being defaced by thoughtless buildings and projects. . . . The inane things that have all but ruined this place have been unchallenged much too long' " (ibid., p. 140). The signers were architect Antonio de Chicchis, designer James Lesko, sculptor Gordon Yee, professor Joe Nicholson, and architects Delbert Highlands and Troy West. See *Pittsburgh Point*, Apr. 6, 1967. Further protest came from the Pittsburgh Regional Planning Association.

194

I refer here to the volume of photographs by Eric Mendelsohn, *Amerika, das Bilderbuch eines Architekten* (Rudolf Mosse Verlag, Berlin, 1926).

195

See Lubove, "The Social Dimensions of the Renaissance," in idem, *Twentieth Century Pittsburgh*, pp. 142ff.

196

See New York City Planning Commission, *Plan for New York City 1969* (M.I.T. Press, Cambridge, Mass., 1969). The City Planning Commission, presided over by Mayor John V. Lindsay, was composed of Donald H. Elliott, chairman, Gerald R. Coleman, Martin Gallant, Walter McQuade, Ivan A. Michael, Chester Rapkin, and Beverly M. Spatt; former members included Lawrence M. Orton, James G. Sweeney, Elinor C. Guggenheimer, and Harmon H. Goldstone. For the Regional Plan Association's detailed plan of Manhattan (elaborated by Rai Y. Okamoto, Frank E. Williams, and Klaus Huboi, assisted by Dietrick Kunkel and Carlisle Towery), see Stanley B. Tankel, Boris Pushkarev, and William B. Shore, eds., *Urban Design Manhattan* (Studio Vista, London, 1969). See also, Monroy, "Piani e progetti per Manhattan."

197

See also the Regional Plan Association's proposal for 42nd Street, considered as a single megastructure, in Tankel, Pushkarev, and Shore, *Urban Design Manhattan*, pp. 86ff.

198

See Francesco Dal Co, "Città senza piani, piani senza città: note a margine della pianificazione urbana negli Stati Uniti," *Contropiano*, no. 1, 1970, pp. 172-188.

199

See Weisman, "New View of Skyscraper History," pp. 153-154. On the transformation and recent history of the Embarcadero Center, see William Marlin, "The Streets of Camelot," *Architectural Forum* 138, no. 3, 1973, pp. 26-38.

200

See Giusi Rapisarda, "Die Stadt und ihr Doppelgänger. Von 'Metropolis' zu 'King Kong'," *Archithese*, no. 17, 1976, pp. 29-36.

INDEX